SCOTLAND

Rick Steves with Cameron Hewitt

CONTENTS

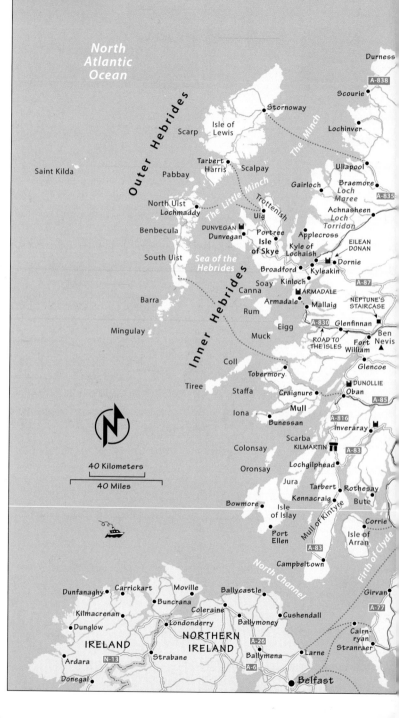

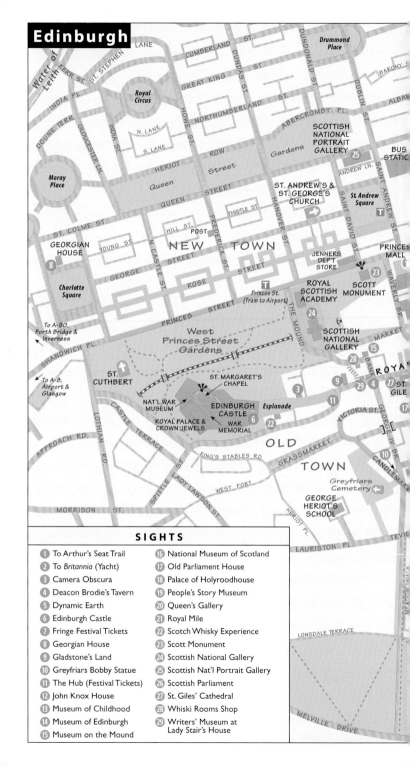

Edinburgh

SIGHTS

1. To Arthur's Seat Trail
2. To *Britannia* (Yacht)
3. Camera Obscura
4. Deacon Brodie's Tavern
5. Dynamic Earth
6. Edinburgh Castle
7. Fringe Festival Tickets
8. Georgian House
9. Gladstone's Land
10. Greyfriars Bobby Statue
11. The Hub (Festival Tickets)
12. John Knox House
13. Museum of Childhood
14. Museum of Edinburgh
15. Museum on the Mound
16. National Museum of Scotland
17. Old Parliament House
18. Palace of Holyroodhouse
19. People's Story Museum
20. Queen's Gallery
21. Royal Mile
22. Scotch Whisky Experience
23. Scott Monument
24. Scottish National Gallery
25. Scottish Nat'l Portrait Gallery
26. Scottish Parliament
27. St. Giles' Cathedral
28. Whiski Rooms Shop
29. Writers' Museum at Lady Stair's House

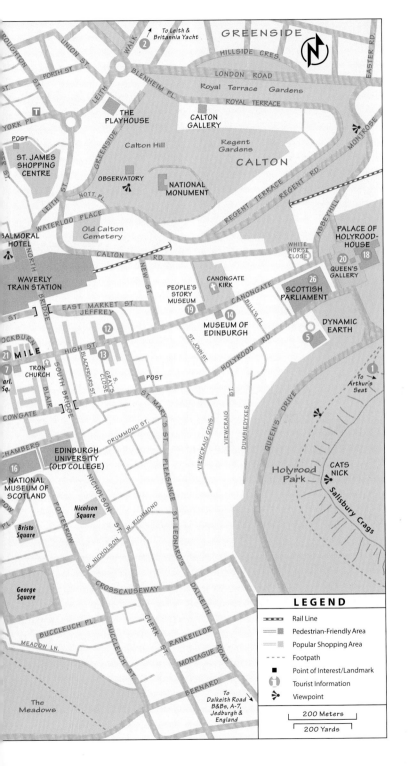

GREENSIDE

To Leith &
Britannia Yacht

HILLSIDE CRES.

LONDON ROAD

Royal Terrace Gardens

ROYAL TERRACE

BOROUGHTON

UNION ST.

FORTH ST.

LEITH WALK

BLENHEIM PL.

GREENSIDE

LEITH ST.

THE PLAYHOUSE

CALTON GALLERY

Calton Hill

Regent Gardens

CALTON

YORK PL.

POST

ST. JAMES SHOPPING CENTRE

OBSERVATORY

NATIONAL MONUMENT

NOTT. PL.

WATERLOO PLACE

Old Calton Cemetery

REGENT TERRACE

REGENT RD.

MONTROSE

ABBEYHILL

PALACE OF HOLYROODHOUSE

BALMORAL HOTEL

NORTH BRIDGE

CALTON RD.

WHITE HORSE CLOSE

20 18

QUEEN'S GALLERY

WAVERLY TRAIN STATION

NEW ST.

PEOPLE'S STORY MUSEUM

CANONGATE KIRK

CANONGATE

BULL'S CL.

26

SCOTTISH PARLIAMENT

EAST MARKET ST.

JEFFREY

19

14

MUSEUM OF EDINBURGH

ST.

COCKBURN ST.

12

HIGH ST.

BLACKFRIARS ST.

GRAY'S CLOSE

ST. JOHN ST.

HOLYROOD RD.

DYNAMIC EARTH

5

To Arthur's Seat

1

MILE

21

7

Parl. Sq.

TRON CHURCH

13

SOUTH BRIDGE

BLAIR ST.

ST. MARY'S ST.

POST

QUEEN'S DRIVE

VIEWCRAIG GDNS

VIEWCRAIG ST.

DUMBIEDYKES

COWGATE

CHAMBERS ST.

DRUMMOND ST.

EDINBURGH UNIVERSITY (OLD COLLEGE)

NICOLSON ST.

PLEASANCE

ST. LEONARD'S ST.

Holyrood Park

CATS NICK

Salisbury Crags

16

NATIONAL MUSEUM OF SCOTLAND

POTTERROW

Nicolson Square

W. RICHMOND

Bristo Square

W. NICHOLSON ST.

George Square

CROSSCAUSEWAY

BUCCLEUCH PL.

MEADOW LN.

BUCCLEUCH ST.

CLERK ST.

RANKEILLOR

MONTAGUE ST.

DALKEITH ROAD

BERNARD

To Dalkeith Road B&Bs, A-7, Jedburgh & England

The Meadows

LEGEND

- ▬▬▬ Rail Line
- ▬▬▬ Pedestrian-Friendly Area
- ▬▬▬ Popular Shopping Area
- - - - Footpath
- ■ Point of Interest/Landmark
- ⊕ Tourist Information
- ✧ Viewpoint

200 Meters

200 Yards

Scotland's national dress: the kilt

Oban's harbor

Isle of Skye

Rick Steves®

SCOTLAND

INTRODUCTION

Scotland is a little land that packs a big punch. From the yin-and-yang cities of Edinburgh and Glasgow to the rugged Highlands and remote islands, this fiercely proud country specializes in showing off its dramatic scenery and unique culture. Scotland's famous clichés—whisky distilleries, moody glens, golf links, bagpipes, kilts, and yes, haggis—offer glimpses of a deeply engaging cultural feast.

This book breaks Scotland into its top big-city, small-town, and rural destinations. It gives you all the information and opinions necessary to wring the maximum value out of your limited time and money in each of these locations. If you plan a month or less for Scotland and have a normal appetite for information, this book is all you need. If you're a travel-info fiend, this book sorts through all the superlatives and provides a handy rack upon which to hang your supplemental information.

Experiencing Scottish culture, people, and natural wonders economically and hassle-free has been my goal for more than three decades of traveling, tour guiding, and travel writing. With this book, I pass on to you the lessons I've learned, updated for your trip.

While including the predictable biggies (such as Edinburgh, Glasgow, Stirling, and the Isle of Skye), this book also mixes in a healthy dose of Back Door intimacy (windswept moors, evocative glens, and small-town Highland Games). It is selective. Scotland has 790 islands, but I recommend just my favorites: Skye, Mull, Iona, Staffa, and Orkney.

The best is, of course, only my opinion. But after spending much of my life researching Europe, I've developed a sixth sense for what travelers enjoy. The places featured in this book will knock your spots off.

INTRODUCTION

Map Legend

⚹ Viewpoint	Ⓣ Taxi Stand	)▨▨▨(Tunnel
↟ Entrance	Ⓑ Bus Stop	‐‐‐‐‐ Railway
ⓘ Tourist Info	Ⓟ Parking	▨▨▨▨ Pedest. Zone
WC Restroom	⚑ Golf Course	+▪Ⓣ▪+ Tram
⋔ Prehistoric Sight	Ⓦ Whisky Distillery/ Tasting	⋯⋯⋯ Ferry/Boat Route
▟ Castle, Manor House		✈ Airport
⌂ Church	▮ Pub	▨▨▨▨ Stairs
▪ Statue/Point of Interest	⛾ Park	‐ ‐ ‐ ‐ Walk/Tour Route
	▲ Peak	‐‐‐‐‐‐ Trail

Use this legend to help you navigate the maps in this book.

ABOUT THIS BOOK

Rick Steves Scotland is a personal tour guide in your pocket. This book is organized by destinations. Each is a mini vacation on its own, filled with exciting sights, strollable neighborhoods, homey and affordable places to stay, and memorable places to eat. Within the destination chapters, you'll find these sections:

Planning Your Time suggests a schedule for how to best use your limited time.

Orientation has specifics on public transportation, helpful hints, local tour options, easy-to-read maps, and tourist information.

Sights describes the top attractions and includes their cost and hours.

Self-Guided Walks take you through interesting neighborhoods, pointing out sights and fun stops.

Sleeping describes my favorite hotels, from good-value deals to cushy splurges.

Eating serves up a buffet of options, from inexpensive pubs to fancy restaurants.

Connections outlines your options for traveling to destinations by train, bus, and plane, plus route tips for drivers.

The **Scotland: Past and Present** chapter gives a quick overview of Scottish history and culture.

Practicalities is a traveler's tool kit, with my best tips about money, sightseeing, sleeping, eating, staying connected, and transportation (trains, buses, ferries, car rentals, driving, and flights). Here you'll also find definitions of typically Scottish terms.

The **appendix** has the nuts-and-bolts: useful phone numbers and websites, a holiday and festival list, recommended books and films, a climate chart, a handy packing checklist, and a fun British-Yankee dictionary.

Key to This Book

Updates

This book is updated regularly, but things change. For the latest, visit www.ricksteves.com/update.

Abbreviations and Times

I use the following symbols and abbreviations in this book:

Sights are rated:

▲▲▲	Don't miss
▲▲	Try hard to see
▲	Worthwhile if you can make it
No rating	Worth knowing about

Tourist information offices are abbreviated as **TI,** and bathrooms are **WC**s. To categorize accommodations, I use a **Sleep Code** (described on page 444).

Like Europe, this book uses the **24-hour clock** for schedules. It's the same through 12:00 noon, then keeps going: 13:00, 14:00, and so on. For anything over 12, subtract 12 and add p.m. (14:00 is 2:00 p.m.).

When giving **opening times,** I include both peak season and off-season hours if they differ. So, if a museum is listed as "May-Oct daily 9:00-16:00," it should be open from 9 a.m. until 4 p.m. from the first day of May until the last day of October (but expect exceptions).

A ⋂ symbol indicates that a free, downloadable self-guided Rick Steves audio tour is available.

For **transit** or **tour departures,** I first list the frequency, then the duration. So, a train connection listed as "2/hour, 1.5 hours" departs twice each hour, and the journey lasts an hour and a half.

Browse through this book, choose your favorite destinations, and link them up. Then have a brilliant trip! Traveling like a temporary local, you'll get the absolute most out of every mile, minute, and dollar. And, as you visit places I know and love, I'm happy that you'll be meeting some of my favorite Scottish people.

Planning

This section will help you get started on planning your trip—with advice on trip costs, when to go, and what you should know before you take off.

TRAVEL SMART

Your trip to Scotland is like a complex play—it's easier to follow and really appreciate on a second viewing. While no one does the

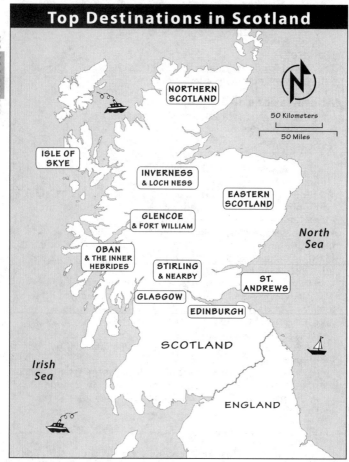

Top Destinations in Scotland

NORTHERN SCOLAND

ISLE OF SKYE

INVERNESS & LOCH NESS

EASTERN SCOTLAND

GLENCOE & FORT WILLIAM

OBAN & THE INNER HEBRIDES

STIRLING & NEARBY

ST. ANDREWS

GLASGOW

EDINBURGH

North Sea

SCOTLAND

Irish Sea

ENGLAND

50 Kilometers

50 Miles

same trip twice to gain that advantage, reading this book in its entirety before your travels accomplishes much the same thing.

Design an itinerary that enables you to visit sights at the best possible times. Note festivals, holidays, specifics on sights, and days when sights are closed. To connect the dots smoothly, read the tips in Practicalities on taking trains and buses, or renting a car and driving. Designing a smart trip is a fun, doable, and worthwhile challenge.

Make your itinerary a mix of intense and relaxed stretches. To maximize rootedness, minimize one-night stands. It's worth a long drive after dinner (or a train or bus ride with a dinner picnic) to be settled into a town for two nights. Every trip—and every traveler—needs slack time (laundry, picnics, people-watching, and so on). Pace yourself. Assume you will return.

Reread this book as you travel, and visit local tourist information offices (abbreviated as TI in this book). Upon arrival in a new town, lay the groundwork for a smooth departure; confirm the train, bus, or road you'll take when you leave.

Even with the best-planned itinerary, you'll need to be flexible. Update your plans as you travel. Get online or call ahead to double-check tourist information, learn the latest on sights (special events, tour schedules, and so on), book tickets and tours, make reservations, reconfirm hotels, and research transportation connections.

Enjoy the friendliness of the Scottish people. Connect with the culture. Set up your own quest for the best hike, castle, or whisky. Slow down and be open to unexpected experiences. You speak the language—use it! Ask questions—most locals are eager to point you in their idea of the right direction. Keep a notepad in your pocket for noting directions, organizing your thoughts, and confirming prices. Wear your money belt, learn the currency, and figure out how to estimate prices in dollars. Those who expect to travel smart, do.

TRIP COSTS

Five components make up your trip costs: airfare, surface transportation, room and board, sightseeing and entertainment, and shopping and miscellany.

Airfare: A basic round-trip flight from the US to Edinburgh can cost, on average, about $1,000-2,000 total, depending on where you fly from and when (cheaper in winter). If your trip extends beyond Scotland, consider saving time and money by flying into one city and out of another—for instance, into Edinburgh and out of Amsterdam. Overall, Kayak.com is the best place to start searching for flights on a combination of mainstream and budget carriers.

Surface Transportation: For a two-week whirlwind trip of all my recommended Scottish destinations, allow $250 per person for public transportation (train and bus tickets). If you'll be renting a car, allow at least $230 per week, not including tolls, gas, and supplemental insurance. If you'll be keeping the car for three weeks or more, look into leasing, which can save you money on insurance and taxes for trips of this length. Car rentals and leases are cheapest when arranged from the US. For more on public transportation and car rental, see "Transportation" in Practicalities.

Room and Board: You can thrive in Scotland on $120 a day per person for room and board (more in big cities). This allows $15 for lunch, $35 for dinner, and $70 for lodging (based on two people splitting the cost of a $140 double room that includes breakfast). Students and tightwads can enjoy Scotland for as little as $60 ($30 for a bed, $30 for meals and snacks).

Sightseeing and Entertainment: Figure about $12-25 per

INTRODUCTION

Scotland at a Glance

This book's destinations are organized roughly south (the Lowlands) to north (the Highlands).

The Lowlands

▲▲▲**Edinburgh** Proud and endlessly entertaining Scottish capital, with an imposing castle, attraction-studded Royal Mile, excellent museums, and atmospheric neighborhoods.

▲▲**Glasgow** Scotland's fun and funky biggest city—gritty but gentrifying, and packed with gregarious locals, edgy culture, and a treasure trove of 20th-century architecture.

▲**Stirling and Nearby** Site of one of Scotland's top castles (home of the Stuart kings) overlooking a historic plain, with great sights nearby—from giant horse heads and a Ferris wheel for boats at Falkirk to Highland scenery in the Trossachs.

▲▲**St. Andrews** Beach town that hosts Scotland's top university and the world's most famous golf course, plus top-notch industrial museums in nearby Dundee and charming coastal scenery in the East Neuk.

The Highlands

▲▲**Oban and the Inner Hebrides** Handy home-base town of Oban, with boat trips to the isles of Mull, Iona, and Staffa.

---

major sight (Edinburgh Castle-$27, Stirling Castle-$23, around $12-15 for whisky distillery tours), $5-8 for minor ones (St. Andrew's Cathedral tower climb-$7.20), and $35-80 for splurge experiences (e.g., bus tours and concerts). For information on various sightseeing passes, see page 442. An overall average of $30 a day works for most people. Don't skimp here. After all, this category is the driving force behind your trip—you came to sightsee, enjoy, and experience Scotland.

Shopping and Miscellany: Figure roughly $2 per postcard, $3 for tea or an ice-cream cone, and $5 per pint of beer. Shopping can vary in cost from nearly nothing to a small fortune. Good budget travelers find that this category has little to do with assembling a trip full of lifelong memories.

SIGHTSEEING PRIORITIES

So much to see, so little time. How to choose? Depending on the length of your trip, and taking geographic proximity into account, here are my recommended priorities:

▲**Glencoe and Fort William** Stirring "Weeping Glen" of Glencoe offering some of the Highlands' best scenery and hikes, plus the transit-hub town of Fort William and the historic "Road to the Isles."

▲▲**Inverness and Loch Ness** Regional capital with easy access to more Highland sights, including Culloden Battlefield (Scotland's Alamo) and monster-spotting at the famous Loch Ness.

▲**Eastern Scotland** Grab-bag of sights between Inverness and Edinburgh, including the whisky and hillwalking mecca of Pit-lochry, a look at early Iron Age crannog life on Loch Tay, the distilleries of Speyside, the Queen's Scottish retreat at Balmoral Castle, and cliff-capping Dunnottar Castle.

▲▲**Isle of Skye** Dramatically scenic island with craggy Cuillin Hills, jagged Trotternish Peninsula, castles, a distillery, dynamic clan history, and the colorful harbor town of Portree.

Northern Scotland Some of the Highlands' best get-away-from-it-all scenery along Wester Ross and the north coast, plus the fascinating Orkney Islands—with Scotland's best prehistoric sites, evocative Old Norse history, and WWI/WWII naval harbor.

3 days:	Edinburgh
5 days, add:	Glasgow, Stirling
7 days, add:	Oban, Glencoe
9 days, add:	Inverness, Loch Ness, Culloden
11 days, add:	Isle of Skye
13 days, add:	St. Andrews, Mull/Iona/Staffa
15 days, add:	Your choice of sights near Stirling or in Eastern Scotland
17 days, add:	Orkney
21 days, add:	More sights near Stirling, Wester Ross and the north coast, and slow down

The top 15 days include everything on my "Scotland's Best Two-Week Trip by Car" itinerary and map (see page 8). If you're traveling here in summer, check schedules for Highland Games in the areas you're visiting, and plan your time accordingly.

Build your itinerary to match your interests. Golfers make a pilgrimage to St. Andrews; nature lovers add extra time for hiking in Glencoe; whisky aficionados appreciate Speyside and Pitlochry;

Scotland's Best Two-Week Trip by Car

Day	Plan	Sleep in
1	Arrive Edinburgh	Edinburgh
2	Edinburgh	Edinburgh
3	Edinburgh	Edinburgh
4	More time in Edinburgh, then train to Glasgow	Glasgow
5	Glasgow	Glasgow
6	Pick up car, drive to Oban	Oban
7	Side-trip to Mull and Iona	Oban
8	Drive through Glencoe this morning, then to Isle of Skye	Isle of Skye
9	Isle of Skye	Isle of Skye
10	Drive along Caledonian Canal and Loch Ness to Inverness	Inverness
11	Inverness and side-trip to Culloden and other sights	Inverness
12	Head south, enjoying your choice of sights in Eastern Scotland or St. Andrews	Pitlochry, Ballater, or St. Andrews
13	More Eastern Scotland or St. Andrews sightseeing; spend evening in Stirling	Stirling
14	Stirling Castle and nearby sights	Stirling
15	Drive to Edinburgh for your flight home	

While this two-week itinerary is designed to be done by car after leaving Glasgow, most connections can be done by bus with a few modifications: You may want to rent a car for your day on Skye; consider a package tour for Highland side-tripping from Inverness; and at the end, go from Inverness straight to Stirling (skipping Eastern Scotland sights, which are out of the way by public transit).

If cities aren't your thing, consider skipping Glasgow (or

royalists tour Balmoral and Glamis castles; prehistorians prioritize Orkney, Kilmartin Glen, and Clava Cairns; and those interested in Scotland's industrial heritage check out the Caledonian Canal, Falkirk Wheel, and excellent museums in Dundee.

WHEN TO GO

In most of Scotland, July and August are peak season—with very long days, the best weather, and the busiest schedule of tourist fun. (Edinburgh is especially swamped throughout August, during the city's festival season.) While it never quite feels "crowded," Scot-

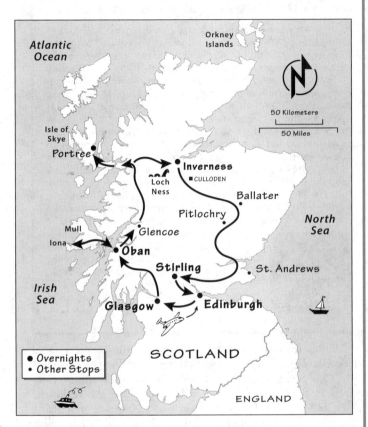

Atlantic
Ocean

Orkney
Islands

50 Kilometers

50 Miles

Isle of
Skye

Portree

Inverness

■ CULLODEN

Loch
Ness

Ballater

Pitlochry

North
Sea

Mull

Glencoe

Iona

Oban

Stirling

St. Andrews

Irish
Sea

Glasgow

Edinburgh

SCOTLAND

● Overnights
• Other Stops

ENGLAND

doing it at the end, as a side-trip from Stirling) to make more time
for the countryside.

With more time, slow down and linger—or enjoy additional
scenery by looping around the north of Scotland: Wester Ross,
the north coast, and the Orkney Islands.

land has a finite number of B&Bs and restaurants—and they are
jam-packed in July and August.

Travel during "shoulder season" (May, early June, Sept, and
early Oct) is easier and can be a bit less expensive. In fact, many
travelers' favorite time to visit Scotland is May and June: smaller
crowds, the full range of sights and tourist fun spots, and the
ability to grab a room almost whenever and wherever they like—
often at a flexible price. Even in the peak of summer, Scotland's
damp and chilly climate means that sunny weather is far from
guaranteed—you may do just as well in shoulder season.

INTRODUCTION

∩ **Rick Steves Audio Europe** ∩

My free **Rick Steves Audio Europe app** is a great tool for enjoying Europe. This app makes it easy to download my audio tours of top attractions, plus hours of travel interviews, all organized into destination-specific playlists.

My self-guided **audio tours** of major sights and neighborhoods are free, user-friendly, fun, and informative. Among these tours is my Royal Mile Walk in Edinburgh, which is marked with this symbol: ∩. You can choose whether to follow the written tour in this book, or pop in your earbuds and listen to essentially the same information—freeing up your eyes to appreciate the sights along the walk. My audio tours are hard to beat: Nobody will stand you up, the quality is reliable, you can take the tour exactly when you like, and the price is right.

The Rick Steves Audio Europe app also offers a far-reaching library of insightful **travel interviews** from my public radio show with experts from around the globe—including many of the places in this book.

This app and all of its content are entirely free. You can download Rick Steves Audio Europe via Apple's App Store, Google Play, or the Amazon Appstore. For more information, see www.ricksteves.com/audio europe.

Winter travelers find absolutely no crowds and soft room prices, but sightseeing hours are shorter and the weather is reliably bad. Some attractions open only on weekends or close entirely in the winter (Nov-Feb). The weather can be cold and dreary, and nightfall draws the shades on sightseeing well before dinnertime. While rural charm falls with the leaves, city sightseeing is fine in the winter.

Plan for rain no matter when you go. Just keep traveling and take full advantage of bright spells. The weather can change several times in a day, but rarely is it extreme. As the locals say, "There is no bad weather, only inappropriate clothing." Bring a jacket and dress in layers. Temperatures below 32°F cause headlines, and days that break 80°F—while more frequent in recent years—are still rare in Scotland. (For more information, see the climate chart in the appendix.) While sunshine may be rare, summer days are very long. The midsummer sun is up from 6:30 until 22:30. It's not uncommon to have a gray day, eat dinner, and enjoy hours of sunshine afterward.

KNOW BEFORE YOU GO
Check this list of things to arrange while you're still at home.

You need a **passport**—but no visa or shots—to travel in Scotland. You may be denied entry into certain European countries if your passport is due to expire within three months of your ticketed date of return. Get it renewed if you'll be cutting it close. It can take up to six weeks to get or renew a passport (for more on passports, see www.travel.state.gov). Pack a photocopy of your passport in your luggage in case the original is lost or stolen.

Book rooms well in advance if you'll be traveling during peak season or any major **holidays or festivals** (see list on page 490).

Call your **debit- and credit-card companies** to let them know the countries you'll be visiting, to ask about fees, to request your PIN code (it will be mailed to you), and more. See page 436 for details.

Do your homework if you want to buy **travel insurance.** Compare the cost of the insurance to the cost of your potential loss. Also, check whether your existing insurance (health, homeowners, or renters) covers you and your possessions overseas. For more tips, see www.ricksteves.com/insurance.

Consider buying a **rail pass** after researching your options (see page 473 and www.ricksteves.com/rail for all the specifics).

Tickets to **Edinburgh's Military Tattoo** (Aug) sell out early—book as far ahead as possible (www.edintattoo.co.uk; for details, see page 97).

If you'll be in **Edinburgh at festival time** (most of Aug), check the schedule for theater and music ahead of time. If there's something you just have to see, consider buying tickets before you go (for tips, see page 96, and for a current festival schedule, visit www.eif.co.uk and www.edfringe.com). Other good places for live shows are Glasgow and even little Pitlochry (with its hardworking Festival Theatre, www.pitlochryfestivaltheatre.com).

To **golf at St. Andrews' famous Old Course,** you'll need to reserve the previous fall, or put your name in for the "ballot" two days before (see page 214).

If you plan to hire a **local guide,** reserve ahead by email. Popular guides can get booked up.

If you're bringing a **mobile device,** consider signing up for an international plan for cheaper calls, texts, and data (see page 462). Download any apps you might want to use on the road, such as maps, transit schedules, and **Rick Steves Audio Europe** (see page 10).

How Was Your Trip?

Were your travels fun, smooth, and meaningful? If you'd like to share your tips, concerns, and discoveries, please fill out the survey at www.ricksteves.com/feedback. To check out readers' hotel and restaurant reviews—or leave one yourself—visit my travel forum at www.ricksteves.com/travel-forum. I value your feedback. Thanks in advance.

Traveling as a Temporary Local

We travel all the way to Scotland to enjoy differences—to become temporary locals. You'll experience frustrations. Certain truths that we find "God-given" or "self-evident," such as cold beer, ice in drinks, bottomless cups of coffee, "the customer is king," and bigger being better, are suddenly not so true. One of the benefits of travel is the eye-opening realization that there are logical, civil, and even better alternatives. A willingness to go local ensures that you'll enjoy a full dose of Scottish hospitality.

Europeans generally like Americans. But if there is a negative aspect to the Scottish image of Americans, it's that we are loud, wasteful, ethnocentric, too informal (which can seem disrespectful), and a bit naive.

The Scots (and Europeans in general) place a high value on speaking quietly in restaurants and on trains. Listen while on the bus or in a restaurant—the place can be packed, but the decibel level is low. Try to adjust your volume accordingly to show respect for their culture.

While the Scots look bemusedly at some of our Yankee excesses—and worriedly at others—they nearly always afford individual travelers all the warmth we deserve.

Judging from all the happy feedback I receive from travelers who have used this book, it's safe to assume you'll enjoy a great, affordable vacation—with the finesse of an independent, experienced traveler.

Thanks, and have a brilliant holiday!

Rick Steves

Back Door Travel Philosophy

From *Rick Steves Europe Through the Back Door*

Travel is intensified living—maximum thrills per minute and one of the last great sources of legal adventure. Travel is freedom. It's recess, and we need it.

Experiencing the real Europe requires catching it by surprise, going casual..."through the Back Door."

Affording travel is a matter of priorities. (Make do with the old car.) You can eat and sleep—simply, safely, and enjoyably—anywhere in Europe for $100 a day plus transportation costs. In many ways, spending more money only builds a thicker wall between you and what you traveled so far to see. Europe is a cultural carnival, and time after time, you'll find that its best acts are free and the best seats are the cheap ones.

A tight budget forces you to travel close to the ground, meeting and communicating with the people. Never sacrifice sleep, nutrition, safety, or cleanliness to save money. Simply enjoy the local-style alternatives to expensive hotels and restaurants.

Connecting with people carbonates your experience. Extroverts have more fun. If your trip is low on magic moments, kick yourself and make things happen. If you don't enjoy a place, maybe you don't know enough about it. Seek the truth. Recognize tourist traps. Give a culture the benefit of your open mind. See things as different, but not better or worse. Any culture has plenty to share. When an opportunity presents itself, make it a habit to say "yes."

Of course, travel, like the world, is a series of hills and valleys. Be fanatically positive and militantly optimistic. If something's not to your liking, change your liking.

Travel can make you a happier American, as well as a citizen of the world. Our Earth is home to seven billion equally precious people. It's humbling to travel and find that other people don't have the "American Dream"—they have their own dreams. Europeans like us, but with all due respect, they wouldn't trade passports.

Thoughtful travel engages us with the world. It reminds us what is truly important. By broadening perspectives, travel teaches new ways to measure quality of life.

Globetrotting destroys ethnocentricity, helping us understand and appreciate other cultures. Rather than fear the diversity on this planet, celebrate it. Among your most prized souvenirs will be the strands of different cultures you choose to knit into your own character. The world is a cultural yarn shop, and Back Door travelers are weaving the ultimate tapestry. Join in!

SCOTLAND

One of the three countries that make up Great Britain, rugged, feisty, colorful Scotland stands apart. Whether it's the laid-back, less-organized nature of the people, the stony architecture, the unmanicured landscape, or simply the haggis, go-its-own-way Scotland is distinctive.

Scotland encompasses about a third of Britain's geographical area (30,400 square miles), but has less than a tenth of its population (about 5.3 million). This sparsely populated chunk of land stretches to Norwegian latitudes. Its Shetland Islands, at about 60°N (similar to Anchorage, Alaska), are the northernmost point in Britain. You may see Scotland referred to as "Caledonia" (its ancient Roman name) or "Alba" (its Gaelic name). Scotland's fortunes were long tied to the sea; all of its leading cities are located along firths (estuaries), where major rivers connect to ocean waters.

The southern part of Scotland, called the Lowlands, is relatively flat and urbanized. The northern area—the Highlands—features a wild, severely undulating terrain, punctuated by lochs (lakes) and fringed by sea lochs (inlets) and islands.

The Highland Boundary Fault that divides Scotland geologically also divides it culturally. Historically, there were two distinct identities: rougher Highlanders in the northern wilderness and the more refined Lowlanders in

Scotland Almanac

Official Name: Scotland.

Population: About 5.3 million. Scotland is mostly English-speaking, though about 1.5 million people use the Scots "language," and about 60,000 speak Scottish Gaelic.

Latitude and Longitude: 57° N and 4° W. The Shetland Islands are Scotland's northernmost point, at 60°N (similar to Anchorage, Alaska).

Area: 30,400 square miles, about the size of South Carolina.

Geography: Scotland's flatter southern portion is the Lowlands; the Highlands to the north are more wild and hilly, and the country boasts over 6,000 miles of coastline and 787 islands (only about 130 are inhabited). Ben Nevis in western Scotland (at 4,406 feet) is Great Britain's highest peak.

Biggest Cities: Glasgow has 600,000 people, Edinburgh 490,000.

Economy: The gross domestic product is about $141 billion, and the GDP per capita is $26,400. The Scottish service sector (including retail and financial services) has become an increasingly significant part of its economy, producing 72 percent of all economic activity in 2011.

Scotland's main exports include food and drink, as well as chemicals and petroleum products. Scotch whisky comprises a quarter of all UK food and drink exports; exports to the US represent the biggest market for Scotch by value, though France is the biggest market by volume.

Scotland uses the same currency as UK countries England, Wales, and Northern Ireland: the pound sterling.

Government: Queen Elizabeth II officially heads the country—but for Scots she is simply Queen Elizabeth, not Queen Elizabeth II. (Scotland and England were separate monarchies when England had their first Elizabeth.) David Cameron is the UK's prime minister, and Nicola Sturgeon is Scotland's first minister.

Flag: The Saltire, with a diagonal, X-shaped white cross on a blue field, is meant to represent the crucifixion of Scotland's patron saint, the apostle Andrew.

The Average Scot: The average Scottish person will live to age 79 and doesn't identify with an organized religion. He or she has free health care, gets 28 vacation days a year (versus 16 in the US), lives within a five-minute walk of a park or green space, and gets outdoors at least once a week.

the southern flatlands and cities. Highlanders represented the stereotypical image of "true Scots," speaking Gaelic, wearing kilts, and playing bagpipes, while Lowlanders spoke languages of Saxon origin and wore trousers. After the Scottish Reformation, the Lowlanders embraced Protestantism, while the Highlanders stuck to Catholicism. Although this Lowlands/Highlands division has faded over time, some Scots still cling to it.

The Lowlands are dominated by a pair of rival cities: Edinburgh (on the east coast's Firth of Forth) and Glasgow (on the west

coast's Firth of Clyde) mark the endpoints of Scotland's 75-mile-long "Central Belt," where three-quarters of the country's population resides. Edinburgh, the old royal capital, teems with Scottish history and is the country's best tourist attraction. Glasgow, once a gloomy industrial city, is becoming a hip, laid-back city of art, music, and architecture. In addition to these two cities—both of which warrant a visit—the Lowlands' highlights include the medieval university town and golf mecca of St. Andrews, the small city of Stirling (with its castle and many nearby historic sites), and selected countryside stopovers.

Generally, the Highlands are hungry for the tourist dollar, and everything overtly Scottish is exploited to the kilt; you need to spend some time here to get to know

the area's true character. You can get a feel for the Highlands with a quick drive to Oban, through Glencoe, then up the Caledonian Canal to Inverness. With more time, the Isles of Iona, Staffa, and Mull (an easy day trip from Oban); the Isle of Skye; the handy distillery town of Pit-

lochry; and countless brooding countryside castles will flesh out your Highlands experience. And for those really wanting to get off the beaten path, continue north—all the way up the dramatic west coast (called Wester Ross) to John O'Groats, at Britain's northeastern tip. To go farther, cross the Pentland Firth to Orkney, with its own unique culture and history.

At these northern latitudes, cold and drizzly weather isn't uncommon—even in midsummer. The blazing sun can quickly be covered over by black clouds and howling wind. Your B&B host will warn you to prepare for "four seasons in one day." Because Scots feel personally responsible for bad weather, they tend to be overly optimistic about forecasts. Take any Scottish promise of "sun by the afternoon" with a grain of salt—and bring your raincoat, just in case.

Americans and Canadians of Scottish descent enjoy coming "home" to Scotland. If you're Scottish, your surname will tell you which clan your ancestors likely belonged to. The prefix "Mac" (or "Mc") means "son of"—so "MacDonald" means the same thing as "Donaldson." Tourist shops everywhere are happy to help you track down your clan's tartan (distinctive plaid pattern). For more on how these "clan tartans" don't go back as far as you might think, see the sidebar on page 35.

Scotland shares a monarchy with the rest of the United Kingdom, though to Scots, Queen Elizabeth II is just "Queen Elizabeth"; the first Queen Elizabeth ruled England, but not Scotland. (In this book, I use Great Britain's numbering.) Scotland is not a sovereign state, but it is a "nation" in that it has its own traditions, ethnic identity, languages (Gaelic and Scots), and football league. To some extent, it even has its own government.

Recently, Scotland has enjoyed its greatest measure of political autonomy in centuries—a trend called "devolution." In 1999, the Scottish parliament convened in Edinburgh for the first time in almost 300 years; in 2004, it moved into its brand-new building near the foot of the Royal Mile. Though the Scottish parliament's powers are limited (most major decisions are still made in London), the Scots are enjoying the refresh-

ing breeze of increased self-governance. In a 2014 independence referendum, the Scots favored staying in the United Kingdom by a margin of 10 percent. The question of independence will likely remain a pivotal issue in Scotland for many years to come. (For more on Scotland's rocky history with British rule and devolution, see page 428.)

Scotland even has its own currency...sort of. Scots use the same coins as England, Wales, and Northern Ireland, but Scotland also prints its own bills (featuring Scottish rather than English people and landmarks). Just to confuse tourists, three different banks print Scottish pound

SCOTLAND

Scotland

Orkney Islands

Durness •
Thurso •
John O'Groats
Wick •

OUTER HEBRIDES

Lewis

Harris

50 Kilometers
50 Miles

Isle of Skye
Portree •
• Applecross

North Atlantic

Ullapool •

Inverness
■ CULLODEN
■ CLAVA CAIRNS

Loch Ness

INNER HEBRIDES

Mallaig •
Fort Willliam

▲ Ben Nevis

HIGHLANDS

BALMORAL ■
• Ballater

• Aberdeen

North Sea

• Glencoe

• Pitlochry

Iona   Mull

• Oban

Loch Lomond

Stirling

FALKIRK ■ WHEEL

Dundee

• St. Andrews

Glasgow   Edinburgh

Irish Sea

Arran

Ayr •

Jedburgh •

LOWLANDS

NORTHERN IRELAND

• Cairnryan

Dumfries •

Newcastle •

Belfast •

ENGLAND

notes, each with a different design. In the Lowlands (around Edinburgh and Glasgow), you'll receive both Scottish and English pounds from ATMs and in change. But in the Highlands, you'll almost never see English pounds. Bank of England notes are legal and widely used; Northern Ireland bank notes are legal but less common.

The Scottish flag—a diagonal, X-shaped white cross on a blue field—represents the cross of Scotland's patron saint, the Apostle Andrew (who was crucified on an X-shaped cross). You may not realize it, but you see the Scottish flag every time you look at the Union Jack: England's flag (the red St. George's cross on a white field) superimposed on Scotland's (a blue field with a white diagonal cross). The diagonal

British, Scottish, and English

Scotland and England have been tied together for more than 300 years, since the Act of Union in 1707. For a century and a half afterward, Scottish nationalists rioted for independence in Edinburgh's streets and led rebellions ("uprisings") in the Highlands. In this controversial union, history is clearly seen through two very different filters.

If you tour a British-oriented sight, such as Edinburgh's National War Museum Scotland, you'll find things told in a "happy union" way, which ignores the long history of Scottish resistance—from the ancient Picts through the time of Robert the Bruce. The official line: In 1706-1707, it was clear to England and certain parties in Scotland (especially landowners from the Lowlands) that it was in their mutual interest to dissolve the Scottish government and fold it into Britain, to be ruled from London.

But talk to a cabbie or your B&B host, and you may get a different spin. Scottish independence is still a hot-button issue. Since 2007, the Scottish National Party (SNP) has owned the largest majority in the Scottish Parliament. During a landmark referendum in September 2014, the Scots voted to remain part of the union—but many polls, right up until election day, suggested that things could easily have gone the other way.

The rift shows itself in sports, too. While the English may refer to a British team in international competition as "English," the Scots are careful to call it "British." If a Scottish athlete does well, the English call him "British." If he screws up... he's a clumsy Scot.

red cross (St. Patrick's cross) over Scotland's white one represents Northern Ireland. (Wales gets no love on the Union Jack.)

Here in "English-speaking" Scotland, you may still encounter a language barrier. First is the lovely, lilting Scottish accent—which many linguists consider to be a separate language, called "Scots." You may already know several Scots words: lad, lassie, wee, bonnie, glen, loch, aye. On menus, you'll see neeps and tatties (turnips and potatoes). And in place names, you'll see ben (mountain), brae (hill), firth (estuary), and kyle (strait). Second is Gaelic (pronounced "gallic" here; Ireland's closely related Celtic language is pronounced "gaylic")—the ancient Celtic language of the Scots. While only one percent of the population speaks Gaelic, it's making a comeback—particularly in the remote and traditional Highlands. For more on the languages of Scotland—including a glossary of Scots words—see page 468.

While soccer is as popular here as anywhere, golf is Scotland's other national sport. But in Scotland, it's not necessarily considered an exclusively upper-class pursuit; you can generally play a round at a basic course for about £15. While Scotland's best scenery is along the west coast, its best golfing is on the east coast—home to many of its most prestigious golf courses. Most of these are links courses, which use natural sand from the beaches for the bunkers. For tourists, these links are more authentic, more challenging, and more fun than the regular-style courses (with artificial landforms) farther inland. If you're a golfer, St. Andrews—on the east coast—is a pilgrimage worth making.

Outside of the main cities, Scotland's sights are subtle, but its misty glens, brooding countryside castles, and warm culture are plenty engaging. Whether toasting with beer, whisky, or Scotland's favorite soft drink Irn-Bru, enjoy meeting the Scottish people. It's easy to fall in love with the irrepressible spirit and beautiful landscape of this faraway corner of Britain.

EDINBURGH

Edinburgh is the historical, cultural, and political capital of Scotland. For nearly a thousand years, Scotland's kings, parliaments, writers, thinkers, and bankers have called Edinburgh home. Today, it remains Scotland's most sophisticated city.

Edinburgh (ED'n-burah—only tourists pronounce it like "Pittsburgh") is Scotland's showpiece and one of Europe's most entertaining cities. It's a place of stunning vistas—nestled among craggy bluffs and studded with a prickly skyline of spires, towers, domes, and steeples. Proud statues of famous Scots dot the urban landscape. The buildings are a harmonious yellow-gray, all built from the same local sandstone.

Culturally, Edinburgh has always been the place where Lowland culture (urban and English) met Highland style (rustic and Gaelic). Tourists will find no end of traditional Scottish clichés: whisky tastings, kilt shops, bagpipe-playing buskers, and gimmicky tours featuring Scotland's bloody history and ghost stories.

Edinburgh is two cities in one. The Old Town stretches along the Royal Mile, from the grand castle on top to the palace on the bottom. Along this colorful labyrinth of cobbled streets and narrow lanes, medieval skyscrapers stand shoulder to shoulder, hiding peaceful courtyards.

A few hundred yards north of the Old Town lies the New Town. It's a magnificent planned neighborhood (from the 1700s). Here, you'll enjoy upscale shops, broad boulevards, straight streets, square squares, circular circuses, and Georgian mansions decked out in Greek-style columns and statues.

Today's Edinburgh is big in banking, scientific research, and scholarship at its four universities. Since 1999, when Scotland regained a measure of self-rule, Edinburgh reassumed its place as home of the Scottish Parliament. The city hums with life. Students and professionals pack the pubs and art galleries. It's especially lively in August, when the Edinburgh Festival takes over the town. Historic, monumental, fun, and well organized, Edinburgh is a tourist's delight.

PLANNING YOUR TIME

While the major sights can be seen in a day, I'd give Edinburgh two days and three nights.

Day 1: Tour the castle, then consider catching a city bus tour for a one-hour loop (departing from a block below the castle at the Hub/Tolbooth Church; you could munch a sandwich from the top deck if you're into multitasking). Back near the castle, take my self-guided Royal Mile walk, stopping in at shops and museums that interest you (Gladstone's Land is tops). At the bottom of the Mile, consider visiting the Scottish Parliament, the Palace of Holyroodhouse, or both. If the weather's good, you could hike back to your B&B along the Salisbury Crags.

Day 2: Visit the National Museum of Scotland. After lunch (several great choices nearby, on Forrest Road), stroll through the Princes Street Gardens and the Scottish National Gallery. Then follow my self-guided walk through the New Town, visiting the Scottish National Portrait Gallery and the Georgian House—or squeeze in a quick tour of the good ship *Britannia* (check last entry time before you head out).

Evenings: Options include various "haunted Edinburgh" walks, literary pub crawls, or live music in pubs. Sadly, full-blown traditional folk performances are just about extinct, surviving only in excruciatingly schmaltzy variety shows put on for tour-bus groups. Perhaps the most authentic evening out is just settling down in a pub to sample the whisky and local beers while meeting the locals...and attempting to understand them through their thick Scottish accents (see "Nightlife in Edinburgh," page 105).

Orientation to Edinburgh

A VERBAL MAP

With 490,000 people (835,000 in the metro area), Edinburgh is Scotland's second-biggest city (after Glasgow). But the tourist's Edinburgh is compact: Old Town, New Town, and the Dalkeith Road B&B area.

Edinburgh's **Old Town** stretches across a ridgeline slung between two bluffs. From west to east, this "Royal Mile" runs from the Castle Rock—which is visible from anywhere—to the base of the 822-foot extinct volcano called Arthur's Seat. For visitors, this east-west axis is the center of the action. Just south of the Royal Mile are the university and the National Museum of Scotland; farther to the south is a handy B&B neighborhood that lines up along **Dalkeith Road.** North of the Royal Mile ridge is the **New Town,** a neighborhood of grid-planned streets and elegant Georgian buildings.

In the center of it all—in a drained lake bed between the Old and New Towns—sit the Princes Street Gardens park and Waverley Bridge, where you'll find the Waverley train station, TI, Princes Mall, bus info office (starting point for most city bus tours), Scottish National Gallery, and a covered dance-and-music pavilion.

TOURIST INFORMATION

The crowded TI is as central as can be, on the rooftop of the Princes Mall and Waverley train station (Mon-Sat 9:00-18:00, Sun 10:00-18:00, July-Aug daily until 19:00, tel. 0131-473-3868, www.visitscotland.com). While the staff is helpful, be warned that much of their information is skewed by tourism payola (and booking seats on bus tours seems to be a big priority). There's also a TI at the airport (tel. 0131-344-3120).

For more information than what's included in the TI's free map, buy the excellent *Collins Discovering Edinburgh* map (which comes with opinionated commentary and locates almost every major sight). If you're interested in evening music, ask for the free monthly entertainment *Gig Guide* or buy the more comprehensive entertainment listing, *The List.* Also consider buying Historic Scotland's Explorer Pass, which can save you some money if you visit the castles at both Edinburgh and Stirling (for details, see page 442).

ARRIVAL IN EDINBURGH

By Train: Arriving by train at Waverley Station puts you in the city center and below the TI. Taxis queue almost trackside (near platform 11); the ramp they come and go on leads to Waverley Bridge. From the station, follow *Way Out-1-Princes Street* signs and ride up several escalators to Princes Street. From here, the TI is to your left, and the city bus stop is two blocks to your right (for bus directions from here to my recommended B&Bs, see "Sleeping in Edinburgh," later).

By Bus: Scottish Citylink, Megabus, and National Express

Greater Edinburgh

To St. Andrews, Inverness & John O'Groats

To Culross

FIRTH OF FORTH BRIDGES

A-90

Firth of Forth

2 km
2 miles

ROYAL YACHT BRITANNIA

LEITH

M-90

QUEENSFERRY ROAD

A-902 Water of Leith

A-90

WAVERLY TRAIN STN.

To Falkirk & Stirling

M-9

AIRPORT

CORSTORPHINE ROAD

See Edinburgh detail maps

CENTER

Holyrood Park

Arthur's Seat

A-8

M-8

See Dalkeith Road detail map

DALKEITH ROAD

EDINBURGH

To Glasgow

A-720

A-71

To Berwick-upon-Tweed, Newcastle & Durham (England)

Water of Leith

A-70

HILLEND

A-720

MIDLOTHIAN SKI CENTRE

Pentland Hills Regional Park

A-702

A-701

ROSSLYN CHAPEL

Roslin

To A-74, Carlisle & Lake District (England)

buses use the bus station (with luggage lockers) in the New Town, two blocks north of the train station on St. Andrew Square.

By Plane: Edinburgh's slingshot of an airport is located eight miles northwest of the center (tel. 0844-481-8989, www .edinburghairport.com).

Taxis between the airport and city center are pricey (£20-25, 20 minutes to downtown or Dalkeith Road). Fortunately, the airport is well connected to central Edinburgh by tram and bus. Just follow signs outside; the tram tracks are straight ahead, and the bus stop is to the right, along the main road in front of the terminal. **Trams** make several stops in town, including along Princes Street and at St. Andrew Square (£5, 6/hour, 35 minutes, early morning until 23:30, www.edinburghtrams.com). The Lothian **Airlink bus #100** drops you at Waverley Bridge (£4.50, £7.50 round-trip,

6/hour, 30 minutes, buses run all day and 2/hour through the night, tel. 0131/555-6363, www.flybybus.com). Whether you take the tram or bus to the center, to continue on to my recommended B&Bs near Dalkeith Road, you can either take a taxi (about £7), or hop on a city bus (£1.50; see "Sleeping in Edinburgh," later).

To get from the Dalkeith Road B&Bs *to* the Airlink or tram stops downtown, you can take a taxi...or ride a city bus to North Bridge, turn left at the grand Balmoral Hotel, and walk a short distance down Princes Street. Turn right up St. Andrew Street to catch the tram at St. Andrew Square, or continue up to the next bridge, Waverley, for the Airlink bus.

By Car: If you're arriving from the north, rather than drive through downtown Edinburgh to my recommended B&Bs, circle the city on the A-720 City Bypass road. Approaching Edinburgh on the M-9, take the M-8 (direction: Glasgow) and quickly get onto the A-720 City Bypass (direction: Edinburgh South). After four miles, you'll hit a roundabout. Ignore signs directing you into *Edinburgh North* and stay on the A-720 for 10 more miles to the next and last roundabout, named *Sheriffhall*. Exit the roundabout at the first left *(A-7 Edinburgh)*. From here it's four miles to the B&B neighborhood. After a while, the A-7 becomes Dalkeith Road (you'll pass the Royal Infirmary hospital complex). If you see the huge Royal Commonwealth Pool, you've gone a couple of blocks too far (avoid this by referring to the map on page 110).

If you're driving in on the A-68 from the south, first follow signs for *Edinburgh South & West* (A-720), then exit at *A-7(N)/Edinburgh* and follow the directions above.

HELPFUL HINTS

Sunday Activities: Many Royal Mile sights close on Sunday (except in Aug), but other major sights and shops are open. Sunday is a good day to catch a guided walking tour along the Royal Mile or a city bus tour (buses go faster in light traffic). The slopes of Arthur's Seat are lively with hikers and picnickers on weekends.

Festivals: August is a crowded, popular month to visit Edinburgh thanks to the multiple festivals hosted here, including the official Edinburgh International Festival, the Fringe Festival, and the Military Tattoo. Book ahead for hotels, events, and restaurant dinners if you'll be visiting in August, and expect to pay significantly more for your room. Many museums and shops have extended hours in August. For more festival details, see page 490.

Internet Access: Virtually all B&Bs and coffee shops offer free Wi-Fi, and all local public transit has fast, free Wi-Fi on board.

Baggage Storage: At the train station, you'll find pricey, high-

EDINBURGH

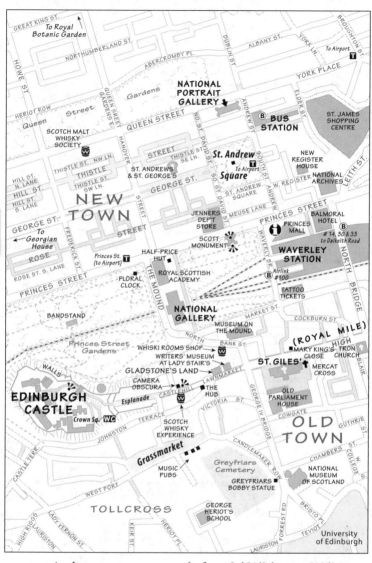

security luggage storage near platform 2 (£6/3 hours, £10/24 hours, daily 7:00-23:00). There are also lockers at the bus station on St. Andrew Square, just two blocks north of the train station.

Laundry: The **Ace Cleaning Centre** launderette is located near my recommended Dalkeith Road B&Bs, where they'll collect and drop off your laundry for a small extra fee (self-serve or full-serve, Mon-Fri 8:00-20:00, Sat 9:00-17:00, Sun 10:00-16:00,

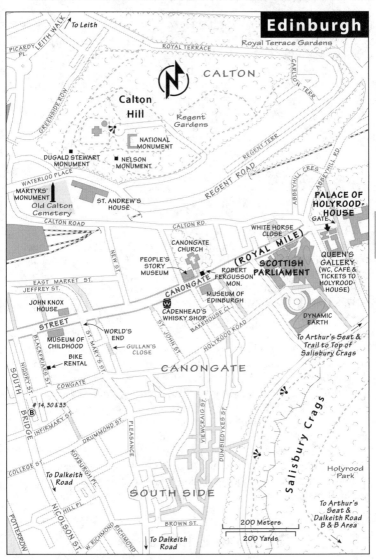

Edinburgh

To Leith

LEITH WALK

PICARDY PL.

Royal Terrace Gardens

ROYAL TERRACE

CALTON

GREENSIDE ROW

Calton Hill

Regent Gardens

NATIONAL MONUMENT

DUGALD STEWART MONUMENT

NELSON MONUMENT

WATERLOO PLACE

REGENT TERR.

REGENT ROAD

ABBEYHILL CRES.

ABBEYHILL RD.

MARTYRS' MONUMENT

Old Calton Cemetery

ST. ANDREW'S HOUSE

CARLTON TERR.

PALACE OF HOLYROOD-HOUSE

GATE

CALTON ROAD

CALTON RD.

WHITE HORSE CLOSE

QUEEN'S GALLERY (WC, CAFE & TICKETS TO HOLYROOD-HOUSE)

NEW ST.

CANONGATE CHURCH

(ROYAL MILE)

SCOTTISH PARLIAMENT

PEOPLE'S STORY MUSEUM

ROBERT FERGUSSON MON.

EAST MARKET ST.

JEFFREY ST.

CANONGATE

MUSEUM OF EDINBURGH

JOHN KNOX HOUSE

CADENHEAD'S WHISKY SHOP

BAKEHOUSE CL.

DYNAMIC EARTH

STREET

ST. MARY'S ST.

ST. JOHN ST.

HOLYROOD ROAD

To Arthur's Seat & Trail to Top of Salisbury Crags

BLACKFRIARS ST.

MUSEUM OF CHILDHOOD

WORLD'S END

GULLAN'S CLOSE

CANONGATE

BIKE RENTAL

NIDDRY ST.

COWGATE

VIEWCRAIG ST.

DUMBIEDYKES ST.

Salisbury Crags

SOUTH BRIDGE

14, 30 & 33

INFIRMARY ST.

DRUMMOND ST.

PLEASANCE

Holyrood Park

COLLEGE ST.

ROXBURGH PL.

To Dalkeith Road

SOUTH SIDE

To Arthur's Seat & Dalkeith Road B & B Area

POTTERROW

NICOLSON ST.

HILL PL.

W. RICHMOND

RICHMOND

BROWN ST.

To Dalkeith Road

200 Meters

200 Yards

EDINBURGH

along bus route to city center at 13 South Clerk Street, opposite Queens Hall, tel. 0131/667-0549).

Bike Rental: The laid-back crew at **Cycle Scotland** offers bike tours and happily recommends good bike routes (£15/3 hours, £20/day, daily 10:00-18:00, just off Royal Mile at 29 Blackfriars Street, mobile 07796-886-899, www.cyclescotland.co.uk).

Car Rental: These places have offices both in the town center and at the airport: **Avis** (24 East London Street, tel. 0844-544-6059, airport tel. 0844-544-6004), **Europcar** (Waverley Station, near platform 2, tel. 0871-384-3453, airport tel. 0871-384-3406), **Hertz** (10 Picardy Place, tel. 0843-309-3026, airport tel. 0843-309-3025), and **Budget** (24 East London Street, tel. 0844-544-9064, airport tel. 0844-544-4605). Some downtown offices close or have reduced hours on Sunday, but the airport locations tend to be open daily. If you plan to rent a car, pick it up on your way out of Edinburgh—you won't need it in town.

Dress for the Weather: Weather blows in and out—bring your sweater and be prepared for rain. Locals say the bad weather is one of the disadvantages of living so close to England.

Updates to This Book: For the latest, see www.ricksteves.com/update.

GETTING AROUND EDINBURGH

Many of Edinburgh's sights are within walking distance of one another, but **buses** come in handy—especially if you're staying at a B&B in the Dalkeith Road area. Double-decker buses come with fine views upstairs. It's easy once you get the hang of it: Buses come by frequently (screens at bus stops show wait times) and have free, fast Wi-Fi on board. The only hassle is that you must pay with exact change (£1.50/ride, £4/all-day pass). As you board, tell your driver where you're going (or just say "single ticket") and drop your change into the box. Ping the bell as you near your stop. Buses run from about 6:00 (9:00 on Sun) to 23:00. You can pick up a route map at the TI or at the transit office at Old Town end of Waverley Bridge (tel. 0131/555-6363, www.lothianbuses.com). Edinburgh's single **tram** line (also £1.50/ride) is designed more for locals than tourists; it's most useful for reaching the airport (described earlier).

The 1,300 **taxis** cruising Edinburgh's streets are easy to flag down (£2.10 to start, then about £2.20/mile, rates go up after 18:00 and on weekends; a ride between downtown and the B&B neighborhood costs about £7). They can turn on a dime, so hail them in either direction.

Tours in Edinburgh

Royal Mile Walking Tours

Walking tours are an Edinburgh specialty; you'll see groups trailing entertaining guides all over town. Below I've listed good all-purpose walks; for **literary pub crawls** and **ghost tours**, see "Nightlife in Edinburgh" on page 105.

Edinburgh Tour Guides offers a good historical walk (without all the ghosts and goblins). Their Royal Mile tour is a gentle two-hour downhill stroll from the castle to the palace (£15; daily at 9:30 and 19:00; meet outside Gladstone's Land, near the top of the Royal Mile—see map on page 37, must reserve ahead, mobile 0785-888-0072, www.edinburghtourguides.com, info@edinburghtourguides.com).

Mercat Tours offers a 1.5-hour "Secrets of the Royal Mile" walk that's more entertaining than intellectual (£12; £17 more for optional, 45-minute guided Edinburgh Castle visit; daily at 13:30, leaves from Mercat Cross on the Royal Mile, tel. 0131/225-5445, www.mercattours.com). The guides, who enjoy making a short story long, ignore the big sights and take you behind the scenes with piles of barely historical gossip, bully-pulpit Scottish pride, and fun but forgettable trivia. They also offer several ghost tours, as well as tours that take you to the 18th-century underground vaults on the southern slope of the Royal Mile.

The **Voluntary Guides Association** offers free two-hour walks, but only during the Edinburgh Festival. You don't need a reservation, but it's a good idea to confirm the details on their website (daily at about 10:00 and 14:00, generally depart from City Chambers across from St. Giles' Cathedral on the Royal Mile, www.edinburghfestivalguides.org). You can also hire their guides (for a small fee) for private tours outside of festival time.

Blue Badge Local Guides

The following guides charge similar prices and offer half-day and full-day tours: **Jean Blair** (a delightful teacher and guide, £180/day, £420/day with car, mobile 0798-957-0287, www.travelthroughscotland.com, jean@travelthroughscotland.com); **Sergio La Spina** (an Argentinean who adopted Edinburgh as his hometown more than 20 years ago, £195/day, tel. 0131/664-1731, mobile 0797-330-6579, sergiolaspina@aol.com); **Ken Hanley** (who wears his kilt as if pants don't exist, £100/half-day, £175/day, extra charge if he uses his car—seats up to six, tel. 0131/666-1944, mobile 0771-034-2044, www.small-world-tours.co.uk, kennethhanley@me.com); and **Liz Everett** (£145/half-day, £190/day, mobile 07821-683-837, liz.everett@live.co.uk).

Edinburgh Bus Tours

Four different one-hour hop-on, hop-off bus tour routes, all run by the same company, circle the town center, stopping at the major sights. **MacTours** (vintage red-and-yellow buses) and **Edinburgh Tour** (green buses) run nearly identical routes that focus on the city center, with live guides. The other options— **City Sightseeing** (red buses, focuses on Old Town) and **Majestic Tour**

Edinburgh at a Glance

▲▲▲**Royal Mile** Historic road—good for walking—stretching from the castle down to the palace, lined with museums, pubs, and shops. **Hours:** Always open, but best during business hours, with walking tours daily. See page 33.

▲▲▲**Edinburgh Castle** Iconic hilltop fort and royal residence complete with crown jewels, Romanesque chapel, memorial, and fine military museum. **Hours:** Daily April-Sept 9:30-18:00, Oct-March 9:30-17:00. See page 56.

▲▲▲**National Museum of Scotland** Intriguing, well-displayed artifacts from prehistoric times to the 20th century. **Hours:** Daily 10:00-17:00. See page 78.

▲▲**Gladstone's Land** Seventeenth-century Royal Mile merchant's residence. **Hours:** Daily July-Aug 10:00-18:30, April-June and Sept-Oct 10:00-17:00, closed Nov-March. See page 67.

▲▲**St. Giles' Cathedral** Preaching grounds of Calvinist John Knox, with spectacular organ, Neo-Gothic chapel, and distinctive crown spire. **Hours:** May-Sept Mon-Fri 9:00-19:00, Sat 9:00-17:00; Oct-April Mon-Sat 9:00-17:00; Sun 13:00-17:00 year-round. See page 68.

▲▲**Scottish Parliament Building** Striking headquarters for parliament, which returned to Scotland in 1999. **Hours:** Sept-June (when parliament is in session)—Mon and Fri-Sat 10:00-17:00, Tue-Thu 9:00-18:30; July-Aug and holidays (when parliament is in recess)—Mon-Sat 10:00-17:00; closed Sun year-round. See page 74.

▲▲**Palace of Holyroodhouse** The Queen's splendid home away from home, with lavish rooms, 12th-century abbey, and gallery with rotating exhibits. **Hours:** Daily April-Oct 9:30-18:00, Nov-March until 16:30, closed during royal visits. See page 75.

▲▲**Scottish National Gallery** Choice sampling of European masters and Scotland's finest. **Hours:** Daily 10:00-17:00, Thu until 19:00; longer hours in Aug: Sun-Wed 10:00-18:00, Thu-Sat 10:00-19:00. See page 82.

(blue-and-yellow buses, includes a stop at the *Britannia* and Royal Botanic Garden)—have recorded commentary. You can pay for just one tour (£14/24 hours), but most people pay a few pounds more for a ticket covering all four buses (£20). Each of the four lines runs all day long (April-Oct roughly 9:30-19:00, shorter off-season; every

▲▲**Scottish National Portrait Gallery** Beautifully displayed *Who's Who* of Scottish history. **Hours:** Daily 10:00-17:00, Thu until 19:00. See page 87.

▲▲**Georgian House** Intimate peek at upper-crust life in the late 1700s. **Hours:** Daily April-Oct 10:00-17:00, July-Aug until 18:00, March and Nov 11:00-16:00; may be open Thu-Sun in Dec, otherwise closed Dec-Feb. See page 90.

▲▲**Royal Yacht *Britannia*** Ship for the royal family with a history of distinguished passengers, a 15-minute trip out of town. **Hours:** Daily April-Sept 9:30-16:30, Oct 9:30-16:00, Nov-March 10:00-15:30 (these are last entry times). See page 90.

▲**Scotch Whisky Experience** Gimmicky but fun and educational introduction to Scotland's most famous beverage. **Hours:** Generally daily 10:00-18:00. See page 66.

▲**The Real Mary King's Close** Tour of underground street and houses last occupied in the 17th century, viewable by guided tour. **Hours:** April-Oct daily 10:00-22:00; Nov-March Sun-Thu until 17:00, Fri-Sat until 21:00 (these are last tour times). See page 72.

▲**Museum of Childhood** Five stories of historic fun. **Hours:** Mon-Sat 10:00-17:00, Sun 12:00-17:00. See page 73.

▲**People's Story Museum** Everyday life from the 18th to 20th century. **Hours:** Mon-Sat 10:00-17:00, closed Sun except during Festival 12:00-17:00. See page 74.

▲**Museum of Edinburgh** Historic mementos, from the original National Covenant inscribed on animal skin to early golf balls. **Hours:** Mon-Sat 10:00-17:00, closed Sun except during Festival 12:00-17:00. See page 74.

▲**Rosslyn Chapel** Small 15th-century church chock-full of intriguing carvings. **Hours:** Mon-Sat 9:30-18:00, until 17:00 Oct-March, Sun 12:00-16:45 year-round. See page 92.

EDINBURGH

10-15 minutes, buy tickets on board, tel. 0131/220-0770, www.edinburghtour.com). On sunny days the buses go topless, but come with increased traffic noise and exhaust fumes. For £50, the Royal Edinburgh Ticket covers two days of unlimited travel on all four tour buses, as well as admission (and line-skipping privileges) at

Edinburgh Castle, the Palace of Holyroodhouse, and the *Britan-nia*. This could save you a few pounds if you plan to visit all these sights and use a tour bus both days (www.royaledinburghticket. co.uk).

Weekend Tour Packages for Students

Andy Steves (Rick's son) runs **Weekend Student Adventures** (WSA Europe), offering three-day and longer guided and unguid-ed packages—including accommodations, sightseeing, and unique local experiences—for student travelers in top European cities, in-cluding Edinburgh (guided trips from €199, see www.wsaeurope. com).

DAY TRIPS FROM EDINBURGH

Many companies run a variety of day trips to regional sights, as well as multiday and themed itineraries. (Several of the private guides listed earlier have cars, too.)

By far the most popular tour is the all-day **Highlands trip.** The standard Highlands tour gives those with limited time a chance to experience the wonders of Scotland's wild and legend-soaked Highlands in a single long day (about £40-50, roughly 8:00-20:30). Itineraries vary but you'll generally visit the vast and brutal Rannoch Moor; Glencoe, still evocative with memories of the clan massacre; views of Britain's highest mountain, Ben Nevis; Fort Au-gustus on Loch Ness (some tours have a 1.5-hour stop here with an optional boat ride); and pause for a 45-minute tea or pub break in Pitlochry. You also learn a bit about Edinburgh as you drive in and out. To save time, look for a tour that gives you a short glimpse of Loch Ness rather than driving its entire length or doing a boat trip. (Once you've seen a little of it, you've seen the whole shebang.)

Larger outfits, typically using bigger buses, include **Timber-bush Highland Tours** (tel. 0131/226-6066, www.timberbushtours. com) and **Gray Line** (tel. 0131/555-5558, www.graylinescotland. com). Other companies pride themselves on keeping group sizes small, with 16-seat minibuses; these include **Rabbie's Trail Burn-ers** (tel. 0131/226-3133, www.rabbies.com) and **Heart of Scot-land Tours: *The Wee Red Bus*** (10 percent Rick Steves discount on full-priced day tours—mention when booking, occasionally can-celed off-season if too few sign up—leave a contact number, tel. 0131/228-2888, www.heartofscotlandtours.co.uk, run by Nick Roche). For young backpackers, **Haggis Adventures** runs over-night trips of up to 10 days (office at 60 High Street, tel. 0131/557-9393, www.haggisadventures.com).

At **Discreet Scotland**, Matthew Wight and his partners specialize in tours of greater Edinburgh and Scotland in spacious

SUVs—good for families (£360/9 hours, mobile 0798-941-6990, www.discreetscotland.com).

Edinburgh Walks

I've outlined two walks in Edinburgh: along the Royal Mile, and through the New Town. Many of the sights we'll pass on these walks are described in more detail later, under "Sights in Edinburgh."

THE ROYAL MILE

The Royal Mile is one of Europe's most interesting historic walks—it's worth ▲▲▲. The following self-guided stroll is also available as a 🎧 downloadable Rick Steves audio tour; see page 10.

EDINBURGH

Overview

Start at Edinburgh Castle at the top and amble down to the Palace of Holyroodhouse. Along the way, the street changes names—Castlehill, Lawnmarket, High Street, and Canongate—but it's a straight, downhill shot totaling just over one mile. And nearly every step is packed with shops, cafés, and lanes leading to tiny squares.

The city of Edinburgh was born on the easily defended rock at the top, where the castle stands today. Celtic tribes (and maybe the Romans) once occupied this site.

As the town grew, it spilled downhill along the sloping ridge that became the Royal Mile. Because this strip of land is so narrow, there was no place to build but up. So in medieval times, it was densely packed with multistory "tenements"—large edifices under one roof that housed a number of tenants.

As you walk, you'll be tracing the growth of the city—its birth atop Castle Hill, its Old Town heyday in the 1600s, its expansion in the 1700s into the Georgian New Town (leaving the old quarter an overcrowded, disease-ridden Victorian slum), and on to the 21st century at the modern Scottish parliament building (2004).

In parts, the Royal Mile feels like one long Scottish shopping mall, selling all manner of kitschy souvenirs (known locally as "tartan tat"), shortbread, and whisky. But the streets are also packed with history, and if you push past the postcard racks into one of the many side alleys, you can still find a few surviving rough edges of the old city. Despite the drizzle, be sure to look up—spires, carvings, and towering Gothic "skyscrapers" give this city its unique urban identity.

This walk covers the Royal Mile's landmarks, but skips the many museums and indoor attractions along the way. These and other sights are described in walking order under "Sights in Edinburgh" on page 56. You can stay focused on the walk (which takes about 1.5 hours, without entering sights), then return later to visit the various indoor attractions; or review the sight descriptions beforehand and pop into those that interest you as you pass them.

• *We'll start at the Castle Esplanade, the big parking lot at the entrance to...*

❶ Edinburgh Castle

Edinburgh was born on the bluff—a big rock—where the castle now stands. Since before recorded history, people have lived on this strategic, easily defended perch.

The **castle** is an imposing symbol of Scottish independence. Flanking the entryway are statues of the fierce warriors who battled English invaders, William Wallace (on the right) and Robert the Bruce (left). Between them is the Scottish motto, *Nemo me impune lacessit*—roughly, "No one messes with me and gets away with it." (For a self-guided tour of Edinburgh Castle, see page 57.)

The esplanade—built as a military parade ground (1816)—is now the site of the annual Military Tattoo. This spectacular massing of regimental bands fills the square nightly for most of August. Fans watch from temporary bleacher seats to see kilt-wearing bagpipers marching against the spectacular backdrop of the castle. TV crews broadcast the spectacle to all corners of the globe.

When the bleachers aren't up, there are fine views in both directions from the esplanade. Facing north, you'll see the body of water called the Firth of Forth, and Fife beyond that. (The Firth of Forth is the estuary where the Forth River flows into the North Sea.) Still facing north, find the lacy spire of the Scott Memorial and two Neoclassical buildings housing art galleries. Beyond them, the stately buildings of Edinburgh's New Town rise. (For a self-guided walk of the New Town, see page 48.) Panning to the right, find the Nelson Monument and some faux Greek ruins atop Calton Hill (see page 95).

The city's many bluffs, crags, and ridges were built up by volcanoes, then carved down by glaciers—a city formed in "fire and ice," as the locals say. So, during the Ice Age, as a river of glaciers swept in from the west (behind today's castle), it ran into the super-hard volcanic basalt of Castle Rock and flowed around it, cutting valleys

The Kilt

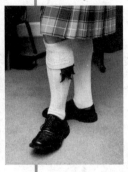

The kilt, Scotland's national dress, is intimately tied in with the country's history. The six-foot-by-nine-foot bolt of fabric originated in the 1500s as a multipurpose robe, toga, tent, poncho, and ground cloth. A wearer would lay it on the ground to scrunch up pleats, then wrap it around the waist and belt it. Extra fabric was thrown over the shoulder or tucked into the belt, creating both a rakish sash and a rucksack-like pouch.

The kilt was standard Highlands dress and became a patriotic statement during conflicts with England. After the tragic-for-Scotland Battle of Culloden in 1746, the British government wanted to end the Scottish clan system. Wearing the kilt, speaking Gaelic, and playing the bagpipes were all outlawed.

In 1782, kilts were permitted again, but had taken on an unrefined connotation, so many Scots no longer wanted to wear one. This changed in 1822 when King George IV visited Edinburgh, wearing a kilt to send the message that he was king of Scotland. Scottish aristocrats were charmed by the king's pageantry, and the kilt was in vogue once more.

During the king's visit, Sir Walter Scott organized a Highland festival that also helped change the image of traditional Scottish culture, giving it a newfound respectability. A generation later, Queen Victoria raised the image of Scottish culture even higher. She loved Scotland and wallpapered her palace at Balmoral with tartan patterns.

The colors and patterns of the original kilts were determined by what dyes were available and who wove them. Because members of one clan tended to live in the same areas, they often wore similar patterns—but the colors were muted, and the patterns weren't necessarily designed to represent a single clan. The "clan tartans" you'll see in Scottish souvenir shops—with a specific, brightly colored design for each family—started as a scam by fabric salesmen in Victorian times. Since then, tartanry has been embraced as if it were historic. (By the way, Scots use these key terms differently than Americans do: "Tartan" is the pattern itself, while "plaid" is the piece of cloth worn over the shoulder with a kilt.)

As Highlanders moved to cities and took jobs in factories, the smaller kilt, or philibeg, replaced the traditional kilt, which could become dangerously snagged by modern machinery. Half the weight of old-style kilts, the practical philibeg is more like a wraparound skirt.

Other kilt-related gear includes the sporran, the leather pouch worn around the waist, and the *sgian dubh* ("black knife"), the short blade worn in the top of the sock. If you're in the market for a kilt, see page 102.

on either side and leaving a tail that became the Royal Mile you're about to walk.

At the bottom of the esplanade, where the square hits the road, look left to find a plaque on the wall above the tiny **witches' well** (now a planter). This memorializes 300 women who were accused of witchcraft and burned here. Below was the Nor' Loch, the swampy lake where those accused of witchcraft (mostly women) were tested: Bound up, they were dropped into the lake. If they sank and drowned, they were innocent. If they floated, they were guilty, and were burned here in front of the castle, providing the city folk a nice afternoon out. The plaque shows two witches: one good and one bad. Tickle the serpent's snout to sympathize with the witches. (I just made that up.)

• Start walking down the Royal Mile. The first block is a street called...

❷ Castlehill

You're immediately in the tourist hubbub. The big tank-like building on your left was the Old Town's **reservoir.** You'll see the wellheads it served all along this walk. While it once held 1.5 million gallons of water, today it's filled with the touristy Tartan Weaving Mill and Exhibition. While it's interesting to see the mill at work,

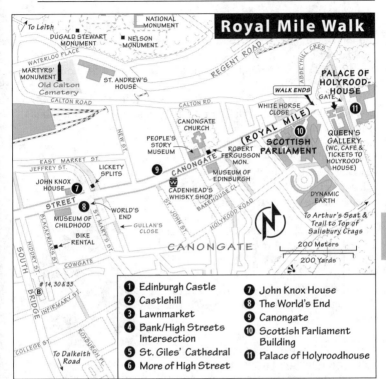

Royal Mile Walk

To Leith
NATIONAL MONUMENT
DUGALD STEWART MONUMENT
NELSON MONUMENT
WATERLOO PLACE
REGENT ROAD
ABBEYHILL CRES.
PALACE OF HOLYROOD-HOUSE
MARTYRS' MONUMENT
Old Calton Cemetery
ST. ANDREW'S HOUSE
CALTON ROAD
CALTON RD.
WALK ENDS
GATE
❶❶
CALTON ROAD
NEW ST.
CANONGATE CHURCH
WHITE HORSE CLOSE
(ROYAL MILE)
❿
SCOTTISH PARLIAMENT
QUEEN'S GALLERY (WC, CAFE & TICKETS TO HOLYROOD-HOUSE)
EAST MARKET ST.
JEFFREY ST.
LICKETY SPLITS
PEOPLE'S STORY MUSEUM
CANONGATE
❾
ROBERT FERGUSSON MON.
MUSEUM OF EDINBURGH
JOHN KNOX HOUSE
❼
CADENHEAD'S WHISKY SHOP
BAKEHOUSE CL.
DYNAMIC EARTH
STREET
❽
WORLD'S END
ST. MARY'S ST.
GULLAN'S CLOSE
ST. JOHN ST.
HOLYROOD ROAD
To Arthur's Seat & Trail to Top of Salisbury Crags
BLACKFRIARS ST.
MUSEUM OF CHILDHOOD
BIKE RENTAL
CANONGATE
200 Meters
200 Yards
NIDDRY ST.
COWGATE
SOUTH BRIDGE
14, 30 & 33
❶ B
INFIRMARY ST.
COLLEGE ST.
ROXBURGH PL.
To Dalkeith Road

❶ Edinburgh Castle
❷ Castlehill
❸ Lawnmarket
❹ Bank/High Streets Intersection
❺ St. Giles' Cathedral
❻ More of High Street
❼ John Knox House
❽ The World's End
❾ Canongate
❿ Scottish Parliament Building
❶❶ Palace of Holyroodhouse

EDINBURGH

you'll have to twist your way down through several floors of tartanry and Chinese-produced Scottish kitsch to reach it at the bottom level.

The black-and-white tower ahead on the left has entertained visitors since the 1850s with its **camera obscura,** a darkened room where a mirror and a series of lenses capture live images of the city surroundings outside. (Giggle at the funny mirrors as you walk fatly by. Across the street, filling the old Castlehill Primary School, is a gimmicky-if-intoxicating whisky-sampling exhibit called the **Scotch Whisky Experience** (a.k.a. "Malt Disney"). Both of these are described later, under "Sights in Edinburgh."

• *Just ahead, in front of the church with the tall, lacy spire, is the old market square known as...*

❸ Lawnmarket

During the Royal Mile's heyday, in the 1600s, this intersection was bigger and served as a market for fabric (especially "lawn," a linen-like cloth). The market would fill this space with bustle, hustle, and lots of commerce. The round white hump in the middle of the roundabout is all that remains of the official weighing beam called the Butter Tron—where all goods sold were weighed for honesty and tax purposes.

Towering above Lawnmarket, with the tallest spire in the city, is the former **Tolbooth Church.** This impressive Neo-Gothic structure (1844) is now home to the Hub, Edinburgh's festival-ticket and information center. The world-famous Edinburgh Festival fills the month of August with cultural action. The various festivals feature classical music, traditional and fringe theater (especially comedy), art, books, and more. Drop inside the building to get festival info (see also page 96). This is a handy stop for its WC, café, and free Wi-Fi.

In the 1600s, this—along with the next stretch, called High Street—was the city's main street. At that time, Edinburgh was bursting with breweries, printing presses, and banks. Tens of thousands of citizens were squeezed into the narrow confines of the Old Town. Here on this ridge, they built **tenements** (multiple-unit residences) similar to the more recent ones you see today. These tenements, rising 10 stories and more, were some of the tallest domestic buildings in Europe. The living arrangements shocked class-conscious English visitors to Edinburgh because the tenements were occupied by rich and poor alike—usually the poor in the cellars and attics, and the rich in the middle floors.

• *Continue a half-block down the Mile.*

Gladstone's Land (at #477b, on the left), a surviving original tenement, was acquired by a wealthy merchant in 1617. Stand in front of the building and look up at this centuries-old skyscraper. This design was standard for its time: a shop or shops on the

ground floor, with columns and an arcade, and residences on the floors above. Because window glass was expensive, the lower halves of window openings were made of cheaper wood, which swung out like shutters for ventilation—and were convenient for tossing out garbage. (For more on Gladstone's, see page 67.)

Notice the snoozing pig by the front door. Just as every house has a vacuum cleaner today, in the good old days a snorting rubbish collector was a standard feature of any well-equipped house. Out front, you may also see trainers with live birds of prey. While this is mostly just a fun way to show off for tourists (and raise donations for the bird of prey center), docents explain the connection: The building's owner was named Thomas Gledstanes—and *gled* is the Gaelic word for "hawk."

Branching off the spine of the Royal Mile are a number of narrow alleyways that go by various local names. A "wynd" (rhymes with "kind") is a narrow, winding lane. A "pend" is an arched gateway. "Gate" is from an Old Norse word for street. And a "close" is a tiny alley between two buildings (originally with a door that "closed" at night). A "close" usually leads to a "court," or courtyard.

To explore one of these alleyways, head into **Lady Stair's Close** (on the left, 10 steps downhill from Gladstone's Land). This alley pops out in a small courtyard, where you'll find the **Writers' Museum** (described on page 67). It's well worth a visit for fans of the city's holy trinity of writers (Robert Burns, Sir Walter Scott, and Robert Louis Stevenson), but it's also a free glimpse of what a typical home might have looked like in the 1600s. Burns actually lived for a while in this neighborhood, in 1786, when he first arrived in Edinburgh.

Opposite Gladstone's Land (at #322), another close leads to **Riddle's Court.** Wander through here and imagine Edinburgh in the 17th and 18th centuries, when tourists came here to marvel at its skyscrapers. Some 40,000 people were jammed into the few blocks between here and the World's End pub (which we'll reach soon). Visualize the labyrinthine maze of the old city, with people scurrying through these back alleyways, buying and selling, and popping into taverns.

No city in Europe was as densely populated—or perhaps as filthy. Without modern hygiene, it was a living hell of smoke, stench, and noise, with the constant threat of fire, collapse, and disease. The dirt streets were soiled with sewage from bedpans emptied out windows. By the 1700s, the Old Town was rife with poverty and cholera outbreaks. The smoky home fires rising from tenements and the infamous smell (or "reek" in Scottish) that wafted across the city gave it a nickname that sticks today: "Auld Reekie."

• *Return to the Royal Mile and continue down it a few steps to take in some sights at the...*

❹ Bank/High Streets Intersection

A number of sights cluster here, where Lawnmarket changes its name to High Street and intersects with Bank Street and George IV Bridge.

EDINBURGH

Begin with **Deacon Brodie's Tavern.** Read the "Doctor Jekyll and Mr. Hyde" story of this pub's notorious namesake on the wall facing Bank Street. Then, to see his spooky split personality, check out both sides of the hanging signpost. Brodie—a pillar of the community by day but a burglar by night—epitomizes the divided personality of 1700s Edinburgh. It was a rich, productive city—home to great philosophers and scientists, who actively contributed to the Enlightenment. Meanwhile, the Old Town was riddled with crime and squalor. The city was scandalized when a respected surgeon—driven by a passion for medical research and needing corpses—was accused of colluding with two lowlifes, named Burke and Hare, to acquire freshly murdered corpses for dissection. (In the

next century, in the late 1800s, novelist Robert Louis Stevenson would capture the dichotomy of Edinburgh's rich-poor society in his *Strange Case of Dr. Jekyll and Mr. Hyde.*)

In the late 1700s, Edinburgh's upper class moved out of the Old Town into a planned community called the New Town (a quarter-mile north of here). Eventually, most tenements were torn down and replaced with newer **Victorian buildings.** You'll see some at this intersection.

Look left down Bank Street to the green-domed **Bank of Scotland.** This was the headquarters of the bank, which had practiced modern capitalist financing since 1695. The building now houses the Museum on the Mound, a free exhibit on banking history (see page 67), and it's also the Scottish headquarters for Lloyds Banking Group—which swallowed up the Bank of Scotland after the financial crisis of 2008.

If you detour left down Bank Street toward the bank, you'll find the recommended **Whiski Rooms Shop.** If you head in the opposite direction, down George IV Bridge, you'll reach some recommended eateries (The Elephant House and The Outsider), as well as the excellent **National Museum of Scotland,** the famous Greyfriars Bobby statue, restaurant-lined Forrest Road, and photogenic Victoria Street, which leads to the pub-lined Grassmarket square (all described later in this chapter).

Otherwise, continue along the Royal Mile. As you walk, be careful crossing the streets along the Mile. Edinburgh drivers—especially cabbies—have a reputation for being impatient with jaywalking tourists. Notice and heed the pedestrian crossing signals, which don't always turn at the same time as the car signals.

Across the street from Deacon Brodie's Tavern is a seated green statue of hometown boy **David Hume** (1711-1776)—one of the most influential thinkers not only of Scotland, but in all of Western philosophy. The atheistic Hume was one of the tower-

ing figures of the Scottish Enlightenment of the mid-1700s. Thinkers and scientists were using the experimental method to challenge and investigate everything, including religion. Hume questioned cause and effect in thought puzzles such as this: We can see that when one billiard ball strikes another, the second one moves, but how do we know the collision "caused" the movement? Notice his shiny toe: People on their way to trial (in the high court just behind the statue) or students on their way to exams (in the nearby university) rub it for good luck.

Follow David Hume's gaze to the opposite corner, where a **brass H** in the pavement marks the site of the last public execution in Edinburgh in 1864. Deacon Brodie himself would have been hung about here (in 1788, on a gallows whose design he had helped to improve—smart guy).

• *From the brass H, continue down the Royal Mile, pausing just before the church square at a stone wellhead with the pyramid cap.*

All along the Royal Mile, **wellheads** like this (from 1835) provided townsfolk with water in the days before buildings had plumbing. This neighborhood well was served by the reservoir up at the castle. Imagine long lines of people in need of water standing here, gossiping and sharing the news. Eventually buildings were retrofitted with water pipes—the ones you see running along building exteriors.

• *Ahead of you (past the Victorian statue of some duke), embedded in the pavement near the street, is a big heart.*

The **Heart of Midlothian** marks the spot of the city's 15th-century municipal building and jail. In times past, in a nearby open space, criminals were hanged, traitors were decapitated, and witches were burned. Citizens hated the rough justice doled out here. Locals still spit on the heart in the pavement. Go ahead...do as the locals do—land one right in the heart of the heart. By the way, Edinburgh has two soccer teams—Heart of Midlothian (known as "Hearts") and Hibernian ("Hibs"). If you're a Hibs fan, spit again.

• *Make your way to the entrance of the church.*

❺ St. Giles' Cathedral

This is the flagship of the Church of Scotland (Scotland's largest denomination)—called the "Mother Church of Presbyterianism."

The interior serves as a kind of Scottish Westminster Abbey, filled with monuments, statues, plaques, and stained-glass windows dedicated to great Scots and moments in history.

A church has stood on this spot since 854, though this structure is an architectural hodgepodge, dating mostly from the 15th through 19th century. In the 16th century, St. Giles' was a kind of national stage on which the drama of the Reformation was played out. The reformer John Knox (1514-1572) was the preacher here. His fiery sermons helped turn once-Catholic Edinburgh into a bastion of Protestantism. During the Scottish Reformation, St. Giles' was transformed from a Catholic cathedral to a Presbyterian church. The spacious interior is well worth a visit, and described in my self-guided tour on page 68.

• *Facing the church entrance, curl around its right side, into a parking lot.*

Sights Around St. Giles'

The grand building across the parking lot from St. Giles' is the **Old Parliament House.** Since the 13th century, the king had ruled a rubber-stamp parliament of nobles and bishops. But the Protestant Reformation promoted democracy, and the parliament gained real power. From the early 1600s until 1707, this building evolved to become the seat of a true parliament of elected officials. That came to an end in 1707, when Scotland signed an Act of Union, joining what's known today as the United Kingdom and giving up their right to self-rule. (More on that later in the walk.) If you're curious to peek inside, head through the door at #11 (free, described on page 72).

The great reformer **John Knox** is buried—with appropriate austerity—under parking lot spot #23. The statue among the cars shows King Charles II riding to a toga party back in 1685.

• *Continue on through the parking lot, around the back end of the church.*

Every Scottish burgh (town licensed by the king to trade) had three standard features: a "tolbooth" (basically a town hall, with a courthouse, meeting room, and jail); a "tron" (official weighing scale); and a "mercat" (or market) cross. The **mercat cross** standing just behind St. Giles' Cathedral has a slender column decorated

with a unicorn holding a flag with the cross of St. Andrew. Royal proclamations have been read at this mercat cross since the 14th century. In 1952, a town crier heralded the news that Britain had a new queen—three days after the actual event (traditionally the time it took for a horse to speed here from London). Today, Mercat Cross is the meeting point for many of Edinburgh's walking tours—both historic and ghostly.

• *Circle around to the street side of the church.*

The statue to **Adam Smith** honors the Edinburgh author of the pioneering *Wealth of Nations* (1776), in which he laid out the economics of free market capitalism. Smith theorized that an "invisible hand" wisely guides the unregulated free market. Stand in front of Smith and imagine the intellectual energy of Edinburgh in the mid-1700s, when it was Europe's most enlightened city. Adam Smith was right in the center of it. He and David Hume were good friends. James Boswell, the famed biographer of Samuel Johnson, took classes from Smith. James Watt, inventor of the steam engine, was another proud Scotsman of the age. With great intellectuals like these, Edinburgh helped create the modern world. The poet Robert Burns, geologist James Hutton (who's considered the father of modern geology), and the publishers of the first *Encyclopedia Britannica* all lived in Edinburgh. Steeped in the inquisitive mindset of the Enlightenment, they applied cool rationality and a secular approach to their respective fields.

• *Head on down the Royal Mile.*

❻ More of High Street

A few steps downhill, at #188 (on the right), is the **Police Information Center.** This place provides a pleasant police presence (say that three times) and a little local law-and-order history to boot. Ask the officer on duty about the impact of modern technology and budget austerity on police work today. Seriously—drop in and discuss whatever law-and-order issue piques your curiosity (free, open daily 10:00-17:30, Aug until 21:30).

Continuing down this stretch of the Royal Mile, which is traffic-free most of the day (notice the bollards that raise and lower for permitted traffic), you'll see the Fringe Festival office (at #180), street musicians, and another wellhead (with horse "sippies," dating from 1675).

Notice those **three red boxes.** In the 20th century, people used

EDINBURGH

these to make telephone calls to each other. (Imagine that!) These cast-iron booths are produced for all of Britain here in Scotland. As phone booths are decommissioned, some are finding new use as tiny shops, ATMs, and even showing up in residential neighborhoods as nostalgic garden decorations.

At the next intersection, on the left is **Cockburn Street** (pronounced "COE-burn"). This was cut through High Street's dense wall of medieval skyscrapers in the 1860s to give easy access to the Georgian New Town and the train station. Notice how the sliced buildings were thoughtfully capped with facades that fit the aesthetic look of the Royal Mile. In the Middle Ages, only tiny lanes (like Fleshmarket Close just uphill from Cockburn Street) interrupted the long line of Royal Mile buildings. These days, Cockburn Street has a reputation for its eclectic independent shops and string of trendy bars and eateries.

• *When you reach the* **Tron Church** *(17th century, currently housing a shopping center), you're at the intersection of* **North and South Bridge streets.** *These major streets lead left to Waverley Station and right to the Dalkeith Road B&Bs. Several handy bus lines run along here.*

This is the halfway point of this walk. Stand on the corner diagonally across from the church. Look up to the top of the Royal Mile at the Hub and its 240-foot spire. Notwithstanding its turret and 16th-century charm, the **Radisson Blu Hotel** just across the street is entirely new construction (1990), built to fit in. The city is protecting its historic look. The **Inn on the Mile** next door was once a fancy bank with a lavish interior. As modern banks are moving away from city centers, sumptuous buildings like these are being converted into ornate pubs and restaurants.

In the next block downhill are three **characteristic pubs,** side by side, that offer free traditional Scottish and folk music in the evenings. Notice the chimneys. Tenement buildings shared stairways and entries, but held individual apartments, each with its own chimney. Take a look back at the spire of St. Giles' Cathedral—inspired by the Scottish crown and the thistle, Scotland's national flower.

• *Go down High Street another block, passing near the* **Museum of Childhood** *(on the right, at #42, and worth a stop; see page 73) and a fragrant* **fudge shop** *a few doors down, where you can sample various flavors (tempting you to buy a slab).*

Directly across the street, just below another wellhead, is the...

❼ John Knox House

Remember that Knox was a towering figure in Edinburgh's history, converting Scotland to a Calvinist style of Protestantism. His religious bent was "Presbyterianism," in which parishes are governed by elected officials rather than appointed bishops. This more democratic brand of Christianity also spurred Scotland toward political democracy. If you're interested in Knox or the Reformation, this sight is worth a visit (see page 73). Full disclosure: It's not certain that Knox ever actually lived here. Attached to the Knox House is the Scottish Storytelling Centre, where locals with the gift of gab perform regularly; check the posted schedule.

• *A few steps farther down High Street, at the intersection with St. Mary's and Jeffrey streets, you'll reach...*

❽ The World's End

For centuries, a wall stood here, marking the end of the burgh of Edinburgh. For residents within the protective walls of the city, this must have felt like the "world's end," indeed. The area beyond

was called Canongate, a monastic community associated with Holyrood Abbey. At the intersection, find the brass bricks in the street that trace the gate (demolished in 1764). Look to the right down St. Mary's Street about 200 yards to see a surviving bit of that old wall, known as the **Flodden Wall.** In the 1513 Battle of Flodden, the Scottish king James IV made the disastrous decision to invade northern England. James and 10,000 of his Scotsmen were killed. Fearing a brutal English counterattack, Edinburgh scrambled to reinforce its broken-down city wall.

The pub on the corner, **No. 1 High Street,** is a centrally located venue for live traditional music—pop in and see what's on tonight. Several other interesting shops are within a few steps of this spot. To the left, down Jeffrey Street, you'll see Scotland's top tattoo parlor, and a supplier for a different kind of tattoo (the Scottish Regimental Store). Across the street from those is the recommended **Lickety Splits,** a fine candy (or "sweets") shop and art gallery.

• *Continue down the Royal Mile—leaving old Edinburgh—as High Street changes names to...*

❾ Canongate

About 10 steps down Canongate, look left down Cranston Street (past the train tracks) to a good view of the Calton Cemetery up on **Calton Hill.** The obelisk, called Martyrs' Monument, remembers a group of 18th-century patriots exiled by London to Australia for their reform politics. The round

EDINBURGH

building to the left is the grave of philosopher David Hume. And the big, turreted building to the right was the jail master's house. Today, the main reason to go up Calton Hill is for the fine views (described on page 95).

The giant, blocky building that dominates the lower slope of the hill is **St. Andrew's House,** headquarters of the Scottish Government—including the office of the first minister of Scotland. According to locals, the building has also been an important base for MI6, Britain's version of the CIA. Wait a minute—isn't James Bond Scottish? Hmmm...

• *A couple of hundred yards farther along the Royal Mile (on the right at #172) you reach **Cadenhead's,** a serious place to sample and buy whisky (see page 99). About 30 yards farther along, you'll pass two worthwhile and free museums, the **People's Story Museum** (on the left, in the old tollhouse at #163) and **Museum of Edinburgh** (on the right, at #142; for more on both, see page 74). But our next stop is the church just across from the Museum of Edinburgh.*

The 1688 **Canongate Kirk** (Church)—located not far from the royal residence of Holyroodhouse—is where Queen Elizabeth II

and her family worship whenever they're in town. (So don't sit in the front pew, marked with her crown.) The gilded emblem at the top of the roof, high above the door, has the antlers of a stag from the royal estate of Balmoral (see page 344). The Queen's granddaughter married here in 2011.

The church is open only when volunteers have signed up to welcome visitors. Chat them up and borrow the description of the place. Then step inside the lofty blue and red interior, renovated with royal money; the church is filled with light and the flags of various Scottish regiments. In the narthex, peruse the photos of royal family events here, and find the list of priests and ministers of this parish—it goes back to 1143 (with a clear break with the Reformation in 1561).

Outside, turn right as you leave the church and walk up into the graveyard. The large, gated grave (abutting the back of the People's Story Museum) is the affectionately tended tomb of **Adam Smith,** the father of capitalism.

Just outside the churchyard, the statue on the sidewalk is of the poet **Robert Fergusson.** One of the first to write verse in the Scots language, he so inspired Robert Burns that Burns paid for Fergusson's tombstone in the Canongate churchyard and composed his epitaph.

Now look across the street at the **gabled house** next to the Museum of Edinburgh. Scan the facade to see shells put there in the 17th century to defend against the evil power of witches yet to be drowned.

• *Walk about 300 yards farther along. In the distance you can see the Palace of Holyroodhouse (the end of this walk) and soon, on the right, you'll come to the modern Scottish parliament building.*

Just opposite the parliament building is **White Horse Close** (on the left, in the white arcade). Step into this 17th-century court-

yard. It was from here that the Edinburgh stagecoach left for London. Eight days later, the horse-drawn carriage would pull into its destination: Scotland Yard. Note that bus #35 leaves in two directions from here—downhill for the Royal Yacht *Britannia,* and uphill along the Royal Mile (as far as South Bridge) and on to the National Museum of Scotland.

• *Now walk up around the corner to the flagpoles (flying the flags of Europe, Britain, and Scotland) in front of the...*

➓ Scottish Parliament Building

Finally, after centuries of history, we reach the 21st century. And finally, after three centuries of London rule, Scotland has a parlia-

ment building...in Scotland. When Scotland united with England in 1707, its parliament was dissolved. But in 1999, the Scottish parliament was reestablished, and in 2004, it moved into this striking new home. Notice how the eco-friendly build-ing, by the Catalan architect Enric Miralles, mixes wild angles, lots of light, bold windows, oak, and native stone into a startling complex. (People from Catalunya—another would-be breakaway nation—have an affinity for Scotland.) From the front of the parliament building, look in the distance at the rocky Salisbury Crags, with people hiking the traverse up to the dramatic next summit called Arthur's Seat. Now look at the building in relation to the craggy cliffs. The architect envisioned the building as if it were rising right from the base of Arthur's Seat, almost bursting from the rock.

Since it celebrates Scottish democracy, the architecture is not a statement of authority. There are no statues of old heroes. There's not even a grand entry. You feel like you're entering an office park.

Given its neighborhood, the media often calls the Scottish Parliament "Holyrood" for short (similar to calling the US Congress "Capitol Hill"). For details on touring the building and seeing parliament in action, see page 74.

• *Across the street is the* **Queen's Gallery,** *where she shares part of her amazing personal art collection in excellent revolving exhibits (see page 77). Finally, walk to the end of the road (Abbey Strand), and step up to the impressive wrought-iron gate of the Queen's palace. Look up at the stag with its holy cross, or "holy rood," on its forehead, and peer into the palace grounds. (The ticket office and palace entryway, a fine café, and a handy WC are just through the arch on the right.)*

⓫ Palace of Holyroodhouse

Since the 16th century, this palace has marked the end of the Royal Mile. An abbey—part of a 12th-century Augustinian monastery—originally stood in its place. While most of that old building is gone, you can see the surviving nave behind the palace on the left. According to one legend, it was named "holy rood" for a piece of the cross, brought here as a relic by Queen (and later Saint) Margaret. (Another version of the story is that King

David I, Margaret's son, saw the image of a cross upon a stag's head while hunting here and took it as a sign that he should build an abbey on the site.) Because Scotland's royalty preferred living at Holyroodhouse to the blustery castle on the rock, the palace grew over time. If the Queen's not visiting, the palace welcomes visitors (see page 75 for details).

• *Your walk—from the castle to the palace, with so much Scottish history packed in between—is complete. And, if your appetite is whetted for more, don't worry; you've just scratched the surface. Enjoy the rest of Edinburgh.*

BONNIE WEE NEW TOWN WALK

Many visitors, mesmerized by the Royal Mile, never venture to the New Town. And that's a shame. With some of the city's finest Georgian architecture (from its 18th-century boom period), the New Town has a completely different character than the Old Town. This self-guided walk—worth ▲▲—gives you a quick orientation. "Part 1" takes about 45 minutes and helps you get your bearings; "Part 2" is more lightly narrated and connects you to one of the New Town's best sights, the Georgian House, in another 30 minutes.

Part 1: Into the New Town

• *Begin on Waverley Bridge, spanning the gully between the Old and New towns; to get there from the Royal Mile, just head down the curved Cockburn Street near the Tron Church (or cut down any of the "close" lanes opposite St. Giles' Cathedral). Stand on the bridge overlooking the train tracks, facing the castle.*

View from Waverley Bridge: From this vantage point, you can enjoy fine views of medieval Edinburgh, with its 10-story-plus "skyscrapers." It's easy to imag-

ine how miserably crowded this area was, prompting the expansion of the city during the Georgian period. Pick out landmarks along the Royal Mile, most notably the open-work steeple of St. Giles'.

A big lake called the **Nor' Loch** once was to the north (nor') of the Old Town; now it's a valley between Edinburgh's two towns. The lake was drained around 1800 as part of the expansion. Before that, the lake was the town's water reservoir...and its sewer. Much has been written about the town's infamous stink (a.k.a. the "flowers of Edinburgh"). The town's nickname, "Auld Reekie," referred to both the smoke of its industry and the stench of its squalor.

The long-gone loch was also a handy place for drowning witches. With their thumbs tied to their ankles, they'd be lashed to dunking stools. Those who survived the ordeal were considered "aided by the devil" and burned as witches. If they died, they were innocent and given a good Christian burial. Edinburgh was Europe's witch-burning mecca—any perceived "sign," including a small birthmark, could condemn you. Scotland burned more witches per capita than any other country—17,000 souls between 1479 and 1722.

Visually trace the train tracks as they disappear into a tunnel below the **Scottish National Gallery** (with lesser-known paint-

ings by great European artists; you can visit at the end of Part 1 of this walk—see page 82). The two fine Neoclassical buildings of the National Gallery date from the 1840s and sit upon a mound that's called, well, **The Mound.** When the New Town was built, tons of rubble from the excavations were piled here (1781-1830), forming a dirt bridge that connected

Bonnie Wee New Town Walk

1. Princes Street Gardens
2. Scott Monument
3. Jenners Department Store
4. St. Andrew Square
5. George Street
6. St. Andrew's and St. George's Church
7. The Dome Restaurant
8. King George IV Statue
9. Thistle Street
10. William Pitt Statue
11. Rose Street
12. Charlotte Square
13. Georgian House

the new development with the Old Town to allay merchant concerns about being cut off from the future heart of the city.

Turning 180 degrees (and facing the ramps down into the train station), notice the huge, turreted building with the clock tower. **The Balmoral** was one of the city's two grand hotels during its glory days (its opposite bookend, The Caledonian, sits at the far end of the former lakebed—near the end of this walk). Aristocrats arriving by train could use a hidden entrance to go from the platform directly up to their plush digs. (Today The Balmoral is known mostly as the place where J. K. Rowling completed the final Harry Potter book.)

• *Now walk across the bridge toward the New Town. Before the corner, enter the gated gardens on the left, and head toward the big, pointy monument. You're at the edge of...*

❶ **Princes Street Gardens:** This grassy park, filling the former lakebed, offers a wonderful escape from the bustle of the city. Once the private domain of the wealthy, it was opened to the public around 1870—not as a democratic gesture, but in hopes of increasing sales at the Princes Street department stores. Join the office workers for a picnic lunch break.

• *Take a seat on the bench indicated by the Livingstone (Dr. Livingstone, I presume?) statue. (The Victorian explorer is well equipped with a guidebook, but is hardly packing light—his lion skin doesn't even fit in his rucksack carry-on.)*

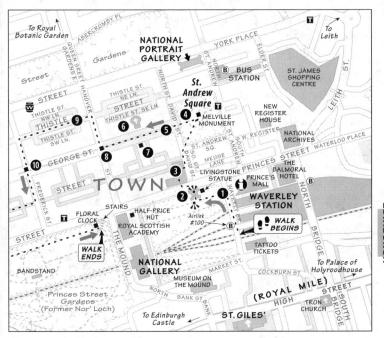

Look up at the towering...

❷ Scott Monument: Built in the early 1840s, this elaborate Neo-Gothic monument honors the great author Sir Walter Scott, one of Edinburgh's many illustrious sons. When Scott died in 1832, it was said that "Scotland never owed so much to one man." Scott almost singlehandedly created the Scotland we know. Just as the country was in danger of being assimilated into England, Scott celebrated traditional songs, legends, myths, architecture, and kilts, thereby reviving the Highland culture and cementing a national identity. And, as the father of the Romantic historical novel, he contributed to Western literature in general. The 200-foot monument shelters a marble statue of Scott and his favorite pet, Maida, a deerhound who was one of 30 canines this dog lover owned during his lifetime. They're surrounded by busts of 16 great Scottish poets and 64 characters from his books. Climbing the tight, stony spiral staircase of 287 steps earns you a peek at a tiny museum midway, a fine city view at the top, and intimate encounters going up and down (£4; daily 10:00-

19:00, until 16:00 Oct-March, tel. 0131/529-4068). For more on Scott, see page 69.

• *Exit the gate near Livingstone and head across busy Princes Street to the venerable...*

❸ Jenners Department Store: As you wait for the light to change (and wait...and wait...), notice how statues of women support the building—just as real women support the business. The arrival of new fashions here was such a big deal in the old days that they'd announce it by flying flags on the Nelson Monument atop Calton Hill.

Step inside and head upstairs into the grand, skylit atrium. The central space—filled with a towering tree at Christmas—is classic Industrial Age architecture. The Queen's coat of arms high on the wall indicates she shops here.

• *From the atrium, turn right and exit onto South St. David Street. Turn left and follow this street uphill one block up to...*

❹ St. Andrew Square: This green space is dedicated to the patron saint of Scotland. In the early 19th century, there were no shops around here—just fine residences; this was a private garden for the fancy people living here. Now open to the public, the square is a popular lunch hangout for workers. The Melville Monument honors a power-monger member of parliament who, for four decades (around 1800), was nicknamed the "uncrowned king of Scotland."

At the far corner of the park is the city's bus station and, beside it, the St. James Shopping Centre. And one block to the left is the excellent **Scottish National Portrait Gallery,** which introduces you to all of the biggest names in Scottish history (for a self-guided tour, see page 87).

• *Follow the Melville Monument's gaze straight ahead out of the park. Cross the street and stand at the top of...*

❺ George Street: This is the main drag of Edinburgh's grid-planned New Town. Laid out in 1776, when King George III was busy putting down a revolution in a troublesome overseas colony, the New Town was a model of urban planning in its day. The architectural style is "Georgian"—British for "Neoclassical." And the street plan came with an unambiguous message: to celebrate the union of Scotland with England into the United Kingdom. (This was particularly important, since Scotland was just two decades re-moved from the failed Jacobite uprising of Bonnie Prince Charlie.)

St. Andrew Square (patron saint of Scotland) and Charlotte Square (George III's queen) bookend the New Town, with its three main streets named for the royal family of the time (George, Queen, and Princes). Thistle and Rose streets—which we'll see on Part 2 of this walk—are named for the national flowers of Scotland and England.

The plan for the New Town was the masterstroke of the 23-year-old urban designer James Craig. George Street—20 feet wider than the others (so a four-horse carriage could make a U-turn)—was the main drag. Running down the high spine of the area, it afforded grand, unobstructed views (thanks to the parks on either side) of the River Forth in one direction and the Old Town in the other. As you stroll down the street, you'll notice that Craig's grid is a series of axes designed to connect monuments new and old; later architects made certain to continue this harmony. For example, notice that the Scott Monument lines up perfectly with this first intersection.

• Halfway down the first block of George Street, on the right, is...

❻ **St. Andrew's and St. George's Church:** Designed as part of the New Town plan in the 1780s, the church is a product of the Scottish Enlightenment. It has an elliptical plan (the first in Britain) so that all can focus on the pulpit. If it's open, step inside. A fine leaflet tells the story of the church, and a handy cafeteria downstairs serves cheap and cheery lunches.

Directly across the street from the church is another temple, this one devoted to money. This former bank building (now housing the recommended restaurant ❼ **The Dome**) has a pediment filled with figures demonstrating various ways to make money, which they do with all the nobility of classical gods. Consider scurrying across the street and ducking inside to view the stunning domed atrium.

Continue down George Street to the intersection with a ❽ statue commemorating the visit by **King George IV.** Notice the particularly fine axis formed by this cross-street: The National Gallery lines up perfectly with the Royal Mile's skyscrapers and the former Tolbooth Church, creating a Gotham City collage.

• Part 1 of our walk is finished; by now you've gotten your New Town bearings. If you were to turn left and head down Hanover Street, in

EDINBURGH

a block you'd run into the Scottish National Gallery; the street behind it curves back up to the Royal Mile.

But to see more of the New Town—including the Georgian House, offering an insightful look inside one of these fine 18th-century homes—stick with me for a few more long blocks through the rest of the New Town.

Part 2: Zigzag Through New Town to the Georgian House

You could continue straight down George Street—lined with ritzy hotels and glitzy bars—to Charlotte Square and the Georgian House. But we'll detour just a bit, zigzagging through side streets to see the various personalities that inhabit this rigid grid.

• *Turn right on Hanover Street; after just one (short) block, cross over and go down...*

❾ **Thistle Street:** Of the many streets in the New Town, this has perhaps the most vivid Scottish character. And that's fitting, as it's named after Scotland's national flower. At the beginning and end of the street, also notice that Craig's street plan included tranquil cul-de-sacs within the larger blocks. Thistle Street seems sleepy, but holds characteristic shops—especially fashionable clothing boutiques—and enticing restaurants (several are recommended later, under "Shopping in Edinburgh" and "Eating in Edinburgh"). For example, halfway down the street on the left, Howie Nicholsby's shop 21st Century Kilt updates traditional Scottish menswear.

You'll pop out at Frederick Street. Turning left, you'll see a ❿ statue of **William Pitt,** prime minister under King George III. (Pitt's father gave his name to the American city of Pittsburgh—which Scots pronounce as "Pitts-burrah"...I assume.)

• *For an interesting contrast, we'll continue down another side street. Pass the statue of Pitt (heading toward Edinburgh Castle), and turn right onto...*

⓫ **Rose Street:** As a rose is to a thistle, and as England is to Scotland, so is brash, boisterous Rose Street to sedate, thoughtful Thistle Street. This stretch of Rose Street feels more commercialized, jammed with chain stores; the second block is packed with pubs and restaurants. As you walk, keep an eye out for the cobbled Tudor rose embedded in the brick sidewalk. When you cross the aptly named Castle Street, linger over the grand views to Edinburgh Castle. It's almost as if they planned it this way... just for the views.

• *Popping out at the far end of Rose Street, across the street and to your right is...*

⓬ Charlotte Square: The building of the New Town started cheap with St. Andrew Square, but finished well with this stately space. In 1791, the Edinburgh town council asked the prestigious Scottish architect Robert Adam to pump up the design for Charlotte Square. The council hoped that Adam's plan would answer criticism that the New Town buildings lacked innovation or ambition—and they got what they wanted. Adam's design, which raised the standard of New Town architecture to "international class," created Edinburgh's finest Georgian square.

• *Along the right side of Charlotte Square, at #7 (just left of the pointy pediment), you can pay a visit to the* **⓭** *Georgian House, which gives you a great peek behind all of these harmonious Neoclassical facades (see page 90).*

When you're done touring the house, you can head back through the New Town grid, perhaps taking some different streets than the way you came. Or, for a restful return to our starting point, consider this...

Return Through Princes Street Gardens: From Charlotte Square, drop down to busy Princes Street (noticing The Caledonian hotel—the grand twin sister of The Balmoral at the start of our walk). But rather than walking along the busy bus-and-tram-lined shopping drag, head into **Princes Street Gardens** instead. With the castle looming overhead, you'll pass a playground, a fanciful Victorian fountain, more monuments to great Scots, war memorials, and a bandstand (which hosts Scottish country dancing—see page 106—as well as occasional big-name acts). Finally you'll reach a staircase up to the Scottish National Gallery; notice the oldest **floral clock** in the world on your left as you climb up.

• *Our walk is over. From here, you can tour the gallery; head up Bank Street just behind it to reach the Royal Mile; hop on a bus along Princes Street to your next stop (or B&B); or continue through another stretch of the Princes Street Gardens to the Scott Monument and our starting point.*

EDINBURGH

Sights in Edinburgh

▲▲▲EDINBURGH CASTLE

The fortified birthplace of the city 1,300 years ago, this imposing symbol of Edinburgh sits proudly on a rock high above you. The

home of Scotland's kings and queens for centuries, the castle has witnessed royal births, medieval pageantry, and bloody sieges. Today it's a complex of various buildings, some dating from the 12th century, linked by cobbled roads that survive from its more recent use as a military garrison. The castle—with expansive views, plenty of history, and the stunning crown jewels of Scotland—is a fascinating and multifaceted sight that deserves several hours of your time.

Cost and Hours: £16.50, daily April-Sept 9:30-18:00, Oct-March 9:30-17:00, last entry one hour before closing, tel. 0131/225-9846, www.edinburghcastle.gov.uk.

Avoiding Lines: The castle is usually least crowded after 14:00 or so; if planning a morning visit, the earlier the better. To avoid ticket lines (worst in Aug), book online and print your ticket at home. You can also pick up your prebooked ticket at machines just inside the entrance or at the Visitor Information desk a few steps uphill on the right. You can also skip the ticket line with a Historic Scotland Explorer Pass (see page 442 for details).

Getting There: Simply walk up the Royal Mile (if arriving by bus from the Dalkeith Road B&B area, get off at South Bridge and huff up the Mile for about 15 minutes).

Taxis get you closer, dropping you a block below the esplanade at the Hub/Tolbooth Church.

Tours: Thirty-minute introductory **guided tours** are free with admission (2-4/hour, depart from Argyle Battery, see clock for next departure; fewer off-season). The informative **audioguide** provides four hours of descriptions, including the National War Museum Scotland (£3 if you purchase with your ticket; £3.50 if you rent it once inside).

Services: The clean WC at the entry routinely wins "British Loo of the Year" awards. For lunch, you have two choices. **The Redcoat Café**—located within Ed-

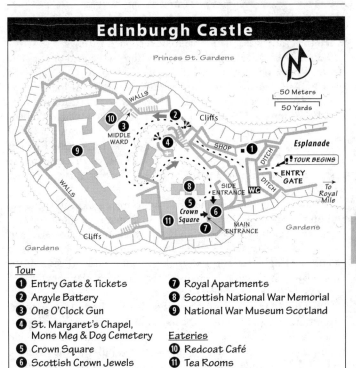

Edinburgh Castle

Princes St. Gardens

WALLS

Cliffs

50 Meters

50 Yards

MIDDLE WARD

SHOP

Esplanade

TOUR BEGINS

ENTRY GATE

To Royal Mile

WALLS

DITCH

DITCH

SIDE ENTRANCE

WC

Crown Square

MAIN ENTRANCE

Gardens

Cliffs

Gardens

Tour

❶ Entry Gate & Tickets
❷ Argyle Battery
❸ One O'Clock Gun
❹ St. Margaret's Chapel, Mons Meg & Dog Cemetery
❺ Crown Square
❻ Scottish Crown Jewels (Honours of Scotland)
❼ Royal Apartments
❽ Scottish National War Memorial
❾ National War Museum Scotland

Eateries

❿ Redcoat Café
⓫ Tea Rooms

EDINBURGH

inburgh Castle—is a big, bright, efficient cafeteria with great views (£6-10 quick, healthy meals). Punctuate the two parts of your castle visit (the castle itself and the impressive National War Museum) with a smart break here. The **Tea Rooms,** at the top of the hill directly across from the crown jewels, serves £10-15 sit-down meals in its tight space.

● Self-Guided Tour

From the ❶ **entry gate,** start winding your way uphill toward the main sights—the crown jewels and the Royal Palace—located near the summit. Since the castle was protected on three sides by sheer cliffs, the main defense had to be here at the entrance. During the castle's heyday in the 1500s, a 100-foot tower loomed overhead, facing the city.

• *Passing through the portcullis gate, you reach the...*

❷ **Argyle (Six-Gun) Battery, with View:** These front-loading, cast-iron cannons are from the Napoleonic era (c. 1800), when the castle was still a force to be reckoned with.

From here, look north across the valley to the grid of the New Town. The valley sits where the Nor' Loch once was; this lake was drained and filled in when the New Town was built in the late 1700s, its swamps replaced with gardens. Later the land provided sites for the Greek-temple-esque Scottish National Gallery and Waverley Station. Looking farther north, you can make out the port town of Leith with its high-rises and cranes, the Firth of Forth, the island of Inchkeith, and—in the far, far distance (to the east)—the cone-like mountain of North Berwick Law, a former volcano.

Now look down. The sheer north precipice looks impregnable. But on the night of March 14, 1314, 30 armed men silently scaled this rock face. They were loyal to Robert the Bruce and determined to recapture the castle, which had fallen into English hands. They caught the English by surprise, took the castle, and—three months later—Bruce defeated the English at the Battle of Bannockburn.

• *A little farther along, near the café, is the...*

❸ **One O'Clock Gun:** Crowds gather for the 13:00 gun blast, a tradition that gives ships in the bay something to set their navigational devices by. Before the gun, sailors set their clocks with help from the Nelson Monument—that's the tall pillar in the distance on Calton Hill. The monument has a "time ball" affixed to the cross on top, which drops precisely at the top of the hour. But on foggy days, ships couldn't see the ball, so the cannon shot was instituted instead (1861). The tradition stuck, every day at 13:00. (Locals joke that the frugal Scots don't fire it at high noon, as that would cost 11 extra rounds a day.)

• *Continue uphill, winding to the left and passing through Foog's Gate. At the very top of the hill, on your left, is...*

❹ **St. Margaret's Chapel:** This tiny stone chapel is Edinburgh's oldest building (around 1120) and sits atop its highest point (440 feet). It represents the birth of the city.

In 1057, Malcolm III murdered King Macbeth (of Shakespeare fame) and assumed the Scottish throne. Later, he married Princess Margaret, and the family settled atop this hill. Their marriage united Malcolm's Highland Scots with Margaret's Lowland Anglo-Saxons—the cultural mix that would define Edinburgh.

Step inside the tiny, unadorned church—a testament to Margaret's reputed piety. The style is Romanesque. The nave is wonderfully simple, with classic Norman zigzags decorating the round arch that separates the tiny nave from the sacristy. You'll see a facsimile of St. Margaret's 11th-century gospel book. The small (modern) stained-glass windows feature St. Margaret herself, St. Columba and St. Ninian (who brought Christianity to Scotland via Iona), St. Andrew (Scotland's patron saint), and William Wallace (the defender of Scotland). These days, the place is popular for weddings. (As it seats only 20, it's particularly popular with brides' parents.)

Margaret died at the castle in 1093, and her son King David I built this chapel in her honor (she was sainted in 1250). David expanded the castle and also founded Holyrood Abbey, across town. These two structures were soon linked by a Royal Mile of buildings, and Edinburgh was born.

Mons Meg, in front of the church, is a huge and once-upon-a-time frightening 15th-century siege cannon that fired 330-pound

stones nearly two miles. Imagine. It was a gift from Philip the Good, duke of Burgundy, to his great-niece's husband King James II of Scotland.

Nearby, belly up to the banister and look down to find the **Dog Cemetery,** a tiny patch of grass with a sweet little line of doggie tombstones, marking the graves of soldiers' faithful canines in arms.

• *Continue on, curving downhill into...*

❺ **Crown Square:** This courtyard is the center of today's Royal Castle complex. Get oriented. You're surrounded by the crown jewels, the Royal Palace (with its Great Hall), and the Scottish National War Memorial.

The castle has evolved over the centuries, and Crown Square is relatively "new." After the time of Malcolm and Margaret, the castle was greatly expanded by David II (1324-1371), complete with tall towers, a Great Hall, dungeon, cellars, and so on. This served as the grand royal residence for two centuries. Then, in 1571-1573, the Protestant citizens of Edinburgh laid siege to the castle and its Catholic/monarchist holdouts, eventually blasting it to smithereens. (You can tour the paltry remains of the medieval castle in nearby **David's Tower.**) The palace was rebuilt nearby—around what is today's Crown Square.

• *We'll tour the buildings around Crown Square. First up: the crown jewels. The main year-round entry to the jewels is on Crown Square. In summer, there's a second option that avoids the long line: Head to the left as you face the main entrance and find another entry (near the WCs). This route takes you through the Honours of Scotland exhibition—an interesting, Disney-esque series of displays (which often moves at a shuffle) telling the story of the crown jewels and how they survived the harrowing centuries, but without any actual artifacts.*

❻ Scottish Crown Jewels (Honours of Scotland): For centuries, Scotland's monarchs were crowned in elaborate rituals involving three wondrous objects: a jewel-studded crown, scepter, and sword. These objects—along with the ceremonial Stone of Scone (pronounced "skoon")—are known as the "Honours of Scotland." Scotland's crown jewels may not be as impressive as England's, but they're treasured by locals as a symbol of Scottish nationalism. They're also older than England's; while Oliver Cromwell destroyed England's jewels, the Scots managed to hide theirs.

History of the Jewels: The Honours of Scotland exhibit that leads up to the Crown Room traces the evolution of the jewels, the ceremony, and the often turbulent journey of this precious regalia. Here's the SparkNotes version:

In 1306, Robert the Bruce was crowned with a "circlet of gold" in a ceremony at Scone—a town 40 miles north of Edinburgh, which Scotland's earliest kings had claimed as their capital. Around 1500, King James IV added two new items to the coronation ceremony—a scepter (a gift from the pope) and a huge sword (a gift from another pope). In 1540, James V had the original crown augmented by an Edinburgh goldsmith, giving it the imperial-crown shape it has today.

These Honours were used to crown every monarch: nine-month-old Mary, Queen of Scots (she cried); her one-year-old son James VI (future king of England); and Charles I and II. But the days of divine-right rulers were numbered.

In 1649, the parliament had Charles I (king of both England and Scotland) beheaded. Soon Cromwell's rabid English antiroyalists were marching on Edinburgh. Quick! Legend says two women scooped up the crown and sword, hid them in their skirts and belongings, and buried them in a church far to the northeast until the coast was clear.

When the monarchy was restored, the regalia were used to crown Scotland's last king, Charles II (1660). Then, in 1707, the Treaty of Union with England ended Scotland's independence. The Honours came out for a ceremony to bless the treaty, and were then

William Wallace (c. 1270-1305)

In 1286, Scotland's king died without an heir, plunging the prosperous country into a generation of chaos. As Scottish nobles bickered over naming a successor, the English King Edward I—nicknamed "Longshanks" because of his height—invaded and assumed power (1296). He placed a figurehead on the throne, forced Scottish nobles to sign a pledge of allegiance to England (the "Ragman's Roll"), moved the British parliament north to York, and took the highly symbolic Stone of Scone to London, where it would remain for centuries.

WILLIAM WALLACE.

A year later, the Scots rose up against Edward, led by William Wallace (popularized in the film *Braveheart*). A mix of history and legend portrays Wallace as the son of a poor-but-knightly family that refused to sign the Ragman's Roll. Exceptionally tall and strong, he learned Latin and French from two uncles, who were priests. In his teenage years, his father and older brother were killed by the English. Later, he killed an English sheriff to avenge the death of his wife, Marion. Wallace's rage inspired his fellow Scots to revolt.

In the summer of 1297, Wallace and his guerrillas scored a series of stunning victories over the English. On September 11, a well-equipped English army of 10,000 soldiers and 300 horsemen began crossing Stirling Bridge. Wallace's men attacked, and in the chaos, the bridge collapsed, splitting the English ranks in two. The ragtag Scots drove the confused English into the river. The Battle of Stirling Bridge was a rout, and Wallace was knighted and appointed guardian of Scotland.

All through the winter, King Edward's men chased Wallace, continually frustrated by the Scots' hit-and-run tactics. Finally, at the Battle of Falkirk (1298), they drew Wallace's men out onto the open battlefield. The English with their horses and archers easily destroyed the spear-carrying Scots. Wallace resigned in disgrace and went on the lam, while his successors negotiated truces with the English, finally surrendering unconditionally in 1304. Wallace alone held out.

In 1305, the English tracked him down and took him to London, where he was convicted of treason and mocked with a crown of oak leaves as the "king of outlaws." On August 23, they stripped him naked and dragged him to the execution site. There he was strangled to near death, castrated, and dismembered. His head was stuck on a spike atop London Bridge, while his body parts were sent on tour to spook would-be rebels. But Wallace's martyrdom only served to inspire his countrymen, and the torch of independence was picked up by Robert the Bruce (see page 65). Despite the *Braveheart* movie, Robert the Bruce, not Wallace, was considered the original "Braveheart." (For the full story, see page 188.)

locked away in a strongbox in the castle. There they lay for over a century, until Sir Walter Scott—the writer and great champion of Scottish tradition—forced a detailed search of the castle in 1818. The box was found...and there the Honours were, perfectly preserved. Within a few years, they were put on display, as they have been ever since.

The crown's most recent official appearance was in 1999, when it was taken across town to the grand opening of the reinstated parliament, marking a new chapter in the Scottish nation. As it represents the monarchy, the crown is present whenever a new session of parliament opens. (And if Scotland ever secedes, you can be sure that crown will be in the front row.)

The Honours: Finally, you enter the Crown Room to see the regalia itself. The four-foot steel **sword** was made in Italy under orders of Pope Julius II (the man who also commissioned Michelangelo's Sistine Chapel and St. Peter's Basilica). The **scepter** is made of silver, covered with gold, and topped with a rock crystal and a pearl. The gem- and pearl-encrusted **crown** has an imperial arch topped with a cross. Legend says the band of gold in the center is the original crown that once adorned the head of Robert the Bruce.

The **Stone of Scone** (a.k.a. the "Stone of Destiny") sits plain and strong next to the jewels. It's a rough-hewn gray slab of sandstone, about 26 by 17 by 10 inches. As far back as the ninth century, Scotland's kings were crowned atop this stone, when it stood at the medieval capital of Scone. But in 1296, the invading army of Edward I of England carried the stone off to Westminster Abbey. For the next seven centuries, English (and subsequently British) kings and queens were crowned sitting on a coronation chair with the Stone of Scone tucked in a compartment underneath.

In 1950, four Scottish students broke into Westminster Abbey on Christmas Day and smuggled the stone back to Scotland in an act of foolhardy patriotism. But what could they do with it? After three months, they abandoned the stone, draped in Scotland's national flag. It was returned to Westminster Abbey, where (in 1953) Queen Elizabeth II was crowned atop it. In 1996, in recognition of increased Scottish autonomy, Elizabeth agreed to let the stone go home, on one condition: that it be returned to Westminster Abbey for all British coronations. One day, the next monarch of the United Kingdom—Prince Charles is first in line—will sit atop it, re-enacting a coronation ritual that dates back a thousand years.

• *Exit the crown jewel display, heading down the stairs. But just before exiting into the courtyard, turn left through a door that leads into the...*

❼ **Royal Apartments:** Scottish royalty lived in the Royal Palace only when safety or protocol required it (they preferred the Palace of Holyroodhouse at the bottom of the Royal Mile). Here you can see several historic but unimpressive rooms. The first

one, labeled **Queen Mary's Chamber,** is where Mary, Queen of Scots (1542-1587), gave birth to James VI of Scotland, who later became King James I of England. Nearby **Laich Hall** (Lower Hall) was the dining room of the royal family.

The **Great Hall** (through a separate entrance on Crown Square) was built by James IV to host the castle's official banquets and meetings. It's still used for such purposes today. Most of the interior—its fireplace, carved walls, pikes, and armor—is Victorian. But the well-constructed wood ceiling is original. This hammer-beam roof (constructed like the hull of a ship) is self-supporting. The complex system of braces and arches distributes the weight of the roof outward to the walls, so there's

no need for supporting pillars or long cross beams. Before leaving, look for the big iron-barred peephole above the fireplace, on the right. This allowed the king to spy on his subjects while they partied.

• *Across the Crown Square courtyard is the...*

❽ Scottish National War Memorial: This commemorates the 149,000 Scottish soldiers lost in World War I, the 58,000 who died

in World War II, and the nearly 800 (and counting) lost in British battles since. This is a somber spot (stow your camera and phone). Paid for by public donations, each bay is dedicated to a particular Scottish regiment. The main shrine, featuring a green Italian-marble memorial that contains the original WWI rolls of honor, sits on an exposed

chunk of the castle rock. Above you, the archangel Michael is busy slaying a dragon. The bronze frieze accurately shows the attire of various wings of Scotland's military. The stained glass starts with Cain and Abel on the left, and finishes with a celebration of peace on the right. To appreciate how important this place is, consider that Scottish soldiers died at twice the rate of other British soldiers in World War I.

• *Our final stop is worth the five-minute walk to get there. Backtrack to the café (and One O'Clock Gun), then head downhill to the...*

❾ **National War Museum Scotland:** This thoughtful museum covers four centuries of Scottish military history. Instead of

the usual musty, dusty displays of endless armor, there's a compelling mix of videos, uniforms, weapons, medals, mementos, and eloquent excerpts from soldiers' letters.

Here you'll learn the story of how the fierce and courageous Scottish warrior changed from being a symbol of resistance against Britain to being a champion of that same empire. Along the way, these military men received many decorations for valor and did more than their share of dying in battle. But even when fighting alongside—rather than against—England, Scottish regiments still promoted their romantic, kilted-warrior image.

Queen Victoria fueled this ideal throughout the 19th century. She was infatuated with the Scottish Highlands and the culture's untamed, rustic mystique. Highland soldiers, especially officers, went to great personal expense to sport all their elaborate regalia, and the kilted men fought best to the tune of their beloved bagpipes. For centuries the stirring drone of bagpipes accompanied Highland soldiers into battle—raising their spirits and announcing to the enemy that they were about to meet a fierce and mighty foe.

This museum shows the human side of war as well as the cleverness of government-sponsored ad campaigns that kept the lads enlisting. Two centuries of recruiting posters make the same pitch that still works today: a hefty signing bonus, steady pay, and job security with the promise of a manly and adventurous life—all spiked with a mix of pride and patriotism.

Stepping outside the museum, you're surrounded by cannons that no longer fire, stony walls that tell an amazing story, dramatic views of this grand city, and the clatter of tourists (rather than soldiers) on cobbles. Consider for a moment all the bloody history and valiant struggles, along with British power and Scottish pride, that have shaped the city over which you are perched.

• *The statue in the courtyard in front of the War Museum is **Earl Haig**—the Scotsman who commanded the British Army through the horrifying WWI trench warfare of Flanders Fields.*

From here, there's only one way out—the same way you came in.

Robert the Bruce (1274-1329)

In 1314, Robert the Bruce's men attacked Edinburgh's Royal Castle, recapturing it from the English. It was just one of many

intense battles between the oppressive English and the plucky Scots during the Wars of Independence.

In this era, Scotland had to overcome not only its English foes but also its own divisiveness—and no one was more divided than Robert the Bruce. As earl of Carrick, he was born with blood ties to England and a long-standing family claim to the Scottish throne.

When England's King Edward I ("Longshanks") conquered Scotland in 1296, the Bruce family welcomed it, hoping Edward would defeat their rivals and put Bruce's father on the throne. They dutifully signed the "Ragman's Roll" of allegiance—and then Edward chose someone else as king.

Twentysomething Robert the Bruce (the "the" comes from his original family name of "de Bruce") then joined William Wallace's revolt against the English. Legend has it that it was he who knighted Wallace after the victory at Stirling Bridge. When Wallace fell from favor, Bruce became a guardian of Scotland (caretaker ruler in the absence of a king) and continued fighting the English. But when Edward's armies again got the upper hand in 1302, Robert—along with Scotland's other nobles—diplomatically surrendered and again pledged loyalty.

In 1306, Robert the Bruce murdered his chief rival and boldly claimed to be king of Scotland. Few nobles supported him. Edward crushed the revolt and kidnapped Bruce's wife, the Church excommunicated him, and Bruce went into hiding on a distant North Sea island. He was now the king of nothing. Legend says he gained inspiration by watching a spider patiently build its web.

The following year, Bruce returned to Scotland and wove alliances with both nobles and the Church, slowly gaining acceptance as Scotland's king by a populace chafing under English rule. On June 24, 1314, he decisively defeated the English (now led by Edward's weak son, Edward II) at the Battle of Bannockburn. After a generation of turmoil (1286-1314), England was finally driven from Scotland, and the country was united under Robert I, king of Scotland.

As king, Robert the Bruce's priority was to stabilize the monarchy and establish clear lines of succession. His descendants would rule Scotland for the next 400 years, and even today, Bruce blood runs through the veins of Queen Elizabeth II, Prince Charles, princes William and Harry, and wee George and Charlotte.

EDINBURGH

SIGHTS ON AND NEAR THE ROYAL MILE
Camera Obscura

A big deal when it was built in 1853, this observatory topped with a mirror reflected images onto a disc before the wide eyes of people

who had never seen a photograph or a captured image. Today, you can climb 100 steps for an entertaining 20-minute demonstration (3/hour). At the top, enjoy the best view any-where of the Royal Mile. Then work your way down through five floors of illusions, holograms, and early pho-tos. This is a big hit with kids, but very overpriced. (It's less impressive on cloudy days.)

Cost and Hours: £14, daily July-Aug 9:00-21:00, April-June and Sept-Oct 9:30-18:00, Nov-March 10:00-17:00, last demo one hour before closing, tel. 0131/225-4239, www.camera-obscura.co.uk.

▲The Scotch Whisky Experience

This gimmicky attraction—consisting of a "Malt Disney" whisky-barrel ride through the whisky production process followed by an

explanation of Scotland's four main whisky regions—seems designed only to distill £14 out of your pocket. It does succeed in providing an entertaining yet informative orientation to the creation of Scottish fire-water (things get pretty psy-chedelic when you hit the yeast stage). The 50-minute experience includes sampling a wee dram and the chance to stand amid the world's largest Scotch whisky collection (almost 3,500 bottles). At the end, you'll find yourself in the bar, with a fascinating wall of unusually shaped whisky bottles. Serious connoisseurs should stick with the more substantial shops in town (for ideas, see page 99), but this place can be worthwhile for beginners—particularly those who won't take a more serious Scotland distillery tour elsewhere. (For more on whisky and whisky tastings, see page 461).

Cost and Hours: £14 "silver tour" includes one sample, £24.50 "gold tour" includes four samples—one from each main region, generally daily 10:00-18:00, tel. 0131/220-0441, www.scotchwhiskyexperience.co.uk.

▲▲Gladstone's Land

This is a typical 16th- to 17th-century merchant's "land," or tenement building. These multistory structures—in which merchants

ran their shops on the ground floor and lived upstairs—were typical of the time (the word "tenement" didn't have the slum connotation then that it has today). At six stories, this one was still just half the height of the tallest "Gothic skyscrapers." Gladstone's Land comes complete with an almost-lived-in, furnished interior. The downstairs cloth shop and upstairs kitchen and living quarters are brought to life by talkative guides. Keep this place in mind as you stroll the rest of the Mile, imagining other houses as if they still looked like this on the inside. (For a comparison of life in the Old Town versus the New Town, also visit the Georgian House, described later.)

EDINBURGH

Cost and Hours: £6.50, daily July-Aug 10:00-18:30, April-June and Sept-Oct 10:00-17:00, closed Nov-March, no photos, tel. 0844-493-2120, www.nts.org.uk.

Writers' Museum at Lady Stair's House

This aristocrat's house, built in 1622, is filled with well-described manuscripts and knickknacks of Scotland's three greatest literary figures: Robert Burns, Robert Louis Stevenson, and Sir Walter Scott. If you'd like to see Scott's pipe and Burns' snuffboxes, you'll love this little museum. You'll wind up steep staircases through a maze of rooms as you peruse first editions and keepsakes of these celebrated writers. Edinburgh's high society gathered in homes like this in the 1780s to hear the great poet Robbie Burns read his work—it's meant to be read aloud rather than to oneself. In the Burns room, you can hear his poetry—worth a few minutes for anyone, and essential for fans.

Cost and Hours: Free, Mon-Sat 10:00-17:00, closed Sun except during Festival 12:00-17:00, tel. 0131/529-4901, www.edinburghmuseums.org.uk.

Museum on the Mound

Located in the basement of the grand Bank of Scotland building, this exhibit tells the story of the bank, which was founded in 1695 (making it only a year younger than the Bank of England, and the longest operating bank in the world). Featuring displays on cash production, safe technology, and bank robberies, this museum struggles mightily to make banking interesting (the case holding £1 million is cool). It's worth popping in if you have extra time or find the subject appealing.

Cost and Hours: Free, Tue-Fri 10:00-17:00, Sat-Sun from

EDINBURGH

Scotland's Literary Greats

Edinburgh was home to Scotland's three greatest literary figures, pictured above: Robert Burns (left), Robert Louis Stevenson (center), and Sir Walter Scott (right).

Robert Burns (1759-1796), known as "Rabbie" in Scotland and quite possibly the most famous and beloved Scot of all time, moved to Edinburgh after achieving overnight celebrity with his first volume of poetry (staying in a house on the spot where Deacon Brodie's Tavern now stands). Even though he wrote in the rough Scots dialect and dared to attack social rank, he was a favorite of Edinburgh's high society, who'd gather in fine homes to hear him recite his works. For more on Burns, see the sidebar on page 424.

One hundred years later, **Robert Louis Stevenson** (1850-1894) also stirred the Scottish soul with his pen. An avid traveler who always packed his notepad, Stevenson created settings that are vivid and filled with wonder. Traveling through Scotland, Europe, and around the world, he distilled his adventures into Romantic classics, including *Kidnapped* and *Treasure Island* (as well as *The Strange Case of Dr. Jekyll and Mr. Hyde*). Stevenson, who

13:00, closed Mon, down Bank Street from the Royal Mile—follow the street around to the left and enter through the gate, tel. 0131/243-5464, www.museumonthemound.com.

▲▲St. Giles' Cathedral

This is Scotland's most important church. Its ornate spire—the Scottish crown steeple from 1495—is a proud part of Edinburgh's skyline. The fascinating interior contains nearly 200 memorials honoring distinguished Scots through the ages.

Cost and Hours: Free but donations encouraged; May-Sept Mon-Fri 9:00-19:00, Sat 9:00-17:00; Oct-April Mon-Sat 9:00-17:00;

EDINBURGH

was married in San Francisco and spent his last years in the South Pacific, wrote, "Youth is the time to travel—both in mind and in body—to try the manners of different nations." He said, "I travel not to go anywhere...but to simply go." Travel was his inspiration and his success.

Sir Walter Scott (1771-1832) wrote the *Waverley* novels, including *Ivanhoe* and *Rob Roy*. He's considered the father of the Romantic historical novel. Through his writing, he generated a worldwide interest in Scotland, and reawakened his fellow countrymen's pride in their heritage. His novels helped revive interest in Highland culture—the Gaelic language, kilts, songs, legends, myths, the clan system—and created a national identity. An avid patriot, he wrote, "Every Scottish man has a pedigree. It is a national prerogative, as unalienable as his pride and his poverty." Scott is so revered in Edinburgh that his towering Neo-Gothic monument dominates the city center. With his favorite hound by his side, Sir Walter Scott overlooks the city that he inspired, and that inspired him.

The best way to learn about and experience these literary greats is to visit the Writers' Museum at Lady Stair's House (see page 67) and to take Edinburgh's Literary Pub Tour (see page 105).

While just three writers dominate your Edinburgh sightseeing, consider also the other great writers with Edinburgh connections: J. K. Rowling (who captures the "Gothic" spirit of Edinburgh with her Harry Potter series); current resident Ian Rankin (with his "tartan noir" novels); J. M. Barrie (who attended University of Edinburgh and later created Peter Pan); Sir Arthur Conan Doyle (who was born in Edinburgh, went to medical school here, and is best known for inventing Sherlock Holmes); and James Boswell (who lived 50 yards away from the Writers' Museum, in James Court, and is revered for his biography of Samuel Johnson).

Sun 13:00-17:00 year-round; audioguide-£3, tel. 0131/225-9442, www.stgilescathedral.org.uk.

Concerts: St. Giles' busy concert schedule includes organ recitals and visiting choirs (frequent free events at 12:15, concerts Sun at 18:00 and sometimes Wed at 20:00, see schedule or ask for

Music at St. Giles' pamphlet at welcome desk or gift shop).

➋ **Self-Guided Tour:** Today's facade is 19th-century Neo-Gothic, but most of what you'll see inside is from the 14th and 15th centuries. Engage the cathedral guides in conversation; you'll be glad you did.

EDINBURGH

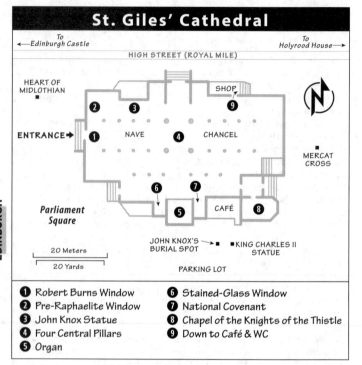

St. Giles' Cathedral

← To Edinburgh Castle

To Holyrood House →

HIGH STREET (ROYAL MILE)

HEART OF MIDLOTHIAN

SHOP

❷   ❸   ❾

ENTRANCE →   ❶   NAVE   ❹   CHANCEL

MERCAT CROSS

❻   ❼

Parliament Square

❺   CAFÉ   ❽

20 Meters

20 Yards

JOHN KNOX'S BURIAL SPOT →   ▪ KING CHARLES II STATUE

PARKING LOT

❶ Robert Burns Window
❷ Pre-Raphaelite Window
❸ John Knox Statue
❹ Four Central Pillars
❺ Organ
❻ Stained-Glass Window
❼ National Covenant
❽ Chapel of the Knights of the Thistle
❾ Down to Café & WC

Just inside the entrance, turn around to see the modern stained-glass ❶ **Robert Burns window,** which celebrates Scotland's favorite poet (see page 424). It was made in 1985 by the Icelandic artist Leifur Breidfjord. The green of the lower level symbolizes the natural world—God's creation. The middle zone with the circle shows the brotherhood of man—Burns was a great internationalist. The top is a rosy red sunburst of creativity, reminding Scots of Burns' famous line, "My love is like a red, red rose"—part of a song near and dear to every Scottish heart.

To the right of the Burns window is a fine ❷ **Pre-Raphaelite window.** Like most in the church, it's a memorial to an important patron (in this case, John Marshall). From here stretches a great swath of war memorials.

As you walk along the north wall, find ❸ **John Knox's statue** (standing like a six-foot-tall bronze chess piece). Look into his eyes for 10 seconds from 10 inches away, and think of the Reformation struggles of the 16th century. Knox, the great religious reformer and founder of austere Scottish Presbyterianism, first preached here in 1559. His insistence that every person should be able to personally read the word of God—notice that he's pointing to a book—gave Scotland an educational system 300 years ahead of the rest of Europe (for more on Knox, see "The Scottish Reformation" on page 208). Thanks partly to Knox, it was Scottish minds that led the way in math, science, medicine, and engineering. Voltaire called Scotland "the intellectual capital of Europe."

Knox preached Calvinism. Consider that the Dutch and the Scots both embraced this creed of hard work, frugality, and strict ethics. This helps explain why the Scots are so different from the English (and why the Dutch and the Scots—both famous for their thriftiness and industriousness—are so much alike).

The oldest parts of the cathedral—the ❹ **four massive central pillars**—are Norman and date from the 12th century. They supported a mostly wooden superstructure that was lost when an invading English force burned it in 1385. The Scots rebuilt it bigger and better than ever, and in 1495 its famous crown spire was completed.

During the Reformation—when Knox preached here (1559-1572)—the place was simplified and whitewashed. Before this, when the emphasis was on holy services provided by priests, there were lots of little niches. With the new focus on sermons rather than rituals, the grand pulpit took center stage.

Knox preached against anything that separated you from God, including stained glass (considered the poor man's Bible, as illiterate Christians could learn from its pictures). Knox had the church's fancy medieval glass windows replaced with clear glass, but 19th-century Victorians took them out and installed the brilliantly colored ones you see today.

Cross over to the ❺ **organ** (1992, Austrian-built, one of Europe's finest) and take in its sheer might.

Immediately to the right of the organ (as you're facing it) is a tiny chapel for silence and prayer. The dramatic ❻ **stained-glass window** above shows the commotion that surrounded Knox when

he preached. The bearded, fiery-eyed Knox had a huge impact on this community. Notice how there were no pews back then. The church was so packed, people even looked through clear windows from across the street. With his hand on the holy book, Knox seems to conduct divine electricity to the Scottish faithful.

To the left of the organ as you face it, in the next alcove, is a copy of the ❼ **National Covenant** (if it's not here, it may be in the chapel described next). It was signed in blood in 1638 by Scottish heroes who refused to compromise their religion for the king's. Most who signed were martyred (their monument is nearby in Grassmarket). You can see the original National Covenant in the Edinburgh Museum, described later.

Head toward the east (back) end of the church, and turn right to see the Neo-Gothic ❽ **Chapel of the Knights of the Thistle** (entry may be possible only with escorted tour—next tour time posted at entrance, £2 donation requested). The interior is filled with intricate wood carving. Built in two years (1910-1911), entirely with Scottish materials and labor, it is the private chapel of the Knights of the Thistle, the only Scottish chivalric order. It's used about once a year for the knights to gather (and, if one dies, to inaugurate a new member). Scotland recognizes its leading citizens by bestowing a membership upon them. The Queen presides over the ritual from her fancy stall, marked by her Scottish coat of arms—a heraldic zoo of symbolism. Are there bagpipes in heaven? Find the tooting stone angel at the top of a window to the left of the altar, and the wooden one to the right of the doorway you came in.

❾ **Downstairs** (enter stairs near the chapel entry) is an inviting, recommended café, along with handy public toilets.

Old Parliament House

The building now holds the civil law courts, so you'll need to go through security first. Step in to see the grand hall, with its fine 1639 hammer-beam ceiling and stained glass. This space housed the Scottish parliament until the Act of Union in 1707. The biggest stained-glass window depicts the initiation of the first Scottish High Court in 1532. The building now holds the civil law courts and is busy with wigged and robed lawyers hard at work in the old library (peek through the door) or pacing the hall deep in discussion. The cleverly named Writz Café, in the basement, is literally their supreme court's restaurant (cheap, Mon-Fri 9:00-14:00, closed Sat-Sun).

Cost and Hours: Free, public welcome Mon-Fri 9:00-16:30, closed Sat-Sun, no photos, borrow info sheet next to security, enter behind St. Giles' Cathedral at door #11; open-to-the-public trials are just across the street at the High Court—the doorman has the day's docket.

▲The Real Mary King's Close

For an unusual peek at Edinburgh's gritty, plague-ridden past, join a costumed performer on an hour-long trip through an excavated underground street and buildings on the northern slope of the Royal Mile. Tours cover the standard goofy, crowd-pleasing ghost stories, but also provide authentic and historical insight into a part of town entombed by later construction. It's best to book ahead (online up to the day before, or by phone or in person for a same-day booking)—even though tours leave every 15 minutes, groups are small and the sight is popular.

Cost and Hours: £14; April-Oct daily 10:00-22:00, Nov-March Sun-Thu until 17:00, Fri-Sat until 21:00; these are last tour times, across from St. Giles' at 2 Warriston's Close—but enter through well-marked door facing High Street, tel. 0845-070-6244, www.realmarykingsclose.com.

▲Museum of Childhood

This five-story playground of historical toys and games is rich in nostalgia and history. Each well-signed gallery is as jovial as a Norman Rockwell painting, highlighting the delights and simplicity of childhood. The museum does a fair job of representing culturally relevant oddities, such as ancient Egyptian, Peruvian, and voodoo dolls, and displays early versions of toys it's probably best didn't make the final cut (such as a grim snake-centered precursor to the popular board game Chutes and Ladders).

Cost and Hours: Free, Mon-Sat 10:00-17:00, Sun 12:00-17:00, 42 High Street.

John Knox House

Intriguing for Reformation buffs, this fine medieval house dates back to 1470 and offers a well-explained look at the life of the great 16th-century reformer. Al-though most contend he never actually lived here, preservationists called it "Knox's house" to save it from the wrecking ball in the 1840s. Regardless, the place has good information on Knox and his intellectual sparring partner, Mary, Queen of Scots. Imagine the Protestant firebrand John Knox and the devout Catholic Mary sitting face-to-face in old rooms like these, discussing the most intimate matters of their spiritual lives as they decided the course of Scotland's religious future. The sparsely furnished house contains some period furniture and exhibits on printing—an essential tool for early reformers. On the top floor there's a fun photo op with a dress-up cape, hat, and feather pen. Mind your head.

Cost and Hours: £5, Mon-Sat 10:00-18:00, closed Sun except in July-Aug 12:00-18:00, 43 High Street, tel. 0131/556-9579, www.tracscotland.org.

▲People's Story Museum

This engaging exhibit traces the working and social lives of ordinary people through the 18th, 19th, and 20th centuries. You'll see

tools, products, and objects related to important Edinburgh trades (printing, brewing), a wartime kitchen, and a circa-1989 trip to the movies. On the top floor, a dated but endearing 22-minute film offers insight into the ways people have lived in this city for generations. On the ground floor, peek into the former jail, an original part of the historic building (the Canongate Tolbooth, built in 1591).

Cost and Hours: Free, Mon-Sat 10:00-17:00, closed Sun except during Festival 12:00-17:00, 163 Canongate, tel. 0131/529-4057, www.edinburghmuseums.org.uk.

▲Museum of Edinburgh

Another old house full of old stuff, this one is worth a stop for a look at its early Edinburgh history (and its handy ground-floor WC). Near the entrance, be sure to see the original copy of the National Covenant—written in 1638 on animal skin. Scottish leaders signed this, refusing to adopt the king's religion—and were killed because of it. Exploring the rest of the collection, keep an eye out for Robert Louis Stevenson's antique golf ball, James Craig's architectural plans for the Georgian New Town, an interactive kids' area with dress-up clothes, a sprawling top-floor exhibit on Edinburgh-born Earl Haig (who led the British Western Front efforts in World War I), and locally made glass and ceramics.

Cost and Hours: Free, same hours as People's Story Museum (listed above), 142 Canongate, tel. 0131/529-4143, www.edinburghmuseums.org.uk.

▲▲Scottish Parliament Building

Scotland's parliament originated in 1293 and was dissolved when Scotland united with England in 1707. But after the Scottish electorate and the British parliament gave their consent, in 1997 it was decided that there should again be "a Scottish parliament guided by justice, wisdom, integrity, and compassion." Formally reconvened by Queen Elizabeth II in 1999, the Scottish parliament now enjoys self-rule in many areas (except for matters of defense, foreign policy, immigration, and taxation). The current

government, run by the Scottish Nationalist Party (SNP), is pushing for even more independence.

The innovative building, opened in 2004, brought together
all the functions of the fledgling parliament in one complex. It's
a people-oriented structure (conceived by Catalan architect Enric
Miralles; for more on the building, see page 47). Signs are written
in both English and Gaelic (the Scots' Celtic tongue).

For a peek at the building and a lesson in how the Scottish
parliament works, drop in, pass through security, and find the visitors' desk. You're welcome in
the public parts of the building,
including a small ground-floor
exhibit on the parliament's history and function and, up several flights of stairs, a viewing
gallery overlooking the impressive Debating Chambers.

Cost and Hours: Free;
Sept-June (when parliament is in session) Mon and Fri-Sat 10:00-
17:00, Tue-Thu 9:00-18:30; July-Aug and holidays (when parliament is in recess) Mon-Sat 10:00-17:00; closed Sun year-round;
www.scottish.parliament.uk. For a complete list of recess dates or
to book tickets for debates, check their website or call their visitor
services line at tel. 0131/348-5200.

Tours: Free worthwhile hour-long tours are offered by proud
locals (2/hour, except when parliament is in session). While you
can try just dropping in, these tours can book up—call or check
online for times and reserve a spot.

Seeing Parliament in Session: You can call or sign up online
to witness the Scottish parliament's hugely popular debates (usually
Tue-Thu 14:00-18:00). On Thursdays from 12:00-12:30 the First
Minister is on the hot seat and has to field questions from members
across all parties.

▲▲Palace of Holyroodhouse

Built on the site of the abbey/monastery founded in 1128 by King
David I, this palace was the true home, birthplace, and coronation

spot of Scotland's Stuart kings
in their heyday (James IV; Mary,
Queen of Scots; and Charles I).
It's particularly memorable as the
site of some dramatic moments
from the short reign of Mary,
Queen of Scots—including the
murder of her personal secretary,
David Rizzio, by agents of her

jealous husband. Today, it's one of Queen Elizabeth II's official residences. She usually manages her Scottish affairs here during Holyrood Week, from late June to early July (and generally stays at Balmoral in August). Holyrood is open to the public outside of the Queen's visits. Touring the interior offers a more polished contrast to Edinburgh Castle, and is particularly worth considering if you don't plan to go to Balmoral. The one-way audioguide route leads you through the fine apartments and tells some of the notable stories that played out here.

Cost: £11.60, includes quality one-hour audioguide; £16.40 combo-ticket includes the Queen's Gallery; £20 combo-ticket adds guided tour of palace gardens—summer only, ask for schedule when buying tickets; tickets sold in Queen's Gallery to the right of the castle entrance (see next listing).

Hours: Daily April-Oct 9:30-18:00, Nov-March until 16:30, last entry 1.5 hours before closing, tel. 0131/556-5100, www.royalcollection.org.uk. It's still a working palace, so it's closed when the Queen or other VIPs are in residence.

Visiting the Palace: The building, rich in history and decor, is filled with elegantly furnished Victorian rooms and a few darker, older rooms with glass cases of historic bits and Scottish pieces that locals find fascinating. Bring the palace to life with the audioguide. The tour route leads you into the grassy inner courtyard, then up to the royal apartments: dining rooms, *Downton Abbey*-style drawing rooms, and royal bedchambers. Along the way, you'll learn the story behind the 96 portraits of Scottish leaders (some real, others imaginary) that line the Great Gallery; why the king never slept in his official "state bed"; why the exiled Comte d'Artois took refuge in the palace; and how the current Queen puts her Scottish subjects at ease when she receives them here. Finally you'll twist up a tight spiral staircase to the private chambers of Mary, Queen of Scots, where conspirators stormed in and stabbed her secretary 56 times.

After exiting the palace, you're free to stroll through the evocative **ruined abbey** (destroyed by the English during the time of Mary, Queen of Scots, in the 16th century) and the **palace gardens** (closed Oct-April except some weekends). Some 8,000 guests—including many honored ladies sporting fancy hats—gather here every July when the Queen hosts a magnificent tea party. (She gets help pouring.)

Nearby: Hikers, note that the wonderful trail up Arthur's Seat starts just across the street from the gardens (see page 94 for details).

Queen's Gallery

This small museum features rotating exhibits of artwork from the royal collection. For more than five centuries, the royal family has amassed a wealth of art trea-sures. While the Queen keeps most in her many private palaces, she shares an impressive load of it here, with exhibits changing about every six months. Though the gallery occupies just a few rooms, its displays can be exquisite. The entry fee includes an excellent audioguide, written and read by the curator.

Cost and Hours: £6.60, £16.40 combo-ticket includes Palace of Holyroodhouse, daily 9:30-18:00, until 16:30 Nov-March, last entry one hour before closing, café, on the palace grounds, to the right of the palace entrance, www.royalcollection.org.uk. Buses #35 and #36 stop outside, saving you a walk to or from Princes Street/North Bridge.

Our Dynamic Earth

Located about a five-minute walk from the Palace of Holyroodhouse, this immense exhibit tells the story of our planet, filling several underground floors under a vast, white Gore-Tex tent. It's pitched, appropriately, at the base of the Salisbury Crags. The exhibit is designed for younger kids and does the same thing an American science exhibit would do—but with a charming Scottish accent. You'll learn about the Scottish geologists who pioneered the discipline, then step into a "time machine" to watch the years rewind, from cave dwellers to dinosaurs to the Big Bang. After viewing several short films on stars, tectonic plates, ice caps, and worldwide weather (in a "4-D" exhibit), you're free to wander past salty pools and a re-created rain forest.

Cost and Hours: £12.50, kids-£8, daily 10:00-17:30, until 18:00 July-Aug, closed Mon-Tue Nov-March, last entry 1.5 hours before closing, on Holyrood Road, between the palace and mountain, tel. 0131/550-7800, www.dynamicearth.co.uk.

SIGHTS SOUTH OF THE ROYAL MILE

▲▲▲National Museum of Scotland

This huge museum has amassed more historic artifacts than every other place I've seen in Scotland combined. It's all wonderfully displayed, with fine descriptions offering a best-anywhere hike through the history of Scotland.

Cost and Hours: Free, daily 10:00-17:00; free one-hour "Highlights" tours daily at 11:00 and 13:00, themed tours at 15:00—confirm tour schedule at info desk or on TV screens; two long blocks south of St. Giles' Cathedral and the Royal Mile, on Chambers Street off George IV Bridge, tel. 0131/247-4422, www.nms.ac.uk.

Eating: On the museum's fifth floor, the dressy and upscale **Tower restaurant** serves good food with a castle view (£19 lunch/early bird special, £16 afternoon tea, £35 three-course dinner special, fancy £18-32 meals; daily 10:00-23:00—later than the museum itself, tel. 0131/225-3003).

➲ **Self-Guided Tour:** The place gives you two museums in one. One wing houses a popular natural history collection, with everything from kid-friendly T. Rex skeletons to Egyptian mummies. But we'll focus on the other wing, which sweeps you through Scottish history covering Roman and Viking times, Edinburgh's witch-burning craze and clan massacres, the struggle for Scottish independence, the Industrial Revolution, and right up to Scotland in the 21st century.

Get oriented on level 1, in the impressive glass-roofed Grand Gallery. This part of the building houses the natural history collection.

• *To reach the Scottish history wing, exit the Grand Gallery at the far right end, under the clock.*

On the way, you'll pass the newly renovated science and technology wing, where you might see Dolly the sheep—the world's first cloned mammal—born in Edinburgh and now stuffed and on display. Continue into Hawthornden Court (level 1), where our tour begins. (It's possible to detour downstairs from here to level -1 for Scotland's prehistoric origins—geologic formation, Celts, Romans, Vikings.)

• *Enter the door marked...*

Kingdom of the Scots (c. 1300-1700): From its very start, Scotland was determined to be free. You're greeted with proud quotes from what's been called the Scottish Declaration of Independence—the Declaration of Arbroath, a defiant letter written to the pope in 1320. As early as the ninth century, Scotland's patron saint, Andrew (see the small statue in the next room), had—according to legend—miraculously intervened to help the Picts and Scots of Scotland remain free by defeating the Angles of England. Andrew's X-shaped cross still decorates the Scottish flag today.

Turning right, enter the first room on your right, with imposing swords and other objects related to Scotland's most famous patriots—William Wallace and Robert the Bruce. Bruce's descendants, the Stuarts, went on to rule Scotland for the next 300 years. Eventually, James VI of Scotland (see his baby cradle) came to rule England as well (as King James I of England).

In the next room, a big guillotine recalls the harsh justice meted out to criminals, witches, and "Covenanters" (17th-century political activists who opposed interference of the Stuart kings in affairs of the Presbyterian Church of Scotland). Nearby, also check out the tomb (a copy) of Mary, Queen of Scots, the 16th-century Stuart monarch who opposed the Presbyterian Church of Scotland. Educated and raised in Renaissance France, Mary brought refinement to the Scottish throne. After she was imprisoned and then executed by Elizabeth I of England in 1587, her supporters rallied each other by invoking her memory. Pendants and coins with her portrait stoked the irrepressible Scottish spirit. Near the replica of Mary's tomb are tiny cameos, pieces of jewelry, and coins with her image.

Browse the rest of level 1 to see everyday objects from that age: carved panels, cookware, and clothes.

• *Backtrack to Hawthornden Court and take the elevator to level 3.*

Scotland Transformed (1700s): You'll see artifacts related to Bonnie Prince Charlie and the Jacobite rebellions as well as the ornate Act of Union document, signed in 1707 by the Scottish parliament. This act voluntarily united Scotland with England under the single parliament of Great Britain. For some Scots, this move was an inevitable step in connecting to the wider world, but for others it symbolized the end of Scotland's existence.

Union with England brought stability and investment to Scotland. In this same era, the advances of the Industrial Revolution were making a big impact on Scottish life. Mechanized textile looms (on display) replaced hand craftsmanship. The huge Newcomen steam-engine water pump helped the mining industry to develop sites with tricky drainage. (The museum puts the device in motion a few times a day.) Nearby is a model of a coal mine (or "colliery"); coal-rich Scotland exploited this natural resource to fuel its textile factories.

How the parsimonious Scots financed these new, large-scale enterprises is explained in an exhibit on the Bank of Scotland. Powered by the Scottish work ethic and the new opportunities that came from the Industrial Revolution, the country came into relative prosperity. Education and medicine thrived. With the dawn of the modern age came leisure time, the concept of "healthful sports," and golf—a popular Scottish pastime. On display are some early golf balls, which date from about 1820, made of leather and stuffed with feathers.

• *Return to the elevator and journey up to level 5.*

Industry and Empire (1800s): Turn right and do a counterclockwise spin around this floor to survey Scottish life in the 19th century. Industry had transformed the country. Highland farmers left their land to find work in Lowland factories and foundries. Modern inventions—the phonograph, the steam-powered train—revolutionized everyday life. In Glasgow, architect Charles Rennie Mackintosh helped to define Scottish Art Nouveau. Scotland was at the forefront of literature (Robert Burns, Sir Walter Scott, Robert Louis Stevenson, the first printing of the Encyclopedia Britannica), science (Lord Kelvin, James Watt, Alexander Graham Bell... he was born here, anyway!), and world exploration (David Livingstone in Africa, Sir Alexander Mackenzie in Canada).

• *Climb the stairs to level 6.*

Scotland: A Changing Nation (1900s): Turn left and do a clockwise spin through this floor to bring the story to the present day. The two world wars decimated the population of this already wee nation. In addition, hundreds of thousands emigrated, especially to Canada (where one in eight Canadians has Scottish origins). The small country has made a big mark on the world: You'll learn how Scots have gone global in the world of entertainment (early boy band Bay City Rollers, funk masters Average White Band, and the Proclaimers, who swore they'd walk a thousand miles to fall down at your door), to an impressive variety of films (gritty *Trainspotting*, fanciful *Harry Potter* blockbusters), to actor-comedians Billy Connolly and Craig Ferguson. The exhibit takes a sober look at the recent trend of devolution from the United Kingdom, especially the 1999 opening of Scotland's own parliament and the landmark 2014 referendum on Scottish independence. Finally, in the Sports Hall of Fame, you'll see the pioneers of modern golf (Tom Morris, from St. Andrews), auto racing (Jackie Stewart and Jim Clark), and a signed baseball by Glasgow-born Bobby (1951 home run) Thomson.

• *Finish your visit on level 7, the rooftop.*

Garden Terrace: Don't miss the great views of Edinburgh from this well-described roof garden, growing grasses and heathers from every corner of Scotland. When you're done, simply ride the elevator down to level 1 and the exit.

Greyfriars Bobby Statue and Greyfriars Cemetery

This famous **statue** of Edinburgh's favorite dog is across the street from the National Museum of Scotland. Every business nearby, it seems, is named for this Victorian Skye terrier, who is reputed to have stood by his master's grave in Greyfriars Cemetery for 14 years. The story was immortalized in a 1960s Disney flick, but recent research suggests that 19th-century businessmen bribed a stray to hang out in the cemetery to attract sightseers. If it was a ruse, it still works.

Just behind Bobby is the entrance to his namesake **cemetery**. Stepping through the gate, you'll see the pink-marble grave of Bobby himself. The well-tended cemetery is an evocative place to stroll, and a nice escape from the city's bustle. Harry Potter fans could turn it into a scavenger hunt: J. K. Rowling sketched out her saga just around the corner at The Elephant House Café—and a few of the cemetery's weather-beaten headstones bear familiar names, including McGonagall and Thomas Riddell. Beyond the cemetery fence are the frilly Gothic spires of posh George Heriot's School, said to have inspired Hogwarts. And just a few short blocks to the east is a street called...Potterrow.

Grassmarket

Once Edinburgh's site for hangings (residents rented out their windows—above the rudely named "Last Drop" pub—for the view), today Grassmarket is a people-friendly piazza. It was

originally the city's garage, a depot for horses and cows (hence the name). It's rowdy here at night—a popular place for "hen dos" and "stag dos" (bachelorette and bachelor parties). In the early evening, the Literary Pub Tour departs from here (see page 105). Some great shopping streets branch off from Grassmarket: Victoria Street, built in the Victorian Age, is lined with colorful little shops and eateries; angling off in the other direction, Candlemaker's Row has one of central Edinburgh's most creative arrays of design shops (and leads, in just a couple of minutes' walk, up to Greyfriars Bobby and the National Museum; for more shopping tips in this area, see page 98).

Hiding in the blur of traffic is a monument to the "Covenanters." These strict 17th-century Scottish Protestants were killed for refusing to accept the king's Episcopalian prayer book. To this day, Scots celebrate their national church's emphatically democratic government. Rather than big-shot bishops (as in the Anglican or Roman Catholic Church), they have a low-key "moderator" who's elected each year.

MUSEUMS IN THE NEW TOWN

These sights are linked by the "Bonnie Wee New Town Walk" on page 48.

▲▲Scottish National Gallery

This delightful, small museum has Scotland's best collection of paintings. In a short visit, you can admire well-described works by

Old Masters (Raphael, Rembrandt, Rubens), Impressionists (Monet, Degas, Gauguin), and a few underrated Scottish painters. (Scottish art is better at the National Portrait Gallery, described next.) Although there are no iconic masterpieces, it's a surprisingly enjoyable collection that's truly world-class.

Cost and Hours: Free; daily 10:00-17:00, Thu until 19:00; longer hours in Aug: Sun-Wed until 18:00, Thu-Sat until 19:00; The Mound (between Princes and Market streets), tel. 0131/624-6200, www.nationalgalleries.org.

Expect Changes: The gallery often loans artwork, including its finest paintings. Ask one of the friendly tartan-sporting attendants or at the info desk downstairs (near the WCs and gallery shop) if you can't find a particular item.

Next Door: The skippable **Royal Scottish Academy** hosts temporary art exhibits and is connected to the Scottish National

Gallery at the Gardens level (underneath the gallery) by the Weston Link building (same hours as gallery, fine café and restaurant).

⊃ **Self-Guided Tour:** Start at the gallery entrance (at the north end of the building). Climb the stairs to the upper level (north end), and take a left. You'll run right into...

Van der Goes—*The Trinity Panels* (c. 1473-1479): For more than five centuries, these panels have stood on this spot in Ed-

inburgh—first in a church, then (when the church was leveled to build Waverley train station) in this museum. The panels likely flanked a central scene of the Virgin Mary that was destroyed by Protestant vandals during the Reformation.

In the left panel is the Trinity: God the Father, in a rich red robe, cradles a spindly, just-crucified Christ, while the dove of the Holy Spirit hovers between them. On the right, the church's director (the man who commissioned the painting from the well-known Flemish painter) kneels and looks on while an angel plays a hymn on the church organ. In typically medieval fashion, the details are meticulous—expressive faces, intricate folds in the robes, Christ's pallid skin, observant angels. The donor's face is a remarkable portrait, with realistic skin tone and a five-o'clock shadow. But the painting lacks true 3-D realism—God's gold throne is overly exaggerated, and Christ's cardboard-cutout body hovers weightlessly.

The flip side of the panels depicts Scotland's king and queen, who are best known to history as the parents of the boy kneeling alongside them. (You can ask the guard to open the panels.) He grew up to become James IV, the Renaissance king who made Edinburgh a cultural capital.

• *Go back across the top of the skylight, to a room where the next two paintings hang facing each other.*

Botticelli—*The Virgin Adoring the Sleeping Christ Child* (c. 1490): Mary looks down at her baby, peacefully sleeping in a flower-filled garden. It's easy to appreciate Botticelli's masterful style: the precisely drawn outlines, the Virgin's pristine skin, the translucent glow. Botticelli creates a serene world in which no shadows are cast. The scene is painted on canvas—unusual at a time when wood panels were the norm. For the Virgin's rich cloak, Botticelli used ground-up lapis lazuli (a very pricey semiprecious stone), and her hem is decorated with gold leaf.

Renaissance-era art lovers would instantly catch the symbolism. Mary wears a wispy halo and blue cloak that recalls the sky blue of heaven. The roses without thorns and enclosed garden are both symbols of virginity, while the violet flowers (at bottom) represent humility. Darker symbolism hints at what's to come. The strawberries (lower right) signify Christ's blood, soon to be shed, while the roses—though thornless now—will become the Crown of Thorns. For now, Mary can adore her sleeping, blissful baby in a peaceful garden. But in a few decades she'll be kneeling again to weep over the dead, crucified Messiah.

Raphael—*Holy Family with a Palm Tree* (1506-1507): Mary, Joseph, and the Christ Child fit snugly within a round frame (a

tondo), their pose symbolizing geometric perfection and the perfect family unit. Joseph kneels to offer Jesus flowers. Mary curves toward him. Baby Jesus dangles in between, linking the family together. Raphael also connects the figures through eye contact: Mary eyes Joseph, who locks onto Jesus, who gazes precociously back. Like in a cameo, we see the faces incised in profile, while their bodies bulge out toward us.

• *Back downstairs at ground level is the main gallery space. Circle around the collection chronologically, watching for works by Bellini, Titian, Velázquez, and El Greco. In Room 7, look for...*

Rubens—*Feast of Herod* (c. 1635-1638): All eyes turn to watch the dramatic culmination of the story of John the Baptist. Salome (standing in center) presents John's severed head on a platter to a horrified King Herod, who clutches the tablecloth and buries his hand in his beard to stifle a gag. Meanwhile, Herod's wife—who cooked up the nasty plot—pokes spitefully at John's head with a fork. A dog tugs at Herod's foot like a nasty conscience. The canvas—big, colorful, full of motion and drama—is totally Baroque. Some have suggested that the features of Herod's wife and Salome are those of Rubens' wife and ex-wives, and the head is Rubens himself.

• *Next, in Room 8, look for...*

Rembrandt—*Self-Portrait, Aged 51* (c. 1657): It's 1657, and 51-year-old Rembrandt has just declared bankruptcy. Besides financial hardship and the auctioning-off of his personal belongings, he's also facing social stigma and behind-his-back ridicule. Once Holland's most renowned painter, he's begun a slow decline into poverty and obscurity.

His face says it all. Holding a steady gaze, he stares with matter-of-fact acceptance, with his lips pursed. He's dressed in dark clothes against a dark background, with the only spot of light shining on the worry lines of his forehead. Get close enough to the canvas to see the thick paste of paint he used for the wrinkles around his eyes—a study in aging.

• *In Room 11, find...*

Gainsborough—*The Honorable Mrs. Graham* (1775-1777): The slender, elegant, lavishly dressed woman was the teenage

bride of a wealthy Scottish landowner. She leans on a column, ostrich feather in hand, staring off to the side (Thoughtfully? Determinedly? Haughtily?). Her faultless face and smooth neck stand out from the elaborately ruffled dress and background foliage. This 18th-century woman wears a silvery dress that echoes 17th-century style—Gainsborough's way of showing how, though she was young, she was classy. Thomas ("Blue Boy") Gainsborough—the product of a clothes-making father and a flower-painting mother—uses aspects of both in this lush portrait. The ruby brooch on her bodice marks the center of this harmonious composition.

• *Climb the stairs to the upper level (south end, opposite from where you entered) and turn right for the Impressionists and Post-Impressionists.*

Impressionist Collection: The gallery has a smattering of (mostly smaller-scale) works from all the main artists of the Impressionist and Post-Impressionist eras. You'll see Degas' ballet scenes, Renoir's pastel-colored family scenes, Van Gogh's peasants, and Seurat's pointillism.

• *Keep an eye out for these three paintings (if you can't find them, ask an attendant).*

Monet's *Poplars on the Epte* (1891) was part of the artist's famous "series" paintings. He set up several canvases in a floating studio near his home in Giverny. He'd start on one canvas in the morning (to catch the morning light), then move to the next as the light changed. This particular canvas captures a perfect summer day, showing both the poplars on the riverbank and their mirror image in the still water. The subject matter begins to dissolve into a pure pattern of color, anticipating abstract art.

Gauguin's *Vision of the Sermon* (1888) shows French peasant women imagining the miraculous event they've just heard preached about in church—when Jacob wrestles with an angel. The painting is a watershed in art history, as Gauguin throws out the rules of "realism" that had reigned since the Renaissance. The colors are surreal, there are no shadows, the figures are arranged almost randomly, and there's no attempt to make the wrestlers appear distant. The diagonal tree branch is the only thing separating the everyday world from the miraculous. Later, when Gauguin moved to Tahiti (see his *Three Tahitians* nearby), he painted a similar world, where the everyday and magical coexist, with symbolic power.

Sargent's *Lady Agnew of Lochnaw* (1892) is the work that launched the career of this American-born portrait artist. Lady

Agnew—the young wife of a wealthy old Scotsman—lounges back languidly and gazes out self-assuredly. The Impressionistic smudges of paint on her dress and the chair contrast with her clear skin and luminous eyeballs. Her relaxed pose (one arm hanging down the side) contrasts with her intensity: head tilted slightly down while she gazes up, a corner of her mouth askew, and an eyebrow cocked seductively.

• *End your visit downstairs on the lower level, home to the...*

Scottish Collection: Though Scotland has produced few "name" painters, this small wing lets you sample some of the best. It's all in one room, designed to be toured chronologically (clockwise). At the end of the first (upper) concourse, look for paintings by **Allan Ramsay.** The son of the well-known poet of the same name, Ramsay painted portraits of curly-wigged men of the Enlightenment era (the philosopher David Hume, King George III) as well as likenesses of his two wives. Ramsay's portrait of the duke of Argyll—founder of the Royal Bank of Scotland—appears on the front of notes printed by this bank.

Downstairs, **Sir Henry Raeburn** chronicled the next generation: Sir Walter Scott, the proud kilt-wearing Alastair Macdonell, and the ice-skating Reverend Robert Walker, minister of the Canongate Church.

Sir David Wilkie's forte was small-scale scenes of everyday life. *The Letter of Introduction* (1813) captures Wilkie's own experience of trying to impress skeptical art patrons in London; even the dog is sniffing the Scotsman out. *Distraining for Rent* (1815) shows the plight of a poor farmer about to lose his farm—a common occurrence during 19th-century industrialization.

Pause and swoon before **William Dyce's** *Francesca da Rimini* (1837). The star-crossed lovers—a young wife and her husband's kid brother—can't help but indulge their passion. The husband later finds out and kills her; at the far left, you see his ominous hand.

Finally, take in **William McTaggart's** impressionistic landscape scenes from the late 1800s for a glimpse of the unique light, powerful clouds, and natural wonder of the Highlands.

▲▲Scottish National Portrait Gallery

Put a face on Scotland's history by enjoying these portraits of famous Scots from the earliest times until today. From its Neo-Gothic facade to a grand entry hall featuring a *Who's Who* of Scotland, to galleries highlighting the great Scots of each age, this impressive museum will fascinate anyone interested in Scottish culture. The gallery also hosts temporary exhibits highlighting the work of more contemporary Scots. Because of its purely Scottish focus, many travelers prefer this to the (pan-European) main branch of the National Gallery.

Cost and Hours: Free, daily 10:00-17:00, Thu until 19:00—occasional live music at 18:00, good cafeteria serving healthy £5-7 meals, 1 Queen Street, tel. 0131/624-6490, www.nationalgalleries.org.

Visiting the Gallery: In the stirring **entrance hall** you'll find busts of great Scots and a full-body statue of Robbie "Rabbie" Burns, as well as (up above) a glorious frieze showing a parade of important historical figures and murals depicting important events in Scottish history. (These are better viewed from the first floor and its mezzanine—described later.) We'll start on the **second floor**, right into the thick of the struggle between Scotland and England over who should rule this land.

Reformation to Revolution (gallery 1): The collection starts with a portrait of **Mary, Queen of Scots** (1542-1587), her cross and rosary prominent. This controversial ruler set off two centuries of strife. Mary was born with both Stuart blood (the ruling family of Scotland) and the Tudor blood of England's monarchs (Queen Elizabeth I was her cousin). Catholic and French-educated, Mary felt alienated from her own increasingly Protestant homeland. Her tense conversations with the reformer John Knox must have been epic. Then came a series of scandals: She married unpopular Lord Darnley, then (possibly) cheated on him, causing Darnley to (possibly) murder her lover, causing Mary to (possibly) murder Darnley, then (possibly) run off with another man, and (possibly) plot against Queen Elizabeth.

Amid all that drama, Mary was forced by her own people to relinquish her throne to her infant son, **James VI.** Find his portraits as a child and as a grown-up. James grew up to rule Scotland, and when Queen Elizabeth (the "virgin queen") died without an heir, he also became king of England (James I). But James' son, **Charles I,** after a bitter civil war, was arrested and executed in 1649: See the large *Execution of Charles I* painting high on the far wall, his blood-dripping head displayed to the crowd; nearby is a portrait of Charles in happier times, as a 12-year-old boy. His son, Charles II, restored the Stuarts to power. He was then succeeded by his Catholic brother James VII of Scotland (II of England), who was sent into exile in France. There the Stuarts stewed, planning a return to power, waiting for someone to lead them in what would come to be known as the Jacobite rebellions.

The Jacobite Cause (gallery 4): The biggest painting in the room is *The Baptism of Prince Charles Edward Stuart*. Born in 1720, this heir to the thrones of Great Britain and Ireland is better known to history as "Bonnie Prince Charlie." (See his bonnie features in various portraits nearby, as a child, young man, and grown man.) Charismatic Charles convinced France to invade Scotland and put him back on the throne there. In 1745, he entered Edinburgh in triumph. But he was defeated at the tide-turning Battle of Culloden (1746). The Stuart cause died forever, and Bonnie Prince Charlie went into exile, eventually dying drunk and wasted in Rome, far from the land he nearly ruled.

Citizens of the World (galleries 5-6): The two biggest paintings here are of King George III and Queen Charlotte (namesakes of the New Town's main street and square). In the late 18th century, Scotland was doing just fine being ruled from England. Paintings here show the confidence of this age, when the New Town of Edinburgh was designed and built. In the 1760s, Edinburgh was the center of Europe's Enlightenment, powered by philosophers such as David Hume (find his portrait, by Allan Ramsay, who also painted the likeness of George III) and his economist friend Adam Smith (depicted in a cameo medallion).

The Age of Improvement (gallery 7): The faces portrayed here belonged to a new society whose hard work and public spirit achieved progress with a Scottish accent. Social equality and the Industrial Revolution "transformed" Scotland—you'll see portraits of the great poet Robert Burns, the son of a farmer (Burns was heralded as a "heaven-taught ploughman" when his poems were first published), and the inventor of the steam engine, James Watt.

Playing for Scotland (gallery 10): Lighten things up with a swing through old-time sports in Scotland, including early golf, curling, Highland Games (including "putting the stone"—similar to shot put), fox hunting, and croquet.

• *Now head back down to the first floor for a good look at the...*

Central Atrium (first floor): Great Scots! The atrium is decorated in a parade of late 19th-century Romantic Historicism. The

frieze (working counterclockwise) is a visual encyclopedia, from an ax-wielding Stone Age man and a druid, to the early legendary monarchs (Macbeth), to warriors William Wallace and Robert the Bruce, to many kings (James I, II, III, and so on), to great thinkers, inventors, and artists (Allan Ramsay, Flora MacDonald, David Hume, Adam Smith, James Boswell, James Watt), the three greatest Scottish writers (Robert Burns, Sir Walter Scott, Robert Louis Stevenson), and culminating with the historian Thomas Carlyle, who was the driving spirit (powered by the fortune of a local newspaper baron) behind creating this portrait gallery.

Best viewed from the first-floor mezzanine are the large-scale **murals** depicting great events in Scottish history, including the landing of St. Margaret at Queensferry in 1068, the Battle of Stirling Bridge in 1297, the Battle of Bannockburn in 1314, and the marriage procession of James IV and Margaret Tudor through the streets of Edinburgh in 1509.

• *Also on this floor is...*

Gallery 11: Artwork rotates in and out, but it always highlights Scots who are making an impact in the world today. You may see Annie Lennox, Ian Rankin, or distinguished Scottish scientists such as physicist Peter Higgs (theorizer of the Higgs boson, the so-called God particle). One constant is the stirring *Three Oncologists,* a ghostly painting depicting the anxiety and terror of cancer and the dedication of those working so hard to conquer it.

▲▲Georgian House

This refurbished Neoclassical house, set on Charlotte Square, is a trip back to 1796. It recounts the era when a newly gentrified

and well-educated Edinburgh was nicknamed the "Athens of the North." Begin on the second floor, where you'll watch an interesting 16-minute video dramatizing the upstairs/downstairs lifestyles of the aristocrats and servants who lived here. Try on some Georgian outfits, then head downstairs to tour period rooms and even peek into the fully stocked medicine cabinet. A volunteer guide shares stories and trivia: You'll learn why Georgian bigwigs had to sit behind a screen while enjoying a fire. A walk down George Street after your visit here can be fun for the imagination.

Cost and Hours: £7, daily April-Oct 10:00-17:00—July-Aug until 18:00, March and Nov 11:00-16:00, may be open Thu-Sun in Dec, otherwise closed Dec-Feb, last entry 45 minutes before closing, 7 Charlotte Square, tel. 0131/226-3318, www.nts.org.uk.

SIGHTS NEAR EDINBURGH
▲▲Royal Yacht *Britannia*

This much-revered vessel, which transported Britain's royal fam-

ily for more than 40 years on 900 voyages (an average of once around the world per year) before being retired in 1997, is permanently moored in Edinburgh's port of Leith. Queen Elizabeth II said of the ship, "This is the only place I can truly relax." Today it's open to the curious public, who have access to its many decks—from engine rooms to drawing rooms—and offers a fascinating time-warp look into the late-20th-century lifestyles of the rich and royal. It's worth the half-hour bus or taxi ride from the center; figure on spending about 2.5 hours total on the outing.

Cost and Hours: £14, includes 1.5-

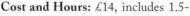

hour audioguide, daily April-Sept 9:30-16:30, Oct 9:30-16:00, Nov-March 10:00-15:30, these are last entry times, tearoom; at the Ocean Terminal Shopping Mall, on Ocean Drive in Leith; tel. 0131/555-5566, www.royalyachtbritannia.co.uk.

Getting There: From central Edinburgh, catch Lothian bus #11 or #22 from Princes Street (just above Waverley Station), or #35 from the bottom of the Royal Mile (alongside the parliament building) to Ocean Terminal. The Majestic Tour hop-on, hop-off bus stops here as well. Drivers can park free in the blue parking garage. Take the shopping center elevator to level E, then follow the signs.

Visiting the Ship: First, explore the **museum,** filled with engrossing royal-family-afloat history. You'll see lots of family photos that evoke the fine times the Windsors enjoyed on the *Britannia,* as well as some nautical equipment and uniforms. Then, armed with your audioguide, you're welcome aboard.

This was the last in a line of royal yachts that stretches back to 1660. With all its royal functions, the ship required a crew of more than 200. Begin in the captain's bridge, which feels like it's been preserved from the day it was launched in 1953. Then head down a deck to see the officers' quarters, then the garage, where a Rolls Royce was hoisted aboard to use in places where the local transportation wasn't up to royal standards. The Veranda Deck at the back of the ship was the favorite place for outdoor entertainment. Ronald Reagan, Boris Yeltsin, Bill Clinton, and Nelson Mandela all sipped champagne here. The Sun Lounge, just off the back Veranda Deck, was the Queen's favorite, with Burmese teak and the same phone system she was used to in Buckingham Palace. When she wasn't entertaining, the Queen liked it quiet. The crew wore sneakers, communicated in hand signals, and (at least near the Queen's quarters) had to be finished with all their work by 8:00 in the morning.

Take a peek into the adjoining his-and-hers bedrooms of the Queen and the Duke of Edinburgh (check out the spartan twin beds), and the honeymoon suite where Prince Charles and Lady Di began their wedded bliss.

Heading down another deck, walk through the officers' lounge (and learn about the rowdy games they played) and past

the galleys (including custom cabinetry for the fine china and silver) on your way to the biggest room on the yacht, the state dining room. Now decorated with gifts given by the ship's many noteworthy guests, this space enabled the Queen to entertain a good-size crowd. The drawing room, while rather simple (the Queen specifically requested "country house comfort"), was perfect for casual relaxing among royals. Princess Diana played the piano, which is bolted to the deck. Note the contrast to the decidedly less plush crew's quarters, mail room, sick bay, laundry, and engine room.

▲Rosslyn Chapel

This small but fascinating countryside church, about a 20-minute drive outside Edinburgh, is a riot of carved iconography. The patterned ceiling and walls have left scholars guessing about the symbolism for centuries.

Cost and Hours: £9, Mon-Sat 9:30-18:00, until 17:00 Oct-March, Sun 12:00-16:45 year-round, no photos allowed, located in Roslin Village, www.rosslynchapel.org.uk.

Getting There: Ride Lothian bus #37 from Princes Street (stop PJ) or North Bridge (1-2/hour, 45 minutes). By car, take the A-701 to Penicuik/Peebles, and follow signs for *Roslin;* once you're in the village, you'll see signs for the chapel.

Background: After it was featured in the climax of Dan Brown's 2003 bestseller *The Da Vinci Code,* the number of visitors to Rosslyn Chapel more than quadrupled. But the chapel's allure existed well before the books, and will endure long after they move from bargain bin to landfill. Founded in 1446 as the private mausoleum of the St. Clair family—who wanted to be buried close to God—the church's interior is carved with a stunning mishmash of Christian, pagan, family, Templar, Masonic, and other symbolism. After the Scottish Reformation, Catholic churches like this fell into disrepair. But in the 18th and 19th centuries, Romantics such as Robert Burns and Sir Walter Scott discovered these evocative old ruins, putting Rosslyn Chapel back on the map. Even Queen Victoria visited, and gently suggested that the chapel be restored to its original state. Today, after more than a century of refits and refurbishments, the chapel transports visitors back to a distant and mysterious age.

Visiting the Chapel: From the ticket desk and visitors center, head to the chapel itself. Ask about docent lectures (usually at the top of the hour). If you have time to kill, pick up the good laminated descriptions for a clockwise tour of the carvings. In the crypt—where the stonemasons worked—you can see faint architectural drawings engraved in the wall, used to help them plot out their master design.

Elsewhere, look for these fun details: In the corner to the left of the altar, find the angels playing instruments—including one with bagpipes. Nearby, you'll see a person dancing with a skeleton. This "dance of death" theme—common in the Middle Ages—is a reminder of mortality: We'll all die eventually, so we might as well whoop it up while we're here. On the other side of the nave are carvings of the seven deadly sins and the seven acts of mercy. One inscription reads: "Wine is strong. Kings are stronger. Women are stronger still. But truth conquers all."

Flanking the altar are two carved columns that come with a legend: The more standard-issue column, on the left, was executed by a master mason, who soon after (perhaps disappointed in his lack of originality) went on a sabbatical to gain inspiration. While he was gone, his ambitious apprentice carved the beautiful cork-screw-shaped column on the right. Upon returning, the master flew into an envious rage and murdered the apprentice with his carving hammer.

Scattered throughout the church, you'll also see the family's symbol, the "engrailed cross" (with serrated edges). Keep an eye out for the more than one hundred "green men"—chubby faces with leaves and vines growing out of their orifices, symbolizing nature. This paradise/Garden of Eden theme is enhanced by a smattering of exotic animals (monkey, elephant, camel, dragon, and a lion fighting a unicorn) and some exotic foliage: aloe vera, trillium, and corn. That last one (framing a window to the right of the altar) is a mystery: It was carved well before Columbus sailed the ocean blue, at a time when corn was unknown in Europe. Several theories have been suggested—some far-fetched (the father of the man who built the chapel explored the New World before Columbus), and others more plausible (the St. Clairs were of Norse descent, and the Vikings are known to have traveled to the Americas well before Columbus). Others simply say it's not corn at all—it's stalks of wheat. After all these centuries, Rosslyn Chapel's mysteries still inspire the imaginations of historians, novelists, and tourists alike.

Royal Botanic Garden

Britain's second-oldest botanical garden (after Oxford) was established in 1670 for medicinal herbs, and this 70-acre refuge is now one of Europe's best.

Cost and Hours: Gardens-free, greenhouse-£5, daily March-Sept 10:00-18:00, until 17:00 Feb and Oct, until 16:00 Nov-Jan, greenhouse closes one hour earlier, café, a mile north of the city center at Inverleith Row, tel. 0131/552-7171, www.rbge.org.uk.

Getting There: It's a 10-minute bus ride from the city center: Take bus #8 from North Bridge, or #23 or #27 from George IV Bridge (near the National Museum) or The Mound. The Majestic Tour hop-on, hop-off bus also stops here.

EDINBURGH

Scottish National Gallery of Modern Art

This museum, set in a beautiful parkland, houses Scottish and international paintings and sculpture from 1900 to the present, including works by Matisse, Duchamp, Picasso, and Warhol. The grounds include a pleasant outdoor sculpture park and a café.

Cost and Hours: Free, daily 10:00-17:00, Aug until 18:00—until 19:00 Thu-Sat, 75 Belford Road, tel. 0131/624-6336, www.nationalgalleries.org.

Getting There: It's about a 20-minute walk west from the city center. Public transportation options aren't good, but a shuttle bus runs hourly between this museum and the Scottish National Gallery (£1 donation requested, confirm times on website).

URBAN HIKES

▲▲Holyrood Park: Arthur's Seat and the Salisbury Crags

Rising up from the heart of Edinburgh, Holyrood Park is a lush green mountain squeezed between the parliament/Holyroodhouse (at the bottom of the Royal Mile) and the Dalkeith Road B&B neighborhood. For an exhilarating hike, connect these two zones with a moderately strenuous 30-minute walk along the Salisbury Crags—reddish cliffs with sweeping views over the city. Or, for a more serious climb, make the ascent to the summit of Arthur's Seat, the  822-foot-tall remains of an extinct volcano. You can run up like they did in *Chariots of Fire*, or just stroll—at the summit, you'll be rewarded with commanding views of the town and surroundings. On May Day, be on the summit at dawn and wash your face in the morning dew to commemorate the Celtic holiday of Beltane, the celebration of spring. (Morning dew is supposedly very good for your complexion.)

You can do this hike either from the bottom of the Royal Mile, or from the B&B neighborhood.

From the Royal Mile: Begin in the parking lot below the Palace of Holyroodhouse. Facing the cliff, you'll see two trailheads. For the easier hike along the base of the **Salisbury Crags,** take the trail to the right. At the far end, you can descend into the Dalkeith Road area or—if you're up for more hiking—continue steeply up the switchbacked trail to the Arthur's Seat summit. If you know you'll want to ascend **Arthur's Seat** from the start, take the wider path on the left from the Holyroodhouse parking lot (easier grade, through the abbey ruins and "Hunter's Bog").

From the Dalkeith Road B&B Neighborhood: If you're

sleeping in this area, enjoy a pre-breakfast or late-evening hike starting from the other side (in June, the sun comes up early, and it stays light until nearly midnight). From the Commonwealth Pool, take Holyrood Park Road, bear left at the first roundabout, then turn right at the second

roundabout (onto Queen's Drive). Soon you'll see the trailhead, and make your choice: Bear right up the steeper "Piper's Walk" to **Arthur's Seat** (about a 20-minute hike from here, up a steeply switchbacked trail). Or bear left for an easier ascent up the "Radial Road" to the **Salisbury Crags,** which you can follow—with great views over town—all the way to Holyroodhouse Palace.

By Car: If you have a car, you can drive up most of the way to Arthur's Seat from behind (follow the one-way street from the palace, park safely and for free by the little lake, and hike up).

▲Calton Hill

For an easy walk for fine views over all of Edinburgh, head up to Calton Hill—the monument-studded bluff that rises up from the eastern end of the New Town. From the Waverley Station area, simply head east on Princes Street (which becomes Waterloo Place).

About five minutes after passing North Bridge, watch on the right for the gated entrance to the **Old Calton Cemetery**—worth a quick walk-through for its stirring monuments to great Scots. The can't-miss-it round monument honors the philosopher David Hume; just next to that is a memorial topped by Abraham Lincoln, honoring Scottish-American troops who were killed in combat. The obelisk honors political martyrs.

The views from the cemetery are good, but for even better ones, head back out to the main road and continue a few more min-

utes on Waterloo Place. Across the street, steps lead up into **Calton Hill.** Explore. Informational plaques identify the key landmarks. At the summit of the hill is the giant, unfinished replica of the Parthenon, honoring those lost in the Napoleonic Wars. Donations to finish it never materialized, leaving it with the nickname "Edinburgh's Disgrace." Nearby, the old observatory is filled with an avant-garde art gallery, and the back of the hillside boasts sweeping views over the Firth of Forth and Edinburgh's sprawl. Back toward the Old Town, the tallest tower celebrates Admiral

Horatio Nelson—the same honoree of the giant pillar on London's Trafalgar Square. The best views are around the smaller, circular Dugald Stewart Monument, with postcard panoramas overlooking the spires of the Old Town and the New Town.

More Hikes

You can hike along the river (called the Water of Leith) through Edinburgh. Locals favor the stretch between Roseburn and Dean Village, but the 1.5-mile walk from Dean Village to the Royal Botanic Garden is also good. For more information on these and other hikes, ask at the TI.

ACTIVITIES

Several enjoyable activities cluster near the B&B area around Dalkeith Road. For details, check their websites.

The **Royal Commonwealth Pool** is an indoor fitness and activity complex with a 50-meter pool, gym/fitness studio, and kids' soft play zone (daily, tel. 0131/667-7211, www.edinburghleisure. co.uk).

The **Prestonfield Golf Club,** also an easy walk from the B&Bs, has golfers feeling like they're in a country estate (dress code, 6 Priestfield Road North, tel. 0131/667-9665, www.prestonfieldgolf. com).

Farther out at **Midlothian Snowsports Centre** (a little south of town in Hillend; better for drivers), try brush-skiing—skiing without any pesky snow. It feels like snow-skiing on a slushy day, even though you're schussing over what seems like a million toothbrushes. Beware: Doctors are used to treating an ailment called "Hillend Thumb"—thumbs dislocated when people fall here and get tangled in the brush. Locals say that skiing here is like falling on a carrot grater (open evenings only—call to confirm hours, bus #4 or #15, tel. 0131/445-4433, www.midlothian.gov.uk).

Festivals in Edinburgh

Every summer, Edinburgh's annual festivals turn the city into a carnival of the arts. The season begins in June with the international film festival (www.edfilmfest.org.uk); then the jazz and blues festival in July (www.edinburghjazzfestival.com).

In August a riot of overlapping festivals known collectively as the **Edinburgh Festival** rages simultaneously—international, fringe, book, and art, as well as the Military Tattoo. There are enough music, dance, drama, and multicultural events to make even the most jaded traveler giddy with excitement. Every day is jammed with formal and spontaneous fun. Many city sights run on extended hours. It's a glorious time to be in Edinburgh...*if* you have (and can afford) a room.

If you'll be in town in August, book your room and tickets for major events (especially the Tattoo) as far ahead as you can lock in dates. Plan carefully to ensure you'll have time for festival activities as well as sightseeing. Check online to confirm dates; the best overall website is www.edinburghfestivals.co.uk. Several publications—including the festival's official schedule, the *Edinburgh Festivals Guide Daily, The List, Fringe Program,* and *Daily Diary*—list and evaluate festival events.

The official, more formal **Edinburgh International Festival** is the original. Major events sell out well in advance (ticket office at the Hub, in the former Tolbooth Church near the top of the Royal Mile, tel. 0131/473-2000, www.hubtickets.co.uk or www.eif.co.uk).

The less formal **Fringe Festival,** featuring edgy comedy and theater, is huge—with 2,000 shows—and has eclipsed the original festival in popularity (ticket/info office just below St. Giles' Cathedral on the Royal Mile, 180 High Street, bookings tel. 0131/226-0000, www.edfringe.com). Tickets may be available at the door, and half-price tickets for some events are sold on the day of the show at the Half-Price Hut, located at The Mound, near the Scottish National Gallery.

The **Military Tattoo** is a massing of bands, drums, and bagpipes, with groups from all over the former British Empire and beyond. Displaying military finesse with a stirring lone-piper finale, this grand spectacle fills the Castle Esplanade (nightly except Sun: Aug 5-27 in 2016, Aug 4-26 in 2017; performances Mon-Fri at 21:00, Sat at 19:30 and 22:30, £25-63, booking starts in Dec, Fri-Sat shows sell out first, all seats generally sold out by early summer, some scattered same-day tickets may be available; office open Mon-Fri 10:00-16:30, closed Sat-Sun, during Tattoo open until show time and closed Sun; 32 Market Street, behind Waverley Station, tel. 0131/225-1188, www.edintattoo.co.uk). Some performances are filmed by the BBC and later broadcast as a big national television special.

The **Festival of Politics,** adding yet another dimension to Edinburgh's festival action, is held in August in the Scottish parliament building. It's a busy weekend of discussions and lectures on environmentalism, globalization, terrorism, gender, and other issues (www.festivalofpolitics.org.uk).

Other summer festivals cover books (mid-late Aug, www.edbookfest.co.uk) and art (late July-Aug, www.edinburghartfestival.com).

EDINBURGH

Shopping in Edinburgh

Edinburgh is bursting with Scottish clichés for sale: kilts, short-bread, whisky...if they can slap a tartan on it, they'll sell it. Locals dismiss the touristy trinket shops, which are most concentrated along the Royal Mile, as "tartan tat." Your challenge is finding something a wee bit more authentic. If you want to be sure you are taking home local merchandise, check if the labels read: "Made in Scotland." "Designed in Scotland" actually means "Made in China." Shops are usually open 10:00-18:00 (later on Thu).

SHOPPING STREETS AND NEIGHBORHOODS
Near the Royal Mile

The Royal Mile is intensely touristy, mostly lined with inter-changeable shops selling made-in-China souvenirs. (While they seem different, most of the shops along the Royal Mile are actually owned by the same family.) I've listed a few worthwhile spots along here later, under "What to Shop For." But in general, the two connecting streets listed next—an easy stroll from the top of the Royal Mile—offer more originality.

Victoria Street, which climbs steeply downhill from the Royal Mile (near the Hub/Tolbooth Church) to Grassmarket, has a fine concentration of creative shops. You'll see I.J. Mellis Cheesemonger (#30A, described later), The Red Door Gallery (fun and hip design—from prints to jewelry, #42), Walker Slater (designer tweed, #16 and #44, described later), Calezat (quality textiles), and more.

Candlemaker Row, exiting Grassmarket opposite Victoria Street, continues the fun lineup, but amps up the creative design. First, where the street meets Grassmarket, look for a pair of funky shops: Fabhatrix hat shop—with everything from dapper men's caps to outrageous fascinators—and Mr. Wood's Fossils. Then head up Candlemaker Row toward the National Museum, passing a fun-to-browse collection of funky galleries. Two of the best galleries, on the left, are the Hannah Zakari boutique (#43) and the PI-KU Collective (#39). Also worth a look are Maple Arts (prints and other artsy design, #62), Joyce Forsyth (designer knitwear, #42), and Little Ox Gallery (pop culture-inspired prints, #23). Greyfriars Bobby awaits you at the top of the street (see page 81).

In the New Town

Thistle Street, lined with some fun eateries, also has a great collection of shops. You'll see some fashion boutiques (Covet, Biscuit), jewelry (Alchemia Studio for modern stuff, Joseph Bonnar for antiques), shoes (Pam Jenkins), and Howie Nicolsby's 21st Century

Kilts, which attempts to bring traditional Scottish menswear into the present day.

For mass-market shopping in the New Town, you'll find plenty of big chain stores along **Princes Street,** facing Princes Street Gardens and the Royal Mile from across the glen. In addition to Marks & Spencer, H&M, BHS, Zara, Primark, and a glitzy Apple Store, you'll also see the granddaddy of Scottish department stores, Jenners (Mon-Sat 9:30-18:30 or later, Sun 10:00-18:00; described on page 52). A couple of blocks up from Jenners, near St. Andrew Square, is the sprawling St. James Shopping Centre, where you can find just about anything you need.

WHAT TO SHOP FOR
Whisky

You can order whisky in just about any bar in town, and whisky shops are a dime a dozen around the Royal Mile. But the places I've listed here distinguish themselves by their tradition and helpful staff. Before sampling or buying whisky, read all about Scotland's favorite spirit on page 460.

Cadenhead's Whisky Shop is not a tourist sight—don't expect free samples. Founded in 1842, this firm prides itself on bottling good whisky straight from casks at the distilleries, without all the compromises that come with profitable mass production (coloring with sugar to fit the expected look, watering down to reduce the alcohol tax, and so on). Those drinking from Cadenhead-bottled whiskies will enjoy the pure product as the distilleries' owners themselves do, not as the sorry public does. The staff explains the some-

times-complex whisky storyboard and talks you through flavor profiles. Buy the right bottle to enjoy in your hotel room night after night (prices start around £14 for about 7 ounces)—unlike wine, whisky has a long shelf life after it's opened. The bottles are extremely durable; ask them to demonstrate (but get a second cap and twist off carefully, as they can break; Mon-Sat 10:30-17:30, closed Sun, 172 Canongate, tel. 0131/556-5864, www.wmcadenhead. com). They host whisky tastings a couple of times a month (posted in the shop)—a hit with aficionados.

Whiski Rooms Shop, just off the Royal Mile, comes with a knowledgeable, friendly staff that happily assists novices and experts alike to select the right bottle. Their adjacent bar usually has about 300 open bottles: Serious purchasers can get a sample. Even better, try one of their tastings. You have two options: You can

EDINBURGH

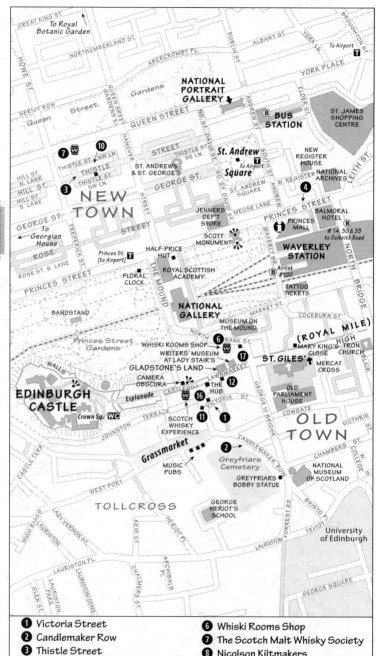

1 Victoria Street
2 Candlemaker Row
3 Thistle Street
4 Princes Street
5 Cadenhead's Whisky Shop
6 Whiski Rooms Shop
7 The Scotch Malt Whisky Society
8 Nicolson Kiltmakers
9 The Scottish Regimental Store

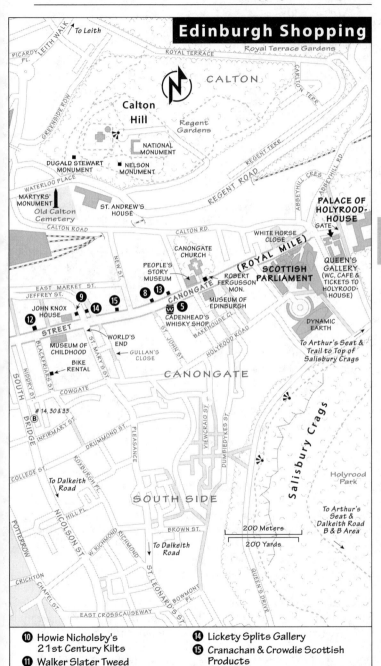

Edinburgh Shopping

To Leith

PICARDY PL.
LEITH WALK
GREENSIDE ROW

ROYAL TERRACE
Royal Terrace Gardens

CALTON

Calton Hill

Regent Gardens

NATIONAL MONUMENT

DUGALD STEWART MONUMENT
NELSON MONUMENT

WATERLOO PLACE

REGENT TERR.

REGENT ROAD

MARTYRS' MONUMENT

Old Calton Cemetery

ST. ANDREW'S HOUSE

CARLTON TERR.

ABBEYHILL CRES.
ABBEYHILL RD.

CALTON ROAD

CALTON RD.

PALACE OF HOLYROOD-HOUSE
GATE

NEW ST.

WHITE HORSE CLOSE

CANONGATE CHURCH

PEOPLE'S STORY MUSEUM

EAST MARKET ST.
JEFFREY ST.

9

⑧ ⑬

⑭ ⑮

ROBERT FERGUSSON MON.

(ROYAL MILE)

SCOTTISH PARLIAMENT

QUEEN'S GALLERY (WC, CAFE & TICKETS TO HOLYROOD-HOUSE)

MUSEUM OF EDINBURGH

CANONGATE

⑤

CADENHEAD'S WHISKY SHOP

BAKEHOUSE CL.

ST. JOHN ST.

HOLYROOD ROAD

DYNAMIC EARTH

To Arthur's Seat & Trail to Top of Salisbury Crags

JOHN KNOX HOUSE

⑫

STREET

WORLD'S END

GULLAN'S CLOSE

MUSEUM OF CHILDHOOD

BIKE RENTAL

BLACKFRIARS ST.
ST. MARY'S ST.

NIDDRY ST.

SOUTH BRIDGE

14, 30 & 33
B

COWGATE

INFIRMARY ST.

DRUMMOND ST.

PLEASANCE

VIEWCRAIG ST.

DUMBIEDYKES RD.

Salisbury Crags

Holyrood Park

COLLEGE ST.

To Dalkeith Road

SOUTH SIDE

To Arthur's Seat & Dalkeith Road B & B Area

HILL PL.

NICOLSON ST.

ROXBURGH PL.

W. RICHMOND
RICHMOND
ST. LEONARD'S ST.

BROWN ST.

200 Meters

200 Yards

POTTERROW

CRICHTON
CHAPEL ST.

To Dalkeith Road

BOWMONT PL.

QUEEN'S DRIVE

EAST CROSSCAUSEWAY

EDINBURGH

⑩ Howie Nicholsby's 21st Century Kilts

⑪ Walker Slater Tweed

⑫ Ness Clothing (2)

⑬ Jewelry Shops

⑭ Lickety Splits Gallery

⑮ Cranachan & Crowdie Scottish Products

⑯ I.J. Mellis Cheesemonger

⑰ Coda Music

order a flight in the bar, which comes with written information about each whisky you're sampling (12 options for £15-22, available anytime the bar is open). Or you can pay a few pounds more for a guided tasting (£20 introductory tasting, £38 premium tasting with the really good stuff, chocolate and cheese pairings also available; takes about one hour, reserve ahead). If you're doing a flight or a tasting, you'll get a small discount voucher for buying a bottle in the store (shop open daily 10:00-19:00, bar until 24:00, both open later in Aug, 4 North Bank Street, tel. 0131/225-1532, www. whiskirooms.com). There's a second location of the bar (but not the shop) farther down the Royal Mile, tucked in the row of pubs at 119 High Street.

Near the Dalkeith Road B&Bs: Perhaps the most accessible place to learn about local whiskies is conveniently located in the B&B neighborhood. **WoodWinters** is a nondescript shop with a passion both for traditional spirits and for the latest innovations in Edinburgh's booze scene. It's well stocked with 300 whiskies and gins (a recently en vogue alternative to Scotch), as well as wines and local craft beers. Manager Rob invites curious browsers to sample a wee dram; he loves to introduce customers to something new (Mon-Wed and Sat 10:00-19:00, Tue-Fri 10:00-

20:00, Sun 13:00-17:00, 91 Newington Road, www.woodwinters. com, tel. 0131/667-2760). For location, see the map on page 111.

In the New Town: **The Scotch Malt Whisky Society,** formerly a private club, recently opened its doors to the general public. While this place's shrouded-in-mystery pretense will be lost on novices, aficionados enjoy signing in at the front desk downstairs, then heading up to a bright, contemporary whisky bar with anonymous, numbered bottles of single malts from all over Scotland. In this "blind tasting" approach, you have to read each number's exacting description in the binder to make your choice...or enlist the help of the bartender (£5-36 glasses, Mon-Sat 11:00-23:00, closed Sun, bar serves light dishes, on-site restaurant, 28 Queen Street, tel. 0131/220-2044, www.smws.com).

Kilts and Other Traditional Scottish Gear

Many of the kilt outfitters you'll see along the Royal Mile are selling cheap knock-offs, made with printed rather than woven tartan material. If you want a serious kilt—or would enjoy window-shopping for one—try one of the places below. These have a few off-the-rack options, but to get a kilt in your specific tartan and size, they'll probably take your measurements, custom-make it, and ship it to you. For a good-quality outfit (kilt, jacket, and accessories), plan on spending in the neighborhood of £1,000.

Nicolson Kiltmakers has a respect for tradition and quality. Owner Gordon enlists and trains local craftspeople who special-

ize in traditionally manufac-
tured kilts and accessories.
He prides himself on keeping
the old ways alive (in the face
of deeply discounted "tartan
tat") and actively cultivates the
next generation of kiltmakers
(daily 9:30-17:30, 189 Canongate, tel. 0131/558-2887, www.
nicolsonkiltmakers.co.uk).

EDINBURGH

The Scottish Regimental Store, run by Nigel, is the official outfitter for military regiments. They sell top-of-the-line, formal kiltwear, as well as medals and pins that can be a more affordable souvenir (Mon-Sat 10:30-17:00, closed Sun, 9 Jeffrey Street, tel. 0131/557-0249, www.scottishregimentalstore.co.uk).

Howie Nicholsby's 21st Century Kilts, in the New Town, brings this traditional craft into the present day. It's fun to peruse his photos of both kilted celebrities (from Alan Cumming to Vin Diesel) and wedding albums—which make you wish you were Scottish, engaged, and wealthy enough to hire Howie to outfit your bridal party (closed Sun-Mon, 48 Thistle Street, tel. 0131/220-9450, www.21stcenturykilts.com).

Tweed and Other Fashionwear

Several places around town sell the famous Harris Tweed (the au-
thentic stuff is handwoven on the Isle of Harris). But these shops put a modern spin on a Scottish classic.

Walker Slater is the place to go for top-quality tweed at top prices. They have two locations tucked down Victoria Street, just

below the Royal Mile: menswear (at
#16) and womenswear (#44). At both
places, you'll find a rich interior and
a wide variety of gorgeous jackets,
scarves, bags, and more. This place
feels elegant and exclusive (Mon-Sat
10:00-18:00, later on Thu, Sat until
17:00, usually closed Sun, www.
walkerslater.com).

Ness, a women's clothing store, gives Scottish tweed a playful, colorful, contemporary spin. You'll find bags, scarves, and knit-wear at two Royal Mile locations: across from the Hub at 367 High

Street, and farther down, across from St. Giles' at 60 High Street (both open daily, www.ness.com).

Jewelry

Jewelry with Celtic designs, mostly made from sterling silver, is a popular and affordable souvenir. While you'll see these sold around town, two convenient shops face each other near the bottom of the Royal Mile: **Hamilton and Young,** which has a line of Outlander-inspired designs (173 Canongate), and **Celtic Design** (156 Canongate).

Food and Treats

Lickety Splits Gallery is part art, part candy, and all character. Naomi, who specializes in everything sweet, stocks her shelves with traditional candies and local crafts, including several map-based items ideal for globetrotters. Naomi also loves to share fascinating historical tidbits on the origins of Scotland's favorite childhood treats—from lucky tatties, soor plooms, and Edinburgh rock to parma violets, humbugs, and fizzy fangs... not to mention the epic scandal over how Chelsea Whoppers became Tootsie Rolls. Candy lovers can mix and match a little bag of goodies to go (Mon-Sat 11:00-17:30, Sun 12:00-16:00—but likely closed Sun in winter, 6 Jeffrey Street, mobile 07415-985-913).

Cranachan & Crowdie collects products (mostly edibles, some crafts) from more than 200 small, independent producers all over Scotland. The selection goes well beyond the mass-produced clichés, and American Beth and Scottish Fiona love to explain the story behind each item (daily 11:00-18:00, on the Royal Mile at 263 Canongate, tel. 07951/587-420).

I.J. Mellis Cheesemonger, tucked down Victoria Street just off the top of the Royal Mile, stocks a wide variety of Scottish, English, and international cheeses. They're as knowledgeable about cheese as they are generous with samples (Mon-Sat 9:30-18:00, Thu-Fri until 19:00, Sun 11:00-17:00, 30A Victoria Street, tel. 0131/226-6215).

Music

Coda, specializing in folk music—both old and new—sits just a few steps below the Royal Mile. This is the place to learn more about Celtic roots music (daily 9:30-17:30, 12 Bank Street, tel. 0131/622-7246).

Nightlife in Edinburgh

▲▲Literary Pub Tour

This two-hour walk is interesting even if you think Sir Walter Scott won an Oscar for playing General Patton. You'll follow the witty dialogue of two actors as they debate whether the great literature of Scotland was high art or the creative re-creation of fun-loving louts fueled by a passion for whisky. You'll wander from the Grassmarket over the Old Town and New Town, with stops in three pubs, as your guides share their takes on Scotland's literary greats. The tour meets at the Beehive pub on Grassmarket (£14, book online and save £2, May-Sept nightly at 19:30, April and Oct Thu-Sun, Jan-March Fri and Sun, Nov-Dec Fri only, www.edinburghliterarypubtour.co.uk).

▲Ghost Walks

A variety of companies lead spooky walks around town, providing an entertaining and affordable night out (offered nightly, most around 19:00 and 21:00, easy socializing for solo travelers). These two options are the most established.

The theatrical and creatively staged **The Cadies & Witchery Tours,** the most established outfit, offers two different 1.25-hour walks: "Ghosts and Gore" (April-Aug only, in daylight and following a flatter route) and "Murder and Mystery" (year-round, after dark, hillier, more surprises and scares). The cost for either tour is the same (£9, includes book of stories, leaves from top of Royal Mile, outside the Witchery Restaurant, near Castle Esplanade, reservations required, tel. 0131/225-6745, www.witcherytours.com).

Auld Reekie Tours offers a scary array of walks daily and nightly (£9-12, 45-90 minutes, leaves from front steps of the Tron Church building on Cockburn Street, tel. 0131/557-4700, www.auldreekietours.com). Auld Reekie focuses on the paranormal, witch covens, and pagan temples, taking groups into the "haunted vaults" under the old bridges "where it was so dark, so crowded, and so squalid that the people there knew each other not by how they looked, but by how they sounded, felt, and smelt." If you want more, there's plenty of it (complete with screaming Gothic "jumpers").

Scottish Folk Evenings

A variety of £35-40 dinner shows, generally for tour groups intent on photographing old cultural clichés, are held in the huge halls of expensive hotels. (Prices are bloated to include 20 percent commissions.) Your "traditional" meal is followed by a full slate of swirling kilts, blaring bagpipes, and Scottish folk dancing with an old-time music hall emcee. If you like Lawrence Welk, you're in for a treat. But for most travelers, these are painfully cheesy. You can some-

EDINBURGH

times see the show without dinner for about two-thirds the price. The TI has fliers on all the latest venues.

Prestonfield House, a luxurious venue near the Dalkeith Road B&Bs, offers its kitschy "Taste of Scotland" folk evening with or without dinner Sunday to Friday. For £49, you get the show with two drinks and a wad of haggis; £62 buys you the same, plus a three-course meal and a half-bottle of wine (be there at 18:45, dinner at 19:00, show runs 20:00-22:00, April-Oct only). It's in the stables of "the handsomest house in Edinburgh," which is now home to the recommended Rhubarb Restaurant (Priestfield Road, a 10-minute walk from Dalkeith Road B&Bs, tel. 0131/225-7800, www.scottishshow.co.uk).

For something more lowbrow—and arguably more authentic—in summer, you can watch the **Princes Street Gardens Dancers** perform a range of Scottish country dancing. The volunteer troupe will demonstrate each dance, then invite spectators to give it a try (£4, June-July Mon 19:30-21:30, at Ross Bandstand in Princes Street Gardens—in the glen just below Edinburgh Castle, tel. 0131/228-8616, www.princesstreetgardensdancing.org.uk). The same group offers summer programs in other parts of town (see website for details).

Theater

Even outside festival time, Edinburgh is a fine place for lively and affordable theater. Pick up *The List* for a complete rundown of what's on (sold at newsstands, may be free at the TI; also online at www.list.co.uk).

▲▲Live Music in Pubs

While traditional music venues have been eclipsed by beer-focused student bars, Edinburgh still has a few good pubs that can deliver a traditional folk-music fix. The monthly *Gig Guide* (free at TI, accommodations, and various pubs, www.gigguide.co.uk) lists several places each night that have live music, divided by genre (pop, rock, world, and folk).

South of the Royal Mile: **Sandy Bell's** is a tight little pub with live folk music nightly from 21:30 (just outside the tourist zone, a few minutes' walk from the Greyfriars Bobby statue and the National Museum of Scotland at 25 Forrest Road, tel. 0131/225-2751). Food is very simple (toasted sandwiches and soup), drinks are cheap, tables are small, and the vibe is local. They also have weekend afternoon sessions (Sat at 14:00, Sun at 16:00).

Captain's Bar is a cozy, music-focused pub with live sessions of folk and traditional music nightly around 21:00 (4 South College Street, http://captainsedinburgh.webs.com).

The Royal Oak is another good—if small—place for a dose of

Celtic music (just off South Bridge opposite Chambers Road at 1 Infirmary Street, tel. 0131/557-2976).

The **Grassmarket** neighborhood (below the castle) bustles with live music and rowdy people spilling out of the pubs and into what was (once upon a time) a busy market square. While it used to be a mecca for Scottish folk music, today it's more youthful with a heavy-drinking, rockin' feel. It's fun to just wander through this area late at night and check out the scene. Thanks to the music and crowds, you'll know where to go...and where not to. Have a beer and follow your ear to places like **Biddy Mulligans** or **White Hart Inn** (both on Grassmarket). **Finnegans Wake,** on Victoria Street (which leads down to Grassmarket), also has live folk and rock each night.

On the Royal Mile: Three characteristic pubs within a few steps of each other on High Street (opposite Radisson Hotel) offer a fun setting, classic pub architecture and ambience, and live music for the cost of a beer: **Whiski Bar** (trad and folk nightly at 22:00), **Royal Mile** (nightly at 22:00, pop and folk music, trad most likely on Thu), and **Mitre Bar** (Fri-Sun at 21:00 or 21:30).

Just a block away (on South Bridge) is **Whistlebinkies Live Music Bar.** While they rarely do folk or Scottish trad, this is the most serious of the music pubs, with an actual stage and several acts nightly (schedule posted outside the door makes the genre clear: rock, pop, jazz or blues, music starts at 19:00 or earlier, young crowd, fun energy, no cover, tel. 0131/557-5114). **No. 1 High Street** is an accessible little pub with a love of folk and traditional music and free performances many nights from 21:00 (Scottish trad on Tue-Wed, bluegrass on Thu). Drop by during your sightseeing as you walk the lower part of the Royal Mile, and ask what's on tonight (across from World's End, 1 High Street, tel. 0131/556-5758).

In the New Town: All the beer drinkers seem to head for the pedestrianized Rose Street, famous for having the most pubs per square inch anywhere in Scotland—and plenty of live music.

Pubs near Dalkeith Road B&Bs

The pubs in the Dalkeith Road B&B area don't typically have live music, but some are fun evening hangouts. **Leslie's Pub,** sitting between a working-class and an upper-class neighborhood, has two sides. Originally, the gang would go in on the right to gather around the great hardwood bar, glittering with a century of *Cheers* ambience. Meanwhile, the more delicate folks would slip in on the left, with its discreet doors, plush snugs (cozy private booths), and ornate ordering windows. Since 1896, this Victorian classic has been appreciated for both its real ales and its huge selection of fine whiskies (listed on a lengthy menu). Dive into the whisky mosh pit on the right, and let them show you how whisky can become "a very good friend." (Leslie's is at 49 Ratcliffe Terrace, daily 11:00-24:00, tel. 0131/667-7205.)

Other good pubs in this area include **The Old Bell** (uphill from Leslie's, popular and cozy, with big TV screens), **The Salisbury Arms** (bigger, more sprawling, feels upscale), and **Reverie Bar** (bright, open space with frequent live music); all three are described later, under "Eating in Edinburgh."

Sleeping in Edinburgh

Book ahead, especially in August, when the annual Festival fills Edinburgh. Conventions, rugby matches, school holidays, and weekends can make finding a room tough at almost any time of year. For the best prices, book direct.

B&Bs NEAR DALKEITH ROAD

South of town near the Royal Commonwealth Pool, these B&Bs—just off Dalkeith Road—are nearly all top-end, sport-

ing three or four stars. While pricey, they come with uniformly friendly hosts and great cooked breakfasts, and are a good value for people with enough money. At these not-quite-interchangeable places, character is provided by the personality quirks of the hosts.

Most listings are on quiet streets and within a few minutes' walk of a bus stop, and most can provide triples or even quads for families.

Prices listed are for most of peak season; if there's a range, prices slide up with summer demand. During the Festival in August, prices are higher; B&Bs also do not accept bookings for one-night stays during this time. In winter, when demand is light, prices get really soft. Expect a 3-5 percent fee on top of these prices for using your credit card.

Near the B&Bs, you'll find plenty of great eateries (see "Eating in Edinburgh," later) and some good, classic pubs (see "Nightlife in Edinburgh," earlier). A few places have their own private parking; others offer access to easy, free street parking (ask when booking—or better yet, don't rent a car for your time in Edinburgh). The nearest launderette is Ace Cleaning Centre (which picks up and drops off; see page 26).

Getting There: This comfortable, safe neighborhood is a ten-minute bus ride from the Royal Mile. From the train station, the nearest place to catch the bus is around the corner on North Bridge: Exit the station onto Princes Street, turn right, cross the street, and walk up the bridge to the bus stop in front of the Marks & Spencer department store (£1.50, use exact change, tell the driver you want a single ticket; bus #14, #30, or #33). About 10 minutes into the ride, after following South Clerk Street for a while, the bus makes a left turn, then a right. Depending on where you're staying, you'll get off at the first or second stop after the turn (confirm specifics with your B&B). Note that the hotels near Mayfield Gardens are reachable by a different set of buses (see listings). Taxi fare between the train station or Royal Mile and the B&Bs is about £7. Taxis are easy to hail on Dalkeith Road if it isn't raining. When heading from the B&Bs into the city, hop off at the South Bridge stop for the Royal Mile.

$$ Gil Dun Guest House, with eight rooms on a quiet cul-de-sac just off Dalkeith Road, is comfortable, pleasant, and managed with care by Gerry and Bill; Maggie helps out, and keeps things immaculate (Sb-£40-50, Db-£85-90, family deals, pleasant garden, 9 Spence Street, tel. 0131/667-1368, www.gildun.co.uk, gildun.edin@btinternet.com).

$$ Dunedin Guest House (dun-EE-din) is bright, plush, and elegantly Scottish, with seven nice, airy rooms, an angelic atrium, and a spacious breakfast room (S with private b on hall-£60, Db-£84-87, Tb-£114, family rooms for up to 4, 8 Priestfield Road, tel. 0131/668-1949, www.dunedinguesthouse.co.uk, reservations@dunedinguesthouse.co.uk, David and Irene Wright).

$$ Ard-Na-Said B&B is an elegant 1875 Victorian house with a comfy lounge. It offers seven bright, spacious rooms with modern bathrooms—including one ground-floor room with a pleasant patio (Sb-£35-55, Db-£65-95, huge four-poster Db-£70-110, Tb-£90-120, prices depend on size of room and season, free parking, 5 Priestfield Road, tel. 0131/667-8754, www.ardnasaid.co.uk, enquiries@ardnasaid.co.uk, Jim and Olive Lyons).

$$ AmarAgua Guest House is an inviting Victorian home away from home, with five welcoming rooms and a Japanese garden. It's given a little extra sparkle by its energetic proprietors, former entertainers Dawn-Ann and Tony Costa (Db-£70-85, Tb-£103-112, more for fancy four-poster rooms, 2-night minimum, 10 Kilmaurs Terrace, tel. 0131/667-6775, www.amaragua.co.uk, reservations@amaragua.co.uk).

$$ Gifford House, on busy Dalkeith Road, is a bright, flowery, creaky-floor retreat with six peaceful rooms—some with ornate cornices, super-king-size beds, and views of Arthur's Seat (Sb-£70-80, Db-£80-90, Tb-£114-120, Qb-£130-140, street parking, 103 Dalkeith Road, tel. 0131/667-4688, www.giffordhouseedinburgh.com, giffordhouse@btinternet.com, David and Margaret).

$$ Aonach Mòr B&B's eight decent rooms have views of either nearby Arthur's Seat or walled gardens (Db-£95, 10 percent

EDINBURGH

Dalkeith Road Hotels & Restaurants

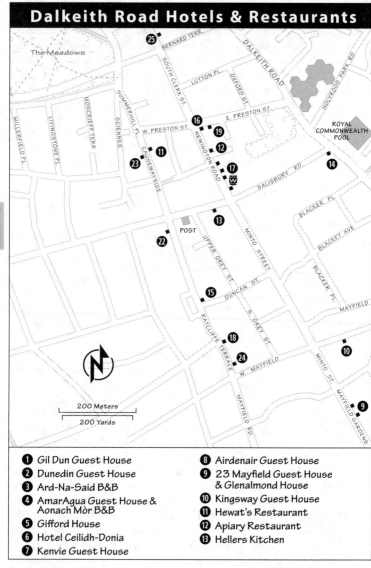

- ❶ Gil Dun Guest House
- ❷ Dunedin Guest House
- ❸ Ard-Na-Said B&B
- ❹ AmarAgua Guest House & Aonach Mòr B&B
- ❺ Gifford House
- ❻ Hotel Ceilidh-Donia
- ❼ Kenvie Guest House
- ❽ Airdenair Guest House
- ❾ 23 Mayfield Guest House & Glenalmond House
- ❿ Kingsway Guest House
- ⓫ Hewat's Restaurant
- ⓬ Apiary Restaurant
- ⓭ Hellers Kitchen

Rick Steves discount if you book by email, 14 Kilmaurs Terrace, tel. 0131/667-8694, www.aonachmor.com, info@aonachmor.com, Callum and Jen).

$$ Hotel Ceilidh-Donia, bigger and more impersonal than the others listed here, rents 17 contemporary rooms with a pleasant back deck, a quiet bar, and a variety of breakfast choices (Sb-£50-66, Db-£70-120, 14 Marchhall Crescent, tel. 0131/667-2743, www. hotelceilidh-donia.co.uk, reservations@hotelceilidh-donia.co.uk).

EDINBURGH

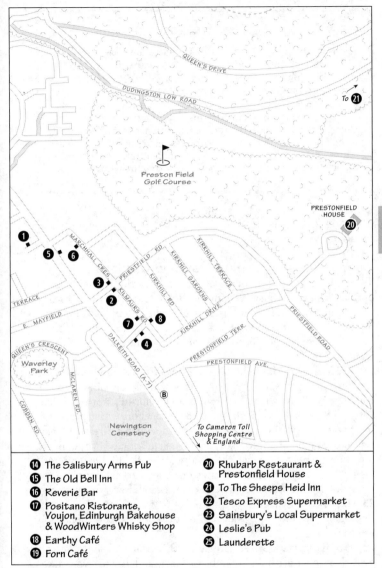

14 The Salisbury Arms Pub
15 The Old Bell Inn
16 Reverie Bar
17 Positano Ristorante, Voujon, Edinburgh Bakehouse & WoodWinters Whisky Shop
18 Earthy Café
19 Forn Café

20 Rhubarb Restaurant & Prestonfield House
21 To The Sheeps Heid Inn
22 Tesco Express Supermarket
23 Sainsbury's Local Supermarket
24 Leslie's Pub
25 Launderette

$ Kenvie Guest House, expertly run by Dorothy Vidler, comes with five older but lovingly maintained rooms (D-£66-70, Db-£74-80, these prices with cash and this book—may close in 2016, family deals, 16 Kilmaurs Road, tel. 0131/668-1964, www. kenvie.co.uk, dorothy@kenvie.co.uk).

$ Airdenair Guest House has five straightforward rooms on the second floor with a lofty above-it-all feeling. While getting a bit long in the tooth, it's a decent budget option (Sb-£40-45,

---

Sleep Code

Abbreviations   (£1=about $1.60, country code: 44)
S=Single, D=Double/Twin, T=Triple, Q=Quad, b=bathroom
Price Rankings
   $$$ Higher Priced—Most rooms £100 or more
    $$ Moderately Priced—Most rooms £80-100
     $ Lower Priced—Most rooms £80 or less
Unless otherwise noted, credit cards are accepted, breakfast
is included, and free Wi-Fi and/or a guest computer is gener-
ally available. Prices change; verify current rates online or by
email. For the best prices, always book directly with the hotel.

Db-£70-80, Tb-£85-95, less off-season, 29 Kilmaurs Road, tel.
0131/668-2336, www.airdenair.com, jill@airdenair.com, Jill and
Doug McLennan).

Guesthouses on or near Mayfield Gardens

These places are just a couple of blocks from the Dalkeith Road
options, along the busy Newington Road thoroughfare. To reach
them, you could take the buses listed for Dalkeith Road earlier,
but it's easier to hop on bus #3, #7, #8, #29, #31, #37, or #49. Note:
Some of these buses depart from the second bus stop, a bit farther
along North Bridge.

$$$ At **23 Mayfield Guest House,** Ross (and Grandma
Mary) rent eight splurge-worthy, thoughtfully appointed rooms
complete with high-tech bathrooms and a hot tub in the garden.
Little extras—such as locally sourced gourmet breakfasts, an invit-
ing guest lounge outfitted with leather-bound Sir Arthur Conan
Doyle books, an "honesty bar," and classic black-and-white movie
screenings—make you feel like royalty (Sb-£79-110, Db-£80-140,
bigger Db-£90-160, price depends on room size, family room for
up to 4, Rick Steves discount with cash, swap library, free parking,
23 Mayfield Gardens, tel. 0131/667-5806, www.23mayfield.co.uk,
info@23mayfield.co.uk). They also rent two apartments (details on
website).

$$ Kingsway Guest House, with seven stylish rooms, is
owned by conscientious, delightful Gary and Lizzie, who have
thought of all the little touches—from a cozy leather-sofa lounge
to the latest advice on neighborhood eats (Sb-£50-70, Db-£65-
90, Tb-£80-120, Qb-£90-130, ask for Rick Steves discount when
you book direct and pay cash, free parking, 5 East Mayfield, tel.
0131/667-5029, www.edinburgh-guesthouse.com, booking@
kingswayguesthouse.com).

$$ Glenalmond House, run by Jimmy and Fiona Mackie,
has nine elegantly decorated rooms, modern bathrooms, and high

prices (Db-£80-100, bigger four-poster Db-up to £130, Tb-£80-130, Qb-£120-169, ask for Rick Steves discount when you book by email or phone and pay cash, discount for longer stays, free parking, 25 Mayfield Gardens, tel. 0131/668-2392, www.glenalmondhouse.com, enquiries@glenalmondhouse.com).

BIG, MODERN HOTELS

The first listing's a splurge. The rest are cheaper than most of the city's other chain hotels, and offer more comfort than character. In each case, I'd skip the institutional breakfast and eat out. To locate these hotels, see the map on page 115. You'll generally pay about £10 a day to park near these hotels.

$$$ Macdonald Holyrood Hotel is a four-star splurge, with 156 rooms up the street from the parliament building and Holyroodhouse Palace. With its classy marble-and-wood decor, fitness center, and pool, it's hard to leave. On a gray winter day in Edinburgh, this could be worth it (rates vary with demand, Db-£110-160, £50 more for recently renovated "feature" rooms, breakfast costs extra, check for specials online, family deals, air-con, elevator, valet parking-£25, near bottom of Royal Mile, across from Dynamic Earth, 81 Holyrood Road, tel. 0131/528-8000, www.macdonaldhotels.co.uk).

$$$ The Inn on the Mile is your trendy, central option, filling a renovated old bank building right in the heart of the Royal Mile (at North Bridge/South Bridge). The nine bright and stylish rooms are an afterthought to the busy upmarket pub, which is where you'll check in. If you don't mind some noise (from the pub and the busy street) and climbing lots of stairs, it's a handy home base (Db-£80-200 depending on season, breakfast-£9, air-con, 82 High Street, tel. 0131/556-9940, www.theinnonthemile.co.uk).

$$$ Handy but Impersonal Chain Hotels: Several cookie-cutter chain hotels sit close to the Royal Mile. These are more convenient for sightseeing than the B&Bs, but have far less character and warmth. Each hotel has complex "dynamic pricing" that fluctuates wildly with demand; to comparison-shop, check each one's website for the prevailing rate during your stay: **Motel One Edinburgh Royal,** part of a stylish German budget hotel chain, is between the train station and the Royal Mile; it feels upscale and trendy for its price range (208 rooms, pay more for a park view or less for a windowless "budget" room with skylight, elevator, 18 Market Street, tel. 0131/220-0730, www.motel-one.com, edinburgh-royal@motel-one.com; second location in the New Town/shopping zone at 134 Princes Street). **The Inn Place,** part of a small chain, fills the former headquarters of *The Scotsman* newspaper—a few steep steps below the Royal Mile—with 27 characterless, minimalist rooms at

EDINBURGH

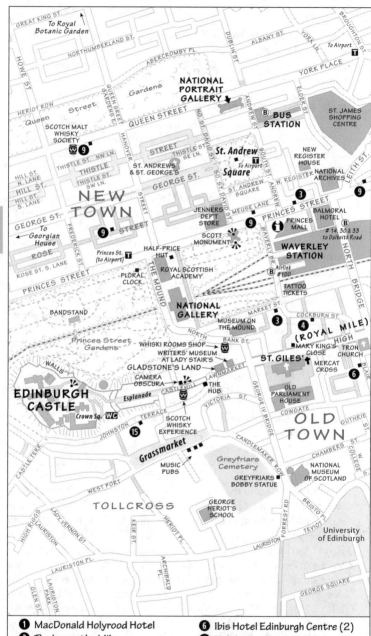

1 MacDonald Holyrood Hotel	**6** Ibis Hotel Edinburgh Centre (2)
2 The Inn on the Mile	**7** Holiday Inn Express Edinburgh Royal Mile
3 Motel One Edinburgh Royal (2)	
4 The Inn Place	**8** Travelodge Central
5 Jurys Inn	**9** Travelodges (4)

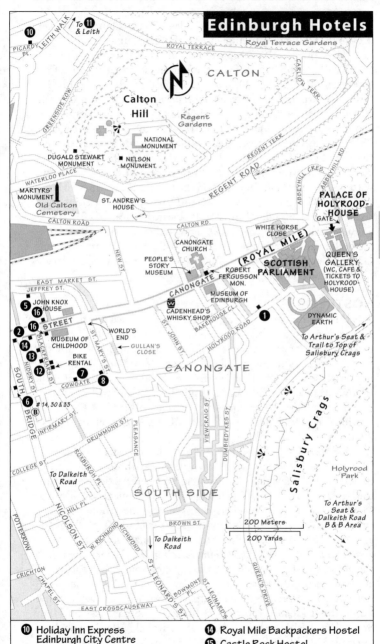

Edinburgh Hotels

EDINBURGH

- **10** Holiday Inn Express Edinburgh City Centre
- **11** To Edinburgh Central Youth Hostel
- **12** Smart City Hostel
- **13** High Street Hostel
- **14** Royal Mile Backpackers Hostel
- **15** Castle Rock Hostel
- **16** Brodie's Hostels (2)

reasonable prices (best deals on weekdays, 20 Cockburn Street, tel. 0131/526-3780, www.theinnplaceedinburgh.co.uk).

Jurys Inn has 186 bright rooms on a quiet street just off the Royal Mile, a short walk from the station (some views, 43 Jeffrey Street, tel. 0131/200-3300, www.jurysinns.com). **Ibis Hotel Edinburgh Centre** has two convenient branches near the Tron Church, smack in the middle of the Royal Mile (99 rooms just behind the church at 6 Hunter Square, tel. 0131/240-7000, h2039@accor.com; 259 rooms in a bigger, less appealing branch around the corner along the busy South Bridge at #77, tel. 0131/292-0000, h8484@accor.com). **Holiday Inn Express Edinburgh Royal Mile** rents 78 rooms with stark modern efficiency just off the Royal Mile down St. Mary's Street (300 Cowgate, tel. 0131/524-8400, www.hiexpressedinburgh.co.uk; another Holiday Inn is at 16 Picardy Place, tel. 0131/558-2300, www.hieedinburgh.co.uk). **Travelodge Central** fills a hulking building just below the Royal Mile with 193 no-nonsense rooms (33 St. Mary's Street, tel. 0871-984-8484, www.travelodge.co.uk; four additional locations in the New Town).

HOSTELS

$ Edinburgh Central Youth Hostel rents 300 beds in rooms accommodating one to eight people (all with private bathrooms and lockers). Guests can eat cheaply in the cafeteria, or cook for the cost of groceries in the members' kitchen (£20-30/bunk depending on season, private rooms available, 15-minute downhill walk from Waverley Station—head down Leith Walk, pass through two roundabouts, hostel is on your left—or take Lothian bus #22 or #25 to Elm Rowe, 9 Haddington Place off Leith Walk, tel. 0131/524-2090, www.syha.org.uk).

$ Smart City Hostel rents 620 bunks in austere, industrial-strength dorms, each with its own private bathroom. But it can get crazy with raucous weekend stag and hen parties. Bar 50 in the basement has an inviting lounge with cheap meals. Half of the rooms function as a university dorm during the school year, becoming available just in time for the tourists (£10-20, 50 Blackfriars Street, tel. 0131/524-1989, http://www.smartcityhostels.com).

Cheap and Scruffy Bohemian Hostels in the Center: These first three sister hostels—popular crash pads for young, hip backpackers—are beautifully located in the noisy center (£12-20, some locations also have private rooms, http://www.macbackpackers.com/): **High Street Hostel** (130 beds, 8 Blackfriars Street, just off High Street/Royal Mile, tel. 0131/557-3984); **Royal Mile Backpackers** (40 beds, 105 High Street, tel. 0131/557-6120); and **Castle Rock Hostel** (300 beds, just below the castle and above the pubs, 15 Johnston Terrace, tel. 0131/225-9666). **Brodie's Hostels,** somewhere between spartan and dumpy in the middle of the Royal Mile, rents 130 cheap beds (£13-17, 93 High Street, second branch across the street at 12 High Street, tel. 0131/556-2223, www.brodieshostels.co.uk).

Eating in Edinburgh

Reservations for restaurants are essential in August and on weekends, and a good idea anytime. Children aren't allowed in many of the pubs.

IN THE OLD TOWN

Pricey places abound on the Royal Mile (listed later). While those are tempting, I prefer the two areas described first, each within a few minutes' walk of the Mile—just far enough to offer better value and a bit less touristy crush.

On Victoria Street

Grainstore Restaurant, a sedate and dressy world of wood, stone, and candles tucked away above busy Victoria Street, has served Scottish produce with a French twist for more than two decades. While they have inexpensive £12.50 two-course lunch specials, dinner is à la carte. Reservations are recommended (£10-14 starters, £17-26 main dishes, Mon-Sat 12:00-14:00 & 18:00-22:00, Sun 18:00-22:00 only, 30 Victoria Street, tel. 0131/225-7635, www.grainstore-restaurant.co.uk).

Maison Bleue Restaurant is popular for their à la carte French/Scottish/North African menu and £20 dinner special before 19:00 (£8-10 small plates, £15-23 main dishes, daily 12:00-22:00, 36 Victoria Street, tel. 0131/226-1900).

Oink carves from a freshly roasted pig each afternoon for sandwiches that come in £4 "oink" or £5 "grunter" sizes. Watch the pig shrink in the front window throughout the day (daily 11:00-18:00 or whenever they run out of meat, cash only, 34 Victoria Street, tel. 01890/761-355). There's another location at the bottom end of the Royal Mile, near the parliament building (at 82 Canongate).

Near the National Museum

These restaurants, located along George IV Bridge and Forrest Road (near the National Museum), are happily removed from the Royal Mile melee.

The Elephant House, two blocks out of the touristy zone, is a comfy neighborhood coffee shop where relaxed patrons browse newspapers in the stay-awhile back room, listen to soft rock, enjoy the castle and cemetery vistas, and sip coffee or munch a light meal. During the day, you'll pick up food at the counter and grab your own seat; after 17:00, the café switches to table service. It's easy to imagine J. K. Rowling spending long afternoons here writing the

EDINBURGH

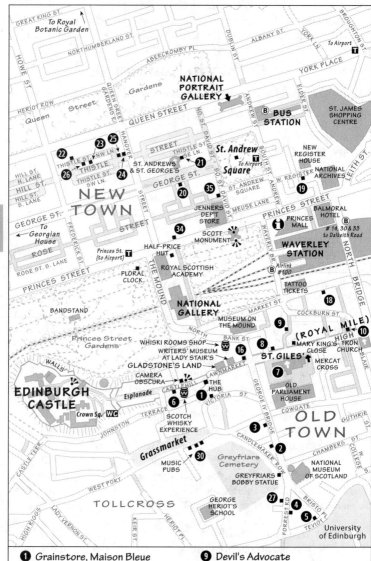

1 Grainstore, Maison Bleue & Oink
2 The Elephant House
3 The Outsider Restaurant
4 Union of Genius, Mums, and Frisky
5 Ting Thai Caravan
6 The Witchery by the Castle
7 St. Giles' Cathedral Café
8 Angels with Bagpipes
9 Devil's Advocate
10 The Baked Potato Shop
11 Edinburgh Larder
12 Mimi's Bakehouse Picnic Parlour
13 Wedgwood Restaurant
14 David Bann Restaurant
15 Clarinda's Tea Room
16 Deacon Brodie's Tavern
17 The World's End Pub
18 The Doric

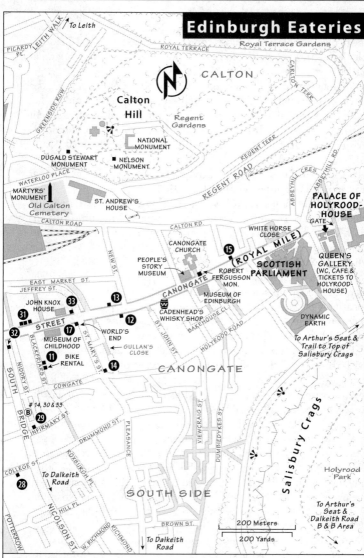

Edinburgh Eateries

EDINBURGH

first Harry Potter book (£5-6 lunches, £8 dinner plates, traditional meat pies, vegetarian options, great desserts, daily 8:00-22:00, 2 blocks south of Royal Mile near National Museum of Scotland at 21 George IV Bridge, tel. 0131/220-5355).

The Outsider, also without a hint of Royal Mile tourism, is a sleek spot serving creative and trendy cuisine (good fish and grilled meats and vegetables) in a minimalist, stylish, hardwood, candlelit castle-view setting. It's noisy with enthusiasm, and the service is crisp and youthful. Reserve for dinner (£7 specials until 17:00, £15-18 main dishes, always a vegetarian course, good wines by the glass, daily 12:00-23:00, 30 yards up from The Elephant House at 15 George IV Bridge, tel. 0131/226-3131).

Just Past the National Museum, on Forrest Road: After passing the Greyfriars Bobby statue and the National Museum, fork left onto Forrest Road. As this is approaching the university campus, here you'll find a few more creative places that skew to a youthful clientele, with virtually no tourists.

Union of Genius is a creative soup kitchen with a strong identity. They cook up six delicious soups each morning at their main location in Leith, then deliver them to this shop by bicycle (for environmental reasons). These are supplemented with good salads and fresh-baked breads (various combos run £4-6). Everything is delicious, with fun foodie twists. Can't decide? Go for the "flight," with three small cups of soup and three types of bread. Line up at the counter, then either take your soup to go, or squeeze into a seat at the two small, shared tables (Mon-Fri 8:30-16:00, Sat 12:00-16:00, closed Sun, 8 Forrest Road, tel. 0131/226-4436).

Next door, **Mums** is a kitschy diner serving up comfort food just like mum used to make. The menu runs to huge portions of heavy, greasy Scottish/British standards—bangers (sausages), meat pies, burgers, and artery-clogging breakfasts (served until 12:00)—all done with a foodie spin, including vegetarian options (£8-10 meals, Mon-Sat 9:00-22:00, Sun from 10:00, 4A Forrest Road, tel. 0131/260-9806). The **Frisky** frozen yogurt shop, nearby, is also great.

Just around the corner, **Ting Thai Caravan** is a casual, industrial-mod, food-focused eatery selling adventurous Thai street food (£5-10 meals, daily 11:30-22:00, Fri-Sat until 23:00, 8 Teviot Place, tel. 0131/225-9801).

Along the Royal Mile

Historic pubs and doily cafés with reasonable, unremarkable meals abound. Though the eateries along this most-crowded stretch of the city are invariably touristy, the scene is fun, and competition makes a well-chosen place a good value. Here are some handy, affordable options for a good bite to eat (listed roughly in downhill order; for locations, see map on page 119). Sprinkled in this list are some places a block or two off the main drag offering better values—and correspondingly filled with more locals than tourists.

The Witchery by the Castle is set in a lushly decorated 16th-century building just below the castle on the Royal Mile, with wood paneling, antique candlesticks, tapestries, and opulent red leather upholstery. Frequented by celebrities, tourists, and locals out for a splurge, the restaurant's emphasis is on pricey Scottish meats and seafood. Reserve ahead, dress smartly, and bear in mind you're paying a premium for the ambience (£19 two-course lunch specials—also available before 18:30 and after 22:30, £35 three-course dinner menu, £22-42 main dishes, daily 12:00-23:30, tel. 0131/225-5613, www.thewitchery.com).

St. Giles' Cathedral Café, hiding under the landmark church, is *the* place for paupers to munch prayerfully. Stairs on the back side of the church lead into the basement, where you'll find simple, light lunches from 11:30 and coffee with cakes all day (Mon-Sat 9:00-17:00, Sun 11:00-17:00, tel. 0131/225-5147).

Angels with Bagpipes, conveniently located across from St. Giles' Cathedral, serves sophisticated Scottish staples in its plush, sleek interior (lunch specials, £15-18 main dishes, daily 12:00-22:00, 343 High Street, tel. 0131/220-1111).

Devil's Advocate is a popular new gastropub that hides down the narrow lane called Advocates Close, directly across the Royal Mile from St. Giles'. With an old cellar setting—exposed stone and heavy beams—done up in modern style, it feels like a mix of old and new Edinburgh. Creative whisky cocktails kick off a menu that dares to be adventurous, but with a respect for Scottish tradition (£13-15 meals, daily 12:00-22:00, later for drinks, 8 Advocates Close, tel. 0131/225-4465).

The Baked Potato Shop is a handy spot to grab a hot, cheap, fast meal along the Royal Mile. They sell "the hottest tattie in town": baked potatoes with a wide variety of vegetarian fillings. It's best for takeaway, but they do have a few cramped seats (£5-7 meals, Mon-Sat 9:00-19:00, in summer until 21:00 or later, 56 Cockburn Street, tel. 0131/225-7572).

Edinburgh Larder promises "a taste of the country" in the center of the city. They focus on high-quality, locally sourced ingredients, available from a display case or as part of an enticing menu of breakfast and lunch dishes. It's a convivial space with rustic tables filled by local families (£5 soups, £7-9 sandwich plates, Mon-Fri 8:00-17:00, Sat-Sun from 9:00, 15 Blackfriars Street, tel. 0131/556-6922).

Mimi's Bakehouse Picnic Parlour, a handy Royal Mile outpost of a prizewinning bakery, serves up baked goods—try the scones—and sandwiches in their cute and modern shop (also £5 takeaway lunches, Mon-Fri 8:00-18:00, Sat-Sun from 10:00, 250 Canongate, tel. 0131/556-6632).

Wedgwood Restaurant is romantic, contemporary, chic, and as gourmet as possible with no pretense. Paul Wedgwood cooks while his wife Lisa serves with appetizing charm. The cuisine: creative, modern Scottish with an international twist and a whiff of Asia. The pigeon and haggis starter is scrumptious. Paul and Lisa believe in making the meal the event of the evening—don't come here to eat and run. I like the ground level with the Royal Mile view, but the busy kitchen ambience in the basement is also fine (£9-10 starters, £18-24 main courses, fine wine by the glass, daily 12:00-15:00 & 18:00-22:00, reservations advised, 267 Canongate on Royal Mile, tel. 0131/558-8737, www.wedgwoodtherestaurant.co.uk).

David Bann, just a three-minute walk off the Royal Mile, is a worthwhile stop for well-heeled vegetarians in need of a break from the morning fry-up. While vegetarian as can be, this place doesn't have even a hint of hippie. It's upscale (it has a cocktail bar), sleek, minimalist, and stylish (gorgeously presented dishes), serious about quality, and organic—they serve polenta, tartlets, soups, and light meals. Reserve ahead (£11-13 main dishes, decadent desserts, Mon-Fri 12:00-22:00, Sat-Sun from 11:00, vegan options, 56 St. Mary's Street, tel. 0131/556-5888).

Clarinda's Tea Room, near the bottom of the Royal Mile, is a charming and girlish time warp—a fine and tasty place to relax after touring the Mile or the Palace of Holyroodhouse. Stop in for a £6 quiche, salad, or soup lunch. It's also great for sandwiches and tea and cake anytime (Mon-Sat 8:45-16:45, Sun 9:30-16:45, 69 Canongate, tel. 0131/557-1888).

Historic Pubs Along the Mile: To drink a pint or grab some forgettable pub grub in historic surroundings, consider one of the landmark pubs described on my self-guided walk: **Deacon Brodie's Tavern,** at a dead-center location on the Royal Mile (a sloppy pub on the ground floor with a sloppy restaurant upstairs) or **The World's End Pub,** farther down the Mile at Canongate (a colorful old place dishing up hearty meals from a creative menu in a fun, dark, and noisy space, 4 High Street). Both serve £8-12 pub meals and are open long hours daily. **The Doric,** less in-your-face but a notch up in quality, sits between the Royal Mile and the train station. Choose between the atmospheric pub or the classy upstairs bistro (£10-16 pub grub, daily 12:00-late, 15 Market Street, tel. 0131/225-1084).

IN THE NEW TOWN

While most of your sightseeing will be along the Royal Mile, it's important that your Edinburgh experience stretches beyond this happy tourist gauntlet. Just a few minutes away, in the Georgian part of town, you'll find a bustling world of office workers, students, and pensioners doing their thing. And at midday, that includes eating. Simply hiking over to one of these places will give you a good helping of modern Edinburgh. All these eateries are within a few minutes' walk of the TI and main Waverley Bridge tour-bus depot.

Elegant Spaces near Princes Street

For a staid glimpse at grand old Edinburgh, these are good choices.

Café Royal is a movie producer's dream pub—the perfect *fin de siècle* setting for a coffee, beer, or light meal. (In fact, parts of *Chariots of Fire* were filmed here.) Drop in, if only to admire the 1880 tiles featuring famous inventors (daily 12:00-14:30 & 17:00-21:30, bar food available all day, two blocks from Princes Mall on 19 West Register Street, tel. 0131/556-1884). There are two eateries here: the noisy pub (£10-15 main dishes) and the dressier restaurant, specializing in oysters, fish, and game (£17-22 plates, reserve for dinner—it's quite small and understandably popular).

The Dome Restaurant, in what was a fancy bank, serves modern international cuisine around a classy bar and under the elegant 19th-century skylight dome. With soft jazz and chic, white-tablecloth ambience, it feels a world apart. Come here not for the food, but for the opulent atmosphere (£13-15 plates until 17:00, £14-23 dinners until 21:45, daily 12:00-23:00, reserve for dinner, open for a drink any time under the dome; the adjacent, more intimate Club Room serves food Mon-Wed 10:00-17:00, Thu-Sat until late, closed Sun; 14 George Street, tel. 0131/624-8634).

Quick and Cheap Eats

St. Andrew's and St. George's Church Undercroft Café, in the basement of a fine old church, is the cheapest place in town for lunch—under £5 for a sandwich and soup. Your tiny bill helps support the Church of Scotland (Mon-Fri lunch only, closed Sat-Sun, at 13 George Street, just off St. Andrew Square, tel. 0131/225-3847).

Supermarkets: **Marks & Spencer Food Hall** offers an assortment of tasty hot foods, prepared sandwiches, fresh bakery items, a wide selection of wines and beverages, and plastic utensils at the checkout queue. It's just a block from the Scott Monument and the picnic-perfect Princes Street Gardens (Mon-Sat 8:00-19:00, Thu until 20:00, Sun 11:00-18:00, Princes Street 54—separate stairway next to main M&S entrance leads directly to food hall, tel. 0131/225-2301). **Sainsbury's** supermarket, a block off Princes Street, also offers grab-and-go items for a quick lunch (Mon-Sat 7:00-22:00, Sun 9:00-20:00, on corner of Rose Street on St. Andrew Square, across the street from Jenners, the classy department store).

Hip Eateries on and near Thistle Street

For something a little more modern and food-focused, head a few more minutes deeper into the New Town to find Thistle Street. This strip and its surrounding lanes are packed with more enticing eateries than the rest of the New Town put together. Browse the options here, but tune into these favorites.

Le Café St. Honoré, tucked away like a secret bit of old Paris, is a charming place with friendly service and walls lined by tempting wine bottles. It serves French-Scottish cuisine in tight, Old World, cut-glass elegance to a dressy crowd (£18 two-course and £24 three-course lunch and dinner specials, daily 12:00-14:00 plus Mon-Fri 17:15-22:00 and Sat-Sun 18:00-22:00, reservations smart—ask to sit upstairs, down Thistle Street from Hanover Street, 34 Northwest Thistle Street Lane, tel. 0131/226-2211, www.cafesthonore.com).

The Bon Vivant is woody, youthful, and candlelit, with a rotating menu of eclectic Mediterranean/Asian dishes and a companion wine shop serving 50 wines by the glass. They have fun £2 tapas plates and heartier £15-17 dishes, served either in the bar up front or in the restaurant in back (daily 12:00-22:00, 55 Thistle Street, tel. 0131/225-3275, www.bonvivantedinburgh.co.uk).

Fishers in the City is a bright, modern, high-energy, casual fish restaurant (£16-21 main dishes, daily 12:00-22:00, 58 Thistle Street, reservations smart, tel. 0131/225-5109, www.fishersrestaurantgroup.co.uk).

Henderson's of Edinburgh has fed a generation of New Town vegetarians hearty cuisine and salads. Even carnivores love this place for its delectable salads and desserts. Henderson's has two separate eateries: Their main restaurant, facing Hanover Street, is self-service by day but has table service after 17:00. Each evening after 19:00, they have pleasant live music—generally guitar or jazz (£12 meals, Mon-Wed 8:00-22:00, Thu-Sat until 23:00, closed Sun except in Aug, between Queen and George streets at 94 Hanover Street, tel. 0131/225-2131). Just around the corner on Thistle Street, **Henderson's Vegan** has a strictly vegan menu and feels a bit more casual (£9-10 plates, daily 12:00-21:30, tel. 0131/225-2605).

El Cartel is a youthful place serving up good tacos and other Mexican dishes in a cramped, edgy atmosphere (£5-8 small plates, daily 12:00-22:00, 64 Thistle Street).

IN THE B&B NEIGHBORHOOD, NEAR DALKEITH ROAD

Nearly all of these places (except for The Sheeps Heid Inn) are within a 10-minute walk of my recommended B&Bs. Reserve on weekends and during the Festival. For locations, see the map on page 110. For a cozy drink after dinner, visit the recommended pubs in the area (see "Nightlife in Edinburgh," earlier).

Sit-Down Restaurants

Hewat's Restaurant, welcoming and popular, is the neighborhood hit. Sample Scottish cuisine or their popular steak dishes in this elegantly whimsical dining space (Mon-Sat dinner only, closed Sun, early-bird specials before 19:00; weeknights: £19/2 courses, £23/3 courses; weekends: £12-17 à la carte dishes; 19 Causewayside, tel. 0131/466-6660, www.hewatsedinburgh.com).

Apiary brings a bit of hipster flair to this otherwise stodgy neighborhood, with an inviting, casual interior and a hit-or-miss, eclectic menu that mingles various international flavors (£10 lunch deals, £15 early-bird specials, £11-15 dinners, daily 10:00-15:30 & 17:30-22:00, 33 Newington Road, tel. 0131/668-4999, www.apiaryrestaurant.co.uk).

Hellers Kitchen is a casual blond-wood space specializing in dishes using local produce and fresh-baked breads. Check the big chalkboard to see what's on (£5-7 light bites and sandwiches, £9-13 main dishes, Mon-Sat 9:00-21:00, Sun 10:00-15:30, next to post office at 15 Salisbury Road, tel. 0131/667-4654).

Pub Grub

The Salisbury Arms Pub, with a nice garden terrace, serves upscale, pleasing traditional classics with yuppie flair in a space that exudes more Martha Stewart and Pottery Barn than traditional public house (£11-17 main dishes, evening specials, food served daily 12:00-22:00, across from the pool at 58 Dalkeith Road, tel. 0131/667-4518).

The Old Bell Inn, with an old-time sports-bar ambience—fishing, golf, horses—serves £9-11 pub meals. This is a classic "snug pub"—all dark woods and brass beer taps, littered with evocative knickknacks. It comes with sidewalk seating and a mixed-age crowd (food served daily until 22:00, 233 Causewayside, tel. 0131/668-1573).

Reverie Bar is just your basic, fun traditional pub with a focus on food rather than drinking. The big windows let in a lot of light, and there's free live music many nights from 21:30 (every other Sun-jazz, Mon-quiz night, Tue-traditional/folk; £11-14 main dishes, food served daily 12:00-15:00 & 17:00-21:00, real ales, 1 Newington Road, tel. 0131/667-8870).

Ethnic Options

Positano Ristorante has a spirited Italian ambience, as manager Donato injects a love of life and food into his little restaurant. The moment you step through the door, you know you're in for good, classic Italian cuisine (£9-11 pizzas and pastas, £14-17 plates, daily 12:00-14:00 & 17:00-23:00, 85 Newington Road, tel. 0131/662-9977).

Voujon Restaurant serves a fusion menu of Bengali and Indian cuisines. Vegetarians appreciate the expansive yet inexpensive offerings for £8 (£10-17 main dishes, daily 12:00-14:00 & 17:30-23:30, 107 Newington Road, tel. 0131/667-5046, www.voujonedinburgh.co.uk).

Fast Eats

At **Edinburgh Bakehouse,** award-winning baker James Lynch makes £1-2 fresh breads, sweets, and meat pies from scratch in this laid-back, nondescript shop. Locals line up for his morning rolls—which earned him the title "baker of the year." Stop by to see the friendly staff and open kitchen in action and judge for yourself (cash only, daily 7:00-18:00, 101 Newington Road).

Earthy is an organic, farm-fresh café and grocery store with a proudly granola attitude. In the café, step up to the counter and take your pick of freshly prepared salads, sandwiches, and baked goods (£6-7). Sit in the industrial-mod interior, with rustic picnic benches, or out in the ragtag back garden. In the well-stocked store, assemble a pricey but top-quality picnic, or just grab some snacks for your B&B room (Mon-Fri 9:00-18:00, Sat 9:00-17:00, Sun 10:00-17:00, store open a bit later, 33 Ratcliffe Terrace, tel. 0131/667-2967).

Forn, a simple but classy Catalan-themed café, has the best espresso drinks in this neighborhood, as well as baked goods and light meals (Tue-Sat 10:00-18:00, Sun 11:00-17:00, closed Mon, 1 East Preston Street, tel. 0131/667-4098).

Groceries: The nearest grocery stores are **Tesco Express** (daily 10:00-22:00, 158 Causewayside) and **Sainsbury's Local** (daily 6:30-23:00, 80 Causewayside). Cameron Toll Shopping Centre, about a half-mile south on your way out of town, houses a **Sainsbury's** superstore for more substantial supplies and gasoline.

Memorable Meals Farther Out

Rhubarb Restaurant specializes in Old World elegance. It's in "Edinburgh's most handsome house"—an over-the-top riot of antiques, velvet, tassels, and fringes. The plush dark-rhubarb color theme reminds visitors that this was the place where rhubarb was first grown in Britain. It's a 10-minute walk past the other recommended eateries behind Arthur's Seat, in a huge estate with big, shaggy Highland cattle enjoying their salads al fresco. At night, it's a candlelit wonder. While most spend a wad here (£18-35 plates), they offer a £20 two-course lunch and a £35 three-course dinner. Reserve in advance and dress up if you can (daily 12:00-

14:00 & 18:00-22:00, £23 afternoon tea served daily 14:00-19:00, in Prestonfield House, Priestfield Road, tel. 0131/662-2303, www. prestonfield.com). For details on their schmaltzy Scottish folk evening, see "Nightlife in Edinburgh," earlier.

The Sheeps Heid Inn, Edinburgh's oldest and most inviting public house, is equally notable for its history, date-night appeal, and hearty portions of affordable, classy dishes. Though it requires a cab ride, it is worth the fare to dine in this dreamy setting in the presence of past queens and kings—or, if you prefer, outside in the classic garden courtyard (£11-18 main dishes, Mon-Sat 11:00-23:00 or 24:00, Sun 12:00-23:00, 43 The Causeway, tel. 0131/661-7974, www.thesheepheidedinburgh.co.uk).

Edinburgh Connections

BY TRAIN OR BUS

From Edinburgh by Train to: Glasgow (4/hour, 50 minutes), **St. Andrews** (train to Leuchars, 1-2/hour, 1 hour, then 10-minute bus into St. Andrews), **Stirling** (roughly 2/hour, 1 hour), **Pitlochry** (8/day direct, 2 hours), **Inverness** (every 1-2 hours, 3.5-4 hours, some with change in Perth), **Oban** (5/day, 4.5 hours, change in Glasgow), **York** (2/hour, 2.5 hours), **London** (1-2/hour, 4.5 hours), **Durham** (hourly direct, 2 hours, more with changes, less frequent in winter), **Newcastle** (2/hour, 1.5 hours), **Keswick/Lake District** (8-10/day to Penrith—some via Carlisle, 1.75 hours, then 40-minute bus ride to Keswick), **Birmingham** (at least hourly, 4-5 hours, some with change in Newcastle or York), **Crewe** (every 2 hours, 3 hours), **Bristol,** near Bath (hourly, 6-6.5 hours), **Blackpool** (roughly hourly, 3-3.5 hours, transfer in Preston). Train info: Tel. 0345-748-4950, www.nationalrail.co.uk.

By Bus: Edinburgh's bus station is in the New Town, just off St. Andrew Square, two blocks north of the train station. Direct buses go to **Glasgow** (bus #900, 4/hour, 1-1.5 hours depending on traffic) and **Inverness** (about hourly, 4-5 hours). To reach other destinations in the Highlands—including **Oban, Fort William, Glencoe,** or **Portree** on the Isle of Skye—you'll have to transfer. It's usually fastest to take the train to Glasgow and change to a bus there. For details, see "Getting Around the Highlands" on page 238. For bus info, stop by the station or call Scottish Citylink (tel. 0871-266-3333, www.citylink.co.uk). Additional long-distance routes may be operated by National Express (www.nationalexpress. com) or Megabus (www.megabus.com).

ROUTE TIPS FOR DRIVERS HEADING SOUTH

It's 100 miles south from Edinburgh to Hadrian's Wall; to Durham, it's another 50 miles.

To Hadrian's Wall: From Edinburgh, Dalkeith Road leads south and eventually becomes the A-68 (handy Cameron Toll supermarket with cheap gas is on the left as you leave Edinburgh Town, 10 minutes south of Edinburgh; gas and parking behind store). The A-68 road takes you to Hadrian's Wall in 2.5 hours. You'll pass Jedburgh and its abbey after one hour. (For one last shot of Scotland shopping, there's a coach tour's delight just before Jedburgh, with kilt makers, woolens, and a sheepskin shop.) Across from Jedburgh's lovely abbey is a free parking lot, a good visitors center, and pay toilets. The England/Scotland border is a fun, quick stop (great view, ice cream, and tea caravan). Just after the turn for Colwell, turn right onto the A-6079, and roller-coaster four miles down to Low Brunton. Then turn right onto the B-6318, and stay on it by turning left at Chollerford, following the Roman wall westward.

To Durham: If you're heading straight to Durham, you can take the scenic coastal route on the A-1 (a few more miles than the A-68, but similar time), which takes you near Holy Island and Bamburgh Castle.

GLASGOW

Glasgow (GLAS-goh)—astride the River Clyde—is a surprising city. In its heyday, Glasgow was one of Europe's biggest cities and the second-largest in Britain, right behind London. A century ago it had 1.2 million people, twice the size (and with twice the importance) of today. It was an industrial powerhouse producing 25 percent of the world's oceangoing ships. But in the mid-20th century, tough times hit Glasgow, giving it a rough edge and a run-down image.

At the city's low point during the Margaret Thatcher years (1980s), its leaders embarked on a systematic rejuvenation designed to again make Glasgow appealing to businesses, tourists...and locals. Today the city feels revitalized and goes out of its way to offer a warm welcome. Glaswegians (rhymes with "Norwegians") are the chattiest people in Scotland—and have the most entertaining (and impenetrable) accent.

Many travelers give Glasgow a miss, but that's a shame: I consider it Scotland's single-most underrated destination. Glasgow is

a workaday Scottish city as well as a cosmopolitan destination, with an unpretentious friendliness, an energetic dining and nightlife scene, top-notch museums (most of them free), and a unique flair for art and design. It's also a pilgrimage site for architecture buffs, thanks to a cityscape packed with Victorian facades, early 20th-century touches, and bold and glassy new construction. Most beloved are the works by hometown boy Charles Rennie Mackintosh, the visionary—and now very trendy—architect who left his mark all over Glasgow at the turn of the 20th century.

Many more tourists visit Edinburgh, a short train trip away. But for a more complete look at urban Scotland, be sure to stop off in Glasgow. Edinburgh may have the royal aura, but Glasgow's down-to-earth appeal is captivating. In Glasgow, there's no upper-crust history, and no one puts on airs. In Edinburgh, people identify with the quality of the school they attended; in Glasgow, it's their soccer team allegiance. One Glaswegian told me, "The people of Glasgow have a better time at a funeral than the people of Edinburgh have at a wedding." In this newly energized city, friendly locals do their best to introduce you to the fun-loving, laid-back Glaswegian way of life.

PLANNING YOUR TIME

While many visitors blitz Glasgow as a day trip from Edinburgh (and a first day in Glasgow is certainly more exciting than a fourth day in Edinburgh)—or even from Stirling—the city can easily fill two days of sightseeing.

On a quick visit, follow my "Get to Know Glasgow" self-guided walk of the city center, tying together the most important sights in the city's core. If your time is short, the interiors most worth considering are the Tenement House and the Piping Centre.

With additional time, your options open up. Follow my West End walk to get a taste of Glasgow's most appealing residential zone, which has the city's best restaurants as well as a number of appealing sights. Fans of Art Nouveau and Charles Rennie Mackintosh can lace together a busy day's worth of sightseeing (the TI has a brochure laying it out). At a minimum, those interested in Mackintosh should visit the Mackintosh House at the Hunterian Gallery (in the West End), the Glasgow School of Art (which he designed), and the Mackintosh exhibit at the Kelvingrove Museum. (The first two are by tour only—call ahead to confirm the schedule.)

Regardless of how long you're staying, consider the two-hour hop-on, hop-off bus tour, which is convenient for getting the bigger picture and reaching three important sights away from the center (the Cathedral Precinct, the Riverside Museum, and the Kelvingrove Museum).

Day Trip from Edinburgh: For a full day, catch the 9:30 train to Glasgow (morning trains every 15 minutes; discount for same-day round-trip if leaving after 9:15 or on weekend); it arrives at Queen Street Train Station before 10:30. To fill your Glasgow

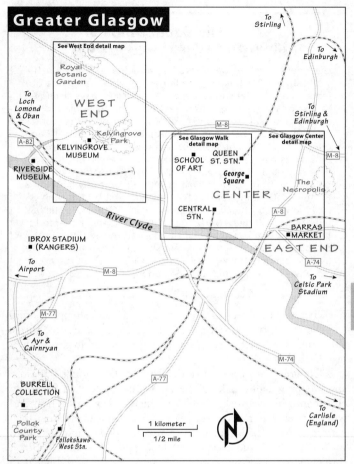

Greater Glasgow

See West End detail map

Royal Botanic Garden

To Loch Lomond & Oban

WEST END

Kelvingrove Park

A-82

KELVINGROVE MUSEUM

RIVERSIDE MUSEUM

River Clyde

IBROX STADIUM ■ (RANGERS)

To Airport

M-8

M-77

To Ayr & Cairnryan

BURRELL COLLECTION

Pollok County Park

Pollokshaws West Stn.

To Stirling

To Edinburgh

M-8

To Stirling & Edinburgh

See Glasgow Walk detail map

See Glasgow Center detail map

SCHOOL OF ART

QUEEN ST. STN.

George Square

CENTER

CENTRAL STN.

M-8

The Necropolis

A-8

BARRAS ■ MARKET

EAST END

A-74

To Celtic Park Stadium

M-74

A-77

To Carlisle (England)

1 kilometer

1/2 mile

N

GLASGOW

hours smartly, I'd do the entire hop-on, hop-off bus tour circuit (two hours), then follow my self-guided walk through downtown (finishing with the Tenement House). If you have time left, head to the West End for dinner or follow my self-guided West End Walk. Then hop the subway back to Queen Street Station (use the Buchanan Street stop) and catch the 21:00 train back to Edinburgh (evening trains depart every 30 minutes).

Orientation to Glasgow

Although it's often thought of as a "second city," Glasgow is actually Scotland's biggest (pop. 600,000, swelling to 1.2 million within Greater Glasgow—that's one out of every five Scots).

The tourist's Glasgow has two parts: the businesslike down-

When the Great Ships of the World Were "Clyde-Built"

Glasgow's River Clyde shipyards were the mightiest in the world, famed for building the largest moving man-made objects on earth. The shipyards, once 50 strong, have dwindled to just 3. Yet a few giant cranes still stand to remind locals and visitors that from 1880 to 1950, a quarter of the world's ships were built here and "Clyde-built" meant reliability and quality. For 200 years, shipbuilding was Glasgow's top employer—as many as 100,000 workers at its peak, producing a new ship every two days. The glamorous Cunard ships were built here—from the *Lusitania* in 1906 (infamously sunk by a German U-boat in World War I, which almost brought the US into the war) to the *Queen Elizabeth II* in 1967. People still talk about the day when over 200,000 Glaswegians gathered for the launch, the Queen herself smashed the champagne bottle on the prow, and the magnificent ship slid into the harbor. To learn lots more about shipbuilding in Glasgow, visit the excellent Riverside Museum (described under "Sights in Glasgow").

GLASGOW

town (train stations, commercial zone, and main shopping drag) and the residential West End (B&Bs, restaurants, and nightlife). Both areas have great sights, and both are covered in this chapter by self-guided walks.

Glasgow's **downtown** is a tight grid of boxy office buildings and shopping malls, making it feel more like a midsized American city than a big Scottish one—like Cincinnati or Pittsburgh, but with shorter skyscrapers made of Victorian sandstone rather than glass and steel. The walkable city center has two main drags, both lined with shops and crawling with shoppers: Sauchiehall Street (pronounced "Suckyhall," running west to east) and Buchanan Street (running north to south). These two pedestrian malls—part of a shopping zone nicknamed the Golden Zed—make a big zig and zag through the heart of town (the third street of the Zed, Argyle Street, is busy with traffic and less appealing).

The **West End** is Glasgow's poshest suburb, with big homes and upscale apartment buildings, lots of green space, and the city's best B&Bs, shops, and restaurants. The area has three pockets of interest: near the Hillhead subway stop, with a lively restaurant scene and the Botanic Gardens; the University of Glasgow campus, with its stately buildings and fine museums; and, just downhill through a sprawling park, the area around the Kelvingrove Museum, with a lively nearby strip of trendy bars and restaurants (Finnieston).

TOURIST INFORMATION

The TI is next to the Glasgow Royal Concert Hall, where Buchanan Street swings left and becomes Sauchiehall (facing the concert hall's steps, it's to your left). While their main function seems to be booking day trips for various tour companies, they will answer questions and also hand out a good, free map and brochures on Glasgow and the rest of Scotland (Mon-Sat 9:00-18:00, Sun 10:00-17:00, until 16:00 Oct-April, www.visitscotland.com).

Mackintosh Trail Ticket: This ticket, sold at the TI, covers entry to all Charles Rennie Mackintosh sights and public transportation to those outside the city limits (£10/day, www.crmsociety.com).

ARRIVAL IN GLASGOW

By Train: Glasgow, a major Scottish transportation hub, has two main train stations, which are just a few blocks apart in the heart of town: **Central Station** (with a grand, genteel interior under a vast steel-and-glass Industrial Age roof) and **Queen Street Station** (more functional, with better connections to Edinburgh, and closer to the TI—take the exit marked *Buchanan Street* to reach the main shopping drag; the TI is at the top of the street and to the left). Both stations have pay WCs and pricey baggage storage. If going between the stations to change trains, you can walk five minutes or take the free roundabout "RailLink" bus #398. Trainspotters may enjoy the guided, behind-the-scenes tours of Central Station, including a spooky, abandoned Victorian train platform (book ahead, www.glasgowcentraltours.co.uk).

By Bus: Buchanan bus station is at Killermont Street, two blocks up the hill behind Queen Street train station.

By Car: Glasgow's downtown streets are steep, mostly one-way, and congested with buses and pedestrians. It may well be the most stressful place to drive in Scotland. Parking downtown is also a hassle: Metered street parking is very expensive (£3/hour) and limited to two hours during the day; garages are even more expensive (figure £22 for 24 hours). Ideally, do Glasgow without a car—for example, tour Edinburgh and Glasgow by public transit, then pick up your rental car on your way out of town. If you are stuck with a car in Glasgow, try to sleep in the West End, where driving and parking are easier (and commuting into downtown for sightseeing is a snap on the subway and buses).

The M-8 motorway, which slices through downtown Glasgow, is the easiest way in and out of the city. Ask your hotel for directions to and from the M-8, and connect with other highways from there.

By Air: For information on Glasgow's two airports, see "Glasgow Connections," at the end of this chapter.

HELPFUL HINTS

Safety: The city center, which is packed with ambitious career types during the day, can feel deserted at night. While the area between Argyle Street and the River Clyde has been cleaned up in recent years, parts can still feel sketchy. As in any big city, use common sense and don't wander down dark, deserted alleys. The Golden Zed shopping drag, the Merchant City area (east of the train stations), and the West End all bustle with crowded restaurants well into the evening and feel well populated in the wee hours.

If you've picked up a football (soccer) jersey or scarf as a souvenir, don't wear it in Glasgow; passions run very high, and most drunken brawls in town are between supporters of Glasgow's two rival soccer clubs: Celtic in green, and Rangers in blue and red. (For more on the soccer rivalry, see page 138.)

Sightseeing: Almost every sight in Glasgow is free, but request £2-3 donations (www.glasgowmuseums.com). One exception is the Glasgow School of Art, but even there all proceeds go back to the school.

Sunday Travel: Bus and train schedules are dramatically reduced on Sundays—most routes have only half the departure times they have during the week. And trains run less frequently in the off-season; so if you want to get to the Highlands by bus on a Sunday in winter, forget it.

Internet Access: Wi-Fi is readily available in Glasgow; the main shopping drag is a big, free hotspot. Many pubs and coffee shops offer free Wi-Fi as well.

Laundry: Majestic Launderette will pick up your dirty clothes at your B&B or hotel, then return them clean (call to arrange, figure around £12-15/load); they also have a self-service launderette near the Kelvingrove Museum in the West End (self-serve or full-serve, Mon-Fri 8:00-18:00, Sat 8:00-16:00, Sun 10:00-16:00, 1110 Argyle Street, tel. 0141/334-3433).

Local Guides: Joan Dobbie, a native Glaswegian and registered Scottish Tourist Guide, will give you the insider's take on Glasgow's sights (£120/half-day, £140/day, tel. 01355/236-749, mobile 07773-555-151, joan.leo@lineone.net). **Colin Mairs** is youthful, knowledgeable, and fun to be with (£100/half-day, £150/day, mobile 07716-232-001, www.ExcursionScotland. com, ExcursionScotland@gmail.com).

Highlands Day Trips: Most of the same companies that do Highlands side-trips from Edinburgh also operate trips from Glasgow. If you'd like to spend an efficient day away from the city, skim the descriptions and listings on page 232, and then check each company's website or browse the brochures at the TI for details.

GETTING AROUND GLASGOW

By City Bus: Most city-center routes are operated by First Bus Company (£2/ride, £4.50 for all-day ticket on First buses, buy tickets from driver, exact change required). Buses run every few minutes down Glasgow's main thoroughfares (such as Sauchiehall Street) to the downtown core (train stations).

By Hop-On, Hop-Off Bus Tour: This tour connects Glasgow's far-flung historic sights in a two-hour loop and lets you hop on and off as you like for two days. Buses are frequent (every 10-20 minutes) and punctual, and alternate between live guides and recorded narration (both are equally good). The route covers the city very well, and the guide does a fine job of describing activities at each stop. While the first stop is on George Square, you can hop on and pay the driver anywhere along the route (£13, tel. 0141/204-0444, www.citysightseeingglasgow.co.uk).

By Taxi: Taxis are affordable, plentiful, and often come with nice, chatty cabbies—all speaking in the impenetrable Glaswegian accent. Just smile and nod. Most taxi rides within the downtown area cost about £6; to the West End is about £8. Use taxis or public transport to connect Glasgow's more remote sights; splurge for a taxi (for safety) any time you're traveling late at night.

By Subway: Glasgow's cute little single-line subway system, nicknamed The Clockwork Orange, makes a six-mile circle that has 15 stops. While simple today, when it opened in 1896 it was the bee's knees (it's the world's third-oldest subway system, after those in London and Budapest). Though the subway is essentially useless for connecting city-center sightseeing (Buchanan Street and St. Enoch are the only downtown stops), it's ideal for reaching sights farther out, including the Kelvingrove Museum (Kelvinhall stop) and West End restaurant/nightlife neighborhood (Hillhead stop; £1.60 single trip, £4 for all-day ticket, subway runs Mon-Sat 6:30-23:30, Sun 10:00-18:00, www.spt.co.uk/subway).

Glasgow Walks

These two self-guided walks introduce you to Glasgow's most interesting (and very different) neighborhoods: the downtown zone and the residential and university sights of the West End.

GET TO KNOW GLASGOW:
THE DOWNTOWN CORE

Glasgow isn't romantic, but it has an earthy charm, its people are a hoot to chat with, and architecture buffs love it. The more time you spend here, the more you'll feel the edgy, artsy vibe. The trick is to always look up—above the chain restaurants and mall stores, you'll discover a wealth of imaginative facades, complete with ornate

GLASGOW

Central Glasgow

To Edinburgh ↗

M Cowcaddens

TENEMENT
HOUSE
MUSEUM

NAT'L
PIPING
CENTRE

FOOTBRIDGE

To
West End

CHARING
CROSS
STATION

SCHOOL
OF ART

WILLOW
TEA ROOMS

CONCERT
HALL

To
Kelvingrove
Museum

Blythswood
Square

Buchanan M

FOOTBRIDGE

GOMA

MURALS

THE
LIGHTHOUSE

CELTIC
TEAM SHOP

CENTRAL
STATION

St Enoch M

To
Riverside
Museum

BROOMIELAW

ST. ENOCH
CENTRE

See Glasgow Walk detail map

River Clyde

To Airport &
Oban via A-82

To Burrell
Collection

friezes and expressive sculptures. These buildings transport you to the heady days around the turn of the 20th century—when the rest of Great Britain was enthralled by Victorianism, but Glasgow set its own course, thanks largely to the artistic bravado of Charles Rennie Mackintosh and his Art Nouveau friends (the "Glasgow Four"). This walking tour takes about 1.5 hours, not including time at any of the sights along the route.

• Start at the St. Enoch subway station, at the base of the pedestrian shopping boulevard, Buchanan Street. (This is a short walk from Cen-

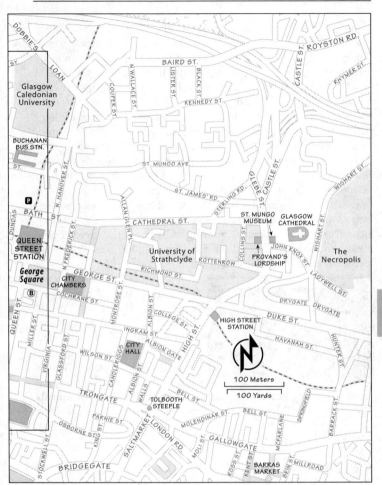

tral Station, a longer walk or quick cab ride from Queen Street Station.)
Take a moment to get oriented.

❶ Argyle Street and Nearby

The "Golden Zed" is the nickname for a Z-shaped pedestrian boulevard made of three streets: Sauchiehall, Buchanan, and Argyle.
Always coming up with marketing slogans to goose the shopping
metabolism of the city, this district (with the top shops in town) is
also called the "Style Mile."

Of the three streets, Argyle (the busy cross street) is the least
appealing, and Buchanan (the pedestrian mall straight ahead) is
the best. But before heading up Buchanan, take a quick detour
down Argyle to see a couple of slices of Glasgow life.

From the subway station, cross the busy street, then turn left along Argyle. A few doors down (on the right, at #154), notice the **Celtic Shop.** This shop is extreme green. That's the color of Glasgow's dominant (for now) soccer team. It's hard for outsiders to fathom the intensity of the rivalry between Glasgow's Celtic and Rangers. Celtic, founded by an Irish Catholic priest to raise money for poor Irish immigrants in the East End, is—naturally—green and favored by Catholics. (For reasons no one can explain, the Celtic team name is pronounced "sell-tic"—like it is in Boston. In all other cases, such as when referring to music, language, or culture, this word is pronounced "kell-tic.") Rangers, with team colors of the Union Jack (red, white, and blue), are more likely to be supported by Unionist and Protestant families. Today Celtic is in the major league and Rangers (wracked by scandals) have fallen into a lower division. Wander into the shop (minimizing or hiding any red or blue you might be wearing). Check out the energy in the photos and shots of the stadium filled with 60,000 fans. You're in a world where red and blue don't exist.

Now head a few steps down the alley (Mitchell Street) just past the Celtic Shop. While it seems a bit seedy, it should be safe...but look out for giant magnifying glasses and taxis held aloft by balloons. City officials have cleverly co-opted street artists by sanctioning huge, fun, and edgy **graffiti murals** like these. (You'll see even more if you side-trip down alleys along the Style Mile.)

• *Now backtrack to the base of...*

❷ Buchanan Street

Buchanan Street has a friendly Ramblas-style vibe with an abundance of street musicians. As you stroll uphill, keep an eye out for a few big landmarks: **Frasers** (#45, on the left) is a vast and venerable department store, considered the "Harrods of Glasgow." The **Argyll Arcade** (#30, opposite Frasers), dating from 1827, is the oldest arcade in town. It's filled mostly with jewelry and comes with security guards dressed in Victorian-era garb. Eager couples—  whether they're engaged or about to be—can be heard to say, "Let's take a shortcut through here." **Princes Square** (at #48, just past Argyll Arcade) is a classic old building dressed with a modern steel

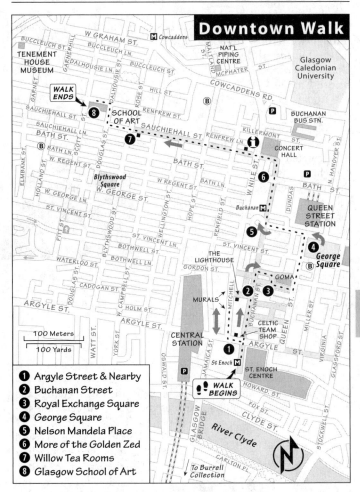

Downtown Walk

- ❶ Argyle Street & Nearby
- ❷ Buchanan Street
- ❸ Royal Exchange Square
- ❹ George Square
- ❺ Nelson Mandela Place
- ❻ More of the Golden Zed
- ❼ Willow Tea Rooms
- ❽ Glasgow School of Art

peacock and foliage. Step inside to see the delightfully modernized Art Nouveau atrium.

At #97 (50 yards up, on the left) is one of two Mackintosh-designed **Willow Tea Rooms** (other location described later in this walk).

• *Just past the tearooms, turn down the alley on the right, called Exchange Place. You'll pass the recommended Rogano restaurant on your right before emerging onto...*

❸ Royal Exchange Square

The centerpiece of this square—which marks the entrance to the shopping zone called Merchant City—is a stately, Neoclassical, bank-like building. This was once the **private mansion** of one of the tobacco lords, the super-rich businessmen who reigned here through the 1700s, stomping through the city with gold-tipped canes. During the port's heyday, these entrepreneurs helped Glasgow become Europe's sixth-biggest city—number two in the British Empire.

Today the mansion houses the **Glasgow Gallery of Modern Art,** nicknamed GoMA. Circle around the building to the main entry (at the equestrian statue of the

Duke of Wellington, often creatively decorated as Glasgow's favorite cone-head), and step back to take in the full Neoclassical facade. On the pediment, notice the funky, mirrored mosaic celebrating the miracles of St. Mungo—an example of how Glasgow refuses to take itself too seriously. The temporary exhibits inside GoMA are generally forgettable, but the museum does have an unusual charter: It displays only the work of living artists (free, £2 suggested donation, Mon-Wed and Sat 10:00-17:00, Thu 10:00-20:00, Fri and Sun 11:00-17:00).

• *Facing the fanciful GoMA facade, turn right up Queen Street. Within a block, you'll reach...*

❹ George Square

This square, the centerpiece of Glasgow, is filled with statues and lined with notable buildings, such as the Queen Street train sta-

tion and the Glasgow City Chambers (the big Neoclassical building standing like a secular church to the east, open by tour, generally Mon-Fri 10:30 and 14:30, free). In front of the City Chambers stands a monument to Glaswegians killed fighting in the World Wars. The square is decorated with a *Who's Who* of statues depicting great Glaswegians. Find James Watt (who perfected the steam engine that helped power Europe into the Industrial Age), as well as Scotland's two top poets: Robert Burns and Sir Walter Scott (capping the tallest pillar in the center). The two equestrian statues are of Prince Albert and a surprisingly skinny Queen Victoria—a rare image of her in her more svelte youth.

• *Just past skinny Vic and Robert Peel, turn left onto West George Street, and cross Buchanan Street to the tall church in the middle of...*

❺ Nelson Mandela Place

This is the first public space named for Nelson Mandela—honoring the man who, while still in prison, helped bring down apartheid in

South Africa. Glasgow, nicknamed Red Clyde Side for its socialist politics and empathy for the working class, has been quick to jump on progressive causes.

The area around this church features some interesting bits of architectural detail. Facing the church's left side are the three circular friezes of the former **Stock Exchange** (built in 1875). These idealized heads represent the industries that made Glasgow prosperous during its prime: building, engineering, and mining.

Around the back of the church find the **Athenaeum**, the sandy-colored building at #8 (notice the low-profile label over the door). Now a law office, this was founded in 1847 as a school and city library during Glasgow's Golden Age. (Charles Dickens gave the building's inaugural address.) Like Edinburgh, Glasgow was at the forefront of the 18th-century Scottish Enlightenment, a celebration of education and intellectualism. The Scots were known for their extremely practical brand of humanism; all members of society, including the merchant and working classes, were expected to be well educated. (Tobacco lords, for example, often knew Latin and Greek.) Look above the door to find the symbolic statue of a reader sharing books with young children, an embodiment of this ideal.

• *Return to the big, pedestrianized Buchanan Street in front of the church. Just downhill, to the right, is a huge Apple Store in a grand old building. But we'll head the opposite direction and start up...*

❻ Buchanan Street to Sauchiehall Street (More of the Golden Zed)

A short distance uphill is the glass entry to Glasgow's subway (from here you could ride directly to the Hillhead stop for the West End restaurant district; see "Eating in Glasgow," later). Soon after, on the right, you'll pass the Buchanan Galleries, an indoor mall that sprawls through several city blocks (offering a refuge in rainy weather).

At the top of Buchanan Street stands the **Glasgow**

Charles Rennie Mackintosh (1868-1928)

Charles Rennie Mackintosh brought an exuberant Art Nouveau influence to the architecture of his hometown. His designs challenged the city planners of this otherwise practical, working-class port city to create beauty in the buildings they commissioned.

As a student traveling in Italy, Mackintosh ignored the paintings inside museums and set up his easel to paint the exteriors of churches and buildings instead. He rejected the architectural traditions of ancient Greece and Rome. In Venice and Ravenna, he fell under the spell of Byzantine design, and in Siena he saw a unified, medieval city design he would try to import—but with a Scottish flavor and palette—to Glasgow.

When Mackintosh was at the Glasgow School of Art, the Industrial Age dominated life. Factories belched black soot as they burned coal and forged steel. Mackintosh and his artist friends drew inspiration from nature and created some of the first Art Nouveau buildings, paintings, drawings, and furniture. His first commission came in 1893, to design an extension to the Glasgow Herald building. More work followed, including the Glasgow School of Art and the Willow Tea Rooms.

A radical thinker, Mackintosh shared credit with his artist wife, Margaret MacDonald (who specialized in glass and metal-

Royal Concert Hall. Its steps are a favorite perch where local office workers munch lunch and enjoy the street scene. The statue is of **Donald Dewar,** who served as Scotland's first ever "First Minister" after the Scottish Parliament reconvened in 1999 (previously they'd been serving in London—as part of the British Parliament—since 1707).

• *From here, the Golden Zed zags left, Buchanan Street becomes Sauchiehall Street—look for the* **TI** *on your right—and the shopping gets cheaper and less elegant. While there's little of note to see, it's still a pleasant stroll. Walk a few blocks and enjoy the people-watching. Just before the end of the pedestrian zone, on the left side (at #217), are the...*

❼ Willow Tea Rooms

Tearooms were hugely popular during the industrial boom of the late 19th century. As Glasgow grew, more people moved to the suburbs, meaning that office workers couldn't easily return home for lunch. And during this age of Victorian morals, the temperance

work). He once famously said, "I have the talent...Margaret has the genius." The two teamed up with another husband-and-wife duo—Herbert MacNair and Margaret's sister, Frances MacDonald—to define a new strain of Scottish Art Nouveau, called the "Glasgow Style." These influential couples were known as "the Glasgow Four."

Mackintosh's works show a strong Japanese influence, particularly in his use of black-and-white contrast to highlight the idealized forms of nature. He also drew inspiration from the Arts and Crafts movement, with an eye to simplicity, clean lines, respect for tradition, and an emphasis on precise craftsmanship over mass production. While some of his designs appear to be repeated, no two motifs are exactly alike—just as nothing is exactly the same in nature.

Mackintosh insisted on designing every element of his commissions—even the furniture, curtains, and cutlery. As a furniture and woodwork designer, Mackintosh preferred to use cheaper materials, then paint them with several thick coats, hiding seams and imperfections and making the piece feel carved rather than built. His projects often went past deadline and over budget, but resulted in unusually harmonious spaces.

Mackintosh inspired other artists, such as painter Gustav Klimt and Bauhaus founder Walter Gropius, but his vision was not appreciated in his own time as much as it is now. He died with only £88 to his name. Now, a century after Scotland's greatest architect set pencil to paper, his hometown is at last celebrating his unique vision.

GLASGOW

movement was trying to discourage the consumption of alcohol. Tearooms were designed to be an appealing alternative to eating in pubs.

These tearooms are also an Art Nouveau masterpiece by Charles Rennie Mackintosh. Visitors are welcome to browse. Mackintosh made his living from design commissions, including multiple tearooms for businesswoman Kate Cranston. Mackintosh designed everything here—down to the furniture, lighting, and cutlery. He took his theme for the café from the name of the street it's on—*saugh* is Scots for willow.

In the design of these tearooms, there was a meeting of the (very modern) minds. In addition to giving office workers an alternative to pubs, Cranston also wanted a place where women could gather while unescorted—in a time when traveling solo could give a woman a less-than-desirable reputation. An ardent women's rights supporter, Cranston requested that the rooms be bathed in white, the suffragettes' signature color.

On the ground floor, peruse the Mackintosh-inspired jewelry and the exhibit about his design in back. Then climb the stairs to find 20 tables run like a diner from a corner kitchen, serving simple meals to middle-class people—just as this place has since it opened in 1903. Be sure to look for the almost-hidden Room de Luxe dining room (upstairs). While most features of the Room de Luxe are reproductions (such as the chairs and the doors, which were too fragile to survive), it appears just as it did in Mackintosh's day (for details, see listing on page 156).

• From here it's a five-minute, mostly uphill walk to the must-see Mackintosh sight in the town center. Leaving the pedestrian zone, continue two more blocks on Sauchiehall, and make a right onto Dalhousie Street; the big, blond sandstone building on the left at the top of the hill is the...

❽ Glasgow School of Art

When he was just 28 years old—and still a no-name junior draughtsman for a big architectural firm—Charles Rennie Mackintosh won the contest to create a new home for the Glasgow School of Art. He threw himself into the project, designing every detail of the building, inside and out.

While at first glance the School of Art seems to merge with all the other red sandstone in Glasgow, its unique details begin to pop out on closer inspection. Mackintosh blended the zeitgeist for curvy, organic Art Nouveau with his own taste for the clean black lines of Japanese minimalism. He also threw in some features evocative of the Romantic "Scottish Baronial" style of medieval Highland castles (unadorned sandstone, towers and turrets, and slit-like windows). And at the same time, the architect—not long out of school himself—ensured that the building served the needs of his patrons, the students. For example, notice the huge, north-side windows (today facing a glassy green building); these were designed to bathe the painting studio in an even, natural light all day long.

Mackintosh—who loved the hands-on ideology of the Arts and Crafts movement but was also a practical Scot—brought all the most recent technologies to this work. Those protruding wrought-iron brackets that hover outside the multipaned windows were invented during the Industrial Revolution and reinforce the big, fragile glass windows. Remember that this work was the Art Nouveau original, and that Frank Lloyd Wright, the Art Deco Chrysler Building, and everything that resembles it came well after Charles Rennie Mack's time.

The interior is even more impressive. Unfortunately, the building was badly damaged by a fire in May 2014. It likely won't open again until 2018 or 2019 at the earliest. But you can still get a taste of Mackintosh's genius inside the school's **Reid Building,** the glassy green structure across the street. Inside is a shop highlighting students' works and a small, free exhibition about Mackintosh, his masterpiece (including an impressive model of the School of Art), and his contemporaries (shop, exhibition, and tour desk open daily 10:00-16:30).

Tours: To learn more, sign up for a one-hour guided tour (likely £10). These include the exterior of the School of Art (with a clear explanation of its architecture and symbolism), a brief walk through the modern Reid Building, and a guided visit to a small but impressive collection of original furniture designed by Mackintosh and his wife and collaborator, Margaret MacDonald. Usually, three or four tours run each day, but the schedule is in flux due to the fire damage and tours can book up, so it's best to check the school's website (www.gsa.ac.uk/tours), call ahead (tel. 0141/353-4526), or email (tours@gsa.ac.uk) to find out your options and book ahead. (Or just drop by and ask.) The tour fees help fund the conservation of Mackintosh's work, and, as a bonus, you get to meet and enjoy the accent of a smart, young Glasgow art student. Serious admirers can ask about the 2.25-hour Mackintosh-themed city walking tours given by students (£20, 4/week).

• *Our walk is finished, but two additional sights lie within a five-minute stroll (in different directions). The remarkably preserved* **Tenement House** *offers a fascinating glimpse into Glasgow lifestyles in the early 1900s. And the* **National Piping Centre** *is ideal for those who want to go beyond the clichés and gain a better appreciation for the history and musicality of Scotland's favorite instrument. Both are described on page 151, and either one is a good place to pass the time while you're waiting for your tour of the School of Art.*

WEST END WALK

Glasgow's West End—just a quick subway, bus, or taxi ride from downtown—is the city's top residential neighborhood. As in so many British cities, the western part of town—upwind of industrial pollution—was the most desirable. This area has great restaurants and nightlife (see "Eating in Glasgow," later), fine accommodations (see "Sleeping in Glasgow," later), and some lesser-known but worthwhile museums. This lightly narrated walk provides a

GLASGOW

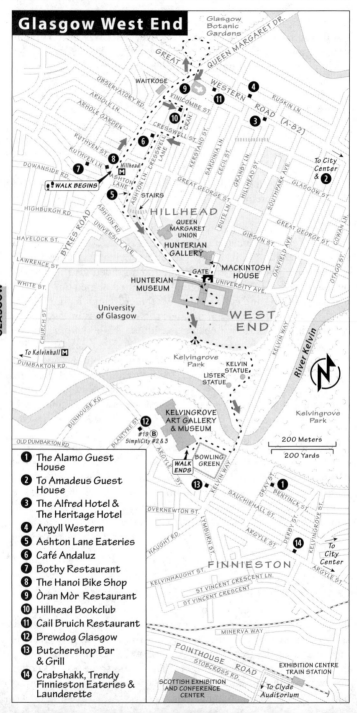

Glasgow West End

1 The Alamo Guest House
2 To Amadeus Guest House
3 The Alfred Hotel & The Heritage Hotel
4 Argyll Western
5 Ashton Lane Eateries
6 Café Andaluz
7 Bothy Restaurant
8 The Hanoi Bike Shop
9 Òran Mòr Restaurant
10 Hillhead Bookclub
11 Cail Bruich Restaurant
12 Brewdog Glasgow
13 Butchershop Bar & Grill
14 Crabshakk, Trendy Finnieston Eateries & Launderette

framework for exploring the West End. It begins at the Hillhead subway stop, meanders through dining and residential zones, explores some grand old university buildings (and related museums), and ends with a wander through the park to the Kelvingrove Museum—one of Glasgow's top sights.

• *Ride the subway to the Hillhead stop. Exiting the station, turn right and walk four short blocks up...*

Byres Road: A *byre* is a cow shed. So back when this was farmland outside the big city, cattle were housed along here. Not anymore: Today, Byres Road is a main thoroughfare through a trendy district. A block before the big intersection, notice the **Waitrose** supermarket on the left. In Britain, this is a sure sign of a posh neighborhood—like a Whole Foods in the US.

Approaching the corner with Great Western Road, you'll see a church spire on the right. Dating from 1862, this church was recently converted into a restaurant and music venue called **Òran Mòr** (Gaelic for "The Great Music"). Step into the entryway to see the colorful murals (by Alasdair Gray, a respected Glaswegian artist and novelist) and the multilingual "Welcome" and "Farewell" messages in the foyer floor. Consider a drink or meal in their pub or a pricier meal in their brasserie. Also check what's on while you're in town, as this is a prime music and theater venue. Glasgow prides itself on its ambitious live music scene, with an average of 130 musical events per week; Glaswegians claim that the city has more music venues than anywhere else north of London. In keeping with Glasgow's unpretentious spirit, the people at Òran Mòr like to keep things accessible. They created a combo-deal called "a play, a pie, and a pint"—all for just £10-15 (and now being copied by other venues around town).

• *If the weather's good, cross Great Western Road and head into the...*

Glasgow Botanic Gardens: This inviting parkland is Glaswegians' favorite place to enjoy a break from the bustling city. And,

like so many things in Glasgow, it's free. Locals brag about their many parks, claiming that—despite their industrial reputation—they have more green space per capita than any other city in Europe. And even the city's name comes from the Gaelic for "the dear green place."

Before going into the park, pause at the red-brick entrance gate. On the gate on the left, look for Glasgow's quite busy **city seal,** which honors St. Mungo, the near-legendary town founder. The jumble of symbols (a bird, a tree, a bell, and a salmon with a ring in its mouth) recall Mungo's four key miracles. Ask any Glaswegian to tell you the tales of St. Mungo—they learn it all by heart. The city motto, "Let Glasgow Flourish," is apt—particularly given its recent rejuvenation following a long, crippling period of industrial rot. Glasgow's current renaissance was kicked off with an ambitious 1989 garden festival in a disused former shipyard. Now the city is one of Europe's trendiest success stories. Let Glasgow flourish, indeed.

Head farther into the park. If the sun's out, it'll be jammed with people enjoying some rare rays. Young lads wait all winter for the day when they can cry, "Sun's oot, taps aff!" and pull off their shirts to make the most of it.

In addition to the finely landscaped gardens, the park has two inviting greenhouse pavilions—both free and open to the public. The big white one on the right is the most elegant, with classical statues scattered among the palm fronds (but beware the killer plants, to the left as you enter). When the clouds roll in and the weather turns rotten—which is more the status quo—these warm, dry areas become quite popular.

When you're done in the park, head back out the way you came in. Back out on the street, before crossing Great Western Road, go right a few steps to find the blue **police call box.** Once an icon of British life, these were little neighborhood mini offices where bobbies could store paperwork and equipment, use the telephone, and catch up with each other. These days, some of the call boxes are being repurposed as coffee shops, ice-cream stands, and time machines. (They're surprisingly spacious inside.)

• Cross back over Great Western Road and backtrack (past the Òran Mòr church/restaurant) one block down Byres Road. Turn left down Vinicombe Street (across from the Waitrose). Now we'll explore...

Back-Streets West End: Peek inside the **Hillhead Bookclub**—a former cinema that's been converted into a hipster bar/restaurant serving affordable food (described later, under "Eating in Glasgow"). Just after that, turn right and walk (on Crawnworth Street) along the row of red-sandstone **tenements**. While that word has negative connotations stateside, here a "tenement" is simply an apartment building. And judging from the grand

size, bulging bay windows, and prime location of these, it's safe to say they're far from undesirable. Many are occupied by a single family, while others are subdivided into five or six rooms for students (the university is right around the corner). Across the street from this tenement row (at #12) is a **baths club**—a private swimming pool, like an exclusive health club back home. Historically, most people couldn't afford bathing facilities in their homes, so they came to central locations like this one to get clean every few days (or weeks). Today, it's the wealthy—not the poor—who come to places like this.

After the baths, turn right down Cresswell Street. A half-block down on the right, turn left down **Cresswell Lane**—an inviting, traffic-free, brick-floored shopping and dining zone. While the Golden Zed downtown is packed with chain stores, this is where you'll find charming one-off boutiques.

Browse your way to the end of the lane, cross the street, and head down the similar, but even more appealing, **Ashton Lane.**

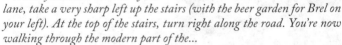

Scout this street and pick a place to return for dinner tonight—you can't go wrong. Fancy a film? Halfway down the street on the right, the Grosvenor Cinema shows both blockbusters and art-house fare (see listing on page 161).

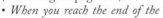

• *When you reach the end of the lane, take a very sharp left up the stairs (with the beer garden for Brel on your left). At the top of the stairs, turn right along the road. You're now walking through the modern part of the...*

University of Glasgow Campus: Founded in 1451, this is Scotland's second-oldest university (after St. Andrews). Its 24,000 students sprawl through the West End. Unlike the fancy "old university" buildings, this area is gloomy and concrete. The hulking building on your left is the Queen Margaret Union, with a music venue that has hosted several big-name bands before they were famous—from Nirvana to Franz Ferdinand. (If you think Franz Ferdinand is an Austrian archduke rather than a Scottish alternative rock band...you've been out of college too long.)

Eventually you'll reach a wide cross street, University Avenue. Turn left up this street and walk two more blocks uphill. At the traffic light, the **Hunterian Gallery and Mackintosh House** are just up the hill on your left, and the **Hunterian Museum** is across the street on the right. Both are free, well worth a visit, and described on page 156.

• *First, stop in at the Hunterian Gallery to sign up for the next (free) tour of the Mackintosh House. Spend any waiting time exploring the gallery's fine art collection—or, with a longer wait, jump ahead to the Hunterian Museum and come back to the Mackintosh House later.*

When you're done here, cross University Avenue. Instead of going through the main gate, go to the left end of the building facing the street to find a more interesting decorative gate.

University of Glasgow Main Building: Take a good look at the gate, which is decorated with the names of illustrious alums.

Pick out the great Scots you're familiar with: James Watt, King James II, Adam Smith, Lord Kelvin, William Hunter (the namesake of the university's museums), and Donald Dewar, a driving force behind devolution who became Scotland's first "First Minister" in 1999.

Go through the gate and face the main university building. Stretching to the left is Graduation Hall, where commencement takes place. Head straight into the building, ride the elevator to floor 4, and take a walk through the **Hunterian Museum.**

After you visit the Hunterian Museum, find the grand staircase down (in the room with the Antonine Wall exhibit). You'll

emerge into one of the twin quads enclosed by the enormous ensemble of university buildings. Veer right to find your way into the atmospheric, Neo-Gothic **cloisters** that support the wing separating the two quads. These are modeled after the Gothic cloisters in the lower chapel of Glasgow Cathedral, across town. On the other side, you'll pop out into the adjoining quad. Enjoy pretending you're a student for a few minutes, then head out the door at the bottom of the quad.

Leaving the university complex, head for the tall flagpole. The turreted building just below is the Kelvingrove Museum, where this walk ends. (If you get turned around in the park, just head for those spires.) To the right, off in the distance, you'll see two silvery, modern structures. Both are concert halls, part of an ambitious rejuvenation project along Glasgow's River Clyde waterfront.

• *From the flagpole, turn left and head to the end of the big building. Head down the stairs leading through the woods on your right (marked* James Watt Building*). When you reach the busy road, turn right along it for a short distance, then—as soon as you can—angle to the right back into the green space of...*

Kelvingrove Park: Another of Glasgow's favorite parks, this originated in the Victorian period, when there was a renewed

focus on trying to get people out into green spaces. One of the first things you'll come to is a big statue of **Lord Kelvin** (1824-1907). Born William Thomson, he chose to take the name of the River Kelvin, which runs through Glasgow (and gives its name to many other things here, including the museum we're headed to). One of the most respected scientists of his time, Kelvin was a pioneer in the field of thermodynamics, and gave his name (or, actually, the river's) to a new, absolute unit of temperature measurement designed to replace Celsius and Fahrenheit.

Just past Kelvin, bear left at the statue of **Joseph Lister** (1827-1912, of "Listerine" fame—he pioneered the use of antiseptics to remove infection-causing germs from the surgical environment), and take the bridge across the River Kelvin. Once across the bridge, turn right toward the museum. You'll walk along a pleasant bowling green that was built for the Commonwealth Games that Glasgow hosted in 2014. They needed lots of people to play here to help "season" the new court, so for a time it was free and open to anyone—creating a surge of popular interest in this very old and genteel sport.

Now's the time to explore the **Kelvingrove Museum,** described on page 157.

• *When you're finished at the museum, exit out the back end, toward the busy road. Several recommended restaurants are ahead and to the left, in the Finnieston neighborhood (see page 169). Or, if you'd like to hop on the subway, just turn right along Argyle Street and walk five minutes to the Kelvinhall station.*

Sights in Glasgow

JUST NORTH OF THE GLASGOW SCHOOL OF ART

Both of these sights are close to the end of my "Get to Know Glasgow" walk, earlier.

▲▲Tenement House

Here's a chance to drop into a perfectly preserved 1930s-era middle-class residence. The National Trust for Scotland bought this otherwise ordinary row home, located in a residential neighborhood, because of the peculiar tendencies of Miss Agnes Toward (1886-1975). For five decades, she kept her home essentially unchanged. The kitchen calendar is still set for 1935, and canisters of licorice powder (a laxative) still sit on the bathroom shelf. It's a time-warp experience, where Glaswegian old-timers enjoy coming to reminisce about how they grew up.

Cost and Hours: £6.50, £3 guidebook, March-Oct daily 13:00-17:00, closed Nov-Feb, no photos allowed, 145 Buccleuch Street (pronounced "ba-KLOO") down off the top of Garnethill, tel. 0141/333-0183, www.nts.org.uk.

Visiting the House: Buy your ticket on the main floor, and poke around the little museum. You'll learn that in Glasgow, a "tenement" isn't a slum—it's simply an apartment house. In fact, tenements like these were typical for every class except the richest. Then head upstairs to the apartment, which is staffed by caring volunteers. Ring the doorbell to be let in. Ask them why the bed is in the kitchen, why the rooms still smell like natural gas, or why there are studs on the banisters. As you look through the rooms laced with Victorian trinkets—such as the ceramic dogs on the living room's fireplace mantle—consider how different they are from Mackintosh's stark, minimalist designs from the same period.

▲National Piping Centre

If you consider bagpipes a tacky Scottish cliché, think again. At this small but insightful museum, you'll get a scholarly lesson in the proud and fascinating history of the bagpipe. For those with a healthy attention span for history or musical instruments—ideally both—it's fascinating. On Thursdays and Fridays (usually 10:00-17:00), a piper is on hand to perform, answer questions, and show you around the collection. At other times, if it's quiet, ask the ticket-sellers to tell you more—some are bagpipe students at the music school across the street. The center also offers a shop, lessons, a restaurant, and accommodations.

Cost and Hours: £4.50, includes audioguide, Mon-Thu 9:00-19:00, Fri 9:00-17:00, Sat 9:00-15:00, closed Sun, 30 McPhater Street, tel. 0141/353-5551, www.thepipingcentre.co.uk.

Visiting the Museum: The collection is basically one big room packed with well-described exhibits, including several historic bagpipes. You'll learn that bagpipes from as far away as Italy, Spain, and Bohemia predated Scottish ones; that Lowlands bagpipes were traditionally bellows-blown rather than lung-powered; and why bagpipes started being used to inspire Scottish soldiers on the battlefield. At the back of the room, look for the hand-engraved, backward printing plates for bagpipe sheet music (which didn't exist until the 19th century). The thoughtful, beautifully produced audioguide—which mixes a knowledgeable commentary with sound bites of bagpipes being played and brief interviews with performers—feels like a 40-minute audio-documentary on the BBC. The 15-minute film shown at the end of the room sums up the collection helpfully. They also have a practice set of bagpipes in case you want to try your hand. The chanter fingering is easy if you play the recorder, but keeping the bag inflated is exhausting.

CATHEDRAL PRECINCT, WITH A HINT OF MEDIEVAL GLASGOW

Very little remains of medieval Glasgow, but a visit to the cathedral and the area around it is a visit to the birthplace of the city. The first church was built here in the 7th century. Today's towering cathedral is mostly 13th century—the only great Scottish church to survive the Reformation intact. In front you'll see an attention-grabbing statue of **David Livingstone** (1813-1873). Livingstone—the Scottish missionary/explorer/cartographer who discovered a huge waterfall in Africa and named it in honor of his queen, Victoria—was born eight miles from here.

Nearby, the Provand's Lordship is Glasgow's only secular building dating from the Middle Ages. The St. Mungo Museum of Religious Life and Art, built on the site of the old Bishop's Castle, is a unique exhibit covering the spectrum of religions. And the Necropolis, blanketing the hill behind the cathedral, provides an atmospheric walk through a world of stately Victorian tombstones. From there you can scan the city and look down on the brewery where Tennent's Lager (a longtime Glasgow favorite) has been made since 1885.

The four main sights, including the cathedral, are within close range of each other. As you face the cathedral, the St. Mungo Museum is on your right (with handy public WCs), the Provand's Lordship is across the street from St. Mungo, and the Necropolis is behind the cathedral and toward the right.

To reach these sights from Buchanan Street, turn east on Bath Street, which soon becomes Cathedral Street, and walk about 15 minutes (or hop a bus along the main drag—try bus #38, or #57, confirm with driver that the bus stops at the cathedral). To head to the Kelvingrove Museum after your visit, from the cathedral, walk two blocks up Castle Street and catch bus #19 (on the cathedral side).

▲Glasgow Cathedral

This blackened, Gothic cathedral is a rare example of an intact pre-Reformation Scottish cathedral. (It was once known as "the Pink Church" for the tone of its stone. But with Industrial Age soot and modern pollution, it blackened. Cleaning would damage the integrity of the stone structure, so it was left black.) The zealous Reformation forces of John Knox ripped out the stained glass and ornate chapels of the Catholic age, but they left the church standing.

Cost and Hours: Free, £3 suggested donation; Mon-Sat 9:30-17:30, Sun 13:00-17:00; until 16:30 Oct-March, ask about free guided tours, near junction of Castle and Cathedral Streets, tel. 0141/552-8198, www.glasgowcathedral.org.uk.

Visiting the Cathedral: Inside, look up to see the wooden barrel-vaulted ceiling, and take in the beautifully decorated sec-

tion over the choir ("quire"). The choir screen is the only pre-Reformation screen surviving in Scotland. It divided the common people from the priests and big shots of the day, who got to worship closer to the religious action. Standing at the choir, turn around to look down the nave at the west wall, and notice how the right wall lists. (Don't worry; it's been listing—and still standing—for 800 years.) The cathedral's glass dates mostly from the 19th century. One window on the right side of the choir, celebrating the 14 trades of Glasgow, dates from 1951.

Step into the lower church (down stairs on right as you face the choir), where the central altar sits upon St. Mungo's tomb. Mungo was the seventh-century Scottish monk and mythical founder of Glasgow who established the first wooden church on this spot and gave Glasgow its name. Notice the ceiling bosses (decorative caps where the ribs come together) with their colorfully carved demons, dragons, and skulls.

▲Necropolis

From the cathedral, a lane leads over the "bridge of sighs" into the park filled with grand tombstones. Glasgow's huge burial hill has a wistful, ramshackle appeal. A stroll among the tombstones of the eminent Glaswegians of the 19th century gives a glimpse of Victorian Glasgow and a feeling for the confidence and wealth of the second city of the British Empire in its glory days.

With the Industrial Age (in the early 1800s), Glasgow's population tripled to 200,000. The existing churchyards were jammed and unhygienic. The city needed a beautiful place in which to bury its beautiful citizens, so this grand necropolis was established. Because Presbyterians are more into simplicity, the statuary is simpler than in a Catholic cemetery. Wandering among the disintegrating memorials to once-important people, I thought about how, someday, everyone's tombstone will fall over and no one will care.

The highest pillar in the graveyard is a memorial to John Knox. The Great Reformer (who's actually buried in Edinburgh) looks down at the cathedral he wanted to strip of all art, and even tear down. (The Glaswegians rallied to follow Knox, but saved the church.) If the cemetery's main black gates are closed, see if you can get in and out through a gate off the street to the right.

▲St. Mungo Museum of Religious Life and Art

This interesting museum, just in front of the cathedral, aims to promote religious understanding. Built in 1990 on the site of the old Bishop's Castle, it provides a handy summary of major and minor world religions, showing how each faith handles various rites of passage across the human life span: birth, puberty, marriage, death, and everything in between and after. Start with the 10-minute video overview on the first floor, and finish with a great view from the top floor of the cathedral and Necropolis.

Cost and Hours: Free, £3 suggested donation, Tue-Thu and Sat 10:00-17:00, Fri and Sun 11:00-17:00, closed Mon, free WCs downstairs, cheap ground-floor café, 2 Castle Street, tel. 0141/276-1625, www.glasgowmuseums.com.

Provand's Lordship

With low beams and medieval decor, this creaky home—supposedly the "oldest house in Glasgow"—is the only secular building surviving in Glasgow from the Middle Ages. It displays the *Lifestyles of the Rich and Famous*...circa 1471. The interior, while sparse and stony, shows off a few pieces of furniture from the 16th, 17th, and 18th centuries. Out back, explore the St. Nicholas Garden, which was once part of a hospital that dispensed herbal remedies. The plaques in each section show the part of the body each plant is used to treat.

Cost and Hours: Free, small donation requested, Tue-Thu and Sat 10:00-17:00, Fri and Sun 11:00-17:00, closed Mon, across the street from St. Mungo Museum at 3 Castle Street, tel. 0141/552-8819, www.glasgowmuseums.com.

THE WEST END

These sights are linked by my West End Walk on page 145.

GLASGOW

▲Hunterian Gallery and Mackintosh House

Here's a sightseeing twofer: an art gallery offering a good look at some Scottish artists relatively unknown outside their homeland, and the chance to take a guided tour through the reconstructed home of Charles Rennie Mackintosh, decorated exactly the way he liked it. For Charles Rennie Mack fans—or anyone fascinated by the worlds artists create for themselves to live in—it's worth ▲▲▲, and arguably provides a more intimate look at Mackintosh than does any other sight in town.

Cost and Hours: Gallery—free, Tue-Sat 10:00-17:00, Sun 11:00-16:00, closed Mon, across University Avenue from the main Hunterian Museum, tel. 0141/330-4221, www.gla.ac.uk/hunterian. Mackintosh House—entry only with free tour, departs every 30 minutes during gallery hours, last tour departs 30 minutes before closing.

Visiting the Museum: First, check in at the reception desk to sign up for a tour of the Mackintosh House. Spend your waiting time visiting the gallery, or, with a longer wait, head across the street to the Hunterian Museum (described later).

You'll take a 30-minute blitz tour through the **Mackintosh House**. In 1906, Mackintosh and his wife, Margaret MacDonald, moved into the end unit of a Victorian row house. Mackintosh gutted the place and redesigned it to his own liking—bathing the interior in his trademark style, a mix of curving, organic lines and rigid, proto-Art Deco functionalism. They moved out in 1914, and the house was demolished in the 1960s—but the university wisely documented the layout and carefully removed and preserved all of Mackintosh's original furnishings. In 1981, when respect for Mackintosh was on the rise, they built this replica house and re-installed everything just as Mackintosh had designed it. On the tour, you'll see the entryway, dining room, drawing room, and bedroom—each one offering fascinating glimpses into the minds of these great artists. You'll see original furniture and decorations by Mackintosh and MacDonald, providing keen insight into their creative process. And in the top-floor exhibition, you'll see some Mackintosh works from other commissions.

The Hunterian's **art gallery** is manageable and worth exploring. One highlight is the modern Scottish art (1850-1960), focusing on two groups: the "Glasgow Boys," who traveled to France to study during the waning days of Realism (1880s), and, a generation later, the Scottish Colourists, who found a completely different inspiration in circa-1910 France—bright, bold, with an almost Picasso-like exuberance. The gallery also has an extensive collection of portraits by American artist James Whistler—Whistler's wife was of Scottish descent, as was Whistler's mother. (Hey, that has a nice ring to it.) The painter always found great support in Scotland, and his heir donated his estate to the University of Glasgow.

▲Hunterian Museum

The oldest public museum in Scotland was founded by William Hunter (1718-1783), a medical researcher. Today his natural sci-

ence collection is housed in a huge and gorgeous space inside the university's showcase building. Everything is well presented and well explained. You'll see a perceptive exhibit on the Antonine Wall (the lesser-known cousin of Hadrian's Wall), built in A.D. 142 to seal off the Picts from the Roman Empire. The eclectic collec-

tion also includes musical instruments, a display on the Glasgow-built *Lusitania*, and a fine collection of fossils, including the aquatic dinosaur called plesiosaur (possibly a distant ancestor of the Loch Ness monster). But most people can't get enough of the endless examples of deformities—two-headed animals, babies in jars, and so on. Ever the curious medical researcher, Hunter collected these for study, and today they still intrigue, titillate, and nauseate visitors to his museum.

Cost and Hours: Free, Tue-Sat 10:00-17:00, Sun 11:00-16:00, closed Mon, Gilbert Scott Building, University Avenue, tel. 0141/330-4221, www.gla.ac.uk/hunterian.

▲▲Kelvingrove Art Gallery and Museum

This "Scottish Smithsonian" displays everything from a stuffed elephant to fine artwork by the great masters. The well-described

contents are impressively displayed in a grand, 100-year-old, Spanish Baroque-style building. The Kelvingrove claims to be one of the most-visited museums in Britain—presumably because of all the field-trip groups you'll see here. Watching all the excited Scot-

tish kids—their imaginations ablaze—is as much fun as the collection itself.

Cost and Hours: Free, £3 suggested donation, Mon-Thu and Sat 10:00-17:00, Fri and Sun 11:00-17:00, free tours at 11:00 and

14:30, Argyle Street, tel. 0141/276-9599, www.glasgowmuseums.com.

Getting There: My self-guided West End Walk leads you here from the Hillhead subway stop, or you can ride the **subway** to the Kelvinhall stop. When you exit, turn left and walk five minutes. **Buses** #2 and #3 run from Hope Street downtown to the museum. It's also on **the hop-on, hop-off bus** route. No matter how you arrive, just look for the huge, turreted red-brick building.

Organ Concerts: At the top of the main hall, the huge pipe organ booms with a daily 30-minute recital at 13:00 (15:00 on Sunday).

Visiting the Museum: Built to house the city collection in 1902, the museum is divided into two sections.

The "Life" section, in the West Court, features a menagerie of stuffed animals (including a giraffe, kangaroo, ostrich, and moose) with a WWII-era Spitfire fighter plane hovering overhead. Branching off are halls with exhibits ranging from Ancient Egypt to "Scotland's First People" to weaponry ("Conflict and Consequence").

The more serene "Expression" section, in the East Court, focuses on artwork, including Dutch, Flemish, French, and local artists (from Mackintosh to the late-Realist "Glasgow Boys"). Upstairs, near the main hall, you'll find the museum's most famous painting, Salvador Dalí's *Christ of St. John of the Cross,* which brought visitors to tears when it was first displayed here in the 1950s. This section also has exhibits on "Scottish Identity in Art," letting you tour the country's scenic wonders and history on canvas.

AWAY FROM THE CENTER
▲▲Riverside Museum

Located along the River Clyde, this high-tech, extremely kid-friendly museum—nostalgic and modern at the same time—is dedicated to all things transportation-related. It was named the European museum of the year in 2013, and visiting here is a must for anyone interested in transportation and how it has shaped society.

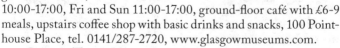

Cost and Hours: Free, £3 suggested donation, Mon-Thu and Sat 10:00-17:00, Fri and Sun 11:00-17:00, ground-floor café with £6-9 meals, upstairs coffee shop with basic drinks and snacks, 100 Pointhouse Place, tel. 0141/287-2720, www.glasgowmuseums.com.

Getting There: It's on the riverfront promenade, two miles west of the city center. **Bus** #100 runs between the museum and George Square (2/hour, last departure from George Square at

15:02, operated by McColl's), or you can take a **taxi** (£6-8, 10-minute ride from downtown). The museum is also included on the **hop-on, hop-off sightseeing bus** route (described earlier, under "Getting Around Glasgow").

Visiting the Museum: Most of the collection is strewn across one huge, wide-open floor. Upon entering, visit the info desk (to the right as you enter, near the shop) to ask about today's free tours and activities—or just listen for announcements. Also pick up a map from the info desk, as the museum's open floor plan can feel a bit like a traffic jam at rush hour.

Diving in, explore the vast collection: stagecoaches, locomotives, double-decker trolleys, and an entire wall stacked with vintage automobiles. Learn about the

opening of Glasgow's old-timey subway (Europe's third oldest). Explore the collections of old toys and prams, and watch a film about 1930s cinema. Stroll the re-creation of a circa-1900 street, with video clips of local seniors in time-warp shops reminiscing (like about the time the little girl noticed her daddy was selling things to the pawn shop to pay the rent). A highlight is the shipping section, commemorating Glasgow's shipbuilding era. On the giant screen, exhilarating newsreels show that proud moment when "the band plays, the minister prays, the lady sponsor gives the name, the crowds cheer, and seconds later a new ship takes to the water for the first time."

Don't miss the much smaller upstairs section, with great views over the River Clyde, additional exhibits about ships built here in Glasgow, and what may or may not be the world's oldest bicycle. The description explains that two different inventors have tried to take credit for the bike—and both of them are Scottish.

Nearby: Be sure to head to the River Clyde directly behind the museum (just step out the back door). The ***Glenlee,*** one of five

remaining tall ships built in Glasgow in the 19th century, invites visitors to come aboard (free, daily 10:00-17:00, Nov-Feb until 16:00, tel. 01413/573-699, www.thetallship.com). Good exhibits illustrate what it was like to live and work aboard the ship. Explore the officers' living quarters, then head below deck to the café and more exhibits. Below that, the cargo hold has kids' activities and offers the chance to peek into the engine room. .

Shopping in Glasgow

Downtown, the **Golden Zed**—a.k.a. "Style Mile"—has all the predictable chain stores, with a few Scottish souvenir stands mixed in. For more on this, see the start of my self-guided "Get to Know Glasgow" Walk.

The West End also has some appealing shops. Many are concentrated on **Cresswell Lane** (covered in my self-guided West End Walk). Browsing here, you'll find an eclectic assortment of gifty shops, art galleries, design shops, hair salons, record stores, home-decor shops, and lots of vintage. Be sure to poke into De Courcy's Arcade, a two-part warren of tiny offbeat shops.

▲Burrell Collection

This eclectic art collection of a wealthy local shipping magnate includes sculpture (from Roman to Rodin), stained glass, tapestries, furniture, Asian and Islamic works, and halls of paintings—starring Cézanne, Renoir, Degas, and a Rembrandt self-portrait. It's three miles outside the city center: Plan to make an afternoon of it, and leave time to walk around the surrounding park, where Highland cattle graze.

Cost and Hours: Free, Mon-Thu and Sat 10:00-17:00, Fri and Sun 11:00-17:00, Pollok Country Park, 2060 Pollokshaws Road, tel. 0141/287-2550, www.glasgowmuseums.com.

Getting There: From downtown, take **bus** #57 to Pollokshaws Road, or take a **train** to the Pollokshaws West train station; the entrance is a 10-minute walk from the bus stop and the train station. By **car**, follow the M-8 to exit at Junction 22 onto the M-77, then take the first exit and follow brown signs.

Nightlife in Glasgow

Glasgow has a youthful vibe, and its nightlife scene is renowned. The city is full of live music acts and venues. Walking through the city center, you'll pass at least one club or bar on every block. For the latest, *The Skinny* is Glasgow's information-packed alternative weekly (www.theskinny.co.uk). Or check out *The List* (www.list.co.uk) or the *Gig Guide* (www.gigguide.co.uk). All three are also available in print form around town.

DOWNTOWN

Glasgow's central business and shopping district is pretty sleepy after hours, but there are a few pockets of activity—each with its own personality. **Bath Street**'s bars and clubs are focused on young professionals as well as students; the recommended Pot Still is a perfect place to sample Scotch whisky (see page 167). Nearby, running just below the Glasgow School of Art, **Sauchiehall Street** is younger, artsier, and more student-oriented. The recently revitalized **Merchant City** zone, stretching just east of the Buchanan Street shopping drag, has a slightly older crowd and a popular gay scene.

IN THE WEST END

There's no shortage of after-hours fun in the West End.

In Hillhead: For a mainstream vibe with easy pickings, ride the subway to Hillhead and look around. **Òran Mòr** (a former church) and **Hillhead Bookclub** (a former cinema) are popular live music venues; check their websites for what's on (see listings on page 168). **Ashton Lane** and surrounding streets are another lively zone where you'll find engaging bars and music venues. **The Grosvenor Cinema,** right on Ashton Lane in the heart of the bustling West End restaurant scene, is a particularly inviting movie theater, with cushy leather seats in two theaters showing films big and small (most movies £10) and lots of special events. Bring in a drink from the cozy bar, or grab some Italian food at the upstairs restaurant (21 Ashton Lane, www.grosvenorcinema.co.uk, tel. 0845-166-6002).

In Finnieston: Glasgow's most up-and-coming hipster quarter, just below the Kelvingrove Museum, is packed with trendy bars and restaurants (for some recommendations, see page 169). But it also has an old-school selection of **Gaelic pubs.** If you're intrigued by Scotland's Gaelic-language culture, you don't need to travel deep into the Highlands to experience it. Finnieston's Argyle Street has a handful of spit-and-sawdust Gaelic pubs, some of which have live music in the evenings: check out **The Islay Inn** (at #1256), **The Park Bar** (at #1202), and **The Ben Nevis** (#1147).

Sleeping in Glasgow

For accommodations, choose between downtown (bustling by day, nearly deserted at night, close proximity to main shopping zone and some major sights, very expensive parking and one-way streets that cause headaches for drivers) and the West End (neighborhoody, best variety of restaurants, easier parking, easy access to West End sights and parks but a bus or subway ride from the center and train station).

GLASGOW

Sleep Code

Abbreviations   **(£1=about $1.60, country code: 44)**
S=Single, **D**=Double/Twin, **T**=Triple, **Q**=Quad, **b**=bathroom
Price Rankings
  $$$ Higher Priced—Most rooms £80 or more
   $$ Moderately Priced—Most rooms £60-80
    $ Lower Priced—Most rooms £60 or less
Unless otherwise noted, credit cards are accepted, and free Wi-Fi and/or a guest computer is generally available. Prices change; verify current rates online or by email. For the best prices, always book directly with the hotel.

GLASGOW

DOWNTOWN

These accommodations are scattered around the city center. I've focused my listings on affordable chain hotels (prices vary from day to day—I've listed an average peak-season price for a standard double) and the best of the few independent hotels in this area. For locations, see the map on page 164. Glasgow also has all of the predictable chains—**Premier Inn, Travelodge, Novotel, Mercure, Jurys Inn**—check online for deals.

$$$ Grasshoppers is a cheerful, above-it-all retreat on the sixth floor of a building overlooking Central Station. The 29 rooms are tight, with small "efficiency" bathrooms, but the welcome is warm and there's 24-hour access to fresh cupcakes, shortbread, and ice cream (Db-£85-125 depending on demand, optional buffet dinner-£17, elevator, 87 Union Street, tel. 0141/222-2666, www.grasshoppersglasgow.com, info@grasshoppersglasgow.com).

$$$ Pipers' Tryst has eight simple rooms done up in good tartan style above a restaurant in the National Piping Centre (described on page 152). It's in a grand, old former church building overlooking a busy intersection, across the street from the downtown business, shopping, and entertainment district. The location is handy, if not romantic, and it's practically a pilgrimage for fans of bagpipes (Db-£89, includes continental breakfast, 30 McPhater Street, tel. 0141/353-5551, www.thepipingcentre.co.uk, hotel@thepipingcentre.co.uk).

$$ Adelaides Guest House rents eight clean and cheerful rooms in a multitasking church building that also houses a theater and nursery school. Ted and Lisa run the place with warmth and quirky humor (S-£40, Sb-£55, Db-£75, family deals, includes continental breakfast, cooked breakfast-£6, 209 Bath Street, tel. 0141/248-4970, www.adelaides.co.uk, reservations@adelaides.co.uk).

$$ Z Hotel, part of a small "compact luxury" chain, offers 104 sleek, efficiency-priced, yet still very stylish rooms. It's welcoming and handy to Queen Street Station, just a few steps off George's Square (Db-£58-90 depending on size—cheapest rooms don't have windows, breakfast-£8, air-con, elevator, free wine-and-cheese buffet each afternoon, 36 North Frederick Street, tel. 0141/212-4550, www.thezhotels.com).

$$ Ibis Glasgow, part of the modern hotel chain, has 141 cookie-cutter rooms with blond wood and predictable comfort (Sb/Db-£58 on weeknights, £85 on weekends, £125 "event rate" during festivals and in Aug, breakfast-£9, elevator, restaurant, hiding behind a big Novotel at 220 West Regent Street, tel. 0141/225-6000, www.ibishotel.com, h3139@accor.com).

$$ Babbity Bowster, named for a traditional Scottish dance, is a pub and restaurant renting five simple, mod rooms up top. It's located in the trendy Merchant City on the eastern fringe of downtown, near several clubs and restaurants (Sb-£50, Db-£65, no breakfast, lots of stairs and no elevator, 10-minute walk from Central Station, 16 Blackfriars Street, tel. 0141/552-5055, www.babbitybowster.com, babbity@btinternet.com). The ground-floor pub serves £5-9 pub grub (daily 12:00-22:00); the first-floor restaurant, run by a French chef, offers £14-17 main dishes (Fri-Sat only 18:30-21:30, closed Sun-Thu).

$ easyHotel is part of the no-frills hotel chain. Its 124 miniscule bedrooms have super-tight bathrooms that feel popped out of a plastic mold. Like its easyJet airline parent company, its pricing is variable and à la carte. Book a room online (for the best deals—often Db-£25-39—book well in advance; the smallest, windowless rooms are cheapest). Then pick and choose which services you want to pay for (Wi-Fi, TV remote control, room cleaning during your stay)—each comes with an additional fee. Stay here only if you want to save money and don't intend to hang out in your room. It's located on the northern edge of downtown, not far from the Glasgow School of Art and downtown shopping zone (no breakfast, 1 Hill Street; view rooms, check prices, and book online: www.easyhotel.com).

IN THE WEST END

For a more appealing neighborhood experience, consider bunking in the West End—the upper-middle-class neighborhood just a few subway stops (or a 15-minute, £8 taxi ride) from downtown. As this is also one of the city's best dining zones, you'll likely come here for dinner anyway—so why not sleep here? The first two listings—my favorites in this area—are a longish walk away from the epicenter of the restaurant scene, while the last three, with less personality and lower prices, are right around the corner from it (at the Hillend subway stop). For locations, see the map on page 164.

$$$ The Alamo Guest House, energetically run by Steve

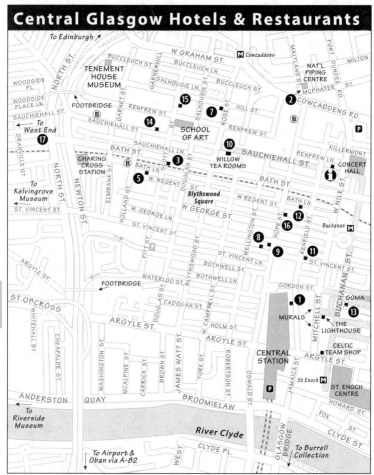

Central Glasgow Hotels & Restaurants

and Emma, faces a bowling green and tennis court in an inviting residential area near the Kelvingrove Museum (not as handy to the subway, but still easy by bus). It has rich, lavishly decorated public spaces and 12 comfortable rooms, half of which have bathrooms on the hall (D-£69-79, Db-£89-109, 46 Gray Street, tel. 0141/339-2395, www.alamoguesthouse.com, info@alamoguesthouse.com).

$$ Amadeus Guest House, a classy refuge overlooking the River Kelvin with nine modern rooms and artistic flourishes, is conveniently located near the Kelvinbridge subway stop—just a 10-minute walk or one subway stop from the restaurant zone (Db-£80, includes continental breakfast, 411 North Woodside Road, tel. 0141/339-8257, www.amadeusguesthouse.co.uk, reservations@amadeusguesthouse.co.uk, Alexandra).

$$ The Alfred, run by the landmark Òran Mòr restaurant/

1. Grasshoppers Hotel
2. Pipers' Tryst
3. Adelaides Guest House
4. Z Hotel
5. Ibis Glasgow
6. Babbity Bowster Rooms
7. easyHotel
8. Martha's
9. Mussel Inn Restaurant
10. Willow Tea Rooms
11. Bread Meats Bread
12. Burger Meats Bun
13. Rogano Restaurant
14. CCA Saramago Bar & Courtyard Vegetarian Café
15. The Vic
16. The Pot Still Bar
17. To West End Eateries & Nightlife
18. Bus to West End

pub (located in the former church just up the street), brings a contemporary elegance to the neighborhood, with 12 new-feeling, stylish rooms (Db-£70, larger Db-£90, 1 Alfred Terrace, tel. 0141/357-3445, www.thealfredhotelglasgow.co.uk, alfred@thealfredhotelglasgow.co.uk).

$$ Argyll Western, with 17 sleek and tartaned Scottish-themed rooms, feels modern, efficient, and a bit impersonal (Db-£70, breakfast-£5, 6 Buckingham Terrace, tel. 0141/339-2339, www.argyllwestern.co.uk, info@argyllwestern.co.uk).

$$ The Heritage Hotel is a lesser value—it's modern but characterless, and the 27 rooms are worn. But the location is convenient and the rates are reasonable (Db-£60, 4 Alfred Terrace, tel. 0141/339-6955, www.theheritagehotel.net, bookings@heritagehotel.fsbusiness.co.uk).

Eating in Glasgow

DOWNTOWN

Martha's is a dream come true for hungry, hurried sightseers (and local office workers) in search of a healthy and satisfying lunch. They serve a seasonal menu of fresh, flavorful wraps, rice boxes, soups, and other great meals made with Scottish ingredients but with eclectic, exotic, international flavors (Indian, Thai, Mexican, and so on). It's understandably popular: Just line up (it moves fast), order at the counter, and then find a table or take your food to go (£5-6 meals, Mon-Fri 7:30-18:00, Sat 9:00-16:00, closed Sun, 142A St. Vincent Street, tel. 0141/248-9771).

Mussel Inn offers light, good-value fish dinners and seafood plates in an airy, informal environment. The restaurant is a cooperative, owned and run by shellfish farmers. Their £10 "kilo pot" of Scottish mussels is popular with locals and big enough to share (£8 "lunchtime quickie" deals, £15-19 dinners, daily 12:00-14:30 & 17:00-22:00 except no afternoon closure Sat-Sun, 157 Hope Street, tel. 0141/572-1405).

The **Willow Tea Rooms,** designed by Charles Rennie Mackintosh, has a diner-type eatery and a classy Room de Luxe (described on page 156). The cheap and cheery menu covers both dining areas (£6-9 meals, £13 afternoon tea, Mon-Sat 9:00-17:00, Sun from 10:30, 217 Sauchiehall Street, tel. 0141/332-0521, www.willowtearooms.co.uk).

Bread Meats Bread is your place for trendy, satisfying, decadent burgers, sandwiches, and fries. The tight interior and few sidewalk tables are always hopping, and the greasy comfort food hits the spot (£7-10 sandwiches, Mon-Sat 11:00-22:00, Sun 11:00-20:00, 104 St. Vincent Street, tel. 0141/249-9898). **Burger Meats Bun,** a few blocks away, is an even younger-feeling cellar restaurant with what Glaswegians would call "dead excellent burgers" (£8-10 burgers and chicken sandwiches, daily 12:30-21:30, 48A West Regent Street, tel. 0141/353-6712).

Rogano is a time-warp Glasgow institution that retains much of the same classy Art Deco interior it had when it opened in 1935. You half-expect to see Bacall and Bogart at the next table. The restaurant has three parts. The bar in front has outdoor seating (£7 lunch sandwiches, £10-13 meals). The fancy dining room at the back of the main floor smacks of the officers' mess on the *Queen Mary*, which was built here on the Clyde during the same period (£20-31 meals with a focus on seafood, £15 afternoon tea). A more casual yet still dressy bistro in the cellar is filled with 1930s-Hollywood glamour (£11-14 meals; daily 12:00-21:30, fancy restaurant closed 16:00-18:00, 11 Exchange Place—just before giant archway from

Buchanan Street, reservations smart, tel. 0141/248-4055, www.
roganoglasgow.com).

Cheap Eats near the Glasgow School of Art: **CCA Saramago
Bar and Courtyard Vegetarian Café,** located on the first floor of
Glasgow's edgy contemporary art museum, charges art-student
prices for its designer, animal-free food. An 18th-century facade,
discovered when the site was excavated to build the gallery, looms
over the atrium restaurant (£3-5 small plates, £6-7 sandwiches and
salads, £9-11 main courses, food served daily 12:00-22:00, free
Wi-Fi, 350 Sauchiehall Street, tel. 0141/332-7959). For a student
hangout within the Glasgow School of Art itself, face the modern
Reid Building and hook around the left side to find the easy-to-
miss entrance to **The Vic**—a funky bar/café with £4-7 starving-
artist fare from an eclectic, international menu (Mon-Sat 12:00-
22:00, closed Sun).

And More: Dozens of restaurants line the main commercial
areas of town: Sauchiehall Street, Buchanan Street, and the Merchant City area. Many are similar, with trendy interiors, Euro
disco-pop soundtracks, and dinner for about £15-20 per person.

For Your Whisky: **The Pot Still** is an award-winning malt
whisky bar from 1835 that boasts a formidable array of more than
600 choices. You'll see locals of all ages sitting in its leathery interior, watching football (soccer) and discussing their drinks. They
have whisky aged in sherry casks, whisky preferred by wine drinkers, and whisky from every region of Scotland. Give the friendly
bartenders a little background on your beverage tastes, and they'll
narrow down a good choice for you from their long list (whisky
runs £3-75 per glass, average price £4-5, £2.50 pasties and pies,
daily 11:00-24:00, 154 Hope Street, tel. 0141/333-0980).

IN THE WEST END
This hip, lively residential neighborhood/university district is
worth exploring, particularly in the evening. The restaurant scene
focuses on two areas (at opposite ends of my West End Walk): near
the Hillhead subway stop and, farther down, in the Finnieston
neighborhood below the Kelvingrove Museum. For locations, see
the map on page 146.

Near Hillhead
There's a fun concentration of restaurants in the streets that fan
out from the Hillhead subway stop (pay £8 for a taxi here from
downtown). Most have tables out front to let you watch the parade
of people, and also convivial gardens in the back. Before choosing
a place, take a stroll and scout the whole scene, focusing on the
streets noted below.

Along Ashton Lane: The top choice along here is **Ubiquitous**

Chip, a beloved local landmark with various pubs and restaurants sprawling through a deceptively large building. The pricey restaurant fills a garden atrium (£23-28 main courses), but it's less expensive to opt for the upstairs brasserie, which overlooks that genteel scene, or the nondescript pub (£10-17 meals; daily 11:00-24:00, 12 Ashton Lane, tel. 0141/334-5007, www.ubiquitouschip. co.uk).

You can also check out the eclectic Ashton Lane lineup, including **Ketchup** (American-style diner), **Brel** (Belgian beer bar), **Vodka Wódka** (Polish vodka bar), **The Wee Curry Shop** (Indian), and **Jinty McGuinty's** (Irish pub and beer garden). The recommended **Grosvenor Cinema** also has its own upstairs café, overlooking the Ashton Lane bustle.

On Cresswell Lane: Of the eateries along here, one favorite is **Café Andaluz,** which offers £5-7 tapas and sangria behind lacy wooden screens, as the waitstaff clicks past on the cool tiles (Mon-Sat 12:00-23:00, Sun 12:30-22:30, 2 Cresswell Lane, tel. 0141/339-1111).

Along Ruthven Lane: Down this characteristic little lane, across Byres Road from the subway station, are two fine options: one Scottish and one Vietnamese, both with inside and outside seating. **Bothy Restaurant** offers tasty, traditional Scottish fayre in an inviting garden courtyard or a rustic-contemporary interior (£12-20 main dishes, daily 12:00-22:00, 11 Ruthven Lane, tel. 0141/334-4040). **The Hanoi Bike Shop,** a rare-in-Scotland Vietnamese "street food" restaurant, serves Asian tapas that are healthy and tasty, using local produce. With tight seating and friendly service, the place has a nice energy (small plates for around £6 each, £8-9 bigger plates, daily 12:00-23:00, 8 Ruthven Lane, tel. 0141/334-7165).

Dining/Nightlife Venues Farther North, near Great Western Road: **Òran Mòr,** a converted 1862 church overlooking a busy intersection, is one of Glasgow's most popular hangouts. It's a five-minute walk from the recommended restaurants (at the intersection of Byres and Great Western roads). In addition to hosting an outdoor beer garden, atmospheric bar (£7-10 pub grub, £4-5 lighter fare), and a pair of upscale-feeling restaurants (£25 meals), the building's former nave hosts a nightclub featuring everything from rock shows to traditional Scottish music nights—check the schedule on their website (bar open daily 9:00-very late; pub food served Mon-Sat 9:00-21:00, Sun 10:00-22:00; restaurants have slightly different hours, top of Byres Road at 731 Great Western Road, tel. 0141/357-6200, www.oran-mor.co.uk). **Hillhead Book-**

club is a historic cinema building cleared out to make room for fun, disco, pub grub, and lots of booze. It's a youthful and quirky art-school scene, with lots of beers on tap, creative cocktails, retro computer games, ping-pong, and theme evenings (£5-7 lunches, £8-10 dinners, Mon-Fri 11:00-24:00, Sat-Sun from 10:00, just off Byres Road at 17 Vinicombe Street, tel. 0141/576-1700).

Upscale Option: For a well-regarded upscale choice in this area, try **Cail Bruich**—serving award-winning classic Scottish dishes with an updated spin in an unpretentious setting. Reservations are smart (£16-21 lunches, £19-25 dinners, lunch Wed-Sun 12:00-14:00, dinner nightly 17:30-21:30, 725 Great Western Road, tel. 0141/334-6265, www.cailbruich.co.uk).

In Finnieston

This very trendy, up-and-coming neighborhood—with the most hipster charm in this very hipster city—stretches east from in front of the Kelvingrove Museum. It's a 15-minute downhill walk from the area described above, or you can ride the subway to the Kelvinhall stop and walk 10 minutes from there. I've listed these roughly in the order you'll reach them as you walk east from the Kelvingrove.

Brewdog Glasgow is a great place to sample Scottish microbrews—from their own brewery in Aberdeen, as well as guest brews—in an industrial-mod setting reminiscent of American brewpubs. Also American-style, they serve many of their beers cold—unlike the room temp of most British brews (also £8-9 burgers and pub grub, Mon-Sat 12:00-24:00, Sun from 12:30, directly across the street from Kelvingrove Museum at 1397 Argyle Street, tel. 0141/334-7175, www.brewdog.com).

Butchershop Bar & Grill is a casual, rustic, American-style steak house, but featuring Scottish products—focusing on dry-aged Scottish steaks (£12-16 main courses, £18-29 steaks, lunch and early-bird deals, daily 12:00-22:00, 1055 Sauchiehall Street, tel. 0141/339-2999, www.butchershopglasgow.com).

Trendy Finnieston Eateries on and near Argyle Street: **Crabshakk,** specializing in fresh seafood, is a foodie favorite, with a very tight bar-and-mezzanine seating area and tables spilling out onto the sidewalk. It's casual but still respectable, and worth reserving ahead (£8-16 meals plus seafood splurges, Tue-Sun 12:00-22:00, closed Mon, 1114 Argyle Street, tel. 0141/334-6127, www.crabshakk.com). Crabshakk anchors a strip of copycat funky/foodie eateries. Survey the choices along here (which change from week to week), but pay special attention to these three: **The Gannet** has £5-8 small plates and £15-20 meals, emphasizing Scottish ingredients with a modern spin (Tue-Sun 12:00-14:00 & 17:00-21:30, closed Mon, 1155 Argyle Street, tel. 0141/204-2081, www.

thegannetgla.com). **Kelvingrove Café and Cocktails** is an unpretentious, rustic-chic bar serving creative £8-10 cocktails and £10-13 Scottish comfort food (daily 10:00-24:00, 1161 Argyle Street, tel. 0141/221-8988, www.kelvingrovecafe.com). **Ox and Finch**, a block up toward the main drag, is another good choice, serving £5-8 small plates in a more upscale, rustic wood-meets-industrial atmosphere (daily 12:00-22:00, 920 Sauchiehall Street, tel. 0141/339-8627, www.oxandfinch.com). Several other fun bars and eateries are in this area—browsing is a delight.

Glasgow Connections

Traveline Scotland has a journey planner that's linked to all of Scotland's train and bus schedule info. Go online (www.travelinescotland.com), call them at tel. 0871-200-2233, or use the individual websites listed below. If you're connecting with Edinburgh, note that the train is faster but the bus is cheaper.

BY TRAIN

From Glasgow's Queen Street Station by Train to: Oban (6/day, fewer on Sun, 3 hours), **Inverness** (11/day, 3 hours, 4 direct, others change in Perth), **Edinburgh** (4/hour, 50 minutes), **Stirling** (3/hour, 30-45 minutes), **Pitlochry** (9/day, 2 hours, some transfer in Perth).

From Glasgow's Central Station by Train to: Keswick in England's Lake District (roughly hourly, 1.5 hours to Penrith, then catch a bus to Keswick, 45 minutes), **Cairnryan** and ferry to Belfast (take train to Ayr, 2/hour, 1 hour; then ride bus to Cairnryan, 1 hour), **Blackpool** (hourly, 3.5-4 hours, transfer in Preston), **Liverpool** (1-2/hour, 3.5-4 hours, change in Wigan or Preston), **Durham** (2/hour, 3 hours, may require change in Edinburgh), **York** (2/hour, 3.5 hours, may require change in Edinburgh), **London** (1-2/hour, 4.5-5 hours direct). Train info: Tel. 0345-748-4950, www.nationalrail.co.uk.

BY BUS

Glasgow's Buchanan bus station is a hub for reaching the Highlands. If you're coming from Edinburgh, you can take the bus to Glasgow and transfer here. Or, for a speedier connection, zip to Glasgow on the train, then walk a few short blocks to the bus station. (Ideally, try to arrive at Glasgow's Queen Street Station, which is closer to the bus station.) For more details on these connections, see "Getting Around the Highlands" on page 238.

From Glasgow by Bus to: Edinburgh (bus #900, 4/hour, 1-1.5 hours depending on traffic), **Oban** (buses #976 and #977; 5/day, 3 hours), **Fort William** (buses #914, #915, and #916; 8/

day, 3 hours), **Glencoe** (buses #914, #915, and #916; 8/day, 2.5 hours), **Inverness** (express bus #G10, 5/day, 3.5 hours, additional options with transfer in Perth), **Portree** on the Isle of Skye (buses #915 and #916, 3/day, 7 hours), **Pitlochry** (5/day, 2.5 hours, transfer in Perth—train is faster). Bus info: Tel. 0871-266-3333, www. citylink.co.uk.

BY PLANE

Glasgow International Airport: Located eight miles west of the city, this airport (code: GLA) has currency-exchange desks, a TI, Internet access, luggage storage, and ATMs (tel. 0844-481-5555, www.glasgowairport.com). Taxis connect downtown to the airport for about £20. Your hotel can likely arrange a private taxi service for £14. Bus #500 zips to central Glasgow (daily at least 4/hour 5:00-23:00, then hourly through the night, £6.50/one-way, £9/round-trip, 15-20 minutes to both train stations, 25 minutes to the bus station, catch at bus stop #1).

Prestwick Airport: A hub for Ryanair (as well as the US military, which refuels planes here), this airport (code: PIK) is about 30 miles southwest of the city center (tel. 0871-223-0700, ext. 1006, www.gpia.co.uk). The best connection is by train, which runs between the airport and Central Station (Mon-Sat 3/hour, 50 minutes, half-price with Ryanair ticket). Stagecoach buses link the airport with Buchanan Bus Station (£10, daily 4/hour plus a few nighttime buses, 45-60 minutes, check schedules at www. travelinescotland.com). If you're wondering about the Elvis Presley Bar, this airport is said to be the only piece of Britain that Elvis ever set foot on. (Elvis' manager, the Dutch-born Colonel Tom Parker, had a legal problem with British immigration.)

ROUTE TIPS FOR DRIVERS

From England's Lake District to Glasgow: From Keswick, take the A-66 for 18 miles to the M-6 and speed north nonstop (via Penrith and Carlisle), crossing Hadrian's Wall into Scotland. The road becomes the M-74 just north of Carlisle. To slip through Glasgow quickly, leave the M-74 at Junction 4 onto the M-73, following signs to *M-8/Glasgow*. Leave the M-73 at Junction 2, exiting onto the M-8. Stay on the M-8 west through Glasgow, exit at Junction 30, cross Erskine Bridge, and turn left on the A-82, following signs to *Crianlarich* and *Loch Lomond*. (For a scenic drive through Glasgow, take exit 17 off the M-8 and stay on the A-82 toward Dumbarton.)

GLASGOW

STIRLING AND NEARBY

Stirling • William Wallace Monument • Bannockburn •
Falkirk • Culross • Doune • Loch Lomond and the Trossachs

The historic city of Stirling is the crossroads of Scotland: Equidistant from Edinburgh and Glasgow (less than an hour from both), and rising above a plain where the Lowlands meet the Highlands, it's no surprise that Stirling has hosted many of the biggest names (and biggest battles) of Scottish history. Everyone from Mary, Queen of Scots to Bonnie Prince Charlie has passed through the gates of its stately, strategic castle.

From those cliff-capping ramparts, you can see where each of the three pivotal battles of Scotland's 13th- and 14th-century Wars of Independence took place: the Battle of Stirling Bridge, where against all odds, the courageous William Wallace defeated the English army; the Battle of Falkirk, where Wallace was toppled by a vengeful English king; and the Battle of Bannockburn, when—in the wake of Wallace's defeat—Robert the Bruce rallied to kick out the English once and for all (well, at least for a few generations). The William Wallace Monument and Bannockburn Visitors Centre—on the outskirts of Stirling, in opposite directions—are practically pilgrimage sites for patriotic Scots.

Stirling itself is sleepy, but it's an ideal home base for a variety of side-trips. In Falkirk, take a spin in a fascinating Ferris wheel for boats, and ogle the gigantic horse heads called The Kelpies. Sitting on the nearby estuary known as the Firth of Forth—on the way to Edinburgh or St. Andrews—is the gorgeously preserved time-warp village of Culross. To the north, fans of Monty Python and *Outlander* flock to Doune Castle. And drivers seeking a low-impact peek at the Highlands make a loop through the Trossachs and along the bonnie, bonnie banks of Loch Lomond.

Stirling Area

Crieff
Muthill • Gleneagles
Auchterarder •
To Perth & Pitlochry
Strathyre •
A-84
Loch Katrine
Brig o'Turk
Callander
Braco • A-9
To Inveraray & Oban
Ben Lomond
The Trossachs
Drumvaich
Doune
DOUNE CASTLE
DEANSTON
WALLACE MONUMENT
A-91
Tarbet •
Aberfoyle •
Lake of Menteith
A-84
Stirling
Buchlyvie •
A-811
BANNOCKBURN
See detail map
M-9
THE KELPIES
Culross
Luss •
Balmaha
Loch Lomond
A-82
M-80
M-876
Bo'ness
Helens-burgh
HILL HOUSE
Balloch
Forth & Clyde Canal
Bonnybridge •
Falkirk
Firth of Clyde
A-8
Dumbarton
Kirkin-tilloch • M-80
Cumbernauld
FALKIRK WHEEL
Union Canal
To Edinburgh
Clydebank
Bathgate

PLANNING YOUR TIME

You'll likely pass near Stirling at least once (and, quite possibly, multiple times) as you travel through Scotland. Skim this chapter to learn about your options and select the stops that interest you. If you can't fit it all in on a pass-through, spend the night. Just as Stirling was ideally situated for monarchs and armies of the past, it's handy for present-day visitors seeking a home base: It's much smaller, and arguably even more conveniently located, than Edinburgh or Glasgow, and it has a variety of good accommodations. You'd need a solid three days to see all of the big sights within an hour's drive of Stirling—but most people are (and should be) more selective.

Stirling

Every Scot knows the city of Stirling (pop. 41,000) deep in their bones. This patriotic heart of Scotland is like Bunker Hill, Gettysburg, and the Alamo, all rolled into one. Stirling perches on a ridge overlooking Scotland's most history-drenched plain: a flat expanse—cut through by the twisting River Forth and the meandering stream called Bannockburn—that divides the Lowlands from the Highlands. And capping that ridge is Stirling's formidable castle, the seat of the final kings of Scotland.

From a traveler's perspective, Stirling is a pleasant mini-Edinburgh, with a steep spine leading up to that grand castle. It's busy with tourists by day, but sleepy at night. The town, and its castle, lack personality—but both are striking and strategic.

Orientation to Stirling

Stirling's old town is situated along a long, narrow, steep hill. At its base are the train and bus stations and a thriving (but characterless) commercial district; at its apex is the castle. The old town feels like a steeper, shorter, less touristy, and far less characteristic version of Edinburgh's Royal Mile.

Tourist Information: The TI is a five-minute walk below the castle, just inside the gates of the Old Town Jail (daily 10:00-17:00, free Wi-Fi, St. Johns Street, tel. 01786/475-019).

Getting Around: While you can walk to Stirling Castle and other in-town sights, it's a long hike to the William Wallace Monument and Bannockburn Heritage Centre; instead, take a frequent public bus or a taxi (about £5-10 to either sight).

Sightseeing Deal: This area's three big historical sights—Stirling Castle, the William Wallace Monument, and Bannockburn Heritage Centre—offer a 10 percent discount if you show a ticket from any of the others.

Sights in Stirling

▲▲STIRLING CASTLE

"He who holds Stirling, holds Scotland." These fateful words have been proven, more often than not, to be true. Stirling Castle's prized position—perched on a volcanic crag overlooking a bridge over the River Forth, the primary passage between the Lowlands and the Highlands—has long been the key to Scotland. This castle was the preferred home of Scottish kings and queens in the Middle Ages; today it's one of the most historic—and most popular—castles in Scotland. Although it was recently renovated and lacks soul, it still has plenty to offer: spectacular views over a gentle countryside, tales of the dynamic Stuart monarchs, and several exhibits that try to bring the place to life.

Cost and Hours: £14.50, daily April-Sept 9:30-18:00, Oct-March 9:30-17:00, last entry 45 minutes before closing, Regimental

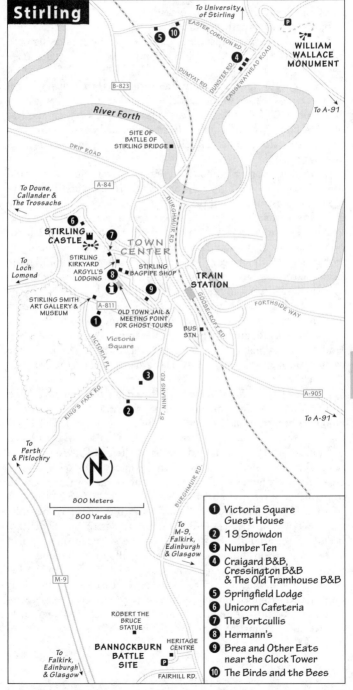

Stirling

To University of Stirling

EASTER CORNTON RD.

⑤ ⑩

④

DUMYAT RD.

DUNSTER RD.

CAUSEWAYHEAD ROAD

P

WILLIAM WALLACE MONUMENT

To A-91

B-823

River Forth

DRIP ROAD

SITE OF BATTLE OF STIRLING BRIDGE ■

To Doune, Callander & The Trossachs

A-84

BURGHMUIR RD.

⑥

STIRLING CASTLE

⑦

TOWN CENTER

To Loch Lomond

STIRLING KIRKYARD
ARGYLL'S LODGING

⑧

STIRLING BAGPIPE SHOP

⑨

TRAIN STATION

FORTHSIDE WAY

STIRLING SMITH ART GALLERY & MUSEUM

ⓘ

A-811

①

OLD TOWN JAIL & MEETING POINT FOR GHOST TOURS

Victoria Square

BUS STN.

GOOSECROFT RD.

VICTORIA PL.

③

ST. NINIANS RD.

A-905

②

KING'S PARK RD.

To A-91

To Perth & Pitlochry

N

800 Meters
800 Yards

BURGHMUIR RD.

To M-9, Falkirk, Edinburgh & Glasgow

M-9

ROBERT THE BRUCE STATUE ■

HERITAGE CENTRE

BANNOCKBURN BATTLE SITE

P

To Falkirk, Edinburgh & Glasgow

FAIRHILL RD.

① Victoria Square Guest House
② 19 Snowdon
③ Number Ten
④ Craigard B&B, Cressington B&B & The Old Tramhouse B&B
⑤ Springfield Lodge
⑥ Unicorn Cafeteria
⑦ The Portcullis
⑧ Hermann's
⑨ Brea and Other Eats near the Clock Tower
⑩ The Birds and the Bees

STIRLING & NEARBY

Museum closes one hour before castle, good café, tel. 01786/450-000, www.stirlingcastle.gov.uk.

Crowd-Beating Tips: Skip the ticket line by purchasing tickets online or using a Historic Scotland Explorer Pass (see page 442).

Tours: The included 30-minute **guided tour** helps you get your bearings—both to the castle, and to Scottish history (generally hourly 10:00-16:00, likely more often in peak season and less off-season, departs from well outside the Fort Major's House). Docents posted throughout can tell you more, and you can rent a £3 **audioguide**.

Getting There: Stirling Castle sits at the very tip of a steep old town. Drivers should follow the *Stirling Castle* signs uphill through town to the esplanade and park at the £4 lot just outside the castle gate. To save a little money, you can leave your car at the Castleview Park-and-Ride off the A-84 and hop on the shuttle bus (2/hour, none on Sun, 15-minute ride, drops you near the TI—walk up from there). Without a car, you can hike the 20-minute uphill route from the train or bus station to the castle, or take a taxi (about £5).

Background: The first castle was built here in the 12th century by King David I (1083-1153). But Stirling Castle's glory days were in the 16th century, when it became the primary residence of the Stuart monarchs, who turned it into a showpiece of Scotland—and a symbol of one-upmanship against England. (At the castle, you may also see the dynasty's name spelled the old way, "Stewart.")

James IV (1473-1513) married the sister of England's King Henry VIII, thereby knitting together the royal families of Scotland (the Stuarts) and England (the Tudors). James V (1512-1542) further expanded the castle. And the France-raised Mary, Queen of Scots (1542-1587) struggled against the rise of Protestantism in her realm. But when Mary's son, King James VI (1566-1625), was crowned King James I of England, he took his royal court with him—never to return to Stirling.

During the Jacobite rebellions of the 18th century, the military took over the castle—bulking it up and destroying its delicate beauty. Even after the Scottish threat had subsided, it remained a British garrison, home base of the Argyll and Sutherland regiments. (It still flies the Union Jack of the United Kingdom.) Finally, in 1964, work began to renovate the castle—an ambitious project that wrapped up just a few years ago. Today, while Stirling Castle is fully restored and gleaming, it feels new and fairly empty—with almost no historic artifacts.

◑ Self-Guided Tour

Begin on the esplanade, just outside the castle entrance, with its grand views.

The Esplanade: The castle's esplanade, a military parade ground in the 19th century, is a tour-bus parking lot in the 21st century. As you survey this site, remember that Stirling Castle bore witness to some of the most important moments in Scottish history. To the right as you face the castle, **King Robert the Bruce** looks toward the plain called Bannockburn, where he defeated the English army in 1314. Squint off to the horizon on Robert's left to spot the pointy stone monument capping the hill called Abbey Craig. This is the **William Wallace Monument,** marking the spot where the Scottish warrior surveyed the battlefield before his victory in the Battle of Stirling Bridge (1297). (Another major battle—one that Scots don't like to talk about as much—also took place nearby: Wallace's defeat at the Battle of Falkirk, in 1298.)

These great Scots helped usher in several centuries of home rule. In 1315, Robert the Bruce's daughter married into an on-the-rise noble clan called the Stuarts, who had distinguished themselves fighting at Bannockburn. When their son Robert became King Robert II of Scotland in 1371, he kicked off the Stuart dynasty. Over the next few generations, their headquarters—Stirling Castle—flourished. The fortified grand entry showed all who approached that James IV (r. 1488-1513) was a great ruler with a powerful castle.

• *Head through the first gate into Guardroom Square, where you can buy your ticket, ask about tour times, and consider renting the audioguide. Then continue up through the inner gate.*

Gardens and Battlements: Once through the gate, follow the passage to the left into a delightful grassy courtyard called the

Queen Anne Garden. This was the royal family's playground in the 1600s. Imagine doing a little lawn bowling with the queen here.

In the casemates lining the garden is the **Castle Exhibition.** Its "Come Face to Face with 1,000 Years of History" exhibit provides an entertaining and worthwhile introduction to the castle. You'll meet each of the people who left their mark here, from the first Stuart kings to William Wallace and Robert the Bruce. Mind your head. The video leaves you thinking that re-enactors of Jacobite struggles are even more spirited than our Civil War re-enactors.

Leaving the garden the way you came, make a sharp U-turn

up the ramp to the top of the **battlements.** From up here, this castle's strategic position is evident: Defenders had a 360-degree view of enemy armies approaching from miles away. These battlements were built in 1710, long after the castle's Stuart glory days, in response to the Jacobite rebellions (from the Latin word for "James"). By this time, the successes of William Wallace and Robert the Bruce were a distant memory; through the 1707 Act of Union, Scotland had become welded to England. Bonnie Prince Charlie—descendant of those original Stuart "King Jameses" who built this castle—was staging a series of uprisings to try to reclaim the throne of Great Britain for the Stuart line, frightening England enough to further fortify the castle. And sure enough, Bonnie Prince Charlie found himself—ironically—laying siege to the fortress that his own ancestors had built: Facing the main gate (with its two round towers), notice the pockmarks from Jacobite cannonballs in 1746.

• *Now head back down to the ramp and pass through that main gate, into the...*

Outer Close: As you enter this courtyard, straight ahead is James IV's yellow **Great Hall.** That brilliant hue—which historians believe is similar to the original color of the building—is known as "king's gold." While today the vivid color makes the building stick out from the rest of the castle, keep in mind that most of the buildings were built of sandstone—so their original color likely matched this yellow quite well. (Scanning the old

gray walls all around, you can still see a few yellow patches that are less weathered.)

To the left as you face James IV's yellow hall is his son **James V's royal palace,** lined with finely carved Renaissance statues. In 1540, King James V, inspired by French Renaissance châteaux he'd seen, had the castle covered with about 200 statues and busts to "proclaim the peace, prosperity and justice of his reign" and to validate his rule. Imagine the impression all these classical gods and goddesses made on visitors. The message: James' rule was a Golden Age for Scotland.

The **guided tours** of the castle depart from just to your right, near the well. Beyond that is the Grand Battery, with its cannons and rampart views and, underneath that, the Great Kitchens. We'll see both at the end of this tour.

• *Hike up the ramp between James V's palace and the Great Hall (under the crenellated sky bridge connecting them). You'll emerge into the...*

Inner Close: Standing at the center of Stirling Castle, you're surrounded by Scottish history. This courtyard was the core of the 12th-century castle. From there, additional buildings were added—each by a different monarch. While all are historic, they are entirely rebuilt and none have the patina of age. Facing downhill, you'll see the Great Hall. The Chapel Royal—where Mary, Queen of Scots was crowned in 1543—is to your left. The royal palace (containing the Royal Apartments) is to your right—notice the "I5" monogram above the windows (for the king who built it: James, or Iacobus in Latin, V). The Stirling Heads Gallery is above that. And behind you is the Regimental Museum.

• *We'll visit each of these in turn. First, at the far-left end of the gallery with the coffee stand, step into...*

The Great Hall: This is the largest secular space in medieval Scotland. Dating from 1503, this was a grand setting for the great banquets of Scotland's Renaissance kings. One such party, to which all of the crowned heads of Europe were invited, reportedly went on for three full days. This was also where kings and queens would hold court, earning it the nickname "the parliament." The impressive hammerbeam roof is a modern reconstruction, modeled on the early 16th-century roof at Edinburgh Castle. It's made of 400 local oak trees, joined by wooden pegs. If you flipped it over, it would float.

• *At the far end of the hall, walk across the sky bridge into James V's palace. Here you can explore...*

The Royal Apartments: Six ground-floor apartments are colorfully done up as they might have looked in the mid-16th century,

when James V and his queen, Mary of Guise, lived here. Costumed performers play the role of palace attendants, happy to chat with you about medieval life. You'll begin in the King's Inner Hall, where he received guests. Notice the 60 carved and colorfully painted oak medallions on the ceiling in the king's presence chamber. The medallions are carved with the faces of Scottish and European royalty. These are copies, painstakingly reconstructed after expert research. You'll soon see the originals up close in the Stirling Heads Gallery.

Continue into the other rooms: the King's Bedchamber, with a four-poster bed supporting a less-than-luxurious rope mattress; and then the Queen's Bedchamber, the Inner Hall, and the Outer Hall, offering a more vivid example of what these rich spaces would have looked like.

• *From the queen's apartments, you'll exit into the top corner of the Inner Close. Directly to your left, up the stairs, is...*

The Stirling Heads Gallery: This is, for me, the castle's highlight—a chance to see the originals of the elaborately carved and

painted portrait medallions that decorated the ceiling of the king's presence chamber. Each one is thoughtfully displayed and lovingly explained.

• *If you were to leave this gallery through the exit, you'd wind up back down in the Queen Anne Garden. Instead, backtrack and exit the way you came in to return to the Inner Close, and visit the two remaining sights.*

The Chapel Royal: One of the first Protestant churches built in Scotland, the Chapel Royal was constructed in 1594 by James VI for the baptism of his first son, Prince Henry. The faint painted frieze high up survives from Charles I's coronation visit to Scotland in 1633. Clearly the holiness of the chapel ended in the 1800s when the army moved in.

Regimental Museum: At the top of the Inner Close, in the King's Old Building, is the excellent **Argyll and Sutherland Highlanders Museum.** Another highlight of the castle, it's barely mentioned in castle promotional material because it's run by a different organization. With lots of tartans, tassels, and swords, it shows how the spirit of Scotland was absorbed by Britain. The two regiments, established in the 1790s to defend Britain in the Napoleonic age and combined in the 1880s, have served with distinction in British military campaigns for more than two centuries. Their pride shows here in the building that's their headquarters, where they've been stationed since 1881. The "In the Trenches" exhibit is a powerful look at World War I, with accounts from the battlefield. Up the spiral stairs, the exhibit continues through World War II and conflicts in the Middle East to the present day.

• *When you're ready to move on, consider the following scenic route back to the castle exit.*

Rampart Walk to the Kitchen: The skinny lane between church and museum leads to the secluded Douglas Gardens at the rock's highest point. From here you can walk the ramparts down-hill to the Grand Battery, with its cannon rampart at the Outer Close. The Outer Close was the service zone, with a well and the kitchen (below the cannon rampart). The great banquets of James VI didn't happen all by themselves, as you'll appreciate when you explore the fine medieval kitchen exhibit (where mannequin cooks oversee medieval recipes); to find it, head down the ramp and look for the *Great Kitchens* sign.

• *Your castle visit ends here, but your castle ticket includes Argyll's Lodging, a fortified noble mansion. Or, for a scenic route down into town, consider a detour through an old cemetery (both described next).*

MORE SIGHTS IN STIRLING
Old Kirkyard Stroll

Stirling has a particularly evocative old cemetery in the kirkyard (churchyard) just below the castle. For a soulful stroll, go down

the stairs where the esplanade meets the parking lot (near the statue of the Scotsman fighting in the South African War). From here, you can wander through the tombstones—Celtic crosses, Victorian statues, and faded headstones—from centuries gone by. The rocky crag in the middle of the graveyard is a fine viewpoint. Work your way over to the Church of the Holy Rude, where you can re-enter the town. From here, Argyll's Lodging and the castle parking lot are just to the left, and the TI and Old Town Jail are just to the right.

Argyll's Lodging

Just below the castle esplanade is this 17th-century nobleman's fortified mansion. European aristocrats wanted to live near power—making this location, where the Earl of Argyll's family resided for about a century, prime real estate. You'll get oriented with a historical display on the first floor, then see the kitchens, dining room, drawing room, and bedchambers. Pick up the descriptions in each room, or ask the docents if you have any questions. Argyll's Landing is less sterile than the castle and worth a few minutes.

Cost and Hours: Included in castle ticket, daily 12:45-17:30.

▲Historic and Haunted Walks

These entertaining and informative walking tours around Stirling are led by a local actor/historian. By day, the walks focus on the history of this royal burgh (£8, July-Aug Wed-Sun at 14:00 and 16:00, May-June and Sept Sat-Sun at 14:00 and 16:00, meets at Cowane's Hospital near the old church). By night, the guide plays the role of the "Happy Hangman," and spends most of the tour leading you through the old kirkyard's evocative cemetery (£6, July-Aug Tue-Sat at 20:30, Sept-June Fri-Sat at 20:00, meet in front of TI, www. stirlingghostwalk.com). Either walk takes about 1.25 hours and enhances your appreciation of Stirling beyond its famous castle.

Old Town Jail

Stirling's historic jail was built during the Victorian Age, when the purpose of imprisonment was shifting from punishment to rehabilitation. And today, theatrical 30-minute tours of the old building offer an insightful look at this page in history. Your hardworking guide changes costumes several times throughout the tour, giving you the perspectives of the old-school hangman, the idealistic new warden, and various prisoners. You'll see some of the old cells, and end at the top of the tower, offering perhaps the best 360-degree views in town of the surrounding countryside. As this is a relatively new attraction, details may change; confirm before you go.

Cost and Hours: £5, likely July-Sept only, tours every 30 minutes daily 10:15-16:15, St. John Street, www.destinationstirling. com.

▲Stirling Bagpipes

This fun little shop, just a block below the castle on Broad Street, is worth a visit for those curious about this uniquely Scottish instrument. Owner Alan refurbishes old bagpipes here, but also makes new ones from scratch, in a workshop on the premises. The pleasantly cluttered shop, which is a bit of a neighborhood hangout, is littered with bagpipe components—chanters, drones, bags, covers, and cords. If he's not too busy, Alan can answer your questions and tell you more about bagpipes. He'll explain how the most expensive parts of the bagpipe are the "sticks"—the chanter and drones, carved from blackwood—while the bag and cover are cheap. A serious set costs £700...beginners should instead consider a £40 starter kit that includes a practice chanter (like a recorder) with a book of sheet music and a CD. Alan hopes to open a wee museum next door to show off his collection of historic bagpipes.

Cost and Hours: Free, Mon-Tue and Thu-Sat 10:00-18:00, closed Wed and Sun, 8 Broad Street, tel. 01786/448-886, www. stirlingbagpipes.com.

Nearby: On the wide street in front of the shop, look for Stirling's **mercat cross**. A standard feature of any Scottish town, this was the place where townsfolk would gather for the market, and where royal proclamations and executions took place. Today the commercial metabolism of this once-thriving street is at a low ebb. Locals joke that every 100 years, the shopping bustle moves one block farther down the road. These days, it's squeezed into the modern shopping mall between the old town and the river.

Stirling Smith Art Gallery and Museum

Tucked at the edge of the grid-planned, Victorian Age neighborhood just below the castle, this endearing and eclectic museum is a hodgepodge of artifacts from Stirling's past: art gallery (where you can meet historical figures with connections to this proud little town), pewter collection, local history exhibits, items from world cultures, a steam-powered carriage, the mutton bone shard removed in the world's first documented tracheotomy (1853), and a 19th-century executioner's cloak and ax. The museum's prized piece is what they claim is the world's oldest surviving soccer ball—a 16th-century stitched-up pig's bladder that restorers found stuck in the rafters of Stirling Castle (presumably kicked up there in a spirited soccer game and forgotten). The building is surrounded by a garden filled with public art.

Cost and Hours: Free, Tue-Sat 10:30-17:00, Sun 14:00-17:00, closed Mon, Dumbarton Road, tel. 01786/471-917, www.smithartgalleryandmuseum.co.uk.

Sleeping in Stirling

IN THE VICTORIAN TOWN, SOUTH OF THE CASTLE

When Stirling expanded beyond its old walls during the Victorian Age, a modern, grid-planned town sprouted just to the south. Today, this posh-feeling area holds a few B&Bs that are within a (long) walk of Stirling's old town and castle. These are all in large, spacious homes with easy parking.

$$$ Victoria Square Guest House has seven plush rooms in a beautiful location facing a big, grassy park. While the prices are high, it's neat as a pin, and Kari and Phil keep things running smoothly. Of my listings, it's the closest to the old town—about a 10-minute walk to the lower part of town, or 20 minutes up to the castle (Db-£110-140, 12 Victoria Square, tel. 01786/473-920, www.victoriasquareguesthouse.com, info@vsgh.co.uk).

$$ 19 Snowdon is a roomy, modern-feeling home with two simply furnished rooms and a fine garden out back (D with private b on the hall-£85, Db-£95, 19 Snowdon Terrace, tel. 01786/396-522, www.stirlingguesthouse.co.uk, janet.storrar@stirlingguesthouse.co.uk, Janet).

$ Number Ten rents three traditional rooms in an older but Scottish-feeling home (with tartan carpets and a nice garden) a bit farther from the town center (Db-£75, 10 Gladstone Place, tel. 01786/472-681, www.cameron-10.co.uk, cameron-10@tinyonline.co.uk, Carol and Donald Cameron).

ALONG CAUSEWAYHEAD ROAD, NORTH OF THE CASTLE

More than a dozen B&Bs offering slightly lower prices line Causewayhead Road, a busy thoroughfare that connects Stirling to the William Wallace Monument. From here, it's a long walk into town (or the Wallace Monument), but the location is handy for drivers (each place has free parking). While this modern residential area lacks charm, it's convenient.

$ Craigard B&B has three small, modern, tidy, and proper rooms that offer good value (Db-£70, 40 Causewayhead Road, tel. 01786/460-540, mobile 0784-040-1551, www.craigardstirling.co.uk, craigard@hotmail.co.uk, Liz).

$ Cressington B&B has four bright, simple rooms—modern, but with classy touches (Db-£65, 34 Causewayhead Road, tel. 01786/462-435, Janie and Allan Neill).

$ The Old Tramhouse is the frilliest of the bunch, with four rooms that are elegantly decorated with a delicate charm (Db-£60-80, 42 Causewayhead Road, tel. 01786/449-774, mobile 0759-054-0604, www.theoldtramhouse.com, enquiries@theoldtramhouse.com, Alison Cowie).

$ Springfield Lodge sits at the back end of the residential zone that lines up along Causewayhead Road. It's across the street from farm fields, giving it a countryside feeling. The four neat rooms fill a spacious modern house (Db-£75-80, Easter Cornton Road—near the recommended Birds and Bees pub, tel. 01786/474-332, mobile 0795-469-2412, www.springfieldlodgebandb.co.uk, springfieldlodgebandb@gmail.com).

Eating in Stirling

Stirling isn't a place to go looking for high cuisine; eateries here tend to be satisfying but functional. All of these are open daily unless otherwise noted.

UP NEAR THE CASTLE

The **Unicorn Cafeteria,** within the castle itself, is excellent, going beyond basic cafeteria fare with tasty £6-10 meals and sandwiches (same hours as castle). Just below the Esplanade, **The Portcullis** is a pub that aches with history, from its dark, wood-grained bar area to its stony courtyard. The food, like the setting, is old-school (£5-7 light fare, £10-15 meals). For something more distinctive, head a few more steps down Broad Street to **Hermann's.** A bit more dressy, it serves a mix of Scottish and Austrian food (though thankfully, not on the same plate)—perfect for those times when you've got a hankering for haggis, but your travel partner wants Wiener schnitzel (£11-14 lunch specials, £19-22 dinner specials, £12-19 main courses à la carte, top of Broad Street, tel. 01786/450-632, www.hermanns-restaurant.co.uk).

LOWER DOWN IN THE TOWN

Lots of interchangeable eateries cluster around the clock tower at the bottom of town. King Street, below the tower, has a few options (including good Indian fare at **Maharaja**), while several more choices abound on Baker Street, above and to the right of the tower. Along here—tucked between several mostly chain pubs and ethnic eateries (Thai, Italian, Indian)—is **Brea,** a popular all-around eatery with an unpretentious vibe and an eclectic, crowd-pleasing menu (£10 pizzas and burgers, £14-17 main courses, closed for lunch Mon, 5 Baker Street, tel. 01786/446-277).

COUNTRY PUB

The Birds and the Bees is a countryside pub, a short walk through a residential neighborhood from the Causewayhead Road B&Bs. It's a sprawling complex; the interior has dark wood and country-kitschy decor (such as cowhide cushions), and there are also several outdoor seating areas in good weather (£10-14 pub grub, Easter Cornton Road, tel. 01786/473-663).

Stirling Connections

From Stirling by Train to: Edinburgh (roughly 2/hour, 1 hour), **Glasgow** (3/hour, 30-45 minutes), **Pitlochry** (5/day direct, 1 hour, more with transfer in Perth), **Inverness** (every 1-2 hours, 3 hours, some transfer in Perth). Train info: Tel. 0345-748-4950, www.nationalrail.co.uk.

STIRLING & NEARBY

Near Stirling

The William Wallace Monument is just outside of town. Sights within side-trip distance include The Kelpies horse-head sculptures, the Falkirk Wheel boat "elevator," the stuck-in-time village of Culross, Doune Castle, and the Trossachs National Park.

JUST OUTSIDE OF STIRLING
▲William Wallace Monument

Commemorating the Scottish hero better known to Americans as "Braveheart," this sandstone tower—built during a wave of Scot-

tish nationalism in the mid-19th century—marks the Abbey Craig hill on the outskirts of Stirling. This is where in 1297 Wallace gathered forces and secured his largest-scale victory against England's King Edward I at the Battle of Stirling Bridge. The victory was a huge boost to the Scottish cause, but England came back to beat the Scots the next year. (For more on William Wallace, see page 61.)

Cost and Hours: £9.50, daily July-Aug 10:00-18:00, April-June and Sept-Oct 10:00-17:00, Nov-March 10:30-16:00, last entry 45 minutes before closing, café at visitors center, vending machines up top, tel. 01786/472-140, www.nationalwallacemonument.com. Skip the £2 audioguide, which repeats posted information.

Getting There: It's two miles northeast of Stirling on the A-8, signposted from the city center. Frequent public buses go from the Stirling bus station to the roundabout below the monument (10-15-minute ride). From there, it's about a 15-minute hike up to the visitors center, then an additional hike up to the monument. Taxis cost about £6-8 one-way. From the visitors center parking lot, you'll need to hike (a very steep 15 minutes) or take a shuttle bus up the hill to the monument itself (depart every 10-15 minutes).

Visiting the Monument: Buy your ticket at the visitors center. Then hike or ride the shuttle bus up to the monument's base. Gazing up, think about how this fanciful structure, like Bavaria's famous Neuschwanstein Castle, was created in the 19th century and designed to evoke (and romanticize) earlier architectural styles—in this case, medieval Scottish castles. The crown-shaped top—reminiscent of St. Gile's on the Royal Mile in Edinburgh—and the dynamic sculpture of William Wallace are patriotic to the max.

Entering, show your ticket and head up the very tight stone spiral staircases (claustrophobes be warned). You'll ascend a total of 246 steps, stopping at three levels partway up to catch your breath and see museum displays. The first level, the Hall of Arms, tells the story of William Wallace and the Battle of Stirling Bridge, including a dramatized post-battle debrief between Wallace and his right-hand man, Andrew de Moray (who would later die from his injuries). Next up is the Hall of Heroes, adorned with busts of great Scots—suggesting the debt this nation owes to Wallace. In the middle of the room, ogle Wallace's five-and-a-half-foot-long broadsword (and try to imagine drawing it from a scabbard on your back at a dead run). But it's not just hero worship: A thoughtful video presentation considers the role of Wallace in both Scottish and English history, and raises the point that one person's freedom fighter is another person's terrorist. The third level's exhibits are about the monument itself: when, why, and how it was built.

Finally you reach the top of the tower, with stunning views over Stirling, its castle, the River Forth (which twists back on itself in an almost 360-degree curve), and Stirling Bridge—a stone version that replaced the original wooden one. Looking out from the same vantage point as Wallace, imagine how the famous battle played out. But if you find yourself picturing

Braveheart—with berserker Scots, their faces painted blue, running across a field to take on the English cavalry—you have the wrong idea. While that portrayal was cinematically powerful, in reality the battle took place on a bridge in a narrow valley (see sidebar).

▲Bannockburn Heritage Centre

On the southern outskirts of Stirling is the Bannockburn Heritage Centre, commemorating what many Scots view as their nation's most significant military victory over the invading English: the Battle of Bannockburn, won by a Scottish army led by Robert the Bruce against England's King Edward II in 1314. The high-tech experience, with 3-D screens and a re-creation of the battle, basically reduces Bannockburn to a video game. But for those interested in the history, it's a good way to really understand, blow by blow, what happened here. While Bannockburn's website recommends reservations, they're rarely needed (except on very busy weekends); just sign up for the next available slot when you arrive, and pass any waiting time (never more than an hour) by exploring

Debunking *Braveheart*

The 1995 multiple-Oscar-winner movie *Braveheart* informs many travelers' impressions of William Wallace and the battles near Stirling. But Mel Gibson's much-assailed Scottish accent may very well be the most authentic thing about the film.

In the 1297 Battle of Stirling Bridge, William Wallace and his ragtag Scottish forces hid out in the forest overlooking the bottleneck bridge, waiting until the perfect moment to ambush the English. Thanks to the tight quarters and the element of surprise, the Scots won an unlikely victory. *Braveheart* serves up an entirely different version of events: armies lining up across an open field, with blue-faced, kilted Highlanders charging at top speed toward heavily armored English troops. The filmmakers left out the bridge entirely, calling it simply "The Battle of Stirling." And the blue face paint? Never happened. A millennium before William Wallace, the ancient Romans did encounter war-painted fighters in Scotland, whom they called the Picts ("painted ones"). But painting faces in the late 13th century would be like WWII soldiers suiting up in chain mail.

Braveheart takes many other liberties with history. William Wallace was *not* the rugged-born Highlander depicted in the movie—he was born in Elderslie, next to Paisley, in the Lowlands. Wallace did *not* vengefully kill Andrew de Moray for deserting him at Falkirk (Moray fought valiantly by Wallace's side at Stirling, and died from battle wounds). Robert the Bruce did *not* betray Wal-

the exhibit, grabbing a snack in the café, or walking out to the monument.

Cost and Hours: £11.50, daily 10:00-17:30, Nov-Feb until 17:00, café, tel. 0844/493-2139, www.battleofbannockburn.com.

Getting There: It's two miles south of Stirling on the A-872, off the M-80/M-9. For non-drivers, it's an easy bus ride from the Stirling bus station (a short walk south from the train station; several buses run on this route, 8/hour, 9-15 minutes).

Background: In simple terms, Robert the Bruce—who was first and foremost a politician—found himself out of political options after years of failed diplomatic attempts to make peace with the strong-arming English. William Wallace's execution left a vacuum in military leadership, and eventually Robert stepped in, waging a successful guerrilla campaign that came to a head as young Edward's army marched to Stirling. Although the Scots were greatly outnumbered, their

lace to the English. And William Wallace most certainly did *not* impregnate the future King Edward II's French bride...who was 10 years old, not yet married to Edward, and still living in France at the time of Wallace's death.

Also, the modern concept of national "Freee-dooooom!" was essentially unknown during the divine-right Middle Ages. Wallace wasn't fighting for "democracy" or "liberty"; he simply wanted to trade one authoritarian, aristocratic ruler (from London) for another authoritarian, aristocratic ruler (from Scotland).

Even the film's title is a falsehood: No Scottish person ever referred to Wallace as "Braveheart," which was actually the nickname of one of the film's villains, Robert the Bruce. After Robert's death, his heart was taken (in a small casket) on a crusade to the Holy Land by his friend Sir James Douglas. During one battle, Douglas threw the heart at an oncoming army and shouted, "Lead on, brave heart, I will follow thee!" Gibson's title is a bit like naming a film about Abraham Lincoln *Old Hickory*.

Scottish people have mixed feelings about *Braveheart*. They appreciate the boost it gave to their underdog nation's profile—and to its tourist industry—juuust enough that they're willing to overlook the film's historical gaffes. For travelers, it can be enjoyable to watch *Braveheart* to prep for your trip...as entertainment. Then go to Stirling and get the real story. (For a fact-based account of Wallace's life, see the sidebar on page 61.)

strategy and use of terrain at Bannockburn—with its impossibly twisty stream presenting a natural barrier for the invading army—allowed them to soundly beat the English and drive Edward out of Scotland...for the time being. (For more about Robert the Bruce, see page 65.) This victory is so legendary among the Scots that the country's unofficial national anthem, "Flower of Scotland"—written 600 years after the battle—focuses on this one event: Robert the Bruce's ragtag squad "stood against him, proud Edward's army, and sent him homeward to think again." (The definitive version of this song was recorded in 1974 by the Scottish folk group The Corries. Look locally for a Corries CD—or buy the song online—and you might soon find yourself singing along at a pub.)

Visiting Bannockburn: Your visit is like preparing for, then playing, an intricate and computerized version of the war game Risk. For the main event, in the "battle room," you'll huddle around a large model of the terrain around Bannockburn and watch a virtual re-creation of troop movements. When buying your ticket, you'll have two choices: "Battle Show," a basic, 15-minute recap of the battle; or "Battle Game," a 45-minute simulation where you actually get to take charge of one of the armies and direct their movements...

before finding out how things actually turned out. Unless you're into strategy games, the "Battle Show" is plenty for most.

You'll begin by watching two short films to set the stage, then head into the main exhibition area, where giant screens show life-size soldiers at pivotal moments in the battle. Behind the screens you can interact with figures from both sides: Move your hand to get them to talk. Because there are no real artifacts on display, most of the exhibit is preparation for your time in the battle room. At the appointed time, report for battle. You'll come away with a very detailed, tactical understanding of the battle that shaped this important moment in Scottish and English history.

Leaving the center, hike out into the field behind, where you can see a **monument** to those lost in the fight. Nearby, on a plinth, stands an equestrian statue of **Robert the Bruce**—surveying the place where he lived his most important moment.

FALKIRK

Two engaging landmarks sit just outside the town of Falkirk, about 12 miles south of Stirling. Taken together, The Kelpies and the Falkirk Wheel offer a welcome change of pace from Scottish countryside kitsch. These flank Falkirk's otherwise unexciting town center, about a 5-mile, 20-minute drive apart (depending on traffic; it's a riddle of roundabouts); ask for a flier illustrating directions between them at either site.

▲The Kelpies

Unveiled in 2014 and standing over a hundred feet tall ("the largest equine sculptures in the world"), these two giant steel horse heads have quickly become a symbol of this town and region. They may seem whimsical, but they're rooted in a mix of mythology and real history: Kelpies are magical, waterborne, shape-shifting sprites of Scottish lore, who often took the form of a horse. And historically, horses—the ancestors of today's  Budweiser Clydesdales—were used as beasts of burden to power Scotland's industrial output. These statues stand over old canals where hardworking horses towed heavily laden barges. But if you prefer, you can just forget all that and ogle the dramatic, energy-charged statues (particularly thrilling to Denver Broncos fans). A café nearby sells drinks and light meals, and a visitors center shows how the heads were built. You can take a 45-minute guided tour through the inside of one of the great beasts, to see how they're supported by a sleek steel skeleton: 300 tons of steel apiece, sitting upon a foundation of 1,200 tons of steel-reinforced concrete, and gleaming with 990 steel panels.

Cost and Hours: Always open and free to view (£2 to park at the horse heads, free to park elsewhere); visitors center open daily 10:00-17:00. Tours—£6.95, daily at the bottom of every hour 10:30-16:30, fewer tours Oct-March, tel. 01324/506-850, www.thehelix.co.uk.

Getting There: The Kelpies are in a park called The Helix, just off the M-9 motorway—you'll spot them as you zip past. For a closer look, exit the M-9 for the A-905 (Falkirk/Grangemouth), then follow *Falkirk/A-904* and brown *Helix Park & Kelpies* signs.

▲▲Falkirk Wheel

At the opposite end of Falkirk stands this remarkable modern incarnation of Scottish technical know-how. You can watch the beautiful, slow-motion contraption as it spins—like a nautical Ferris wheel—to efficiently shuttle ships between two canals separated by 80 vertical feet. With a visitors center, boat trips, hands-on kids' activity zone, and other amusements, the Falkirk Wheel makes engineering fun.

Cost and Hours: Wheel is free to view, visitors center open Mon-Fri 10:00-17:30, Sat-Sun until 18:30, shorter hours Nov-mid-March, park open until 20:00, tel. 0870-050-0208, www.thefalkirkwheel.co.uk.

Getting There: Exit the M-876 motorway for *A-883/Falkirk/Denny*, then follow brown *The Falkirk Wheel* signs. You'll park in a huge, free lot, then stroll about 10 minutes along a canal and across a bridge to reach the visitors center and wheel.

Background: Scotland was a big player in the Industrial Revolution, thanks partly to its network of shipping canals (including the famous Caledonian Canal—see page 322). Using dozens of locks to lift barges up across Scotland's hilly spine, these canals were effective...but excruciatingly slow.

The 115-foot-tall Falkirk Wheel, opened in 2002, is a modern take on this classic engineering challenge: linking the Forth and Clyde Canal below with the aqueduct of the Union Canal, 80 feet above. Rather than using rising and lowering water, the wheel simply picks boats up and—ever so slowly—takes them where they need to go, like a giant waterborne elevator. In the 1930s, it took

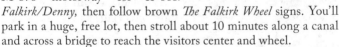

STIRLING & NEARBY

half a day to ascend or descend through 11 locks; now it takes only five minutes.

The Falkirk Wheel is the critical connection in the Millennium Link project, an ambitious £78 million initiative to restore the long-neglected Forth and Clyde and Union canals connecting Edinburgh and Glasgow. Today this 70-mile-long aquatic connection between Scotland's leading cities is a leisurely traffic jam of pleasure craft, and canalside communities have been rejuvenated.

Visiting the Wheel: Twice an hour, the wheel springs (silently) to life: Gates rise up to seal off each of the water-filled gondolas, and then the entire structure slowly rotates a half-turn to swap the positions of the lower and upper boats—each of which stays comfortably upright. The towering structure is not only functional, but beautiful: The wheel's elegantly sweeping shape—with graceful cogs and pointed tips that slice into the water as they spin—was inspired by the Celtic double-headed ax. Or maybe it's a propeller, evoking Glasgow's shipbuilding heritage.

The big, slick **visitors center** has food, souvenirs, free WCs, and a few (not enough) exhibits explaining the wheel. The Falkirk **TI**, just steps away, has similar hours and free Wi-Fi. Kids love exploring the **activity zone** that sprawls across the lake from the visitors center, with plenty of hands-on activities illustrating how human ingenuity has solved the problem of moving water from place to place (from the lock to the Archimedes screw to the piston pump). Around the far side of the basin, you can rent electric **boats** and canoes, or go **"waterwalking"** (stroll—or stumble—in inflated plastic balls across the water's surface).

Cruises: While it's fun just to watch the wheel in action, for a complete experience consider taking a one-hour boat trip. These begin at the basin in front of the visitors center, and include a ride up and down the wheel with a short boat trip on either end—all narrated by your skipper (£8.95, about hourly in summer, call visitors center or check website to confirm schedule and book ahead).

▲CULROSS

This time warp of a village, sitting across the Firth of Forth from Edinburgh (about a 30-minute drive from Stirling), is a perfectly preserved artifact from the 17th and 18th centuries. If you're looking to let your pulse slow, stroll through a steep and sleepy hamlet, and tour a creaky old manor house, Culross is your place. Filmmakers often use Culross to evoke Scottish villages of yore (you've seen it in everything from *Captain America: The First Avenger* to

Outlander). While not worth a long detour, it's a workable stop for drivers connecting Edinburgh to either the Stirling area or St. Andrews (free parking lots flank the town center—an easy, 5-minute waterfront stroll away).

The story of Culross (which locals pronounce KOO-russ) is the story of Sir George Bruce, who, in the late 16th century, figured out a way to build coal mines beneath the waters of the Firth of Forth. The hardworking town flourished, Bruce built a fine mansion, and the town was granted coveted "royal burgh" status by the king. But several decades later, with Bruce's death and the flooding of the mines, the town's fortunes tumbled—halting its development and trapping it as if in amber for centuries. Rescued and rehabilitated by the National Trust for Scotland, today the entire village feels like one big open-air folk museum.

The main sightseeing attraction here is the misnamed **Culross "Palace,"** the big-but-creaky, half-timbered home of George Bruce (£10.50, June-Aug daily 12:00-17:00, April-May and Sept closed Tue-Wed, shorter hours in Oct and closed Nov-March, tel. 01383/880-359, www.nts.org. uk/culross). Buy your ticket at the office under the town hall's clock tower, pick up the included audioguide, then head a few doors down to the ochre-colored palace. Follow-ing a 10-minute orientation

film, you'll walk through several creaky floors to see how a small town's big shots lived four centuries ago. Docents in each room are happy to answer questions. You'll see the great hall, the "principal stranger's bedchamber" (guest room for VIPs), George Bruce's bedroom and stone strong room (where he stored precious—and flammable—financial documents), and the highlight, the painted chamber. The wood slats of its barrel-arched ceiling are painted with whimsical scenes illustrating Scottish virtues and pitfalls. You can also poke around the densely planted, lovingly tended garden out back. (Plants are sold at a table in the front courtyard.)

Your ticket also includes a 45-minute **guided walk** through the town itself (3/day, check website for schedule).

The only other real sight, a steep hike up the cobbled lanes to the top of town, is the partially ruined **abbey.** While there are far more evocative ruins in Scotland, it's fun to poke into the stony, mysterious-feeling interior of this church. But the stroll up the town's cobbled streets past pastel houses, with their carefully tended flower boxes, is even better than the church itself.

IN DOUNE, BETWEEN STIRLING AND THE TROSSACHS

The village of Doune (pronounced "doon") is just a 15-minute drive north of Stirling. While there's not much to see in town, on its outskirts are a pair of attractions: a castle and a distillery. In the village of Doune itself, notice the town seal: a pair of crossed pistols. Aside from its castle and whisky, the town is known for its historic pistol factory. Locals speculate that the first shot of the American Revolution was fired with a Doune pistol.

Getting There: Bus #1 runs from Stirling to Doune (Main Street), from which it's a 10-minute walk to the castle or a 20-minute walk to the distillery (both sit along the River Teith, but in different directions). Drivers head to Doune, then follow castle signs on pretty back roads from there.

Doune Castle

Doune Castle is worth considering for its pop-culture connections: Most recently, Doune stands in for Castle Leoch in the TV series *Outlander*. But well before that, parts of *Monty Python and the Holy Grail* were filmed here. And, while the castle may underwhelm *Outlander* fans (only some exterior scenes were shot here, and currently there's only one paltry display about the show on site), Python fans—and anyone who appreciates British

comedy—will be tickled by the included audioguide, narrated by Python troupe member Terry Jones and featuring sound clips from the film. (If you're not into Python or *Outlander*, Scotland has better castles to visit.)

Cost and Hours: £5.50, daily April-Sept 9:30-17:30, Oct-March 10:00-16:00, tel. 01786/841-742.

Visiting the Castle: Buy your ticket and pick up the 45-minute audioguide, which explains that the castle's most important resident was not Claire Randall or the Knights Who Say Ni, but Robert Stewart, the Duke of Albany (1340-1420)—a man so influential he was called the "uncrowned king of Scotland." You'll see the cellars, ogle the empty-feeling courtyard, then scramble through the two tall towers and the great hall that connects them. The castle rooms are almost entirely empty, but they're brought to life by the audioguide. You'll walk into the kitchen's ox-sized fireplace to peer up the gigantic chimney, and visit the guest room's privy to peer down the medieval toilet. You'll finish your visit at the top of the main tower, with 360-degree views that allow you to fart in just about anyone's general direction.

Deanston Distillery

This big, attractive red-brick industrial complex (formerly a cotton mill) sits facing the river just outside of Doune. While Deanston has been long respected for its fruity, slightly spicy Highland single-malt whisky, the 2012 movie *The Angels' Share*, filmed partly at this distillery, helped put it on the map for tourists. The complex boasts a slick visitors center that's open for tours. On the 50-minute visit, you'll see the equipment used to make the whisky and enjoy a sample. (For more on whisky and the distillation process, see page 460.) A bit more corporate-feeling than some of my favorite Scottish distilleries, Deanston has the advantage of being handy to Stirling.

Cost and Hours: £8-10 depending on number of tastings, tours depart at the top of each hour daily 10:00-16:00 (last tour), best to call ahead to reserve, tel. 01786/843-010, www.deanstonmalt.com.

LOCH LOMOND AND THE TROSSACHS NATIONAL PARK

Within about an hour's drive of half the population of Scotland is the country's leading national park. Though it's a single park, it encompasses two separate areas: The famous lake called Loch Lomond and, just to the east, the Trossachs—a hilly terrain that pleases hikers and joyriders. The Highland Boundary Fault—the geologic line separating the flat Lowlands from the rugged Highlands—runs right through the middle of this area, and in several places you can actually see the terrain in transition.

To be honest, the charms of Loch Lomond and the Trossachs are subtle. Scottish scenery crescendos dramatically as you head north (at Glencoe, the Cairngorms, and the Isle of Skye, for starters). But this area's proximity to Stirling and Glasgow—and its many entertaining connections to Scottish history, literature, and folk culture—make it worth knowing about. For those on a quick, targeted visit to Scotland's Central Belt, Loch Lomond and the Trossachs offer a glimpse of "the Highlands in miniature."

Loch Lomond

Twenty-four miles long and speckled with islands, Loch Lomond is Great Britain's biggest lake by surface area, and second in volume only to Loch Ness. Thanks largely to its easy proximity to Glasgow

(about 15 miles away), this scenic lake is a favorite retreat for Scots as well as foreign tourists. The southernmost of the Munros, Ben Lomond (3,196 feet), looms over the eastern bank.

Loch Lomond's biggest claim to fame is its role in a beloved folk song: "Ye'll take the high road, and I'll take the low road, and I'll be in Scotland afore ye... For me and my true love will never meet again, on the bonnie, bonnie banks of Loch Lomond." As you'll now be humming that all day (you're welcome), here's one interpretation of the song's poignant meaning: Celtic culture believes that fairies return the souls of the deceased to their homeland through the soil. After the disastrous Scottish loss at the Battle of Culloden, Jacobite ringleaders were arrested and taken for trial in faraway London. In some cases, accused pairs were given a choice: One of you will die, and the other will live. The song is a bittersweet reassurance, sung from the condemned to the survivor, that the soon-to-be-deceased will take the spiritual "low road" back to his Scottish homeland—where his soul will be reunited with the living, who will return on the physical "high road" (over land).

Visiting Loch Lomond: There's not much to see, aside from some lochside scenery. You can get a fair dose simply driving by. People traveling from Glasgow toward Oban (or other points north) will get a good look at the loch's **west bank** as they follow the A-82 north (see "Route Tips for Drivers" on page 290).

To see the **east bank** of the lake, it's an easy detour from the Trossachs loop described below, or from Glasgow. Take the A-811 west from Stirling, or the A-809 north from Glasgow, to the village of Drymen (DRIM-men). From here, carry on westward (along the B-837) to Balmaha. In this wide spot in the road, you'll find a visitors center with free geology and wildlife exhibits and advice about various hikes in the region. One easy and popular option is the ascent to Craigie Fort viewpoint (1 mile, 45 minutes round-trip), offering views over the southern part of the lake. For a more ambitious hike, you can follow part of the West Highland Way up to Conic Hill (2.5 miles, 3 hours round-trip).

▲The Trossachs

The hills-and-lochs terrain of the Trossachs, just northwest of Stirling (and due north of Glasgow), is a gently scenic, tourist-clogged corner of Highlands beauty. While the views here pale in comparison to more scenic areas farther north, this well-trod route is packed with interesting footnotes in Scottish history—from Rob Roy to Sir Walter Scott to the Beatles. The Trossachs makes for an easy, pretty spin close to Glasgow or Stirling, but can also be used as a slow-but-scenic connection to points in northern and eastern Scotland (see the options at the end of this drive). I've lightly narrated this loop in a clockwise order, coming from Stirling. But you can go in either direction, and begin or end wherever you like. I've focused on real history rather than silly legends...but sometimes the myths are hard to resist.

◑ Self-Guided Driving Tour: From Stirling, head west on the A-84, then turn off to the left onto the A-873 (marked for *Thornhill*; watch for brown *Trossachs* signs). Carry on through Thornhill and then, in the village of Blairhoyle, turn left onto the A-81.

Soon you'll pass the **Lake of Menteith.** Many Scots are quick to point out that this is the only "lake" (as opposed to "loch") in all of Scotland, and have cooked up an explanation: Its namesake, Sir John Menteith, was a Scot who betrayed William Wallace, leading to his arrest and execution. To punish the traitor, "loch" became "lake." But, like most trumped-up Trossachs legends, this is bogus: The "lake" is likely derived from the Lowland Scots word *laich*— meaning simply "low place."

Continue along the A-81, then bear right onto the A-821 to **Aberfoyle.** Approaching the town, notice the landscape heaving up just beyond it—you can actually see where the Highland Boundary Fault marks the start of the Highlands. The town itself is attractive, if something of a tour bus hell—with more parking lot than town. But it's a convenient place to take a break and grab picnic supplies. At the corner of the parking lot, the Scottish Wool Centre is a tacky tourist mall with a few free attractions out front that are worth a peek: sheep, noisy goats, birds of prey, and a fun little sheepdog demonstration (3/day in summer), in which the clever dogs herd geese on a virtual "tour of Scotland." Across the parking lot, the TI has free Wi-Fi and a small exhibit touting Aberfoyle's literary connections: Sir Walter Scott's *The Lady of the Lake* was inspired by nearby Loch Katrine (which we'll reach soon). This was also the home of Robert Kirk, who (in 1691) wrote *The Secret Commonwealth of Elves, Fauns, and Fairies,* which remains the definitive compendium of Scottish superstition. Soon after, Kirk died mysteriously in a forest glen supposedly inhabited by fairies. (Locals love to share stories, theories, and superstitions about Kirk.)

Leaving Aberfoyle, carry on north along the A-821, following a twisty road called the **Duke's Pass.** This was built by the Duke of Montrose (the villain of the Rob Roy story) to access his mountain estates and to levy tolls. You'll wind your way up into a thickly forested hillscape; watch on the right for the turnoff for the Queen Elizabeth Forest Park visitors center. Here you can get maps and hiking advice, and peruse good exhibits on local geology and wildlife—including live cameras showing osprey nests. They share a parking lot with Go Ape, a popular zip-line and high-ropes course (best to book ahead, full course takes 2.5-3 hours, www. goape.com).

As you crest the Duke's Pass, you'll get a small taste of the **Highland moor** terrain. For a good look at this landscape (and a parking lot with a handy viewpoint), pull off on the right at the start of the Three Lochs Forest Drive. You're surrounded by heather—the scrubby plant (with vibrant purple flowers in the late summer) that blankets much of the Highlands. The oldest pines around you are mostly Scotch (or "Scots") pines; more recently, these have been replaced by faster-growing pines that are better for harvesting. Meanwhile, the deciduous trees (with red berries or white flowers, depending on the season) are rowan trees, also called "mountain ash." Superstitious Highlanders believe that rowans keep witches away and prevent fairies from switching out babies for changelings. If you're bothered by the distant sight of wind farms from this viewpoint, you can commiserate with Donald Trump—the American magnate lobbied the Scottish government to outlaw these structures within sight of his Scottish golf courses.

Back on the main road, you'll start working your way downhill. On your right are glimpses of **Loch Drunkie.** Just ignore tour guides who tell you this was named for the practice of chugging and dumping illegal homebrew whis-ky here when the police showed up.

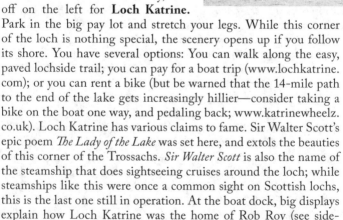

Farther down, you'll pass briefly along the banks of **Loch Achray.** Across the lake is the former Trossachs Hotel, which has hosted everyone from Queen Victoria to the Beatles. In the Fab Four's landmark 1964 tour around the UK, they'd do big shows in cities, then retreat to countryside getaways like this one.

At the end of Loch Achray, turn off on the left for **Loch Katrine.** Park in the big pay lot and stretch your legs. While this corner of the loch is nothing special, the scenery opens up if you follow its shore. You have several options: You can walk along the easy, paved lochside trail; you can pay for a boat trip (www.lochkatrine.com); or you can rent a bike (but be warned that the 14-mile path to the end of the lake gets increasingly hillier—consider taking a bike on the boat one way, and pedaling back; www.katrinewheelz.co.uk). Loch Katrine has various claims to fame. Sir Walter Scott's epic poem *The Lady of the Lake* was set here, and extols the beauties of this corner of the Trossachs. *Sir Walter Scott* is also the name of the steamship that does sightseeing cruises around the loch; while steamships like this were once a common sight on Scottish lochs, this is the last one still in operation. At the boat dock, big displays explain how Loch Katrine was the home of Rob Roy (see side-

Rob Roy MacGregor (1671-1734)

The Trossachs region is Rob Roy country. This near-mythic Scottish folk hero was wounded fighting for the Jacobite cause, then became a trader of Highland cattle. He borrowed money from the Duke of Montrose (for whom Duke's Pass is named), but when one of his men ran off with the cash, Rob Roy had to resort to stealing cattle and harassing the duke, who now called for his head. In his new life as a lovable Robin Hood-type rogue, who stole from the rich and kept for himself, Rob Roy embodied the Scottish suspicion of authority. Immortalized in novels, verse, music, and film by everyone from Sir Walter Scott and William Wordsworth to Hector Berlioz and Liam Neeson, Rob Roy's reputation looms larger than his actual life. And today, visitors enjoy seeing his former stomping grounds, from Loch Katrine to his grave in Balquhidder.

bar). Loch Katrine is also a primary water supply for Glasgow. In 1885, engineers harnessed the power of gravity to pipe the clean mountain waters into the big city. (Glaswegians of the time—accustomed to extremely polluted well water—were unimpressed. As one joke goes, a Glaswegian poured his first glass of water, eyed it suspiciously, and said, "It's got nae color, nae taste—nae good!") And finally, the US president's theme song also has a connection to this unassuming Scottish loch: "Hail to the Chief" came from a musical based on Scott's *Lady of the Lake*. It was played for George Washington to celebrate the end of the War of 1812, and the tradition stuck.

When you're done at Loch Katrine, return to the main A-821 and head toward Callander. You'll go along the other bank of **Loch Achray** (and get a closer look at the Trossachs Hotel—now a time-share). Then you'll pass through **Brig O'Turk** (Gaelic for "Bridge of the Wild Boar") and drive along **Loch Venachar** before reaching a junction with the A-84. It's time to make your decision: Head north for more scenery and access to Loch Tay (Crannog Centre, Kenmore), Pitlochry, and other sights. Or head south for a speedy return to Stirling, by way of Callander and Doune Castle. Both options are outlined below.

To the North: If you head north on the A-84, you'll pass another pretty loch (Lubnaig), and soon after, you'll see the turnoff for **Balquhidder.** Fans of Rob Roy—or anyone named MacGregor—may want to take the two-mile detour (on single-track roads) to

Balquhidder's humble stone church. In the kirkyard, look for the grave of the famous MacGregor clan chieftain. Rob Roy lived most of his life in these hills overlooking Loch Voil (visible in the distance). Back on the main A-84, carry on north (in Lochearnhead, it becomes the A-85); eventually you'll reach the junction with the A-827. From here, you can stick with the main A-85 all the way to **Oban.** Or you can turn right onto the A-827 (toward Killin) to reach the dramatic **Falls of Dochart,** which tumble through a tiny village, and then follow the north bank of Loch Tay to **Kenmore** and the **Crannog Centre;** farther along the A-827, you'll rejoin the main A-9 highway, which heads north to **Pitlochry** and several other attractions on the way up to **Inverness.** (For details on all of these sights, see the Eastern Scotland chapter.) Turning south on the A-9 zips you back toward Perth, then Stirling.

To the South: To complete our loop more directly, head south on the A-84. Just after you make the turn, watch on the left for the Wool Center, with a pair of hairy coos (shaggy Highland cattle) around back who love to pose for photos. Soon after, you'll pass through **Callander,** which feels like a very slightly less touristy version of Aberfoyle. Carrying on through town on the A-84, you'll pass through the village of Doune, where you can stop off for a tour of **Doune Castle** and/or the **Deanston Distillery** (both described earlier in this chapter). **Stirling** is just down the road.

ST. ANDREWS

St. Andrews • Dundee • Glamis Castle • The East Neuk

St. Andrews is synonymous with golf. But there's much more to this charming town than its famous links. Dramatically situated at the edge of a sandy bay, St. Andrews is the home of Scotland's most important university—think of it as the Scottish Cambridge. And centuries ago, the town was the religious capital of the country.

In its long history, St. Andrews has seen two boom periods. First, in the early Middle Ages, the relics of St. Andrew made the town cathedral one of the most important pilgrimage sites in Christendom. The faithful flocked here from all over Europe, leaving the town with a medieval all-roads-lead-to-the-cathedral street plan that survives today. But after the Scottish Reformation, the cathedral rotted away and the town became a forgotten backwater. A new wave of visitors arrived in the mid-19th century, when a visionary mayor (with the on-the-nose name Provost Playfair) began to promote the town's connection with the newly in-vogue game of golf. Most buildings in town date from this Victorian era.

Today St. Andrews remains a popular spot for students, golf devotees (from amateurs to professional golfers to celebrities), and occasionally Britain's favorite royal couple, Will and Kate (college sweethearts, U. of St. A. class of '05). With vast sandy beaches, golfing opportunities for pros and novices alike, playgrounds of castle and cathedral ruins, and a fun-loving student vibe, St. Andrews is an appealing place to take a vacation from your busy vacation. It's also a handy home base for a variety of worthwhile side-trips: interesting museums in the big city of Dundee, the castle home of the late Queen Mother, and a string of relaxing fishing villages (the East Neuk).

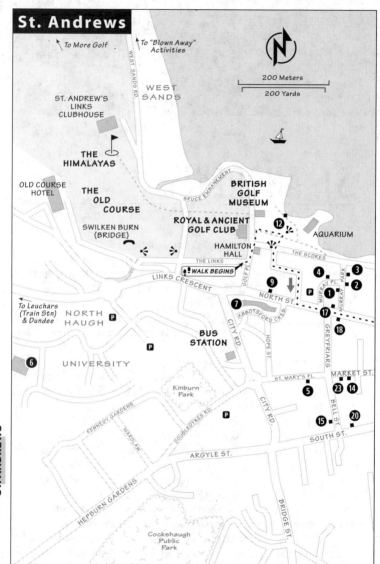

St. Andrews

To More Golf

To "Blown Away" Activities

WEST SANDS RD

WEST SANDS

200 Meters
200 Yards

N

ST. ANDREW'S LINKS CLUBHOUSE

THE HIMALAYAS

OLD COURSE HOTEL

THE OLD COURSE

BRUCE EMBANKMENT

BRITISH GOLF MUSEUM

SWILKEN BURN (BRIDGE)

ROYAL & ANCIENT GOLF CLUB

12

AQUARIUM

HAMILTON HALL

THE SCORES

THE LINKS

WALK BEGINS

GOLF PL.

4

3

MURRAY PL.

2

To Leuchars (Train Stn) & Dundee

LINKS CRESCENT

LINKS CRESCENT

NORTH ST.

9

1

P

7

ABBOTSFORD CRES.

CITY RD

17

MURRAY PL.

GREYFRIARS

18

NORTH HAUGH

P

BUS STATION

HOPE ST.

P

6

UNIVERSITY

Kinburn Park

ST. MARY'S PL.

5

MARKET ST.

23 **14**

BELL ST.

KENNEDY GARDENS

WARDLAW

DOUBLEDYKES RD

P

CITY RD

15

20

SOUTH ST.

ARGYLE ST.

HEPBURN GARDENS

BRIDGE ST.

Cockshaugh Public Park

PLANNING YOUR TIME

St. Andrews, hugging the east coast of Scotland, is a bit off the main tourist track. But it's well connected by train to Edinburgh (via bus from nearby Leuchars), making it a worthwhile day trip from the capital. Better yet, spend a night (or more, if you're a golfer) to enjoy this university town after dark.

If you're not here to golf, this is a good way to spend a day:

1. Hoppity House B&B
2. Cameron House & Glenderran Guest House
3. Montague Guest House & Lorimer House
4. Doune Guest House
5. St. Andrews Tourist Hostel & The Grill House Restaurant
6. Agnes Blackadder Hall
7. McIntosh Hall
8. Forgan's Restaurant
9. Playfair's Restaurant
10. The Glass House Restaurant
11. The Doll's House Restaurant
12. The Seafood Restaurant
13. Cromars Fish & Chips
14. Tailend Fish & Chips
15. Aikmans Pub
16. The Central Pub
17. Greyfriars Pub
18. Taste Coffee
19. Luvians Bottle Shop
20. I.J. Mellis Cheesemonger
21. Fisher and Donaldson Pastries
22. B. Jannettas Ice Cream
23. Groceries (2)

ST. ANDREWS

Follow my self-guided walk, which connects the golf course, the university quad, the castle, and the cathedral. Dip into the Golf Museum, watch the golfers on the Old Course, and play a round at "the Himalayas" putting green. With more time, walk along the West Sands beach, take a spin by car or bus to the nearby East Neuk, or drive up to the museums in Dundee. Dundee and Glamis Castle are also great stops for those connecting St. Andrews to points north.

Orientation to St. Andrews

St. Andrews (pop. 16,000, plus several-thousand more students during term) is situated at the tip of a peninsula next to a broad bay. The town retains its old medieval street plan: Three main streets (North, Market, and South) converge at the cathedral, which overlooks the sea at the tip of town. The middle street—Market Street—has the TI and many handy shops and eateries. North of North Street, the seafront street called The Scores connects the cathedral with the golf scene, which huddles along the West Sands beach at the base of the old town. St. Andrews is compact: You can stroll across town—from the cathedral to the historic golf course—in about 15 minutes.

TOURIST INFORMATION

St. Andrews' helpful TI is on Market Street, about two blocks in front of the cathedral (July-Aug Mon-Sat 9:15-18:00, Sun 10:00-17:00; April-June and Sept-mid-Oct Mon-Sat 9:15-17:00, Sun 11:00-16:00; mid-Oct-March Mon-Sat 9:15-17:00, closed Sun; free Wi-Fi, 70 Market Street, tel. 01334/472-021, www.visitfife.com or www.visitscotland.com).

ARRIVAL IN ST. ANDREWS

By Train and Bus: The nearest train station is in the village of Leuchars, five miles away. From there, a 10-minute bus ride takes you right into St. Andrews (buy ticket from driver, buses meet most trains—see schedule at bus shelter for next bus to St. Andrews; while waiting, read the historical info under the nearby flagpole). St. Andrews' bus station is near the base of Market Street—a short walk from most B&Bs and the TI. A taxi from Leuchars into St. Andrews costs about £14.

By Car: For a short stay, drivers can simply head into the town center and park anywhere along the street. Easy-to-use meters dispense stickers (£1/hour, coins only, 2-hour limit, monitored Mon-Sat 9:00-17:00). For longer stays, you can park for free along certain streets near the center (such as the small lot near the B&B neighborhood around Murray Place, and along The Scores), or use one of the long-stay lots near the entrance to town.

HELPFUL HINTS

Golf Events: Every five years, St. Andrews is swamped with about 100,000 visitors when it hosts the British Open (called simply "The Open" around here; the next one—celebrating The Open's 150th anniversary—is in 2021). The town also fills up every year in early October for the Alfred Dunhill Links

Championship. Unless you're a golf pilgrim, avoid the town at these times (as room rates skyrocket).

School Term: The University of St. Andrews has two terms: spring semester ("Candlemas"), from mid-February through May; and fall semester ("Martinmas"), from mid-September until December. St. Andrews has a totally different vibe in the summer, when most students leave and are replaced by upper-crust golfers and tourists.

Sand Surfing and Adventure Activities: Nongolfers who want to stay busy while their travel partners play the Old Course may enjoy some of the adventure activities offered by **Blown Away**—including "land yachting" (zipping across the beach in wind-powered go-carts), kayaking, and paddle boarding. Brothers Guy and Jamie McKenzie set up shop at the northern tip of West Sands beach (sporadic hours—typically Mon-Fri only—so call first, tel. 07784/121-125, www.blownaway. co.uk, ahoy@blownaway.co.uk).

St. Andrews Walk

This walk links all of St. Andrews' must-see sights and takes you down hidden medieval streets. Allow a couple of hours, or more if you detour for the sights along the way.

• *Start at the base of the seaside street called The Scores, overlooking the famous golf course. (There are benches with nice views by the Links Golf Shop for those with a sandwich to munch.)*

▲The Old Course

You're looking at the mecca of golf. The 18th hole of the world's first golf course is a few yards away, on your left (for info on playing the course, see "Golfing in St. Andrews," later).

The gray Neoclassical building to the right of the 18th hole is the **Royal and Ancient Golf Club** (or "R&A" for short), which is the world's governing body for golf (like the British version of the PGA). The R&A is a private club with membership by invitation only; it was men-only until 2014, but now—finally!—women are also allowed to join. (In Scotland, men-only clubs lose tax benefits, which is quite costly, but they generally don't care about expenses because their membership is wealthy.) Their shop is a great spot to buy a souvenir for the golf lover back home. Even if you're not golfing, watch the action for a while. (Serious fans can walk around to the low-profile stone bridge across the creek called the Swilken Burn, with golf's single most iconic view: back over the 18th hole and the R&A.)

Overlooking the course is the big, red-sandstone **Hamilton Hall,** an old hotel that was turned into university dorms and then swanky apartments (rumor has it Samuel L. Jackson owns one). According to town legend, Hamilton Hall was originally built to upstage the R&A by an American upset over being declined membership to the exclusive club.

Between Hamilton Hall and the beach is the low-profile **British Golf Museum** (described on page 216).

• *Now turn your back to the golf course and walk through the park (along the street called The Scores) a few steps to the obelisk.*

Beach Viewpoint

The broad, two-mile-long sandy beach that stretches below the golf course is the **West Sands.** It's a wonderful place for a relaxing and/or invigorating walk. Or do a slo-mo jog, humming the theme to *Chariots of Fire*—this is the beach on which the characters run in the movie's famous opening scene.

Walk to the benches on the bluff for a good look at the **cliffs** on your right. The sea below was once called "Witches' Lake" because of all the women and men pushed off the cliff on suspicion of witchcraft.

The big obelisk is a **martyrs' monument,** commemorating all those who died for their Protestant beliefs during the Scottish Reformation. (We'll learn more about that chapter of St. Andrews history farther along this walk.)

The Victorian bandstand **gazebo** (between here and the Old Course) recalls the town's genteel heyday as a seaside resort, when the train line ran all the way to town.

Just opposite the obelisk, across The Scores and next to Alexander's Restaurant, walk down the tiny **Gillespie Wynd alleyway.** It winds through the back gardens of the city's stone houses. Notice how the medieval platting gave each landowner a little bit of street front and a long back garden. St. Andrews' street plan typifies that of a medieval pilgrimage town: All main roads lead to the cathedral; only tiny lanes, hidden alleys, and twisting "wynds" (rhymes with "minds") such as this one connect the main east-west streets.

• *The wynd pops you out onto North Street. Make like a pilgrim and head left toward the cathedral—look for its ruined facade in the distance. We'll eventually end up at the cathedral, but we'll take a few interesting detours along the way.*

Walk about 100 yards to the small cinema, from where you'll see the church tower with the red clock face (our next stop). It's on the corner of North Street and Butts Wynd. For some reason, this street sign often goes missing.

St. Salvator's College

The tower with the red clock marks the entrance to St. Salvator's College. If you're a student, be careful not to stand on the **initials PH** in the pink cobbles in front of the gate. These mark the spot where St. Andrews alum and professor Patrick Hamilton—the Scottish Reformation's most famous martyr—was burned at the stake. According to student legend, as he suffered in the flames, Hamilton threatened that any students who stood on this spot would fail their exams. (And you thought you had dramatic professors.)

Now enter the grounds by walking through the arch under the tower. (If the entrance is closed, you can go halfway down Butts Wynd and enter, or at least look, through the gate to the green square.) This grassy square, known to  students as **Sally's Quad,** is the heart of the university. As most of the university's classrooms, offices, and libraries are spread out across the medieval town, this quad is the one focal point for student gatherings. It's where graduation is held every July, where the free-for-all food fight of Raisin Monday takes place in November (see sidebar on page 210), and where almost the entire student body gathered to celebrate the wedding day of their famous alumni couple—Prince William and Kate—complete with military flybys.

On the outside wall of St. Salvator's Chapel, under the arcade, are **display cases** holding notices and university information; if you're here in spring, you might see students nervously clustered here, looking to see if they've passed their exams.

Go through the simple wooden door and into the **chapel.** Dating from 1450, this is the town's most beautiful medieval church. It's a Gothic gem, with a wooden ceiling, 19th-century stained glass, a glorious organ, and what's supposedly the pulpit of reformer John Knox.

Stroll around Sally's Quad counterclockwise. If you're feeling curious, push a few doors (some seemingly off-limits university buildings, many marked by blue doors, are actually open to the public). On the east (far) side, stop to check out the crazy faces on the heads above the second-floor windows. Find the **university's shield** over the door marked *School 6.* The diamonds are from the coat of arms of the bishop who issued the first university charter in 1411; the crescent moon is a shout-out to Pope Benedict XIII, who gave the OK in 1413 to found the university (his given name was

The Scottish Reformation

It's easy to forget that during the 16th-century English Reformation—when King Henry VIII split with the Vatican and formed the Anglican Church (so he could get an officially recognized divorce)—Scotland was still its own independent nation. Like much of northern Europe, Scotland eventually chose a Protestant path, but it was more gradual and grassroots than Henry VIII's top-down, destroy-the-abbeys approach. While the English Reformation resulted in the Church of England (a.k.a. the Anglican Church, called "Episcopal" outside of England), with the monarch at its head, the Scottish Reformation created the Church of Scotland, which had groups of elected leaders (called "presbyteries" in church jargon).

One of the leaders of the Scottish Reformation was John Knox (1514-1572), who studied under the great Swiss reformer John Calvin. Returning to Scotland, Knox hopped from pulpit to pulpit, and his feverish sermons incited riots of "born-again" iconoclasts who dismantled or destroyed Catholic churches and abbeys (including St. Andrew's Cathedral). Knox's newly minted Church of Scotland gradually spread from the Lowlands to the Highlands. The southern and eastern part of Scotland, around St. Andrews—just across the North Sea from the Protestant countries of northern Europe—embraced the Church of Scotland long before the more remote and Catholic-oriented part of the country to the north and west. Today about 40 percent of Scots claim affiliation with the Church of Scotland, compared with 20 percent who are Catholic (still mostly in the western Highlands). Glasgow and western Scotland are more Catholic partly because of the Irish immigrants who settled there after fleeing the potato famine in the 1840s.

Peter de Luna); the lion is from the Scottish coat of arms; and the X-shaped cross is a stylized version of the Scottish flag (a.k.a. St. Andrew's Cross). On the next building to the left, facing the chapel, is St. Andrew himself (above door of building labeled *Upper & Lower College Halls*).

• *Exit the square at the west end—opposite the university shield—and turn right into Butts Wynd. (If the gate's closed, backtrack out the main gate and hang a right into Butts Wynd.) When the alley ends, you're back at The Scores. Across the street and a few steps to the right is the...*

Museum of the University of St. Andrews (MUSA)

This free museum is worth a quick stop. The first room has some well-explained medieval artifacts. Find the copy of the earliest-known map of the town, made in 1580—back when the town walls led directly to the countryside and the cathedral was intact. Notice that the street plan within the town walls has remained the same—but no golf course. The next room has some exhibits on student life, including the "silver arrow competition" (which determines the best archer on campus from year to year) and several of the traditions explained in the "Student Life in St. Andrews" sidebar. The next room displays scientific equipment, great books tied to the school, and an exhibit on the Scottish Reformation. The final room has special exhibits. For a great view of the West Sands, climb to the rooftop terrace.

Cost and Hours: Free; April-Oct Mon-Sat 10:00-17:00, Sun 12:00-16:00; Nov-March Thu-Sun 12:00-16:00, closed Mon-Wed; 7 The Scores, tel. 01334/461-660, www.st-andrews.ac.uk/musa.

• *Leaving the museum, walk left toward the castle. The turreted stone buildings along here (including one fine example next door to the museum) are built in the Neo-Gothic Scottish Baronial style, and most are academic departments. About 100 yards farther along, the grand building on the right is St. Salvator's Hall, the most prestigious of the university residences and former dorm of Prince William.*

Just past St. Salvator's Hall on the left are the remains of...

St. Andrews Castle

Overlooking the sea, the castle is an evocative empty shell—another casualty of the Scottish Reformation. With a small museum and good descriptions peppered around a mostly empty shell, it

offers a quick king-of-the-castle experience in a striking setting.

Cost and Hours: £5.50, £8 combo-ticket includes cathedral exhibit, daily April-Sept 9:30-17:30, Oct-March 10:00-16:00, tel. 01334/477-196, www. historic-scotland.gov.uk.

Visiting the Castle: Your visit starts with a colorful, kid-friendly exhibit about the history of the castle. Built by a bishop to entertain visiting diplomats in the late 12th century, the castle was home to the powerful bishops, archbishops, and cardinals of St. Andrews. In 1546, the cardinal burned a Protestant preacher at the stake in front of the castle. In retribution, Protestant reformers took the castle and killed the cardinal. In 1547, the French came to attack the castle on behalf of their Catholic ally, Mary, Queen of Scots. During the ensuing siege, a young Protestant refugee named John Knox was captured and sent to France to row on a galley ship. Eventually he traveled to Switzerland and met the Swiss Protestant ringleader, John Calvin. Knox brought Calvin's ideas back home and became Scotland's greatest reformer.

Next, head outside to explore. The most interesting parts are underground: the "bottle dungeon," where prisoners were sent,

Student Life in St. Andrews

St. Andrews is first and foremost a university town. Scotland's most prestigious university, founded in 1411, is the third-oldest in the English-speaking world after Oxford and Cambridge. While U. of St. A. is sometimes called "England's northernmost university" due to the high concentration of English students—as numerous as the Scottish ones—a quarter of the 6,000 undergrads and 1,000 grad students hail from overseas.

Some Scots resent the preponderance of upper-crust English students (disparagingly dubbed "Yahs" for the snooty way they say "yes"). However, these southerners pay the bills—they are on the hook for tuition, unlike Scots and most EU citizens. And no one seems to mind that the school's most famous graduates, Prince William and Kate Middleton (class of '05), are the definition of upper-class. Soon after "Wills" started studying art history here, the number of female art history majors skyrocketed. (He later switched to geography.)

As with any venerable university, St. Andrews has its share of quirky customs. Most students own traditional red academic "gowns" (woolen robes) to wear on special occasions, such as graduation. In medieval times, however, they were the daily uniform—supposedly so students could be easily identified in brothels and pubs. (In a leap of faith, divinity students—apparently beyond temptation—wear black.) The way the robe is worn indicates the student's status: First-year students (called "bejants") wear them normally, on the shoulders; second-years ("semi-bejants") wear them slightly off the shoulders; third-years ("tertians") wear them off one shoulder (right for "scientists," left for "artists"); and fourth-years ("magistrands") wear them off both shoulders.

The best time to see these robes is during the Pier Walk on Sundays during the university term. After church services (around noon), gown-clad students parade out to the end of the lonesome pier beyond the cathedral ruins. The tradition dates so far back that no one's sure how it started (probably to bid farewell to a visiting dignitary). Today, students just enjoy being a part of the visual spectacle of a long line of red robes flapping in the North Sea wind.

Another age-old custom is a social-mentoring system in which underclassmen choose an "academic family." On Raisin Monday, in mid-November, students give treats to their upperclassmen "parents"—traditionally raisins, but these days more often indulgences like wine and lingerie. Then the "parents" dress up their "children" in outrageous costumes and parade them through town. The underclassmen are obliged to carry around "receipts" for their gifts—written on unlikely or unwieldy objects like plastic dinosaurs, microwave ovens, or even refrigerators—and to sing the school song in Latin on demand. This oddball scenario invariably degenerates into a free-for-all food fight on Sally's Quad.

never to return (peer down into it in the Sea Tower); and the tight "mine" and even tighter "counter-mine" tunnels (follow the signs, crawling is required to reach it all; go in as far as your claustrophobia allows). This shows how the besieging pro-Catholic Scottish government of the day dug a mine to take (or "undermine") the castle—but were followed at every turn by the Protestant counter-miners.

Nearby: Just below the castle is a small beach called the **Castle Sands,** where university students take a traditional and chilly morning dip on May 1. Supposedly, doing this May Day swim is the only way to reverse the curse of having stepped on Patrick Hamilton's initials (explained earlier).

• *Leaving the castle, turn left and continue along the bluff on The Scores, which soon becomes a pedestrian lane leading directly to the gate to the cathedral graveyard. Enter it to stand amid the tombstone-strewn ruins of...*

▲St. Andrew's Cathedral

Between the Great Schism and the Reformation (roughly the 14th-16th centuries), St. Andrews was the ecclesiastical capital of Scotland—and this was its showpiece church. Today the site features the remains of the cathedral and cloister (with walls and spires pecked away by centuries of scavengers), a graveyard, and a small exhibit and climbable tower.

Cost and Hours: Cathedral ruins-free, exhibit and tower-£4.50, £8 combo-ticket includes castle; daily April-Sept 9:30-17:30, Oct-March 10:00-16:00, tel. 01334/472-563, www.historic-scotland.gov.uk.

Background: It was the relics of the Apostle Andrew that first put this town on the map and gave it its name. There are numerous legends associated with the relics. According to one version, in the fourth century, St. Rule was directed in a dream to bring the relics northward from Constantinople. When the ship wrecked offshore from here, it was clear that this was a sacred place. Andrew's bones (an upper arm, a kneecap, some fingers, and a tooth) were kept on this site, and starting in 1160, the cathedral was built and pilgrims began to arrive. Since St. Andrew had a direct connection to Jesus, his relics were believed to possess special properties, making them worthy of pilgrimages on par with St. James' relics in Santiago de Compostela, Spain (of Camino de Santiago fame). St. Andrew became Scotland's patron saint; in fact, the white "X" on the blue Scottish flag evokes the diagonal cross on which St. Andrew was crucified (he chose this type of cross because he felt unworthy to die as Jesus had).

➔ Self-Guided Tour: You can stroll around the cathedral **ruins**—the best part of the complex—for free. First walk between

the two ruined but still towering ends of the church, which used to be the apse (at the sea end, where you entered) and the main entry (at the town end). Visually trace the gigantic footprint of the former church in the ground, including the bases of columns—like giant sawed-off tree trunks. Plaques identify where elements of the church once stood.

Looking at the one wall that's still standing, you can see the architectural changes that were made over the 150 years the cathedral was built—from the rounded, Romanesque windows at the front to the more highly decorated, pointed Gothic arches near the back. Mentally rebuild the church, and try to imagine it in its former majesty, when it played host to pilgrims from all over Europe.

The church wasn't destroyed all at once, like all those ruined abbeys in England (demolished in a huff by Henry VIII when he broke with the pope). Instead, because the Scottish Reformation was more gradual, this church was slowly picked apart over time. First just the decorations were removed from inside the cathedral. Then the roof was pulled down to make use of its lead. Without a roof, the cathedral fell further and further into disrepair, and was quarried by locals for its handy precut stones (which you'll still find in the walls of many old St. Andrews homes). The elements—a big storm in the 1270s and a fire in 1378—also contributed to the cathedral's demise.

The surrounding **graveyard,** dating from the post-Reformation Protestant era, is much more recent than the cathedral. In this golf-obsessed town, the game even infiltrates the cemeteries: Many notable golfers from St. Andrews are buried here (such as Young Tom—or "Tommy"—Morris, four-time British Open winner).

Go through the surviving wall into the former **cloister,** marked by a gigantic grassy square in the center. You can still see the cleats up on the wall, which once supported beams. Imagine the cloister back in its heyday, its passages filled with strolling monks.

At the end of the cloister is a small **exhibit** (entry fee required), with a relatively dull collection of old tombs and other carved-stone relics that have been unearthed on this site. Your ticket also includes entry to the surviving **tower of St. Rule's Church** (the rectangular tower beyond the cathedral ruins that was built to hold the precious relics of St. Andrew about a thousand years ago). If you feel like hiking up the 157 very claustrophobic steps for the view over St. Andrews' rooftops, it's worth the price. Up top, you can also look out to sea to find the pier where students traditionally walk out in their robes (see sidebar on page 210).

• *Leave the cathedral grounds on the town side of the cathedral. Angling right, head down North Street. Just ahead, on the left, is the adorable...*

▲St. Andrews Preservation Trust Museum and Garden

Filling a 17th-century fishing family's house that was protected from developers, this museum is a time capsule of an earlier, simpler era. The house itself seems built for Smurfs, but once housed 20 family members. The ground floor features replicas of a grocer's shop and a "chemist's" (pharmacy), using original fittings from actual stores. Upstairs are temporary exhibits. Out back is a tranquil garden (dedicated to the memory of a beloved professor) with "great-grandma's washhouse," featuring an exhibit about the history of soap and washing. Lovingly presented, this quaint, humble house provides a nice contrast to the big-money scene around the golf course at the other end of town.

Cost and Hours: Free but donation requested, generally open early June-early Oct daily 14:00-17:00, closed off-season, 12 North Street, tel. 01334/477-629, www.standrewspreservationtrust.org.

• *From the museum, hang a left around the next corner to South Castle Street. Soon you'll reach...*

Market Street

At the top of Market Street—one of the most atmospheric old streets in town—look for the tiny white house on your left, with the cute curved staircase. What's that chase scene on the roof?

Now turn right down Market Street (which leads directly to the town's center, but we'll take a curvier route). Notice how the streets and even the buildings are smaller at this oldest end of town, as if the whole city is shrinking as the streets close in on the cathedral. Homeowners along Market Street are particularly proud of their address, and recently pooled their money to spiff up the cobbles and sidewalks.

Passing an antique bookstore on your right, take a left onto Baker Lane, a.k.a. Baxter Wynd. You'll pass a tiny and inviting public garden on your right before landing on South Street.

• Turn right and head down South Street. After 50 yards, cross the street and enter a gate marked by a cute gray facade and a university insignia.

St. Mary's College
This is the home of the university's School of Divinity (theology). If the gate's open, find the peaceful quad, with its gnarled tree that was purportedly planted by Mary, Queen of Scots. To get a feel of student life from centuries past, try poking your nose into one of the old classrooms.

• Back on South Street, continue to your left. Some of the plainest buildings on this stretch of the street have the most interesting history—several of them were built to fund the Crusades. Turn right on Church Street. You can end this walk at charming Church Square—perhaps while enjoying a decadent pastry from the recommended Fisher and Donaldson bakery (closed Sun).

But if you want to do more exploring, continue a few more yards down Church Street to Market Street, and turn right to find the TI, grocery stores, and the recommended Luvians Bottle Shop (whisky).

Golfing in St. Andrews

St. Andrews is the Cooperstown of golf. While St. Andrews lays claim to founding the sport (the first record of golf being played

here was in 1553), nobody knows exactly where and when people first hit a ball with a stick for fun. In the Middle Ages, St. Andrews traded with the Dutch; some historians believe they picked up a golf-like Dutch game on ice, and translated it to the bonnie rolling hills of Scotland's east coast. Since the grassy beachfront strip just outside St. Andrews was too poor to support crops, it was used for playing the game—and, centuries later, it still is. Why do golf courses have 18 holes? Because that's how many fit at the Old Course in St. Andrews, golf's single most famous site. While you putt-er around the course, keep in mind this favorite Scottish say-it-aloud joke: "Balls," said the queen. "If I had two, I'd be king." The king laughed—he had to.

The Old Course
The Old Course hosts the British Open every five years (next in 2021). At other times it's open to the public for golfing. The famous Royal and Ancient Golf Club (R&A) doesn't actually own the course, which is public and managed by the St. Andrews Links

Trust. Drop by their clubhouse, overlooking the beach near the Old Course (open long hours daily, www.standrews.com). They have a well-stocked shop, a restaurant, and a rooftop garden with nice views over the Old Course.

Teeing Off at the Old Course: Playing at golf's pinnacle course is pricey (£170/person, less off-season), but open to the public—subject to lottery drawings for tee times and reserved spots by club members. You can play the Old Course only if you have a handicap of 24 (men) or 36 (women and juniors) or better; bring along your certificate or card. If you don't know your handicap—or don't know what "handicap" means—then you're not good enough to play here (they want to keep the game moving). If you play, you'll do nine holes out, then nine more back in—however, all but four share the same greens.

Reserving a Tee Time: To ensure a specific tee time at the Old Course, you'll have to reserve a year ahead. You can fill out the form at www.standrews.com during a brief window between late August and mid-September, for tee times the following year. By late October, they'll confirm your date. Otherwise, some tee times are determined each day by a lottery called the "daily ballot." You can put your name in for this—on their website, in person, or by calling 01334/466-666—by 14:00 two days before (2 players minimum, 4 players max). They post the results online at 16:00. Note that no advance reservations are taken on Saturdays or in September, and the courses are closed on Sundays—which is traditionally the day reserved for townspeople to stroll.

Singleton Strategies: Single golfers aren't eligible to reserve or ballot. If you're golfing solo, you could try to team up with someone (try asking your B&B for tips). Or there's a Hail-Mary, last-minute strategy for the very determined: Each day, a few single golfers fill gaps in the schedule on a first-come, first-served basis. You have to show up in person at the starter's hut (with the small practice putting green, in front of the R&A). The starter generally arrives at 6:00 (yes, that's in the morning); die-hard golfers start lining up several hours before (prepared to doze in the drizzle). This is a very long shot: You may get lucky...or you may get up early for nothing. The best advice is to swing by the starter's hut the day before, when they should have a sense of how likely a spot is to open up, and can advise you on how early to arrive.

Other Courses: The trust manages six other courses (including two right next to the Old Course—the New Course and the Jubilee Course), plus the modern cliff-top Castle Course just outside the city. These are cheaper, and it's much easier to get a tee time (£75 for New and Jubilee, £120 for Castle Course, £15-45 for others). It's usually possible to get a tee time for the same day or next day (if you want a guaranteed reservation, make it at least 2 weeks in advance). The Castle Course has great views overlooking the town, but even more wind to blow your ball around.

Club Rental: You can rent decent-quality clubs around town for about £30. The **Auchterlonies** shop has a good reputation (on Golf Place—a few doors down from the R&A, tel. 01334/473-253, www.auchterlonies.com); you can also rent clubs from the Old Course links clubhouse for a few pounds more.

▲The Himalayas

Named for its dramatically hilly terrain, "The Himalayas" is basically a very classy (but still relaxed) game of minigolf. Techni-

cally the "Ladies' Putting Green," this cute little patch of undulating grass presents the perfect opportunity for nongolfers (female or male) to say they've played the links at St. Andrews—for less than the cost of a Coke. It's remarkable how the contour of the land can present even more challenging obstacles than the tunnels, gates, and distractions of a corny miniature golf course back home. Flat shoes are required (no high heels). You'll see it on the left as you walk toward the clubhouse from the R&A.

Cost and Hours: £3 for 18 holes. The putting green is open to nonmembers (tourists like you) Mon-Tue and Fri 10:30-16:45, Wed 10:30-12:00 & 16:00-18:30, Thu 11:00-18:30, Sat 10:30-18:00, and Sun 12:00-18:00, tel. 01334/475-196.

British Golf Museum

This exhibit, which started as a small collection in the R&A across the street, is the best place in Britain to learn about the Scots' favorite sport. It's fascinating for golf lovers.

Cost and Hours: £7, includes informative book about the history of golf; April-Oct Mon-Sat 9:30-17:00, Sun 10:00-17:00; Nov-March daily 10:00-16:00; last entry 45 minutes before closing; café upstairs; Bruce Embankment, in the blocky modern building squatting behind the R&A by the Old Course, tel. 01334/460-046, www.britishgolfmuseum.co.uk.

Visiting the Museum: The compact, one-way exhibit reverently presents a meticulous survey of the game's history. At the entrance, a constant two-hour loop film shows highlights of the British Open from 1923 to the present. From here, follow the counterclockwise route to learn about the evolution of golf—

Sleep Code

Abbreviations   (£1=about $1.60, country code: 44)
S=Single, D=Double/Twin, T=Triple, Q=Quad, b=bathroom
Price Rankings
   $$ Higher Priced—Most rooms £70 or more
   $ Lower Priced—Most rooms less than £70
Unless otherwise noted, credit cards are accepted, breakfast
is included, and free Wi-Fi and/or a guest computer is gener-
ally available. Prices change; verify current rates online or by
email. For the best prices, always book directly with the hotel.

---

from the monarchs who loved and hated golf (including the king
who outlawed it because it was distracting men from church and
archery practice), to Tom Morris and Bobby Jones, all the way up
to the "Golden Bear" and a randy Tiger. Along the way, you'll see
plenty of old clubs, balls, medals, and trophies, and learn about
how the earliest "feathery" balls and wooden clubs were made.
Touchscreens invite you to learn more, and you'll also see a "hall of
fame" with items donated by today's biggest golfers. Finally you'll
have a chance to dress up in some old-school golfing duds and try
out some of that antique equipment for yourself.

Sleeping in St. Andrews

Owing partly to the high-roller golf tourists flowing through the
town, St. Andrews' accommodations are quite expensive. I've list-
ed high-season rates (June-Sept); most of these places are cheaper
off-season. During graduation week in June, hotels often require
a four-night stay and book up quickly. All of the ones I've listed,
except the hostel and the dorms, are on the streets called Murray
Park and Murray Place, between North Street and The Scores in
the old town. If you need to find a room on the fly, head for this
same neighborhood, which has far more options than just the ones
I've listed below.

   $$ Hoppity House is a bright and contemporary place, with
attention to detail and built-in furniture that makes good use of
space. You may find a stuffed namesake bunny or two hiding out
among its six rooms. Helpful Gordon and Heather are fun to talk
with and generous with travel tips (Sb-£45-65, Db-£75-90, deluxe
Db-£90-110, price depends on size, family room, fridges in rooms,
4 Murray Park, tel. 01334/461-116, mobile 07701-099-100, www.
hoppityhouse.co.uk, enquiries@hoppityhouse.co.uk).

   $$ Cameron House has five old-fashioned, paisley, mas-
culine-feeling rooms around a beautiful stained-glass atrium (S/

Sb-£48, Db-£96, 11 Murray Park, tel. 01334/472-306, www. cameronhouse-sta.co.uk, info@cameronhouse-sta.co.uk, Donna).

$$ **Montague Guest House** has richly furnished public spaces—with a cozy, leather-couches lounge—and eight straight-forward rooms (Sb-£60, Db-£80-100 depending on size, 21 Murray Park, tel. 01334/479-287, www.montaguehouse.com, info@montagueguesthouse.com, Andrew and Gillian).

$$ **Doune Guest House** is golfer-friendly, with seven comfortable rooms (S-£49, Db-£98, cash only, 5 Murray Place, tel. 01334/475-195, www.dounehouse.com, info@dounehouse.com).

$$ **Lorimer House** has five comfortable, tastefully decorated rooms, including one on the ground floor (Db-£100, deluxe Db-£120, 19 Murray Park, tel. 01334/476-599, www.lorimerhouse.com, info@lorimerhouse.com, Mick and Chris Cordner).

$$ **Glenderran Guest House** offers five plush rooms (including two true singles) and a few nice breakfast extras (Sb-£60, Db-£115, same-day laundry-£10/load, 9 Murray Park, tel. 01334/477-951, www.glenderran.com, info@glenderran.com, Ray and Maggie).

Hostel: $ **St. Andrews Tourist Hostel** has 44 beds in colorful 4- to 8-bed rooms about a block from the base of Market Street. The high-ceilinged lounge is a comfy place for a break, and the friendly staff is happy to recommend their favorite pubs (bunk in dorm room-£20, St. Mary's Place, tel. 01334/479-911, www. standrewshostel.com).

UNIVERSITY ACCOMMODATIONS

In the summer (early June-Aug), some of the University of St. Andrews' student-housing buildings are tidied up and rented out to tourists. I've listed the most convenient options below (website for both: www.discoverstandrews.com; pay when reserving). Both of these include breakfast and Wi-Fi. Because true single rooms are rare in St. Andrews' B&Bs, these dorms are a good option for solo travelers.

$$ **Agnes Blackadder Hall** has double beds and private bathrooms; it's more comfortable, but also more expensive and less central (Sb-£55, Db-£75, family Qb-£109, North Haugh, tel. 01334/467-000, agnes.blackadder@st-andrews.ac.uk).

$ **McIntosh Hall** is cheaper and more central, but it only has twin beds and shared bathrooms (S-£40, D-£65, Abbotsford Crescent, tel. 01334/467-035, mchall@st-andrews.ac.uk).

Eating in St. Andrews

Forgan's is tempting and popular, tucked back in a huge space behind Market Street in what feels like a former warehouse. It's done up country-kitschy, with a rollicking energy, and serves up hearty food (£9-13 meals, Mon-Fri 12:00-22:00, Sat-Sun 10:00-22:00, 110 Market Street, tel. 01334/466-973, www.forgansstandrews. co.uk). On Friday and Saturday nights after 22:30, they have live *ceilidh* (traditional Scottish) music, and everyone joins in the dancing; consider reserving a booth for a late dinner, then stick around for the show.

Playfair's, a restaurant and steakhouse downstairs in the Ardgowan Hotel between the B&B neighborhood and the Old Course, has a cozy/classy interior and outdoor seating at rustic tables set just below the busy street (£6-8 lunches, £10-14 dinners, daily 12:00-late, off-season weekdays open for dinner only, 2 Playfair Terrace on North Street, tel. 01334/472-970).

The Glass House serves pizza, pasta, and salads in a two-story glass building with an open-style layout (£8 lunches, £9-12 dinners, early-bird specials, daily 12:00-22:00, second-floor outdoor patio, near the castle on 80 North Street, tel. 01334/473-673). The same company operates a couple other restaurants in town, with similar hours, prices, and early-bird deals, but each with its own personality: **The Grill House** offers Mexican-style food in a vibrantly colored space (St. Mary's Place, tel. 01334/470-500), while **The Doll's House** serves up cuisine with a French flair; its sidewalk seating out front is across from Holy Trinity Church (3 Church Square, tel. 01334/477-422). Comparing their early-dinner specials may help you choose (http://dollshousestandrews.co.uk).

The Seafood Restaurant is St. Andrews' favorite splurge. Situated in a modern glassy building overlooking the beach near the Old Course, it's like dining in an aquarium. The place serves locally caught seafood to a room full of tables that wrap around the busy open kitchen. Dinner reservations are recommended; at both lunch and dinner, you'll choose from a set-price menu—no à la carte (lunch: £22/2 courses, £28/3 courses; dinner: £40/2 courses, £50/3 courses; daily 12:00-14:30 & 18:00-21:30, The Scores, tel. 01334/479-475, www.theseafoodrestaurant.com).

On Market Street: In the area around the TI, you'll find a concentration of good restaurants—pubs, grill houses, coffee shops, Asian food, fish-and-chips (see later), and more...take your pick. Also on Market Street, you can stock up for a picnic at **Tesco** or **Sainsbury's Local.**

Fish-and-Chips: **Cromars** is a local favorite for takeaway fish-and-chips, centrally located on Market Street near the TI. At the counter, you can order yours to go, or—in good weather—enjoy it at the sidewalk tables (£6-10 fish-and-chips and burgers); farther in is a small sit-down restaurant with slightly higher prices and more choices (£9-14 main dishes; both open daily 10:30 until late, at the corner of Union and Market, tel. 01334/475-555). **Tailend,** owned by the same people, is a few blocks up Market Street. They also have a takeaway counter up front (£6-8 fish-and-chips) and a nicer sit-down area in the back (£12-15 main courses, £8-10 burgers, daily 11:30-late, 130 Market Street, tel. 01334/474-070).

Pubs: There's no shortage in this college town. These aren't "gastropubs," but they all serve straightforward pub fare (all open long hours daily). **Aikmans,** run by Barbara and Malcolm (two graduates from the university who couldn't bring themselves to leave), features a cozy wood-table ambience, a focus on ales, live music (traditional Scottish music occasionally, other live music Fri-Sat), and simple soups, sandwiches, and snacks (£3-6 basic grub, 32 Bell Street, tel. 01334/477-425). **The Central,** right along Market Street, is a St. Andrews standby, with old lamps and lots of brass (£5-7 sandwiches, £9-13 pub grub, 77 Market Street, tel. 01334/478-296). **Greyfriars,** with forgettable food, is in a classy, modern hotel near the Murray Park B&Bs (£5-6 light meals, £8-13 main dishes, 129 North Street, tel. 01334/474-906).

Coffee: **Taste,** a little café just across the street from the B&B neighborhood, has the best coffee in town and a laid-back, borderline-funky ambience that feels like a big-city coffeehouse back home. It also serves cakes and light food (daily 7:00-22:00, 148 North Street, tel. 01334/477-959).

Whisky Shop: **Luvians Bottle Shop**—run by three brothers (**Lu**igi, **Vi**ncenzo, and **An**tonio)—is a friendly place to talk, taste, and purchase whisky. Distilleries bottle unique single-cask vintages exclusively for this shop to celebrate the British Open every five years (ask about the 21-year-old Springbank they received in 2015 to commemorate the tournament). With nearly 50 bottles open for tastings, a map of Scotland's whisky regions, and helpful team members, this is a handy spot to learn about whisky. They also sell a wide range of microbrews and offer guided tastings, such as the "Grand Tour" of Scottish whiskies for £15 per person (must arrange in advance, see website for details; daily 10:00-22:00 except Sun opens at 12:30, 66 Market Street, tel. 01334/477-752, www.luvians.com).

Cheese: **I.J. Mellis Cheesemonger,** the excellent Edinburgh cheese shop with a delectable array of Scottish, English, and international cheeses, has a branch on South Street (Mon-Sat 9:00-19:00, Sun 10:00-17:00, 149 South Street, tel. 01334/471-410).

Dessert: **Fisher and Donaldson** is beloved for its rich, affordable pastries and chocolates. Listen as the straw-hatted bakers chat with their regular customers, then try their Coffee Tower—like a giant cream puff filled with rich, lightly coffee-flavored cream—or their number-one seller, the fudge doughnut (Mon-Fri 6:00-17:15, Sat until 17:00, closed Sun, just around the corner from the TI at 13 Church Street, tel. 01334/472-201). **B. Jannettas,** which has been around for more than a century, features a creative range of 52 tasty ice-cream flavors (daily 9:00-22:00, 31 South Street, tel. 01334/473-285, www.jannettas.co.uk).

St. Andrews Connections

Trains don't go into St. Andrews—instead, use the Leuchars station (5 miles from St. Andrews, connected by buses coordinated to meet most trains, 2-4/hour, see "Arrival in St. Andrews" on page 204). The TI has useful train schedules, which also list bus departure times from St. Andrews.

From Leuchars by Train to: Edinburgh (1-2/hour, 1 hour), **Glasgow** (2/hour, 2 hours, transfer in Haymarket), **Inverness** (roughly hourly, 3.25-4 hours, 1-2 changes). Trains run less frequently on Sundays. Train info: Tel. 0345-748-4950, www.nationalrail.co.uk. To reach **Dundee,** take bus #99 from St. Andrews bus station near the base of Market Street (every 10 minutes, 30 minutes).

Near St. Andrews

Two starkly different destinations are within a half-hour's drive of St. Andrews, in opposite directions. To the north is the up-and-coming city of Dundee, with a pair of excellent museums (offering more-interesting-than-they-sound, in-depth exhibits on the local jute industry and Antarctic exploration); just beyond is Glamis Castle, the childhood home of Queen Elizabeth's mother, known as the Queen Mother. And to the south is the charming string of seaside villages called the East Neuk. Either one makes a good half-day side-trip, or you can squeeze them in on your way between St. Andrews and other destinations.

DUNDEE

The once-prosperous, then decrepit, and now steadily rejuvenating city of Dundee (Scotland's fourth-largest, with about 150,000 people) sits at the mouth of the River Tay. In its heyday, Dundee was known for the "Three J's": jute (turning the raw fiber into rope, burlap, and canvas), jam (importing that orange marmalade that's on every B&B breakfast table), and journalism (as the home of the respected publishing company of D. C. Thomson & Co., respon-

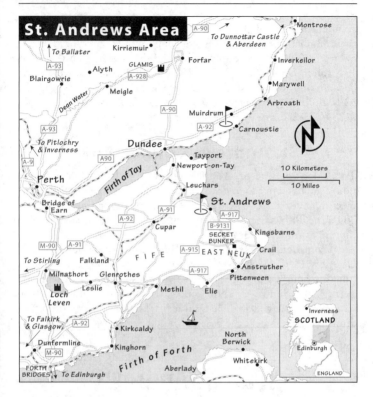

St. Andrews Area

To Ballater · Kirriemuir · Forfar · To Dunnottar Castle & Aberdeen · Montrose · Inverkeilor · Marywell · Arbroath · Blairgowrie · Alyth · GLAMIS · A-93 · A-928 · Meigle · Dean Water · A-90 · Muirdrum · A-92 · Carnoustie · To Pitlochry & Inverness · A-93 · Dundee · Tayport · Newport-on-Tay · Firth of Tay · A90 · Perth · Leuchars · 10 Kilometers · 10 Miles · Bridge of Earn · St. Andrews · A-91 · A-917 · A-92 · Cupar · B-9131 · SECRET BUNKER · Kingsbarns · M-90 · A-91 · A-915 · EAST NEUK · Crail · To Stirling · Falkland · FIFE · Anstruther · Milnathort · Glenrothes · A-917 · Pittenweem · Leslie · Methil · Elie · Loch Leven · To Falkirk & Glasgow · A-92 · Kirkcaldy · North Berwick · Dunfermline · Kinghorn · Whitekirk · M-90 · Firth of Forth · FORTH BRIDGES · To Edinburgh · Aberlady · Inverness · SCOTLAND · Edinburgh · ENGLAND

sible for the *Sunday Post*—and for creating many beloved Scottish cartoon characters).

But, like many Industrial Age British boomtowns, Dundee fell on hard times in the 20th century. Today Dundee is working to reinvent its downtown core and its waterfront. It's also remaking its economy, adding a fourth "J": joysticks. Rockstar Games' Dundee office was the birthplace of the wildly popular "Grand Theft Auto" computer game series. While the city still has a ways to go—for now, it merits only a quick stop for two great museums—it's clear that Dundee's trajectory is promising.

Getting There: Drivers can make a strategic strike at one or both of the city's museums, both of which have parking nearby. They're in different parts of town: Discovery Point, right along the waterfront, is well signed, while the Verdant Works Jute Museum is buried in a mostly deserted industrial area higher up in town (though it's marked with brown signs, it's more reliable to use GPS to find it). **Train** travelers find that Discovery Point is easy (it's right across the street from the train station), but the Verdant Works Jute Museum, just under a mile away, isn't well connected by public transit; walk or take a taxi from Discovery Point.

▲▲Discovery Point and the RRS *Discovery*

At the turn of the 20th century—long after the Age of Discovery—Antarctica was the world's last great mystery. With fervor matched

a half-century later in the Space Race, ambitious countries set out to learn more about the unexplored continent. This museum tells the story of the Royal Research Ship (RRS) *Discovery*, which was built in Dundee and set sail for Antarctica in 1901. It was one of the most successful scientific expeditions of its time.

This attraction, on Dundee's riverfront, has two parts: First, you'll tour a museum about the ship and the expeditions that it undertook. Then you'll head outside and explore the actual ship, restored to how it was in 1924.

Cost and Hours: £9, £15.50 combo-ticket with Verdant Works/Jute Museum; April-Oct Mon-Sat 10:00-18:00, Sun 11:00-18:00, closes one hour earlier off-season; Riverside Drive, tel. 01382/309-060, www.rrsdiscovery.com.

Visiting the Museum: While everything in the museum is well described, the ship itself has only a few brief informational plaques; consider renting the £3 audioguide.

Begin by touring the **museum** to better appreciate the ship and the role it played in navigation history. You'll learn how the ship was built and provisioned, and how the crew (led by Commander Robert Falcon Scott, who died a decade later in a race to the South Pole) planned and perilously executed their icy journey. The exhibit explains that when the ship set sail in 1901, less was known about Antarctica than was known about the moon when the first Apollo mission landed in 1969. A good 10-minute film helps provide historical context.

Head outside to the **ship** itself. You'll walk across the decks, then delve below to see the engine room, galley, mess deck, and living quarters. The photographic darkroom, drawing table, and vials for scientific samples illustrate the ship's mission: opening up a new continent to human understanding.

Nearby: You'll see a huge mess of construction surrounding the *Discovery*. They're building an £80 million branch of the **Victoria & Albert Museum** next door (due to open in 2018), along with other improvements.

▲Verdant Works and Scotland's Jute Museum

Hardworking, industrious Scotland has several fine museums about how things are made—and this is one of the best. Filling a for-

mer jute processing factory called Verdant Works, it's located in a run-down but gentrifying zone of brick factories. This museum explores every facet of the jute industry that put Dundee on the map. Especially worthwhile for those with a healthy interest in engineering, the well-presented museum accomplishes the remarkable task of making jute interesting even to those less mechanically inclined.

Cost and Hours: £9, £15.50 combo-ticket with Discovery Point; April-Oct Mon-Sat 10:00-18:00, Sun 11:00-18:00; shorter hours off-season; West Henderson's Wynd, tel. 01382/309-060, www.verdantworks.com.

Background: Starting in the 1830s, Dundee businessmen—who came to be known as "jute barons"—developed a local industry around processing the fiber of a plant called jute, which could be used to make rope, burlap sacks, sails, canvases, carpeting, and even clothing. In an age before plastics, versatile jute was a prized material...and virtually all of the world's supply came through Dundee. Great Britain's nautical expansion further boosted the industry: Dundee-made materials sailed to every corner of the earth. Coinciding with the Highland Clearances and the decline of traditional rural lifestyles, the jute boom lured many floundering farmers and peasants into urban factories. By century's end, Dundee's population had tripled.

As in other Industrial Age cities, Dundee's rapid changes created a sharply stratified society, with a tiny and obscenely wealthy upper class and a huge, desperately poor lower class. But before long, the jute industry fell victim to "outsourcing," a century before its time: By 1875, a jute factory opened in India (where the raw materials were harvested), and by 1900, more jute products were produced in Calcutta than in Dundee. The rise of plastics and other synthetic fibers in the 1970s drove the final nail into the industry's coffin; Dundee's last remaining jute factory closed in 1999.

Visiting the Museum: First watch the excellent, 15-minute *Juteopolis* film, which sets the stage for the museum and helps explain why you're spending your vacation learning about jute. Then head across the courtyard to the Works Office and follow the one-way route through the exhibit. The highlight is the "From Fibre to Fabric" exhibit in the machine hall, where you'll see the actual machinery used for each of the several steps required to turn this tropical fiber into practical products. On some days (most likely

Wed-Fri), volunteer docents are standing by to explain more and even to demonstrate some of the century-old equipment. Don't miss the upstairs section (access from outside, in the courtyard) about the social history of the city, showing different walks of life relating to the jute industry. The museum also recently opened the cavernous High Mill, with even more exhibits delving into different facets of the industry and a huge Boulton and Watt steam engine from 1801, still in working order.

Downtown Dundee

With a little time to spare, it's worth walking 10 minutes from Discovery Point to the town center. In front of the city's landmark Caird Hall concert venue (with the TI next door), you'll find a bustling, traffic-free people zone, with cafés, public tables, fountains, and a glitzy shopping mall. Find the life-sized statues of Desperate Dan and Minnie the Minx (Dundee-born cartoon characters who are as beloved among Scots as they are unknown to Americans). A quick walk here offers an inspiring peek into the Dundee of the future.

North of Dundee
▲Glamis Castle

A 20-minute drive north of Dundee (or 45 minutes north of St. Andrews) is the residence of the Earls of Strathmore—best known

as the childhood-home castle of the Queen Mother (a.k.a. Elizabeth Bowes-Lyon, 1900-2002). Glamis (pronounced "glahms") is a proper castle inside and out: You'll drive down a grand, tree-lined driveway to a majestic palace bristling with turrets and filled with elaborately decorated rooms that drip with history and blue-blood quirk. Coming here just seems the right way to pay respects to the Queen Mother, who gave birth to the longest-reigning monarch in British history and supported her husband, King George VI, as he rallied Britain through World War II (as depicted in *The King's Speech*). Their second daughter, Princess Margaret, was born right here at Glamis—the first royal baby born in Scotland in 300 years. The "Queen Mum" always had a deep affection for her home at Glamis, and always clad herself in a distinctive hue that she liked to call "Strathmore blue."

Cost and Hours: £11, April-Oct daily 10:00-17:30, closed Nov-March, last entry one hour before closing, tel. 01307/840-393, www.glamis-castle.co.uk.

Getting There: From Dundee, head north on the A-90 expressway (toward Aberdeen); the exit is well marked with brown *Glamis Castle* signs (also marked for *Kirriemuir*). From the exit, follow the A-928 seven miles to the castle.

Visiting the Castle: You can only visit the interior on a 50-minute guided tour. You'll see both grand state rooms and intimate quarters—including the private rooms of the Queen Mother, which her parents installed after she married the prince to ensure she'd keep coming home for visits. The tour is packed with fun insights into aristocratic eccentricities, from the paintings of one earl who simply adored his leather body armor (painted to resemble a sculpted Greek god), to a rare painting of Jesus wearing a hat. Glamis also loves to tout its title as the "most haunted castle in Scotland"—though the ghost tales your guide imparts are more silly than scary. (Even more suspect are boasts that Glamis inspired Shakespeare as the setting for *Macbeth*—a claim also made by Cawdor Castle.) After your tour, you can visit a few more exhibits and explore the grounds on your own—a handout suggests four walking routes.

THE EAST NEUK

On the lazy coastline meandering south from St. Andrews, the cute-as-a-pin East Neuk (pronounced "nook") is a collection of tidy fishing villages. While hardly earth-shattering, the East Neuk is

a pleasant detour if you've got the time. The villages of Crail and Pittenweem have their fans, but Anstruther is worth most of your attention. The East Neuk works best as a half-day side-trip (by either car or bus) from St. Andrews, though drivers can use it as a scenic detour between Edinburgh and St. Andrews.

Getting There: It's an easy **drive** from St. Andrews. For the scenic route, follow the A-917 south of town along the coast, past Crail, on the way to Anstruther and Pittenweem. For a shortcut directly to Anstruther, take the B-9131 across the peninsula (or return that way after driving the longer coastal route there). **Buses** connect St. Andrews to the East Neuk: Bus #95 goes hourly from St. Andrews to Crail and Anstruther (50 minutes to Anstruther, catch bus at St. Andrews bus station or from Church Street, around the corner from the TI). The hourly #X60 bus goes directly to Anstruther, then on to Edinburgh (25 minutes to Anstruther, 2.25 hours more to Edinburgh). Bus info: Tel. 0871-200-2233, www.travelinescotland.com.

▲Anstruther

Stretched out along its harbor, colorful Anstruther (AN-stru-ther; pronounced ENT-ster by locals) is the centerpiece of the East Neuk. The main parking lot and bus stop are both right on the harbor. Anstruther's handy **TI,** which offers lots of useful information for the entire East Neuk area, is located next door to the town's main sight, the Scottish Fisheries Museum (April-Oct Mon-Sat 10:00-17:00, Sun 11:00-16:00, closed Nov-March, tel. 01333/311-073). Stroll the harborfront to the end, detouring inland around the little cove (or crossing the causeway at low tide) to reach some colorful old houses, including one encrusted with seashells.

Anstruther's **Scottish Fisheries Museum** is true to its slogan: "We are bigger than you think!" The endearingly hokey exhibit sprawls through several harborfront buildings, painstakingly tracing the history of Scottish seafaring from primitive dugout dinghies to modern vessels. You'll learn the story of Scotland's "Zulu" fishing boats and walk through vast, boat-filled rooms. For a glimpse at humble fishing lifestyles, don't miss the Fisherman's Cottage, hiding upstairs from the courtyard (£8; April-Sept Mon-Sat 10:00-17:30, Sun 11:00-17:00; shorter hours off-season; last entry one hour before closing, tearoom, Harbourhead, tel. 01333/310-628, www.scotfishmuseum.org).

Eating in Anstruther: Anstruther's claim to fame is its fish-and-chips. Though there are several good chippies in town, the famous one is the **Anstruther Fish Bar,** facing the harbor just a block from the TI and Fisheries Museum (takeout or dine in for a few pounds more, open long hours daily, 42-44 Shore Street, tel. 01333/310-518).

Scotland's Secret Bunker

Among the rolling farm fields between St. Andrews and the East Neuk, a blink-and-you'll-miss-it stone farmhouse conceals a sprawling network of corridors: 24,000 square feet, 100 feet under the ground, protected by 10-foot-thick reinforced concrete walls. You'll climb down the stairs and hike through a long tunnel to explore a warren of Cold War-era control rooms, dormitories, and telecommunications centers, plus a chapel and the office of the Minister of State of Scotland (who would command the military in the event of an attack). You'll also watch black-and-white films that calmly explain to homeowners how to prepare for—and cope with—a nuclear attack.

The exhibit itself is overpriced and frustratingly hokey—a jumble of 1970s technology, scarcely explained other than by the melodramatic £2 audioguide. But for those interested in the Cold War, simply exploring this space is a powerful experience (and a somber contrast to the links and beaches of St. Andrews).

The most striking part of the experience is watching the 46-minute BBC-produced film *The War Game,* a harrowing dramatization of what would happen in the event of a nuclear attack. Its "Keep Calm and Carry On," pull-no-punches straightforwardness is a haunting reminder of an age when global nuclear holocaust seemed not only possible, but likely. (Produced in 1965, the film was immediately branded too disturbing to broadcast, and was not shown on the BBC for 20 years.)

Cost and Hours: £11, March-Oct daily 10:00-18:00, closed Nov-Feb, last entry one hour before closing, tel. 01333/310-301, www.secretbunker.co.uk.

Getting There: Head out of St. Andrews toward Crail, but just outside of town, turn off on the right toward *Dunino* and *Anstruther* (on the B-9131). Then follow brown *Secret Bunker* signs about six miles through farmland.

THE SCOTTISH HIGHLANDS

Filled with more natural and historical mystique than people, the Highlands are where Scottish dreams are set. Legends of Bonnie Prince Charlie linger around crumbling castles as tunes played by pipers in kilts swirl around tourists. Intrepid Munro baggers scale bald mountains, grizzled islanders man the drizzly ferry crossings, and midges make life miserable (bring bug spray). The Highlands are the most mountainous, least inhabited, and—for many—most scenic and romantic part of Scotland.

The Highlands are covered with mountains, lochs, and glens, scarcely leaving a flat patch of land for building a big city. Geographically, the Highlands are defined by the Highland Boundary Fault, which slashes 130 miles diagonally through the middle of Scotland just north of the big cities of the more densely populated "Central Belt" (Glasgow and Edinburgh).

This geographical and cultural fault line is clearly visible on maps, and you can even see it in the actual landscape—especially around Loch Lomond and the Trossachs, where the transition from rolling Lowland hills to bald Highland mountains is almost too-on-the-nose. Just beyond the fault, the Grampian Mountains curve across the middle of Scotland; beyond that, the Caledonian Canal links the east and west coasts (slicing diagonally through the Great Glen, another geological fault, from Oban to Inverness), with even more mountains to the north.

Though the Highlands' many "hills" are technically too short to be called "mountains," they do a convincing imitation. (Just don't say that to a Scot.) Scotland has 282 hills over 3,000 feet. A list of these was first compiled in 1891 by Sir Hugh Munro, and to this day the Scots still call their high hills "Munros." (Hills

Hiking the Highlands

Scotland is a hiker's paradise...as long as you bring rain gear. I've recommended a few hikes of varying degrees of difficulty throughout this book. Remember: Wear sturdy (ideally waterproof) shoes, and be prepared for any weather. For serious hikes, pick up good maps and get advice at local TIs or from a knowledgeable resident (such as your B&B host). A good resource for hiking route tips is www.walkhighlands.co.uk.

For a more in-depth experience, consider one of Scotland's famous multiday walks. These are the most popular:

West Highland Way: 95 miles, 5-10 days, Milngavie to Fort William by way of Loch Lomond, Glencoe, and Rannoch Moor

Great Glen Way: 79 miles, 5-6 days, Fort William to Inverness along the Caledonian Canal, Fort Augustus, and Loch Ness

John Muir Way: 134 miles, 9-10 days, newer route—from 2014—that runs coast to coast through the Central Belt of Scotland, from Helensburgh to Dunbar via Falkirk, the Firth of Forth, and Edinburgh

from 2,500-3,000 feet are known as "Corbetts," and those from 2,000-2,500 are "Grahams.") Avid hikers—called "Munro baggers"—love to tick these mini-mountains off their list. According to the Munro Society, more than 5,000 intrepid hikers can brag that they've climbed all of the Munros. (To get started, you'll find lots of good information at www.walkhighlands.co.uk/munros).

The Highlands occupy more than half of Scotland's area, but are populated by less than five percent of its people—a population density comparable to Russia's. Scotland's Hebrides Islands (among them Skye, Mull, Iona, and Staffa) are often included in the Highlands, simply because they share much of the same culture, clan history, and Celtic ties. (Orkney and Shetland, off the north coast of Scotland, are a world apart—they feel more Norwegian than Highlander.)

Inverness is the Highlands' de facto capital, and often claims to be the region's only city. (The east coast port city of Aberdeen—Scotland's third largest, and quadruple the size of Inverness—has its own Doric culture and dialect, and is usually considered its own animal.)

The Highlands are where you'll most likely see Gaelic—the old Celtic language that must legally accompany English on road signs. While few Highlanders actually speak Gaelic—and virtually no one speaks it as a first language—certain Gaelic words are used as a nod of respect to their heritage. *Fàilte* (welcome), *Slàinte mhath!* (cheers!—literally "good health"), and *tigh* (house—featured in many business names) are all common. If you're making friends in a Highland pub, ask your new mates to teach you some Gaelic words.

The Highlands are also the source of many Scottish superstitions, some of which persist in remote communities, where mischievous fairies and shape-shifting kelpies are still blamed for trouble. Many superstitions surround babies. New parents were gripped with a fear that their newborn could be replaced by a devilish imposter called a changeling. Well into the 20th century, a midwife called a "howdie" would oversee key rituals: Before a birth, doors and windows would be unlocked and mirrors would be covered. And the day of the week a baby is born was charged with significance ("Monday's child is fair of face, Tuesday's child is full of grace...").

Many American superstitions and expressions originated in Scotland (such as "black sheep," based on the idea that a black sheep was terrible luck for the flock). Just as a baseball player might refuse to shave during a winning streak, many perfectly modern Highlanders carry a sprig of white heather for good luck at their wedding (and are careful not to cross two knives at the dinner table). And let's not even start with the Loch Ness monster...

In the summer, the Highlands swarm with tourists...and midges. These miniature mosquitoes—like "no-see-ums"—are bloodthirsty and determined. They can be an annoyance from late May through September, depending on the weather. Hot sun or a stiff breeze blows the tiny buggers away, but they thrive in damp, shady areas. Locals suggest blowing or brushing them off, rather than swatting them—since killing them only seems to attract more (likely because of the smell of fresh blood). Scots say, "If you kill one midge, a million more will come to his funeral." Even if you don't usually travel with bug spray, consider bringing or buying some for a summer visit. Locals recommend Avon's Skin So Soft, which is effective against midges, but less potent than DEET-based bug repellants.

Keep an eye out for another Scottish animal: shaggy Highland

The Scottish Highlands

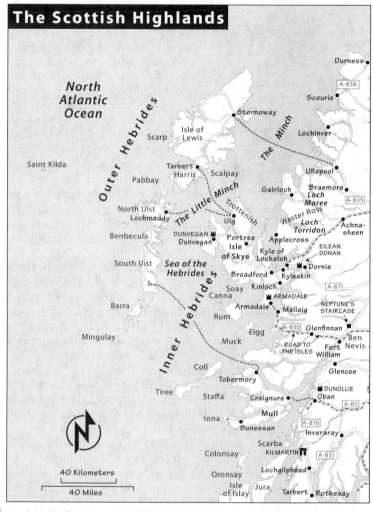

North Atlantic Ocean

Durness

A-838

Scourie

Lochinver

Ullapool

A-835

Stornoway

The Minch

Isle of Lewis

Scarp

Saint Kilda

Outer Hebrides

Tarbert
Harris   Scalpay

Pabbay

The Little Minch

Gairloch   Braemore
Loch
Maree
Wester Ross
Loch
Torridon   Achna-
sheen

North Uist
Lochmaddy

Trottenish

Uig

Applecross

EILEAN
DONAN

Benbecula

DUNVEGAN
Dunvegan   Portree
Isle
of Skye

Kyle of
Lochalsh   Dornie

Kyleakin

Broadford   A-87

South Uist

Sea of the
Hebrides

Soay   Kinloch

Canna   ARMADALE

Barra   Armadale   Mallaig   NEPTUNE'S
STAIRCASE

Rum

Mingulay   Muck   Eigg   A-830   Glenfinnan   Ben
Nevis

ROAD TO
THE ISLES   Fort
William

Inner Hebrides

Coll   Glencoe

Tobermory   DUNOLLIE

Tiree   Staffa   Craignure   Oban

Mull   A-85

Iona   A-816

Bunessan   Inveraray

Scarba
KILMARTIN   A-83

Colonsay   Lochgilphead

Oronsay
Isle
of Islay   Jura   Tarbert   Rothesay

40 Kilometers

40 Miles

cattle called "hairy coos." They're big and have impressive horns, but are best known for their adorable hair falling into their eyes (the hair protects them from Scotland's troublesome insects and unpredictable weather). Hairy coos graze on sparse vegetation that other animals ignore, and, with a heavy coat (rather than fat) to keep them insulated, they produce a lean meat that resembles venison. (Highland cattle meat is not commonly eaten, and

the relatively few hairy coos you'll see are kept around mostly as a national symbol.)

While the prickly, purple thistle is the official national flower, heather is the unofficial national shrub. This scrubby vegetation blankets much of the Highlands. It's usually a muddy reddish-brown color, but it bursts with purple flowers in the late summer; the less common bell heather blooms in July. Heather is one of the few things that will grow in the inhospitable terrain of a moor, and it can be used to make dye, rope, thatch, and even beer (look for Fraoch Heather Ale).

Highlanders are an outdoorsy bunch. For a fun look at local athletics, check whether your trip coincides with one of the Highland Games that enliven Highland communities in summer (see the sidebar on page 236). And keep an eye out for the unique Highland sport of shinty: a brutal, fast-paced version of field hockey played for keeps. Similar to Irish hurling, shinty is a full-contact sport that encourages tackling and fielding airborne balls, with players swinging their sticks (called camans) perilously through the air. The easiest place to see shinty is at Bught Park in Inverness (see page 297), but it's played across the Highlands.

PLANNING YOUR TIME

Here are three recommended Highland itineraries: two days, four days, or a full week or more. These plans assume you're driving, but can be done (with some modifications) by bus.

Two- to Three-Day Highland Highlights Blitz

This almost ridiculously fast-paced option squeezes the maximum Highland experience out of a few short days, and assumes you're starting from Glasgow or Edinburgh.

Day 1: In the morning, head up to the Highlands. (If coming from Edinburgh, consider a stop at Stirling Castle en route.) Drive along Loch Lomond and pause for lunch in Inveraray. Try to get to Oban in time for the day's last distillery tour (see hours on page 247 smart to book ahead). Have dinner in Oban.

Day 2: Get an early start from Oban and make a beeline for Glencoe, where you can visit the folk museum and enjoy a quick, scenic drive up the valley. Then drive to Fort William and follow the Caledonian Canal to Inverness, stopping at Fort Augustus to see the locks (and have a late lunch). Drive along Loch Ness to search for monsters, then wedge in a visit to the Culloden Battlefield (just outside Inverness) in the late afternoon. Finally, make good time southward on the A-9 back to Edinburgh (3 hours, arriving late).

Day 3: To extend this plan a bit, take your time getting to Inverness on Day 2 and spend the night there. Follow my self-guided Inverness Walk either that evening or the next morning. Leaving Inverness, tour Culloden Battlefield, visit Clava Cairns, then head south, stopping off at any place that appeals: The best options near the A-9 are Pitlochry and the Scottish Crannog Centre on Loch Tay, or take the more rugged eastern route to see the Speyside whisky area, Balmoral Castle and Ballater village, and Cairngorms mountain scenery. Or, if this is your best chance to see Stirling Castle or the Falkirk sights (Falkirk Wheel, Kelpies sculptures), fit them in on your way south.

Six-Day Highlands and Islands Loop

While you'll see the Highlands on the above itinerary, you'll whiz past the sights in a misty blur. This more reasonably paced plan is for those who want to slow down a bit.

Day 1: Follow the plan for Day 1, above, sleeping in Oban (2 nights).

Day 2: Do an all-day island-hopping tour from Oban, with visits to Mull, Iona, and (if you choose) Staffa.

Day 3: From Oban, head up to Glencoe for its museum and valley views. Consider lingering for a (brief) hike. Then zip up to Fort William and take the "Road to the Isles" west (pausing in Glenfinnan to see its viaduct) to Mallaig. Take the ferry over the sea to Skye, then drive to Portree to sleep (2 nights).

Day 4: Spend today enjoying the Isle of Skye. In the morning, do the Trotternish Peninsula loop; in the afternoon, take your pick of options (Talisker Distillery, Dunvegan Castle, Fairy Pools hike in the Cuillins).

Day 5: Leaving Portree, drive across the Skye Bridge for a photo-op pit stop at Eilean Donan Castle. The A-87 links you over to Loch Ness, which you'll follow to Inverness. If you get in early enough, consider touring Culloden Battlefield this evening. Sleep in Inverness (1 night).

Day 6: See the Day 3 options for my Highlands Highlights Blitz, earlier.

10-Day (or More) Highlands Explorer Extravaganza

Using the six-day Highlands and Islands Loop as a basis, pick and choose from these possible modifications (listed in order of where they'd fit into the itinerary):

• Add an overnight in **Glencoe** to make more time for hiking there.
• Leaving the Isle of Skye, drive north along **Wester Ross** (the scenic northwest coast). Go as far as Ullapool, then cut back down to Inverness, or...
• Take another day or two (after spending the night in Ullapool) to carry on northward through remote and rugged scenery to Scotland's **north coast.** Drive east along the coast all the way to John O'Groats; then either take the ferry from Scrabster across to Orkney, or shoot back down to Inverness on the A-9 (about 3 hours).
• Visit **Orkney** (2-night minimum). This can fit into the above plan after John O'Groats. Or, to cut back on the remote driving, simply zip up on the A-9 from Inverness (about 3 hours)— or fly up from Inverness, Edinburgh, or Aberdeen.
• On the way south from Inverness, follow the **Speyside whisky**

Scottish Highland Games

Throughout the summer, Highland communities host traditional festivals of local sport and culture. These Highland Games (sometimes called Highland Gatherings) combine the best elements of a track meet and a county fair. They range from huge and glitzy (such as Braemar's world-famous games, which the Queen attends, or the Cowal Highland Gathering, Scotland's biggest) to humble and small-town. Some of the more modern games come with loud pop music and corporate sponsorship, but still manage to celebrate the Highland spirit.

Most Highland Games take place between mid-June and late August (usually on Saturdays, but occasionally on weekdays). The games are typically a one-day affair, kicking off around noon and winding down in the late afternoon. At smaller games, you'll pay a nominal admission fee (typically around £5-7). Events are rain or shine (so bring layers) and take place in a big park ringed by a running track, with the heavy events and Highland dancing stage at opposite ends of the infield. Surrounding the whole scene are junk-food stands, a few test-your-skill carnival games, and local charities raising funds by selling hamburgers, fried sausage sandwiches, baked goods, and bottles of beer and Irn-Bru. The emcee's running commentary is a delightful opportunity to just sit back and enjoy a lilting Scottish accent.

The day's events typically kick off with a **pipe band** parading through town—often led by the local clan chieftain—and ending with a lap around the field. Then the sporting events begin.

In the **heavy events**—or feats of Highland strength—brawny, kilted athletes test their ability to hurl various objects of awkward shapes and sizes as far as possible. In the weight throw, competitors spin like ballerinas before releasing a 28- or 56-pound ball on a chain. The hammer throw involves a similar technique with a 26-pound ball on a long stick, and the stone put (with a 20- to 25-pound ball) has been adopted in American sports as the shot put. In the "weight over the bar" event, Highlanders swing a 56-pound weight over a horizontal bar that begins at 10 feet high and ends at closer to 15 feet. (That's like tossing a 5-year-old child over a double-decker bus.) And, of course, there's the caber toss: Pick up a giant log (the caber), get a running start, and release it end-over-end with enough force to (ideally) make the caber flip all the way over and land at the 12 o'clock position. (Most competitors wind up closer to 6.)

Meanwhile, the **track events** run circles around the muscle: the 90-meter dash, the 1,600-meter, and so on. The hill race adds a Scottish spin: Combine a several-mile footrace with the ascent of a nearby summit. The hill racers begin with a lap in the stadium before disappearing for about an hour. Keep an eye on nearby hillsides to pick out their colorful jerseys bobbing up and down a distant peak. This custom supposedly began when an 11th-century king staged a competition to select his personal letter carrier. After about an hour—when you've forgotten all about them—the hill racers start trickling back into the stadium to cross the finish line.

The **Highland dancing** is a highlight. Accompanied by a lone piper, the dancers (in groups of two to four) toe their routines

with intense concentration. Dancers remain always on the balls of their feet, requiring excellent balance and stamina. While some men participate, most competitors are female—from wee lassies barely out of nappies, all the way to poised professionals. Common steps are the Highland fling (in which the goal is to keep the feet as close as possible to one spot), sword dances (in which the dancers step gingerly over crossed swords on the stage), and a variety of national dances.

Other events further enliven the festivities. The pipe band periodically assembles to play a few tunes, often while marching around the track (giving the runners a break). Larger games may have a massing of multiple pipe bands, or bagpipe and drumming competitions. You may also see re-enactments of medieval battles, herd dog demonstrations, or dog shows (grooming and obedience). Haggis hurling—a relatively new event in which participants stand on a whisky barrel and attempt to throw a cooked haggis as far as possible—has caught on recently. And many small-town events end with the grand finale of a town-wide tug-of-war, during which everybody gets bruised, muddy, and hysterical.

If you're traveling to Scotland in the summer, before locking in your itinerary, check online schedules to see if you'll be near any Highland Games. Rather than target the big, famous gatherings, I make a point of visiting the smaller clan games. One helpful website—listing dates for most but not all of the games around Scotland—is www.shga.co.uk. For many travelers to Scotland, attending a Highland Games can be a trip-capping highlight. And, of course, many communities in the US and Canada also host their own Highland Games.

trail, cut through the **Cairngorms,** visit **Balmoral Castle,** and sleep in **Ballater.** Between Balmoral and Edinburgh, consider visiting Glamis Castle (Queen Mum's childhood home), Dundee (great industrial museums), or Culross (scenic firthside village).

• Add an overnight wherever you'd like to linger; the best options are the **Isle of Skye** (to allow more island explorations) or **Inverness** (to fit in more side-trips).

GETTING AROUND THE HIGHLANDS

By Car: The Highlands are made for joyriding. There are a lot of miles, but they're scenic, the roads are good, and the traffic is light. Drivers enjoy flexibility and plenty of tempting stopovers. Be careful, but don't be too timid about passing; otherwise, diesel fumes and large trucks might be your main memory of driving in Scotland. The farther north you go, the more away-from-it-all you'll feel, with few signs of civilization. Even on a sunny weekend, you can go miles without seeing another car. Don't wait too long to gas up—village gas stations are few and far between, and can close unexpectedly. Get used to single-lane roads: While you can make good time when they're empty (as they often are), don't let your guard down, and slow down on blind corners—you never know when an oncoming car (or a road-blocking sheep) is right around the bend. If you do encounter an oncoming vehicle, unspoken rules of the road dictate that the driver closest to a pullout will use it—even if they have to back up. A little "thank-you" wave (or even just an index finger raised off the steering wheel) is the customary end to these encounters.

By Public Transportation: Glasgow is the gateway to this region (so you'll most likely have to transfer there if coming from Edinburgh). The **train** zips from Glasgow to Fort William, Oban, and Kyle of Lochalsh in the west; and up to Stirling, Pitlochry, and Inverness in the east. For more remote destinations (such as Glencoe), the bus is better.

Most of the **buses** you'll need are operated by Scottish Citylink. You can pay the driver in cash when you board. But in peak season—when these buses fill up—it's smart to buy tickets in advance: Book online at www.citylink.co.uk, call 0871-216-3333, or stop by a bus station or TI. Booking the day before generally guarantees a seat; otherwise, you may get bumped to the next departure.

Glasgow's Buchanan Station is the main Lowlands hub for reaching Highlands destinations. From Edinburgh, it's best to transfer in Glasgow (fastest by train, also possible by bus)—though there are direct buses from Edinburgh to Inverness, where you can connect to Highlands buses. Once in the Highlands, Inverness and Fort William serve as the main bus hubs.

Note that bus frequency can be substantially reduced on Sundays and in the off-season (Oct-mid-May). Unless otherwise noted, I've listed bus information for summer weekdays. Always carefully confirm schedules locally.

These buses are particularly useful for connecting the sights in this book:

Buses **#976** and **#977** connect Glasgow with Oban (5/day, 3 hours).

Buses **#914, #915,** and **#916** go from Glasgow to Fort William, stopping at Glencoe (8/day, 2.5 hours to Glencoe, 3 hours total to Fort William). From Fort William, buses **#915** and **#916** continue all the way up to Portree on the Isle of Skye (3/day, 7 hours for the full run).

Bus **#918** goes from Oban to Fort William, stopping en route at Ballachulish near Glencoe (3/day, 1 hour to Ballachulish, 1.5 hours total to Fort William).

Bus **#44**—operated by Stagecoach, not Scottish Citylink—is a cheaper alternative for connecting Glencoe to Fort William (hourly Mon-Sat, none Sun, www.stagecoachbus.com).

Buses **#19** and **#919** connect Fort William with Inverness (7-9/day, 2 hours).

Buses **#M90** (express, 4 hours) and **#M91** (many stops including Pitlochry, 5 hours) run from Edinburgh to Inverness; these depart about hourly, alternating between express and slow.

Bus **#917** connects Inverness with Portree, on the Isle of Skye (3-4/day, 3.5 hours).

Bus **#G10** is an express connecting Inverness and Glasgow (5/day, 3.5 hours; many additional connections possible with change in Perth).

SCOTTISH HIGHLANDS

OBAN AND THE INNER HEBRIDES

Oban • Isles of Mull, Iona, and Staffa • Near Oban (Inveraray and Kilmartin Glen)

For a taste of Scotland's west coast, the port town of Oban is equal parts endearing and functional. This busy little ferry-and-train terminal has no important sights, but makes up the difference in character, in scenery (with its low-impact panorama of overlapping islets and bobbing boats), and with one of Scotland's best distillery tours. But Oban is also convenient: It's midway between the Lowland cities (Glasgow and Edinburgh) and the Highland riches of the north (Glencoe, Isle of Skye). And it's the "gateway to the isles," with handy ferry service to the Hebrides Islands.

If time is tight and serious island-hopping is beyond the scope of your itinerary, Oban is ideally situated for a busy and memorable full-day side-trip to three of the most worthwhile Inner Hebrides: big, rugged Mull; pristine little Iona, where buoyant clouds float over its historic abbey; and Staffa, a remote, grassy islet inhabited only by sea birds. (The best of the Inner Hebrides—the Isle of Skye—is covered in its own chapter.) Sit back, let someone else do the driving, and enjoy a tour of the Inner Hebrides.

This chapter also includes a few additional sights near Oban, handy for those connecting the dots: the most scenic route between Glasgow and Oban (along the bonnie, bonnie banks of Loch Lomond and through the town of Inveraray, with its fine castle); and the faint remains of Kilmartin Glen, the prehistoric homeland of the Scottish people.

PLANNING YOUR TIME

If you're on a speedy blitz tour of Scotland, Oban is a strategic and pleasant place to spend the night. But you'll need two nights to enjoy Oban's main attraction: the side-trip to Mull, Iona, and Staffa. There are few actual sights in Oban itself, beyond the distillery tour, but—thanks to its manageable size, scenic waterfront setting, and great restaurants—the town is an enjoyable place to linger.

Oban

Oban (pronounced OH-bin) is a low-key resort. Its winding promenade is lined by gravel beaches, ice-cream stands, fish-and-chip joints, a tourable distillery, and a surprising diversity of good restaurants. Everything in Oban is close together, and the town seems eager to please its many visitors: Wool and tweed are perpetually on sale, and posters announce a variety of day tours to Scotland's wild and wildlife-strewn western islands. When the rain clears, sun-starved Scots sit on benches along the Esplanade, leaning back to catch some rays. Wind,
boats, gulls, layers of islands, and the promise of a wide-open Atlantic beyond give Oban a rugged charm.

Orientation to Oban

Oban, with about 10,000 people, is where the train system of Scotland meets the ferry system serving the Hebrides islands. As "gateway to the isles," its center is not a square or market, but its harbor. Oban's business action, just a couple of streets deep, stretches along the harbor and its promenade.

TOURIST INFORMATION

Oban's TI, located at the North Pier, sells bus and ferry tickets and is well stocked with brochures (flexible hours, generally July-Aug Mon-Sat 9:00-19:00, Sun 10:00-17:00; April-June Mon-Sat 9:00-17:30, Sun 10:00-17:00; Sept-Oct daily 10:00-17:00; Nov-

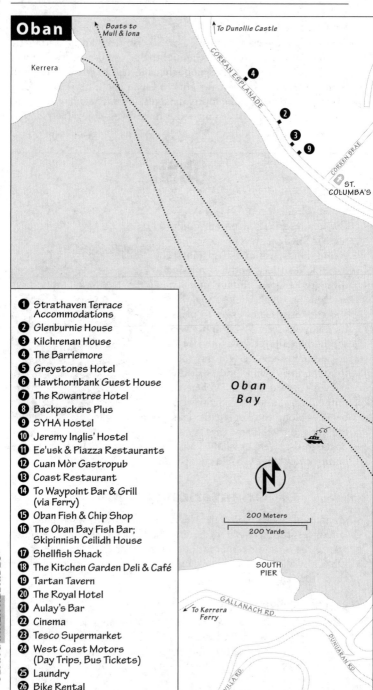

Oban

Boats to Mull & Iona

To Dunollie Castle

Kerrera

CORRAN ESPLANADE

4

2

3

9

CORREN BRAE

ST. COLUMBA'S

Oban Bay

200 Meters

200 Yards

SOUTH PIER

GALLANACH RD.

To Kerrera Ferry

DUNUARAN RD.

VILLA RD.

1 Strathaven Terrace Accommodations
2 Glenburnie House
3 Kilchrenan House
4 The Barriemore
5 Greystones Hotel
6 Hawthornbank Guest House
7 The Rowantree Hotel
8 Backpackers Plus
9 SYHA Hostel
10 Jeremy Inglis' Hostel
11 Ee'usk & Piazza Restaurants
12 Cuan Mòr Gastropub
13 Coast Restaurant
14 To Waypoint Bar & Grill (via Ferry)
15 Oban Fish & Chip Shop
16 The Oban Bay Fish Bar; Skipinnish Ceilidh House
17 Shellfish Shack
18 The Kitchen Garden Deli & Café
19 Tartan Tavern
20 The Royal Hotel
21 Aulay's Bar
22 Cinema
23 Tesco Supermarket
24 West Coast Motors (Day Trips, Bus Tickets)
25 Laundry
26 Bike Rental

OBAN & INNER HEBRIDES

To Fort William
& Inverness

CROFT RD.

DUNOLLIE ROAD

LONGSDALE RD.

P

BENVOULIN RD.

DUNOLLIE TER.

BREADALBANE ST.

1

DALRIACH RD.

ATLANTIS
SPORTS &
LEISURE
CENTRE

CORRAN ESPLANADE

P

P

8

6

OBAN
LAWN
BOWLING
CLUB

ARDCONNEL RD.

NURSERY LN.

22

19

7

POST

15

ALBERT RD.

5

CRAIGARD RD.

13

MC CAIG'S
TOWER

LAUREL RD.

LAUREL RD.

DUNCRAGGAN RD.

LONGSDALE RD.

OBAN
WAR & PEACE
MUSEUM

GEORGE ST.

26

OBAN
WHISKY
DISTILLERY
ⓦ

ARDCONNEL TERRACE

ROCKFIELD RD.

11

ℹ

14

NORTH
PIER

12

TWEEDALE ST.

ROCKFIELD RD.

16

25

HILL ST.

18

24

ST. EVENSON ST.

TRAIN
STATION

17

AIRD'S CRES.

21

20

10

Argyll
Square

COMBIE ST.

FERRY
TERMINAL

SHORE ST.

HIGH ST.

ALBANY ST.

P

MARKET ST.

LOCHSIDE ST.

COMBIE ST.

GLENSHELLACH TERRACE

GLENCRUITTEN RD.

23

OBAN & INNER HEBRIDES

March Mon-Sat 10:00-17:00, Sun 11:00-15:00; 3 North Pier, tel. 01631/563-122, www.oban.org.uk).

HELPFUL HINTS

Internet Access: There's free Wi-Fi all over town, including at the TI and many cafés.

Bookstore: Waterstones, a huge bookstore overlooking the harborfront, offers maps and a fine collection of books on Scotland (long hours daily, 12 George Street, tel. 0843/290-8529).

Baggage Storage: The train station has luggage lockers, but is open limited hours (Mon-Sat 5:00-20:30, Sun 10:45-18:00)—confirm the closing time before committing (£3-5 depending on bag size).

Laundry: You'll find **Oban Quality Laundry** tucked a block behind the main drag on Stevenson Street (same-day drop-off service-£8-12/load, no self-service, Mon-Fri 9:00-17:00, Sat 9:00-13:00, closed Sun, tel. 01631/563-554).

Supermarket: Tesco is a five-minute walk from the train station (Mon-Sat 6:00-24:00, Sun 8:00-20:00, WC in front by registers, inexpensive cafeteria; walk through Argyll Square and look for entrance to large parking lot on right, Lochside Street).

Bike Rental: Oban Cycles is on the main drag (Tue-Sat 10:00-17:00, closed Sun-Mon, 87 George Street, tel. 01631/566-033).

Bus Station: The "station" is just a pullout, marked by a stubby clock tower, at the roundabout in front of the train station. In peak season, it's wise to prebook bus tickets the day before—either at the TI, or at the West Coast Motors office (see next).

Bus and Island Tour Tickets: West Coast Motors, a block from the train station in the bright-red building along the harbor at 1 Queens Park Place, has two parts. The travel shop, on the left side, sells bus tickets (Mon-Fri 9:00-17:00, closed Sat-Sun—on those days, go to the other side). On the right side, the West Coast Tours office is where you can book tours to the isles of Mull, Iona, and Staffa (Tue-Sat 6:30-17:30, Sun-Mon 8:30-17:30, tel. 01631/566-809, www.westcoasttours.co.uk).

Highland Games: Oban hosts its touristy Highland Games every August (www.obangames.com), and the more local-oriented Lorne Highland Games each June (www.lorne-highland-games.org.uk). Nearby Taynuilt, a 20-minute drive east, hosts their sweetly small-town Highland Games in mid-July (www.taynuilthighlandgames.com).

Tours from Oban

For the best day trip from Oban, tour the islands of Mull, Iona, and/or Staffa (offered daily Easter-Oct, described later)—or consider staying overnight on remote and beautiful Iona. With more time or other interests, consider one of many other options you'll see advertised.

Wildlife Tours

If you just want to go for a boat ride, the easiest option is the one-hour seal-watching tour (£10, various companies—look for signs at the harbor). But to really get a good look at Scottish coastal wildlife, several groups—including **Coastal Connection** (based in Oban) and **Sealife Adventures** and **SeaFari** (based in nearby coastal towns)—run whale-watching tours that seek out rare minke whales, basking sharks, bottlenose dolphins, and porpoises. For an even more ambitious itinerary, the holy grail is Treshnish Island (out past Staffa), which brims with puffins, seals, and other sea critters. Options abound—check at the TI for information.

Open-Top Bus Tours

If the weather is good and you don't have a car, you can go by bus for a spin out of Oban for views of nearby castles and islands, plus a stop near McCaig's Tower with narration by the driver (£7, departs train station 4/day, no tours Oct-April, 1.5 hours, www.citysightseeingoban.com).

Sights in Oban

▲The Burned-Out Sightseer's Visual Tour from the Pier

If the west coast weather permits, get oriented to the town while taking a break: Head out to the North Pier, just past the TI, and find the benches that face back toward town (in front of the recommended Piazza restaurant). Take a seat and get to know Oban.

Scan the harborfront from left to right, surveying the mix of grand Victorian sandstone buildings and humbler modern storefronts. At the far-right end of town is the ferry terminal and—very likely—a lumbering ferry loading or unloading. Oban has always been on the way to something, and today is no different. The townscape seems dominated by Caledonian-MacBrayne, Scotland's biggest ferry company. CalMac's 30 ships serve 24 destinations and transport over 4 million passengers a year. The town's port has long been a lifeline to the islands.

Hiding near the ferry terminal is the train station. With the arrival of the train in 1880, Oban became the unofficial capital of Scotland's west coast and a destination for tourists. The Caledonian Hotel, the original terminus hotel that once served those train travelers, dominates the harborfront.

Tourism aside, herring was the first big industry. A dozen boats still fish commercially—you'll see them tucked around the ferry terminal. The tourist board, in an attempt to entice tourists to linger longer, is trying to rebrand Oban as a "seafood capital" rather than just the "gateway to the isles." As the ocean's supply has become depleted, most local fish is farmed. There's still plenty of shellfish.

After fishing, big industries here historically included tobacco (imported from the American colonies), then whisky. At the left end of the embankment, find the building marked *Oban Whisky Distillery*. It's rare to find a distillery in the middle of a town, but Oban grew up around this one. With the success of its whisky, the town enjoyed an invigorating confidence, optimism, and, in 1811, a royal charter. Touring Oban's distillery is the best activity in Oban.

Above the distillery, you can't miss the odd mini-Colosseum. This is McCaig's Tower, an employ-the-workers-and-build-me-a-fine-memorial project undertaken by an Oban tycoon in 1900. McCaig died before completing the structure, so his complete vision for it remains a mystery. (This is an example of a "folly"—that uniquely British notion of an idiosyncratic structure erected by a colorful aristocrat.) While the building itself is nothing to see up close, a 10-minute hike through a Victorian residential neighborhood leads you to a peaceful garden and a commanding view.

Now turn and look out to sea, and imagine this: At the height of the Cold War, Oban played a critical role when the world's first two-way transatlantic telephone cable was laid from Gallanach Bay to Newfoundland in 1956—a milestone in global communication. This technology later provided the White House and the Kremlin with the "hotline" that was created after the Cuban Missile Crisis to avoid a nuclear conflagration.

▲▲West Highland Malt Scotch Whisky Distillery Tours

The 200-year-old Oban Whisky Distillery produces more than 25,000 liters a week, and exports much of that to the US. The distillery offers serious and fragrant one-hour tours explaining the process from start to finish, with two smooth samples of their signature product: Oban whisky is moderately smoky, and characterized by notes of sea salt, citrus, and honey. You'll also receive a whisky glass and a discount coupon for the shop. This is the handiest whisky tour you'll encounter—just a block off the harbor—and one of the best. The exhibition that precedes the tour gives a quick, whisky-centric history of Oban and Scotland. Then your guide will walk you through each step of the process: malting, mashing, fermentation, distillation, and maturation. Photos are not allowed inside—supposedly because a spark from your camera could ignite the alcohol fumes. (Or maybe it has more to do with interdistillery competition.) For details on the distilling process and tips on tasting whisky, see page 460.

Cost and Hours: Tours cost £8, are limited to 16 people, depart every 20-30 minutes, and fill up quickly. Because the hours tend to change frequently—and it's best to prebook in any case—check their website or call ahead for the specific schedule. But it's generally open July-Sept Mon-Fri 9:30-19:30, Sat-Sun 9:30-17:00; March-June and Oct-Nov daily 9:30-17:30; Dec-Feb daily 12:30-16:00; last tour 1.25 hours before closing, Stafford Street, tel. 01631/572-004, www.discovering-distilleries.com.

Serious Tasting: Connoisseurs can ask about their "exclusive tour," which adds a visit to the warehouse and four premium tastings in the manager's office (£40, 2 hours, likely July-Sept, Mon, Wed, and Fri at 16:00 only, reserve ahead).

Oban War & Peace Museum

Opened in 1995 on the 50th anniversary of Victory in Europe Day, this charming little museum focuses on Oban's experience during World War II. But it covers more than just war and peace. Photos show Oban through the years, and a 15-minute looped video gives a simple tour around the region. Volunteer staffers love to chat about the exhibit—or anything else on your mind.

Cost and Hours: Free; May-Oct Mon-Sat 10:00-18:00, Sun until 16:00; March-April and Nov daily until 16:00; closed Dec-Feb; Corran Esplanade, next to Regent Hotel on the promenade, tel. 01631/570-007, www.obanmuseum.org.uk.

Dunollie Castle and Museum

In a park just a mile up the coast, this spartan, stocky castle with 10-foot walls is a delightful stroll from the town center. The ruins offer a commanding, windy view of the harbor—a strategic spot back in the days when transport was mainly by water. For more than a thousand years, clan chiefs ruled this region from this ancestral home of Clan MacDougall, but the castle was abandoned in 1746. The adjacent house, which dates from 1745, shows off the MacDougall clan's family heritage—much of it naval; docents explain the charming if humble exhibits.

While the castle and museum are, frankly, not much, the local pride in the display and the walk from town make the visit fun. To get there, stroll out of town along the harborfront promenade. At the war memorial (with inviting seaview benches), cross the street. A gate leads to a little lane, lined with historic and nature boards along the way to the castle.

Cost and Hours: £5, April-Oct Mon-Sat 10:00-16:00, Sun 13:00-16:00, closed Nov-March, tel. 01631/570-550, www. dunollie.org.

OBAN & INNER HEBRIDES

ACTIVITIES IN OBAN
Atlantis Leisure Centre
This industrial-type sports center is a good place to get some exercise on a rainy day or let the kids run wild for a few hours. It has a rock-climbing wall, tennis courts, indoor "soft play centre" (for kids under 5), and an indoor swimming pool with a big water slide. The outdoor playground is free and open all the time.

Cost and Hours: Pool only-£4/adult, £2.50/child, no rental towels or suits, fees for other activities; open Mon-Fri 7:00-21:30, Sat-Sun 9:00-18:30; call or check online for open-swim pool hours, on the north end of Dalriach Road, tel. 01631/566-800, www.atlantisleisure.co.uk.

Oban Lawn Bowling Club
The club has welcomed visitors since 1869. This elegant green is the scene of a wonderfully British spectacle of old men tiptoeing wishfully after their balls. It's fun to watch, and—if there's no match scheduled and the weather's dry—anyone can rent shoes and balls and actually play.

Cost and Hours: £5/person; informal hours, but generally daily 10:00-16:00 & 17:00 to "however long the weather lasts"; just south of sports center on Dalriach Road, tel. 01631/570-808, www.obanbowlingclub.com.

ISLANDS NEAR OBAN
The isles of Mull, Iona, and Staffa are farther out, require a full day to visit, and are described later in this chapter. For a quicker glimpse at the Inner Hebrides, consider these two options.

Isle of Kerrera
Functioning like a giant breakwater, the Isle of Kerrera (KEH-reh-rah) makes Oban possible. Just offshore from Oban, this stark but very green island offers a quick, easy opportunity to get that romantic island experience. While it has no proper roads, it offers nice hikes, a ruined castle, and a few sheep farms. You may see the Kerrera ferry filled with sheep heading for Oban's livestock market.

Getting There: You have two options for reaching the island. Easiest is a boat operated by the recommended Waypoint Bar & Grill, which goes from Oban's North Pier to the Kerrera Marina (£5 round-trip, free if you spend at least £5 at the restaurant, less frequent off-season). The other boat departs from two miles south of town (follow the coast road past the ferry terminal); from here, the boat goes to the middle of the island (passengers only, £4.50 round-trip, bikes free, 5-minute trip, Easter-Oct runs about 2/hour 8:00-18:00 with a break 12:30-14:00, fewer boats Sun and off-season, tel. 01631/563-665, if no answer contact Oban TI for info; www.kerrera-ferry.co.uk).

Sleeping on Kerrera: Your only option is the **$ Kerrera Bunkhouse,** a refurbished 18th-century stable that can sleep up to eight people in four compartments (£15/person, £100 for the entire bunkhouse, includes bedding but not towels, cheaper for 2 nights or more, open year-round but must book ahead, kitchen, tel. 01631/566-367, www.kerrerabunkhouse.co.uk, info@ kerrerabunkhouse.co.uk, Martin and Aideen). They also run a tea garden that serves meals (Easter-Sept daily 10:30-16:30, closed Oct-Easter).

Isle of Seil

Enjoy a drive, a walk, some solitude, and the sea. Drive 12 miles south of Oban on the A-816 to the B-844 to the Isle of Seil (pronounced "seal"), connected to the mainland by a bridge (which, locals like to brag, "crosses the Atlantic"...well, maybe a small part of it).

Just over the bridge on the Isle of Seil is a pub called **Tigh-an-Truish** ("House of Trousers"). After the Jacobite rebellions, a new law forbade the wearing of kilts on the mainland. Highlanders on the island used this pub to change from kilts to trousers before they made the crossing. The pub serves great meals and good seafood dishes to those either in kilts or pants (pub likely open daily—call ahead, tel. 01852/300-242).

Seven miles across the island, on a tiny second island and facing the open Atlantic, is **Easdale,** a historic, touristy, windblown little slate-mining town—with a slate-town museum and an egomaniac's incredibly tacky "Highland Arts" shop (shuttle ferry goes the 300 yards). An overpriced direct ferry runs from Easdale to Iona; but, at twice the cost of the Mull-Iona trip, the same time on the island, and very little time with a local guide, it's hardly worth it. For a better connection to Iona, see page 256.

Nightlife in Oban

Little Oban has a few options for entertaining its many visitors. At the TI, pick up the *What's On* leaflet, or check www.obanwhatson. co.uk. Fun low-key activities may include open-mic, disco, or quiz theme nights in pubs; occasional Scottish folk shows; coffee meetings; and—if you're lucky—duck races. On Wednesday nights, the Oban Pipe Band plays in the square by the train station. Here are a few other ways to entertain yourself while in town.

Live Music: On many summer nights, you can drop into **Skipinnish Ceilidh House** on the main drag for Highland music, song, and dancing. The owners—professional musicians Angus

Sleep Code

Abbreviations   **(£1=about $1.60, country code: 44)**
S=Single, **D**=Double/Twin, **T**=Triple, **Q**=Quad, **b**=bathroom
Price Rankings
   $$$ **Higher Priced**—Most rooms £70 or more
    $$ **Moderately Priced**—Most rooms £30-70
     $ **Lower Priced**—Most rooms £30 or less
Unless otherwise noted, credit cards are accepted at hotels and hostels—but not B&Bs—breakfast is included, and free Wi-Fi and/or a guest computer is generally available. Prices change; verify current rates online or by email. For the best prices, always book directly with the hotel.

and Andrew—invest in talented musicians and put on a good show, featuring live bands, songs sung in Gaelic, Highland dancing, and great Scottish storytelling. For many, the best part is the chance to learn some *ceilidh* (KAY-lee) dancing. These group dances are a lot of fun—wallflowers and bad dancers are warmly welcomed, and the staff is happy to give you pointers (£10 music session, cheaper if prebooked online, pricier for concerts with visiting big-name *ceilidh* bands, music 2-3 nights/week mid-June-mid-Sept usually starting around 20:30, check website for schedule, 34 George Street, tel. 01631/569-599, www.skipinnishceilidhhouse.com). Various pubs and hotels in town have live traditional music in the summer; as specifics change from year to year, ask your B&B host or the TI for the latest (try the **Tartan Tavern,** a block off the waterfront at 3 Albany Terrace; or **The Royal Hotel,** just above the train station on Argyll Square).

Cinema: The Phoenix Cinema closed down for two years and then was saved by the community. It's now volunteer-run and booming (140 George Street, www.obanphoenix.com).

Characteristic Pub: Aulay's Bar, with decor that shows off Oban's maritime heritage, has two sides, each with a different personality. Having a drink here invariably comes with a good "blether" (conversation), and the gang is local (basic £6 pub grub, daily 11:00-24:00, 8 Airds Crescent, just around the corner from the train station and ferry terminal).

Sleeping in Oban

SIMPLE, AFFORDABLE B&Bs ON STRATHAVEN TERRACE

Oban's B&Bs offer a better value than its hotels. The following fine but interchangeable B&Bs line up on a quiet, flowery street that's nicely located two blocks off the harbor, three blocks from the center, and a 10-minute walk from the train station. By car, as you enter town from the north, turn left immediately after King's Knoll Hotel, and take your first right onto Breadalbane Street. ("Strathaven Terrace" is actually just the name for this row of houses on Breadalbane Street.) The alley behind the buildings has tight, free parking for all of these places. None of these B&Bs accept credit cards.

$$ Gramarvin Guest House has four crisp and cheery rooms, one with a private bathroom on the hall (Db-£65-70, Tb-£98-105, at #5, tel. 01631/564-622, www.gramarvin.co.uk, mary@gramarvin.co.uk, Mary).

$$ Raniven Guest House has five simple, tastefully decorated rooms and gracious, fun-loving hosts Moyra and Stuart (Sb-£35-40, Db-£65-70, at #1, tel. 01631/562-713, www.ranivenoban.com, bookings@ranivenoban.com).

$$ Sandvilla B&B rents five fine rooms (Db-£60-70, at #4, tel. 01631/564-483, www.holidayoban.co.uk, sandvilla@holidayoban.co.uk, Josephine and Robert).

GUESTHOUSES AND SMALL HOTELS

These options are a step up from the B&Bs—in terms of both amenities and price. All have tight, free parking.

Along the Embankment

These are along the Esplanade, which stretches north of town above a cobble beach (with beautiful bay views); they are a 10-minute walk from the center.

$$$ Glenburnie House, a stately Victorian home, has an elegant breakfast room overlooking the bay. Its 12 spacious, comfortable, classy rooms feel like plush living rooms. There's a nice lounge and a tiny sunroom with a stuffed "hairy coo" head (Sb-£60, Db-£90-120, price depends on size and view, closed mid-Nov-March, the Esplanade, tel. 01631/562-089, www.glenburnie.co.uk, stay@glenburnie.co.uk, Graeme).

$$$ Kilchrenan House, the turreted former retreat of a textile magnate, has 14 large rooms, most with bay views. The stunning rooms #5, #9, and #15 are worth the few extra pounds, while the "standard" rooms in the newer annex are a good value (Sb-£55, Db-£70-105, price depends on size and views, 2-night minimum, welcome drink of whisky or sherry, different "breakfast special" every day, family rooms, closed Nov-Feb, a few houses past the cathedral on the Esplanade, tel. 01631/562-663, www.kilchrenanhouse.co.uk, info@kilchrenanhouse.co.uk, Colin and Frances).

$$$ The Barriemore, at the very end of Oban's grand waterfront Esplanade, comes with a nice patio, front sitting area, and

14 well-appointed rooms. Some front-facing rooms have views; rooms in the modern addition in the back are cheaper (Sb-£65-75, Db-£90-110, Tb-£100-125, two ground-floor double mini suites with views-£130-165, less off-season, price depends on view, the Esplanade, tel. 01631/566-356, www.barriemore-hotel.co.uk, reception@barriemore-hotel.co.uk, Sue, Jan, and Mark).

Above the Town Center

These places perch a block above the main waterfront zone—a quick (but uphill) walk from all of the action. Many rooms come with views, and are priced accordingly.

$$$ Greystones is the town's most enticing splurge. It fills a big, stately, turreted mansion at the top of town with five spacious rooms that mix Victorian charm and sleek gray-and-white minimalism. Built as the private home for the director of Kimberley Diamond Mine, it later became a maternity hospital, and today Mark and Suzanne have turned it into a stylish and restful retreat. The lounge and breakfast room offer stunning views over Oban and the offshore isles (Db-£120-165 depending on size and view, closed Nov-mid-Feb, 13 Dalriach Road, tel. 01631/358-653, www.greystonesoban.co.uk, stay@greystonesoban.co.uk).

$$$ Hawthornbank Guest House fills a big Victorian sandstone house with seven traditional-feeling rooms. Half of the rooms face bay views, and the other half overlook the town's lawn bowling green (Db-£65-95 depending on size and view, Dalriach Road, tel. 01631/562-041, www.hawthornbank.co.uk, hawthornbank@btinternet.com).

In the Town Center

$$$ The Rowantree Hotel is a group-friendly place with 24 good rooms reminiscent of a budget hotel in the US (with thin walls). They often have rooms when other places are full, and the location is very central—right on Oban's main drag (Sb-£60-90, Db-£100-130, includes breakfast—or skip breakfast to save a few pounds, cheaper off-season, easy parking, George Street, tel. 01631/562-954, www.rowantreehoteloban.co.uk).

HOSTELS

$ Backpackers Plus is central, laid-back, and fun. It fills part of a renovated old church with a sprawling public living room, 47 beds, and a staff generous with travel tips (bed in dorm room-£16, includes breakfast, great shared kitchen, £5 laundry service for guests only, 10-minute walk from station, on Breadalbane Street, tel. 01631/567-189, www.backpackersplus.com, info@backpackersplus.com, Peter). They have two other locations nearby with private rooms (D-£49, Db-£58).

$ The official **SYHA hostel,** on the scenic waterfront Esplanade, is in a grand building with 98 beds and smashing views of the harbor and islands from the lounges and dining rooms. While institutional, this place is quite nice (all rooms en suite, private rooms available, bed in dorm room-£22, bunk-bed Db-£46, Tb-£74, Qb-£96, price varies with demand, also has family rooms and 8-bed apartment with kitchen, £3/night more for nonmembers, breakfast and dinner extra, pay laundry, kitchen, tel. 01631/562-025, www.syha.org.uk, oban@syha.org.uk).

$ Jeremy Inglis' Hostel has 37 beds located two blocks from the TI and train station. This loosely run place feels more like a commune than a youth hostel...and it's cheap (£18/bed, S-£29, D-£36, cash only, includes linens, breakfast comes with Jeremy's homemade jam, kitchen, no curfew, second floor at 21 Airds Crescent, tel. 01631/565-065, jeremyinglis@mctavishs.freeserve.co.uk).

Eating in Oban

Oban brags that it is the "seafood capital of Scotland," and indeed its sit-down restaurants (listed first) are surprisingly high quality for such a small town. For something more casual, consider a fish-and-chips joint.

SIT-DOWN RESTAURANTS

These fill up in summer, especially on weekends. To ensure getting a table, you'll want to book ahead. The first four are generally open daily from about 12:00-21:00, with an afternoon closure (from 14:00 or 15:00 to 17:00).

Ee'usk (a phonetic rendering of *iasg*, Scottish Gaelic for "fish") is a popular, stylish, family-run place on the waterfront. It has a casual-chic atmosphere, a bright and glassy interior, sweeping views on three sides, and fish dishes favored by both natives and tourists. Reservations are recommended every day in summer and on weekends off-season (£9-12 lunches, £14-22 dinners, no kids under age 12 at dinner, North Pier, tel. 01631/565-666, www.eeusk.com, MacLeod family).

Cuan Mòr is a popular, casual restaurant that combines traditional Scottish with modern flair—both in its crowd-pleasing cuisine and in its furnishings, made of wood, stone, and metal scavenged from the beaches of Scotland's west coast (£6 lunches, £9-14 main courses, no afternoon closure, brewery in back, 60 George Street, tel. 01631/565-078).

Coast proudly serves fresh local fish, meat, and veggies in a mod pine-and-candlelight atmosphere. As everything is prepared and presented with care by husband-and-wife team Richard and Nicola—who try to combine traditional Scottish elements in in-

OBAN & INNER HEBRIDES

novative new ways—come here only if you have time for a slow meal (£11 lunches, £16-20 dinners, £15 two-course and £18 three-course specials, closed Sun for lunch, 104 George Street, tel. 01631/569-900).

Piazza, next door to Ee'usk and also run by the MacLeods, has similar decor but dishes up serviceable Italian cuisine and offers a more family-friendly ambience. They have some outdoor seats and big windows facing the sea (£8-12 pizzas and pastas, smart to reserve ahead July-Aug, tel. 01631/563-628, www.piazzaoban.com).

A Ferry Ride Across the Harbor: **Waypoint Bar & Grill,** just across the bay from Oban, is a laid-back patio at the Kerrera Marina with a no-nonsense menu of grilled seafood. It's not fancy, but the food is fresh and inexpensive, and on a nice day the open-air waterside setting is unbeatable (£6-11 lunches, £10-18 dinners, £24 seafood platter, May-Sept daily 11:00-23:00, closed Oct-April, reservations smart, tel. 01631/565-888, www.waypointbarandgrill.com). A free-for-customers ferry to the marina leaves from Oban's North Pier—look for the sign near the Piazza restaurant (departs hourly at :10 past each hour, 10-minute trip).

FISH-AND-CHIP JOINTS

There are plenty of good fish-and-chips places in Oban, but these two are the town favorites. Each has a front counter serving food to go (for a few pounds less) and good seating with table service farther inside.

Oban Fish and Chip Shop, run by husband-and-wife team George and Lillian (with Lewis and Sammy working the fryer), serves praiseworthy haddock and mussels among other tasty options in a cheery blue cabana-like dining room. Consider venturing away from basic fish-and-chips into a world of more creative seafood dishes (£7 haddock-and-chips to go, £9-16 main courses to eat in, sit-down restaurant closes at 21:00, takeaway available later, 116 George Street, tel. 01631/567-000).

At **The Oban Bay Fish Bar,** which is also family-run, Renato serves all things from the sea (plus an assortment of Scottish classics) battered and fried. Choose between the casual restaurant or takeaway counter, where you can give fried haggis a try (£8-10 meals, cheaper for takeaway, daily 12:00-23:00, on the harborfront at 34 George Street, below Skipinnish, tel. 01631/565-855).

LUNCH

The green **shellfish shack** at the ferry dock regularly gets fresh deliveries from local fishermen and is the best spot to pick up a seafood sandwich or a snack. They sell smaller bites (such as cold sandwiches) for £3-6, as well as some bigger cold platters and a few

£7 hot dishes (often free samples, picnic tables nearby, daily from 10:00 until the boat unloads from Mull around 17:45).

The Kitchen Garden is fine for soup, salad, or sandwiches. It's a deli and gourmet-foods store with a charming café upstairs (£4 sandwiches to go, £5-8 dishes upstairs, Mon-Sat 9:00-17:30, Sun 10:00-16:30, closed Sun Jan-mid-Feb, 14 George Street, tel. 01631/566-332).

Oban Connections

By Train from Oban: Trains link Oban to the nearest transportation hub in **Glasgow** (6/day, fewer on Sun, 3 hours); to get to **Edinburgh,** you'll have to transfer in Glasgow (5/day, 4.5 hours). To reach **Fort William** (a transit hub for the Highlands), you'll take the same Glasgow-bound train, but transfer in Crianlarich (3/day, 4 hours)—the direct bus is easier (see next). Oban's small train station has a ticket window and lockers (both open Mon-Sat 5:00-20:30, Sun 10:45-18:00, train info tel. 0345-748-4950, www.nationalrail.co.uk).

By Bus: Bus #918 passes through Ballachulish—a half-mile from **Glencoe**—on its way to **Fort William** (3/day, 1 hour to Ballachulish, 1.5 hours total to Fort William). Take this bus to Fort William, then transfer to bus #919 to reach **Inverness** (4 hours, 20-minute layover in Fort William) or bus #915 or #916 to **Portree** on the Isle of Skye (3/day, 4.5-5 hours). A different bus (#976 or #977) connects Oban with **Glasgow** (5/day, 3 hours), from where you can easily connect by bus or train to **Edinburgh** (figure 4.5 hours). Buses arrive and depart from a roundabout, marked by a stubby clock tower, just before the entrance to the train station (tel. 0871-266-3333, www.citylink.co.uk). You can buy bus tickets at the West Coast Motors shop near the bus stop, or at the TI across the harbor. Book in advance during peak times.

By Boat: Ferries fan out from Oban to the **southern Hebrides** (see information on the islands of Iona and Mull, later). Caledonian MacBrayne Ferry info: Tel. 01631/566-688, free booking tel. 0800-066-5000, www.calmac.co.uk.

ROUTE TIPS FOR DRIVERS

From Glasgow to Oban via Loch Lomond and Inveraray: For details on the most scenic route from Glasgow to Oban, see "Near Oban" at the end of this chapter.

From Oban to Glencoe and Fort William: It's an easy one-hour drive from Oban to Glencoe. From Oban, follow the coastal A-828 toward Fort William. After about 20 miles—as you leave the village of Appin—you'll see the photogenic **Castle Stalker** marooned on a lonely island (you can pull over at the Wildlife Hub's huge parking lot for decent, distant views of the castle). At North Ballachulish, you'll reach a bridge spanning Loch Leven; rather than crossing the bridge, turn off and follow the A-82 into the Glencoe Valley for about 15 minutes. (For tips on the best views and hikes in Glencoe, see the next chapter.) After exploring the valley, make a U-turn and return through Glencoe village. To continue on to Fort William, backtrack to the bridge at North Ballachulish (great view from bridge) and cross it, following the A-82 north.

For a scenic shortcut directly back to Glasgow or Edinburgh, continue south on the A-82 after Glencoe via Rannoch Moor and Tyndrum. Crianlarich is where the road splits, and you'll either continue on the A-82 toward Loch Lomond and Glasgow or pick up the A-85 and follow signs for Stirling, then Edinburgh.

Isles of Mull, Iona, and Staffa

For the easiest one-day look at a good sample of the dramatic and historic Inner Hebrides (HEB-rid-eez) islands, take a tour from Oban to Mull, Iona, and Staffa. Though this trip is spectacular when it's sunny, it's worthwhile in any weather (but if rain or rough seas are expected, I'd skip the Staffa option). For an even more in-depth look at the Inner Hebrides, head north to Skye (see the Isle of Skye chapter).

GETTING AROUND THE ISLANDS
Here's the game plan: Take a ferry from Oban to Mull (45 minutes), ride a West Coast Motors tour bus across Mull (1.25 hours),
then board a quick ferry from Mull to Iona. The total round-trip travel time is 5.5 hours—all of it incredibly scenic—plus about two hours of free time on Iona. With two extra hours and an extra £23, you can add a side-trip to Staffa (yet another boat trip—about 35 minutes each way—plus an hour free on that island). Buy your strip of tick-

ets—one for each leg—at the West Coast Motors office in Oban (£40 for Mull/Iona tour, £63 for Mull/Iona/Staffa tour—£55 "early bird" option described later; April-Oct only—no tours Nov-March, book one day ahead in July-Sept if possible, bus tickets can sell out during busy summer weekends). You can also buy individual tickets for each leg, if you plan to spend extra time (or an overnight) on Iona.

Mull/Iona Tour: You'll leave in the morning from the Oban pier on the huge Oban-Mull **ferry** run by Caledonian MacBrayne (boats depart Mon-Fri at 9:45, Sat at 9:30, Sun at 9:50, board at least 20 minutes before departure). As the schedule can change from year to year, confirm your departure time carefully in Oban. The best inside seats on the ferry—with the biggest windows—are in the sofa lounge on the "observation deck" (level 4) at the back end of the boat. (Follow signs for the toilets, and look for the big staircase to the top floor; this floor also has its own small snack bar with hot drinks and basic sandwiches.) On board, if it's a clear day, ask a local or a crew member to point out Ben Nevis, the tallest mountain in Great Britain. The ferry has a fine cafeteria with hot meals and sandwiches packaged for picnicking, and a bookshop. Five minutes before landing on Mull, you'll see the striking 13th-century Duart Castle on the left.

Walk-on passengers disembark from deck 3, across from the bookshop (port side). Upon arrival in Mull, find your **bus** for the entertaining and informative ride across the Isle of Mull. The right (driver's) side offers better sea views during the second half of the journey to Fionnphort, while the left side has fine views of Mull's rolling wilderness. The driver spends the entire ride chattering away about life on Mull, slowing to point out wildlife, and sharing adages like, "If there's no flowers on the gorse, snogging's gone out of fashion." These hardworking locals make historical trivia fascinating—or at least fun. Your destination is Mull's westernmost ferry terminal, called Fionnphort, where you'll board a small, rocking **ferry** for the brief ride to Iona. Unless you stay overnight, you'll have only about two hours to roam freely around the island before taking the ferry-bus-ferry ride in reverse back to Oban. The return boat arrives in Oban around 17:45.

Staffa Add-On: If you add Staffa, the basic structure is the same as described above. But to fit in the extra island, you'll need to either return two hours later, or depart two hours earlier. Most people return late: Follow the above route, but upon arriving at Fionnphort at the far end of Mull, board the small, orange Staffa Tours boat; after a 35-minute trip, you'll have about an hour of free time on Staffa, then return to Iona. You'll then have about two hours to see Iona before returning: ferry to Fionnphort, bus across Mull, and a ferry back to Oban (arriving in Oban around 19:45). Alternatively, the cheaper "early bird" option takes the crack-of-dawn boat to Mull (departs Tue-Sat at 7:40, Sat at 7:30, not available Sun-Mon) and returns on the ferry that arrives in Mull at 17:45.

Staying Longer on Iona: For a chance to really experience

OBAN & INNER HEBRIDES

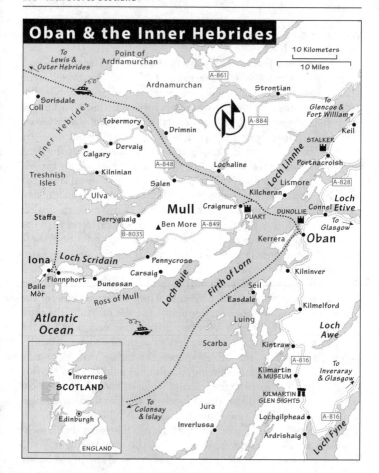

Oban & the Inner Hebrides

peaceful, idyllic Iona, spend a night or two (Scots bring their kids and stay on this tiny island for a week). In this case, don't buy your tickets at the bus-tour office in Oban—they require a same-day return. Instead, buy each leg of the ferry-bus-ferry (and return) trip separately. Get your Oban-Mull ferry ticket at the Oban ferry office (one-way for walk-on passengers-£5.65, round-trip-£9.45, ticket good for 5 days). Once you arrive in Mull (Craignure), follow the crowds to the tour buses and buy a ticket directly from the driver (£14 round-trip). When you arrive at the ferry terminal (Fionnphort), walk into the small trailer ferry office to buy a ticket to Iona (£2.60 each way). If it's closed, you can buy a ticket from the ferry worker at the dock (cash or credit/debit cards accepted; leaving Iona, do the same, as there's no ferry office).

It's also possible to do a one-day trip with more time on Iona (about four hours). Take the first boat of the day (see times in

"Staffa Add-On," earlier), then connect at Mull to bus #496, which takes you to Fionnphort and the Iona ferry (no tour narration, buy each leg separately). The benefit of taking the tour—besides the helpful commentary—is the guarantee of a seat each way. Ask at the bus tour office for details.

Driving: Don't bother trying to do this one-day trip by car—the Oban-Mull ferry crossing is very expensive (£69 round-trip for the car, plus passengers); because of tight ferry timings, you'll wind up basically following the tour buses anyway; and you'll miss all of the commentary. Driving on Mull comes with narrow, single-track roads (with frequent pullouts or "passing places") clogged with sheep. Drive on Mull only if you have extra time to slow down and explore.

Mull

The Isle of Mull, the second largest of the Inner Hebrides (after Skye), has nearly 300 scenic miles of coastline and castles and a 3,169-foot-high mountain, one of Scotland's Munros. Called Ben More ("Big Mountain" in Gaelic), it was once much bigger. At 10,000 feet tall, it made up the entire island of Mull—until a volcano erupted. Things are calmer now, and, similarly, Mull has a

noticeably laid-back population. My bus driver reported that there are no deaths from stress, and only a few from boredom.

With steep, fog-covered hillsides topped by cairns (piles of stones, sometimes indicating graves) and ancient stone circles, Mull has a gloomy, otherworldly charm. Bring plenty of rain protection and wear layers in case the sun peeks through the clouds. As my driver said, Mull is a place of cold, wet, windy winters and mild, wet, windy summers.

On the far side of Mull, the caravan of tour buses unloads at Fionnphort, a tiny ferry town. The ferry to the island of Iona takes about 200 walk-on passengers. Confirm the return time with your bus driver, then hustle to the dock to make the first trip over (otherwise, it's a 30-minute wait; on very busy days, those who dillydally may not fit on the first ferry). At the dock, there's a small ferry-passenger building with a meager snack bar and a pay WC; a more enticing seafood bar is across the street. After the 10-minute ride, you wash ashore on sleepy Iona (free WC on this side), and the ferry mobs that crowded you on the boat seem to disappear up the main road and into Iona's back lanes.

The **About Mull Tours and Taxi** service can also get you around Mull (tel. 01681/700-507 or mobile 0788-777-4550, www.aboutmull.co.uk). They also do day tours of Mull, focusing on local history and wildlife (half-day tours also available, shorter Mull tours can drop you off at Iona ferry dock at 15:00 for a quick Iona visit and pick you up at 18:00, minimum 2 people, must book ahead).

Iona

The tiny island of Iona, just 3 miles by 1.5 miles, is famous as the birthplace of Christianity in Scotland. You'll have about two hours here on your own before you retrace your steps (your bus driver will tell you which return ferry to take back to Mull).

A pristine quality of light and a thoughtful peace pervades the stark, (nearly) car-free island and its tiny community. With buoyant clouds bouncing playfully off distant bluffs, sparkling-white crescents of sand, and lone tourists camped thoughtfully atop huge rocks just looking out to sea, Iona is a place that's perfect for meditation. To experience Iona, it's important to get out and take a little hike; you can follow some or all of my self-guided walk outlined below. And you can easily climb a peak—nothing's higher than 300 feet above the sea.

Orientation to Iona

The ferry arrives at the island's only real village, Baile Mòr, with shops, a restaurant/pub, a few accommodations, and no bank (get cash back with a purchase at the grocery store). The only taxi on Iona is **Iona Taxi** (tel. 07810-325-990, www.ionataxi.co.uk). Up the road from the ferry dock is a little **Spar** grocery (Mon-Sat 9:00-17:00, Sun from 11:00, shorter hours and closed Sun Oct-April, free island maps). Iona's official website (www.isle-of-iona.net) has good information about the island.

Iona Walk

Here's a basic self-guided route for exploring Iona. With the standard two hours on Iona that a day trip allows, you likely won't have time for everything. Either do a thorough visit to the abbey (with a guided tour and/or audioguide) and then a light stroll; or do the

History of Iona

St. Columba (521-597), an Irish scholar, soldier, priest, and founder of monasteries, got into a small war over the posses-

sion of an illegally copied psalm book. Victorious but sickened by the bloodshed, Columba left Ireland, vowing never to return. According to legend, the first bit of land out of sight of his homeland was Iona. He stopped here in 563 and established an abbey.

Columba's monastic community flourished, and Iona became the center of Celtic Christianity. Missionaries from Iona spread the gospel throughout Scotland and northern England, while scholarly monks established Iona as a center of art and learning. The *Book of Kells*—perhaps the finest piece of art from "Dark Ages" Europe—was probably made on Iona in the eighth century.

The island was so important that it was the legendary burial place for ancient Scottish clan chieftains and kings (including Macbeth, of Shakespeare fame) and even some Scandinavian monarchs.

Slowly, the importance of Iona ebbed. Vikings massacred 68 monks in 806. Fearing more raids, the monks evacuated most of Iona's treasures to Ireland (including the *Book of Kells,* which is now in Dublin). Much later, with the Reformation, the abbey was abandoned, and most of its finely carved crosses were destroyed. In the 17th century, locals used the abbey only as a handy quarry for other building projects.

Iona's population peaked at about 500 in the 1830s. In the 1840s, a potato famine hit, and in the 1850s, a third of the islanders emigrated to Canada or Australia. By 1900, the population was down to 210, and today it's only around 200.

But in our generation, a new religious community has given the abbey fresh life. The Iona Community is an ecumenical gathering of men and women who seek new ways of living the Gospel in today's world, with a focus on worship, peace and justice issues, and reconciliation (http://iona.org.uk).

entire walk described below, but skip the abbey (unless you have time for a quick visit on your way back).

From the ferry dock, head directly up the single paved road that passes through the village and up a small hill to visit the **Nunnery Ruins,** one of Britain's best-preserved medieval nunneries (free).

Immediately after the nunnery, turn right on North Road to reach the chapel and abbey. You'll curve up through the fields—

passing the parish church and Heritage Center on your left (see later)—before the road swings right.

Soon, on the right, you'll see **St. Oran's Chapel,** in the graveyard of the Iona Abbey. This chapel is the oldest church building on the island. Inside you'll find a few grave slabs carved in the distinctive Iona School style, which was developed by local stone-carvers in the 14th century. On these tall, skinny headstones, look for the depictions of medieval warrior aristocrats with huge swords. Many more of these carvings have been moved to the abbey, where you can see them in its cloister and museum.

It's free to see the graveyard and chapel; the **Iona Abbey** itself has an admission fee, but it's worth the cost just to sit in the stillness of its lovely, peaceful interior courtyard. (For details, see "Sights on Iona," later.)

Just beyond and across the road from the abbey is the **Iona Community's Welcome Centre** (free WCs), which runs the abbey with Historic Scotland and hosts modern-day pilgrims who come here to experience the birthplace of Scottish Christianity. (If you're staying longer, you could attend a worship service at the abbey—check the schedule here; tel. 01681/700-404, www.iona.org.uk.) Its gift shop is packed with books on the island's important role in Christian history.

Continue past the abbey and welcome center on North Road. A 10-minute walk brings you to the footpath for **Dùn Ì,** a steep but short climb with good views of the abbey looking back toward Mull.

Returning to the main road, walk another 20-25 minutes to the end of the paved road, where you'll arrive at a gate leading through a sheep- and cow-strewn pasture to Iona's pristine white-sand **North Beach.** Dip your toes in the Atlantic and ponder what this Caribbean-like alcove is doing in Scotland. Be sure to allow at least 40 minutes to return to the ferry dock.

Sights on Iona

▲Iona Abbey

This (mostly rebuilt) church marks the site of Christianity's arrival in Scotland. You'll see Celtic crosses, the original shrine of

St. Columba, a big church slathered with medieval carvings, a tranquil cloister, and an excellent museum with surviving fragments of this site's fascinating layers of history.

Cost and Hours: £7.10, not covered by bus tour ticket, daily April-Sept 9:30-17:30, Oct-March until 16:30, museum closes 30 minutes earlier, tel. 01681/700-512, www. historic-scotland.gov.uk.

Visiting the Abbey: While the present abbey, nunnery, and graveyard go back to the 13th century, much of what you'll see was rebuilt in the 20th century. Be sure to read the "History of Iona" sidebar to prepare for your visit.

At the entrance building, pick up your included audioguide, and ask about the good 30-minute guided tours (4/day and well worthwhile). Then head toward the church. You'll pass two faded **Celtic crosses** (and the base of a third); the originals are in the museum at the end of your visit. Some experts believe that Celtic crosses—with their distinctive shape so tied to Christianity on the British Isles—originated right here on Iona.

Facing the entrance to the church, you'll see the original **shrine to St. Columba** on your left—a magnet for pilgrims.

Head inside the **church.** It feels like an active church—with hymnals neatly stacked in the pews—because it is, thanks to the Iona Community (across the street, and explained in the "Welcome to Iona Walk"). While much of this space has been rebuilt, take a moment to look around and you'll find some original decorations. Plenty of original medieval stone carving (especially the capitals of many columns) still survives. To see a particularly striking example, stand near the pulpit in the middle of the church and look back to the entrance. Partway up the left span of the pointed arch framing the transept, look for the eternally screaming face. While interpretations vary, this may have been a reminder for the priest not to leave out the fire-and-brimstone parts of his message. Some of the newer features of the church—including the base of the baptismal font near the entrance, and the main altar—are carved from locally quarried Iona marble: white with green streaks. In the right/south transept is the tomb of George Campbell—the Eighth Duke of Argyll, who donated this property in 1900, allowing it to be restored.

When you're ready to continue, find the poorly marked door into the **cloister**. (As you face the altar, it's about halfway down the nave on the left, before the transept.) This space is filled with harmonious light, additional finely carved capitals (these are modern re-creations), and—displayed along the walls—several more of the tall, narrow tombstones like the ones displayed in St. Oran's Chapel. On these, look for a couple of favorite motifs: the long, intimidating sword  (indicating a warrior of the Highland clans) and the ship with billowing sails (a powerful symbol of this seafaring culture).

Around the far side of the cloister is the shop. But before leaving, don't overlook the easy-to-miss **museum.** (To find it, head outside and walk around the left side of the abbey complex, toward the sea.) This modern, well-presented space exhibits a remarkable collection of original stonework from the abbey—including what's left of the three Celtic crosses out front—all eloquently described.

Take some time to linger and make sure you've seen all you want to see. Then go in peace.

Heritage Centre

This little museum, tucked behind the parish church between the nunnery ruins and the abbey (watch for signs), is small but well done, with displays on local and natural history and a tiny tearoom.

Cost and Hours: £2.50, Mon-Sat 10:30-16:30, closed Sun and Nov-mid-April, www.ionaheritage.co.uk.

Sleeping and Eating on Iona

These are listed roughly in the order you'll reach them as you climb the main road from the ferry dock. The two hotels listed here have some seaview rooms (with small windows) and close in winter (Nov-March). At each one, the price drops for longer stays (more than 4-5 nights). Both also have restaurants. In addition to my suggestions listed below, there are many B&Bs, apartments, and a hostel (for options, see www.isle-of-iona.net/accommodation).

$$$ Argyll Hotel, built in 1867, proudly overlooks the waterfront, with 17 cottage-like rooms and pleasingly creaky hallways lined with bookshelves. Of the two hotels, it feels classier (Sb-£70, D-£85, Db-£99, larger Db-£150, luxury seaview Db-£170, extra bed for kids-£16, reserve far in advance for July-Aug, comfortable lounge and sunroom, tel. 01681/700-334, www.argyllhoteliona. co.uk, reception@argyllhoteliona.co.uk). Its dining room is open to the public for lunch (£6-8, daily 12:15-14:00, tea served until 16:30) and dinner (£12-20, 18:00-20:00).

$$$ St. Columba Hotel, a bit higher up in town and situated in the middle of a peaceful garden with picnic tables, has 27 institutional rooms and spacious lodge-like common spaces—such as a big, cushy seaview lounge (Sb-£74-88, Db-£127-155, huge view Db-£190, extra bed for kids-£15, closed Nov-March, next door to abbey on road up from dock, tel. 01681/700-304, www. stcolumba-hotel.co.uk, info@stcolumba-hotel.co.uk). Their fine 21-table restaurant, overlooking the water, is open to the public for lunch (£8-12, daily 12:15-14:30), tea (14:00-17:00), and dinner (£13-17, 18:30-20:00).

$$ Calva B&B, a five-minute walk past the abbey, has three spacious rooms (Db-£70, second house on left past the abbey, look for sign in window and gnomes on porch, tel. 01681/700-340; friendly Janetta, Ken, and Jack the bearded collie).

Staffa

Those more interested in nature than in church history will enjoy the trip to the wildly scenic Isle of Staffa. Completely uninhabited (except for seabirds), Staffa is a knob of rock draped with a vibrant green carpet of turf. Remote and quiet, it feels like a Hebrides nature preserve.

Most day trips give you an hour on Staffa—barely enough time to see its two claims to fame: The basalt columns of Fingal's

Cave, and (in summer) a colony of puffins. To squeeze in both, be ready to hop off the boat and climb the staircase. Partway up to the left, you can walk around to the cave (about 7 minutes). Or continue up to the top, then turn right and walk across the spine of the grassy island (about 10-15 minutes) to the cove where the puffins gather. (Your captain should point out both options and let you know how active the puffins have been.)

▲▲Fingal's Cave

Staffa's shore is covered with bizarre, mostly hexagonal basalt columns that stick up at various heights. It's as if the earth were offering God his choice of thousands of six-sided cigarettes. (The island's name likely came from the Old Norse word for "stave"—the building timbers these columns resemble.) This is the other end of

Northern Ireland's popular Giant's Causeway. You'll walk along the uneven surface of these columns, curling around the far side of the island, until you can actually step inside the gaping mouth of a cave—where floor-to-ceiling columns and crashing waves combine to create a powerful experience. Listening to the water and air flowing through this otherworldly space inspired Felix Mendelssohn to compose his overture, *The Hebrides*.

While you're ogling the cave, consider this: Geologists claim these unique formations were created by volcanic eruptions more than 60 million years ago. As the surface of the lava flow quickly cooled, it contracted and crystallized into columns (resembling the caked mud at the bottom of a dried-up lakebed, but with deeper cracks). As the rock later settled and eroded, the columns broke off into the many stair-like steps that now honeycomb Staffa.

Of course, in actuality, these formations resulted from a heated rivalry between a Scottish giant named Fingal, who lived on Staffa, and an Ulster warrior named Finn MacCool, who lived across the sea on Ireland's Antrim Coast. Knowing that the giant was coming to spy on him, Finn had his wife dress him as a sleeping infant. The giant, shocked at the infant's size, fled back to Scotland in terror of whomever had sired this giant baby. Breathing a sigh of relief, Finn tore off the baby clothes and prudently knocked down the bridge.

▲▲Puffins

A large colony of Atlantic puffins settles on Staffa each spring and summer during mating season (generally early May through early August). Puffins—with their stout little bodies, penguin-like black-and-white colorings, beady black eyes, and brightly colored beaks and feet—live most of their lives on the open ocean, coming to land only to breed. Puffins mate for life and typically lay just one egg each year, which the male and female take turns caring for. To feed their young, puffins plunge as deep as 200 feet below the sea's surface to catch sand eels and other small fish.

The puffins tend to scatter when the boat arrives. But after the boat pulls out and its passengers hike across the island, the very tame puffins' curiosity gets the better of them. First you'll see them flutter up from the off-shore rocks, with their distinctive, bobbing flight. They'll zip and whirl around, and finally they'll start to land on the lip of the cove. Sit quietly, move slowly, and be patient, and soon they'll get close. (If any seagulls are nearby, shoo them away—puffins are undaunted by humans, who do them no harm, but they're terrified of predator seagulls.)

In the waters around Staffa—on your way to and from the other islands—also keep an eye out for a variety of **marine life**, including seals, dolphins, porpoises, and the occasional minke whale, fin whale, or basking shark (a gigantic fish that hinges open its enormous jaw to drift-net plankton).

Near Oban

The following sights are worth considering for drivers. The first section outlines the best driving route from Glasgow to Oban, including the appealing pit stop at Inveraray. And the second section covers one of Scotland's most important prehistoric sites, Kilmartin Glen.

BETWEEN GLASGOW AND OBAN

The drive from Glasgow (or Edinburgh) to Oban provides dreamy vistas and your first look at the dramatic landscapes of the Highlands.

Driving Tour from Glasgow to Inveraray

Here's a loosely narrated route: Leaving Glasgow on the A-82, you'll soon be driving along the west bank of **Loch Lomond** (described on page 195). The first picnic turnout has the best lake views, benches, a park, and a playground.

Halfway up the loch, at Tarbet, the road forks; keep left to stay on the A-83 (toward *Campbeltown*). You'll pass the village of Arrochar, then drive along the banks of Loch Long. The scenery crescendos as you pull away from the loch and twist up over the mountains and through a pine forest, getting your first glimpse of bald Highlands mountains—it's clear that you've just crossed the Highland Boundary Fault. Enjoy the waterfalls, and notice that the road signs are now in English as well as Gaelic. As you climb into more rugged territory—up the valley called Glen Croe—be mindful that the roads connecting the Lowlands with the Highlands (like the one down in the glen below) were originally a military project designed to facilitate government quelling of the Highland clans.

At the summit, watch for the large parking lot with picnic tables on your left (signed for *Argyll Forest Park*). Stretch your legs at what's aptly named the **Rest-and-Be-Thankful Pass.** The colorful name comes from the 1880s, when second- and third-class coach passengers got out and pushed the coach and first-class passengers up the hill.

Twisting down the far side of the pass, you'll drive through Glen Kinglas and soon reach **Loch Fyne,** a saltwater "sea loch" famous for its shellfish (keep an eye out for oyster farms and seafood restaurants). In fact, Loch Fyne is the namesake of a popular UK restaurant chain.

Looping around Loch Fyne, you reach...

▲Inveraray

Nearly everybody stops at this lovely, seemingly made-for-tourists castle town on Loch Fyne. Park near the pier and browse the wide selection of eateries and tourist shops (**TI** open daily, on Front Street, tel. 01499/302-063; public WCs at end of nearby pier).

As you approach town, keep an eye on the right (when crossing the bridge) for the dramatic **Inveraray Castle.** This stronghold of one of the more notorious branches of the Campbell clan is scenic from afar and, if you can spare the time, fun to tour—it's worth ▲ (£10, April-Oct daily 10:00-17:45, closed Nov-March, last entry 45 minutes before closing, café, free parking—watch for signs from main road, tel. 01499/302-203, www.inveraray-castle.com). This residence of the Dukes of Argyll comes with a dramatic, turreted exterior (one of Scotland's most striking) and a lavishly decorated interior that feels spacious and neatly tended. Public television fans may recognize this as "Duneagle Castle" (a.k.a. Uncle Shrimpy's pad) from one of the *Downton Abbey* Christmas specials—big photos of the Grantham and MacClare clans decorate the genteel rooms. Roam from room to room, reading the laminated descriptions and asking questions of the gregarious docents. The high-

The Irish Connection

The Romans called the people living in what is now Ireland the "Scoti" (meaning pirates). When the Scoti crossed the narrow Irish Sea and invaded the land of the Picts 1,500 years ago, that region became known as Scoti-land. Ireland and Scotland were never fully conquered by the Romans, and they retained similar clannish Celtic traits. Both share the same Gaelic branch of the linguistic tree.

On clear summer days, you can actually see Ireland—just 17 miles away—from the Scottish coastline. The closest bit to Scotland is the boomerang-shaped Rathlin Island, part of Northern Ireland. Rathlin is where Scottish leader Robert the Bruce retreated in 1307 after defeat at the hands of the English. Legend has it that he hid in a cave on the island, where he observed a spider patiently rebuilding its web each time a breeze knocked it down. Inspired by the spider's perseverance, Bruce gathered his Scottish forces once more and finally defeated the English at the decisive battle of Bannockburn (see page 65).

Flush with confidence from his victory, Robert the Bruce decided to open a second front against the English...in Ireland. In 1315, he sent his brother Edward over to enlist their Celtic Irish cousins in an effort to thwart the English. After securing Ireland, Edward hoped to move on and enlist the Welsh, thus cornering England with their pan-Celtic nation. But Edward's timing was bad: Ireland was in the midst of famine. His Scottish troops had to live off the land and began to take food and supplies from the starving Irish. Some of Ireland's crops may have been intentionally destroyed to keep it from being used as a colonial "breadbasket" to feed English troops. The Scots quickly wore out their welcome, and Edward the Bruce was eventually killed in battle near Dundalk in 1318.

It's interesting to imagine how things might be different today if Scotland and Ireland had been permanently welded together as a nation 700 years ago. You'll notice the strong Scottish influence in Northern Ireland when you ask a local a question and he answers, "Aye, a wee bit." And in Glasgow—on Scotland's west coast, closest to Ireland—an Ireland-like division between royalist Protestants and republican Catholics survives today in the form of soccer team allegiances. In  big Scottish cities (like Glasgow and Edinburgh), you'll even see "orange parades" of protesters marching in solidarity with their Protestant Northern Irish cousins. The Irish—always quick to defuse tension with humor—joke that the Scots are just Irish people who couldn't swim home.

light is the Armory Hall that fills the main atrium, where swords and rifles are painstakingly arrayed in starburst patterns. As with many such castles, the aristocratic clan still lives here (*private* signs mark rooms where the family resides). The kids attend school in London, but spend a few months here each year; in the winter, the castle is closed to the public and they have the run of the place. After touring the interior, do a loop through the finely manicured gardens.

Once in town, the main "sight" is the **Inveraray Jail,** an over-priced, corny, but mildly educational former jail converted into a museum. This "living 19th-century prison" includes a courtroom where mannequins argue the fate of the accused. Then you'll head outside and explore the various cells of the outer courtyard. The playful guards may lock you up for a photo op, while they ex-plain how Scotland reformed its prison system in 1839—you'll see both "before" and "after" cells in this complex (£9, open daily, tel. 01499/302-381, www.inverarayjail.co.uk).

Leaving Inveraray: To continue **directly to Oban** (about an hour), leave Inveraray through the gate at the woolen mill and get on the A-819, which takes you through Glen Aray and along Loch Awe. A left turn on the A-85 takes you into Oban. If you have time to kill—and a healthy interest in prehistoric sites—going to Oban by way of **Kilmartin Glen** (described next) adds about 45 minutes of driving. To get there, head straight up Inveraray's main street and get on the waterfront A-83 (marked for *Campbeltown*); after a half-hour, in Lochgilphead, turn right onto the A-816, which takes you through Kilmartin Glen and all the way up to Oban. (To avoid backtracking, be ready to stop at the prehistoric sites lining the A-816 between Lochgilphead and Kilmartin village.)

SOUTH OF OBAN
Kilmartin Glen

Scotland isn't as rich with prehistoric sites as South England is, but the ones in Kilmartin Glen, while faint, are some of Scotland's most accessible—and most important. This wide valley, clearly im-bued with spiritual and/or strategic power, contains reminders of several millennia worth of inhabitants. Today it's a playground for those who enjoy tromping through grassy fields while daydreaming about who moved these giant stones here so many centuries ago.

This isn't worth a long detour, unless you're fascinated by prehistoric sites.

Four to five thousand years ago, Kilmartin Glen was inhabited by Neolithic people who left behind fragments of their giant, stony monuments. And 1,500 years ago, this was the seat of the kings of the Scoti, who migrated here from Ireland around A.D. 500, giving rise to Scotland's own branch of Celtic culture. From this grassy valley, the Scoti kings ruled their empire, called Dalriada (also sometimes written Dál Riata), which encompassed much of Scotland's west coast, the Inner Hebrides, and the northern part of Ireland. The Scoti spoke Gaelic and were Christian; as they overtook the rest of the Highlands—eventually absorbing their rival Picts—theirs became a dominant culture, which is still evident in pockets of present-day Scotland. Today, Kilmartin Glen is scattered with burial cairns, standing stones, and a hill called Dunadd—the fortress of the Scoti kings.

Visiting Kilmartin Glen: Sites are scattered throughout the valley, including some key locations along or just off the A-816 south of Kilmartin village. If you're coming from Inveraray, you'll pass these *before* you reach the village and museum itself. Each one is explained by good informational signs.

The bulbous hill called **Dunadd** sits just west of the A-816, about four miles north of Lochgilphead and four miles south of Kilmartin village (watch for blue, low-profile *Dunadd Fort* signs). A fort stood here since the time of Christ, but it was the Scoti kings—who made it their primary castle from the sixth to ninth centuries—that put Dunadd on the map. Park in the big lot at its base and hike through the faint outlines of terraces to the top, where you can enjoy sweeping views over all of Kilmartin Glen; this southern stretch is a marshland called "The Great Moss" (Moine Mhor). Look for carvings in the rock: early Celtic writing, the image of a boar, and a footprint (carved into a stone crisscrossed with fissures). This "footprint of fealty" (a replica) recalls the inauguration ceremony in which the king would place his foot into the footprint, symbolizing the marriage between the ruler and the land.

About two miles farther north on the A-816, brown *Dunchraigaig* signs mark a parking lot where you can cross the road to the 4,000-year-old, 100-foot-in-diameter **Dunchraigaig Cairn**—the burial place for 10 Neolithic VIPs. Circle around to find the opening, where you can still crawl into a small recess. This is one of at least five such cairns that together created a mile-and-a-half-long "linear cemetery" up the middle of Kilmartin Glen. From this cairn, you can walk five minutes to several more prehistoric structures: Follow signs through the gate, and walk to a farm field with **Ballymeanoch**—an avenue of two stone rows (with six surviving stones), a disheveled old cairn, and a stone circle.

About one more mile north on the A-816, just off the intersection with the B-8025 (toward *Tayvallich*), is the small Kilmartin Burn parking lot. From here, cross the stream to a field where the five **Nether Largie Standing Stones** have stood in a neat north-south line for 3,200 years. Were these stones designed as an astronomical observatory? Burial rituals or other religious ceremonies? Sporting events? Or just a handy place for sheep to scratch themselves? From here, you can hike the rest of the way through the field to the Nether Largie South Cairn and the Temple Wood Stone Circles, described next (which don't have their own parking).

For a quick look at those two, just beyond the Tayvallich turn-off on the A-816, turn left on the tiny road toward Slockavullin (over the stone bridge). You'll pass (in the field on your left) the **Nether Largie South Cairn,** then spot (on your right) the striking **Temple Wood Stone Circles.** The larger, older of these circles dates to more than 5,000 years ago, and both were added onto and modified over the millennia.

To get the big picture, head for the **Kilmartin House Museum,** in the center of Kilmartin village. The cute stone house has a ticket desk, bookshop, and café; the museum—with modern exhibits explaining this area's powerful history—fills the basement of the adjacent modern building (though a new home for the exhibit is in the works). The modest but modern museum features handy explanations, a few original artifacts, and lots of re-creations (£5, daily except closed Christmas-Feb, tel. 01546/510-278, www.kilmartin.org). From the museum, you can look out across the fields to see **Glebe Cairn,** one of the five cairns of the "linear cemetery." Another one, the **Nether Largie North Cairn,** was reconstructed in the 1970s and can actually be entered (a half-mile south of the museum; ask for directions at museum).

Many, many more prehistoric sites fill Kilmartin Glen (more than 800 within a six-mile radius); the museum sells in-depth guidebooks for the curious, and can point you in the right direction for what you're interested in.

GLENCOE AND FORT WILLIAM

Glencoe • Fort William • The Road to the Isles

Scotland is a land of great natural wonders. And some of the most spectacular—and most accessible—are in the valley called Glencoe, just an hour north of Oban and on the way to Fort William, Loch Ness, Inverness, or the Isle of Skye. The evocative "Weeping Glen" of Glencoe aches with both history and natural beauty. Beyond that, Fort William anchors the southern end of the Caledonian Canal, offering a springboard to more Highlands scenery. This is where Britain's highest peak, Ben Nevis, keeps its head in the clouds, and where you'll find a valley made famous by a bonnie prince...and (later) by a steam train carrying a young wizard named Harry.

PLANNING YOUR TIME

On a quick visit, this area warrants just a few hours between Oban and either Inverness or Skye: Wander through Glencoe village, tour its modest museum, then drive up Glencoe valley for views before continuing on your way. But if you have time to linger in the Highlands, Glencoe is an ideal place to do it. Settle in for a night (or more) to make time for a more leisurely drive and to squeeze in a hike or two—I give an overview of the best options, from easy strolls to challenging ascents.

Beyond Glencoe, Fort William—a touristy and overrated transportation hub—is skippable, but can be a handy lunch stop. The Road to the Isles, stretching west from Fort William to the coast, isn't worth a detour, but it's very handy for those connecting to the Isle of Skye. Along the way, the only stop worth more than a quick photo is Glenfinnan, with its powerful ties to Bonnie Prince Charlie and Jacobite history.

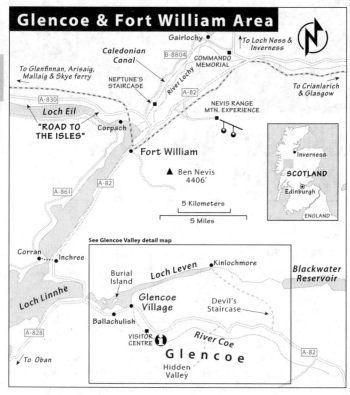

Glencoe & Fort William Area

- Gairlochy
- To Loch Ness & Inverness
- Caledonian Canal
- B-8804
- COMMANDO MEMORIAL
- River Lochy
- To Glenfinnan, Arisaig, Mallaig & Skye ferry
- NEPTUNE'S STAIRCASE
- A-82
- To Crianlarich & Glasgow
- NEVIS RANGE MTN. EXPERIENCE
- A-830
- Loch Eil
- "ROAD TO THE ISLES"
- Corpach
- Fort William
- ▲ Ben Nevis 4406'
- A-861
- A-82
- 5 Kilometers
- 5 Miles
- Inverness
- SCOTLAND
- Edinburgh
- ENGLAND

See Glencoe Valley detail map

- Corran
- Inchree
- Loch Leven
- Kinlochmore
- Blackwater Reservoir
- Burial Island
- Glencoe Village
- Devil's Staircase
- Loch Linnhe
- Ballachulish
- A-828
- VISITOR CENTRE
- River Coe
- A-82
- Glencoe
- To Oban
- Hidden Valley

Glencoe

This valley is the essence of the wild, powerful, and stark beauty of the Highlands. Along with its scenery, Glencoe offers a good dose of bloody clan history: In 1692, government Redcoats (led by a local Campbell commander) came to the valley, and they were sheltered and fed for 12 days by the MacDonalds—whose leader had been late in swearing an oath to the British monarch. Then, on the morning of February 13, the soldiers were ordered to rise up early and kill their sleeping hosts, violating the rules of Highland hospitality and earning the valley the nickname "The Weeping Glen." Thirty-eight men were killed outright; hundreds more fled through a blizzard, and some 40 additional villagers (mostly women and children) died from exposure. It's fitting that such an

Harry Potter Sights

Harry Potter's story is set in a magical, largely fictional Britain, but you can visit real locations used in the film series. **Glencoe** was the main location for outdoor filming in *The Prisoner of Azkaban* and *The Half-Blood Prince,* and many shots of the Hogwarts grounds were filmed in the Fort William and Glencoe areas. The *Hogwarts Express* that carries Harry, Ron, and Hermione to school each year runs along the actual **Jacobite Steam Train** line (between Fort William and Mallaig).

In *The Prisoner of Azkaban*, **Loch Shiel, Loch Eilt,** and **Loch Morar** (near Fort William) were the stand-ins for Hogwarts Lake. **Steal Falls,** at the base of Ben Nevis, is the locale for the Triwizard Tournament in *The Goblet of Fire.*

epic, dramatic incident should be set in this equally epic, dramatic valley, where the cliffsides seem to weep (with running streams) when it rains.

Aside from its tragic history, this place has captured the imaginations of both hikers and artists. Movies filmed here include everything from *Monty Python and the Holy Grail* and *Highlander* to *Harry Potter and the Prisoner of Azkaban* and the James Bond film *Skyfall.* When filmmakers want a stunning, rugged backdrop; when hikers want a scenic challenge; and when Scots want to remember their hard-fought past...they all think of Glencoe.

Orientation to Glencoe

The valley of Glencoe is just off the main A-828/A-82 road between Oban and points north (such as Fort William and Inverness). If you're coming from the north, the signage can be tricky—at the roundabout south of Fort William, follow signs to *Crianlarich* and *A-82.* The most appealing town here is the sleepy one-street village of Glencoe, worth a stop for its folk museum and its status as the gateway to the valley. The town's hub of activity is its grocery store, which has an ATM (daily 8:00-19:00, until 20:00 Fri-Sat). The slightly larger and more modern town of Ballachulish (a half-mile away) has more services, including a nice Co-op grocery store (daily 7:00-22:00).

In the loch just outside Glencoe (near Ballachulish), notice the burial island—where the souls of those who "take the low road" are piped home. (For an explanation of "Ye'll take the high road, and I'll take the low road," see page 196.) The next island was the Island of Discussion—where those in dispute went until they found agreement.

TOURIST INFORMATION

Your best source of information (especially for walks and hikes) is the **Glencoe Visitor Centre,** described later. The nearest **TI** is well signed in Ballachulish; it's buried inside a huge café and gift shop (daily Easter-Oct 9:00-17:00, Nov-Easter 10:00-16:00, tel. 01855/811-866, www.glencoetourism.co.uk). For more information on the area, see www.discoverglencoe.com.

Bike Rental: At **Crank It Up Gear,** Davy rents road and mountain bikes, and can offer plenty of suggestions for where to pedal in the area (£15/half-day, £20/all day, just off the main street to the left near the start of town, 20 Lorn Drive, mobile 07746-860-023, www.crankitupgear.com).

Sights in Glencoe

Glencoe Village

Glencoe village is just a line of houses sitting beneath the brooding mountains. The only real sight in town is the folk museum (described below). But walking the

main street gives a good glimpse of village Scotland. From the free parking lot at the entrance to town, go for a stroll. You'll pass lots of little B&Bs renting two or three rooms, the stony Episcopal church, the folk museum, the town's grocery store, and the village hall.

At the far end of the village, on the left just before the bridge, a Celtic cross **World War I** memorial stands on a little hill. Even this

wee village lost 11 souls during that war—a reminder of Scotland's disproportionate contribution to Britain's war effort. You'll see memorials like this (usually either a Celtic cross or a soldier with bowed head) in virtually every town in Scotland.

If you were to cross the little bridge, you'd head up into Glencoe's wooded parklands, with some easy hikes (described later). But for one more landmark, turn right just before the bridge and walk about five minutes. Standing on a craggy bluff on your right is another memorial—this one to the **Glencoe Massacre,** which still haunts the memories of people here and throughout Scotland.

Glencoe and North Lorn Folk Museum

This gathering of thatched-roof, early 18th-century croft houses is jammed with local history, creating a huggable museum filled

with humble exhibits gleaned from the town's old closets and attics. When one house was being rethatched, its owner found a cache of 200-year-old swords and pistols hidden there from the government Redcoats after the disastrous battle of Culloden. You'll also see antique toys, boxes from old food products, sports paraphernalia, a cabinet of curiosities, and plenty of information on the MacDonald clan. Be sure to look for the museum's little door that leads out back, where additional, smaller buildings are filled with everyday items (furniture, farm tools, and so on) and exhibits on the Glencoe Massacre and Highland doctors.

Cost and Hours: £3, call ahead for hours—generally Easter-Oct Mon-Sat 10:00-16:30, closed Sun and off-season, sometimes closed at lunchtime, tel. 01855/811-664, www.glencoemuseum. com.

Glencoe Visitor Centre

This modern facility, a mile past Glencoe village up the A-82 into the dramatic valley, is designed to resemble a *clachan*, or traditional Highland settlement. The information desk inside the shop at the ranger desk is your single best resource for advice (and maps or guidebooks) about local walks and hikes (several of which are outlined later in this chapter). At the back of the complex you'll find a viewpoint with a handy 3-D model of the hills for orientation. There's also a pricey £6.50 exhibition about the surrounding landscape, the region's history, wildlife, mountaineering, and conservation. It's worth the time to watch the more-interesting-than-it-sounds two-minute video on geology and the 14-minute film on the Glencoe Massacre, which thoughtfully traces the events leading up to the tragedy rather than simply recycling romanticized legends.

Cost and Hours: Free; April-Oct daily 9:30-17:30; Nov-March Thu-Sun 10:00-16:00, closed Mon-Wed; last entry 45 minutes before closing, free Wi-Fi, café, tel. 01855/811-307, www. glencoe-nts.org.uk.

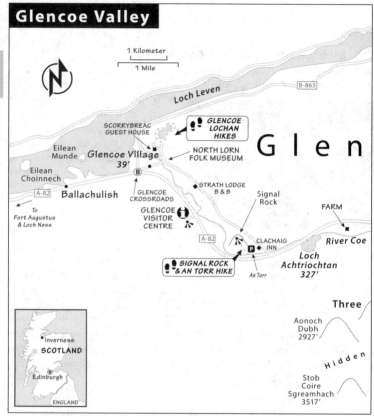

Glencoe Valley Driving Tour

If you have a car, spend an hour or so following the A-82 through the valley, past the Glencoe Visitor Centre, into the desolate moor beyond, and back again. You'll enjoy grand views, dramatic craggy hills, and, if you're lucky, a chance to hear a bagpiper in the wind: Roadside Highland buskers often set up here on good-weather summer weekends. (If you play the recorder—and the piper's not swarmed with other tourists—ask to finger a tune while he does the hard work.)

Here's a lightly narrated explanation of the route. Along the way, I've pointed out sometimes easy-to-miss trailheads, in case you're up for a hike (hikes described in the next section).

🡒 **Self-Guided Driving Tour:** Leaving Glencoe village on the A-82, it's just a mile to the **Glencoe Visitor Centre** (on the right, described earlier). Soon after, the road pulls out of the forested hills and gives you unobstructed views of the U-shaped valley.

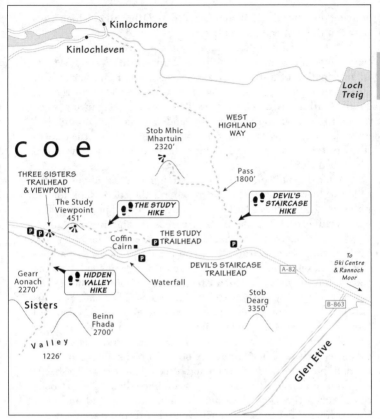

About a mile after the visitors center, on the left, is a parking lot for **Signal Rock and An Torr,** a popular place for low-impact forested hikes. Just beyond, also on the left, is a single-track road leading to the **Clachaig Inn,** a classic hikers' pub (described on page 285). The hillsides above the inn were the setting for Hagrid's hut in the third Harry Potter movie (though nothing remains from filming).

Continuing along the A-82, you'll hit a straight stretch, passing a lake (Loch Achtriochtan), and then a small farm, both on the right. After the farm, the valley narrows a bit as you cut through

Glencoe Pass. On the right, you'll pass two small parking lots. Pull into the second one for perhaps the best viewpoint of the entire valley, with point-blank views of the steep ridge-like mountains known as the **Three Sisters.** This is also the

starting point for the challenging **Hidden Valley hike,** which leads between the first and second sisters.

As you continue, keep an eye out for partially ruined stone buildings—the remains of pillboxes built during World War II in anticipation of a possible Nazi invasion. After another mile or so—through some glorious waterfall scenery—watch on the left for the **Coffin Cairn,** which looks like a stone igloo (parking is just across the road if you want a cairn-and-waterfalls photo op). Just after the cairn, look on the left for pull-out parking for the **hike to The Study,** a viewpoint overlooking the road you just drove down (described later).

After this pull-out, you'll hit a straightaway for about a mile, followed by an S-curve. Just at the end of the curve, look for the pull-out parking on the left, just before the stand of pine trees. This is the trailhead for the **Devil's Staircase** hike, high into the hills.

Continuing past here, you're nearing the end of the valley. The intimidating peak of **Stob Dearg** (on the right) looms like a dour watchman, guarding the far end of the valley. Soon you'll pass the turnoff (on the right) for **Glen Etive,** an even more remote-feeling valley. (This was the setting for the final scenes of *Skyfall*. Yes, this is where James Bond grew up. Of *course* he grew up in Glencoe.) Continuing past that, the last sign of civilization (on the right) is the Glencoe Ski Centre. And from here, the terrain flattens out as you enter the vast **Rannoch Moor**—50 bleak square miles of heather, boulders, and barely enough decent land to graze a sheep.

You could keep driving as far as you like—but the moor looks pretty much the same from here on out. Turn around and head back through Glencoe...it's scenery you'll hardly mind seeing twice.

Hiking in Glencoe

Glencoe is made for hiking. Many routes are not particularly well marked, so it's essential to get very specific instructions (from the rangers at the Glencoe Visitor Centre, or other knowledgeable locals) and equip yourself with a good map (the Ordnance Survey Explorer Map #384, sold at the visitors center, is ideal). Below, I've suggested a few of the most enticing walks and hikes. These vary from easy, level strolls to challenging climbs. Either way, equip yourself with proper footwear (even the easy trails can get swamped in wet weather) and rain gear—you never know when a storm will blow in.

I've listed these roughly in order of how close they are to Glencoe village, and given a rough sense of difficulty for each. Some of them (including the first two) are more forested, but the ones out in the open—which really let you feel immersed in the wonders of Glencoe—are even better.

While you can walk to the first two areas from Glencoe village, the rest are best for drivers. Some of these trailheads are tricky to find; remember, I've designed the driving commentary in the previous section to help you find the hikes off the A-82.

Glencoe Lochan (Easy)

Perched on the forested hill above Glencoe village is an improbable slice of the Canadian Rockies. A century ago, this was the personal playground of Lord Strathcona, a local boy done good when he moved to Canada and eventually became a big Canadian Pacific Railway magnate. In 1894, he returned home with his Canadian wife and built the Glencoe House (which was recently restored into an exclusive, top-of-the-top hotel, with suites starting around £500 a night). His wife was homesick for the Rockies, so he had the grounds landscaped to represent the lakes, trees, and mountains of her home country. They even carved out a manmade lake (Glencoe Lochan), which looks like a slice of Canada tucked under a craggy Scottish backdrop. (She was still homesick—they eventually returned to Canada.)

Today, the house and immediate surroundings are off-limits, but the rest of the area is open for exploration. Head to the end of Glencoe village, cross the bridge, and continue straight up (following signs for *Glencoe Lochan*)—it's a 20-minute uphill walk, or 5-minute drive, from the village center. Once there, a helpful orientation panel in the parking lot suggests three different, color-coded, one-mile walking loops—mostly around that beautiful lake, which reflects the hillsides of Glencoe.

From this area, a good trail network called the **Orbital Recreational Track** follows the river through the forest up the valley, all the way to the Clachaig Inn (about 45 minutes one-way). This links you to the Signal Rock and An Torr areas (described next). Eventually they hope to extend this trail system across the valley and back to the Glencoe Visitor Centre, which would allow a handy loop hike around the valley floor.

Signal Rock and An Torr (Easy to Moderate)

This forested area has nicely tended trails and gives you a better chance of spotting wildlife than the more desolate hikes described later. To explore this area, park at the well-marked lot just off of the A-82 and go for a walk. A well-described panel at the trailhead narrates three options: easy yellow route to the Clachaig Inn; longer blue route to Signal Rock; and strenuous black route along the hillsides of An Torr. The Signal Rock route brings you to a panoramic point overlooking the valley—so named because a fire could be lit here to alert others in case of danger.

Hidden Valley (Challenging)

Three miles east of Glencoe village, this aptly named glen is tucked between two of the dramatic Three Sisters mountains. Also called the Lost Valley (Coire Gabhail in Gaelic), this was supposedly where the MacDonalds hid stolen cattle from their rivals, the Campbells (who later massacred them). This is the most challenging of the hikes I describe—it's strenuous and has stretches with uneven footing. Expect to scramble a bit over rocks, and to cross a river on stepping stones (which may be underwater after a heavy rain). As the rocks can be slippery when wet, skip this hike in bad weather. Figure about two and a half to three hours round-trip (with an ascent of more than 1,000 feet).

Begin at the second parking lot at Glencoe Pass (on the right when coming from Glencoe), with views of the Three Sisters. You're aiming to head between the first and second Sisters (counting from the left). Hike down into the valley between the road and the mountains. Bear left, head down a metal staircase, and cross the bridge over the river. (Don't cross the bridge to the right of the parking lots—a common mistake.) Once across, you'll start the treacherous ascent up a narrow gorge. Some scrambling is required, and at one point a railing helps you find your way. The next tricky part is where you cross the river. You're looking for a pebbly beach and a large boulder; stepping stones lead across the river, and you'll see the path resume on the other side. But if the water level is high, the stones may be covered—though still passable with good shoes and steady footing. (Don't attempt to scramble over the treacherous slopes on the side of the river with the loose rocks called scree.) Once across the stepping stones, keep on the trail into the valley.

Much Easier Alternative: If you'd simply enjoy the feeling of walking deep in Glencoe valley—with peaks and waterfalls overhead—you can start down from the parking lot toward the Hidden Valley trail, and then simply stroll the old road along the valley floor as far as you want in either direction.

The Study
(Easy to Moderate)

For a relatively easy, mostly level hike through the valley with a nice viewpoint at the end, consider walking to the flat rock called "The Study" and back. It takes about 45-60 minutes round-trip. The walk essentially

parallels the main highway, but on the old road a bit higher up. You'll park just beyond the Three Sisters and the Coffin Cairn. From there, cut through the field of stone and marshy turf to the old road—basically two gravel tire ruts—and follow them to your left. You'll hike above the modern road, passing several modest waterfalls, until you reach a big, flat rock with stunning views of the Three Sisters and the valley beyond. (Fellow hikers have marked the spot with a pile of stones.)

The Devil's Staircase (Strenuous but Straightforward)

About eight miles east of Glencoe village, near the end of the valley, you can hike this brief stretch of the West Highland Way. It was built by General Wade, the British strategist who came to Scotland after the 1715 Jacobite rebellion to help secure government rule here. Designed to connect Glencoe valley to the lochside town of Kinlochmore, to the north, it's named for its challenging switchbacks. Most hikers simply ascend to the pass at the top (an 800-foot gain), then come back down to Glencoe. It's challenging, but easier to follow and with more comfortable footing than the Hidden Valley hike. Figure about 45-60 minutes up, and 30 minutes back down (add 45-60 minutes for the optional ascent to the summit of 2,320-foot Stob Mhic Mhartuin).

From the parking lot, a green sign points the way. It's a steep but straightforward hike up, on switchback trails, until you reach the pass—marked by a cairn (pile of stones). From here, you can head back down into the valley. Or, if you have stamina left, consider continuing higher—head up to the peak on the left, called **Stob Mhic Mhartuin.** The 30-40-minute hike to the top (an additional gain of 500 feet) earns you even grander views over the entire valley.

For an even longer hike, it is possible to carry on down the other side of the staircase to **Kinlochmore** (about 2 hours descent)—but your car will still be in Glencoe. Consider this: Leave your car in Glencoe village. Take a taxi to the trailhead. Hike across to Kinlochmore. Then take the hourly Stagecoach bus #44 back to Glencoe and your car.

Sleeping in Glencoe

Glencoe is an extremely low-key place to spend the night between Oban or Glasgow and the northern destinations. You'll join two kinds of guests: one-nighters just passing through and outdoorsy types settling in for several days of hiking.

HUMBLE PLACES IN GLENCOE VILLAGE

The following B&Bs are along the main road through the middle of the village, and all are cash only.

Sleep Code

Abbreviations   (£1=about $1.60, country code: 44)
S=Single, **D**=Double/Twin, **T**=Triple, **Q**=Quad, **b**=bathroom
Price Rankings
  $$$ Higher Priced—Most rooms £70 or more
    $$ Moderately Priced—Most rooms £30-70
      $ Lower Priced—Most rooms £30 or less
Unless otherwise noted, credit cards are accepted at hotels
and hostels—but not B&Bs—breakfast is included, and free
Wi-Fi and/or a guest computer is generally available. Prices
change; verify current rates online or by email. For the best
prices, always book directly with the hotel.

$$ Grianan B&B, across from the grocery store, comes with a homey feeling and two large rooms sharing a bath (D-£50, great for families, also rents self-catering cottage, tel. 01855/811-322, donaldyoung@hotmail.co.uk, Jane and Donald).

$$ Morven Cottage offers two rooms, a breakfast room overlooking the gardens, owners with plenty of character, and a son who was an extra in a Harry Potter movie (Db-£54, can accommodate double/twin/family, dogs welcome, tel. 01855/811-544, www.morvenbnb.com, Freddie and Bob).

$$ Dunire Guest House is a bit bigger—and pricier—than most, with five modern rooms (Db-£66-68, tel. 01855/811-305, www.dunireglencoe.co.uk, dunire.glencoe@hotmail.co.uk, Ann).

$$ Ghlasdrum B&B, next to the police station and set back from the A-82, has four large and modern rooms, a cozy dining room with a fireplace, and the nicest bathrooms (Sb-£40, Db-£60, tel. 01855/811-593, maureen@ken110.orangehome.co.uk, Maureen and Ken).

$$ Tulachgorm B&B has two comfortable rooms sharing a bathroom in a modern house with fine mountain views (D-£50, tel. 01855/811-391, mellow Ann Blake and friendly border collie Jo).

OUTSIDE OF TOWN

These three options—offering more comforts than the simple places listed earlier—are on or near the back road that runs through the forest parallel to the main A-82. Each offers seclusion with good proximity to both the village and the valley (but are best-suited for drivers). To reach them, take the road up through the middle of Glencoe village and cross the bridge. For the Scorrybreac Guest House, head straight up the hill and follow signs. For the other two, turn right just after the bridge and follow the river; first you'll pass the Strath Lodge, and then—after driving about three miles past campgrounds and hostels—you'll reach the Clachaig Inn on the right.

$$$ Strath Lodge, energetically run by Ann and Dan (who are generous with hiking tips), brings a fresh perspective to Glencoe's otherwise stodgy accommodations scene. Their four rooms, upstairs in their modern, light-filled, lodge-like home, are partway down the road to the Clachaig Inn (standard Db-£82, superior Db-£97, tel. 01855/811-337, mobile 07775-826-080, www.strathlodgeglencoe.com, stay@strathlodgeglencoe.com).

$$$ Scorrybreac Guest House enjoys a privileged position just across the road from the restored Glencoe House (now a luxury hotel). From here, walks around the Glencoe Lochan wooded lake park are easy, and it's about a 10-minute walk down into the village. Emma and Graham rent five modern, nondescript rooms (Db-£68-88 depending on size, pay Wi-Fi, family rooms, tel. 01855/811-354, www.scorrybreacglencoe.com, scorrybreac@btinternet.com).

$$$ Clachaig Inn, which runs three popular pubs on site, also rents 23 rooms, all with private bath. It works well for hikers seeking a comfy mountain inn (Db-£104, recommended pub, tel. 01855/811-252, 3 miles from Glencoe, www.clachaig.com).

Eating in Glencoe

Choices around Glencoe are slim—this isn't the place for fine dining. But four options offer decent food a short walk or drive away. For evening fun, take a walk or ask your B&B host where to find music and dancing.

In Glencoe: The only real restaurant is **The Glencoe Gathering & Inn,** with lovely dining areas and a large outdoor deck. Choose between the quirky, fun pub, specializing in seafood with a Scottish twist, or the fancier restaurant (£9-16 main courses, food served daily 12:00-21:00, at junction of A-82 and Glencoe village, tel. 01855/811-265).

The **Glencoe Café,** also in the village, is just right for soups and sandwiches, and Justine's homemade baked goods—especially the carrot loaf—are irresistible (£4 soups, £8.50 soup and *panini* lunch combo, daily 10:00-17:00, last order at 16:00, free Wi-Fi).

Near Glencoe: **Clachaig Inn,** set in a stunning valley a few miles from Glencoe village, serves food all day long to a clientele that's half locals and half tourists. This unpretentious and very popular social hub features billiards, live music, £8-12 pub grub, and a wide range of whiskies and hand-pulled ales. There are three areas, sharing the same menu: The upscale-chic Bidean Lounge, the spit-and-sawdust, pub-around-an-open-fire Boots Bar, and the adjoining former beer cellar aptly called The Snug (all open daily for lunch and dinner, music Sat from 21:00, see hotel listing earlier for driving directions, tel. 01855/811-252).

In Ballachulish: **Laroch Bar & Bistro,** in the next village over from Glencoe (toward Oban), is trying to bring some modern class to this sleepy corner of Scotland. Choose between the fancier bistro or the cozy bar with lighter fare (£15-20 meals, daily 12:00-22:00, tel. 01855/811-940, www.thelarochrestaurantandbar.co.uk). Drive into Ballachulish village, and you'll see it on the left.

Glencoe Connections

Buses don't actually drive down the main road through Glencoe village, though some (most notably those going between Glasgow and Fort William) stop near Glencoe village at a place called **"Glencoe Crossroads"**—a short walk into the village center. Other buses (such as those between Oban and Fort William) stop at the nearby town of **Ballachulish,** which is just a half-mile away (or a £3 taxi ride). Tell the bus driver where you're going ("Glencoe village") and ask to be let off as close as possible.

From **Glencoe Crossroads,** you can catch bus #914, #915, or #916 (8/day) to **Fort William** (30 minutes) or **Glasgow** (2.5 hours).

From **Ballachulish,** you can take bus #918 (3/day) to **Fort William** (30 minutes) or **Oban** (1 hour). Bus info: Tel. 0871-266-3333, www.citylink.co.uk.

There's another, cheaper option for reaching **Fort William** from either Glencoe Crossroads or Ballachulish: Stagecoach bus #44 runs hourly in each direction (Mon-Sat, no buses Sun, www.stagecoachbus.com).

To reach **Inverness** or **Portree** on the Isle of Skye, transfer in Fort William. To reach **Edinburgh,** transfer in Glasgow.

Fort William

Fort William—after Inverness, the second biggest town in the Highlands (pop. 10,000)—is Glencoe's opposite. While Glencoe is a humble one-street village, appealing to hikers and nature-lovers, Fort William's glammed-up main drag feels like one big Scottish shopping mall (with souvenir stands and outdoor stores touting perpetual "70 percent off" sales). The town is clogged with a United Nations of tourists trying to get out of the rain. Big bus tours drive through Glencoe...but they sleep in Fort William.

While Glencoe touches the Scottish soul of the Highlands, Fort William was a steely and intimidating headquarters of the counter-insurgency movement—in many ways designed to crush

that same Highland spirit. After the English Civil War (early 1650s), Oliver Cromwell built a fort here to control his rebellious Scottish subjects. This was beefed up (and named for King William III) in 1690. And following the Jacobite uprising in 1715, King George I dispatched General George Wade to coordinate and fortify the crown's Highland defenses against further Jacobite dissenters. Fort William was the first of a chain of intimidating bastions (along with Fort Augustus on Loch Ness, and Fort George near Inverness) stretching the length of the Great Glen. But Fort William's namesake fortress is long gone, leaving nothing tangible to help today's visitors imagine its militaristic past.

Orientation to Fort William

Given its strategic position—between Glencoe and Oban in the south, Inverness in the east, and the Isle of Skye in the west—you're likely to pass through Fort William at some point during your Highlands explorations. And, while "just passing through" is the perfect plan here, Fort William can provide a good opportunity to stock up on whatever you need (last supermarket before Inverness), grab lunch, and get any questions answered at the TI.

Arrival in Fort William: You'll find pay parking lots flanking the main pedestrian zone, High Street—one is squeezed between town and the loch, and the other is tucked up behind the main drag. The train and bus stations sit side by side just north of the old town center, an easy walk away.

Tourist Information: The TI is on the car-free main drag (generally July-Aug daily 9:30-18:30; Easter-June Mon-Sat 9:00-17:00, Sun 10:00-17:00; shorter hours off-season; free Wi-Fi, 15 High Street, tel. 01397/701-801). Free public WCs are up the street, next to the parking lot.

Sights in Fort William

West Highland Museum

Fort William's only real sight is its humble but well-presented museum. It's a fine opportunity to escape the elements, and—if you take the time to linger over the exhibits—a genuinely insightful about local history and Highland life.

Cost and Hours: Free, £3 suggested donation, guidebook-£1, Mon-Sat 10:00-17:00, Nov-Dec and March until 16:00, closed Sun—but may be open Sun in July-Aug, closed Jan-Feb, on Cam-

GLENCOE & FORT WILLIAM

eron Square, tel. 01397/702-169, www.westhighlandmuseum.org. uk.

Visiting the Museum: Follow the suggested one-way route through exhibits on two floors. You'll begin by learning about the WWII green beret commandos, who were trained in secrecy near here (see "Commando Memorial" listing, later). Then you'll see the historic Governor's Room, decorated with the original paneling from the room in which the order for the Glencoe Massacre was signed. The ground floor also holds exhibits on natural history (lots of stuffed birds and other critters), mountaineering (old equipment), and archaeology (stone and metal tools).

Upstairs, you'll see a selection of old tartans and a salacious exhibit about Queen Victoria and John Brown (her Scottish servant...and, possibly, suitor). The good Jacobite exhibit gives a concise timeline of that complicated history, from Charles I to Bonnie Prince Charlie, and displays a selection of items emblazoned with the prince's bonnie face—including a clandestine portrait that you can only see by looking in a cylindrical mirror. Finally, the Highland Life exhibit collects a hodgepodge of tools, musical instruments (some fine old harps that were later replaced by the much louder bagpipes as the battlefield instrument of choice), and other bric-a-brac.

NEAR FORT WILLIAM
Ben Nevis
From Fort William, take a peek at Britain's highest peak, Ben Nevis (4,406 feet). Thousands walk to its summit each year. On a clear day, you can admire it from a distance. Scotland's only mountain cable cars—at the **Nevis Range Mountain Experience**—can take you to a not-very-lofty 2,150-foot perch on the slopes of Aonach Mòr for a closer look (£12, 15-minute ride, generally open daily but closed in high winds and mid-Nov-mid-Dec—call ahead, signposted on the A-82 north of Fort William, tel. 01397/705-825, www. nevisrange.co.uk).

▲Commando Memorial
This powerful bronze ensemble of three stoic WWII commandos, standing in an evocative mountain setting, is one of Britain's most beloved war memorials. During World War II, Winston Churchill decided that Britain needed an elite military corps. He created the British Commandos, famous for wearing green berets (an accessory—and name—later borrowed

by elite fighting forces in the US and other countries). The British Commandos trained in the Lochaber region near Fort William, in the windy shadow of Ben Nevis. Many later died in combat, and this memorial—built in 1952—remembers those fallen British heroes.

Nearby is the Garden of Remembrance, honoring British Commandos who died in more recent conflicts, from the Falkland Islands to Afghanistan. It's also a popular place to spread Scottish military ashes. Taken together, these sights are a touching reminder that the US is not alone in its distant wars. Every nation has its share of honored heroes willing to sacrifice for what they believe to be the greater good.

Getting There: The memorial is about nine miles outside of Fort William, on the way to Inverness (just outside Spean Bridge); see "Route Tips for Drivers" on page 290.

Sleeping in Fort William

These two B&Bs are on Union Road, a five-minute walk up the hill above High Street. Each place has three rooms, one of which has a private bathroom on the hall.

$$ Glenmorven Guest House is a friendly, flower-bedecked, family-run place at the end of the road. The hospitality, special extras, and views of Loch Linnhe are worth the walk (Db-£65-70, laundry service, welcome whisky, lots of stairs up from the road, tel. 01397/703-236, www.glenmorven.co.uk, glenmorvenguesthouse@gmail.com, Anne and Colin Jamieson).

$$ Gowan Brae B&B ("Hill of the Big Daisy") is a hobbit-cute house with an antique-filled dining room and three rooms with loch or garden views (Db-£70, £60 in off-season, tel. 01397/704-399, www.gowanbrae.co.uk, gowan_brae@btinternet.com, Jim and Ann Clark).

Eating in Fort William

These places are on traffic-free High Street, near the start of town. All (except Deli Craft) are open daily for lunch; The Grog & Gruel also does dinner.

Deli Craft has good, made-to-order deli sandwiches and other prepared foods—a handy place to assemble a tasty, healthy picnic (closed Sun, 61 High Street, tel. 01397/698-100).

Hot Roast Company sells beef, turkey, ham, or pork sandwiches, topped with some tasty extras, along with soup, salad, and coleslaw (£4 takeaway, a bit more for sit-down service, 127 High Street, tel. 01397/700-606).

The Grog & Gruel serves real ales, good £6-12 pub grub,

and Tex-Mex and Cajun dishes, with some unusual choices such as burgers made from boar, haggis, or Highland venison (66 High Street, tel. 01397/705-078).

Fort William Connections

Fort William is a major transit hub for the Highlands, so you'll likely change buses here at some point during your trip.

From Fort William by Bus to: Glencoe (all Glasgow-bound buses—#914, #915, and #916; 8/day, 30 minutes; also Stagecoach bus #44, hourly Mon-Sat, none Sun), **Ballachulish** near Glencoe (Oban-bound bus #918, 3/day, 30 minutes; also Stagecoach bus #44, hourly Mon-Sat, none Sun), **Oban** (bus #918, 3/day, 1.5 hours), **Portree** on the Isle of Skye (buses #915 and #916, 3/day, 4 hours), **Inverness** (buses #19 and #919, 7-9/day, 2 hours), **Glasgow** (buses #914, #915, and #916; 8/day, 3 hours). To reach **Edinburgh,** take the bus to Glasgow, then transfer to a train or bus (figure 5 hours total). Bus info: Citylink—tel. 0871-266-3333, www.citylink.co.uk; Stagecoach—www.stagecoachbus.com.

From Fort William by Train: See the listing for the Jacobite Steam Train on page 294.

ROUTE TIPS FOR DRIVERS

From Fort William to Loch Ness and Inverness: Head north out of Fort William on the A-82. After about eight miles, in the village of Spean Bridge, take the left fork (staying on the A-82). About a mile later, on the left, keep an eye out for the **Commando Memorial** (described earlier and worth a quick stop). From here, the A-82 sweeps north and follows the Caledonian Canal, passing through **Fort Augustus** (a good lunch stop, with its worthwhile Caledonian Canal Visitor Centre), and then follows the north side of Loch Ness on its way to Inverness. Along the way, the A-82 passes **Urquhart Castle** and two **Loch Ness Monster exhibits** in Drumnadrochit (described in the Inverness and Loch Ness chapter).

From Oban to Fort William via Glencoe: See page 255 in the Oban chapter.

From Fort William to the Isle of Skye: You have two options: Head west on the A-830 through **Glenfinnan,** then catch the ferry from Mallaig to Armadale on the Isle of Skye (this "Road to the Isles" area is described in the next section). Or, head north on the A-82 to Invergarry, and turn left (west) on the A-87, which you'll follow (past **Eilean Donan Castle**) to Kyle of Lochalsh and the **Skye Bridge** to the island. Consider using one route one way, and the other on the return trip.

The Road to the Isles

Between Fort William and the Isle of Skye lies a rugged landscape with close ties to the Jacobite rebellions. It was here that Bonnie Prince Charlie first set foot on Scottish soil in 1745, in his attempt to regain the British throne for his father. The village of Glenfinnan, about 30 minutes west of Fort William, is where he first raised the Stuart family standard—and an army of Highlanders. Farther west, the landscape grows even more rugged, offering offshore glimpses of the Hebrides. It's all tied together by a pretty, meandering road—laid out by the great Scottish civil engineer Thomas Telford—that's evocatively (and aptly) named "The Road to the Isles." While these sights aren't worth going out of your way to see, they're ideal for those heading to the Isle of Skye (via the Mallaig-Armadale ferry), or for those who'd enjoy taking the so-called "Harry Potter train" through a Hogwartian landscape.

If you're driving, be sure you allow enough time to make it to Mallaig before the Skye ferry departs (figure at least 1.5 hours

of driving time from Fort William to the ferry, not including stops, and remember to arrive at least 20 minutes before the ferry is scheduled to depart). In summer it's smart to reserve a spot on the ferry the day before, either online or by phone. For more tips on the Mallaig-Armadale ferry, see "Getting to the Isle of Skye" on page 351.

Sights on the Road to the Isles

I've connected these sights with some commentary for those driving from Fort William to Mallaig for the Skye ferry. (If you're interested in the Jacobite Steam Train instead, see the end of this chapter.) In addition to the sights at Glenfinnan, this route is graced with plenty of loch-and-mountain views and, near the end, passes along a beautiful stretch of coast with some fine sandy beaches.

• *From Fort William, head north on the A-82. At the big roundabout, turn left onto the A-830 (marked for* Mallaig *and* Glenfinnan*). You'll pass a big sign listing the next Skye ferry departure. Just after, you'll cross a bridge; look up and to the right to see...*

Neptune's Staircase

This network of eight stair-step locks, designed by Thomas Telford in the early 19th century, offers a handy look at the ingenious locks of the Caledonian Canal. For more on this remarkable engineering accomplishment—which combined natural lochs with manmade locks and canals to connect Scotland's east and west coasts—see the sidebar on page 322. Engineers might want to pull over just after the bridge (well marked) to stroll around the locks for a closer look, but

the rest of us can pretty much get the gist from the road.

• *Continue west on the A-830 for another 14 miles, much of it along Loch Eil. Soon you'll reach a big parking lot and visitors center at...*

▲Glenfinnan

In the summer of 1745, Bonnie Prince Charlie—grandson of James VII of Scotland (and II of England), who was kicked off the British throne in 1688—arrived at Glenfinnan...and waited. He had journeyed a long way to this point, sailing from France by way of the Scottish Isle of Eriskay, and finally making landfall at Loch nan Uamh (just west of here). For the first time in his life, he set foot on his ancestral homeland...the land he hoped that, with his help, his father would soon rule. But to reclaim the thrones of England and Scotland for the Stuart line, the fresh-faced, 24-year-old prince would need the support of the Highlanders. And here at Glenfinnan, he held his breath at the moment of truth. Would the Highland clans come to his aid?

As Charlie waited, gradually he began to hear the drone of bagpipes filtering through the forest. And then, the clan chiefs appeared: MacDonalds. Camerons. MacDonnells. McPhees. They had been holding back—watching and waiting, to make sure they weren't the only ones. Before long, the prince felt confident that he'd reached a clan quorum. And so, here at Glenfinnan, on August 19, 1745, Bonnie Prince Charlie raised his royal standard—officially kicking off the armed Jacobite rebellion that came to be known as "The '45." Two days later, Charlie and his 1,500 clansmen compatriots headed south to fight for control of Scotland. (Sadly, Glenfinnan is also the place where Bonnie Prince Charlie retreated eight months later, after his campaign's crushing defeat at Culloden—see page 312.)

Today Glenfinnan, which still echoes with history, is a wide spot in the road with a big visitors center and two landmarks: a monument to Bonnie Prince Charlie's raising of the standard, and a railroad viaduct made famous by the Hogwarts Express.

Visiting Glenfinnan: Pay to park your car, then head into the **visitors center** (daily July-Aug 9:30-17:30, April-June and Sept-Oct 10:00-17:00, closed Nov-March, café, WCs, tel. 0844-493-

2221). The outdoor areas and the center itself are free, but two sights charge admission: the museum and the monument (£3.50 each).

The **Jacobite Museum** inside the visitors center is small but enlightening, using modern exhibits to explain the story of Bonnie Prince Charlie and "The '45."

The **Glenfinnan Viaduct,** with 416 yards of raised track over 21 supporting arches, is visible from the parking lot. But if you

have time, it's worth hiking 10 minutes up the adjacent hill for much better views. Find the well-marked, steeply switch-backed path behind the visitors center and huff on up. From the viewpoint up top, you'll enjoy sweeping (if distant) views of the viaduct in one direction, and the monument and banks of Loch Shiel in the other. You may even catch a glimpse of the Jacobite Steam Train chugging along (described later).

The **Glenfinnan Monument,** between the visitors center and the loch, is a pillar capped with a stirring statue of a kilted "Unknown Highlander" standing below the standard. You can pay to go up inside the monument (with a guided tour—ask at visitors center), but I'd skip it.

• *Carrying on west along the A-830, the scenery grows more rugged. Shortly you'll begin to catch glimpses of silver sand beaches at the heads of the rocky lochs. Soon you'll reach the village of...*

Arisaig

While there's not much to see in this village, it has an interesting history. Gaelic for "safe place," Arisaig has provided shelter for many seafarers—including the real Long John Silver (Robert Louis Stevenson's father was an engineer who built lighthouses here). In the 20th century, remote Arisaig was a secret training ground for WWII-era spies. The "Special Operations Executive" prepared brave men and women here for clandestine operations in Nazi-occupied Europe. Beach scenes from the classic 1983 Burt Lancaster film *Local Hero* were filmed here.

• *Around Arisaig, signs for the* Alternative Coastal Route *direct you to the B-8008, which parallels the A-830 highway the rest of the way to Mallaig. If you've got ample time to kill, consider taking these back roads for a more scenic approach to the end of the road. Either way, you'll end up at* **Mallaig** *and the* **Skye Ferry.**

The Jacobite Steam Train

The West Highland Railway Line chugs 42 miles from Fort William west to the ferry port at Mallaig. This train (they don't actually call it the "Hogwarts Express") offers a small taste of the Harry Potter experience...but it may be a letdown for those who take this trip only for its wizarding connections. Although one of the steam engines and some of the coaches were used in the films, don't expect a Harry Potter theme ride. However, you can expect beautiful scenery. Along the way, the train stops for 20 minutes at Glenfinnan Station (just after the Glenfinnan Viaduct), and then gives you way too much time (1.75 hours) to poke around the dull port town of Mallaig before heading back to Fort William.

Cost and Hours: One-way—£29 adults, £17 kids; round-trip—£34 adults, £19 kids; more for first class, tickets must be purchased in advance—see details next, 1/day Mon-Fri mid-May-Oct, 2/day Mon-Fri early June-Aug, also 1/day Sat-Sun late-June-late-Sept, departs Fort William at 10:15 and returns at 16:00, afternoon service in summer departs Fort William at 14:30 and returns at 20:30, about a 2-hour ride each way, WCs on board, tel. 0844/850-4680 or 0844/850-4682, www.westcoastrailways.co.uk. Pay lockers for storing luggage are at the Fort William train station (station open long hours daily).

Prebooking Tickets: Trains leave from Fort William's main train station, but you must book ahead online or by phone—you cannot buy tickets for this train at ticket offices. A limited number of seats may be available each day on a first-come, first-served basis (cash only, buy from conductor at coach D), but in summer, trips are often sold out. Rail passes are not accepted.

Cheaper Alternative: The 84-mile round-trip from Fort William takes the better part of a day to show you the same scenery twice. Modern "Sprinter" trains follow the same line and accept rail passes. Consider taking the steam train one-way to Mallaig, then speeding back on a regular train to avoid the long Mallaig layover and slow return (£12.10 one-way between Fort William and Mallaig, 1.5 hours, 2-3/day, to ensure a seat in peak season book by 18:00 the day before, tel. 0845-755-0033, www.nationalrail.co.uk).

Skye Connection: Note that you can use either the steam train or the Sprinter to reach the Isle of Skye: Take the train to Mallaig, walk onto the ferry to Armadale (on Skye), then catch a bus in Armadale to your destination on Skye (bus #52, www.stagecoachbus.com).

INVERNESS AND LOCH NESS

Inverness • Loch Ness • Culloden Battlefield
• Clava Cairns

Inverness, the Highlands' de facto capital, is an almost-unavoidable stop on the Scottish tourist circuit. Fortunately, it's also a pleasant town, and an ideal springboard for some of the country's most famous sights. Hear the music of the Highlands in Inverness and the echo of muskets at Culloden, where government troops drove Bonnie Prince Charlie into exile and conquered his Jacobite supporters. Ponder the mysteries of Scotland's murky prehistoric past at Clava Cairns, and get to know Macbeth's descendants at Cawdor Castle. Just to the southwest of Inverness, explore the locks and lochs of the Caledonian Canal while playing hide-and-seek with the Loch Ness monster.

PLANNING YOUR TIME

Though it has little in the way of sights, Inverness does have a workaday charm and is a handy spot to spend a night or two between other Highland destinations. One night here gives you time to take a quick tour of nearby attractions. With two nights, you can find a full day's worth of sightseeing nearby.

Note that Loch Ness is between Inverness and Oban, Glencoe, and the Isle of Skye. If you're heading to or from one of those places, it makes sense to see Loch Ness en route, rather than as a side-trip from Inverness.

GETTING AROUND THE HIGHLANDS

With a car, the day trips around Inverness are easy. Without a car, you can get to Inverness by train (better from Edinburgh, Stirling, Glasgow, or Pitlochry) or by bus (better from Skye, Oban, and

Glencoe), then side-trip to Loch Ness, Culloden, and other nearby sights by public bus or with a package tour.

Inverness

Inverness is situated on the River Ness at the base of a castle (the town's courthouse, not a tourist attraction). Inverness' charm is its normalcy—it's a nice, midsize Scottish city that gives you a palatable taste of the "urban" Highlands and a contrast to cutesy tourist towns. It has a disheveled, ruddy-cheeked grittiness and is well located for enjoying the surrounding countryside sights. Check out the bustling, pedestrianized downtown, or meander the picnic-friendly riverside paths and islands—best at sunset, when the light hits the castle and couples hold hands while strolling along the water and over the many footbridges.

Orientation to Inverness

Inverness, with about 67,000 people, has been one of the fastest-growing areas of Scotland for the last decade. Marked by its castle,

Inverness clusters along the River Ness. Where the main road crosses the river at Ness Bridge, you'll find the TI; within a few blocks (away from the river) are the train and bus stations and an appealing pedestrian shopping zone. Most of my recommended B&Bs huddle atop a gentle hill behind the castle (a 10-minute uphill walk, or a £5 taxi ride, from the city center).

Tourist Information: At the centrally located TI, you can pick up activity and day-trip brochures, the self-guided *City Centre Trail* walking-tour leaflet, and the *What's On* weekly events sheet for the latest theater and music (all free). The office also has a bulletin board with timely local event information (June-Sept Mon-Sat 8:45-18:30, Sun 9:30-18:00; Oct-May Mon-Sat 9:00-17:00, Sun 10:00-17:00—except Dec-Feb until 15:00; free Wi-Fi, free WCs nearby, Castle Wynd, tel. 01463/252-401, http://www.inverness-scotland.com).

HELPFUL HINTS

Charity Shops: Inverness is home to several pop-up charity shops. Occupying vacant rental spaces, these are staffed by volunteers who are happy to talk about their philanthropy. You can pick up a memorable knickknack, adjust your wardrobe for the weather, and learn about local causes.

Festivals and Events: The summer is busy with special events, which can make it tricky to find a room. Book far ahead during these times, including the Etape Loch Ness bike race (early June), Highland Games (late June), Belladrum Tartan Heart Festival (music, late July), Black Isle farm show (early Aug), and Loch Ness Marathon (late Sept). The big RockNess Music Festival has been on hiatus due to budget cuts, but may return (www.rockness.co.uk).

For a real Highland treat, catch a **shinty match** (a combination of field hockey, hurling, and American football—but without pads). Inverness Shinty Club plays at Bught Park, along Ness Walk (the TI or your B&B can tell you if there are any matches on, or check www.spanglefish.com/invernessshintyclub).

Bookstore: Leakey's Bookshop, located in a converted church built in 1649, is the place to browse through teetering towers of musty old books and vintage maps, warm up by the wood-burning stove, and climb the spiral staircase to the loft for views over the stacks (Mon-Sat 10:00-17:30, closed Sun, in Greyfriar's Hall on Church Street, tel. 01463/239-947, Charles Leakey).

Baggage Storage: The train station has lockers (open Mon-Sat 6:40-20:30, Sun from 10:40), or you can leave your bag at the bus station's ticket desk (small fee, daily 7:45-18:15).

Laundry: New City Launderette is just across the Ness Bridge from the TI (self-service-£5-6/load, same-day full-service-about £10-12/load, priced by weight, Mon-Sat 8:00-18:00, until 20:00 Mon-Fri June-Oct, Sun 10:00-16:00 year-round, last load one hour before closing, 17 Young Street, tel. 01463/242-507). **Thirty Degrees Laundry** on Church Street is another option (full-service only-£10/load, drop off first thing in the morning for same-day service, Mon-Sat 8:30-17:30, closed Sun, 84 Church Street, tel. 01463/710-380).

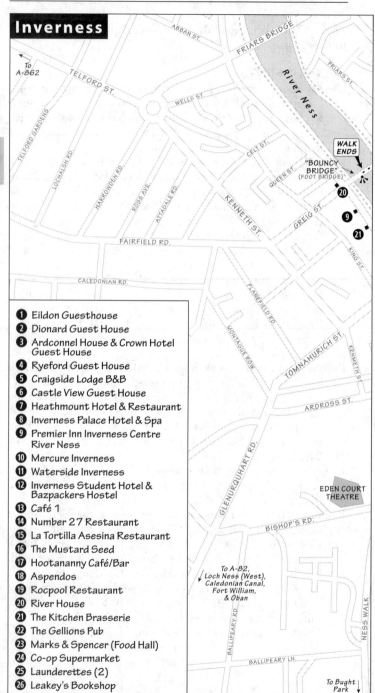

Inverness

1 Eildon Guesthouse
2 Dionard Guest House
3 Ardconnel House & Crown Hotel Guest House
4 Ryeford Guest House
5 Craigside Lodge B&B
6 Castle View Guest House
7 Heathmount Hotel & Restaurant
8 Inverness Palace Hotel & Spa
9 Premier Inn Inverness Centre River Ness
10 Mercure Inverness
11 Waterside Inverness
12 Inverness Student Hotel & Bazpackers Hostel
13 Café 1
14 Number 27 Restaurant
15 La Tortilla Asesina Restaurant
16 The Mustard Seed
17 Hootananny Café/Bar
18 Aspendos
19 Rocpool Restaurant
20 River House
21 The Kitchen Brasserie
22 The Gellions Pub
23 Marks & Spencer (Food Hall)
24 Co-op Supermarket
25 Launderettes (2)
26 Leakey's Bookshop

INVERNESS & LOCH NESS

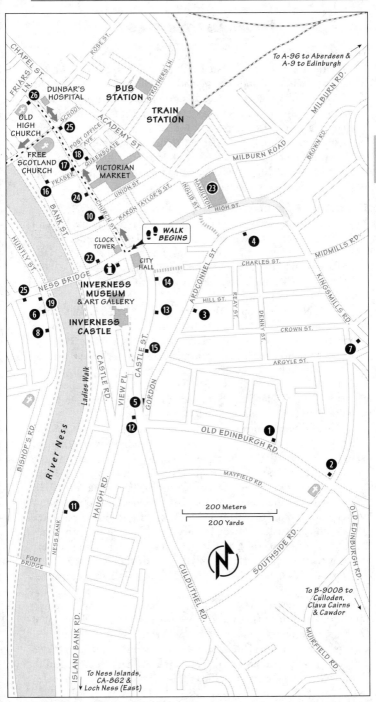

Tours in Inverness

Walking Tours

Cameron—a.k.a. "the man in the kilt"—at **Happy Tours** offers history walks by day, and "Crime and Punishment" tours by night. These one-hour walks are cheeky and peppered with his political opinions—a fun mix of history, local gossip, Scottish culture, and comedy. Cameron also offers other tours, guides bike tours to Loch Ness, and rents bikes for £15 per day (tours-£6/person; history tour daily April-Sept at 11:00, 13:00, and 15:00; Crime and Punishment at 19:00 and 20:30; tours leave from steps of TI, just show up, tel. 07828/154-683, www.happy-tours.biz).

Excursions from Inverness

While thin on sights of its own, Inverness is a great home base for day trips. A variety of tour companies offer day trips—details and tickets are available at the TI. It's smart to book ahead, especially in peak season. Skip the City Sightseeing hop-on, hop-off bus tour (whose main objective is connecting you with cruises run by Jacobite, their sister company).

Loch Ness: The top of this famous lake is a 20-minute drive southwest, so it combines well with other local attractions. **Jacobite Tours** focuses on trips that include Loch Ness, from a one-hour basic boat ride to a 6.5-hour extravaganza. Their 3.5-hour "Sensation" tour includes a guided bus tour with live narration, a half-hour Loch Ness cruise, and visits to Urquhart Castle and the better of the two Loch Ness exhibits (£33, for more options see www. jacobite.co.uk, tel. 01463/233-999).

Isle of Skye: Two companies do day tours to the Isle of Skye. **Wow Scotland**'s ambitious 12-hour itinerary takes you all over the island, including the charming harbor village of Portree and the super-scenic Trotternish Peninsula, as well as a drive along Loch Ness and a view of Eilean Donan Castle (£69, 3/week June-Aug, scattered departures in May and Sept, none Oct-April, www. wowscotland.com, tel. 01463/719-106). **Highland Experience Tours** runs their Isle of Skye itinerary more frequently (daily May-Sept, 4/week off-season), but it's shorter (10 hours) and doesn't make it to the northern parts of the island, such as Portree and Trotternish (£49, tel. 01463/719-222, www.highlandexperience. com).

The Orkney Islands: For a very ambitious itinerary, you can take an all-day tour that departs Inverness at the crack of dawn (7:15), drives you up to John O'Groats to catch the passenger ferry, then takes you on a whistle-stop tour of Orkney's main attractions before returning you to collapse at your Inverness B&B at 21:00. While it's a long day, it's an efficient use of your time if you're determined to see Orkney (£72, daily June-Aug only, www.jogferry.co.uk).

Other Destinations: Highland Experience Tours (mentioned earlier) also offers a variety of other daylong tours, including the Royal Deeside and Malt Whisky Trail, and John O'Groats (tel. 01463/719-222, www.highlandexperience.com).

Inverness Walk

Humble Inverness has meager conventional sights, but its fun history and quirky charm become clear as you take this short self-guided walk.

• *Start at the clock tower and TI.*

Clock Tower and TI: Notice the **Gaelic language** on directional and street signs all around you. While nobody speaks Gaelic as a first language (and few Scottish people speak it at all), this old Celtic language symbolizes the strength of Scottish Highland culture.

The **clock tower** looming 130 feet above you is all that remains of a tollbooth building erected in 1791. This is the highest spire in town, and for generations was a collection point for local taxes. Here, four streets—Church, Castle, Bridge, and High—come together, integrating God, defense, and trade—everything necessary for a fine city.

About 800 years ago, a castle was built on the bluff overhead and the town of Inverness coalesced right about here. For centuries, this backwater town's economy was based on cottage industries. Artisans who made things also sold them. In 1854, the train arrived, injecting energy and money from Edinburgh and Glasgow, and the Victorian boom hit. With the Industrial Age came wholesalers, distributors, mass production, and affluence. Much of the city was built during this era, in Neo-Gothic style—over-the-top and fanciful, like the City Hall (from 1882, kitty-corner to the clock tower). With the Victorian Age also came tourism.

Look for the **Bible quotes** chiseled into the wall across the street from the City Hall. A civic leader, tired of his council members being drunkards, edited these Bible verses for maximum impact, especially the bottom two.

Hiding just up the hill (behind the eyesore concrete home of the Inverness Museum and Art Gallery) is **Inverness Castle.** Although the castle is closed to the public, it's worth hiking up there at some point during your visit to enjoy some of the best views of

Inverness. The courthouse in the castle doesn't see a lot of action. In the last 30 years, there have been only two murders to prosecute. As locals like to say, "no guns, no problems." While hunters can own a gun, gun ownership in Scotland is complicated and tightly regulated.

By the way, every day and night in peak season, Cameron ("the man in the kilt" who gave me the material for this walk) gives entertaining hour-long guided walks that begin from the TI near here (see "Tours in Inverness," earlier).

• *Walk a few steps uphill toward the Scottish hamburger restaurant that caught on big-time in the US.*

Mercat Cross and Old Town Center: Standing in front of the City Hall is a well-worn mercat cross, which designated the market in centuries past. This is where the townspeople gathered to hear important proclamations, share news, watch hangings, gossip, and so on. The scant remains of a prehistoric stone at the base of the cross are what's left of Inverness' "Stone of Destiny." According to tradition, whenever someone moved away from Inverness, they'd take a tiny bit of home with them in the form of a chip of this stone—so it's been chipped and pecked almost to oblivion.

The yellow **Caledonian** building faces McDonald's at the base of High Street. (Caledonia was the ancient Roman name for Scotland.) It was built in 1847, complete with Corinthian columns and a Greek-style pediment, as the leading bank in town, back when banks were designed to hold the money of the rich and powerful... and intimidate working blokes. Notice how nicely pedestrianized High Street welcomes people and seagulls...but not cars.

• *Next we'll head up Church Street, which begins between the clock tower and The Caledonian.*

Church Street: The street art you'll trip over at the start of Church Street is called *Earthquake*— a reminder of the quake that hit Inverness in 1816. As the slabs explain, the town's motto is "Open Heartedness, Insight, and Perseverance."

Stroll down Church Street. Look up above the modern storefronts to see Old World facades. **Union Street** (the second corner on the right)—stately, symmetrical, and Neoclassical—was the fanciest street in the Highlands when it was built in the 19th century. Its buildings had indoor toilets. That was big news.

Midway down the next block of Church Street (on the right), an alley marked by an ugly white canopy leads to the **Victorian**

Market. Explore this gallery of shops under an iron-and-glass domed roof dating from 1876 (closed Sun). The first section seems abandoned, but delve deeper to find some more active areas, where local shops mix with tacky "tartan tat" souvenir stands. If you're seriously into bagpipes, look for **Cabar Fèidh,** where American expat Brian sells CDs and sheet music, and repairs and maintains the precious instruments of local musicians.

Go back out of the market the way you came in, and continue down Church Street. At the next corner you come to **Hootananny,** famous locally for its live music (pop in to see what's on tonight). Just past that is **Abertarff House,** the oldest house in Inverness. It was the talk of the town in 1593 for its "turnpike" (spiral staircase) connecting the floors.

Continue about a block farther along Church Street. The lane on the left leads to the "**Bouncy Bridge**" (where we'll finish this walk). Opposite that lane (on the right) is **Dunbar's Hospital,** with four-foot-thick walls. In 1668, Alexander Dunbar was a wealthy landowner who built this as a poor folks' home. You can almost read the auld script in his coat of arms above the door.

A few steps up Church Street, walk through the iron gate on the left and into the churchyard (we're focusing on the shorter church on the right—ignore the bigger one on the left). Looking at the WWI and WWII memorials on the church's wall, it's clear which war hit Scotland harder. While no one famous is buried here, many tombstones go back to the 1700s. Being careful not to step on a rabbit, head for the bluff overlooking the river.

Old High Church: There are a lot of churches in Inverness (46 Protestant, 2 Catholic, and 2 Gaelic-language), but these days, most are used for other purposes. This one, dating from the 11th century, is the most historic (but is generally closed). It was built on what was likely the site of a pagan holy ground. Early Christians called upon St. Michael to take the fire out of pagan

spirits, so it only made sense that the first Christians would build their church here and dedicate the spot as St. Michael's Mount.

In the sixth century, the Irish evangelist monk St. Columba

brought Christianity to northern England, the Scottish islands (at Iona), and the Scottish Highlands (in Inverness). He stood here amongst the pagans and preached to King Brude and the Picts.

Study the bell tower from the 1600s. The small door to nowhere (one floor up) indicates that back before the castle offered protection, this tower was the place of last refuge for townsfolk under attack. They'd gather inside and pull up the ladder. The church became a prison for Jacobites after the Battle of Culloden, and executions were carried out in the churchyard.

Every night at 20:00, the bell in the tower rings 100 times. It has rung like this since 1730 to remind townsfolk that it's dangerous to be out after dinner.

• *From here, you can circle back to the lane leading to the "Bouncy Bridge" and then hike out onto the bridge. Or you can just survey the countryside from this bluff.*

The River Ness: Emptying out of Loch Ness and flowing seven miles to the sea (a mile from here), this is one of the shortest rivers in the country. While it's shallow (you can almost walk across it), there are plenty of fish in it. A 64-pound salmon was once pulled out of the river right here. In the 19th century, Inverness was smaller, and across the river stretched nothing but open fields. Then, with the Victorian boom, the suspension footbridge (a.k.a. "Bouncy Bridge") was built in 1881 to connect new construction across the river with the town.

• *Your tour is over. Inverness is yours to explore.*

Sights in Inverness

Inverness Museum and Art Gallery

This free, likable town museum is worth poking around on a rainy day to get a taste of Inverness and the Highlands. The ground-floor exhibits on geology and archaeology peel back the layers of Highland history: Bronze and Iron ages, Picts (including some carved stones), Scots, Vikings, and Normans. Upstairs you'll find the "social history" exhibit (everything from Scottish nationalism to hunting and fishing) and temporary art exhibits.

Cost and Hours: Free, April-Oct Tue-Sat 10:00-17:00, shorter hours off-season, closed Sun-Mon year-round, cheap café, in the ugly modern building behind the TI on the way up to the castle, tel. 01463/237-114, www.highlifehighland.com.

Inverness Castle

Inverness' biggest non-sight has nice views from its front lawn, but the building itself isn't worth visiting. A wooden fortress that stood on this spot was replaced by a stone structure in the 15th century. In 1715, that castle was named Fort George to assert English control over the area. In 1745, it was destroyed by Bonnie Prince Charlie's Jacobite army and remained a ruin until the 1830s, when the present castle was built. The statue outside (from 1899) depicts Flora MacDonald, who helped Bonnie Prince Charlie escape from the English (see page 371). The castle was built as the courthouse, and when trials are in session, loutish-looking men hang out here, waiting for their bewigged barristers to arrive.

River Walks

As with most European cities, where there's a river, there's a walk. Inverness, with both the River Ness and the Caledonian Canal, does not disappoint. Consider an early-morning stroll along the Ness Bank to capture the castle at sunrise, or a post-dinner jaunt to Bught Park for a local shinty match (see "Helpful Hints—Festivals and Events," earlier). The forested islands in the middle of the River Ness—about a 10-minute walk south of the center—are a popular escape from the otherwise busy city.

Here's a good plan for your Inverness riverside constitutional: From the Ness Bridge, head along the riverbank under the castle (along the path called "Ladies Walk"). As you work your way up the river, you'll see the architecturally bold Eden Court Theatre (across the river), pass a white pedestrian bridge, see a WWI memorial, and peek into the gardens of several fine old Victorian sandstone riverfront homes. Nearing the tree-covered islands, watch for fly-fishers in hip waders on the pebbly banks. Reaching the first, skinny little island, take the bridge with the wavy, wrought-iron railing and head down the path along the middle of the island. Notice that this is part of the Great Glen Way, a footpath that stretches from here all the way to Fort William (79 miles). Enjoy this little nature break, with gurgling rapids—and, possibly, a few midges. Reaching the bigger bridge, cross it and enjoy strolling through tall forests. After two more green-railinged bridges, traverse yet another island, and find one last white-iron bridge that takes you across to the opposite bank. You'll pop out at the corner of Bught Park, the site of shinty practices and games—are any going on today?

From here, you can simply head back into town on this bank. If you'd like to explore more, you could continue farther south. It's not as idyllic or as pedestrian-friendly, but in this zone you'll find minigolf, a skate park, the Highland Archive building, the free Botanic Gardens (daily 10:00-17:00, until 16:00 Nov-March), and the huge Active Inverness leisure center, loaded with amusements

Sleep Code

Abbreviations   (£1=about $1.60, country code: 44)
S=Single, D=Double/Twin, T=Triple, Q=Quad, b=bathroom
Price Rankings
  $$$ Higher Priced—Most rooms £90 or more
   $$ Moderately Priced—Most rooms £60-90
    $ Lower Priced—Most rooms £60 or less
Unless otherwise noted, credit cards are accepted at hotels and hostels—but not B&Bs—breakfast is included, and free Wi-Fi and/or a guest computer is generally available. Prices change; verify current rates online or by email. For the best prices, always book directly with the hotel.

including a swimming pool with adventure slides, a climbing wall, a sauna and steam area, and a gymnasium (www.invernessleisure. co.uk).

Continuing west from these leisure areas, you'll eventually hit the Caledonian Canal; to the south, this parallels the River Ness, and to the north is where it meets Beauly Firth, then Moray Firth and the North Sea. From the Tomnahurich Bridge, paths on either bank allow you to walk along the Great Glen Way until you're ready to turn around.

Nightlife in Inverness

Scottish Folk Music

While you can find traditional folk music sessions in pubs and hotel bars anywhere in town, two places are well established as *the* music pubs. Neither charges a cover for the music, unless a bigger-name band is playing.

The Gellions has live folk and Scottish music nightly (from 21:30 or 22:00). Just across the street from the TI, it has local ales on tap and brags it's the oldest bar in town (14 Bridge Street, tel. 01463/233-648, www.gellions.co.uk).

Hootananny is an energetic place with several floors of live rock, blues, or folk music, and drinking fun nightly. Music in the main bar usually begins about 21:30 (traditional music sessions Sun-Wed, bands on weekends). On weekends only, upstairs is the Mad Hatter's nightclub, complete with a "chill-out room" (bar open 12:00-24:00, 67 Church Street, tel. 01463/233-651, www. hootananny.co.uk). They also serve good traditional Scottish food (see listing in "Eating in Inverness," later).

Sleeping in Inverness

B&Bs ON AND NEAR ARDCONNEL STREET AND OLD EDINBURGH ROAD

These B&Bs are popular; book ahead for June through August (and during the peak times listed in "Helpful Hints," earlier), and be aware that some require a two-night minimum during busy times. The places I list are all a 10-minute walk from the train station and town center. To get to the B&Bs, either catch a taxi (£5) or walk: From the train and bus stations, go left on Academy Street. At the first stoplight (the second if you're coming from the bus station), veer right onto Inglis Street in the pedestrian zone. Go up the Market Brae steps. At the top, turn right onto Ardconnel Street toward the B&Bs and hostels.

$$ Eildon Guesthouse, set on a quiet corner, offers five tranquil rooms with spacious baths at an excellent value. The cute-as-a-button 1890s countryside brick home exudes warmth and serenity from the moment you open the gate (Db-£80, Tb-£115, family rooms, in-room fridges, parking, 29 Old Edinburgh Road, tel. 01463/231-969, eildonguesthouse@yahoo.co.uk, www.eildonguesthouse.co.uk, Jacqueline).

$$ Dionard Guest House, wrapped in a fine hedged-in garden just up Old Edinburgh Road from Ardconnel Street, has cheerful common spaces and six pleasant, slightly faded rooms, including two on the ground floor (Db-£70-90 depending on size, in-room fridges, 39 Old Edinburgh Road, tel. 01463/233-557, www.dionardguesthouse.co.uk, enquiries@dionardguesthouse.co.uk, Brian and Doris—but they may be selling soon).

$$ Ardconnel House is a classic, traditional place offering a nice, large guest lounge, along with six spacious and comfortable rooms (Sb-£50, Db-£80, family room-£95, no children under 10, slightly cheaper off-season or for 3 or more nights, 21 Ardconnel Street, tel. 01463/240-455, www.ardconnel-inverness.co.uk, ardconnel@gmail.com, John and Elizabeth).

$$ Ryeford Guest House is a decent value, with six flowery rooms and piles of teddy bears (Sb-£47, Db-£74, Tb-£111, vegetarian breakfast available, small twin room #1 in back has fine garden view, Wi-Fi in front lounge, above Market Brae steps, go left on Ardconnel Terrace to #21, tel. 01463/242-871, www.scotland-inverness.co.uk/ryeford, joananderson@uwclub.net, Joan and George Anderson).

$$ Craigside Lodge B&B has five large rooms with tasteful modern flair. Guests share an inviting sunroom and a cozy lounge with a great city view (Sb-£45, Db-£75, just above Castle Street at 4 Gordon Terrace, tel. 01463/231-576, www.craigsideguesthouse.co.uk, enquiries@craigsideguesthouse.co.uk, Paul and Mandy).

$ Crown Hotel Guest House has six clean, bright rooms and an enjoyable breakfast room (Sb-£40, Db-£60, family room, lounge, 19 Ardconnel Street, tel. 01463/231-135, www.crownhotel-inverness.co.uk, reservations@crownhotel-inverness.co.uk, friendly Catriona—pronounced "Katrina"—Barbour).

Across the River: **$$ Castle View Guest House** sits right along the River Ness at the Ness Bridge—and, true to its name, it owns smashing views of the castle. Its eight rooms (half with views) are colorfully furnished, and the place feels a bit more urban than the traditional B&Bs listed earlier (Db-£80-90, 2a Ness Walk, tel. 01463/241-443, www.castleviewguesthouseinverness.com, enquiries@castleviewguesthouseinverness.com).

HOTELS

The following hotels may have rooms when my recommended B&Bs are full.

$$$ Heathmount Hotel's understated facade hides a chic retreat for comfort-seeking travelers. Its eight elegant rooms come with unique decoration, parking, and fancy extras (Sb-£90-110, Db-£105-160, rates depend on size, Kingsmill Road, tel. 01463/235-877, info@heathounthotel.com, www.heathmounthotel.com). Their restaurant is also recommended; see "Eating in Inverness."

$$$ Inverness Palace Hotel & Spa, a Best Western, is a fancy splurge with a pool, a gym, and 88 overpriced rooms. It's located right on the River Ness, across from the castle (rack rates: Db-£209-229, but you can often get a much better rate—even half-price—if you book a package deal on their website, even cheaper last-minute rooms, river/castle view rooms about £40 more than rest, breakfast extra, elevator, free parking, 8 Ness Walk, tel. 01463/223-243, www.invernesspalacehotel.co.uk, palace@miltonhotels.com).

$$$ Premier Inn Inverness Centre River Ness, along the River Ness, offers 99 predictable rooms. What the hotel lacks in charm and glitz it makes up for in affordable rates and location (Db-£60-120, £29 rooms not uncommon if booked online well in advance, air-con, elevator, parking-£10/day, 19-21 Huntly Street, tel. 01463/246-490, www.premierinn.com).

$$$ Mercure Inverness, right in the town center, has 118 rooms and feels less commercial than other chain hotels (Db-£125-175, much cheaper if booked in advance online, elevator, gym, parking-£4/day, entrance is at Church Street, tel. 0844/815-9006, www.mercureinverness.co.uk, sales.mercureinverness@jupiterhotels.co.uk).

$$$ Waterside Inverness, in a nice location along the River Ness, has 35 crisp, recently updated rooms and a river-view restaurant (Sb-£75, Db-£140, superior Db-£170, Qb-£190, call or check website for deals as low as Db-£85, 19 Ness Bank,

tel. 01463/233-065, www.thewatersideinverness.co.uk, info@
thewatersideinverness.co.uk).

HOSTELS ON CULDUTHEL ROAD

For funky and cheap dorm beds near the center and the recommended Castle Street restaurants, consider these friendly side-
by-side hostels, geared toward younger travelers. They're about a
12-minute walk from the train station.

$ **Inverness Student Hotel** has 57 beds in nine rooms and
a laid-back lounge with a bay window overlooking the River
Ness. The knowledgeable, friendly staff welcomes any traveler
over 18. Dorms are a bit grungy, but each bunk has its own playful name (bunk in dorm room-£17-18, price depends on season,
breakfast-£2, free tea and coffee, pay laundry service, kitchen, 8
Culduthel Road, tel. 01463/236-556, www.invernessstudenthotel.
com, info@invernessstudenthotel.com).

$ **Bazpackers Hostel,** a stone's throw from the castle, has
a quieter, more private feel and 20 beds in basic dorms (bunk in
dorm room-£17-19, D-£44, cheaper Oct-May, linens provided,
reception open 7:30-23:00 but available 24 hours, no curfew, pay
laundry service, 4 Culduthel Road, tel. 01463/717-663, www.
bazpackershostel.co.uk). They also rent a small apartment nearby
(£100, sleeps up to 4).

Eating in Inverness

You'll find a lot of traditional Highland fare—game, fish, lamb,
and beef. Reservations are smart at most of these places, especially
on summer weekends.

NEAR THE B&Bs, ON OR NEAR CASTLE STREET

The first three eateries line Castle Street, facing the back of the
castle.

Café 1 serves up high-quality modern Scottish and international cuisine with trendy, chic bistro flair. This popular place fills
up on weekends, so it's smart to call ahead (£13-22 main courses,
lunch and early-bird dinner specials until 18:45, open Mon-Fri
12:00-14:30 & 17:00-21:30, Sat from 12:30 & 18:00, closed Sun,
75 Castle Street, tel. 01463/226-200, www.cafe1.net).

Number 27 has a straightforward, crowd-pleasing menu that
offers something for everyone—burgers, pastas, and more. The
food is surprisingly elegant for this price range (£9-16 main courses, £5-9 lunches, daily 12:00-21:00, generous portions, local ales
on tap, noisy bar up front not separated from restaurant in back, 27
Castle Street, tel. 01463/241-999).

La Tortilla Asesina has Spanish tapas, including spicy king prawns (the house specialty). It's an appealing, colorfully tiled, and vivacious dining option that feels like Spain (£3-7 cold and hot tapas—three make a meal, handy combination lunches, daily 12:00-22:00, 99 Castle Street, tel. 01463/709-809).

The recommended **Heathmount Hotel** serves good food in their quiet dining room (£9-18 meals, Mon-Fri 12:00-14:30 & 17:00-22:00, Sat-Sun 12:30-21:30, 5-minute walk down Argyle Street to Kingsmills Road, tel. 01463/235-877).

IN THE TOWN CENTER

The Mustard Seed serves Scottish food with a modern twist in an old church with a river view. It's pricey, but worth considering for a nice lively-at-lunch, mellow-at-dinner meal. Ask for a seat on the balcony if the weather is cooperating. Reservations are essential on weekends (£9 lunch specials, £13 early-bird specials before 19:00, £15-20 dinners, daily 12:00-15:00 & 17:30-22:00, on the corner of Bank and Fraser Streets, 16 Fraser Street, tel. 01463/220-220, www.mustardseedrestaurant.co.uk).

Hootananny mixes an energetic pub and live music with Scottish staples like lamb stovies (stew) and cullen skink (fish chowder). It's got a great join-in-the-fun vibe at night (£6-8 lunches, £9-10 dinners, food served Mon-Sat 12:00-15:00 & 17:00-20:30, Sun 17:00-21:30 only; see "Nightlife in Inverness," earlier).

Aspendos serves up freshly prepared, delicious Turkish dishes in a spacious, exuberantly decorated dining room (£12-15 main courses, daily 12:00-22:00, 26 Queensgate, tel. 01463/711-950).

Picnic: The **Marks & Spencer** Food Hall is best (you can't miss it—on the main pedestrian mall, near the Market Brae steps at the corner of the big Eastgate Shopping Centre; Mon-Sat 8:00-18:00, Thu until 20:00, Sun 11:00-17:00, tel. 01463/224-844). There's a simpler **Co-op** market a few blocks away (daily 6:00-22:00, 59 Church Street).

ACROSS THE RIVER

Rocpool Restaurant is a hit with locals and good for a splurge. Owner/chef Steven Devlin serves creative modern European food in a sleek—and often crowded—chocolate/pistachio dining room. Reserve ahead or be sorry (£16 lunch specials, £18 early-bird weekday special until 18:45, £13-24 dinners; open Mon-Sat 12:00-14:30 & 17:45-22:00, closed Sun; across Ness Bridge from TI at 1 Ness Walk, tel. 01463/717-274, www.rocpoolrestaurant.com).

River House, a classy, sophisticated, but unstuffy riverside place, is the brainchild of Cornishman Alfie—who prides himself on melding the seafood know-how of both Cornwall and Scotland, with a bit of Mediterranean flair. Reserve ahead for this small, popular splurge (£18-21 main courses, Mon-Sat 17:30-21:30, Fri-

Sat also 12:00-14:00, closed Mon off-season and Sun year-round, 1 Greig Street, tel. 01463/222-033, www.riverhouseinverness.co.uk).

The Kitchen Brasserie is the sister restaurant of The Mustard Seed (directly across the river). Equally good and popular, they serve fantastic homemade comfort food—pizza, pasta, and burgers—in an ultra-modern townhouse (£8 lunch specials, £13 early-bird special until 19:00, £10-16 dinners, daily 12:00-15:00 & 17:00-22:00, 15 Huntly Street, tel. 01463/259-119, www. kitchenrestaurant.co.uk).

Inverness Connections

From Inverness by Train to: Pitlochry (almost hourly, 1.5 hours), **Stirling** (every 1-2 hours, 3 hours, some transfer in Perth), **Kyle of Lochalsh** near Isle of Skye (4/day, 2.5 hours), **Edinburgh** (every 1-2 hours, 3.5-4 hours, some with change in Perth), **Glasgow** (11/day, 3 hours, 4 direct, others change in Perth), **Thurso** (for ferries to Orkney; 4/day, 4 hours). The Caledonian Sleeper provides overnight service to **London** (www.sleeper.scot). Train info: tel. 0345-748-4950, www.nationalrail.co.uk.

By Bus: Inverness has a handy direct bus to **Portree** on the Isle of Skye (bus #917, 3/day, 3.5 hours), but for other destinations in western Scotland, you'll first head for **Fort William** (bus #19 or #919, 7-9/day, 2 hours). For connections onward to **Oban** (figure 4 hours total) or **Glencoe** (3 hours total), see "Fort William Connections" on page 290. Inverness is also connected by direct bus to **Edinburgh** (about hourly, 4-hour express #M90 or 5-hour #M91 with many stops) and **Glasgow** (express bus #G10, 5/day, 3.5 hours, additional options with Perth transfer). These buses are run by Scottish Citylink; for schedules, see www.citylink.co.uk. Tickets are sold in advance online, by phone at tel. 0871-266-3333, or in person at the Inverness bus station (daily 7:45-18:15, baggage storage, 2 blocks from train station on Margaret Street, tel. 01463/233-371). For bus travel to England, check National Express (www.nationalexpress.com) or Megabus (http://uk.megabus.com).

ROUTE TIPS FOR DRIVERS
Inverness to Edinburgh (160 miles, 3.25 hours minimum): Leaving Inverness, follow signs to the A-9 (south, toward Perth). If you haven't seen the Culloden Battlefield yet (described later), it's an easy detour: Just as you leave Inverness, head four miles east off the A-9 on the B-9006. Back on the A-9, it's a wonderfully speedy, scenic highway (A-9, M-90, A-90) all the way to Edinburgh. If you have time, consider stopping en route in Pitlochry (just off the A-9; see the Eastern Scotland chapter).

To Oban, Glencoe, or Isle of Skye: See page 290.

INVERNESS & LOCH NESS

Near Inverness

Inverness puts you in the heart of the Highlands, within easy striking distance of a gaggle of famous and worthwhile sights: Commune with the Scottish soul at the historic Culloden Battlefield, where British history reached a turning point. Wonder at three mysterious Neolithic cairns, which remind visitors that Scotland's history goes back even before Braveheart. And enjoy a homey country castle at Cawdor. Loch Ness—with its elusive monster—is another popular and easy day trip.

In addition to the sights in this section, note that the Speyside Whisky Trail, the Leault Working Sheepdogs farm show, and the Highland Folk Museum are also within side-tripping distance of Inverness (all are covered in the Eastern Scotland chapter).

CULLODEN BATTLEFIELD

Jacobite troops under Bonnie Prince Charlie were defeated at Culloden (kuh-LAW-dehn) by supporters of the Hanover dynasty (King George II's family) in 1746. Sort of the "Scottish Alamo," this last major land battle fought on British soil spelled the end of Jacobite resistance and the beginning of the clan chiefs' fall from power. Wandering the desolate, solemn battlefield, you sense that something terrible occurred here. Locals still bring white roses and speak of "The '45" (as Bonnie Prince Charlie's entire campaign is called) as if it just happened. The

battlefield at Culloden and its high-tech visitors center together are worth ▲▲▲.

Orientation to Culloden

Cost and Hours: £11, £5 guidebook, daily April-Oct 9:00-17:30, June-Aug until 18:00, Nov-Dec and Feb-March 10:00-16:00, closed Jan, café, tel. 01463/796-090, www.nts.org.uk/culloden.

Tours: The good, included **audioguide** leads you through the outdoor areas, using GPS to inform you about important sites on the battlefield (pick up before 17:00 at end of indoor exhibit, earlier off-season).

Getting There: It's a 15-minute **drive** east of Inverness. Follow signs to *Aberdeen*, then *Culloden Moor*—the B-9006 takes you right there (well signed on the right-hand side). Parking is

£2. Public **buses** leave from Inverness' Queensgate Street and drop you off in front of the entrance (£5 round-trip ticket, bus #8C or #8A, roughly hourly—none on Sun, 40 minutes, ask at TI for route/schedule updates). A **taxi** costs around £10-15 one-way.

Length of This Tour: Allow 2-2.5 hours.

Background

The Battle of Culloden (April 16, 1746) marks the steep decline of the Scottish Highland clans and the start of years of repression of Scottish culture by the English. It was the culmination of a year's worth of battles, and at the center of it all was the charismatic, enigmatic Bonnie Prince Charlie (1720-1788).

Charles Edward Stuart, from his first breath, was raised with a single purpose—to restore his family to the British throne. His grandfather was King James II (VII of Scotland), deposed in 1688 by the English Parliament for his tyranny and pro-Catholic bias. The Stuarts remained in exile in France and Italy, until 1745, when young Charlie crossed the Channel from France to retake the throne in the name of his father (James VIII and III to his supporters). He landed on the west coast of Scotland and rallied support for the Jacobite cause. Though Charles was not Scottish-born, he was the rightful heir directly down the line from Mary, Queen of Scots—and so many Scots joined the Stuart family's rebellion out of resentment at being ruled by a foreign king (English royalty of German descent—though they were distantly related to Mary, Queen of Scots, too).

Bagpipes droned, and "Bonnie" (handsome) Charlie led an army of 2,000 tartan-wearing, Gaelic-speaking Highlanders across Scotland, seizing Edinburgh. They picked up other supporters of the Stuarts from the Lowlands and from England. Now 6,000 strong, they marched south toward London—quickly advancing as far as Derby, just 125 miles from the capital—and King George II made plans to flee the country. But anticipated support for the Jacobites failed to materialize in the numbers they were hoping for (both in England and from France). The Jacobites had so far been victorious in their battles against the Hanoverian government forces, but the odds now turned against them. Charles retreated to the Scottish Highlands, where many of his men knew the terrain and might gain an advantage when outnumbered. The English government troops followed closely on his heels.

Against the advice of

his best military strategist, Charles' army faced the Hanoverian forces at Culloden Moor on flat, barren terrain that was unsuited to the Highlanders' guerrilla tactics. The Jacobites—many of them brandishing only broadswords, targes (wooden shields covered in leather and studs), and dirks (long daggers)—were mowed down by King George's cannons and horsemen. In less than an hour, the government forces routed the Jacobite army, but that was just the start. They spent the next weeks methodically hunting down ringleaders and sympathizers (and many others in the Highlands who had nothing to do with the battle), ruthlessly killing, imprisoning, and banishing thousands.

Charles fled with a £30,000 price on his head (an equivalent of millions of today's pounds). He escaped to the Isle of Skye, hidden by a woman named Flora MacDonald (her grave is on the Isle of Skye, and her statue is outside Inverness Castle). Flora dressed Charles in women's clothes and passed him off as her maid. Later, Flora was arrested and thrown in the Tower of London before being released and treated like a celebrity.

Charles escaped to France. He spent the rest of his life wandering Europe trying to drum up support to retake the throne. He drifted through short-lived romantic affairs and alcohol, and died in obscurity, without an heir, in Rome.

Though usually depicted as a battle of the Scottish versus the English, in truth Culloden was a civil war between two opposing dynasties: Stuart (Charlie) and Hanover (George). In fact, about one-fifth of the government's troops were Scottish (joined by many Germans, Swiss, and Dutch), and several redcoat deserters fought along with the Jacobites. However, as the history has faded into lore, the battle has come to be remembered as a Scottish-versus-English standoff—or, in the parlance of the Scots, the Highlanders versus the Strangers.

The Battle of Culloden was the end of 60 years of Jacobite rebellions, the last major battle fought on British soil, and the final stand of the Highlanders. From then on, clan chiefs were deposed; kilts, tartans, and bagpipes were outlawed; and farmers were cleared off their ancestral land, replaced by more-profitable sheep. Scottish culture would never recover from the events of the campaign called "The '45."

Self-Guided Tour

Culloden's visitors center, opened in 2008, is a state-of-the-art £10 million facility. The ribbon was cut by two young local men, each descended from soldiers who fought in the battle (one from either side). On the way up to the door, look under your feet at the memorial stones for fallen soldiers and clans, mostly purchased by their

American and Canadian descendants. Your tour takes you through two sections: the exhibit and the actual battlefield.

The Exhibit

The initial part of the exhibit provides you with some background. As you pass the ticket desk, note the **family tree** of Bonnie Prince Charlie ("Charles Edward Stuart") and George II, who were distant cousins. Next is the first of the exhibit's shadowy-figure **touchscreens,** which connect you with historical figures who give you details from both the Hanoverian and Jacobite perspectives. A **map** shows the other power struggles happening in and around Europe, putting this fight for political control of Britain in a wider context. This battle was no small regional skirmish, but rather a key part of a larger struggle between Britain and its neighbors, primarily France, for control over trade and colonial power. In the display case are **medals** from the early 1700s, made by both sides as propaganda.

From here, your path through this building is cleverly designed to echo the course of the Jacobite army. Your short march gets

under way as Charlie sails from France to Scotland, then finagles the support of Highland clan chiefs. As he heads south with his army to take London, you, too, are walking south. Along the way, maps show the movement of troops, and wall panels cover the buildup to the attack, as seen from both sides. Note the clever division of information: To the left and in red is the story of the "government" (a.k.a. Hanoverians/Whigs/English, led by the Duke of Cumberland); to the right, in blue, is the Jacobites' perspective (Prince Charlie and his Highlander/French supporters).

But you, like Charlie, don't make it to London—in the dark room at the end, you can hear Jacobite commanders arguing over whether to retreat back to Scotland. Pessimistic about their chances of receiving more French support, they decide to U-turn, and so do you. Heading back up north, you'll get some insight into some of the strategizing that went on behind the scenes.

By the time you reach the end of the hall, it's the night before the battle. Round another bend into a dark passage, and listen to the voices of the anxious troops. While the English slept soundly in their tents (recovering from celebrating the Duke's 25th birthday), the scrappy and exhausted Jacobite Highlanders struggled through the night to reach the battlefield (abandoning their plan of a surprise night attack at Nairn and instead retreating back toward Inverness).

At last the two sides meet. As you wait outside the theater for the next showing, study the chart depicting how the forces were ar-

ranged on the battlefield. Once inside the theater, you'll soon be surrounded by the views and sounds of a windswept moor. An impressive four-minute **360° movie** projects the re-enacted battle with you right in the center of the action (the violence is realistic; young kids should probably sit this one out). If it hasn't hit you already, the movie drives home just how outmatched the Jacobites were.

Leave the movie, then enter the last room. Here you'll find **period weapons,** including ammunition and artifacts found on the battlefield, as well as **historical depictions** of the battle. You'll also find a section describing the detective work required to piece together the story from historical evidence. On the far end is a huge map, with narration explaining the combat you've just experienced while giving you a bird's-eye view of the field through which you're about to roam.

The Battlefield

Collect your free **audioguide** and go outside. From the back wall of the visitors center, survey the battlefield. In the foreground is a

cottage used as a makeshift hospital during the conflict. To the east/right (south of the River Nairn) is the site that Lord George Murray originally chose for the action. In the end, he failed to convince Prince Charlie of its superiority, and the battle was held here—with disastrous consequences. Although not far from Culloden, the River Nairn site was miles away tactically, and things might have turned out differently for the Jacobites had the battle taken place there instead.

Bear left up the path, toward the battlefield. Your GPS guide knows where you are, and the attendant will give you directions on where to start. As you walk along the path, stop each time you hear the "ping" sound (if you keep going, you'll confuse the guide). The basic audioguide has 10 stops—including the Jacobite front line, the Hanoverian front line, and more—and takes a minimum of 30 minutes, which is enough for most people. At the third stop, you have the option of detouring along a larger loop (6 extra stops, mostly focusing on the Jacobite line—figure another 30 minutes minimum) before rejoining the basic route. Each stop has additional information on everything from the Brown Bess musket to who was standing on what front line—how long this part of the tour takes depends on how much you want to hear. Notice how uneven and boggy the ground is in parts, and imagine trying to run across this hummocky terrain with all your gear, toward almost-certain death.

As you pass by the **mass graves,** marked by small headstones, realize that entire clans fought, died, and were buried together. (The fallen were identified by the clan badge on their caps.) The Mackintosh grave alone was 77 yards long.

When you've finished your walking tour, reenter the hall, return your audioguide, then catch the last part of the exhibit, which covers the aftermath of the battle. As you leave the building, hang a left to see the wall of **protruding bricks,** each representing a soldier who died. The handful of Hanoverian casualties are on the left

(about 50); the rest of the long wall's raised bricks represent the multitude of dead Jacobites (about 1,500).

If you're having trouble grasping the significance of this battle, play a game of "What if?" If Bonnie Prince Charlie had persevered on this campaign and taken the throne, he likely wouldn't have plunged Britain into the Seven Years' War with France (his ally). And increased taxes on either side of that war led directly to the French and American revolutions. So if the Jacobites had won...the American colonies might still be part of the British Empire today.

CLAVA CAIRNS

Scotland is littered with reminders of prehistoric peoples—especially in Orkney and along the coast of the Moray Firth—but the Clava Cairns, worth ▲, are among the best-preserved, most interesting, and easiest to reach. You'll find them nestled in the spooky countryside just beyond Culloden Battlefield. These "Balnauran of Clava" are Neolithic burial chambers dating from 3,000 to 4,000 years ago. Although they appear to be just some giant piles of rocks in a sparsely forested clearing, a closer look will help you appreciate the prehistoric logic behind them. (The site is well explained by informative plaques.) There are three structures: a central "ring cairn" with an open space in the center but no access to it, flanked by two "passage cairns," which were once covered. The entrance shaft in each passage cairn lines up with the setting sun at the winter solstice. Each cairn is surrounded by a stone circle, and the entire ensemble is framed by evocative trees—injecting this site with even more mystery.

Cost and Hours: Free, always open.

Getting There: Just after passing Culloden Battlefield on the B-9006 (coming from Inverness), signs on the right point to *Clava Cairns.* Follow this twisty road to the free parking lot by the stones. You can also walk from Culloden Battlefield, but it's three miles round-trip and not very appealing (mostly along roads; the Inverness TI has maps). Skip the cairns if you don't have a car or if the weather is bad.

CAWDOR CASTLE

Homey, intimate, and worth ▲, this castle is still the residence of the Dowager (read: widow) Countess of Cawdor, a local aristocrat-

ic branch of the Campbell family. The castle's claim to fame is its connection to Shakespeare's *Macbeth,* in which the three witches correctly predict that the protagonist will be granted the title "Thane of Cawdor." The castle is not used as a setting in the play—which takes place in Inverness, 300 years before this castle was built—but Shakespeare's dozen or so references to "Cawdor" are enough for the marketing machine to kick in. Today, virtually nothing tangibly ties Cawdor to the Bard or to the real-life Macbeth. But even if you ignore the Shakespeare lore, the castle is worth a visit.

Cost and Hours: £10.50, good £5 guidebook explains the

family and the rooms, May-Sept daily 10:00-17:30, closed Oct-April, tel. 01667/404-401, www.cawdorcastle.com.

Getting There: It's on the B-9090, just off the A-96, about 15 miles east of Inverness (6 miles beyond Culloden and the Clava Cairns). In recent years, public transportation to the castle has been nonexistent—but ask at the Inverness TI just in case it has resumed.

Visiting the Castle: The chatty, friendly docents (including Jean at the front desk, who can say "welcome" and "mind your head" in 60 different languages) give the castle an air of intimacy—most are residents of the neighboring village of Cawdor and act as though they're old friends with the Dowager Countess (many probably are). Entertaining posted explanations—written by the countess' late husband, the sixth Earl of Cawdor—bring the castle to life and make you wish you'd known the old chap. While many of today's castles are still residences for the aristocracy, Cawdor feels even more lived-in than the norm—you can imagine the Dowager Countess stretching out in front of the fireplace with a good book. Notice her geraniums in every room.

Stops on the tour include a tapestry-laden bedroom and a "tartan passage" speckled with modern paintings. In another bedroom (just before the stairs back down) is a tiny pencil sketch by Salvador Dalí. Inside the base of the tower, near the end of the tour, is the castle's proud symbol: a holly tree dating from 1372. According to the beloved legend, a donkey leaned against this tree to mark the spot where the castle was to be built—which it was, around the tree. (The tree is no longer alive, but its withered trunk is still propped up in the same position. No word on the donkey.)

The **gardens,** included with the ticket, are worth exploring, with some 18th-century linden trees, a hedge maze (not open to the public), and several surprising species (including sequoia and redwood). In May and June, the laburnum arbors drip with yellow blossoms.

The nine-hole **golf course** on the castle grounds is bigger than pitch-and-putt and fun even for nongolfers (£12.50/person).

Nearby: The close but remote-feeling **village of Cawdor**—with a few houses, a village shop, and a tavern—is also worth a look if you've got time to kill.

INVERNESS & LOCH NESS

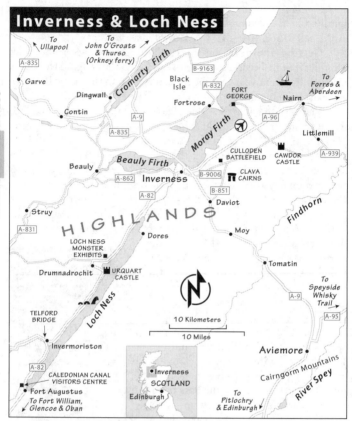

Loch Ness

I'll admit it: I had my zoom lens out and my eyes on the water. The local tourist industry thrives on the legend of the Loch Ness monster. It's a thrilling thought, and there have been several seemingly reliable "sightings" (by monks, police officers, and sonar imaging). But even if you ignore the monster stories, the loch is impressive: 23 miles long, less than a mile wide, 754 feet deep, and containing more water than all of the freshwater bodies of England and Wales combined. It's essentially the vast chasm of a fault line, filled with water. Whoa. I'm thankful the loch is in Scotland—where property laws make it extremely difficult to buy or build along its banks—and not in California.

Getting There: The Loch Ness sights are a 20-minute drive southwest of Inverness. To drive the full length of Loch Ness takes about 45 minutes. Fort William-bound buses #19 and #919 make stops at Urquhart Castle and Drumnadrochit (7-9/day, 35-40 minutes).

Sights on Loch Ness

Loch Ness Monster Exhibits

In July 1933, a couple swore they saw a giant sea monster shimmy across the road in front of their car by Loch Ness. Within days, ancient legends about giant monsters in the lake (dating as far back as the sixth century) were revived—and suddenly everyone was spotting "Nessie" poke its head above the waters of Loch Ness. Further sightings and photographic "evidence" have bolstered the claim that there's

something mysterious living in this unthinkably deep and murky lake. (Most sightings take place in the deepest part of the loch, near Urquhart Castle.) Most witnesses describe a waterbound dinosaur (resembling the real, but extinct, plesiosaur). Others cling to the slightly more plausible theory of a gigantic eel. And skeptics figure the sightings can be explained by a combination of reflections, boat wakes, and mass hysteria. The most famous photo of the beast (dubbed the "Surgeon's Photo") was later discredited—the "monster's" head was actually attached to a toy submarine. But that hasn't stopped various cryptozoologists from seeking photographic, sonar, and other proof.

And that suits the thriving local tourist industry just fine. The Nessie commercialization is so tacky that there are two different monster exhibits within 100 yards of each other, both in the town of Drumnadrochit. Each has a tour-bus parking lot and more square footage devoted to their kitschy shops than to the exhibits. The overpriced exhibits are actually quite interesting—even though they're tourist traps, they'll appease that small part of you that knows the *real* reason you wanted to see Loch Ness.

Loch Ness Centre & Exhibition: This exhibit—the better option of the two, and worth ▲—is headed by a naturalist who has spent many years researching lake ecology and scientific phenomena. With video presentations and special effects, this exhibit

The Caledonian Canal

Two hundred million years ago, two tectonic plates collided, creating the landmass we know as Scotland and leaving a crevice of thin lakes slashing diagonally across the country. This Great Glen Fault, from Inverness to Oban, is easily visible on any map.

British engineer Thomas Telford connected the lakes 200 years ago with a series of canals so ships could avoid the long trip around the north of the country. The Caledonian Canal runs 62 miles from Scotland's east to west coasts; 22 miles of it is manmade. Telford's great feat of engineering took 19 years to complete, opening in 1822 at a cost of one million pounds.

But bad timing made the canal a disaster commercially. Napoleon's defeat in 1815 meant that ships could sail the open seas more freely. And by the time the canal opened, commercial ships were too big for its 15-foot depths. Just a couple of decades after the Caledonian Canal opened, trains made the canal almost useless...except for Romantic Age tourism. From the time of Queen Victoria (who cruised the canal in 1873), the canal has been a popular tourist attraction. To this day the canal is a hit with vacationers, recreational boaters, and lock-keepers who compete for the best-kept lock.

The scenic drive from Inverness along the canal is entertaining, with Drumnadrochit (Nessie centers), Urquhart Castle, Fort Augustus (five locks), and Fort William (under Ben Nevis, with the eight-lock "Neptune's Staircase"). As you cross Scotland, you'll follow Telford's work—22 miles of canals and locks between three lochs, raising ships from sea level to 51 feet (Ness), 93 feet (Lochy), and 106 feet (Oich).

While Neptune's Staircase, a series of eight locks near Fort William, has been cleverly named to sound intriguing (see page 291), the best lock stop is midway, at Fort Augustus, where the canal hits the south end of Loch Ness. In Fort Augustus, the **Caledonian Canal Visitor Centre,** three locks above the main road, gives a good rundown on Telford's work (see page 324). Stroll past several shops and eateries to the top for a fine view.

Seven miles north, in the town of **Invermoriston,** is another Telford structure: a stone bridge, dating from 1805, which spans the Morriston Falls as part of the original road. Look for a small parking lot just before the junction at A-82 and A-887, on your right as you drive from Fort Augustus. Carefully cross the A-82 and walk three minutes back the way you came. The bridge, which took eight years to build and is still in use, is on your right.

explains the geological and historical environment that bred the monster story, as well as the various searches that have been conducted. Refreshingly, it retains an air of healthy skepticism instead of breathless monster-chasing. It also has some artifacts related to the search, such as a hippo-foot ashtray used to fake monster footprints and the *Viperfish*—a harpoon-equipped submarine used in a 1969 Nessie search (£7.45, daily Easter-Oct 9:30-17:45, July-Aug until 18:45, Nov-Easter 10:00-16:15, last entry 45 minutes before closing, in the big stone mansion right on the main road to Inverness, tel. 01456/450-573, www.lochness.com).

Nessieland Castle Monster Centre: The other exhibit (up a side road closer to the town center, affiliated with a hotel) is less serious. It's basically a tacky high-school-quality photo report and a 30-minute *We Believe in the Loch Ness Monster* movie, which features credible-sounding locals explaining what they saw and a review of modern Nessie searches. (The most convincing reason for locals to believe: Look at the hordes of tourists around you.) It also has small exhibits on the area's history and on other "monsters" and hoaxes around the world (£6, daily May-Sept 9:00-19:00, Oct-April 9:00-17:00, tel. 01456/450-342, www.nessieland.co.uk).

▲Urquhart Castle

The ruins at Urquhart (UR-kurt), just up the loch from the Nessie exhibits, are gloriously situated with a view of virtually the entire lake.

Cost and Hours: £8.50, guidebook-£4, daily April-Sept 9:30-18:00, Oct 9:30-17:00, Nov-March 9:30-16:30, last entry 45 minutes before closing, café, tel. 01456/450-551, www.historic-scotland.gov.uk.

Visiting the Castle: The visitors center has a tiny exhibit with interesting castle artifacts and a good eight-minute film taking you on a sweep through a thousand years of tumultuous history—from St. Columba's visit to the castle's final destruction in 1692. The castle itself, while dramatically situated and fun to climb through, is a relatively empty shell. After its owners (who supported the crown) blew it up to keep the Jacobites from taking it, the largest medieval castle in Scotland (and the most important in the Highlands) wasn't considered worth rebuilding or defending, and was abandoned.

Well-placed, descriptive signs help you piece together this once-mighty fortress. As you walk toward the ruins, take a close look at the trebuchet (a working replica of one of the most destructive weapons of English King Edward I), and ponder how this giant slingshot helped Edward grab almost every castle in the country away from the native Scots.

Loch Ness Cruises

Cruises on Loch Ness are as popular as they are pointless. The lake is scenic, but far from Scotland's prettiest—and the time-consuming boat trips show you little more than what you'll see from the road. As it seems that Loch Ness cruises are a mandatory part of every "Highlands Highlights" day tour, there are several options, leaving from the top, bottom, and middle of the loch. The basic one-hour loop costs around £14 and includes views of Urquhart Castle and lots of legends and romantic history (Jacobite is the dominant outfit of the many cruise companies, www.jacobite.co.uk). I'd rather spend my time and money at Fort Augustus or Urquhart Castle.

▲Fort Augustus

Perhaps the most idyllic stop along the Caledonian Canal is the little lochside town of Fort Augustus. It was founded in the 1700s—before there was a canal here—as part of a series of garrisons and military roads built by the English to quell the Highland clansmen, even as the Stuarts kept trying to take the throne in London. Before then, there were no developed roads in the Highlands—and without roads, it's hard to keep indigenous people down.

From 1725 to 1733, the English built 250 miles of hard roads and 40 bridges to open up the region; Fort Augustus was a central Highlands garrison at the southern tip of Loch Ness, designed to awe clansmen. It was named for William Augustus, Duke of Cumberland—notorious for his role in destroying the clan way of life in the Highlands. (When there's no media and no photographs to get in the way, ethnic cleansing has little effect on one's reputation.)

Fort Augustus makes for a delightful stop if you're driving through the area. Parking is easy. There are plenty of B&Bs, charming eateries, and an inviting park along the town's five locks. You can still see the capstans, surviving from the days when the locks were cranked open by hand.

The fine little **Caledonian Canal Visitor Centre** nicely tells the story of the canal's construction (free, daily Easter-Oct, tel. 01320/366-493).

Eating in Fort Augustus: You can eat reasonably at eateries along the canal. Try **The Little Neuk,** a good café serving filled rolls and homemade soups. **The Lock Inn** and **The Bothy** are pubs with decent food, and the **Canalside Chip Shop** offers fish and chips. The only real grocery store in town is the gas station, next to the TI, which is a five-minute walk north from the canal just after crossing the River Oich (also housing the post office, a WC, and an ATM).

EASTERN SCOTLAND

Pitlochry • Loch Tay • Speyside Whisky Trail • Balmoral Castle • Scotland's East Coast

Between Edinburgh and Inverness, the eastern expanse of Scotland bulges out into the North Sea. The main geological landmark is Cairngorms National Park, with gently rugged Highland scenery and great hiking terrain. If your time is limited, Scotland is more satisfying elsewhere. But this region is easily accessible—you'll likely pass through at some point on your trip—and has a lot to offer, especially for those with special interests. I've sorted through the many duds and focused on a few gems.

This chapter is organized geographically: sights west and east of the Cairngorms. Those in a hurry should focus on the west, where the A-9 highway links up some fun choices. Pitlochry has a green-hills-and-sandstone charm, a warm welcome, and a pair of great distilleries, making it the region's best overnight stop. Nearby you'll find a fascinating trip back to prehistory (at the Scottish Crannog Centre on Loch Tay), a fun sheepdog show, and an open-air folk museum.

East of the Cairngorms, the attractions require more of a detour (most convenient for those connecting Inverness and St. Andrews), but an even better look at rural Scotland. Whisky connoisseurs flock to Speyside, royalists visit Balmoral Castle and the nearby home-base village of Ballater, and ruined-castle fans head to Dunnottar.

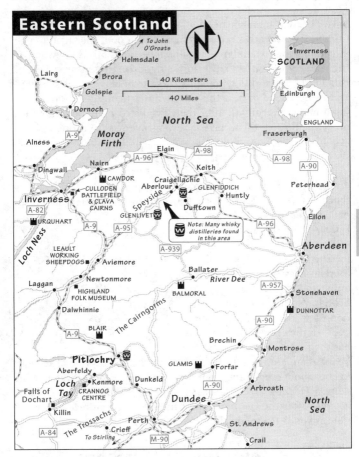

Eastern Scotland

Note: Many whisky distilleries found in this area

West of the Cairngorms

The A-9 highway, connecting Inverness, Stirling, and Edinburgh, may be Scotland's single most touristy road. Heading south on the A-9, soon after leaving Inverness, the highway begins to skirt around the bulging west edge of Cairngorms National Park, which it follows almost all the way to Pitlochry. These bald, heather-covered hills are what many people picture when they imagine Highland scenery. The best look at the Cairngorms is on the east side of the park, around the village of Ballater and Balmoral Castle (see page 344); the A-939, connecting the valley of the River Spey to Ballater, is particularly dramatic. But you'll get a decent glimpse of scenery along the A-9.

As you follow the A-9, it seems every exit is stacked with four or five brown "tourist attraction" signs. For the most part, the options along here are more convenient than good; they tend to pale in comparison to similar—but superior—alternatives elsewhere in the country. But if your trip to Scotland isn't taking you beyond this Highland corridor, some of these may be worth a stop. Pitlochry, described next, is the top town (particularly for those seeking a handy overnight); after that, I've listed more options in the order you'll reach them traveling from Inverness to Edinburgh.

Pitlochry

This likable tourist town, famous for its whisky and its hillwalking (both beloved by Scots), makes an enjoyable overnight stop. Just

outside the craggy Highlands, Pitlochry is set amid pastoral rolling hills that offer plenty of forest hikes. While it seems that tourism is essentially the town's only industry—with perhaps Scotland's highest concentration of woolens shops and outdoor outfitters—Pitlochry also has the feel of a real community. People here are friendly and bursting with town pride: They love to chat about everything from the high-quality local theater to the salmon ladder at the hydroelectric dam. It's also a restful place, where—after the last tour bus pulls out—you can feel your pulse slow as you listen to gurgling streams.

Orientation to Pitlochry

Plucky little Pitlochry (pop. 2,500) lines up along its tidy, tourist-minded main street, Atholl Road, which runs parallel to the River Tummel. The train station is on Station Road, off the main street. Most distilleries are a short drive out of town, but you can walk to the two best (see my self-guided whisky walk). Navigate easily by following the black directional signs to Pitlochry's handful of sights.

Tourist Information: The helpful TI, at one end of town, has free Wi-Fi and public computers, and sells maps for local hill walks and scenic drives. Their good £1 *Pitlochry Path Network* brochure is handy (July-early Sept Mon-Sat 9:00-18:00, Sun 9:30-17:00; April-June and early-Sept-Oct Mon-Sat 9:30-17:30, Sun 10:00-16:00; shorter hours and closed Sun Nov-March; 22 Atholl Road, tel. 01796/472-215).

HELPFUL HINTS

Bike Rental: Escape Route Bikes, located across the street and a
block from the TI (away from town), rents a variety of bikes
(basic bike-£14/5 hours, £24/24 hours, more for better bikes,
includes helmet and lock if you ask, Mon-Sat 9:00-17:30, Sun
10:00-17:00, 3 Atholl Road, tel. 01796/473-859, www.escape-
route.co.uk).

Parking: Drivers who aren't spending the night can park in the
large pay-and-display lot next to the TI, in the center of town.

Pitlochry Whisky Walk

You can spend an enjoyable afternoon hillwalking from downtown
Pitlochry to a pair of top distilleries on this self-guided walk. The
entire loop trip takes two to three hours, depending on how long
you linger in the distilleries (at least an hour of walking each way).
It's a good way to see lush fern forests and a pretty decent waterfall,
especially if you've only experienced urban Scotland. The walk is
largely uphill on the way to the Edradour Distillery; wear good
shoes, bring a rain jacket just in case, and be happy that you'll stroll
easily downhill *after* you've had your whisky samples.

At the TI, pick up the *Pitlochry Path Network* brochure and
follow along with its map. You'll be taking the **Edradour Walk**
(marked on directional signs with yellow hiker icons; on the map
it's a series of yellow dots). Leave the TI and head left along the
busy A-924. The walk can be done in either direction, but I'll describe it counterclockwise.

Within 10 minutes, you'll walk under the railroad tracks and
then come to **Bell's Blair Athol Distillery** on your left. If you're
a whisky buff, stop in here (described later, under "Sights in Pitlochry"). Otherwise, hold out for the much more atmospheric
Edradour. You'll pass a few B&Bs and suburban homes, then a
sign marked *Black Spout*. Just after this, you'll cross a bridge, then
take the next left, walking under another stone rail overpass and
away from the road. Following this path, you'll come to a clearing,
and as the road gets steeper, you'll see signs directing you 50 yards
off the main path to see the "Black Spout"—a wonderful waterfall
well worth the few extra steps.

At the top of the hill, you'll arrive in another clearing, where
a narrow path hugs a huge field on your left. Low rolling hills surround you in all directions. It seems like there's not another person
around for miles, with just the thistles to keep you company. From
here it's an easy 20 minutes to the **Edradour Distillery** (described
later).

Leaving the distillery, to complete the loop, head right, following the paved road (Old North Road). In about 50 yards, a sign

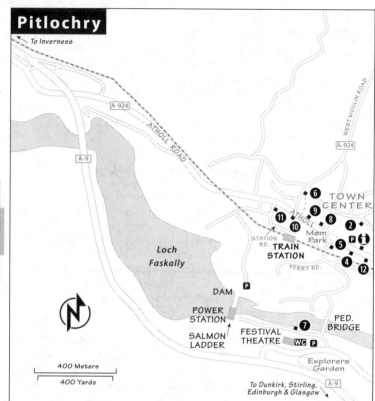

points left into the field. Take the small footpath that runs along the left side of the road. (If you see the driveway with stone lions on both sides, you've gone a few steps too far.) You'll walk parallel to the route you took getting to the distillery, hugging the far side of the same huge field. The trail then swoops back downhill through the forest, until you cross the footbridge and make a left. You'll soon reach Knockfarrie Road—take this downhill; you'll pass a B&B and hear traffic noises as you emerge from the forest. The trail leads back to the highway, with the TI a few blocks ahead on the right.

Sights in Pitlochry

DISTILLERY TOURS

For background on types of whiskies, how whisky is made, and tasting it like a pro, see page 460.

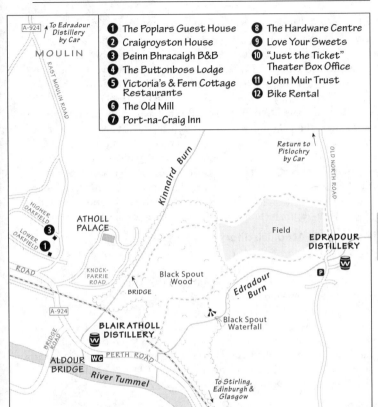

- ❶ The Poplars Guest House
- ❷ Craigroyston House
- ❸ Beinn Bhracaigh B&B
- ❹ The Buttonboss Lodge
- ❺ Victoria's & Fern Cottage Restaurants
- ❻ The Old Mill
- ❼ Port-na-Craig Inn
- ❽ The Hardware Centre
- ❾ Love Your Sweets
- ❿ "Just the Ticket" Theater Box Office
- ⓫ John Muir Trust
- ⓬ Bike Rental

EASTERN SCOTLAND

▲▲Edradour Distillery

This cute distillery (pronounced ED-rah-dower)—the smallest historic distillery in Scotland (est. 1825)—takes pride in making

its whisky with a minimum of machinery. Small white-and-red buildings are nestled in an impossibly green Scottish hillside. ("Edradour"—also the name of the stream that gurgles through the complex—means "land between two rivers.") With its idyllic setting and gregarious spirit, it's one of the most enjoyable distillery tours in Scotland. Unlike the bigger distilleries, they allow you to take photos of the equipment. If you like the whisky, buy some here and support the Pitlochry economy—this is one of the few independently owned distilleries left in Scotland.

Cost and Hours: £7.50 for a one-hour tour, departs 2-3/hour, mid-April-mid-Oct Mon-Sat 10:00-17:00, closed Sun and off-season, last tour departs one hour before closing, tel. 01796/472-095, www.edradour.com.

Getting There: Most come to the distillery by car (follow signs from the main road, 2.5 miles into the countryside), but you can also get there on a peaceful hiking trail that you'll have all to yourself (follow my "Pitlochry Whisky Walk," earlier).

Visiting the Distillery: You'll watch a 10-minute orientation film, then enjoy a guided tour through the facility: from the malt barn (where the barley is germinated and dried) to the still (where giant copper stills turn distiller's beer into whisky) to the warehouse (where 6,000 casks age in the darkness). Take a deep whiff of the rich aroma—you're smelling the so-called "angels' share," the tiny percentage of each cask that's lost to evaporation. And, of course, you'll finish things off with two free sample drams.

Bell's Blair Athol Distillery

This big, ivy-covered facility is more conveniently located (about a half-mile from the town center) and more corporate-feeling, offering 45-minute tours with a wee taste at the end. I'd tour this only if you're a whisky completist, or if you lack the wheels or hiking stamina to reach Edradour.

Cost and Hours: £7, Easter-Oct tours depart 2/hour daily 10:00-17:00, July-Aug until 17:30, possibly closed Sun in spring, last tour departs one hour before closing; shorter hours, fewer tours, and closed Sat-Sun off-season; tel. 01796/482-003, www.discovering-distilleries.com/blairathol.

THE TOWN CENTER

Pitlochry's main street is a pleasant place to wander and window-shop. Starting at the big parking lot by the TI, turn right and walk into town. As you stroll, consider this: The town exists thanks to the arrival of the train, which conveniently brought Romantic Age tourists from the big cities in the south to this lovely bit of Scotland. Queen Victoria herself visited three times in the 1860s, putting Pitlochry on the tourist map. The postcard-perfect Victorian sandstone architecture on the main street makes it clear that this was a delightful escape for city folks back in the 19th century.

Pause when you reach the **memorial park,** with a poignant Celtic cross honoring men from the local parish whose lives were lost fighting in World War I—a reminder of Scotland's disproportionate sacrifices in that conflict. Throughout Scotland, even many tiny villages have similar monuments.

From the park, get oriented. **Ferry Road,** which branches off under the rail bridge (passing two recommended restaurants), eventually leads to a footbridge that will take you to the other side of the river—home to Pitlochry's spunky Festival Theatre, as well as a power station with a salmon ladder (a fun excuse for a lazy walk—for details on these, see later). Across the street, consider stepping into **The Hardware Centre.** In small towns like Pitlochry—without a Wal-Mart (I mean, Tesco)—shops like this serve as catch-all general stores for the community. In addition to hardware, it carries a full range of kitchenware.

Now continue up the main street—checking real-estate prices, browsing for whisky and woolens, or perhaps getting a too-close shave at the gimmicky Sweeny Todd's Demon Barber shop. Look for the purple awning marking the **Love Your Sweets** shop (on the right, at #58), stocking a staggering variety of uniquely Scottish candies in bulk. Step in to buy a mixed bag of some unusual flavors of hard candies, such as clove, rhubarb, or Irn-Bru. At the next little park on the right, a surging stream angles away from the main road and to the recommended Old Mill restaurant.

Farther along the main road, on the left (at #89), watch for the **Just the Ticket** office, where you can learn more about Pitlochry's Festival Theatre. If you're spending the night, drop in to see what's on tonight.

One more block farther along, Station Road runs off to the left, toward the train station that put Pitlochry on the map. On this corner, be sure to step into the **John Muir Trust.** John Muir (1838-1914) was born in Scotland, moved to the US when he was 10, and later helped establish the world's first national park system in the US. Inside is a tiny exhibit called The Wild Space, with a feel-good nature video and a small art gallery. They also sell books, maps, and other conservation-themed souvenirs (free, July-Aug Mon-Sat 10:00-17:00, Sun 11:00-16:00, shorter hours and closed Tue off-season, tel. 01796/470-080, www.jmt.org).

From here, things peter out pretty quickly along the main road. If you're up for a longer stroll—but don't want to tackle the Whisky Walk outlined earlier—double back to the other side of the street and do some more window-shopping on your return to the memorial park, where you can head across the river to see the area described next.

ACROSS THE RIVER

These sights line up (in this order) along the largely undeveloped riverbank opposite Pitlochry's town center. While none are knock-out sights, they're a fine excuse for a pretty stroll or drive. Walkers

EASTERN SCOTLAND

Sleep Code

Abbreviations   (£1=about $1.60, country code: 44)
S=Single, D=Double/Twin, T=Triple, Q=Quad, b=bathroom
Price Rankings
   $$ Higher Priced—Most rooms £80 or more
   $ Lower Priced—Most rooms less than £80
Unless otherwise noted, credit cards are accepted, breakfast is included, and free Wi-Fi and/or a guest computer is generally available. Prices change; verify current rates online or by email. For the best prices, always book directly with the hotel.

---

can reach this area easily in about 15 minutes: Head down Ferry Road (near the memorial park), cross the footbridge, and turn right. Drivers head east out of town (toward Bell's Blair Athol Distillery), then turn right on Bridge Road and cross the river. To reach the power station and salmon ladder, watch for the turnoff for *Port na Craig Historic Hamlet*. For the festival theater (where you can also park to walk up to the Explorers Garden) stay on the main road to the big parking lot, which is just beyond the historic hamlet turnoff.

Pitlochry Power Station and Salmon Ladder

Pitlochry's dam on the River Tummel provides a nice place to go for a stroll, and also comes with a salmon ladder—a series of chambers that allow salmon to "step" their way upstream next to the dam (salmon may run April-Oct, best May-June). Near the ladder, a sporadically open visitors center offers a mildly entertaining exhibit about hydroelectric power in the region. You can also walk all the way across the top of the dam, pausing to read informational plaques and to peer through windows into the hydroelectric plant (dam closed 20:00-8:00).

Pitlochry Festival Theatre

This theater company rotates its productions, putting on a different play every night. Most are classics, with a few musicals and new shows mixed in. The venue has a variety of other programming year-round (£15-30, a few pounds more Fri-Sat nights; plays generally run May-Oct Mon-Sat, closed Sun; purchase tickets online, by phone, or in person; visit Just the Ticket, in town at 89 Atholl Road, or the theater—same price, box office open daily 10:00-20:00, restaurant, tel. 01796/484-626, www.pitlochryfestivaltheatre.com).

Nearby: Just above the theater's parking lot, the six-acre **Explorers Garden** features plants and wildflowers from around the world (£4, April-Oct daily 10:00-17:00, closed Nov-March, tel. 01796/484-626, www.explorersgarden.com).

Sleeping in Pitlochry

I've listed prices for a standard double room in peak season (July-Sept); you'll typically pay less off-season. Of these, the Craigroyston House and the Buttonboss Lodge are easier for train travelers; the others are more plush but a steeper hike from the station (consider a taxi). All of these have free parking.

$$ The Poplars Guest House, perched regally on a meticulously landscaped hill high above the main road, has been stylishly renovated by Jason and Nathalie. The huge, spacious home has eight rooms that combine modern comforts and a respect for tradition (Db-£89, cheaper for 2 or more nights, 27 Lower Oakfield, tel. 01796/472-129, www.poplars-pitlochry.com, info@poplars-pitlochry.com).

$$ Craigroyston House, my sentimental favorite in Pitlochry, is a quaint, large Victorian country house with eight Laura Ashley-style bedrooms. Gretta and Douglas Maxwell are welcoming and generous with local information (Db-£98, family room, cash only, next to the former church at 2 Lower Oakfield, tel. 01796/472-053, www.craigroyston.co.uk, reservations@craigroyston.co.uk). Drivers can reach it on Lower Oakfield Road; walkers can walk up from the huge parking lot next to the TI on Atholl Road (find the small gate at the back of the lot).

$$ Beinn Bhracaigh (to pronounce it, just clear your throat) feels hotelesque, with 13 modern, tasteful rooms and a well-stocked honesty bar. Of my listings, it sits the highest above the main road—still within a (longish, steep) walk, but easier by car. But the location comes with fine views across the town center and river to the hills beyond (Db-£92, more for bigger rooms, 14 Higher Oakfield, tel. 01796/470-355, www.beinnbhracaigh.com, info@beinnbhracaigh.com).

$ The Buttonboss Lodge has a less idyllic setting, right along the busy main road across from the TI (expect some traffic noise). But it's affordable and convenient for train travelers. The eight rooms, managed by Cristian, are straightforward and a bit old-fashioned (Db-£70-80 depending on size, 25 Atholl Road, tel. 01796/472-065, mobile 0790-247-2065, www.buttonbosslodge.co.uk, info@buttonbosslodge.co.uk).

Eating in Pitlochry

Plenty of options line the main drag, including several bakeries selling picnic supplies. **Victoria's** restaurant and coffee shop, a local favorite, feels like a down-home diner, serving up an eclectic menu of comfort food (£9-11 sandwiches at lunch only, £11-12 pizzas, £12-17 dinners, daily 10:00-20:30, patio seating, free Wi-Fi, at corner of memorial park, 45 Atholl Road, tel. 01796/472-670). **Fern Cottage,** just behind Victoria's, feels slightly more dressy and puts a Mediterranean spin on their menu (£14-17 main courses, daily 12:00-15:00 & 17:00-20:30, Ferry Road, tel. 01796/473-840). **The Old Mill,** tucked a block behind the main drag in an actual old mill, is a popular, high-energy, pubby restaurant (£6-10 sandwiches at lunch only, £13-17 meals, food served daily 12:00-21:00, tel. 01796/474-020). **Port-na-Craig Inn** is a fancy option on the river, just downhill from the theater (£13-15 lunch specials, daily 11:00-22:00, tel. 01796/472-777).

Pitlochry Connections

The train station is open Monday to Saturday 8:00-18:30 and Sunday 10:30-18:00 (may have shorter hours in winter).

From Pitlochry by Train to: Inverness (almost hourly, 1.5 hours), **Stirling** (5/day direct, 1 hour, more with transfer in Perth), **Edinburgh** (8/day direct, 2 hours), **Glasgow** (9/day, 2 hours, some transfer in Perth; also 5 buses/day with transfer in Perth—train is faster). Train info: Tel. 0345-748-4950, www.nationalrail.co.uk.

Sights West of the Cairngorms

ALONG THE A-9 HIGHWAY
▲▲Leault Working Sheepdogs

Each afternoon, Neil Ross presents a 45-minute demonstration of his well-trained sheepdogs. The experience is vividly real and fascinating. You'll hunker down in a natural little amphitheater in the turf while Neil describes his work. He'll demonstrate why shepherds have used a crook for thousands of years, and explain why farmers get frustrated when "fancy people with numbers after their names" try to tell them how to manage their land. Then the dogs get to work: With shouts and whistles, each dog follows individual commands, demonstrating an impressive mastery over the sheep. (Watching in awe, you can't help but think: Sheepdogs are smart... and sheep are idiots.) After the presentation, you'll meet (and pet) the border collie stars of the show, and may have the

chance to feed some lambs or to try your hand at shearing sheep. If they happen to have a litter of border collie puppies, even those who dislike dogs may find it hard to resist smuggling one home.

Cost and Hours: £5, demonstration only once per day, May-Oct Sun-Fri at 16:00, closed to the public at other times, no demonstrations Sat or Nov-April, tel. 01540/651-402, www. leaultworkingsheepdogs.co.uk.

Getting There: The entrance to the farm is a gravel road that literally runs across the A-9. But since the little road sneaks up on you, it's safer to exit for Kincraig, then follow the brown signs around to a driveway that takes you (carefully) back across the A-9 and up to the farm.

▲**Highland Folk Museum**

Scotland doesn't have a top-notch open-air folk museum—but this is close enough. Just off the highway on the outskirts of Newtonmore, the museum features re-creations of traditional buildings from the surrounding area from the 1700s through the 1930s. The buildings are a bit spread out, and it's quiet outside of frequent "activity days" (check the schedule online).

Cost and Hours: Free, £4 guidebook, daily April-Aug 10:30-17:30, Sept-Oct 11:00-16:30, closed Nov-March, www. highlifehighland.co.uk.

Getting There: Exit the A-9 in Newtonmore, then follow brown signs for about five minutes through the village to the museum (free parking).

Visiting the Museum: From the entrance, turn right and walk about 10 minutes through a pine forest to the undisputed highlight: a circa-1700, thatched-roof Highland township called **Baile Gean.** Here you'll find a gathering of four primitive stone homes and three barns, each furnished as it would have been in the Jacobite era. Although built for the museum, the township was closely based on an actual settlement a few

miles away that was populated until the 1830s. Costumed docents can explain traditional Highland lifestyles, and you'll likely see—and smell—a peat fire filling one of the homes with its rich smoke. (Because peat doesn't spit or spark, it was much safer to burn than wood—which was too valuable to feed fires anyway, as most tools were made of wood.) This area provided an ideal backdrop for some of the rural-life scenes in the TV production of *Outlander* (see sidebar on page 494).

Hike back to the woods to return to the rest of the open-air museum, which is less interesting (and, if you're short on time, skippable). Consider ducking into the schoolhouse (just below the entrance) to learn about early-20th-century classrooms, or hike to the far end of the complex to see a scattering of other buildings (and some hairy "coos").

Blair Castle

The residence of the Dukes of Atholl (a.k.a. Clan Murray) has less personality than other, similar aristocratic homes in Scotland—

but it's convenient for those zipping past on the A-9. In Gaelic, a "blàr" or "blair" is a flat bit of land surrounded by hills. And sure enough, this stately, white palace rises up from a broad clearing. A stout fortress during the Jacobite wars, it was later renovated and expanded as a mansion in the Scottish Baronial style. The family still lives in the wing to the left as you face the entrance. In the relatively humdrum interior, you'll follow a self-guided, one-way route through a series of aristocratic rooms, decorated with so many portraits that it makes you think the Dukes of Atholl had time for little other than sitting for painters. Neither the docents nor the dry printed descriptions do much to bring the place to life. The highlight is the wood-paneled ballroom at the end, draped in tartan and bristling with antlers. If time allows, explore the grounds—especially the walled Hercules Garden, where rugged plantings surround a lily-padded pond, overlooked by a statue of Hercules (accessed via the trail near the parking lot).

Cost and Hours: £10.50, April-Oct daily 9:30-17:30, closed Nov-March, last entry one hour before closing, tel. 01796/481-207, www.blair-castle.co.uk.

Getting There: From the town of Blair Atholl (just off of the A-9), drive down the long, tree-lined driveway to the free parking lot. From Pitlochry, you can take the more scenic B-8019/B-8079 instead of the A-9.

▲Dunkeld

This charming wee town, just off the A-9, is worth considering for a stretch-your-legs break. While the town center is pleasant—with flower boxes and cleverly named shops—its claim to fame is its partially ruined cathedral, which sits on the banks of the

River Tay. The **Cathedral of St. Columba** was actually Scotland's leading church for a brief time in the ninth century, when that important saint's relics were being stored here during Viking raids. Later it blossomed into a large cathedral complex in a secluded, riverside setting. But it was devastated by the one-two punch of Reformation iconoclasts (who tore down most of the building) and Jacobites (who fought the Battle of Dunkeld near here). Today, after walking through the stony interior (consider borrowing the good audioguide for a £1 donation), be sure to head outside and circle the entire complex. You'll discover that the current church is merely the choir of the original structure—a huge, ruined nave (currently undergoing restoration) stretches behind it.

ON LOCH TAY

A short drive west of the A-9, Loch Tay is worth visiting mostly for its excellent Scottish Crannog Centre—the best place in Scotland to learn about early Iron-Age life. You can also drive along Loch Tay (and past the thundering Falls of Dochart) to connect Pitlochry and the A-9 corridor with the Trossachs and Loch Lomond.

▲▲Scottish Crannog Centre

Across Scotland, archaeologists know that little round islands on the lochs are evidence of crannogs—circular houses on stilts, dating to 500 years before Christ.
Iron-Age Scots built on the water because in an age before roads, people traveled by boat, and because waterways were easily defended against rampaging animals (or people). Scientists have found evidence of 18 such crannogs
on Loch Tay alone. One has been rebuilt, using mostly traditional methods, and now welcomes visitors. Guided by a passionate and well-versed expert, you'll spend about an hour visiting the crannog and learning about how its residents lived.

Cost and Hours: £8.75, daily April-Oct 10:00-17:30, closed Nov-March, well marked just outside Kenmore on the south bank of Loch Tay, tel. 01887/830-583, www.crannog.co.uk.

Visiting the Museum: The visit has three parts. First, while waiting for your guided tour, you'll look around the modest exhibition—explaining the history of crannogs, excavation efforts, and the building of this new one. Then your guide—dressed in prehistoric garb—will take you out across the rustic wooden bridge to the crannog itself, where you'll huddle under the thatched roof and learn about Iron-Age architecture. Your guide explains how families of up to 20 people lived in just one crannog—along with their livestock—and paints a vivid picture of what life was like in those rugged times. Finally you'll have a hands-on opportunity to experience Iron-Age "technology"—turning a lathe, grinding flour, spinning yarn, and even starting a fire using nothing but wood and string.

Kenmore

Located where Loch Tay empties into the River Tay, Kenmore is a sleepy, one-street, black-and-white village with a big hotel, a

church, and a post office/general store. There's not much to do here, other than visit the nearby Scottish Crannog Centre, enjoy the Loch Tay scenery, and consider hiking through the woods to the Taymouth Castle (currently being renovated). With its classic old hotel, Kenmore can be a handy home base for this area.

Sleeping in Kenmore: **$$ Kenmore Hotel,** dominating the village center, feels like a classic Scottish country hotel—it claims to be the oldest inn in Scotland (dating from 1572). The 39 rooms are old-fashioned but cozy, and welcoming lounges, terraces, and other public spaces sprawl through the building. Look for the Robert Burns poem above the fireplace in one of the bars (Db-£89-135 depending on room size, elevator, The Square, Kenmore, tel. 01887/830-205, www.kenmorehotel.com, reception@kenmorehotel.com). The pub, dining room, and various outdoor dining areas all share the same menu (£11-17 meals).

Falls of Dochart

At the far end of Loch Tay from Kenmore, in the village of Killin, the road passes on a stone bridge over a churning waterfall where the peat-brown waters of the River Dochart tumble dramatically into the loch. The romantic bridge is busy with passing motorists enjoying a photo op; eateries and gift shops surround the scene. You can clamber down onto the flat stones

for a closer look. From the bridge, notice the stone archway marking the burial ground of the Clan Macnab.

East of the Cairngorms

While the A-9 corridor to the west is studded with touristy amusements, the area east of the Cairngorms (while hardly undiscovered) feels more rugged and lets you dig deeper into the countryside. In this area, I've focused on two river valleys with very different claims to fame: Speyside, curling along the top of the Cairngorms, is famous for its many distilleries; Royal Deeside, cutting through the middle of the Cairngorms, is the home of the Queen's country retreat at Balmoral and the neighboring village of Ballater. Overnighting in Ballater is an ideal way to linger in this region and sleep immersed in Cairngorms splendor.

Speyside Whisky Trail

Of the hundred or so distilleries in Scotland, half lie near the valley of the River Spey—a small area called Speyside. The ample waters of the river, along with generous peat deposits, have attracted distillers here for centuries. While I prefer some of the smaller, more intimate distillery tours elsewhere (including Oban Distillery in Oban, Talisker on the Isle of Skye, and Edradour near Pitlochry), Speyside is convenient to Inverness and practically a pilgrimage for aficionados. The distilleries here feel bigger and more corporate, but they also include some famous names (including the world's two best-selling brands of single malts, Glenfiddich and Glenlivet). And for whisky lovers, it's simply enjoyable to spend time in a region steeped in such reverence for your favorite drink.

PLANNING YOUR TIME

A quick car tour of Speyside takes about a half-day, and is a scenic way to connect Inverness to Royal Deeside (it also works as a side-trip from Inverness). The biggest hurdle is choosing from among the many distilleries here. Whisky aficionados probably already have their favorites (or can do a little homework); laypeople might as well focus on the big, famous, easy ones: the free Glenlivet tour, or the granddaddy of them all, Glenfiddich. And anyone should fit in a stop at the Speyside Cooperage to see a facet of whisky production that you'll encounter nowhere else. To avoid waiting around during the busy summer months, it's a good idea to call ahead and book a time slot at the distillery of your choice.

Those wanting to linger in Speyside could consider spending

the night in one of the area's towns. For whisky-themed accommodations, consider the Cregallachie Hotel or The Mash Tun B&B in Aberlour.

Because public transit connections aren't ideal, Speyside works best for drivers—though if you're determined, you could take the train from Inverness to Elgin and catch the "whisky bus" from there (Stagecoach bus #38, stops in Craigellachie and Aberlour on the way to Dufftown, about hourly, none Sun).

Orientation to Speyside

The A-95, which parallels the River Spey, is the region's artery (to reach it, take the A-9 south from Inverness and turn off toward Grantown-on-Spey). Brown *Malt Whisky Trail* signs help connect the dots. While several distilleries lie along the main road, even more are a short side-trip away. Three humdrum villages form the nucleus of Speyside: Aberlour (the biggest and most charming), Craigellachie (essentially a wide spot in the road), and Dufftown (with a characteristic crossroads street plan culminating at a clock tower).

A word of caution: In Scotland, DUI standards are very low (0.05 percent) and strictly enforced. Go easy on the tastings, or bring a designated driver.

Sights in Speyside

I've listed these roughly west to east, as you'll reach them approaching Speyside on the A-95. For a good primer on whisky and whisky tastings, see page 460.

Glenlivet Distillery
Sitting five miles south of the A-95 (turn off at Bridge of Avon), this is one of the area's most popular distilleries to tour—though it's hard to know whether that's because of the whisky's famous reputation, or because it's the only free tour. The 45-minute tour takes you through the sprawling production facility—perched on a ridge overlooking Cairngorms National Park—and includes a wee dram. Note: This is just a short detour for those connecting Speyside to Ballater on the scenic route through the mountains (B-9008/A-939).

Cost and Hours: Free tours depart every 20 minutes, mid-

March-mid-Nov Mon-Sat 9:30-17:00, Sun from 12:00, closed in winter, last tour begins one hour before closing, head to the village of Glenlivet and follow signs from there, tel. 01340/821-720, www. theglenlivet.com.

Aberlour

Officially named "Charlestown of Aberlour" for its founder, this attractive sandstone town lines up along the A-95. It's famous both for its namesake whisky distillery (www.aberlour.com) and as the home of Walkers Shortbread, which you'll see sold in red-tartan boxes all over Scotland (you can get some at the factory store in town). **The Mash Tun,** just off the main road, is an atmospheric whisky bar with rooms upstairs (www.mashtun-aberlour.com).

Craigellachie

The blink-and-you'll-miss-it village of Craigellachie (craig-ELL-a-kee) is home to the landmark **$$ Craigellachie Hotel.** This classic old grand hotel, a handy home base for whisky pilgrims, is famous for its whisky bar—stocking more than 800 bottles (opens daily at 17:00, the receptionist may let you in for a peek at other times, 26 rooms, Db-£160, www.craigellachiehotel.co.uk). Just past the hotel on the A-941, keep an eye out on the left for the picturesque **Craigellachie Bridge,** built by the great Scottish industrial architect Thomas Telford.

Note that the A-95 takes a sharp turn to the right in Craigellachie (just before the hotel), leading to the cooperage described next, and beyond that, to the Glenfiddich Distillery and Dufftown; the main road (past the hotel and the bridge) becomes A-941.

▲Speyside Cooperage

The single biggest factor in defining whisky's unique flavor is the barrel it's aged in. At this factory, on the outskirts of Craigellachie,

you can watch master coopers build or refurbish casks for distilleries throughout Scotland. The 14 coopers who work here—and must complete a four-year apprenticeship to get the gig—are the last of a dying breed; while just about everything used to be transported in barrels, today these traditional containers are specialized for booze. First you'll view an engaging 15-minute film, then you'll head up to an observation deck peering down over the factory floor. Oak timber is shaped into staves, which are gathered into metal hoops, then steamed to make them more pliable. Finally the inside is charred with a gas flame, creating a carbonized coating that helps give whisky its golden hue and flavor. Because the vast majority of casks used in Scotland are hand-me-downs from the US (where bourbon laws only allow one use per barrel), you're more likely to see reassembly of old casks (with new ends) rather than from-scratch creation of new ones. But the process is equally fascinating.

Cost and Hours: £3.50, tours depart every 30 minutes, Mon-Fri 9:00-15:30, closed Sat-Sun, Dufftown Road, Craigellachie, tel. 01340/871-108, www.speysidecooperage.co.uk.

Glenfiddich Distillery

As you enter Dufftown, keep an eye out on the left for the home of Scotland's top-selling single malt whisky. This sprawling but still charming factory—with a name that means "Valley of the Deer" (hence the logo)—offers tours and tastings that are a bit more involved (and expensive) than the norm. It's smart to call ahead to understand your options and reserve.

Cost and Hours: Basic £10 "Explorers" visit includes 1.5-hour tour and 4 tastings (departs every 30 minutes), more expensive options available, daily 9:30-16:00 (last tour), tel. 01340/822-373, www.glenfiddich.com.

Dufftown

This charming, sleepy town radiates from its clock-tower-topped main square. A few steps up Conval Street from the tower, the humble, one-room **Whisky Museum** doubles as the TI. You'll see a small selection of historical displays and tools from the whisky trade (free, unpredictable hours but likely daily 10:00-16:00 in summer, tel. 01340/821-591). **The Whisky Shop,** directly behind the tower, is a serious place selling 650 different types of whisky (daily 10:00-18:00,  closed Sun in winter, 1 Fife Street, tel. 01340/821-097, www. whiskyshopdufftown.com).

Balmoral Castle and Royal Deeside

Royal Deeside—the forested valley of the River Dee—is two sights in one: the Scottish home of the British royal family, wrapped in some of the most gorgeous scenery of Cairngorms National Park.

▲Balmoral Castle

The Queen stays at her 50,000-acre private estate, located within Cairngorms National Park, from August through early October.

But in the months leading up to Her Royal Highness' arrival, the grounds and the castle's ballroom are open to visitors. While royalists will enjoy this glimpse into the place where Liz, Chuck, Billy, and Katie unwind, cynics will find the visit overrated and overpriced. Because this is a vacation palace (rather than a state residence), it lacks the sumptuous state rooms you'll see at Holyroodhouse in Edinburgh; this visit is about the grounds and the setting rather than the interior.

Cost and Hours: £11, includes audioguide, April-July daily 10:00-17:00, closed Aug-March, arrive at least an hour before closing, tel. 013397/42534, www.balmoralcastle.com.

Safaris: If you're caught up in the beauty of Balmoral, consider booking a ranger-led Land Rover safari through the grounds (£60, 4 hours, 2/day during the open season).

Background: Queen Victoria and Prince Albert bought Balmoral in 1848. The thickly forested hills all around reminded Albert of his Thuringian homeland, but Victoria adored it as well—calling it her "Highland paradise." They remodeled the castle extensively in the Scottish Baronial style—a romantic, faux-antique look resembling turreted Scottish Renaissance castles from the 16th century—helping to further popularize that look. Ever since, each monarch has enjoyed retreating to this sprawling property, designed for hunting (red deer) and fishing (salmon). The royal family was here when news broke of Princess Diana's death. (Their initial decision not to return to London or to mourn publicly was highly criticized, as depicted in the film *The Queen*.) Today Balmoral has a staff of hundreds, 80 miles of roads, a herd of Highland cattle, and a flock of Highland ponies (stout little miniature horses useful for hauling deer carcasses over the hills).

Visiting the Castle: From the parking lot (with a TI/gift shop, WCs, and the royal church across the street—described later), walk across the River Dee to reach the ticket booth. From here, you can either hike 15 minutes to the palace, or hop on the free trolley.

Once at the stables, pick up your included audioguide and peruse a few exhibits, including a short orientation film. In the main exhibit, you'll see a film of the kilts-and-bagpipes wel-

EASTERN SCOTLAND

come parade, plus wooden corgis, a diorama of local wildlife, and lots and lots of historical photos of royals enjoying Balmoral. Peek into the Queen's garage to see her custom Bentley.

Then follow your audioguide on a short loop through the grounds and gardens before arriving at the palace. (To cut to the chase, or if the weather is bad, you can shortcut past the café to the palace and the one room open to the public.) As you walk through the produce and flower gardens, ponder the unenviable challenge of trying to time all of the flowers to bloom and the produce to ripen at exactly the same time, coinciding with the royal family's arrival the first week of August (especially difficult given Scotland's notoriously uncooperative climate).

Finally you'll reach the somewhat anticlimactic grand finale: the palace ballroom, with carpeting, birch-carved paneling, and stags' heads high on the walls. Display cases show off memorabilia (children's games played by royal tots, and a fully operational mini-Citroën that future kings and queens have enjoyed driving around). Near the exit, a touchscreen offers you a virtual glimpse at the tartaned private quarters that are off-limits to us rabble.

Nearby: For a free peek at another royal landmark, stop at **Crathie Kirk,** the small, stony, charming parish church where the royal family worships when they are at Balmoral, and where Queen Victoria's beloved servant John Brown is buried (£1 donation requested, Mon-Sat 10:00-12:30 & 13:00-16:00, Sun 13:00-16:00, closed Nov-March). The church is just across the highway from the Balmoral parking lot.

The next town past Balmoral Castle (in the opposite direction from Ballater) is **Braemar** (bray-MAR). This tiny village hosts the most famous Highland Games in Scotland, as the Queen is almost always in attendance (first Sun in Sept, www.braemargathering. org). If you swing through town, you can take a look at its big games grandstand and its picturesque castle (not worth touring).

▲▲Ballater

Ballater (BAH-lah-tur) is the place where you'll feel as much royalist sentiment as anywhere in Scotland. For the people of Ballater (many of whom work, either directly or indirectly, with Balmoral Castle), the Windsors are, simply, their neighbors. Royal connections aside, Ballater is a pleasant, unpretentious, extremely tidy little town. Just big enough to have all the essential tourist services—but neatly nestled in the wooded hills of the Cairngorms, and a bit more "away from it all" than Pit-

lochry—Ballater is an ideal home base for those wanting to spend a night in this part of Scotland.

It was local springs—which bubbled up supposedly healing waters—that first put Ballater on the map. But there's no question the town is what it is today thanks to Queen Victoria and Prince Albert, who bought the nearby Balmoral Castle in 1848, then built a train station in Ballater to access it. Today, the town's best attraction may be its residents, who revel in telling tales of royal encounters. Prince Charles, who lives not at Balmoral but at Burke Hall (not open to the public), has a particular affection for this part of the Cairngorms. He supports Ballater charities and has been known to show up unannounced at town events...and locals love him for it. ("Prince Charles is a really nice guy," one of them told me. "Not at all like the chap you see on TV.")

Sights in Ballater: Unfortunately, the town's only real sight—the old **train station** built by Queen Victoria to more easily commute to her new summer home at
Balmoral Castle—suffered a fire in
early 2015. The artifacts housed in
its minimuseum were saved, but it
could be years before the station is
rebuilt and reopened. Even so, the
town is still fun for a wander. Facing
the charred station are two stately
sandstone buildings honoring the
couple that put this little village
on the map: the Prince Albert Hall
(likely housing the TI while the station is being rebuilt) and the Victoria Hall. Exploring the streets nearby, with their characteristic little
shops, you'll notice several boasting

the coveted seals announcing "By Appointment of her Majesty the Queen" or "By Appointment of H.R.H. the Prince of Wales"—meaning that they're authorized to sell their wares directly to the gang at Balmoral.

A block from the station—past the Balmoral Bar, with its turrets that echo its namesake castle—the unusually fine parish church is surrounded by an inviting green, with benches, flower gardens, and royal flourishes...like everything in Ballater.

Sleeping in Ballater: The town has several fine B&Bs; given the royal proximity and generally touristy nature of Ballater, prices are high, but so is quality.

$$ Osborne House is a big and cozy home, with spacious rooms, a lush walled garden, and delightful hosts Heather and Neil (S-£55, Sb-£60, Db-£90, less for 2 or more nights, 4 Dundarroch

Road, tel. 013397/55320, www.osbornehousebedandbreakfast. com, osbornehousebedandbreakfast@gmail.com). Just down the road past the Osborne House garden, look for the white fence surrounding the Victoria barracks—where soldiers tasked with guarding the Queen reside.

$$ Gordon Guest House, right in the center of town facing the historic train station, has five richly furnished rooms (Db-£80-110 depending on size, Station Square, tel. 013397/55996, www.thegordonguesthouse.com, info@thegordonguesthouse.com, Martin and Amanda).

$$ Schoolhouse B&B, in a sleepy, more residential area lower down in the town (near the campground), funnels its profits into the owners' overseas charity work: teaching English and providing critical dental work to disadvantaged people in India, Bangladesh, and Sri Lanka (D-£69, Db-£84, Anderson Road, tel. 013397/56333, www.school-house.eu, Alan and Cathy),

Eating in Ballater: If you're just passing through, consider grabbing lunch at the old-school café **The Bothy;** farther along the main street (toward Aberdeen), near the end of the strip of shops, **Rocksalt & Snails** is a hipper choice. There's also a handy, long-hours **Co-op grocery store** facing the parish church, and nice tables on the green. For a more serious dinner, Ballater has two good Indian restaurants (both facing the green) and a few hotel restaurants and pubs; the food at the landmark **Balmoral Bar** is good and affordable, though the ambience is dominated by huge TV screens playing sports.

Scotland's East Coast

Scotland's inlet-slashed, island-speckled west coast gets all of the attention...and should. But if you're nearby, consider taking a peek at the east coast. While St. Andrews—with its links and beaches—is probably Scotland's finest east coast town, one uniquely hulking castle ruin rises above other coastal choices: Dunnottar Castle. For those who enjoy hiking on coastal bluffs and exploring ruins, it's worth a detour on your way south from Ballater and Balmoral.

Dunnottar Castle

The mostly ruined, empty, and otherwise underwhelming castle of Dunnottar (duh-NAW-tur) owns a privileged position: clinging to the top of a bulbous bluff, flanked by pebbly beaches and surrounded nearly 360 degrees by the North Sea. It's scenic and strategic. From the parking lot, you'll walk five minutes to a fork: To the right, you'll come to a ridge with a panoramic view of the castle's fine setting; to the left, you'll hike steeply down (almost all the way to the beach), then steeply back up, to the castle itself. Inside, there's not much to see. The only important thing that happened here was the Battle for the Honours of Scotland, when the Scottish crown jewels were briefly hidden away in the castle from Oliver Cromwell's army, which laid siege to Dunnottar (unsuccessfully) for three days. But don't worry too much about the history, or the scant posted descriptions—just explore the stately ruins while enjoying the panoramic views, sea spray, and cry of the gulls.

Cost and Hours: The photo-op view is free (and enough for many); entering the castle costs £6, April-Sept daily 9:00-18:00, closes at dusk off-season, tel. 01569/762-173, www.dunnottarcastle.co.uk.

Getting There: It's just off the busy A-90 expressway, which runs parallel to the coast between Aberdeen and Dundee; exit for Stonehaven, and you'll find Dunnottar well signed just to the south.

Nearby: Dunnottar sits just beyond **Stonehaven**, a pleasant, workaday seafront town that's a handy place to stretch your legs or grab some lunch (big pay parking lot right in the town center, ringed by eateries and grocery stores).

EASTERN SCOTLAND

ISLE OF SKYE

Portree • Sights on the Isle of Skye

The rugged, remote-feeling Isle of Skye has a reputation for unpredictable weather ("Skye" comes from the Old Norse for "The Misty Isle"). But it also offers some of Scotland's best scenery, and it rarely fails to charm its many visitors. Narrow, twisty roads wind around Skye in the shadows of craggy, black, bald mountains, and the coastline is ruffled with peninsulas and sea lochs (inlets).

Skye is the largest of the Inner Hebrides, and Scotland's second-biggest island overall (over 600 square miles), but it's still manageable: You're never more than five miles from the sea. The island has only about 13,000 residents; roughly a quarter live in the main village, Portree. Other population centers include Kyleakin (near the bridge connecting Skye with the mainland) and Broadford (a tidy string of houses on the road between Portree and the bridge). The mountain-like Cuillin Hills separate the northern part of the island (Portree, Trotternish, Dunvegan) from the south (Skye Bridge, Kyleakin, Sleat Peninsula).

Set up camp in Portree, Skye's charming, low-key tourism hub (or, to stay closer to the mainland, overnight in Kyleakin). Then dive into Skye's attractions. Drive around the appealing Trotternish Peninsula, enjoying Scotland's scenic beauty: sparsely populated rolling fields, stony homes, stark vistas of jagged rock formations, and the mysterious Outer Hebrides looming on the horizon. Go for a hike in (or near) the dramatic Cuillin Hills, sample a peaty dram of whisky, and walk across a desolate bluff to a lighthouse at the end of the world. Learn about the sordid clan history of Skye, and visit your choice of clan castles: the MacLeods' base at Dunvegan, the MacDonalds' ruins near Armadale, and—nearby but not on Skye—the postcard-perfect Eilean Donan fortress, previously a Mackenzie stronghold but today held by the Macraes. Or just settle in, slow down, and enjoy island life.

The most useful TI is in Portree; shops in smaller towns (including Dunvegan) host more basic "information points."

PLANNING YOUR TIME

With two weeks in Scotland, Skye merits two nights, allowing a full day to hit its highlights: Trotternish Peninsula loop, Dunvegan Castle, the Fairy Pools hike (or another hike in the Cuillin Hills), and the Talisker Distillery tour. Mountaineers need extra time for hiking and hillwalking. Because it takes time to reach, Skye is skippable if you only have a few days in Scotland—instead, focus on the more accessible Highlands sights (Oban and its nearby islands, and Glencoe).

Situated between Oban/Glencoe and Loch Ness/Inverness, Skye fits neatly into a Highlands itinerary. To avoid seeing the same scenery twice, it works well to drive the "Road to the Isles" from Fort William to Mallaig, then take the ferry to Skye; later, leave Skye via the Skye Bridge and follow the A-87 east toward Loch Ness and Inverness, stopping at Eilean Donan Castle en route, or vice versa. With more time, take the very long and scenic route north from Skye, up Wester Ross and across Scotland's north coast, then down to Inverness (see the Northern Scotland chapter).

GETTING TO THE ISLE OF SKYE

By Car: Your easiest bet is the slick, free **Skye Bridge** that crosses from Kyle of Lochalsh on the mainland to Kyleakin on Skye (for more on the bridge, see page 379).

The island can also be reached by **car ferry.** The major ferry line connects the mainland town of Mallaig (west of Fort William along the "Road to the Isles"—see page 291) to Armadale on Skye (£24.30/car, £4.75/passenger, April-late Oct 8/day each way, 4-6/day on Sun, off-season very limited Sat-Sun connections, check-in closes 20 minutes before sailing, can be canceled in rough weather, 30-minute trip, operated by Caledonian MacBrayne, toll-free tel. 0800-066-5000 or tel. 01475/650-397, www.calmac.co.uk). To ensure getting a space for your car in peak season, it's smart to reserve the day before, either online or by phone. A tiny, six-car, proudly local "turntable" ferry crosses the short gap between the mainland Glenelg and Skye's Kylerhea, but it's close enough to the bridge that it's more charming than useful (runs frequently Easter-Oct, http://skyeferry.co.uk).

By Bus: Skye is connected to the outside world by Scottish Citylink buses (www.citylink.co.uk), which use Portree as their Skye hub. From Portree, buses connect to **Inverness** (bus #917, 3/

Isle of Skye

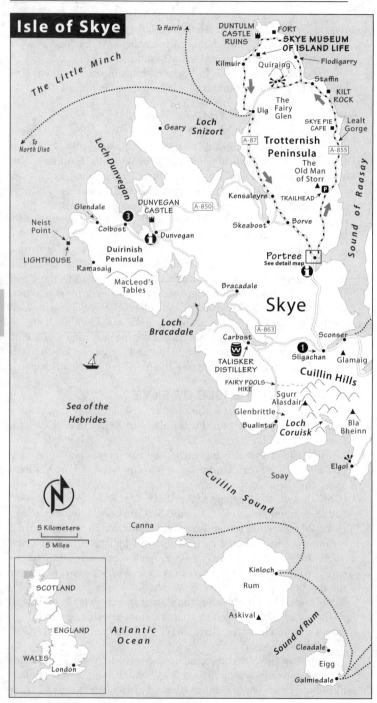

ISLE OF SKYE

To Harris

DUNTULM CASTLE RUINS
FORT
SKYE MUSEUM OF ISLAND LIFE
Kilmuir
Quiraing
Flodigarry
Staffin
KILT ROCK

The Little Minch

The Fairy Glen
Uig
SKYE PIE CAFE
Lealt Gorge

To North Uist

Geary
Loch Snizort
A-87
Trotternish Peninsula

Loch Dunvegan

The Old Man of Storr

Glendale
DUNVEGAN CASTLE
A-850
Kensaleyre
TRAILHEAD

Neist Point
Colbost
③
Dunvegan
Skeabost
Borve

LIGHTHOUSE

Duirinish Peninsula
Ramasaig
MacLeod's Tables

Portree
See detail map

Bracadale

Skye

Loch Bracadale

Sound of Raasay

A-863
Carbost
Sconser

TALISKER DISTILLERY
①
Sligachan
Glamaig

FAIRY POOLS HIKE
Cuillin Hills

Sea of the Hebrides

Sgurr Alasdair
Glenbrittle
Loch Coruisk
Bla Bheinn

Bualintur

Elgol

Soay

Cuillin Sound

5 Kilometers
5 Miles

Canna

Kinloch
Rum

SCOTLAND

Askival

Atlantic Ocean

ENGLAND

Sound of Rum

Cleadale

WALES

Eigg
London
Galmisdale

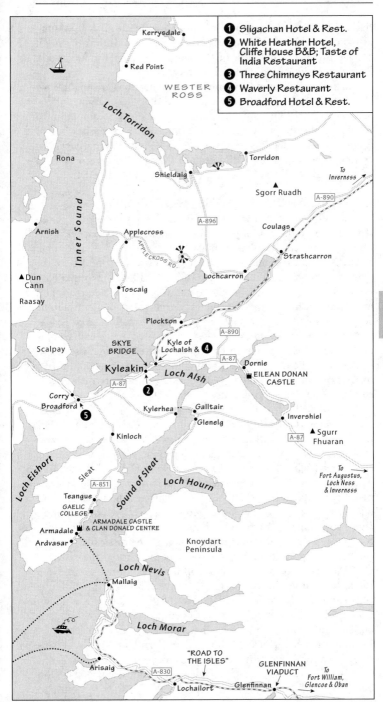

Legend:

1. Sligachan Hotel & Rest.
2. White Heather Hotel, Cliffe House B&B; Taste of India Restaurant
3. Three Chimneys Restaurant
4. Waverly Restaurant
5. Broadford Hotel & Rest.

Kerrysdale

Red Point

WESTER ROSS

Loch Torridon

Torridon

Shieldaig

Sgorr Ruadh

To Inverness

A-890

Rona

A-896

Coulags

Arnish

Applecross

APPLECROSS RD.

Strathcarron

Dun Cann

Toscaig

Lochcarron

Raasay

Plockton

Scalpay

A-890

SKYE BRIDGE

Kyle of Lochalsh & 4

Kyleakin

Loch Alsh

Dornie

EILEAN DONAN CASTLE

2

Corry

A-87

Broadford

Kylerhea

Galltair

Invershiel

5

Glenelg

A-87

Sgurr Fhuaran

Kinloch

Loch Eishort

Sleat

A-851

Loch Hourn

To Fort Augustus, Loch Ness & Inverness

Teangue

GAELIC COLLEGE

Sound of Sleat

ARMADALE CASTLE & CLAN DONALD CENTRE

Armadale

Knoydart Peninsula

Ardvasar

Loch Nevis

Mallaig

Loch Morar

Arisaig

A-830

"ROAD TO THE ISLES"

Lochailort

GLENFINNAN VIADUCT

Glenfinnan

To Fort William, Glencoe & Oban

ISLE OF SKYE

day, 3.5 hours) and **Glasgow** (buses #915 and #916, 3/day, 7 hours, also stops at **Fort William** and **Glencoe**). For **Edinburgh,** you'll transfer in either Inverness or Glasgow (4/day, 7.5-8 hours total). (For connections within the Isle of Skye, see later.)

More complicated **train-plus-bus** connections are possible for the determined: Take the train from Edinburgh, Glasgow, or Inverness to Fort William; transfer to the Jacobite Steam Train to Mallaig; take the ferry across to Armadale; then catch a bus to Portree (Stagecoach bus #52, 5/day, 1.25 hours). Alternatively, you can take the train from Edinburgh or Glasgow to Inverness, take another train to Kyle of Lochalsh, then catch a bus to Portree.

GETTING AROUND THE ISLE OF SKYE

By Car: Once on Skye, you'll need a car to enjoy the island. (Even if you're doing the rest of your trip by public transportation, a car rental is worthwhile here to make maximum use of your time; Portree-based car-rental options are listed on page 356.) If you're driving, a good map is a must (look for a 1:130,000 map that covers the entire island with enough detail to point out side roads and attractions; Philip's and Ordnance Survey are good). You'll be surprised how long it takes to traverse this "small" island: Kyleakin and Skye Bridge to Portree—45 minutes; Portree to Dunvegan—30 minutes; Portree to the tip of Trotternish Peninsula and back again—1.5-2 hours (depending on sightseeing stops); Portree to Armadale/ferry to Mallaig—1 hour; Uig (on Trotternish Peninsula) to Dunvegan—45 minutes.

By Bus: Skye can be frustrating by bus, especially on Sundays, when virtually no local buses run. Portree is the hub for bus traffic. Most buses within Skye are operated by Stagecoach (www.stagecoachbus.com; buy individual tickets or, for longer journeys, consider the £8.50 all-day Dayrider ticket or the £32 weeklong Megarider ticket). From Portree, you can loop around the Trotternish Peninsula on **bus #57A** (counterclockwise route) or **bus #57C** (clockwise route; Mon-Sat 4-5/day in each direction, none on Sun). **Bus #56** connects Portree and Dunvegan (5/day Mon-Fri, 3/day Sat, none on Sun, 40 minutes, goes right to the castle, catch a bus that leaves no later than 12:45 to have enough time at the castle).

The made-for-tourists **open-top bus #60X** loops around the island in summer; in the morning, it circles from Portree to Dunvegan and back (via Sligachan), and in the afternoon, it does a loop from Portree around the Trotternish Peninsula. Along the way, the bus stops just long enough for quick sightseeing at key places (e.g., 10 minutes at Kilt Rock, 1 hour at Dunvegan Castle); to stay longer, you can wait for a different bus following the same route.

To bus it from Portree to **Kyleakin,** you'll need to travel on Scottish Citylink (the Inverness-bound #917, 4/day, 1 hour); to reach **Eilean Donan Castle,** take any Citylink bus heading toward Fort William or Inverness (#915, #916, and #917; get off at Dornie and walk from there, 6-7/day, 1 hour).

By Tour: If you're without a car, consider taking a tour. Several operations on the island take visitors to hard-to-reach spots. Figure £30-40 per person to join an all-day island tour (usually 7-8 hours). Two Portree-based options using smaller 8- or 16-seat minibuses (rather than big coaches) are **Skye Scenic Tours** (www.skyescenictours.com) and **Tour Skye Tours** (www.tourskye.com). Portree-based **Michelle Rhodes** also does tours around the island (see page 357).

Portree

Skye's main attraction is its natural beauty, not its villages. But of those villages, the best home base is Portree (pore-TREE), Skye's largest settlement, transportation hub, and tourism center—ideally located for exploring Skye's highlight, the Trotternish Peninsula.

Portree is nestled deep in its protective, pastel harbor; overlapping peninsulas just offshore guard it from battering west coast storms. The original settlement here had the Gaelic name Kiltaraglen, meaning "the church of St. Talarican." In 1540, King James V arrived at this neutral ground to rally support among the feuding MacDonald and MacLeod clans. The clan chiefs swore allegiance to the Scottish king, earning the village the new name Port-Righ (Gaelic for "the King's Port"). Others propose a less romantic version: It's simply from Port Ruigheadh, "Port with Sloping Land." Either way, most of today's Portree dates from its early-19th-century boom time as a kelp-gathering and herring-fishing center.

If Portree has any disadvantages, it's that it takes at least 45 minutes to drive here (over a mountain pass) from the Skye Bridge (those passing through on a quick visit may prefer overnighting in Kyleakin instead—see page 378). Also, as the most popular town on Scotland's most popular island, Portree is jammed with visitors in the summer. Accommodations book up very early, and restaurants have lines out the door. If here in July or August, book your room as far ahead as you can (ideally a few months out), and try to reserve dinner up to a few days ahead.

Orientation to Portree

Although Portree doesn't have any real sights, it does boast a gorgeous harbor area and—in the streets above—all of the necessary tourist services: a good TI, fine B&Bs, great restaurants, a grocery store, a launderette, and so on. The main business zone of this functional village—the island's biggest, with about 2,850 residents—is in the tight grid of lanes on the bluff just above the harbor, anchored by Portree's tidy main square, Somerled Square. From here, buses fan out across the island and to the mainland. Homes, shops, and B&Bs line the roads leading out of town.

Tourist Information: Portree's helpful TI is a block off the main square (Mon-Sat 9:00-18:00, until 17:00 off-season; Sun 10:00-16:00; free Wi-Fi, Bayfield Road, just south of Bridge Road, tel. 01478/612-137).

HELPFUL HINTS

Internet Access: All Portree accommodations have free Wi-Fi, as do many cafés. You'll also find free hotspots at the TI and at the Aros Centre (on the way out of town).

WCs: Public WCs are across the street and down a block from the TI, across from the hostel.

Laundry: There's a **self-service launderette** below the Independent Hostel—it's next door to the Portree Youth Hostel, just off the main square (about £6/load, usually 11:00-21:00, last load starts at 20:00, The Green, tel. 01478/613-737).

Supermarket: A **Co-op** is on Bank Street (daily 7:00-23:00).

Bike Rental: Island Cycles rents bikes in the middle of town, just off the main square (£8.50/half-day, £17.50/24 hours, Mon-Sat 9:00-17:00, closed Sun, shorter hours in winter, The Green, tel. 01478/613-121, www.islandcycles-skye.co.uk).

Car Rental: To make the most of your time on Skye, rent a car. Several options line up along the road to Dunvegan and charge around £40-60/day (most are closed Sun; smart to call several days ahead in peak season, but worth trying last-minute). The most user-friendly option is **M2 Motors,** which can pick you up at your B&B or the bus station (tel. 01478/613-344, www.m2-motors.co.uk). If they're booked up, try **Jansvans** (tel. 01478/612-087, www.jans.co.uk), **Highland Motors/ HM Hire** (based nearby in Borve but can pick up in Portree, tel. 01470/532-264, www.hm-hire.co.uk), or **Morrison** (tel. 01478/612-688, morrisoncarrental.com).

Parking: As you enter town, you'll see signs on the right directing

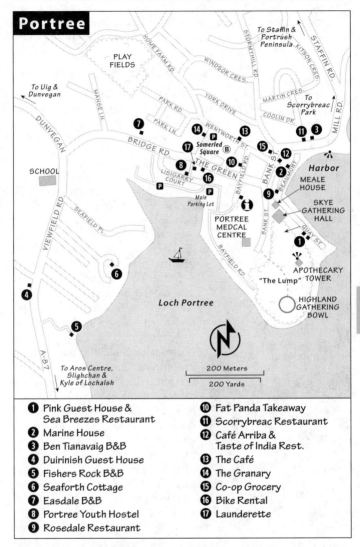

Portree

To Staffin &
Portrush
Peninsula

PLAY
FIELDS

To Uig &
Dunvegan

To
Scorrybreac
Park

SCHOOL

Somerled
Square

Harbor

MEALE
HOUSE

SKYE
GATHERING
HALL

PORTREE
MEDCAL
CENTRE

APOTHECARY
TOWER

"The Lump"

HIGHLAND
GATHERING
BOWL

Loch Portree

Main
Parking Lot

200 Meters

200 Yards

To Aros Centre,
Slighchan &
Kyle of Lochalsh

ISLE OF SKYE

1 Pink Guest House &
Sea Breezes Restaurant

2 Marine House

3 Ben Tianavaig B&B

4 Duirinish Guest House

5 Fishers Rock B&B

6 Seaforth Cottage

7 Easdale B&B

8 Portree Youth Hostel

9 Rosedale Restaurant

10 Fat Panda Takeaway

11 Scorrybreac Restaurant

12 Café Arriba &
Taste of India Rest.

13 The Café

14 The Granary

15 Co-op Grocery

16 Bike Rental

17 Launderette

you to a free parking lot below, at water level—after parking, just head up the stairs to the TI. You can also pay to park in the main town square or in front of the TI.

Town Walk: Michelle Rhodes leads guided 50-minute town walks through Portree most summer weekdays (£5, look for sign near main bus stop on Somerled Square for times; if there's no sign, there's no tour; mobile 07833-073-951, tel. 01478/611-915, www.skyehistoryandheritagetours.co.uk, michellelorrainerhodes@gmail.com). She also offers guided driving tours around the island, specializing in clan battles or fairies, myths, and legends (£75/person, email to arrange).

Sights in Portree

There's not a turnstile in town, but Portree itself is fun to explore. Below I've described the village's three areas: the main square and "downtown," the harborfront, and the hill above the harbor. You can link them up, in any order, for an orientation walk.

Somerled Square and the Town Center

Get oriented to Portree on the broad main square, with its mercat cross, bus stops, parking lot, and highest concentration of park benches. The square is named for Somerled (Old Norse for "Summer Wanderer"), the 12th-century ruler who kicked off the MacDonald clan dynasty and first united Scotland's western islands into the so-called Lordship of the Isles.

It seems every small Scottish town has both a mercat cross and a World War I memorial—and in Portree, they're combined

into one big **monument.** A mercat cross originally indicated the right for a town to host a market, and was the community gathering point for celebrations, public shamings, and executions. The WWI memorial is a reminder of the disproportionate loss of life that particular conflict exacted on Scotland. In the case of wee Portree, 28 local men went to war...and eight came back. (Ten were killed in a single night of fighting.) The WWII memorial was added later, as was a mention of Portree's lone casualty from the Korean War.

Much of present-day Portree was the vision of Sir James MacDonald, who pushed to develop the town in the late 18th century. City leaders imported the impressive engineer Thomas Telford (famous for his many great canals, locks, and bridges) to help design the village's harbor and the roads connecting it to the rest of the island.

Wentworth Street, running from this square to the harbor, is the main shopping drag. Several English-sounding streets in Portree (Wentworth, Bosville, Douglas, Beaumont) are named for aristocratic families that the MacDonalds married into, helping to keep the clan financially afloat. Window-shop your way two blocks along Wentworth Street, until you run into busy Bank Street. To your right is the **Royal Hotel,** built on the site of MacNab's Inn, where Bonnie Prince Charlie bid farewell to Flora MacDonald following his crushing defeat at Culloden, then set sail, never again to return to Scotland.

Quay Street leads down the hill to...

▲▲Portree Harbor

Portree's most pleasant space is its harbor, where colorful homes look out over bobbing boats and the surrounding peninsulas. As

one of the most protected natural harbors on the west coast, it's the reason that Portree emerged as Skye's leading town. Find a scenic perch at the corner of the harbor and take it all in.

While tourism is today's main industry, Portree first boomed in the mid-18th century thanks to kelp—yes, kelp. Seaweed was gathered here, sun-dried, and burned in kilns to create an ashy-blue substance that was rich in soda, an essential ingredient in the production of glass and soap. But with the defeat of Napoleon at Waterloo, international sources of kelp opened up, causing this local industry to crash.

This economic downturn coincided with a potato famine (similar to the one across the sea in Ireland), and by the mid-1800s, many locals were setting sail from this harbor to seek a better life in North America. It was a brutal process: Before leaving Portree, each emigrant's belongings were carefully inspected to ensure they reached a minimum threshold of resources necessary to forge a new life in the New World. (Most didn't.) For those who made it onto the ship, the four-month journey was beset by disease, danger, and miserable living conditions. Tens of thousands of Scottish would-be emigrants perished on the trip in what came to be known as "coffin ships."

But Portree soldiered on, bolstered by its prime location for fishing—especially for herring. By the early 20th century, a nationwide herring boom had again buoyed Portree's economy, with as many as 800 fishing boats crowding its harbor.

Notice the stone building with the sealed-off door at the base of the stairs leading up into town. This was the former **ice house,** which was in operation until the 1970s. The winch at the peak of the building was used to haul big blocks of ice into an enormous subterranean cellar, to preserve Atlantic salmon throughout the summer.

Survey the harbor, enjoying the **pastel homes**—which come

with lots of local gossip. Rumor has it that these used to be more uniform, until a proud gay couple decided to paint their house pink (it's now a recommended B&B). The blue-and-white house next door belongs to a fan of the West Ham United soccer team. Soon the other homeowners followed suit, each choosing their own color. Speaking of bright colors, look for the traffic-cone-orange boat floating in the harbor. This belongs to the Royal National Lifeboat Institution (RNLI), Britain's charity-funded answer to the US Coast Guard.

Go for a stroll along the Telford-built pier. Along here, a couple of different companies offer 1.5-hour excursions out to the sea-eagle nests and around the bay (ask the captains at the port, or inquire at the TI). At the far end of the pier is a BP gas station with huge, underwater tanks for fueling visiting boats.

Ascending "The Lump" (Hill Above the Harbor)

For a different perspective on Portree—and one that gets you away from the tourists—hike up the bluff at the south end of the harbor. From the Royal Hotel, head up Bank Street.

After a few steps, you'll spot the white **Meall House** on your left—supposedly Portree's oldest surviving home (c. 1801) and once the sheriff's office and jail (peek in the window to see how thick the walls are). Today it's a center for the Gaelic cultural organization Fèisean nan Gàidheal, which celebrates the Celtic tongue that survives about as well here on Portree as anywhere in Scotland. Hiding behind the Meall House, along the harborview path, is the stepped-gable, red-sandstone **Skye Gathering Hall** (from 1879). This is where Portree's upper-crust throws big, fancy, invitation-only balls on the days before and after Skye's Highland Games. The rest of the year, it hosts cultural events and—on most days—a fun little market with a mix of crafts and flea market-type items.

Back on Bank Street, continue uphill. Soon you'll approach the **Portree Medical Centre**—one of just two hospitals on the entire Isle of Skye. While they can handle emergencies here, they prefer not to deliver babies; expectant mothers on Skye are strongly urged to go to Inverness a week before the due date, and wait there for the baby to arrive.

Just before the hospital's parking lot, watch on the left for the uphill lane through the trees. Use this to hike on up to the top of the hill that locals call "The Lump" (or, for those with more local pride, "Fancy Hill"). Emerging into the clearing, you'll reach a huge, flat **bowl**

that was blasted out of solid rock to hold 5,000 people during Skye's annual Highland Gathering. (For more on Highland Games, see page 236.) In addition to the typical Highland dancing, footraces, and feats of strength, Skye's games have a unique event: From this spot, runners climb downhill, swim across Loch Portree, ascend the hill on the adjacent peninsula, then swim back again. (And you thought you were tired from climbing up here.)

Curl across the hilltop toward the harbor, and you'll run into a crenellated **apothecary tower.** It was built in 1834, not as a castle

fortification but to alert approaching sailors that a pharmacist was open for business in Portree. If you have any doubt about the power of Scotland's west coast storms, this tower was literally blown over by gale-force winds in a 1991 storm, but has since been rebuilt. It's usually open if you'd like to climb to the top for views over the harbor and the region—on a clear day, you can see all the way to the Old Man of Storr (see page 367).

Outside of Portree
Aros Centre

This visitors center, a mile outside of town on the road to Kyleakin and Skye Bridge, overlooks the sea loch. It's a jack-of-all-trades, with a modern 180-seat theater (featuring both cultural events and first-run movies), big café, free WCs and Wi-Fi, gift shop, and (upstairs) an art gallery showcasing the works of local artists. The center also has a space that hosts long-term temporary exhibits; for the next several years, you'll likely see a fascinating exhibit about the archipelago of St. Kilda—the farthest-flung islands of the Hebrides, uninhabited since the last residents were evacuated by the government in 1930. Today the largest island of the archipelago, Hirta, is an evocative and romantic ghost town, overrun with wildlife and occasional curious human day-trippers (for a very long day trip there from Skye, see www.gotostkilda.co.uk). You'll watch a soothing 20-minute film and enjoy good exhibits on St. Kilda's geology, flora and fauna, prehistoric stone structures, and unique (pre-1930) culture. But given St. Kilda's tentative ties to Skye, most people should view this as a rainy-day alternative.

Cost and Hours: Visitors center-free, exhibit-£5, both open daily 9:00-17:00—but often later because of special events and

---

Sleep Code

Abbreviations   (£1=about $1.60, country code: 44)
S=Single, **D**=Double/Twin, **T**=Triple, **Q**=Quad, **b**=bathroom.
Price Rankings
  $$$ Higher Priced—Most rooms £80 or more.
    $$ Moderately Priced—Most rooms £50-80.
      $ Lower Priced—Most rooms £50 or less.
Unless otherwise noted, credit cards are accepted, breakfast
is included, and free Wi-Fi and/or a guest computer is gener-
ally available. Prices change; verify current rates online or by
email. For the best prices, always book directly with the hotel.

---

movies, check website for events schedule, Viewfield Road, tel.
01478/613-649, www.aros.co.uk.

Walks and Hikes near Portree

The Portree TI can offer advice about hikes in the area; if either of
the below options interests you, get details there before you head
out.

One popular choice, which doesn't require a car, is called the
Scorrybreac Path. To get to the trailhead—three-quarters of a
mile from Somerled Square—walk north out of Portree on Mill
Road, veer right onto Scorrybreac Road when you're just leaving
town (following the sign for *Budhmor*), then follow the coastline
to the start of the hiking trail, marked by signs. From here, you'll
walk along the base of a bluff with views back on Portree's colorful
harborfront.

Drivers can tackle the more ambitious hike up to the **Old Man
of Storr:** You'll drive about 15 minutes north of town (following
the start of my Trotternish Peninsula Driving Tour) and park at
the Old Man of Storr trailhead. Green trail signs lead you through
a gate and up along a well-trod gravel path through a felled woodland. Once you've reached the top of the first bluff, take the right
fork, and continue all the way up to the pinnacle. Plan on about
two hours round-trip.

Sleeping in Portree

Portree is packed to the gills in July and August: Book your room
as far ahead as possible. You may need to check with several places.
The ones lacking websites (Marine House, Seaforth Cottage, Easdale B&B) have old-school charm, and tend to have room when
others are full. Spring and fall (March-June and Sept-Oct) are also
busy, but a bit more manageable.

ON THE HARBOR

$$ At **Pink Guest House,** energetic Robbie and Fiona rent 11 bright, spacious rooms (8 with sea views) on the harbor. The rates include a full Scottish breakfast and the hosts' youthful enthusiasm (Db-£80, £5 extra for view, large family rooms, free Wi-Fi, Quay Street, tel. 01478/612-263, www.pinkguesthouse.co.uk, info@ pinkguesthouse.co.uk).

$$ **Marine House,** a cozy, welcoming, delightful time warp run by sweet Skye native Fiona Stephenson, has three simple, homey rooms (two with a private bathroom down the hall) and fabulous views of the harbor (S-£27, D/Db-£80, cash only, reserved parking right on harbor, 2 Beaumont Crescent, tel. 01478/611-557, stephensonfiona@yahoo.com).

UP IN TOWN

$$ **Ben Tianavaig,** on the busy road through town overlooking the harbor, offers four comfortable rooms (all with views). Charlotte and Bill are generous with travel tips and foster a shoes-off tidiness (smaller Db-£75-78, large Db-£88, street parking out front, 5 Bosville Terrace, tel. 01478/612-152, www.ben-tianavaig.co.uk, info@ben-tianavaig.co.uk).

$ **Portree Youth Hostel,** run by Hostelling Scotland (SYHA), is a modern-feeling, institutional, cinderblock-and-metal building with 57 beds in 17 rooms. In addition to the dorms (£22/bunk), they have several private rooms that may appeal even to nonhostelers (D-£58, Db-£68, no breakfast, kitchen, laundry, tel. 01478/612-231, www.hostellingscotland.com).

ON VIEWFIELD ROAD

A couple of dozen places line Viewfield Road, stretching south from Portree toward the Aros Centre. All offer convenient parking and are within walking distance of town (figure 10-15 minutes). Some are on smaller side lanes that stretch down toward the water, but all are well marked from the main road.

$$ **Duirinish Guest House** feels homey, modern, and tidy. With four rooms, it sits across the main road from the water (only a few obstructed sea views) but comes with a warm welcome (smaller Db-£75, standard Db-£80, tel. 01478/613-728, www.duirinish-bandb-skye.com, ruth.n.prior@hotmail.co.uk, Ruth and Allan).

$$ **Fishers Rock,** a serene retreat with a glassy, contemporary, light-filled waterfront breakfast room, has a soothing energy and three rooms (non-view Db-£72, seaview Db-£78, big seaview Db with balcony-£82, tel. 01478/612-122, www.fishersrock.com, fishersrock@btinternet.com, Heather).

$$ **Seaforth Cottage** feels like a retired sea captain's home. Overlooking tidal flats, its garden is artfully littered with nautical flotsam and jetsam. The three simple rooms come with sea views and are a bit older, but priced accordingly (Db-£70, tel. 01478/612-040, ianskye48@hotmail.co.uk, gentle Ian).

$$ Easdale B&B is another old-school place with three rooms and a bright breakfast room set just above the busy main road; it's a bit closer to town than the places listed above (Db-£72, Bridge Road, tel. 01478/613-244—call to reserve, spunky and plainspoken Chrissie).

SLEEPING IN SLIGACHAN, BETWEEN PORTREE AND KYLEAKIN

$$$ Sligachan Hotel (pronounced SLIG-a-hin), a compound of related sleeping and eating options, is a local institution and a haven for hikers. In the Campbell family since 1913, the hotel's 21 rooms are comfortable, if a bit dated and simple for the price, while the nearby campground and bunkhouse offer a budget alternative. The setting—surrounded by the mighty Cuillin Hills—is remarkably scenic (Sb-£70, Db-£140, £20 more for bigger "superior" room, campground-£7.50/person, bunkhouse-£22/person; cheaper Oct-April, closed Nov-Feb, on the A-87 between Kyleakin and Portree in Sligachan, hotel and campground tel. 01478/650-204, bunkhouse tel. 01478/650-458, www.sligachan.co.uk, reservations@sligachan.co.uk). For location, see the map on page 352.

Eating in Portree

Note that Portree's few eateries tend to close early (21:00 or 22:00), and during busy times, lines begin to form soon after opening (or, at some popular places, even before). Reserve well ahead in peak season...or be prepared to wait.

ON THE WATERFRONT

Portree's little harbor has a scattering of good eateries but none have actual waterfront seating; for that, you'll have to picnic or get takeout.

Sea Breezes is a popular choice, with understated contemporary decor and a seafood-focused menu. While reservations aren't possible at lunch, it's essential to reserve ahead for dinner (£8-13 lunches, £12-20 dinners, popular £27 seafood platter, daily June-Aug 12:30-14:00 & 17:30-21:30, shorter hours April-May and Sept-Oct, closed Nov-March, tel. 01478/612-016, www.seabreezes-skye.co.uk).

Rosedale Restaurant, upstairs in the big Rosedale Hotel with just a dozen tables and serene views of the harbor, is another good place for fresh, local seafood (£14-20 dinners, £50 seafood platter for two, daily 17:30-21:00, reservations smart, tel. 01478/613-131, www.portreerestaurant.co.uk).

Picnicking on the Harbor: The no-name **fish-and-chips stand** facing the harbor is a decent choice for those simply wanting to munch something on the harbor's benches or steps (£7 fish-and-chips). Or grab takeaway up in town—the **Fat Panda** Asian restaurant on Bayfield Road is good, and the **Co-op** grocery has a small selection of sandwiches and other prepared foods.

UP IN TOWN

Scorrybreac is Portree's best splurge, offering a delightful array of well-presented international dishes that draw from local ingredients and traditions. The chef/owner, Callum, is the son of a famous singer who lives in town—but this restaurant is helping him make a name for himself. The cozy, modern, unpretentious dining room fills up quickly, so book ahead (£30/2 courses, £35/3 courses, Thu-Sat 12:00-14:00 & 17:30-22:30, Sun and Tue-Wed 17:30-22:30, closed Mon, 7 Bosville Terrace, tel. 01478/612-069, www.scorrybreac.com).

Café Arriba tries hard to offer eclectic flavors in this small Scottish town. With an ambitious menu that includes local specialties, Mexican, Italian, and more, this youthful, colorful, easygoing eatery's hit-or-miss cuisine is worth trying. Drop in to see what's on the blackboard menu today (£6-10 meals, lots of vegetarian options, daily 7:00-18:00, Quay Brae, tel. 01478/611-830).

The Café, a few steps off the main square, is a busy, popular hometown diner serving good crank-'em-out food to an appreciative local crowd. The homemade ice-cream from the stand in front is a nice way to finish your meal (£9-13 lunches and burgers, £10-16 dinners, also does takeaway, daily 9:00-21:30, Wentworth Street, tel. 01478/612-553). The same people own **The Granary,** with a similar comfort-food approach in a slightly more spacious and contemporary-feeling space; it's just across Somerled Square (£12-17 main courses, long hours daily, tel. 01478/612-873).

The Taste of India, with a nondescript contemporary interior, serves good Indian food and may have tables when other places are full (£8-11 meals, daily 12:00-14:00 & 17:00-23:30, upstairs on Bank Street—look for door across from Co-op grocery, tel. 01478/611-706).

Eating Elsewhere on the Isle of Skye

In addition to the following two destination restaurants, I've described some eateries in and near Kyleakin—where Skye meets the mainland—on page 378.

ISLE OF SKYE

IN SLIGACHAN

Sligachan Hotel (described earlier) is a grand and rustic old hotel in an extremely scenic setting, nestled in the Cuillin Hills. Choose between the lovely dining room (£13-18 local seafood dishes, nightly 18:30-21:00) and the big, open-feeling pub serving micro-brews and mountaineer-pleasing grub (£10-13 meals, long hours daily, food served until 21:30, pub closed Oct-Feb; on the A-87 between Kyleakin and Portree in Sligachan, tel. 01478/650-204).

IN COLBOST, NEAR DUNVEGAN

Three Chimneys Restaurant is known throughout Scotland as a magnet for foodies. Its 16 tables fill an old three-chimney croft house, with a stone-and-timbers decor that artfully melds old and new—a perfect complement to the modern Scottish cuisine. It's cozy, classy, candlelit, and a bit dressy (do your best), but not stuffy. Because of its remote location—and the fact that it's almost always booked up—reservations are absolutely essential, ideally several weeks if not months ahead, although it's worth calling in case of last-minute cancellations (figure £40-50 for lunch, £65-90 for dinner, not including drinks, daily 12:15-14:00 & 18:15-21:30, shorter hours off-season, tel. 01470/511-258, www.threechimneys.co.uk, Eddie and Shirley Spear). They also rent six swanky, pricey suites next door (Db-£345).

Getting There: It's in the village of Colbost, about a 10- to 15-minute drive west of Dunvegan on the Duirinish Peninsula (that's about 45 minutes each way from Portree). To get there, first head for Dunvegan, then follow signs toward Glendale. The Neist Point Lighthouse (described later) is at the end of the same road. For location, see the map on page 352.

Sights on the Isle of Skye

I've organized these sights geographically, roughly from north (near Portree) to south.

THE TROTTERNISH PENINSULA

This inviting peninsula north of Portree is packed with windswept castaway views, unique geological formations, a few offbeat sights, and some of Scotland's most dramatic scenery. Along the way, you'll explore a gaggle of old-fashioned stone homes, learn about Skye's ancient farming lifestyles, and pay homage at the grave of a brave woman who rescued a bonnie prince. In good weather, a spin around Trotternish is the single best Skye activity (and you'll still have time to visit Dunvegan Castle, Talisker Distillery, and/or the Cuillin Hills later on).

▲▲▲Trotternish Peninsula Driving Tour

The following loop tour starts and ends in Portree, circling the peninsula counterclockwise. If you did it with minimal stops, you'd make it back to Portree within two hours—but it deserves the better part of a day. Note that during several stretches, you'll be driving on a paved single-track road; use the occasional "passing places" to pull over and allow faster cars to go by.

○ **Self-Guided Tour:** Begin in the island's main town, Portree (see page 355).

• *Head north of Portree on the A-855, following signs for* Staffin. *About three miles out of town, you'll begin to enjoy some impressive views of the Trotternish Ridge. As you pass the small loch on your right, straight ahead is the distinctive feature called the...*

Old Man of Storr: This 160-foot-tall tapered slab of basalt stands proudly apart from the rest of the Storr. The unusual

landscape of the Trotternish Peninsula is due to massive landslides (the largest in Britain). This block slid down the cliff about 6,500 years ago and landed on its end, where it has slowly been whittled by weather into a pinnacle. An icon of Skye, the Old Man of Storr has been featured in many films—from *Flash Gordon* to *Prometheus* to *Snow White and the Huntsman*. The lochs on your right supply drinking water for the town of Portree and have been linked together to spin the turbines at a nearby hydroelectric plant that once provided all of Skye's electricity.

As you approach the formation, watch on the left for the parking lot marked *Old Man of Storr*. If you'd like to tackle the two-hour hike up to the formation, park here (for details on the hike, see page 362).

• *After passing the Old Man, enjoy the scenery on your right, overlooking...*

Nearby Islands and the Mainland: Some of Skye's most appealing scenery isn't the island itself, but the surrounding terrain. In the distance, craggy mountains recede into the horizon. The long island in the foreground, a bit to the north, is called Rona. This military-owned island and the channel behind it were used to develop and test one of Margaret Thatcher's pet projects, the Sting Ray remote-control torpedo.

As you drive, you'll notice that Skye seems to have more sheep

ISLE OF SKYE

than people. During the Highland Clearances of the early 19th century, many human residents were forced to move off the island to make room for more livestock. The people who remain are some of the most ardently Gaelic Scots in Scotland. While only about one percent of all Scottish people speak Gaelic (pronounced "gallic"), one-third of Skye residents are fluent. A generation ago, it was illegal to teach Gaelic in schools; today, Skye offers its residents the opportunity to enroll in Gaelic-only education, from primary school to college (Sabhal Mòr Ostaig, on Skye's Sleat Peninsula, is the world's only college with courses taught entirely in Scottish Gaelic; see page 381).

• *About four miles after the Old Man parking lot, you'll pass a sign for the River Lealt. Immediately after, the turnoff on the right is an optional stop at the...*

Lealt Gorge: Where the River Lealt tumbles toward the sea, it carves out a long and scenic gorge. To stretch your legs, you can

walk about five minutes along the lip of the gorge to reach a viewpoint overlooking a protected, pebbly cove and some dramatic rock formations. The formations on the left, which look like stacked rocks, are the opposite: they've been weathered by centuries of battering storms, which have peeled back any vegetation and ground the stones to their smooth state. Peering down to the beach, you'll see a smokestack and some other ruins of a plant that once processed diatomite—a crumbly, clay-like substance made from algae fossils, which has hundreds of industrial uses. This factory, which closed in 1960, is a reminder of a time when tourism wasn't the island's only source of income. When this was functioning, no roads connected this point to Portree, so the factory's waterfront location made it possible to ship the diatomite far and wide.

• *About a mile down the road, in the village of Culnacoc, watch for signs on the left to the...*

Skye Pie Café, in the Glenview Bed and Breakfast (just off the main road), is a trendy eatery selling top-quality £4-5 sweet and savory pies (takeaway available). With its café and art gallery, the Glenview has an artsy, almost hipster vibe—it's a refreshingly modern pit stop in this otherwise very remote-feeling area (café open Mon-Fri 11:00-17:00, closed Sat-Sun, tel. 01470/562-248, www.glenviewskye.co.uk).

• *Continue along the road. Just after the village of Valtos (about 2 miles after the Lealt Gorge viewpoint), you'll pass a big loch on the left and a wee loch on the right, next to a parking lot. Park at the well-marked Kilt Rock viewpoint to check out...*

Kilt Rock: So named because of its resemblance to a Scotsman's tartan, this 200-foot-tall sea cliff has a layer of volcanic rock

with vertical lava columns that look like pleats (known as columnar jointing), sitting atop a layer of horizontal sedimentary rock. Don't miss the dramatic formations in the opposite direction, too.

• *Continuing north, as you approach the village of **Staffin**, you'll begin to see interesting rock formations high on the hill to your left. Staffin's name, like that of the isle of Staffa (described on page 265), comes from Old Norse and means "the place of staves or pillars"—both boast dramatic basalt rock pillars. If you need a public WC, partway through town, watch on the left for the Staffin Community Hall (marked Talla Stafainn, sharing a building with a grocer).*

Just after you leave Staffin, watch for signs on the left to turn off and head up to the rock formation called...

The Quiraing: You'll get fine views of this jagged northern end of the Trotternish Ridge—rated ▲▲—as you drive up. Landslides caused the dramatic scenery in this area, and each rock formation has a name, such as "The Needle" or "The Prison." On your left, notice a couple of modern cemeteries high in the hills, far above the village. It seems like a strange spot to bury the dead, in the middle of nowhere. But it's logical—the land here is less valuable for development, and since it's not clay, as it is down by the water, it also provides better drainage.

As you approach the summit of this road, you'll reach a parking area on the left. This marks a popular trailhead for hiking out to

get a closer look at the formations. If you've got the time, energy, and weather for a sturdy 30-minute uphill hike, here's your chance. You can either follow the trail along the base of the rock formations, or hike up to the top of the plateau and follow it to the

end (both paths are faintly visible from the parking area). Once up top, your reward is a view of the secluded green plateau called "The Table," another landslide block, which isn't visible from the road.

• *You could continue on this road all the way to Uig, at the other end of*

ISLE OF SKYE

the peninsula. But it's worth backtracking, then turning left onto the main road (A-855, now single-track), to see the...

Tip of Trotternish: A few miles north, after the village of Flodigarry, you'll pass the **Flodigarry Hotel,** with a cottage on the premises that was once home to Bonnie Prince Charlie's rescuer, Flora MacDonald (the cottage is now part of the hotel and not open to the public).

Soon after, at the top of the ridge at the tip of the peninsula (on the right), you'll see the remains of an old **fort**—not from the Middle Ages or the days of Bonnie Prince Charlie, but from World War II, when the Atlantic was monitored for U-boats from this position.

Farther down the road, you'll pass (on the right) the crumbling remains of another fort, this one much older: **Duntulm Castle,** which was the first stronghold on Skye of the influential MacDonald clan. It was from here that the MacDonalds fought many fierce battles against Clan MacLeod (for more on these clan battles, see the sidebar on page 380). The castle was abandoned around 1730 for Armadale Castle on the southern end of Skye (see page 381). In the distance beyond, you can see the **Outer Hebrides**—the most rugged, remote, and Gaelic part of Scotland.

• *A mile after the castle, watch for the turnoff on the left to the excellent...*

Skye Museum of Island Life: This fine little stand of seven thatched stone huts, organized into a family-run museum and worth

▲▲, explains how a typical Skye family lived a century and a half ago (£2.50, Easter-Oct Mon-Sat 9:30-17:00, closed Sun and Nov-Easter, tel. 01470/552-206, www.skyemuseum.co.uk). Though there are ample posted explanations, the guidebook is worth buying.

The three huts closest to the sea are original (more than 200 years old). Most interesting is The Old Croft House, which was the residence of the Graham family until 1957. Inside you'll find three rooms: kitchen (with peat-burning fire) on the right, parents' bedroom in the middle, and a bedroom for the 12 kids on the left. Nearby, The Old Barn displays farm implements, and the Ceilidh House contains dense but very informative displays about crofting (the traditional tenant-farmer lifestyle on Skye—explained later), Gaelic, and other topics.

The four other huts were reconstructed here from elsewhere on the island, and now house exhibits about weaving and the village smithy (which was actually a gathering place). As you explore, admire the smart architecture of these humble but deceptively well-planned structures. Rocks hanging from the roof keep the thatch from blowing away, and the streamlined shape of the structure embedded in the ground encourages strong winds to deflect around the hut rather than hit it head-on.

• *After touring the museum, drive out to the very end of the small road that leads past the parking lot, to a lonesome cemetery. Let yourself in through the gate to reach the tallest Celtic cross at the far end, which is the...*

Monument to Flora MacDonald: This local heroine supposedly rescued the beloved Jacobite hero Bonnie Prince Charlie at his darkest hour. After his loss at Culloden, and with a hefty price on his head, Charlie retreated to the Outer Hebrides. But the Hanover dynasty, which controlled the islands, was closing in. Flora MacDonald rescued the prince, disguised him as her Irish maid, Betty Burke, and sailed him to safety on Skye. (Charlie pulled off the ruse thanks to his soft, feminine features—hence the nickname "Bonnie," which means "beautiful" or "handsome.") The flight inspired a popular Scottish folk song: "Speed bonnie boat like a bird on the wing, / Onward, the sailors cry. / Carry the lad that's born to be king / Over the sea to Skye." For more on Bonnie Prince Charlie and the Battle of Culloden, see page 312.

• *Return to the main road and proceed about six miles around the peninsula. On the right, notice the big depression.*

The Missing Loch: This was once a large loch, but it was drained in the mid-20th century to create more grazing land for sheep. If you look closely, you may see a scattering of stones in the middle of the field. Once a little island, this is the site of a former monastery...now left as high, dry, and forgotten as the loch. Beyond the missing loch is Prince Charlie's Point, where the bonnie prince is said to have come ashore on Skye with Flora MacDonald.

• *Soon after the loch, you'll drop down over the town of...*

Uig: Pronounced "OO-eeg," this village is the departure point for ferries to the Outer Hebrides (North Uist and Harris islands, 2-3/day). It's otherwise unremarkable, but does have a café with good sandwiches (follow *Uig Pier* signs into town—look for a white building with blue *Café* sign, next to ferry terminal at entrance to town).

• *Continue past Uig, climbing the hill across the bay. To take a brief*

detour to enjoy some hidden scenery, consider a visit to the Fairy Glen.
To find it, just after passing the big Uig Hotel on your left, take the next
left turn (marked for Sheadar *and* Balnaknock*). Follow this single-*
track road about 1.5 miles through the countryside. You'll emerge into an
otherworldly little valley called...

The Fairy Glen: Whether or not you believe in fairies, it's easy
to imagine why locals claim that they live here. With evocatively
undulating terrain—ruffled, conical hills called "fairy towers" reflected in glassy ponds, rising up from an otherwise flat and dull
countryside—it's a magical place. There's little to see on a quick
drive-by, but hikers enjoy exploring these hills, discovering little
caves, weathered stone fences, and concentric stone circles (a relatively recent addition). The higher you go, the better the views.
Hardy hikers enjoy clambering up to the top of the tallest rock
tower, the "Fairy Castle" (also called Castle Ewen). As you explore,
keep an eye out for "Skye landmines" (sheep droppings).

• *Head back the way you came, and continue uphill on the main road*
(A-87), with views down over Uig's port. Near the top is a large parking
strip on the right. Pull over here and look back to Uig for a lesson about
Skye's traditional farming system.

Crofting: You'll hear a lot about crofts during your time on
Skye. Traditionally, arable land on the island was divided into

plots. If you look across to the
hills above Uig, you can see strips
of demarcated land running up
from the water—these are crofts.
Crofts were generally owned by
landlords (mostly English aristocrats or Scottish clan chiefs, and
later the Scottish government)
and rented to tenant farmers. The
crofters lived and worked under
very difficult conditions, and were lucky if they could produce
enough potatoes, corn, and livestock to feed their families. Rights
to farm the croft were passed down from father to son over generations, but always under the auspices of a wealthy landlord.

Finally, in 1976, new legislation kicked off a process of priva-
tization called "decrofting." Suddenly crofters could have their land
decrofted, then buy it for an affordable price (£130 per quarter-
hectare, or about £8,000 for one of the crofts you see here). Many
decroftees would quickly turn around and sell their old family
home for a huge profit, but hang on to most of their land and build
a new house at the other end. In the crofts you see here, notice that
some have a house at the top of a strip of land and another house at
the bottom. Many crofts (like most of these) are no longer cultivat-
ed, but that should change, as crofters are now legally required to

farm their land...or lose it. In many cases, families who have other jobs still hang on to their traditional croft, which they use to grow produce for themselves or to supplement their income.

• *Our tour is finished. From here, you can continue along the main road south toward Portree (and possibly continue from there on to the Cuillin Hills). Or take the shortcut road just after Kensaleyre (B-8036), and head west on the A-850 to Dunvegan and its castle. All of your Skye options are described in the following pages.*

NORTHWEST SKYE
▲Dunvegan Castle

Perched on a rock overlooking a sea loch, Dunvegan Castle is the residence of the MacLeod (pronounced "McCloud") clan. One

of Skye's preeminent clans, the MacLeods often clashed with their traditional rivals, the MacDonalds, whose castle is on the southern tip of the island (see page 380). The MacLeods—who prefer the full name "MacLeod of Mac-Leod"—claim that Dunvegan is the oldest continuously in-habited castle in Scotland. The current clan chief, Hugh Magnus MacLeod of MacLeod, is a film producer who divides his time between London and the castle, where his noble efforts are aimed at preserving Dunvegan for future generations. Worth ▲▲▲ to people named MacLeod, the castle offers an interesting look at Scotland's antiquated clan system, provides insight into rural Scottish aristocratic lifestyles, and has fine gardens that are a delight to explore. Dunvegan feels rustic and a bit worse-for-wear compared to some of the more famous Scottish castles closer to civilization.

Cost and Hours: £11, April-mid-Oct daily 10:00-17:30, closed mid-Oct-March, café in parking lot, tel. 01470/521-206, www.dunvegancastle.com.

Getting There: It's near the small town of Dunvegan in the northwestern part of the island, well signposted from the A-850 (free parking). From Portree, bus #56 takes you right to the castle's parking lot (5/day Mon-Fri, 3/day Sat, none Sun; leave Portree no later than 12:45 to have time to tour the castle).

Visiting the Castle: Follow the one-way route through the castle, borrowing laminated descriptions in each room—and don't hesitate to ask the helpful docents if you have any questions.

You'll head up the main staircase and loop through the left wing. On the **bedroom**'s elegant canopy bed, look for the clan's seal and motto, carved into the headboard. The words "Hold Fast," which you'll see displayed throughout the castle, recall an incident where a MacLeod chieftain saved a man from being gored by a bull by literally taking the bull by the horns and wrestling it to the ground.

Beyond the bedroom, you'll ogle several more rooms, including the dining room, which is overloaded with MacLeod family portraits. The library's shelves are crammed with rich, leather-bound books.

Then you'll be routed back across the top of the stairs to the right wing, with the most interesting rooms. The 14th-century **drawing room** is the oldest part of the castle—it served as the great hall of the medieval fortress. But today it's a far cry from its gloomy, stony, Gothic-vaulted original state. In the 18th century, a clan chief's new bride requested that it be brightened up and modernized, so they added a drop ceiling and painted plaster walls. The only clue to its original bulkiness is how thick the walls are (notice that the window bays are nine feet thick). In the drawing room, look for the tattered silk remains of the Fairy Flag, a mysterious swatch with about a dozen different legends attached to it (explained by the handout).

Leaving the drawing room, notice the entrance to the **dungeon**—a holdover from that stout medieval fortress. Squeeze inside the dungeon and peer down into the deep pit.

At the end of this wing is the **north room,** a mini museum of the clan's most prestigious artifacts. The glass case in the middle of the room holds the Claymore Sword—one of two surviving swords made of extremely heavy Scottish iron rather than steel. Dating from the late 15th or early 16th century, this unique weapon is the bazooka of swords—designed not for dexterous fencing, but for one big kill-'em-all swing. In the display case in the corner, find Rory Mor's Horn—made from a horn of the subdued bull that gave the clan its motto. Traditionally, this horn would be filled with nearly a half-gallon of claret (Bordeaux wine), which a potential heir had to drink in one gulp to prove himself fit for the role. Other artifacts include bagpipes and several relics related to Bonnie Prince Charlie (including a lock of his hair and his vest). Look for a portrait of Flora MacDonald and some items that belonged to her.

At the end of the tour, you can wander out onto the **terrace** overlooking a sea loch. In the cellar, see the scant remains of the **kitchen,** with the base of a hidden stone staircase that leads up to the drawing room. The servants' bell is next to a panel listing the 40 rooms in the house—each one with a flag that would pop up to indicate to which room the servants were being summoned. Nearby, you can watch a **video** about the MacLeod clan.

Between the castle and the parking lot are five acres of enjoyable **gardens** to stroll through while pondering the fading clan system. Circling down to the sea loch, you'll enjoy grand views back up to the castle (and see a dock selling 30-minute boat rides on Loch Dunvegan to visit a seal colony on a nearby island—£6, tel. 01470/521-500). Higher up, don't miss some of the

finer, hidden parts of the gardens: the walled garden, the woodland walk up to the water garden (with a thundering waterfall and a gurgling stream), and the wide-open round garden.

The flaunting of inherited wealth and influence in some English castles rubs me the wrong way. But here, seeing the rough edges of a Scottish clan chief's castle, I had the opposite feeling: sympathy and compassion for a proud way of life that's slipping into the sunset of history. You have to admire the way they "hold fast" to this antiquated system (in the same way the Gaelic tongue is kept on life support). Paying admission here feels more like donating to charity than padding the pockets of a wealthy family. In fact, watered-down McClouds and McDonalds from America, eager to reconnect with their Scottish roots, help keep the Scottish clan system alive.

ISLE OF SKYE

▲Neist Point and Lighthouse

To get a truly edge-of-the-world feeling, consider an adventure on the back lanes of the Duirinish Peninsula, west of Dunvegan.

This trip is best for hardy drivers looking to explore the most remote corner of Skye and undertake a moderately strenuous hike to a lighthouse. Although it looks close on the map, give this trip 30 minutes each way from Dunvegan, plus at least 30 minutes to hike from the parking lot to the lighthouse (with a steep uphill return). After hiking around the cliff, the lighthouse springs into view, with the Outer Hebrides beyond.

Getting There: Head west from Dunvegan, following signs for *Glendale*. You'll cross a moor, then twist around the Dunvegan sea loch, before heading overland and passing through rugged, desolate hamlets that seem like the setting for a BBC sitcom about backwater Britain. After passing through Glendale, carefully track *Neist Point* signs until you reach an end-of-the-road parking lot.

Eating: It's efficient and fun to combine this trek with lunch or dinner at the pricey, recommended **Three Chimneys Restaurant,** on the road to Neist Point at Colbost (reservations essential; see page 366).

WESTERN SKYE
▲Talisker Distillery

Opened in 1830, Talisker is a Skye institution (and the only distillery on the island). This tiny whisky distillery is situated at the

base of a hill with 14 springs, and at the edge of a sea loch—making it easier to ship ingredients in and whisky out. On summer days, the distillery swarms with visitors from all over the world. Call ahead to reserve a tour: You'll sniff both peated and unpeated grains; see the big mash tuns, washbacks, and stills; and sample a wee dram at the end. Island whisky tends to be smokier than mainland whisky due to the amount of peat smoke used during malting. Talisker workers describe theirs as "medium smoky" (which may be easier for nonconnoisseurs to take), with peppery, floral, and vanilla notes.

Cost and Hours: £8 for 45-minute tour, one taste, and a £3 voucher toward a bottle, £35 tasting tour offered selected weekdays—call ahead; Mon-Sat 9:30-17:00, Sun 11:00-17:00 except closed Sun April-May and Oct; tours depart 3-4/hour in summer—last tour one hour before closing; Nov-March open Mon-Fri only, 4 tours/day—call ahead for schedule; on the loch in Carbost village, tel. 01478/614-308, www.discovering-distilleries.com.

Nearby: Note that the **Fairy Pools Hike**—an easy walk that includes some of the best Cuillin views on the island—starts from near Talisker Distillery (see next section).

CENTRAL SKYE
▲▲Cuillin Hills

These dramatic, rocky "hills" (which look more like mountains to me) stretch along the southern coast of the island, dominating Skye's landscape. Unusually craggy and alpine for Scotland, the Cuillin seem to rise directly from the deep. You'll see them from just about anywhere on the southern two-thirds of the island, but no roads actually take you through the heart of the Cuillin—that's reserved for hikers and climbers, who love this area. To get the best views with a car, consider these options.

Sligachan: The road from the Skye Bridge to Portree is the easiest way to appreciate the Cuillin (you'll almost certainly drive along here at some point during your visit). These mountains are all that's left of a long-vanished volcano. As you approach, you'll clearly see that there are three separate ranges (from right to left): red, gray, and black. The steep and challenging Black Cuillin is the most popular for serious climbers; the granite Red Cuillin ridge is more rounded.

The crossroads of Sligachan, with an old triple-arched bridge and a landmark hotel (see page 366), is nestled at the foothills of the Cuillin, and is a popular launch pad for mountain fun. The 2,500-foot-tall cone-shaped hill looming over Sligachan, named Glamaig ("Greedy Lady"), is the site of an annual 4.5-mile hill race in July: Speed hikers begin at the door of the Sligachan Hotel, race to the summit, run around a bagpiper, and scramble back down to the hotel. The record: 44 minutes (30 minutes up, 13 minutes down, 1 minute dancing a jig up top).

Fairy Pools Hike: Perhaps the best easy way to get some Cuillin views—and a sturdy but manageable hike—is to follow the popular trail to the Fairy Pools. This is relatively near Talisker Distillery (in the southwestern part of the island, see page 376).

To reach the hike from the A-863 between Sligachan and Dunvegan, follow signs to *Carbost*. Just before reaching the village of Carbost, watch for signs and a turnoff on the left to *Glenbrittle*. Follow this one-track road through the rolling hills, getting closer and closer to the Cuillin peaks. The well-marked *Fairy Pools* turnoff will be on your right. Parking here, you can easily follow the well-tended trail down across the field and toward the rounded peaks. (While signs suggest a 9.5-mile, 4- to 5-hour loop, most people simply hike 30 minutes to the pools and back; it's mostly level, though there's an uphill stretch on the return.)

Very soon you'll reach a gurgling river, which you'll follow toward its source in the mountains. Because the path is entirely through open fields, you enjoy scenery the entire time (and you can't get lost). Soon the river begins to pool at the base of each waterfall, creating a series of picturesque pools. Although footing can be treacherous, many hikers climb down across the rocks to swim and sunbathe. This is a fun place to linger (bring a picnic, if not a swimsuit). As I overheard one visitor say, "Despite the fact that it's so cold, it's so invitin'!"

Elgol: For the best view of the Cuillin, locals swear by the drive from Broadford (on the Portree-Kyleakin road) to Elgol, at the tip of a small peninsula that faces the Black Cuillin head-on. While it's just 12 miles as the crow flies from Sligachan, give it a half-hour each way to drive to the tip (mostly on single-track roads). For even more scenery, take a boat excursion from Elgol into Loch Coruisk, a sea loch surrounded by the Cuillin (April-Oct, departures several times a day, fewer Sun and off-season, generally 3 hours round-trip including 1.5 hours free time on the shore of the loch).

SOUTH SKYE
Kyleakin

Kyleakin (kih-LAH-kin), the last town in Skye before the Skye Bridge, used to be a big tourist hub...until the bridge connecting

it to the mainland enabled easier travel to Portree and other areas deeper in the island. Today this unassuming little village, with a ruined castle (Castle Moil), a cluster of lonesome fishing boats, and a forgotten ferry slip, still works fine as a home base. If you need to rent a car or call a taxi, contact **Skye Car Hire,** across the bridge in Kyle of Lochalsh (free delivery within 5 miles, tel. 01599/534-323, www.skyecarhire.co.uk).

Sleeping in Kyleakin: $$ **White Heather Hotel,** run by friendly and helpful Gillian and Craig Glenwright, has seven small but nicely decorated rooms with woody pine bathrooms, across from the waterfront and the castle ruins (Sb-£52, Db-£76-80, much bigger and newer "superior" Db-£110, family rooms, cheaper for stays longer than 2 nights, lounges, washer and dryer available, closed late Oct-Feb, The Harbour, tel. 01599/534-577, www.whiteheatherhotel.co.uk, info@whiteheatherhotel.co.uk). $$ **Cliffe House B&B** rents three rooms in a white house perched at the very edge of the water. All of the rooms, including the breakfast room and cozy lounge, enjoy wonderful views over the strait, the bridge...and any passing sea life (Db-£76-82 depending on size, cash only, closed Dec-Jan, tel. 01599/534-019, www.cliffehousebedandbreakfast.co.uk, info@ cliffehousebedandbreakfast.co.uk, Ian and Mary Sikorski).

Eating in and near Kyleakin: Kyleakin has several inter-changeable pubs. For something more creative, head out of town to the **Taste of India,** just past the roundabout on the A-87 toward Broadford (£8-11 main courses, also does takeaway, daily 17:00-23:00, tel. 01599/534-134). Long-hours **Co-op** grocery stores are across the bridge in Kyle of Lochalsh and up the road in Broadford (both along the main road).

Eating in Kyle of Lochalsh: If you can get reservations, eat fresh Scottish cuisine at the **Waverly Restaurant,** a tiny six-table place with locally sourced food, across the bridge from Kyleakin in Kyle of Lochalsh (£18-22 main courses, early-bird specials, open Fri-Tue 17:30-21:30, closed Wed-Thu, reservations essential, Main Street, across from Kyle Hotel and up the stairs, tel. 01599/534-337, www.waverleykyle.co.uk, Dutch chef/owner Ank).

Eating in Broadford: Up the road in Broadford are more eat-eries, including the renovated **Broadford Hotel.** This restaurant, part of an upscale Skye hotel chain, is attempting to bring classy cuisine to this small town, in a nice contemporary setting with har-bor views (£12-23 main courses, daily 12:00-23:00, Torrin Road at junction with Elgol, tel. 01471/822-204, www.broadfordhotel. co.uk). It was at this hotel that a secret elixir—supposedly once concocted for Bonnie Prince Charlie—was re-created by hotelier James Ross after finding the recipe in his father's belongings. Now known as Drambuie, the popular liqueur—which caught on in the 19th century—is made with Scotch whisky, heather honey, and spices. With its wide variety of Drambuie drinks, the Broadford's Spinaker Lounge is the place to try it.

Skye Bridge

Connecting Kyleakin on Skye with Kyle of Lochalsh on the main-land, the Skye Bridge was Europe's most expensive toll bridge per foot when it opened to great controversy in 1995 amid concerns that it would damage B&B business in the towns it connects, and disrupt native otter habitat. Here's the Skye natives' take on things: A generation ago, Lowlanders (city folk) began selling their urban homes and buying cheap property on Skye. Natives had grown to enjoy the slow-paced lifestyle that came with living life according to the whim of the ferry, but these new transplants found their commute into civilization too frustrating by boat. They demanded a bridge be built. Finally a deal was struck to privately fund the bridge, but the toll wasn't established before construction began. So when the bridge opened—and the ferry line it replaced closed—locals were shocked to be charged upward of £5 per car each way to go to the mainland. A few years ago, the bridge was bought by

The Feuding Clans of Skye

Skye is one of the best places to get a taste of Scotland's colorful, violent history of clan clashes. As the largest of the Inner Hebrides Islands, with easy nautical connections to Scotland's west coast and much of northern Ireland, it's logical that Skye was home to two powerful, rival clans: the MacDonalds and the MacLeods.

The MacDonalds (a.k.a. "**Clan Donald**"), with their base at Duntulm Castle (see page 370), were the dominant clan of the Hebrides. In the 12th century, the MacDonalds' ancestral ruler Somerled first unified the disparate islands and western Highlands into a "Lordship of the Isles" that lasted for centuries. Throughout this period, they struggled to maintain control against rival clans—especially the MacLeods.

Clan MacLeod, with its castle at Dunvegan (see page 373), controlled the western half of Skye. Another branch of the MacLeods was based on the Isle of Lewis, in the Outer Hebrides. The MacLeods' ancestor, Olav the Black, had been defeated by Somerled, pulling their territory in to the Lordship of the Isles. But over the centuries, the MacLeods frequently challenged the authority of the MacDonalds, clashing in countless minor skirmishes as well as major clan battles in 1411, 1480, and 1578.

Adding to the volatile mix was **Clan Mackenzie,** which controlled much of the northern Highlands from their base at Eilean Donan Castle (see page 381). The Mackenzies waged battle against the MacDonalds in 1491 and again in 1497.

The epic 1578 clash featured a series of grievous offenses. First, the MacLeods invaded the MacDonald-controlled Isle of Eigg, and, upon finding the islanders huddled in a cave for protection, set a roaring fire at the mouth of the cave—killing virtually the entire population. In retaliation, the MacDonalds barred the door of a church on the MacLeod-controlled Isle of Uist and burned all of the worshippers alive. In the ensuing battle, the furious MacLeods massacred the MacDonalds and buried the dead on a turf dike—earning the conflict the name "Battle of the Spoiling Dike."

The final clan battle on Skye began with a strategic marriage designed to broker a peace between the warring clans. Donald MacDonald married Margaret MacLeod, following a tradition called a "handfast," in which the groom was allowed a "trial period" of one year and one day with his new bride. After Margaret injured her eye, Donald decided to "return" her. Adding insult to injury, he sent her back to Dunvegan Castle on a one-eyed horse, led by a one-eyed man with a one-eyed dog. And so began two years of brutal warfare between the clans (the War of the One-Eyed Woman). In 1601, the Battle of Coire Na Creiche decimated both sides, but the MacDonalds emerged victorious. It would be the last of the great clan battles between the MacDonalds and the MacLeods, and it's said to be the final battle fought in Scotland using only pre-gunpowder weapons (swords and arrows).

the Scottish Executive, the fare was abolished, and the Skye natives were somewhat appeased. There's no denying that the bridge has been a boon for Skye tourism, making a quick visit to the island possible without having to wait for a ferry.

SKYE'S SLEAT PENINSULA
Clan Donald Center and Armadale Castle

Facing the sea just outside Armadale is the ruined castle of Clan Donald, also known as the MacDonalds (Mac/Mc = "son of"), at one time the most pow-erful clan in the Scottish Highlands and Hebrides.

Armadale Castle—more of a mansion than a fortress—was built in 1790, during the relatively peaceful, post-Jacobite age when life at the MacDon-alds' traditional home, Duntulm Castle at the tip of the Trotternish Peninsula, had be-come too rugged and inconvenient. Today the Armadale Castle ruins (which you can view, but not enter) anchor a sprawling visitors center that celebrates the MacDonald way of life. You'll explore its manicured gardens, ogle the castle ruins, and visit the Museum of the Isles. This modern, well-presented museum tells the history of Scotland and Skye through the lens of its most influential clan (only a few artifacts but good descriptions, includes 1.5-hour au-dioguide). While fascinating for people named MacDonald, it's pricey and not worth a long detour for anyone else. But because it's right along the main road near the Armadale-Mallaig ferry (con-necting Skye to the Road to the Isles), it can be an enjoyable place to kill some time while waiting for your ferry. At the parking lot is a big shop and café with free WCs; to see the grounds, castle ruins, and museum, you'll have to pay admission.

Cost and Hours: £8.50, mid-April-Oct daily 9:30-17:30, hours vary off-season—call ahead or check online, Armadale, tel. 01471/844-305, www.clandonald.com.

Nearby: Heading north on the A-851 from the Clan Don-ald Centre, keep an eye out for **Sabhal Mòr Ostaig**. Skye is very proud to host this college, with coursework taught entirely in Gaelic.

ON THE MAINLAND, NEAR THE ISLE OF SKYE
▲Eilean Donan Castle

This postcard castle, watching over a sea loch from its island perch, is scenically (and conveniently) situated on the road be-

tween the Isle of Skye and Loch Ness. While the photo op is worth ▲▲, the interior—with cozy rooms—is worth only a peek and closer to ▲. Famous from such films as Sean Connery's *Highlander* (1986) and the James Bond movie *The World Is Not Enough* (1999), Eilean Donan (EYE-lan DOHN-an) might be Scotland's most photogenic countryside castle (chances are good it's on that Scotland calendar you bought during your trip). Strategically situated at the confluence of three sea lochs, this was the stronghold of the Mackenzies—a powerful clan that was, like the MacLeods at Dunvegan, a serious rival to the mighty MacDonalds (see sidebar). Though it looks ancient, the current castle is actually less than a century old. The original castle on this site (dating from 800 years ago) was destroyed in battle in 1719, then rebuilt between 1912 and 1932 by the Macrae family as their residence. (The Macraes became bodyguards to the Mackenzies in the 14th century and later took over from their bosses as holders of the castle.)

Cost and Hours: £7, good £3.50 guidebook; daily July-Aug 9:00-18:00, March-June & Sept-Oct from 18:00; may open a few days a week Nov-Feb—call ahead, last entry one hour before closing; café, tel. 01599/555-202, www.eileandonancastle.com.

Getting There: It's not actually on the Isle of Skye, but it's quite close, in the mainland town of Dornie. Follow the A-87 about 15 minutes east of Skye Bridge, through Kyle of Lochalsh and toward Loch Ness and Inverness. The castle is on the right side of the road, just after a long bridge. Buses that run between Portree and Inverness (including #915, #916, and #917) stop at Dornie, a short walk from the castle (6-7/day, 1 hour from Portree).

Visiting the Castle: Buy tickets at the visitors center, then walk across the bridge and into the castle complex, and make your way into the big, blocky keep. You'll begin with some audiovisual introductory exhibits, then work through the historic rooms. While the castle is a footnote on a Scottish scale, the exhibits work hard to make its story engaging. Docents posted throughout can tell you more. First you'll see the claustrophobic, vaulted Billeting Room (where soldiers had their barracks), then head upstairs to the inviting Banqueting Room. After the renovation, this was a sort of living room. Another flight of stairs takes you to the circa-1930 bedrooms, which feel more cozy and accessible than those in many other castles—and do a great job of evoking the lifestyles of the aristocrats who built the current version of Eilean Donan as their personal castle playset. Downstairs is the cute kitchen exhibit, with mannequins preparing a meal. Finally, you'll head through a few more humble exhibits (on old guns, bagpipes, and flags) to the exit.

NORTHERN SCOTLAND

Wester Ross • The North Coast • The Orkney Islands

Scotland's far north is its rugged and desolate "Big Sky Country"—with towering mountains, vast and moody moors, achingly desolate glens, and a jagged coastline peppered with silver-sand beaches. Far less discovered than the big destinations to the south, this is where you can escape the crowds and touristy "tartan tat" of the Edinburgh-Stirling-Oban-Inverness rut, and get a picturesque corner of Scotland all to yourself. Even on a sunny summer weekend, you may not pass another car for miles. It's just you and the Munro baggers. Beyond Orkney, there's no real "destination" in the north—it's all about the journey.

This chapter covers everything north of the Isle of Skye and Inverness, divided into three sections: the scenic west coast (called Wester Ross); the sandy north coast; and the fascinating Orkney archipelago just offshore from Britain's northernmost point.

Fully exploring northern Scotland takes some serious time. The roads are narrow, twisty, and slow, and the pockets of civilization are few and far between. With two weeks or less in Scotland, this area doesn't make the cut (except maybe Orkney). But if you have time to linger, and you appreciate desolate scenery and an end-of-the-world feeling, the untrampled north is worth considering.

Even on a shorter visit, Orkney may be alluring for adventurous travelers seeking a contrast to the rest of Scotland. The islands' claims to fame—astonishing prehistoric sites, Old Norse (Norwegian) heritage, and recent history as a WWI and WWII naval base—combine to spur travelers' imaginations.

PLANNING YOUR TIME

For a scenic loop through this area, try this four-day plan:

Day 1   From the Isle of Skye, drive up the west coast (including the Applecross detour, if time permits), overnighting in Torridon or Ullapool.

Day 2   Continue the rest of the way up the west coast, then trace the north coast from west to east, catching the late-afternoon ferry to Orkney.

Day 3   Spend all day on Orkney.

Day 4   Finish up on Orkney and take the ferry back to the mainland; with enough time and interest, squeeze in a visit to John O'Groats before driving three hours back to Inverness (on the relatively speedy A-9).

The above plan includes a borderline-unreasonable amount of driving, on twisty, challenging, often single-track roads (especially on days 1 and 2). If you don't have someone to split the time behind the wheel, or if you want to really slow down, consider adding another overnight to break up the trip.

To reach **Orkney** most efficiently—without all of the slow-going west coast scenery—consider zipping up on a flight (easy and frequent from Inverness, Edinburgh, or Aberdeen), or make good time on the A-9 highway from Inverness up to Thurso (figure 3 hours one-way) to catch the ferry.

It's possible (but very slow) to traverse this area by bus, but I'd skip it without a car. If you're flying to Orkney, consider renting a car for your time here.

NORTHERN SCOTLAND

Wester Ross

North of the Isle of Skye, Scotland's sparsely populated, ruggedly scenic west coast is a big draw for travelers seeking stunning views without the crowds. For casual visitors, the views in Glencoe and on the Isle of Skye are much more accessible and just as good as what you'll find farther north. But diehards enjoy getting away from it all in Wester Ross. This section provides a quick outline of the most scenic route, from south to north.

This area, called Wester Ross (the western part of the region of Ross), is remote, mountainous, and slashed with jagged "sea lochs." (That's "inlets" in American English, or "fjords" in Norwegian.) After seeing its towering peaks, you'll understand why George R.

Northern Scotland

40 Kilometers

40 Miles

Westray

Rousay

SCOTLAND
• Inverness
⊛ Edinburgh
ENGLAND

North Atlantic
Ocean

See Orkney
Islands
detail map

Mainland
SKARA BRAE ⛨ Kirkwall
Stromness
Hoy • Scapa Flow
Orkney Islands

Pentland Firth

Dunnet Head
Scabster
Thurso
Gills
John O'Groats
Halkirk
MEY

Cape Wrath
Smoo Cave
Durness ⛨ *Kyle of Durness* → Loch Eriboll
A-838
Tongue
A-836

Wick
A-9
A-99

Scourie •
Loch Glendhu
A-894
B-869
Kyleaku
Kylesku
ARDVECH ⛨
Lochinver •
Loch Assynt
A-835
Inchnadamph
A-836
Kinbrace

Helmsdale

▲ Knockan Crag
Strathcanaird
Loch Shin
Lairg
Brora
Golspie
North Sea

INTEREWE GARDENS
Ardmare •
Ullapool
Loch Broom
Dornoch

Poolewe ■
Loch Maree
Braemore
A-832
A-835
Alness
A-9
Moray Firth
Elgin

Gairloch
W E S T E R R O S S
Loch Torridon
Kinlochewe
Dingwall
Nairn
CAWDOR ■
Speyside

Applecross
• Torridon
Achnasheen
CULLODEN BATTLEFIELD ■
A-95

APPLECROSS ROAD
A-890
Inverness
⛨ CLAVA CAIRNS
A-939

Loch Carron
EILEAN DONAN
A-82

Kyle •
Kyleakin
• Dornie
Loch Ness
A-9

Isle of Skye
A-87
Fort Augustus •
Aviemore
Ballater

Mallaig •
CALEDONIAN CANAL →
Laggan
Newtonmore
BALMORAL ■
A-830

The Minch

NORTHERN SCOTLAND

R. Martin named the primary setting of his *Game of Thrones* epic "Westeros."

There's a fine variety of scenery—but not many towns—on the way north. Connecting Skye or Glencoe to Ullapool (the logical halfway point up the coast) takes a full day. It may not sound like that many miles (figure 130 miles from Eilean Donan Castle to Ullapool; the Applecross detour adds another 20 slow-going miles)—

but they're twisty and often single-track. If you want to just get a taste of this rugged scenery—without going farther north—you can drive the Wester Ross coastline almost as far as Ullapool, then turn off on the A-835 for a quick one-hour drive to Inverness.

Sights in Wester Ross

▲▲Wester Ross Driving Tour, from Eilean Donan Castle to Ullapool

From the A-87, a few miles east of Kyle of Lochalsh (and the Skye Bridge), follow signs for the A-890 north toward *Lochcarron*. (Note that **Eilean Donan Castle** is just a couple of miles farther east from this turnoff; if coming from Skye, you could squeeze in a visit to that castle before backtracking to this turnoff.) From here on out, you can carefully track the brown *Wester Ross Coastal Trail* signs, which will keep you on track.

You'll follow the A-890 as it cuts across a hilly spine, then twists down and runs alongside **Loch Carron.** At the end of the loch, just after the village of Strathcarron, you'll reach a T-intersection that offers two choices. The faster route up to Ullapool—which skips much of the best scenery—takes you right on the A-890 (toward *Inverness*). But for the scenic route outlined here, instead turn left, following the A-896 (following signs for *Lochcarron*). From here, you'll follow the opposite bank of Loch Carron.

Soon after you pull away from the lochside, you'll cross over a high meadow and see a well-marked turnoff on the left for a super-

scenic—but challenging—alternate route: the **Applecross Road,** over a pass called Bealach na Bà (Gaelic for "Pass of the Cattle"). Intimidating signs suggest a much more straightforward alternate route that keeps you on the A-896 straight up to Loch Torridon (if doing this, skip down to the "Loch Torridon" section, below). But if you're relatively comfortable negotiating steep switchbacks, and have the time to spare (adding about 20 miles to the total journey), this road is drivable. You'll twist up, up, up—hearing your engine struggle up gradients of up to 20 percent—and finally over, with rugged-moonscape views over peaks and lochs. From the summit (at 2,053 feet), the jagged mountains rising from the sea are the Cuillin Hills on the Isle of Skye. Finally you'll corkscrew back down the other side, arriving at the humble seafront town of Applecross.

Once in **Applecross,** you could either return over the same pass to pick up the A-896 (slightly faster), or, for a meandering but very scenic route, carry on all the way around the northern headland of the peninsula. This provides you with further views of Raasay and Skye, through a deserted-feeling landscape on single-track roads. Then, turning the corner at the top of the peninsula, you'll begin to drive above Loch Torridon, with some of the finest views on this drive.

Whether you take the Applecross detour or the direct route, you'll wind up at the stunning sea loch called **Loch Torridon**—

hemmed in by thickly forested pine-covered hills, it resembles the Rockies. You'll pass through an idyllic fjordside town, Shieldaig, then cross over a finger of land and plunge deeper into Upper Loch Torridon. Near the end of the loch, keep an eye out for **The Torridon**—a luxurious lochfront grand hotel with gorgeous Victorian Age architecture, a café serving afternoon tea, and expensive rooms (www.thetorridon.com).

As you loop past the far end of the loch—with the option to turn off for the village of **Torridon** (which has a good youth hostel, www.syha.org.uk)—the landscape has shifted dramatically, from pine-covered hills to a hauntingly desolate glen. You'll cut through this valley—bookended by towering peaks and popular with hikers—before reaching the town of Kinlochewe.

At Kinlochewe, take the A-832 west (following *Ullapool* signs from here on out), and soon you'll be tracing the bonnie, bonnie

banks of **Loch Maree**—considered by many connoisseurs to be one of Scotland's finest lochs. You'll see campgrounds, nature areas, and scenic pull-outs as you make good time on the speedy two-lane lochside road. (The best scenery is near the beginning, so don't put off that photo stop.)

Nearing the end of Loch Maree, the road becomes single-track again as you twist up over another saddle of scrubby land. On the other side, you'll get glimpses of Gair Loch through the trees, before finally arriving at the little harbor of **Gairloch.** Just beyond the harbor, where the road straightens out as it follows the coast, keep an eye out (on the right) for the handy Gale Center. Run as a charity, it has WCs, a small café with treats baked by locals, a fine shop of books and crafts, and comfortable tables and couches for taking a break (www. galeactionforum.co.uk).

True to its name, Gair Loch ("Short Loch") doesn't last long, and soon you'll head up a hill (keep an eye out for the pullout on the left, offering fine views over the village). The next village is Polewe, on **Loch Ewe.** Just after the village, on the left, is the **Interewe Gardens.** These beautiful gardens, run by the National Trust for Scotland, were the pet project of Osgood Mackenzie, who in 1862 began transforming 50 acres of his lochside estate into a subtropical paradise. The warming Gulf Stream and—in some places—stout stone walls help make this oasis possible. If you have time and need to stretch your legs from all that shifting, spend an hour wandering its sprawling grounds. The walled garden, near

the entrance, is a highlight, with each bed thoughtfully labeled (£10.50, daily, www.nts. org.uk).

Continuing on the A-832 toward Ullapool, you'll stay above Loch Ewe, then briefly pass above the open ocean. Soon you'll find yourself following **Little Loch Broom** (with imposing mountains on your right). At the end of that loch, you'll carry on straight and work your way past a lush strip of farmland at the apex of the loch. Soon you'll meet the big A-835 highway; turn left and take this speedy road the rest of the way into Ullapool. (Or you can turn right to zip on the A-835 all the way to Inverness—just an hour away.) Whew!

Ullapool

A gorgeously set, hard-working town of about 1,500 people, Ullapool (ulla-PEWL) is what passes for a metropolis in Wester Ross. Its most prominent feature is its big, efficient ferry dock, connecting the mainland

with Stornoway on the Isle of Lewis (Scotland's biggest, in the Outer Hebrides). Facing the dock is a strip of cute little houses, today housing restaurants, shops, B&Bs, and residences. Behind the waterfront, the town is only a few blocks deep—you can get the lay of the land in a few minutes' stroll. Curving around the back side of the town—along a big, grassy campground—is an inviting rocky beach, facing across the loch in one direction and out toward the open sea in the other.

Orientation to Ullapool: Ullapool has several handy services for travelers. An excellent **bookshop** is a block up, straight ahead from the ferry dock. Many services line Argyle Street, which runs parallel to the harbor one block up the hill: the **TI** is to the right, while a Bank of Scotland **ATM** and the **post office** are to the left. On this same street, the town runs a fine little **museum** with well-done exhibits about local history (closed Sun and Nov-March, www.ullapoolmuseum.co.uk). This street, nicknamed "Art-gyle Street," also has a smattering of local art **galleries.**

Sleeping in Ullapool: Several B&Bs line the harborfront Shore Street, including **Point Cottage B&B** (2 rooms, both with great dormer views and a nice nautical feel, www.pointcottagebandb. co.uk), **Waterside House** (3 rooms, www.waterside.uk.net), and the town's official **youth hostel** (www.syha.org.uk). A block up from the water on West Argyle Street, **West House** has five rooms but requires a two-night minimum stay (www.westhousebandb. co.uk).

Eating in Ullapool: The two most reliable places are the **Ceil-idh Place,** on West Argyle Street a block above the harbor (www. theceilidhplace.com); and **The Arch Inn,** facing the water a half-block from the ferry dock (www.thearchinn.co.uk). Both have a nice pubby vibe as well as sit-down dining rooms with a focus on locally caught seafood. Both also rent rooms and frequently host live music. For a quick meal, two different **chippies** (around the corner from each other, facing the ferry dock) keep the breakwater promenade busy with al fresco budget diners and happy seagulls.

▲Northwest Scotland Driving Tour, from Ullapool to the North Coast

The scenery continues as you head north from Ullapool, all the way up to Scotland's northern coast. Leaving Ullapool, follow signs that read simply *North (A-835).* You'll pass through the cute little beachside village of **Ard-mair,** then pull away from the coast.

About 15 minutes after leaving Ullapool, just after you

exit the village of Strathcanaird and head uphill, watch on the left for a pullout with a handy orientation panel describing the panorama of **towering peaks** that line the road. It looks like a mossy Monument Valley. Enjoy the scenery for about four more miles—surrounded by wee lochs and gigantic peaks—and watch for the **Knockan Crag** visitors center, above you on the right, with exhibits on local geology, flora, and fauna and suggestions for area hikes (unmanned and open daily 24 hours, WCs, www.nnr-scotland.org.uk).

Continuing north along the A-835, you'll soon pass out of the region of Ross and Cromarty and enter Sutherland. At the T-intersection, turn left for *Kylesku* and *Lochinver* (on the A-837). From here on out, you can start following the *North & West Highlands Tourist Route*; you'll also see your first sign for John O'Groats at the northeastern corner of Scotland (152 miles away).

You'll roll through moors, surrounded on all sides by hills. Just after the barely-there village of Inchnadamph, keep an eye

out on the left for the ruins of **Ardvrech Castle,** which sits in crumbled majesty upon its own little island in Loch Assynt, connected to the world by a narrow sandy spit. Just after these ruins, you'll have another choice: For the fastest route to the north coast, turn right to follow A-894 (toward *Kylesku* and *Durness*). If you have some time to spare, you could carry on straight to scenically follow Loch Assynt toward the sleepy fishing village of **Lochinver** (12 miles). After seeing the village, you could go back the way you came to the main road, or continue all the way around the little peninsula on the B-869, passing several appealing sandy beaches and villages.

Back on the main A-894, you'll pass through an almost lunar landscape, with peaks all around, finally emerging at the gorgeous, mountain-rimmed **Loch Glendhu,** which you'll cross on a stout modern bridge. From here, it's a serene landscape of rock, heather, and ferns, with occasional glimpses of the coast—such as at **Scourie,** with a particularly nice sandy beach. Finally (after the road becomes A-838—keep left at the fork, toward *Durness*), you'll head up, over,

and through a vast and dramatic glen. At the end of the glen, you'll start to see sand below you on the left; this is **Kyle of Durness,** which goes on for miles. You'll see the turnoff for the ferry to Cape Wrath, then follow tidy stone walls the rest of the way into **Durness.**

The North Coast

Scotland's north coast, which stretches a hundred miles from Cape Wrath in the northwest corner to John O'Groats in the northeast, is gently scenic, but less dramatic than Wester Ross—the jagged mountains loom far to the south, and your views are dominated by an alternating array of moors and jagged coastline. This is a good place to make up the long miles. I've described the driving route along the north coast from west to east.

NORTH COAST DRIVING TOUR
Durness to Thurso

Durness is a beachy village of cow meadows perched on a bluff above sandy shores. This area has a different feel from Wester Ross—it's less rugged and more manicured, with tidy farms hemmed in by neatly stacked stone walls. There's not much to see or do in the town, but there is a 24-hour gas station (gas up now—this is your last chance for a while...trust me) and a handy TI (by the big parking lot with the "Award Winning Beach," tel. 01971/509-005).

Head east out of the village on the A-838, watching for brown signs on your right to *Durness Village Hall.* Pull over here to stroll through the small **memorial garden for John Lennon,** who enjoyed his boyhood vacations in Durness.

Just after the village hall, on the left, pull over at **Smoo Cave** (free WCs in parking lot). Its goofy-sounding name comes from the Old Norse *smúga,* for cave. (Many places along the north coast—which had a strong Viking

(NORTHERN SCOTLAND)

influence—have Norse rather than Gaelic or Anglo-Saxon place names.) It's free to hike down the well-marked stairs to a protected cove, where an underground river has carved a deep cave into the bluff. Walk inside the cave to get a free peek at the waterfall; for a longer visit, you can pay for a 20-minute boat trip and guided walk (unnecessary for most; sign up at the mouth of the cave).

Back on the road, soon after Smoo Cave, on the left, is the gorgeous **Ceannabeinne Beach** (Gaelic for "End of the Moun-

tains"). Of the many Durness-area beaches, this is the locals' favorite.

Heading east from the Durness area, you'll traverse many sparsely populated miles—long roads that cut in and out from the coast, with scrubby moorland and distant peaks on the other side. You'll emerge at the gigantic **Loch Eriboll,** which you'll circumnavigate—passing lamb farms and crumbling stone walls—to continue your way east. Leaving this fjord, you'll cut through some classic fjord scenery until you finally pop out at the scenic **Kyle of Tongue.** You'll cross over the big modern bridge, then twist up through the village of Tongue and continue your way eastward (the A-838 becomes the A-836)—through more of the same scrubby moorland scenery. Make good time for the next 40 lonely miles. Notice how many place names along here use the term "strath"—a wide valley (as opposed to a narrower "glen"), such as where jagged mountains open up to the sea.

Finally—after going through little settlements like Bettyhill and Melvich—the moors begin to give way to working farms as you approach Thurso.

Thurso, John O'Groats, and Nearby

The main population center of northern Scotland (pop. 8,000), Thurso is a functional transit hub with a charming old core. As you face out to sea, the heavily industrialized point on the left is **Scrabster,** with the easiest ferry crossing to Orkney (for details, see "Getting to Orkney" on page 396).

• *Continuing east from Thurso (following brown* John O'Groats *signs on the A-836), it's about eight miles to the village of Dunnet. If you have time for some rugged scenery, turn off here to drive the four miles (each way) to...*

Dunnet Head

While John O'Groats is often mistakenly called "Britain's north-ernmost point," Dunnet Head pokes up just a bit farther. And, while it lacks the too-cute signpost marking distances to faraway landmarks, views from here are better than from John O'Groats. Out at the tip of Dunnet Head, a lonely lighthouse enjoys panoramic views across the Pentland Firth to Orkney, while a higher vantage point is just up the hill. Keep an eye out for seabirds, including puffins.

• *In the village of Dunnet, between the main road and Dunnet Head, look for the well-signed...*

Mary-Ann's Cottage

This little stone house explains traditional crofting lifestyles—left just as it was when 92-year-old Mary-Ann Calder moved out in 1990 (very limited hours).

• *Back on the main A-836, about four miles farther east is the turnoff for the...*

Castle of Mey

The Queen Mother grew up at Glamis Castle (see page 225), but after her daughter became Queen Elizabeth II, she purchased and

renovated this sprawling property as an escape from the bustle of royal life...and you couldn't get much farther from civilization than this. For nearly 50 years, the Queen Mum stayed here for annual visits in August and October. Today it welcomes visitors to tour its homey interior and 30 acres of manicured gardens (closed Oct-mid-May, www.castleofmey.org.uk).

• *From Mey, it's another six miles east to John O'Groats. About halfway there, in Gills Bay, is another ferry dock for cars heading to Orkney (see "Getting to Orkney" on page 396).*

John O'Groats

A total tourist trap that's somehow also genuinely stirring, John O'Groats marks the northeastern corner of the Isle of Britain—bookending the country with Land's End, 874 miles to the south-

west in Cornwall. People enjoy traversing the length of Britain by motorcycle, by bicycle, or even by foot (it takes about eight weeks to trudge along the "E2E" trail—that's "End to End"). And upon arrival, whether they've walked for two months or just driven up for the day from Inverness, everyone wants to snap a "been there, done that" photo with the landmark signpost. Surrounding that is a huge parking lot, a souvenir stand masquerading as a TI, and lots of tacky "first and last" shops and restaurants. Orkney looms just off the coast.

Nearby: The real target of "End to End" pilgrims isn't the signpost, but the **Duncansby Head Lighthouse**—about two miles to the east, it's the actual northeasternmost point, with an even more end-of-the-world vibe. (By car, head away from the John O'Groats area on A-99, and watch for the Duncansby Head turnoff on the left, just past the Seaview Hotel.) If you have time for a hike, about a mile south of the lighthouse are the **Duncansby Stacks**—dramatic sea stacks rising up above a sandy beach.

• *You made it! Great job. Now to complete your journey, turn around and drive (or walk) 874 miles to Land's End.*

The Orkney Islands

The Orkney Islands are, for seasoned travelers, a holy grail: the remote forbidden fruit dangling over the crown of Scotland. While it takes some effort to reach Orkney, it's worth the trouble.

Crossing the 10-mile Pentland Firth separating Orkney from northern Scotland, you leave the Highlands behind and enter a new

world. With no real tradition for clans, tartans, or bagpipes, Orkney feels not "Highlander" or even "Scottish," but Orcadian (as locals are called). Though Orkney was inhabited by Picts from the sixth century B.C., during most of its formative history—from 875 all the way until 1468—it was a prized trading hub of the Norwegian realm, giving it a feel more Scandinavian than Celtic. The Vikings left their mark, both literally (runes carved into prehistoric stone monuments) and culturally: Many place names are derived from Old Norse, and the Orkney flag looks like the Norwegian flag with a few yellow accents. And given its status as the Royal Navy headquarters during both World Wars, Orkney is one of the most pro-British corners of Scotland. In the 2014 independence referendum, Orkney cast the loudest "no" vote in the entire country (67 percent against).

Orkney's landscape is also a world apart: Aside from some dramatic sea cliffs hiding along its perimeter, it's a mostly flat, bald island, with few trees and lots of tidy farms with gently mooing cows.

For the sightseer, Orkney has two draws unmatched by any place else in Scotland: It has some of the finest prehistoric sites in northern Europe, left behind by an advanced Stone Age civilization that flourished here. And the harbor called Scapa Flow has fascinating remnants of its important military status during the World Wars—from intentional shipwrecks designed to seal off the harbor, to muscular Churchill-built barriers to finish the job a generation later.

GETTING TO ORKNEY

By Car/Ferry: Two different car ferry options depart from near Thurso, which is about a three-hour drive up from Inverness (on the A-9); for the very scenic (and very long) route, you could loop all the way up Wester Ross, and then along the north coast from Durness to Thurso (see earlier in this chapter). Plan on about £55-60 one-way for a car on the Northlink ferry, or £35-40 on the Pentland ferry, plus £15-20 per passenger (depending on route and demand). For either company, it's smart to reserve online at least a day before you plan to travel; check in at the ferry dock a minimum of 30 minutes before departure. The two companies land at opposite corners of Orkney; from either Stromness or St. Margaret's Hope, it's about a 30-minute drive to Kirkwall.

For most, the best choice is the **Scrabster-Stromness** ferry, operated by NorthLink (3/day in each direction in summer, 2/day off-season, 1.5-hour crossing, www.northlinkferries.co.uk). While it's a slightly longer crossing, it's also a bigger boat, with more services (including a good sit-down cafeteria), and it glides past the Old Man of Hoy, giving you an easy glimpse at one of Orkney's top landmarks. This ferry is coordinated with bus #X99, connecting Scrabster to Inverness (www.stagecoachbus.com).

The **Gills Bay-St. Margaret's Hope** route is operated by Pentland Ferries; its main advantage is the proximity of Gills Bay to John O'Groats, making it easy to visit Britain's northeasternmost point on your way to or from the ferry—but Gills Bay is also that much farther from Inverness (2-3/day in each direction, one-hour crossing, www.pentlandferries.co.uk).

There's also a **passenger-only boat** directly from John O'Groats to Burwick, which connects to an onward bus to Kirkwall (3/day July-Aug, 1/day May and Sept, none Oct-April, 40-minute crossing, www.jogferry.co.uk). While this works for those leaving their car at John O'Groats for a quick day trip to Orkney, it's more weather-dependent.

By Plane: To save yourself the long drive and ferry ride, consider a targeted visit to Orkney by plane; Kirkwall's little airport has direct flights to Inverness, Edinburgh, Glasgow, and Aberdeen (www.flybe.com has good deals if you book ahead).

By Tour from Inverness: The John O'Groats foot ferry operates a very long all-day tour from Inverness that includes bus and ferry transfers, and a guided tour around the main sights (£72, daily June-Aug only, www.jogferry.co.uk).

PLANNING YOUR TIME

Orkney merits at least two nights and one full day. To see the best of Orkney in a single day, spend the morning at the prehistoric sites (Maeshowe and nearby sites, Skara Brae), and the afternoon driving along the Churchill Barriers and visiting the Italian Chapel—or vice versa. Spend any remaining time exploring Kirkwall (its one sight worth entering is St. Magnus Cathedral). With more time, explore the farther corners of the archipelago; WWII buffs may want to devote a half-day to the Isle of Hoy and its many wartime sites.

Orkney is Scotland's busiest cruise port; on days when ships are in port, normally sleepy sights can be jammed. Check the cruise schedule at www.orkneyharbours.com and plan accordingly to avoid busy times at popular sights (Skara Brae, the Italian Chapel).

Orientation to Orkney

Orkney (as the entire archipelago is called) is made up of 70 islands, with a total population of 24,500. The main island—with the primary town (Kirkwall) and ferry ports connecting Orkney to northern Scotland (Stromness and St. Margaret's Hope)—is called, confusingly, Mainland. (It just goes to show you: One man's island is another man's mainland.)

Port Towns: Orkney's "second city," with 2,200 people, **Stromness** is worth a stroll while waiting for your ferry. Equal parts fishing town and tourist depot, its traffic-free main drag has a certain salty charm. **St. Margaret's Hope**—named for a 13th-century Norwegian princess who was briefly Queen of Scots until she died en route to Orkney—is even smaller, with a charming seafront village atmosphere.

Getting Around Orkney: While this chapter is designed for travelers with a car (or a driver—see next), **public buses** do connect sites on Mainland (operated by Stagecoach, www.stagecoachbus.com). From Mainland, **ferries** fan out to outlying islets (www.orkneyferries.co.uk); the main ports are Kirkwall (for points north)

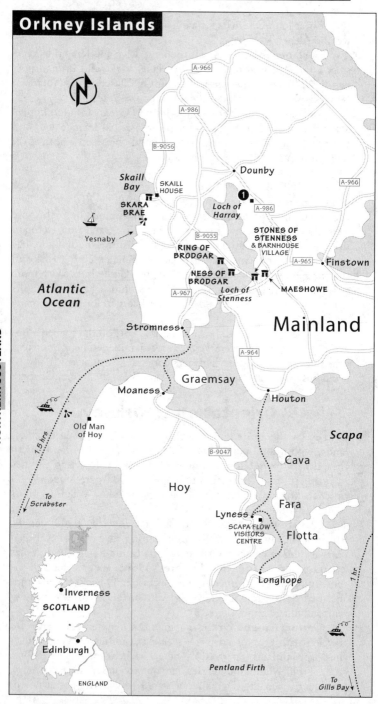

Orkney Islands

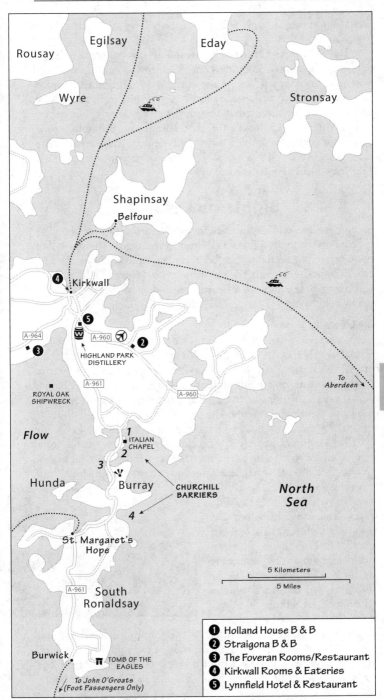

Rousay

Egilsay

Eday

Wyre

Stronsay

Shapinsay

● Belfour

4 Kirkwall

5

A-964

3

W

A-960

HIGHLAND PARK
DISTILLERY

A-961

2 Straigona

A-960

*To
Aberdeen*

ROYAL OAK
SHIPWRECK

Flow

1 ■ ITALIAN
CHAPEL

2

3

Hunda

Burray

CHURCHILL
BARRIERS

4

*North
Sea*

St. Margaret's
Hope

A-961

South
Ronaldsay

5 Kilometers

5 Miles

Burwick ●

Ⓣ TOMB OF THE
EAGLES

*To John O'Groats
(Foot Passengers Only)*

1 Holland House B & B
2 Straigona B & B
3 The Foveran Rooms/Restaurant
4 Kirkwall Rooms & Eateries
5 Lynnfield Hotel & Restaurant

and Houton (for Hoy). If taking a car on a ferry, it's always smart to book ahead.

Local Guide: Orkney Uncovered is run by husband-and-wife team Kinlay (who guides) and Kirsty (who manages the office), who are energetic and passionate about sharing their adopted home with visitors. Their standard itinerary hits both prehistoric and wartime highlights, but they're happy to tailor the itinerary to your interests (£320 for a full-day, 9-hour tour for up to 3 people, more for bigger groups or multiday tours, also offers cruise excursions, tel. 01856/878-822, www.orkneyuncovered.co.uk, enquiries@orkneyuncovered.co.uk).

Sights on Orkney

Some people spend days (or lifetimes) exploring Orkney, but I've focused on the main sights you'll want to see in a short visit—all of them on (or connected to) the big island called Mainland: the Orcadian capital, Kirkwall; the prehistoric sites (especially Maeshowe and Skara Brae); and the evocative reminders of the World Wars (WWI shipwrecks, Churchill Barriers, Italian Chapel).

▲Kirkwall

Orkney's main town (pop. 9,200) is tidy and functional. Like the rest of the island, most of its buildings are more practical than pretty, but some charm hides around its fringes. You'll likely pass through here at some point for logistical reasons (to gas up, change buses, use the airport, or stock up on groceries), but the town also has some worthwhile sights. The handy **TI**, with free Wi-Fi, is at the bus station (daily Easter-Oct, closed Sun off-season).

St. Magnus Cathedral, whose pointy steeple is visible from just about anywhere in town, may be Scotland's most enjoyable church to visit—it's worth ▲▲ (free, open daily except closed Sun morning in summer and all day Sun in winter). The building dates from the 12th century, back when this was part of the Parish of Trondheim, Norway. Built from vibrant red sandstone by many of the same stonemasons who worked on Durham's showpiece cathedral, St. Magnus is harmonious Romanesque

inside and out: stout columns and small, rounded windows and arches. Inside, it boasts a delightful array of engaging monuments, all well described by the self-guided tour brochure: a bell from the *Royal Oak* battleship, sunk in Scapa Flow in 1939 (explained later);

a reclining monument of arctic explorer John Rae, who appears to be enjoying a very satisfying nap; the entrance to a dungeon where suspected witches were held while awaiting trial; the likely bones of St. Magnus (a beloved local saint); and many other characteristic flourishes. But the highlight is the gravestones that line the walls of the nave, each one carved with reminders of mortality: skull and crossbones, coffin, hourglass, and the shovel used by the undertaker. Read some of the poignant epitaphs: "She lived regarded and dyed regreted."

Two other, less thrilling sights are near the cathedral: The **Bishop and Earl's Palaces** are a pair of once-grand, now-empty ruined buildings (fun for a scamper through their sparsely described rubble). And the **Orkney**

Museum is a free, charmingly modest exhibit on the history of the islands, from prehistory through the 20th century. You'll see display cases jammed with lots of old artifacts and dated descriptions.

In front of the cathedral stands Kirkwall's mercat cross (market cross), which is the starting point for the annual event called **The Ba'.** Short for "ball," this is a no-holds-barred, citywide rugby match that takes place every Christmas and New Year's Day. Hundreds of Kirkwall's rough-and-tumble young lads team up based on neighborhood (the Uppies and the Doonies), and attempt to deliver the ball to the opposing team's goal by any means necessary. The only rule: There are no rules. While it's usually just one gigantic scrum pushing back and forth through the streets, other tactics are used (such as the recent controversy when one team simply tossed the ball in a car and drove it to the goal). Ask locals about their stories—or scars—from The Ba'.

From the cathedral area, Kirkwall's shop-lined, pedestrians-only **main drag** heads down to the harbor, changing names several times as it curls through town.

It's a workaday strip, lined with a combination of humble local shops and places trying to be trendy (such as the Brig Larder, a boutique grocery store co-owned by a butcher and a fishmonger). You'll pop out at the little harbor, where fishing boats bob and ferries fan out to the northern islets.

Kirkwall has one more worthwhile sight: the **Highland Park Distillery,** a sprawling stone facility on the way out of town to the south (toward South Ronaldsay and the Scapa Flow WWII sites; £7.50 tour includes one dram, daily in summer, shorter hours off-season, www.highlandpark.co.uk). The one-hour tours are similar to other distilleries, but this is one of only six in all of Scotland that malts its own barley—you'll see the malting floor (where the barley is spread and stirred while germinating) and the peat-fired kilns. Guides love to explain how the distillery's well-regarded whiskies get their flavor from Orkney's unique composition of peat (composed mostly of heather on this treeless island) and its high humidity (which minimizes alcohol "lost to the angels" during maturation).

▲▲▲Prehistoric Sites

Orkney boasts an astonishing concentration of 5,000-year-old Neolithic monuments—one of the best such collections in Great Britain (and that's saying something). And here on Orkney, there's also a unique Bronze Age overlay, during which Picts, and then Vikings, built their own monuments to complement the ones they inherited.

Combo-Ticket: If visiting several prehistoric sites, consider the Orkney Explorer Pass, which includes all of the biggies for £18. All of the sites are managed by Historic Scotland (for cost and hours details, see www.historic-scotland.gov.uk).

Prehistoric Orkney: Five thousand years ago—before the Picts and Celts, before the ancient Greeks or Romans, before the Great Pyramids, and even centuries before Stonehenge—Orkney had a bustling settlement with some 30,000 people (a population even larger than today's). The climate, already milder than most of Scotland thanks to the Gulf Stream, was even warmer then, making this a desirable place to live. Orkney's prehistoric residents left behind structures from every walk of life: humble residential settlements (Skara Brae, Barnhouse Village), mysterious stone circles (Ring of Brodgar, Stenness Stones), more than 100 tombs (Maeshowe, Tomb of the Eagles), and what appears to be a sprawling ensemble of spiritual buildings (the Ness of Brodgar). And, this being the Stone Age, all of this was accomplished using tools made not of metal, but of stone and bone. While you could spend days poring over all of Orkney's majestic prehistoric monuments, on a short visit focus on the following highlights.

Maeshowe: The finest chambered tomb north of the Alps, Maeshowe (mays-HOW) was built around 3500 B.C. From the outside, it looks like yet another big mound. But inside, the burial

chamber is remarkably intact. On the required 30-minute tour, you'll squeeze through the entrance tunnel and emerge into a space designed for ancestor worship, surrounded by three smaller cells. At the winter solstice, the setting sun shines through the entrance tunnel, illuminating the entrance to the main cell. How they managed to cut and transport gigantic slabs of sandstone (up to 30 tons), then assemble this dry-stone, corbeled pyramid—all in an age before metal tools—is a question that still puzzles present-day engineers. Adding to this place's mystique, in the 12th century, a band of Vikings took shelter here for three days during a storm, and entertained themselves by carving runic messages into the walls—many of them still readable ("Ofram Sigurdsson carved these runes"). Reservations are required; call ahead in the morning to book a tour (£5.50, tours depart daily 2/hour, tel. 01856/761-606).

Prehistoric Sites near Maeshowe: A narrow spit of land just a few hundred yards from Maeshowe is lined with several stunning, free-to-visit Neolithic holdovers (from Maeshowe, head south on the A-965 and immediately turn right onto the B-9055, following *Bay of Skaill* signs). Along this road, you'll reach the following sites, in this order (watch for the brown signs). Conveniently, these line up on the way to Skara Brae.

The **Stones of Stenness**—three and a half standing stones, surviving from an original 12—form a 100-foot-diameter ring. Dating from around 3100 B.C., these are some of the oldest standing stones in Britain (a millennium older than Stonehenge). From these stones, a footpath continues through the field to the **Barnhouse Village.** Likely built around the same time as the Stones of Stenness, this was probably a residential area for the priests and custodians of the ceremonial monuments all around. Discovered in 1984, much of what you see today has been reconstructed—making this the least favorite site of archaeological purists. Still, it provides an illuminating contrast to Skara Brae

(described later): While those homes were built underground, the ones at Barnhouse were thatched stone huts not unlike ones you

still see around Great Britain today. The entire gathering was enclosed by a defensive wall.

Back on the road, just before the **causeway** between two
lochs—saltwater on the left and freshwater on the right—two pillars flank the road (one intact, the other stubby). These formed a
gateway of sorts to the important Neolithic structures just beyond.

On the left, look for the scaffolding and tarps of the **Ness of
Brodgar**—an exciting opportunity to observe an actual archaeological dig in progress (discov-
ered only in 2003). The work site
you see covers only one-tenth of
the entire complex, which was
likely an ensemble of important
ceremonial buildings...think of
it as the "Orkney Vatican." The
biggest foundation, nicknamed
"the Cathedral," appears to have
been a focal point for pilgrim-

ages. Don't be surprised if there's no action—due to limited fund-
ing, archaeologists are likely at work here only in July and August
(at other times, it's carefully covered, with nothing to see). The
archaeologists hope to raise enough funds to build a permanent
visitors center. Guided tours are sometimes available; check www.
orkneyjar.com/archaeology/nessofbrodgar for details.

Farther along on the left, you'll begin to see stones capping
a ridge above the road. This is the **Ring of Brodgar,** more than

three times larger than the
Stones of Stenness (and
about 500 years newer).
Of the original 60 to 80
stones—creating a cir-
cle as wide as a football
field—27 still survive. The
ring, which sits amidst a
marshy moor, was sur-
rounded by a henge (moat)
that was 30 feet wide and 20 feet deep. Walking around the ring,
notice that some are carved with "graffiti"—names of visitors from
the late 19th century to the early 20th century, as well as some faint
Norse runes carved by a Viking named Bjorn around A.D. 1150.

Skara Brae: At the far-eastern reaches of Mainland (about a
20-minute drive from Maeshowe), this remarkable site illustrates
how some Neolithic people lived like rabbits in warrens—hun-
kered down in subterranean homes, connected by tunnels and lit
only by whale-oil lamps. Uncovered by an 1850 windstorm, Skara
Brae (SKAH-rah bray, meaning roughly "village under hills") has

been meticulously excavated and is very well presented (£7.10, open daily year-round, café and WCs).

You'll begin your visit in the small exhibition hall, where you'll watch a short film and see displays on Neolithic life. Then you'll head out and walk inside a reconstructed home from Skara Brae—with a hearth, beds, storage area, and live-bait tanks dug into the floor. Finally, you'll walk across a field—passing timeline stones that count down landmarks of human achievement—to reach the site itself. Museum attendants stand by to answer any questions.

The oldest, standalone homes at Skara Brae were built around 3100 B.C.; a few centuries later, the complex was expanded and con-

nected with tunnels. You'll walk on a grassy ridge just above the complex, peering down into 10 partially ruined homes and the tunnels that connect them. All of this was covered with turf, with only two or three entrances and exits. Because sandstone is a natural insulator, these spaces—while cramped and dank—would have been warm and cozy during the frequent battering storms. If you see a grate, squint down into the darkness: A primitive sewer system, flushed by a rerouted stream, ran beneath all of the homes, functioning not too differently from modern sewers. And all of this was accomplished without the use of metal tools. They even created an ingenious system of giant stone slabs on pivots, allowing them to be opened and closed like modern doors.

Before leaving, look out over the nearby bay, and consider that this is only about one-third of the entire size of the original Skara Brae. What's now a beach was once a freshwater loch. But with the rising Atlantic, the water became unusable. About 800 years after it was built, the village was abandoned; since then, most of it has been lost to the sea. This area is called Skaill Bay, from the Old Norse *skål* for "cheers!"—during Viking times, this was a popular place for revelry...but the revelers had no clue they were partying on top of a Neolithic village.

And now for something completely different: Your ticket to Skara Brae also includes the **Skaill House,** the sprawling stone mansion on the nearby hilltop. You'll tour some lived-in rooms (c. 1950) and see a fascinating hodgepodge of items that illustrate Orkney's prime location for passing maritime trade: The dining room proudly displays Captain James Cook's dinner service—bartered by his crew on their return voyage after the captain was killed in Hawaii (Orkney was the first place they made landfall in the UK). You'll also see traditional Orkney chairs (with woven backs); in the library, an Old Norse "calendar"—a wooden stick that you could hold up to the horizon at sunset to determine the exact date; a Redcoat's red coat from the Crimean War; a Spanish chest salvaged from a shipwreck; and some very "homely" (and supposedly haunted) bedrooms.

Nearby: Just south of Skara Brae, drivers can consider a quick visit to the sightseeing twofer of **Yesnaby** (watch for the turnoff on the B-9056). On a bluff overlooking the sea, you'll find an old antiaircraft artillery battery from World War II, and some of Orkney's most dramatic sea cliff scenery.

▲▲▲Scapa Flow: World War II Sites

For a quick and fascinating glimpse of Orkney's World War II locations, you need only drive 10 minutes south from Kirkwall on the A-961 (leave town toward St. Mary's and St. Margaret's Hope, past the Highland Park Distillery)—to the natural harbor called Scapa Flow (see the sidebar). From the village of St. Mary's, you can cross over all four of the Churchill Barriers, with subtle reminders of war all around. The floor of Scapa Flow is littered with shipwrecks, and if you know where to look, you can still see many of them as you drive by.

Barrier #1 crosses from St. Mary's to the Isle of Burray. This narrow channel is where, in the early days of World War II, the German U-47 slipped between sunken ships to attack the *Royal Oak*—demonstrating the need to build these barriers. Notice that the Churchill Barriers have two levels: smaller quarried stone down below, and huge concrete blocks on top.

Just over the first barrier, perched on the little rise on the left, is Orkney's most fascinating wartime site: the **Italian Chapel.** Italian POWs who were captured during the North African campaign (and imprisoned here on Orkney to work on the Churchill Barriers) were granted permission to create a Catholic chapel to remind them of their homeland. While the front view is a pretty Baroque facade, if you circle around you'll see that the core of the structure is two prefab Nissen huts (similar to Quonset huts). Inside, you can see the remarkable craftsmanship of the artists who decorated the church. In 1943, Domenico Chiocchetti led the effort to create this house of worship, and personally painted the frescoes that adorn the interior.

The ethereal *Madonna e Bambino* over the main altar is based on a small votive he had brought with him to war. An experienced ironworker named Palumbi used scrap metal (much of it scavenged from sunken WWI ships) to create the gate and chandeliers, while others used whatever basic materials they could to finish the details. (Notice the elegant corkscrew base of the baptismal font near the entrance; it's actually a suspension spring coated in concrete.) These lovingly crafted details are a hope-filled symbol of the gentility and grace that can blossom even during brutal wartime. (And the British military is proud of this structure as an embodiment of Britain's wartime ethic of treating POWs with care and respect.) Spend some time examining the details—such as the stained-glass windows, which are painted rather than leaded. The chapel was completed in 1944, just two months before the men who built it were sent home. Chiocchetti returned for a visit in

the 1960s, bringing with him the wood-carved Stations of the Cross that now hang in the nave.

Continuing south along the road, you'll cross over two more barriers in rapid succession. You'll see the masts and hulls of

shipwrecks—scuttled here during World War I to block the harbor. As you cross over the bridges, notice that these are solid barriers, with no water circulation—in fact, the water level on each side of the barrier varies slightly, since the tide differs by an hour and a half.

At the far end of **Barrier #3,** on the left, watch for the huge wooden boxes on the beach. These were used in pre-barrier times (WWI) for boom floats, which supported nets designed to block submarines.

After Barrier #3, as you climb the hill, watch for the pullout on the right with an orientation board. From this **viewpoint,** you can see three of the Churchill Barriers in one grand panorama.

Scapa Flow: Britain's Remote Wartime Naval Base

Orkney's arc of scattered islands form one of the world's largest natural harbors, called Scapa Flow (SKAH-pah flow). The Norsemen named this area *skalpi floi*—"scabbard water," where a sword was sheathed—suggesting that they used this area to store their warships when not in use. And in the 20th century, Scapa Flow was the main base for Britain's Royal Navy.

During World War I, to thwart U-boat attacks, dozens of old ships and fishing vessels were requisitioned and intentionally sunk to block the gaps between the islets that define Scapa Flow. You can still see many of these "block ships" underwater today.

At the end of World War I, a fleet of 74 German battleships surrendered at Scapa Flow. On the morning of June 21, 1919—days before the Treaty of Versailles was formally enacted—the British admiral took most of his navy out on a "victory lap" patrol. Once they were gone, the German commander ordered his men to scuttle the entire fleet, rather than turn them over. By the time the British fleet returned five hours later, 52 German ships littered the bottom of the bay. The British opened fire on the remaining German ships, killing nine Germans—the final casualties of World War I. While most of the ships were later salvaged for scrap, to this day, German crockery washes up on Orkney beaches after a storm. Seven ships remain at a depth of 150 feet, making this one of Eu-

Carrying on south, the next barrier isn't a Churchill Barrier at all—it's an ayre, a causeway that was built during the Viking period.

Finally you'll reach **Barrier #4**—hard to recognize because so much sand has accumulated on its east side (look for the giant breakwater blocks). Surveying the dunes along this barrier, notice the crooked concrete shed poking up—actually the top of a shipwreck. The far side of this sand dune is one of Orkney's best beaches—sheltered and scenic.

From here, the A-961 continues south past **St. Margaret's Hope** (where the ferry to Gills Bay departs) and all the way to Burwick, at the southern tip of South

rope's most popular scuba diving destinations.

Scapa Flow also played a critical role in World War II. Even before Britain declared war on Germany, Luftwaffe reconnaissance flights had identified a gap in the sunken-ship barriers around the harbor. And on October 14, 1939—just weeks after war was declared—a Nazi U-47 slipped inside the harbor and torpedoed the HMS *Royal Oak*, killing 834 (including 110 seamen-in-training under the age of 15). To this day, the battleship—which had been fully loaded with fuel and ordnance—sits on the bottom of the bay, marked with a green warning buoy.

In April 1940, Luftwaffe planes flew from German-occupied Norway to bomb Orkney for three days straight in what's termed the "Battle of Orkney." But the islands were bulked up with heavy-duty gun batteries and other defenses, turning Orkney into a fortress. A sea of blimps called "barrage balloons"—designed to interfere with air attacks—clogged the air overhead. They even built a false fleet out of wood (also protected by barrage balloons) as a decoy for the Luftwaffe. The local population of 22,000 was joined by some 80,000 troops. Many surviving fragments from this period can still be seen all over the island.

To ensure that no further surprises would sneak into the bay, First Lord of the Admiralty Winston Churchill visited here (just weeks before becoming prime minister) and hatched a plan to build sturdy barriers spanning the small distances between the islands south of Kirkwall. Throughout the wartime years, British workers and Italian prisoners of war labored to construct the "Churchill Barriers." The roads on top of the barriers opened just a few days after V-E Day, and today tourists use them to island-hop—and to learn about the dramatic history of Scapa Flow.

NORTHERN SCOTLAND

Ronaldsay. From here you can see the tip of Scotland. Nearby is the **Tomb of the Eagles,** a burial cairn similar to Maeshowe, but less accessible (time-consuming visit, www.tomboftheeagles.co.uk).

More WWII Sites: For those really interested in the World War II scene, consider a ferry trip out to the **Isle of Hoy;** the main settlement, Lyness, has the Scapa Flow Visitors Centre and cemetery (www.scapaflow.co.uk). Near Lyness alone are some 37 Luftwaffe crash sites. A tall hill, called Wee Fea, was hollowed out to hold 100,000 tons of fuel oil. Also on Hoy, you can hike seven miles round-trip to the iconic **Old Man of Hoy**—a 450-foot-high sea stack in front of Britain's tallest vertical sea cliffs. (Or you can see the same thing for free from the deck of the Stromness-Scrabster ferry.)

Sleeping on Orkney

($$ = £85 or more; $ = £85 or less)

These accommodations are in or near Kirkwall, close to the center of Mainland—allowing you to easily fan out to the sights on the island's far corners. Orkney's B&Bs are not well marked; be sure to get specific instructions from your host before you arrive, especially for countryside places.

In Kirkwall: With a handy location just behind the cathedral, **$ 2 Dundas Crescent** has three old-fashioned rooms rented by welcoming Ruth, in a big old house that used to be a manse—a preacher's home (Db-£75, tel. 01856/874-805, www.twodundas. co.uk). Across the street and a few doors downhill, **$ 13 Palace Road** has three rooms, one with a private bathroom down the hall (Db-£80, book through www.visitscotland.com or by phone, tel. 01856/872-249). Higher up in town, consider **$ Hildeval B&B,** in a modern home with five contemporary-style rooms (Db-£80, tel. 01856/878-840, www.hildeval-orkney.co.uk). And **$$ Lynnfield Hotel** rents 10 rooms that are a bit old-fashioned in decor, but with modern hotel amenities (Db-£115-155, on Holm Road/A-961, tel. 01856/872-505, www.lynnfieldhotel.com).

In the Countryside: **$$ Holland House,** a classy and inviting retreat with three rooms, offers countryside quiet that's still a short drive from Kirkwall, the main prehistoric sites, and Stromness; thoughtful, welcoming Jan takes great care of her guests (Db-£104, in the Harray district, tel. 01856/771-400, www. hollandhouseorkney.co.uk). **$ Straigona B&B,** about a five-minute drive outside of Kirkwall (just past the airport), has three rooms in a cozy modern home, run by helpful Julie and Mike (Db-£80-85, more for 1 night, tel. 01856/861-328, www.straigona.co.uk). And—for more anonymity and grand views over Scapa Flow—the recommended restaurant **$$ The Foveran** has eight rooms, some with contemporary flourish and others more traditional (Db-£110-120, five minutes from Kirkwall by car, tel. 01856/872-389, www. thefoveran.com).

Eating on Orkney

In Kirkwall: If sightseeing in Kirkwall, you'll find several good lunch spots around the cathedral. The **Strynd Tea Room,** tucked down an alley (look for the sign at Broad Street), is a fine choice for coffee and cakes, afternoon tea, or a light lunch. Nearby, **The Reel** (a music club/café) and **Judith Glue Shop** (a souvenir-and-craft shop) are both touristy but workable. From the cathedral, you can also browse your way down the main street, which is lined with additional options; you'll wind up at the harbor, where **Helgi's** pub serves quality food.

Destination Restaurants near Kirkwall: To splurge at a destination restaurant, consider two choices just outside of Kirkwall, with talented chefs working hard to elevate Orcadian cuisine—using traditional local ingredients, but with international flourish. These are pricey (plan on main courses around £20). **The Foveran,** perched on a bluff with smashing views over Scapa Flow, has a cool, contemporary dining room with a wall of windows (dinner nightly May-Sept, weekends only in winter, about a five-minute drive southwest of Kirkwall on the A-964, www.thefoveran.com, tel. 01856/872-389). **Lynnfield Hotel,** near the Highland Park Distillery on the way out of town (with some views over Kirkwall's rooftops), has a more traditional feel (open daily for lunch and dinner, on Holm Road/A-961, tel. 01856/872-505, www. lynnfieldhotel.com).

SCOTLAND: PAST AND PRESENT

Rugged and remote, Scotland has had a particularly hard-fought history. Split by the Highland Boundary Fault, which separates the flatter, more London-looking Lowlands in the south from the craggy, deeply Celtic Highlands in the north, the two halves have distinct characters. Ringing the country are distant islands—the Hebrides, Orkney, and Shetland—each bringing its own local customs, history, and traditions to the table. Since ancient times, the feisty people of Scotland—Highlanders and Lowlanders alike—have fought to preserve their region's unique identity. Scotland's rabble-rousing national motto is *Nemo me impune lacessit*—"No one provokes me with impunity." In Scotland, perhaps more than most places, legends of national heroes abound.

PREHISTORIC ORIGINS, ROMAN REBELLION, AND HIGHLAND CLANS

Scotland's first inhabitants were hunter-gatherers who came north as the Ice Age receded (7000 B.C.). In Neolithic times (4500-2000 B.C.), a new wave of farmer-herders arrived from the south. They left us stone circles and passage graves (funeral mounds with a burial chamber inside, reached by a passage). While few Neolithic structures survive in Scotland, Orkney—which flourished during this age—has some of the UK's best and oldest (see page 402).

Also during the Stone Age, people began to settle on the waters of Scotland's many lochs, building igloo-shaped homes called crannogs. Made of wood and built upon timber pilings driven deep into the loch's floor, they were linked to the shore only by a removable wooden plank. Crannogs were at once well-protected and easy to access (in an age when most travel was by boat), and they provided unobstructed views across the loch. Many circular "islands" you may notice in lochs today are likely grown-over, abandoned crannogs. (For more on crannogs, visit the excellent Crannog Centre on Loch Tay—see page 339.)

Around 500 B.C., the Celts moved in from Europe, bringing Iron-Age technology and the language that would develop into the

Gaelic tongue. The Celts built hilltop forts, with large stone towers called brochs.

In A.D. 80, Roman legions—having already conquered England—marched north and established a camp near Edinburgh. They called today's Scotland "Caledonia" (a term you'll still see everywhere) and battled the

fierce Celts, whom they dubbed Caledonii—or "Picts" ("painted"; for their war paint). But the Picts would not surrender. Eventually, the Romans decided they had expanded far enough—and Scotland just wasn't worth the effort. It was mountainous, wild, and dangerous—not just with Picts, but with predatory beasts such as bears, wolves, and lynx. The Romans sealed off Caledonia (and the pesky Picts) with two walls—the famous Hadrian's Wall (73 miles long and up to 20 feet high) near Durham, in England, and the lesser-known Antonine Wall (from the Firth of Clyde to the Firth of Forth—essentially from today's Glasgow to Edinburgh). From then on, while England was forever stamped with a Roman/European perspective, Scotland was set on a course that was isolated and Celtic.

Medieval Scotland was a stew of peoples: Picts in the northern Highlands, Anglo-Saxons (Germanic invaders) in the south, and the "Scoti" (Celtic cousins from Ireland) on the west coast. (While little survives from this time, you can still see faint remains of some of the Scoti's important sites in Kilmartin Glen—see page 270.) The Scoti gradually overwhelmed and absorbed the Picts. In their kingdom of Alba (the Gaelic name for Scotland), they established Gaelic as the chief language and Christianity—brought from Ireland by St. Columba in the sixth century—as the dominant religion. Even at this early date, Scotland's geographical/ethnic boundary was already set: Gaelic/Celtic culture in the Highland north, English-friendly Anglo-Saxons in the Lowland south.

Vikings attacked from the north, and succeeded in capturing the northern islands, which remained Norse until the 15th century. (To this day, Orkney and Shetland have a Norwegian flavor and a heritage of Old Norse rune carvings and place names.) But much of the Scottish realm united under a Gaelic warlord named Kenneth MacAlpin. In 843, in his capital at Scone (50 miles north of Edinburgh), MacAlpin was crowned atop the Stone of Scone—making him the first king of Scots.

But this "Scotland" was a tiny and troubled land. In the 11th century (as Shakespeare later recalled it), King Duncan was murdered by one of his own men: Macbeth. King Macbeth was, in turn, killed by Duncan's son, Malcolm Canmore—the man who would establish Edinburgh and bring remote Scotland onto the stage of the wider world.

Meanwhile, in the remote reaches of the Highlands and the Hebrides, communities were based on the clan system: tribes of people sharing a stretch of land managed by a chieftain (or "laird"), who served as a kind of caretaker for the people and future generations. In Gaelic, *clann* means "children"; the clan system was the traditional Scottish way of passing along power—similar to England's dukes, barons, and counts. Although clan members took the chief's name in solidarity, they were not necessarily related by blood. The patrilineal clan system eventually became further subdivided into septs—alliances of families who pledged allegiance to the same chieftain.

Most Highlanders were kilted farmers who lived in humble huts with dirt floors, dry-stone walls, and peaty fires with heavy

smoke that escaped through thatched roofs. (For a glimpse of this lifestyle—which persisted well into the 18th century—visit the Highland Folk Museum south of Inverness, described on page 337, or the Museum of Island Life on the Isle of Skye, described on page 370.) While it's not quite true that each clan had its own carefully designed tartan pattern, clan members did tend to live in a single geographical area, where certain natural dyes and weavers predominated—so they likely dressed in (somewhat) similar colors. (For more on the kilt tradition, see page 35.)

Some clans were allies, either through intermarriage or through shared interests. Others were sworn enemies. The most famous rivalry was a three-way struggle between Clan Donald (or MacDonald), Clan Mackenzie, and Clan MacLeod, who clashed in several epic battles (see sidebar on page 380).

WILLIAM WALLACE, ROBERT THE BRUCE, AND MEDIEVAL INDEPENDENCE

When King Malcolm III married the English Princess Margaret in 1070, it united the culture of the Highland Scots with that of the Lowland Anglo-Saxons. Margaret was exceptionally pious, and she fostered the Christian faith as never before. Increasingly, Scotland became ruled from the southern Lowlands and influenced by its southern neighbor, England. As English settlers moved north, they built castles and abbeys. They also brought with them a new social order—a hierarchical government that went beyond the small social unit of the Highland clan.

But in the far reaches of Scotland, the clan system still flourished. Clan Donald, based on the Isle of Skye's Sleat Peninsula, controlled its own sprawling kingdom: In the 12th century, a great warrior named Somerled took control of the Lordship of the Isles, which included most of Scotland's west coast islands, and penetrated deep into the Highlands and present-day Northern Ireland (Antrim). This fully independent maritime state lasted until 1493, when its territory was finally folded into the holdings of the Stuart kings. (To this day, the British heir apparent carries the title "Lord of the Isles.")

In 1286, the king of Scotland died without an heir. To settle the battle over succession, the Scots invited King Edward I of England ("Longshanks") to arbitrate. Edward seized the moment to assert his power over Scotland. He invaded, defeated the chosen successor, and stole the revered coronation stone—the Stone of Scone—taking it back to London (where it remained, almost untouched, until 1996).

Enraged, the Scots rallied around nobleman William Wallace (see page 61). He defeated the English at Stirling Bridge (1297) and was named the "guardian of Scotland." Wallace marched his army into England, plundered its north, then returned to Scotland—where he was defeated at the Battle of Falkirk in 1298. Disgraced, Wallace retreated to the Highlands and waged guerrilla warfare against the English until he was finally betrayed, arrested, and brutally executed in 1305.

The torch was passed to the earl of Carrick, Robert the Bruce (see page 65), who united Scotland's many clans and defeated the

English at the tide-turning Battle of Bannockburn (1314). Bruce was crowned King Robert, and his heirs would rule Scotland for the next four centuries under the Stewart family name. (Later, when Mary, Queen of Scots, moved to France, she changed the spelling to "Stuart" because the French alphabet of the time lacked the letter "w"—for simplicity, I've used that spelling throughout this book.) Scotland had secured its independence.

Over the next two centuries, Scotland's kings ruled from their castle in Stirling (see page 174), gradually asserting central control over local clans and expanding the country's boundaries into the modern nation. But the Stuart monarchy was still weak, plagued with infighting over succession. Fortunately, England was kept at bay, plagued by its own troubles fighting the French (Hundred Years' War) and each other (Wars of the Roses). Scotland's long-standing "Auld Alliance" with the French existed mainly to support its independence from England.

MARY, QUEEN OF SCOTS; JOHN KNOX; AND THE PROTESTANT REFORMATION

Everything changed when Henry VIII took the English crown, sparking a border war with Scotland. In the Battle of Flodden (1513), Scotland was utterly defeated. Soon Scotland faced an even greater enemy. As the Reformation crept into Scotland (c. 1540-1560), it split the country in two. The Highlands remained Catholic, rural, pro-monarchy, and pro-French. The Lowlands grew increasingly Protestant, urban, anti-monarchy, and pro-English.

When the Scottish King James V died in 1542, his six-day-old daughter Mary was named Queen of Scots (r. 1542-1567). Mary grew up staunchly Catholic and was educated in France, where she married the French crown prince in 1558. By the time the newly widowed Mary arrived back home (in 1561) to rule her native Scotland, the teenage queen found a hostile country in the throes of a Protestant Reformation (for the full story, see the sidebar on page 208).

The leader of the movement was John Knox (1514-1572), who grew up poor outside of Edinburgh. At a young age, he was at the forefront of the Reformation and a disciple of early reformer George Wishart, who was burned at the stake. Knox was arrested and exiled for two years; he spent much of this time among reformers in England, and with John Calvin in Geneva. Upon his return to Scotland (1559), he brought with him crates full of English bibles, which he used to spread both the Word of God and the English language. Knox went on an evangelical kick, preaching fire and brimstone throughout the Lowlands. He spread the message of Protestantism, wrote a Declaration of Independence-type manifesto called the "Confession of the Faith," and (with the help of some powerful supporters) outlawed Catholicism under punishment of prison or even death.

Mary, Queen of Scots' homecoming came just as Reformation fever was at its peak. Mary summoned Knox for a series of debates,

where they hashed out their differences. While they ultimately agreed to disagree on the larger points, they did come to some compromises: Mary insisted on her personal right to say Mass in private, despite the national ban on the Catholic faith.

The Scots soon became disgusted with Mary's messy personal life, starting with her 1565 remarriage. The groom was her first cousin, Lord Darnley—an English-Scottish prince whose claim to both crowns had made him many enemies. Their marriage soured, and rumors flew that Mary was getting fresh with her secretary. The secretary was brutally murdered at Edinburgh's Palace of Holyroodhouse in front of a horrified Mary,

and suspicion fell on Darnley. Then Darnley himself was found strangled in his Edinburgh home, while Mary fled the country with the prime suspect—the earl of Bothwell—soon to be Mary's third husband. Amid all of the drama, Mary gave birth to a son—whether Darnley's or the secretary's, no one knows—who would grow up to be king of both Scotland and England.

KING JAMES VI/I, KING CHARLES I, AND CIVIL WAR

Following an uprising in 1567, Mary was forced to abdicate in favor of her infant son, who became King James VI of Scotland. Raised a Protestant, James assumed official duties at age 17 (1584) and brought a tentative peace to religiously divided Scotland. (Meanwhile, Mary was arrested on suspicion of murder, charged with an unrelated plot against her cousin, Queen Elizabeth I of England, and beheaded in 1587.)

In the 1592 Golden Act, Presbyterianism triumphed, and was

Typical Church Architecture

History comes to life when you visit a centuries-old church. Even if you wouldn't know your apse from a hole in the ground, learning a few simple terms will enrich your experience. Note that not every church has every feature, and a "cathedral" isn't a type of church architecture, but rather a designation for a church that's a governing center for a local bishop.

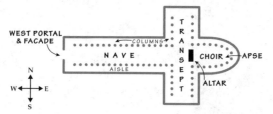

Aisles: The long, generally low-ceilinged arcades that flank the nave.

Altar: The raised area with a ceremonial table (often adorned with candles or a crucifix), where the priest prepares and serves the bread and wine for Communion.

Apse: The space beyond the altar, often bordered with small chapels.

Barrel Vault: A continuous round-arched ceiling that resembles an extended upside-down U.

Choir ("quire" in British English): A cozy area, often screened off, located within the church nave and near the high altar where services are sung in a more intimate setting.

Cloister: Covered hallways bordering a square or rectangular open-air courtyard, traditionally where monks and nuns got fresh air.

Facade: The front exterior of the church's main (west) entrance, usually highly decorated.

Groin Vault: An arched ceiling formed where two equal barrel vaults meet at right angles. Less common usage: term for a medieval jock strap.

Narthex: The area (portico or foyer) between the main entry and the nave.

Nave: The long, central section of the church (running west to east, from the entrance to the altar) where the congregation sits or stands through the service.

Transept: In a traditional cross-shaped floor plan, the transept is one of the two parts forming the "arms" of the cross. The transepts run north-south, perpendicularly crossing the east-west nave.

West Portal: The main entry to the church (on the west end, opposite the main altar).

Typical Castle Architecture

Castles were fortified residences for medieval nobles. Castles come in all shapes and sizes, but knowing a few general terms will help you understand them.

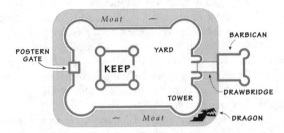

Barbican: A fortified gatehouse, sometimes a stand-alone building located outside the main walls.

Crenellation: A gap-toothed pattern of stones atop the parapet.

Drawbridge: A bridge that could be raised or lowered using counterweights or a chain and winch.

Great Hall: The largest room in the castle, serving as throne room, conference center, and dining hall.

Hoardings (or Gallery or Brattice): Wooden huts built onto the upper parts of the stone walls. They served as watch towers, living quarters, and fighting platforms.

The Keep (or Donjon): A high, strong stone tower in the center of the castle complex; the lord's home and refuge of last resort.

Loopholes (or Embrasures): Narrow wall slits through which soldiers could shoot arrows.

Machicolation: A stone ledge jutting out from the wall, with holes through which soldiers could drop rocks or boiling oil onto wall-scaling enemies below.

Moat: A ditch encircling the wall, often filled with water.

Motte-and-Bailey: A form of early English castle, with a small hilltop fort (motte) and an enclosed, fortified yard (bailey).

Parapet: Outer railing of the wall walk.

Portcullis: A heavy iron grille that could be lowered across the entrance.

Postern Gate: A small, unfortified side or rear entrance from which to launch attacks or escape.

Towers: Tall structures with crenellated tops or conical roofs serving as lookouts, chapels, living quarters, or dungeons.

Turret: A small lookout tower rising up from the top of the wall.

Wall Walk (or Allure): A pathway atop the wall where guards could patrol and where soldiers stood to fire at the enemy.

The Yard (or Bailey): An open courtyard inside the castle walls.

made the rule of law. Scotland went forward as a predominantly Protestant nation. But even among Protestants, there were religious divisions. Scottish Protestants were Presbyterians, members of the newly reorganized Church (or "Kirk") of Scotland. Presbyterian-ism (from the Greek word *prebuteros,* "elder") championed a self-governing congregation with leaders they elected themselves. This was in stark contrast to historic Catholic and Church of England hierarchies, led by a bishop (from the Greek *episkopos*) appointed by the king. The religious divide had political implications: Naturally, monarchs wanted to retain the politically powerful right to appoint bishops and rule congregations, while Presbyterians insisted on separation of kirk and state. Presbyterians also tended to be anti-king and pro-parliament.

In 1603, Queen Elizabeth I—England's "virgin queen"—died without an heir. Her distant cousin, Scotland's King James VI, was

next in line for the English throne. Upon leaving Edinburgh and being crowned England's King James I in London (making him both King James VI and I), he united Scotland and England. The two nations have been tied together, however fitfully, ever since.

James' son Charles I (1600-1649) was born and crowned in Scotland, but otherwise spent most of his life in England. He continued his father's attempts to consolidate the many threads of Protestantism throughout his lands, favoring the

English Episcopalian model. Charles I traveled to St. Giles' Cathedral in Edinburgh; appointed a bishop who, in turn, anointed him; and eventually introduced his own prayer book. This was a bridge too far for the Scots, who rioted and signed the National Covenant, proclaiming that the Scots had a special relationship with God that was outside the control of the crown. These "Covenanters" effectively declared their independence from the Church of England, and insisted that the Church of Scotland was under entirely Scottish control. A revolution was brewing.

The Covenanters went on military raids into northern England. King Charles attempted to quell the uprising with promises of reform, but became distracted by problems closer to home: Civil war broke out in England, pitting Charles (and the monarchy and Anglicanism) against Oliver Cromwell (with his supporters in parliament and the Puritans). Scotland was also divided. The Covenanters backed Cromwell, while many traditional Highlanders backed the king.

A Scottish army of 25,000 Covenanters invaded England, captured Charles I, and turned him over to Cromwell. On January 30, 1649, the English beheaded the king of Scotland.

ENGLAND'S ASCENDANCY AND THE ACT OF UNION

Left without a king, Scotland's landed gentry crowned Charles' son at Scone on January 1, 1651 (the last coronation at Scone). But Cromwell marched north and put a decisive end to any ideas of Scottish independence. It was clear that Scotland could never again be independent without the approval of England.

Charles II (1630-1685) escaped to France, where he spent the next nine years in exile. In 1660 he was invited back to London, and in 1661, the English parliament—suffering from Cromwell remorse—invited him to take the English throne. The monarchy was restored, with Charles II (a Stuart) ruling both England and Scotland.

But the two countries remained bitterly divided over religion. After Charles II died, his Catholic successor—James II (James VII of Scotland)—was ousted by England's parliament in a coup d'etat (called the Glorious Revolution), and replaced by a Protestant noble from the Dutch House of Orange-Nassau and his English wife (King William III and Mary II).

In Scotland, the newly ascendant Lowland Protestants set about forcing Highland Catholics and Episcopalians to swear allegiance to the Protestant king. This culminated in the infamous Glencoe Massacre of 1692, where pro-Protestants of the Campbell clan used the occasion as a pretext to slaughter their centuries-old enemy, the MacDonalds. (For more on Glencoe, see page 274.)

At the same time as Scotland's king was being forced into exile, the world was changing in other ways. England was on the rise as a naval and colonial superpower, and began encroaching on Scotland. Many Scots, particularly in the southern Lowlands, welcomed the English presence. These were people of Anglo-Saxon heritage, Calvinists and parliamentarians (who had like-minded counterparts in England), and traders and industrialists (who wanted to trade with wealthy England).

Due to a failed trading post venture in Panama (the Darien Scheme), Scotland went bankrupt. Members of the Scottish parliament (some of whom were bribed) agreed to accept a bailout from England, which came with one major string attached: the Act of Union. So it was that in 1707, Scotland's parliament (dominated by wealthy Lowlanders) voted itself out of existence, and the Scottish nation was officially joined with England, becoming part of "Great

Britain." The independence of the Scottish nation—led by the Stuart family since the days of Robert the Bruce—was over.

JACOBITE RISINGS AND MASS EMIGRATIONS

Or was it? Many Scots, especially in the Highlands, clung loyally to their ousted King James II (VII of Scotland) and his successors. They were called Jacobites—after the Latin "Jacobus" for James—and saw the Stuarts as their best hope to regain Scotland's independence. On the other side was the ascendant Protestant/urban faction, who supported the British government and monarch.

In the first of two Jacobite "risings," a coalition of traditionalists, Highland clans, and Catholics rallied around James II's son in 1715. But English troops easily routed them at the Battle of Sheriffmuir (10 miles north of Stirling), the grand hopes of "The '15" rebellion sputtered, and James Junior was sent scurrying back to his home-in-exile in France.

In 1745, a second rebellion was led by James II's grandson, known as "Bonnie Prince Charlie." That summer, the exiled Prince

Charles sailed across the sea from France and landed in Scotland near Glenfinnan (see page 292), where he raised an army of Highlanders and set out to re-establish the Stuart monarchy. The terrified king put a price on Charles' bonnie head (the equivalent of £15 million in today's pounds), but the outlaw prince succeeded in rallying many Scots to his cause. Within a few months, inspired by their charismatic leader, the Highlander forces had taken most of Scotland and even much of northern England. In their march toward London, they penetrated as far south as Derby—just 125 miles from the Tower of London. But the gains were ephemeral. Prince Charles' army was small (6,000 men) and disorganized; promised French support failed to materialize; and he had almost no popular support in the Lowlands, much less in England.

As better-equipped British troops advanced, Prince Charles pulled back to the Highlands. The two armies finally met in 1746 for one final, bloody conflict at Culloden Moor, just outside of Inverness, where Bonnie Prince Charlie's ragtag, kilted, bagpipe-bolstered army was routed and massacred. (For more on the prince and his defeat, see page 312.) Charles himself escaped the chaos, dressed as a female servant to sail "over the sea to Skye," and ultimately died in exile in Rome. To this day, patriotic Scots lament the crippling blow dealt to the rebellion they call "The '45."

After Charlie's defeat, the authorities (aristocratic landowners with government assistance) came down brutally on those who had supported the Jacobites, targeting the Highland clans and their traditional way of life. Kilt-wearing was forbidden, the feudal clan system was dismantled, homes were burned, and valuables were plundered. Clan chieftains who hadn't been exiled took over formerly communal lands and treated them as their own.

Landowners decided to make more efficient use of their land, bringing about the so-called "Highland Clearances" (which escalated following The '45, and peaked in the early 19th century). They evicted their farming populations and transformed the agricultural model from croft (subsistence farming of locally used crops) to mass production (more profitable sheep). Many displaced farmers moved to cities for factory work (as this coincided with the burgeoning Industrial Revolution—see the next section). Many others sought a better life in the New World.

From the mid- to late-19th century, an estimated two million Scots emigrated, mostly to North America, Australia, and New Zealand. Many perished in the perilous four-month Atlantic crossing, on vessels so rife with disease they were nicknamed "coffin ships." Those who survived employed their Scottish work ethic and industriousness to help build their adopted nations (concentrated in places like Nova Scotia—"New Scotland"). Some 15 percent of today's Canadians cite Scottish heritage. In fact, the "Scottish" populations of both Canada and the United States rival the population of Scotland.

Meanwhile, back home, Highland culture all but died out. It was a bleak time for traditional life in Scotland.

SCOTLAND REBOUNDS: SCOTTISH ENLIGHTENMENT, INDUSTRIAL REVOLUTION, AND HIGHLAND REVIVAL

Despite the difficult times in the Highlands, Lowlands Edinburgh thrived. In the last half of the 1700s, the city had become one of Europe's (and the world's) most intellectual cities. Edinburgh benefited from a rich university tradition, a strong Protestant work ethic, an educated middle class, connections with a powerful England, and, simply, good genes. Edinburgh was a city of secular, rational thinkers who embraced the scientific method and empirical observation.

Scots of note from this period include philosopher David Hume (who applied cool rationality and a scientific approach to religion, morals, and philosophy); economist Adam Smith (who wrote about division of labor and the free market in *The Wealth of Nations*); James Watt (who developed better steam engines, propelling Great Britain—and the world—into a busy Industrial

Robert Burns (1759-1796)

Robert Burns, Scotland's national poet, holds a unique place in the heart of the Scottish people—a heart that still beats loud and proud thanks, in large part, to Burns himself.

Born on a farm in southwestern Scotland, Robbie (or "Rabbie," as Scots affectionately call him) was the oldest of seven children. His early years were full of literally backbreaking farm labor, which left him with a lifelong stoop. Though much was later made of his ascendance to literary acclaim from a rural, poverty-stricken upbringing, he was actually quite well educated (per Scottish tradition), equally as familiar with Latin and French as he was with hard work.

He started writing poetry at 15, but didn't have any published until age 28—to finance a voyage to the West Indies (which promised better farming opportunities). When that first volume, *Poems, Chiefly in the Scottish Dialect*, became a sudden and overwhelming success, he reconsidered his emigration. Instead, he left his farm for Edinburgh, living just off the Royal Mile. He spent a year and a half in the city, schmoozing with literary elites, who celebrated this "heaven taught" farmer from the hinterlands as Scotland's "ploughman poet."

His poetry, written primarily in the Scots dialect, drew on his substantial familiarity with both Scottish tradition and Western literature. By using the language of the common man to create works of beauty and sophistication, he found himself wildly popular among both rural folk and high society. Hearty poems such as "To a Mouse," "To a Louse," and "The Holy Fair" exalted the virtues of physical labor, romantic love, friendship, natural beauty, and drink—all of which he also pursued with vigor in real life. This further endeared him to most Scots, though considerably less so

Age); and great names in virtually every discipline: geologist James Hutton, chemist Joseph Black, painter Allan Ramsay, and of course the literary greats Robert Burns (see the sidebar) and Sir Walter Scott (see page 69). It's fitting that the *Encyclopedia Britannica*—the pre-Wikipedia authority on all things—was first published in Edinburgh in 1768.

As the Industrial Revolution dawned, Scotland became a power-house: Textiles were woven in large

to Church fathers, who were particularly displeased with his love life (of Burns' dozen children, nine were by his eventual wife, the others by various servants and barmaids).

After achieving fame and wealth, Burns never lost touch with the concerns of the Scottish people, championing such radical ideas as social equality and economic justice. Burns bravely and loudly supported the French and American revolutions, which inspired one of his most beloved poems, "A Man's a Man for A' That," and even an ode to George Washington—all while other writers were being shipped off to Australia for similar beliefs. While his social causes cost him some aristocratic friends, it cemented his popularity among the masses, and not just within Scotland (he became, and remains, especially beloved in Russia).

Intent on preserving Scotland's rich musical and lyrical traditions, Burns traveled the countryside collecting traditional Scottish ballads. If it weren't for Burns, we'd have to come up with a different song to sing on New Year's Eve—he's the one who found, reworked, and popularized "Auld Lang Syne." His championing of Scottish culture came at a critical time: England had recently and finally crushed Scotland's last hopes of independence, and the Highland clan system was nearing its end. Burns lent the Scots dialect a new prestige, and the scrappy Scottish people a reinvigorated identity. (The official Burns website, www.robertburns.org, features a full collection of his works.)

Burns died at 37 of a heart condition likely exacerbated by so much hard labor (all the carousing probably hadn't helped, either). By that time, his fortune was largely spent, but his celebrity was going strong—around 10,000 people attended his burial. Even the Church eventually overcame its disapproval, installing a window in his honor at St. Giles' Cathedral. In 2009, his nation voted Burns "Greatest Ever Scot" in a TV poll. And every January 25 (the poet's birthday), on Burns Night, Scots gather to recite his songs and poems, tuck into some haggis ("chieftain o' the puddin' race," according to Burns), and raise their whisky to friendship, and Scotland.

factories, powered by Watt's steam engine, which were fueled by Lanarkshire coal, then exported on iron ships built in the Clyde shipyards. Scotland was a global leader in pig iron exports and shipbuilding. Glasgow—an industrial center—overtook genteel Edinburgh as Scotland's biggest city. Dundee boomed, thanks to its skill for processing jute, which could be turned into rope, sacks, sails, and other essential items for a seafaring culture (for more, visit Dundee's fascinating Jute Museum—see page 223).

In the early 19th century, the Scottish civil engineer Thomas Telford (1757-1834)—nicknamed "The Colossus of Roads"—designed roadways, bridges, canals, and locks to tie together the

Scottish Castles at a Glance

Scotland is a land of castles. But after seeing several, they start to blend together. To help you choose, here's a rundown of the defining characteristics of the castles listed in this book. These are listed roughly in order of worthiness.

▲▲▲**Edinburgh Castle** The granddaddy of them all, with good exhibits, historic chapels, royal apartments, the "Honours of Scotland" (crown jewels), a very big cannon, and lots of crowds. See page 34.

▲▲**Palace of Holyroodhouse** (Edinburgh) Historic palace at the foot of the Royal Mile, with ties to Mary, Queen of Scots, and still host to Queen Elizabeth II's annual Garden Party. See page 75.

▲▲**Stirling Castle** The historic home of Scotland's Stuart dynasty, with rebuilt rooms, fine exhibits, and a stunning and strategic location overlooking the site of many of Scotland's most important moments. See page 174.

▲**Balmoral Castle** (in eastern Scotland) The Queen's summer Highland home, with great Cairngorms scenery and fine gardens...but only one (ho-hum) room open to the public. See page 344.

▲**Dunvegan Castle** (Isle of Skye) Remote, endearingly ragtag home of Clan MacLeod, with fine rugged gardens. See page 373.

▲**Cawdor Castle** (near Inverness) Charming castle with personality and purported ties to Macbeth. See page 318.

remotest corners of Scotland, effectively shrinking the country for the modern era. (His masterpiece, the Caledonian Canal, is easy to see between Fort William and Inverness—see page 322.)

Meanwhile, just a few decades after the harsh post-Jacobite crackdown, Highland culture began to enjoy a renaissance. By the late 18th century, people were already romanticizing Bonnie Prince Charlie (further spurred by Sir Walter Scott's 1814 historical novel *Waverley*). In the Romantic Age of the 19th century, tartans, kilts, bagpipes, and other aspects of Highland culture made a big comeback. In 1852, Queen Victoria and Prince Albert purchased Balmoral Castle (in the shadow of the Highlands' Cairngorm Mountains—see page 344), and proceeded to renovate it in a fanciful interpretation of the Scottish Baronial style. This signaled not just an acceptance, but a nostalgic embrace, of traditional Highland

▲**Glamis Castle** (north of Dundee) The Queen Mother's home castle, with a striking exterior and an enjoyably idiosyncratic interior. See page 225.

▲**Eilean Donan Castle** (near Isle of Skye) One of Scotland's most scenically set castles, on an islet in a loch. See page 381.

▲**Inveraray Castle** (near Oban) Classic castle exterior and a cozy interior used to film scenes from *Downton Abbey*. See page 268.

▲**Urquhart Castle** (on Loch Ness) Mostly ruined castle perched over Loch Ness. See page 323.

Doune Castle (near Stirling) Otherwise underwhelming castle with ties to *Outlander* and Monty Python, and an entertaining Terry Jones-narrated audioguide. See page 194.

Dunnottar Castle Ruins stunningly set on a huge, bald rock towering over Scotland's east coast. See page 348.

Armadale Castle (Isle of Skye) Ruined Clan Donald mansion with fine gardens and a museum of clan history—fascinating to Mac-Donalds, dull to most others. See page 381.

St. Andrews Castle Ruined shell overlooking the beach and offering an explanation of castle warfare techniques. See page 209.

Blair Castle (near Pitlochry, in eastern Scotland) Crenellated aristocratic residence that's dull inside but handy to see. See page 338.

culture, just a century after it had been dismantled by the same monarchy.

This Scottish Baronial style, popularized by Sir Walter Scott, was a Romantic, Neo-Gothic celebration of medieval Highland castles. It features a stout sandstone structure with pointy turrets,

fanciful finials, round towers, crenellated battlements, and narrow windows—based on Scotland's 16th-century tower houses, which were in turn based on the châteaux of France. In many ways, this is Scotland's signature architectural style: You'll see it everywhere, from the urban streets of Glasgow, to castles on the remotest fringes of Scotland, to a fictional school for witchcraft and wizardry.

THE 20th CENTURY: SCOTLAND AT WAR

By the 20th century, Scotland was the workhorse of Great Britain. And as bastion of the working class, there's little wonder that the

government was typically controlled by the Labour Party. James Ramsay MacDonald was PM of the UK from 1929 until 1935.

Scotland was also the workhorse of the British military—never more so than during World War I, when Scottish lads were disproportionately massacred on the battlefields of Europe. Scotland, with about one-tenth of the UK's population, had double the per-capita deaths of the other parts of Britain. One out of every four Scottish soldiers never came home. Earl Haig of Edinburgh commanded British

troops—victoriously—through some of the most gruesome trench warfare in history, at Flanders Fields in Belgium. As you travel around Scotland, you'll find a WWI memorial in every tiny village—with unsettlingly long lists of local boys who sacrificed the utmost for Britain.

On most of these memorials, you'll find a little "addendum" plaque listing WWII deaths. While the Blitz was devastating to London and other English towns closer to the Continent (such as Coventry), the impact of World War II was less felt in the far-north reaches of Scotland—though Scapa Flow, a natural harbor surrounded by the Orkney Islands, was the remote headquarters of the British navy in both World Wars (see page 406).

SCOTLAND TODAY: DEVOLUTION AND SCOTTISH PRIDE

By the last decades of the 20th century, change was percolating in Scotland. Since the 1980s, the main topic of Scottish political debate has become "devolution": the push to "devolve" authority over Scottish affairs from London to Scotland proper. The general sea change in European

culture over the last few generations of respecting smaller, under-dog nations—even at the expense of big, historically dominant countries—has been felt here as much as anywhere.

For centuries—essentially ever since the crushed Jacobite up-risings—the notion of Scottish independence was rarely taken seri-ously. That began to change in the mid- to late-20th century. The independence-minded Scottish National Party (SNP), which had been founded as a fringe movement in 1934, won its first seat in the UK parliament in 1967. The discovery of North Sea oil in the late 1960s gave this often-overlooked corner of the United King-dom some serious economic clout, and with it, more political pull. Pro-independence factions gained traction with the slogan "It's Scotland's oil," proposing a windfall for Scots suffering through post-industrial rot and economic malaise.

The SNP gained seats in the UK parliament and pushed for a 1979 referendum on devolution. The measure won with 52 per-cent of the vote, but turnout was too low to legitimize the result. Through the 1980s and most of the 1990s, anti-independence UK prime ministers Margaret Thatcher and John Major downplayed devolution talk. But the SNP and other agitators ensured that the idea never completely faded.

When Prime Minister Tony Blair took office in May 1997, his Labour government (mindful of Scotland's strong working-class roots and long-standing support for the Labour Party) was more open to the idea of devolution. And in a referendum in September 1997, three out of every four Scots voted "yes" to the statement, "I agree that there should be a Scottish parliament." In response, the UK parliament passed the Scotland Act 1998, creating a Scot-tish parliament that convened to much fanfare in Edinburgh on May 12, 1999 (with Donald Dewar becoming the first-ever First Minister of Scotland). For the first time since the Act of Union in 1707, Scotland had its own parliament. The Scottish Parliament building—with mind-bending architecture and an inviting gar-den—opened in 2004 across the street from the Queen's residence at the Palace of Holyroodhouse (it's free to tour the interior—see page 48).

With devolution, Edinburgh once again has become the actual self-governing capital of Scotland. The Scotland Act 2012 further expanded the mandate of the Scottish parliament, and today, the list of "devolved" issues (under local Scottish control) includes edu-cation, the environment, health and social services, housing, and tourism. Other matters—including foreign policy, defense, energy policy, and social security—remain "reserved" for the central UK government.

Today the SNP is the most powerful party in Scotland (con-trolling 64 out of 129 seats in the Scottish parliament), and the third-largest party in the UK (controlling 56 out of 650 seats in the UK's House of Commons; there are only 59 House of Commons seats for Scotland). Its leader, Nicola Sturgeon of Glasgow, is the public face of the SNP, giving voice to independence-minded Scots in TV debates during the 2015 UK general election.

Today's supporters of Scottish independence take up ballots, not broadswords. On September 18, 2014, the Scottish people went to the polls to vote on a simple question: "Should Scotland be an independent country?" Right up until the day of the referendum, many observers believed that Scotland was about to declare its independence, which would have opened up a whole range of questions about how two prosperous and powerful countries could peacefully disentangle themselves. But the results were clear: 55.3 percent of Scottish residents voted "no." While Scotland will remain part of the United Kingdom—for now—the referendum signaled to many in the greater UK that Scotland must be taken seriously. During the campaign, the opposition promised Scotland even more political autonomy if it voted "no." While Scottish nationalists want to fast-track these new powers, it's not clear how quickly it will happen. One thing is sure: The vote may be over, but the nationalists aren't done fighting yet.

NOTABLE SCOTS

Throughout Scotland's history, the country has been a center of both scientific and creative thought. The 18th century age of Scottish Enlightenment in particular was a hotbed of intellectual progress—I've listed the greats of that era earlier in this chapter (on page 423).

Famous artistic Scots include royal portraitist Henry Raeburn (whose 1790s ice-skating minister, *The Reverend Robert Walker Skating on Duddington Loch*, still adorns modern-day Christmas cards); 20th-century landscape painter William MacTaggart; and Scotland's greatest architect Charles Rennie Mackintosh (see sidebar on page 142).

Scottish entertainers are everywhere, from the original James Bond (Sean Connery) and the young Obi-Wan Kenobi (Ewan McGregor), to two Dr. Whos (David Tennant and Peter Capaldi). Actors James McAvoy, Gerard Butler, Karen Gillan, Tilda Swinton, Billy Connolly, Craig Ferguson, Robert Carlyle, Robbie Coltrane, and Alan Cumming all hail from Scotland, as do musical artists the Proclaimers, Annie Lennox, Cocteau Twins, the Jesus and Mary Chain, Belle and Sebastian, and Franz Ferdinand; and sports stars Andy Murray (tennis), Catriona Matthews (golfer), and Jackie Stewart (auto racing). Scotland's literary tradition is particularly strong (see sidebar on page 68), with writers from Robert Burns to Sherlock Holmes creator Sir Arthur Conan Doyle making the country proud.

On the scientific front, Peter Higgs was researching at the University of Edinburgh in the 1960s when he speculated on the existence of a subatomic "God particle" that might tie together many other theories on the structure of the universe.

Great people of Scottish descent fill American and Canadian history books, among them James Monroe, Washington Irving, Andrew Carnegie, Alexander Graham Bell, Jack Daniel, Ronald Reagan, Neil Armstrong, and Bill Gates. Whether it's as part of the United Kingdom, or as its own, increasingly independent nation, it's clear that Scotland's impact on the world has only just begun.

PRACTICALITIES

This chapter covers the practical skills of European travel: how to get tourist information, pay for purchases, sightsee efficiently, find good-value accommodations, eat affordably but well, use technology wisely, and get between destinations smoothly. To round out your knowledge, check out "Resources."

Tourist Information

Before your trip, start with the **Visit Scotland website,** which contains a wealth of knowledge on destinations, activities, accommodations, and transport in Scotland (www.visitscotland.com).

In Scotland, a good first stop is generally the tourist information office (abbreviated **TI** in this book). Officially called Visit Scotland Information Centres, these are all operated by the national tourist board (look for the purple signs). They're found even in very small and remote places, where they're called "information points."

Be aware that TIs are in business to help

you enjoy spending money in their town. (Once upon a time, they were actually information services, but today some have become promoters masquerading as TIs.) While this corrupts much of their advice—and you can get plenty of information online—I still make a point to swing by the local TI upon arrival in a new town. Even if they are overly commercial, TIs continue to be good places to confirm opening times, pick up a city map, and get information on public transit (including bus and train schedules), walking tours, special events, and nightlife. Stop in with a list of questions and a proposed plan to double-check. Many TIs have information on the entire country or at least the region, so try to pick up maps for destinations you'll be visiting later in your trip. If you're arriving in town after the TI closes, call ahead or pick up a map in a neighboring town.

For all the help TIs offer, steer clear of their room-finding services (bloated prices, booking fees, no opinions, and commissions that come from the pocket of your B&B host).

Other Helpful Websites for Scotland: To learn more about places around Scotland, see www.undiscoveredscotland.co.uk. For hiking advice, see www.walkhighlands.co.uk.

Travel Tips

Emergency and Medical Help: In Scotland, dial 999 or 112 for police help or a medical emergency. If you get sick, do as the locals do: Go to a pharmacy and see a "chemist" (pharmacist) for advice. Or ask at your hotel for help—they know of the nearest medical and emergency services.

Theft or Loss: To replace a passport, you'll need to go in person to a US embassy (see page 489). If your credit and debit cards disappear, cancel and replace them (see "Damage Control for Lost Cards" on page 437). File a police report, either on the spot or within a day or two; you'll need it to submit an insurance claim for lost or stolen rail passes or travel gear, and it can help with replacing your passport or credit and debit cards. For more information, see www.ricksteves.com/help. To minimize the effects of loss, back up your digital photos and other files frequently.

Time Zones: Scotland, which is one hour earlier than most of continental Europe, is five/eight hours ahead of the East/West Coasts of the US. The exceptions are the beginning and end of Daylight Saving Time: Scotland and Europe "spring forward" the last Sunday in March (two weeks after most of North America) and "fall back" the last Sunday in October (one week before North America). For a handy online time converter, see www. timeanddate.com/worldclock.

Business Hours: Most stores are open Monday through Saturday (roughly 9:00 or 10:00 to 17:00 or 18:00). In cities, some stores stay open later on Wednesday or Thursday (until 19:00 or 20:00). Some big-city department stores are open later throughout the week (Mon-Sat until about 21:00). Sundays have the same pros and cons as they do for travelers in the US: Sightseeing attractions are generally open, many street markets are lively with shoppers, banks and many shops are closed, public transportation options are fewer (for example, no bus service to or from smaller towns), and there's no rush hour. Friday and Saturday evenings are lively; Sunday evenings are quiet.

Watt's Up? Scotland's electrical system is 220 volts, instead of North America's 110 volts. Most newer electronics (such as laptops, battery chargers, and hair dryers) convert automatically, so you won't need a converter, but you will need an adapter plug with three square prongs, sold inexpensively at travel stores in the US. Avoid bringing older appliances that don't automatically convert voltage; instead, ask to borrow one from your B&B or buy a cheap replacement in Scotland. Low-cost hairdryers and other small appliances are sold at Superdrug and Boots (ask your hotelier for the closest branch). Or pop into a department store.

Discounts: Discounts (called "concessions" or "concs" in Scotland) are not listed in this book. However, many sights, buses, and trains offer discounts to youths (up to age 18), students (with proper identification cards, www.isic.org), families, seniors (loosely defined as retirees or those willing to call themselves seniors), and groups of 10 or more. Always ask. Some discounts are available only for citizens of the European Union (EU).

Money

This section offers advice on how to pay for purchases on your trip (including getting cash from ATMs and paying with plastic), dealing with lost or stolen cards, VAT (sales tax) refunds, and tipping.

WHAT TO BRING

Bring both a credit card and a debit card. You'll use the debit card at cash machines (ATMs) to withdraw local cash for most purchases, and the credit card to pay for larger items. Some travelers carry a third card, in case one gets demagnetized or eaten by a temperamental machine.

Exchange Rate

1 British pound (£1) = about $1.60

While the euro (€) is now the currency of most of Europe, Scotland (and all of Britain) is sticking with its pound sterling. The British pound (£), also called a "quid," is broken into 100 pence (p). Pence means "cents." You'll find coins ranging from 1p to £2 and bills from £5 to £50.

While the pound sterling is used throughout the UK, Scotland prints its own bills, which are decorated with Scottish landmarks and VIPs. These are interchangeable with British pound notes, which are widely circulated here. The coins are the same throughout the UK.

To convert prices from pounds to dollars, add about 60 percent: £20 = about $32, £50 = about $80. (Check www. oanda.com for the latest exchange rates.)

For an emergency stash, bring several hundred dollars in hard cash in $20 bills. If you need to exchange the bills, go to a bank; avoid using currency-exchange booths because of their lousy rates and/or outrageous (and often hard-to-spot) fees.

CASH

Cash is just as desirable in Scotland as it is at home. Small businesses (B&Bs, mom-and-pop cafés, shops, etc.) prefer that you pay your bills with cash. Some vendors will charge you extra for using a credit card, some won't accept foreign credit cards, and some won't take any credit cards at all. Cash is the best—and sometimes only—way to pay for cheap food, bus fare, taxis, and local guides.

Throughout Europe, ATMs are the standard way for travelers to get cash. They work just like they do at home. To withdraw money from an ATM (known as a "cashpoint" in Scotland), you'll need a debit card (ideally with a Visa or MasterCard logo for maximum usability), plus a PIN code (numeric and four digits). For increased security, shield the keypad when entering your PIN code, and don't use an ATM if anything on the front of the machine looks loose or damaged (a sign that someone may have attached a "skimming" device to capture account information). Try to withdraw large sums of money to reduce the number of per-transaction bank fees you'll pay.

When possible, use ATMs located outside banks—a thief is less likely to target a cash machine near surveillance cameras, and if your card is munched by a machine, you can go inside for help. Stay away from "independent" ATMs such as Travelex, Euronet, YourCash, Cardpoint, and Cashzone, which charge huge commissions, have terrible exchange rates, and may try to trick users with "dynamic currency conversion" (described at the end of "Credit and Debit Cards," next). Although you can use a credit card to withdraw cash at an ATM, this comes with high bank fees and only makes sense in an emergency.

While traveling, if you want to monitor your accounts online to detect any unauthorized transactions, be sure to use a secure connection (see page 463).

Even in bonnie Scotland, pickpockets target tourists. To safeguard your cash, wear a money belt—a pouch with a strap that you buckle around your waist like a belt and tuck under your clothes. Keep your cash, credit cards, and passport secure in your money belt, and carry only a day's spending money in your front pocket.

CREDIT AND DEBIT CARDS

For purchases, Visa and MasterCard are more commonly accepted than American Express. Just like at home, credit or debit cards work easily at larger hotels, restaurants, and shops. I typically use my debit card to withdraw cash to pay for most purchases. I use my credit card sparingly: to book hotel reservations, to buy advance tickets for events or sights, to cover major expenses (such as car rentals or plane tickets), and to pay for things online or near the end of my trip (to avoid another visit to the ATM). While you could instead use a debit card for these purchases, a credit card offers a greater degree of fraud protection.

Ask Your Credit- or Debit-Card Company: Before your trip, contact the company that issued your debit or credit cards.

• Confirm that your **card will work overseas,** and alert them that you'll be using it in Europe; otherwise, they may deny transactions if they perceive unusual spending patterns.

• Ask for the specifics on transaction **fees.** When you use your credit or debit card—either for purchases or ATM withdrawals—you'll typically be charged additional "international transaction" fees of up to 3 percent (1 percent is normal) plus $5 per transaction. If your card's fees seem high, consider getting a different card just for your trip: Capital One (www.capitalone.com) and most credit unions have low-to-no international fees.

• Verify your daily ATM **withdrawal limit,** and if necessary, ask your bank to adjust it. I prefer a high limit that allows me to take out more cash at each ATM stop and save on bank fees; some travelers prefer to set a lower limit in case their card is stolen. Note that foreign banks also set maximum withdrawal limits for their ATMs (£300 is usually the maximum).

• Get your bank's emergency **phone number** in the US (but not its 800 number, which isn't accessible from overseas) to call collect if you have a problem.

• Ask for your credit card's **PIN** in case you need to make an emergency cash withdrawal or encounter Europe's chip-and-PIN system; the bank won't tell you your PIN over the phone, so allow time for it to be mailed to you.

Magnetic-Stripe Versus Chip-and-PIN Credit Cards: Europeans are increasingly using chip-and-PIN credit cards embedded with an electronic security chip and requiring a four-digit PIN. Your American-style card (with just the old-fashioned magnetic stripe) will work fine in most places. But it might not work at unattended payment machines, such as those at train and subway stations, toll plazas, parking garages, bike-rental kiosks, and gas pumps. If you have problems, try entering your card's PIN, look for a machine that takes cash, or find a clerk who can process the transaction manually.

Major US banks are beginning to offer credit cards with chips. Many of these are not true chip-and-PIN cards, but instead are chip-and-signature cards, for which your signature verifies your identity. These cards should work for live transactions and at most payment machines, but won't work for offline transactions such as at unattended gas pumps. If you're concerned, ask if your bank offers a true chip-and-PIN card. Andrews Federal Credit Union (www.andrewsfcu.org) and the State Department Federal Credit Union (www.sdfcu.org) offer these cards and are open to all US residents.

No matter what kind of card you have, it pays to carry pounds; you can always use an ATM to withdraw cash with your magnetic-stripe debit card.

Dynamic Currency Conversion: If merchants or hoteliers offer to convert your purchase price into dollars (called dynamic currency conversion, or DCC), refuse this "service." You'll pay even more in fees for the expensive convenience of seeing your charge in dollars. If your receipt shows the total in dollars only, ask for the transaction to be processed in the local currency. If the clerk refuses, pay in cash—or mark the receipt "local currency not offered" and dispute the DCC charges with your bank.

Some ATMs and retailers try to confuse customers by presenting DCC in misleading terms. If an ATM offers to "lock in" or "guarantee" your conversion rate, choose "proceed without conversion." Other prompts might state, "You can be charged in dollars: Press YES for dollars, NO for GBP." Always choose the local currency in these situations.

DAMAGE CONTROL FOR LOST CARDS

If you lose your credit, debit, or ATM card, you can stop people from using your card by reporting the loss immediately to the respective global customer-assistance centers. Call these 24-hour

US numbers collect: Visa (tel. 303/967-1096), MasterCard (tel. 636/722-7111), and American Express (tel. 336/393-1111). In Scotland, to make a collect call to the US, dial 0-800-89-0011. Press zero or stay on the line for an operator. European toll-free numbers (listed by country) can be found at the websites for Visa and MasterCard. Diner's Club has offices in Britain (tel. 0845-862-2937) and the US (tel. 514/877-1577; call collect).

Try to have this information ready: full card number, whether you are the primary or secondary cardholder, the cardholder's name exactly as printed on the card, billing address, home phone number, circumstances of the loss or theft, and identification verification (your birth date, your mother's maiden name, or your Social Security number—memorize this, don't carry a copy). If you are the secondary cardholder, you'll also need to provide the primary cardholder's identification-verification details. You can generally receive a temporary card within two or three business days in Europe (see www.ricksteves.com/help for more).

If you report your loss within two days, you typically won't be responsible for any unauthorized transactions on your account, although many banks charge a liability fee of $50.

TIPPING

Tipping in Scotland isn't as automatic and generous as it is in the US. For special service, tips are appreciated, but not expected. As in the US, the proper amount depends on your resources, tipping philosophy, and the circumstances, but some general guidelines apply.

Restaurants: If a service charge is included in the bill, it's not necessary to tip. Otherwise, it's appropriate to tip about 10-12.5 percent. (For more information, see page 453).

Taxis: For a typical ride, round up your fare a bit (for instance, if the fare is £4.50, pay £5). If the cabbie hauls your bags and zips you to the airport to help you catch your flight, you might want to toss in a little more. But if you feel like you're being driven in circles or otherwise ripped off, skip the tip.

Services: In general, if someone in the service industry does a super job for you, a tip of a pound or so is appropriate...but not required. If you're not sure whether (or how much) to tip for a service, ask a local for advice.

GETTING A VAT REFUND

Wrapped into the purchase price of your Scottish souvenirs is a Value-Added Tax (VAT) of about 20 percent. You're entitled to get most of that tax back if you purchase more than £30 (about $48) worth of goods at a store that participates in the VAT-refund scheme (although individual stores can require that you spend more). Typically, you must ring up the minimum at a single retailer—you can't add up your purchases from various shops to reach the required amount.

Getting your refund is straightforward and, if you buy a substantial amount of souvenirs, well worth the hassle. If you're lucky, the merchant will subtract the tax when you make your purchase. (This is more likely to occur if the store ships the goods to your home.) Otherwise, you'll need to:

Get the paperwork. Have the merchant completely fill out the necessary refund document (either an official VAT customs form, or the shop or refund company's own version of it). You'll have to present your passport at the store. Get the paperwork done before you leave the shop to ensure you'll have everything you need (including your original sales receipt).

Get your stamp at the border or airport. Process your VAT document at your last stop in the European Union (such as at the airport) with the customs agent who deals with VAT refunds. Arrive an additional hour early before you need to check in for your flight to allow time to find the local customs office—and to stand in line. It's best to keep your purchases in your carry-on. If they're too large or dangerous to carry on (such as knives), pack them in your checked bags and alert the check-in agent. You'll be sent (with your tagged bag) to a customs desk outside security; someone will examine your bag, stamp your paperwork, and put your bag on the belt. You're not supposed to use your purchased goods before you leave. If you show up at customs wearing your new Highland kilt, officials might look the other way—or deny you a refund.

Collect your refund. You'll need to return your stamped document to the retailer or its representative. Many merchants work with a service that has offices at major airports, ports, or border crossings. These services, which extract a 4 percent fee, can refund your money immediately in cash or credit your card (within two billing cycles). If the retailer handles VAT refunds directly, it's up to you to contact the merchant for your refund. You can mail the documents from home, or more quickly, from your point of departure (using an envelope you've prepared in advance or one that's been provided by the merchant). You'll then have to wait—it can take months.

CUSTOMS FOR AMERICAN SHOPPERS

You are allowed to take home $800 worth of items per person duty-free, once every 31 days. As for food, you can take home many processed and packaged foods: vacuum-packed cheeses, dried herbs, jams, baked goods, candy, chocolate, oil, vinegar, mustard, and honey. Fresh fruits and vegetables and most meats are not allowed, with exceptions for some canned items. As for alcohol, you can bring in one liter duty-free (it can be packed securely in your checked luggage, along with any other liquid-containing items).

To bring alcohol (or liquid-packed foods) in your carry-on bag on your flight home, buy it at a duty-free shop at the airport. You'll increase your odds of getting it onto a connecting flight if it's packaged in a "STEB"—a secure, tamper-evident bag. But stay away from liquids in opaque, ceramic, or metallic containers, which usually cannot be successfully screened (STEB or no STEB).

For details on allowable goods, customs rules, and duty rates, visit www.cbp.gov.

Sightseeing

Sightseeing can be hard work. Use these tips to make your visits to Scotland's finest sights meaningful, fun, efficient, and painless.

PLAN AHEAD

Set up an itinerary that allows you to fit in all your must-see sights. Most sights keep stable hours, but you can easily confirm the latest by checking with the TI or visiting museum websites.

Don't put off visiting a must-see sight—you never know when a place will close unexpectedly for a holiday, strike, or royal audience. Many museums are closed or have reduced hours at least a few days a year, especially on holidays such as Christmas, New Year's, and Bank Holiday Mondays in May and August. A list of holidays is on page 490; check online for possible museum closures during your trip. Off-season, many museums have shorter hours.

Going at the right time helps avoid crowds. This book offers tips on the best times to see specific sights. Try visiting popular sights very early or very late. Evening visits are usually peaceful, with fewer crowds. For tips on sights or events that should be booked in advance, see page 11.

Study up. To get the most out of the self-guided tours and sight descriptions in this book, read them before you visit.

AT SIGHTS

Here's what you can typically expect:

Entering: Be warned that you may not be allowed to enter if you arrive 30 to 60 minutes before closing time. And guards start ushering people out well before the actual closing time, so don't save the best for last.

Some important sights have a security check, where you must open your bag or send it through a metal detector. Some sights require you to check daypacks and coats. (If you'd rather not check your daypack, try carrying it tucked under your arm like a purse as you enter.)

At admission desks, you may see references to "Gift Aid"—a tax-deduction scheme that benefits museums—but this only concerns UK taxpayers.

Photography: If the museum's photo policy isn't clearly posted, ask a guard. Generally, taking photos without a flash or tripod is allowed. Some sights ban photos altogether, including whisky distilleries, supposedly because "a spark from your camera could ignite the alcohol fumes." (It may have more to do with inter-distillery competition.)

Special Exhibits: Museums may show special exhibits in addition to their permanent collection. An extra fee, which may not be optional, might be assessed for these shows.

Expect Changes: Artwork can be on tour, on loan, out sick, or shifted at the whim of the curator. Pick up a floor plan as you enter, and ask museum staff if you can't find a particular item.

Audioguides and Apps: Many sights rent audioguides, which generally offer excellent recorded descriptions (about £4). If you bring your own earbuds, you can enjoy better sound and avoid holding the device to your ear. To save money, bring a Y-jack and share one audioguide with your travel partner. Increasingly, museums and sights offer apps—often free—that you can download to your mobile device (check their websites). I've produced a free, downloadable ∩ audio tour for Edinburgh's Royal Mile. For more on my audio tours, see page 10.

Guided tours are most likely to occur during peak season (usually £3-8 and widely ranging in quality). Some sights also run short introductory videos featuring their highlights and history. These are generally well worth your time and a great place to start your visit.

Services: Important sights and cathedrals may have an on-site café or cafeteria (usually a handy place to rejuvenate during a long visit). The WCs at sights are free and nearly always clean.

Before Leaving: At the gift shop, scan the postcard rack or thumb through a guidebook to be sure you haven't overlooked something that you'd like to see.

Every sight or museum offers more than what is covered in this book. Use the information in this book as an introduction—not the final word.

SIGHTSEEING MEMBERSHIPS

Many sights in Scotland are managed by either Historic Scotland or the National Trust for Scotland. Each organization has a combo-deal that can save some money for busy sightseers.

Historic Scotland's Explorer Pass covers its 78 properties, including Edinburgh Castle, Stirling Castle, and several sites on Orkney (£30/3 days out of any 5, £40/7 days out of any 14, www.historic-scotland.gov.uk/explorer). This pass allows you to skip the ticket-buying lines at Edinburgh and Stirling castles.

Membership in the **National Trust for Scotland** covers more than 350 historic houses, manors, and gardens throughout Great Britain, including 100 properties in Scotland. From the US, it's easy to join online through the Royal Oak Foundation, the National Trust's American affiliate (one-year membership: $65 for one person, $95 for two, family and student memberships, www.royal-oak.org). For more on National Trust for Scotland properties, see www.nts.org.uk.

Factors to Consider: An advantage to these deals is that you'll feel free to dip into lesser sights without considering the cost of admission. But remember that your kids already get in free or cheaply at most places, and people over 60 get discounted prices at many sights. If you're traveling by car and can get to the remote sights, you're more likely to get your money's worth out of a pass or membership, especially during peak season (Easter-Oct), when all the sights are open.

Sleeping

I favor hotels and restaurants that are handy to your sightseeing activities. Rather than list accommodations scattered throughout a town, I choose places in my favorite neighborhoods. My recommendations run the gamut, from dorm beds to fancy rooms with all the comforts. In Scotland, small bed-and-breakfast places (B&Bs) generally provide the best value, though I also include some bigger hotels. Outside of pricey big cities, you can expect to find good B&B doubles for £70-110, including cooked breakfast and tax. Bigger cities, swanky splurge B&Bs, and big hotels may cost 20-30 percent more.

A major feature of the Sleeping sections in this book is my extensive and opinionated listing of good-value rooms. I like places that are clean, central, relatively quiet at night, reasonably priced, friendly, small enough to have a hands-on owner and stable staff, run with a respect for Scottish traditions, and not listed in other guidebooks. (For me, meeting six out of these eight criteria means it's a keeper.) I'm more impressed by a convenient location and a fun-loving philosophy than flat-screen TVs and a pricey laundry service.

Scotland has a rating system for hotels and B&Bs. Its stars are supposed to imply quality, but I find they mean only that the place is paying dues to the tourist board. Rating systems often have little to do with value.

Book your accommodations well in advance, especially if you want to stay at one of my top listings or if you'll be traveling during busy times. See page 490 for a list of major holidays and festivals; for tips on making reservations, see page 450.

Some people make reservations as they travel, calling hotels and B&Bs a few days to a week before their arrival. If you'd rather travel without any reservations at all, you'll have greater success snaring rooms if you arrive at your destination early in the day. If you anticipate crowds (weekends are worst) on the day you want to check in, call hotels at about 9:00 or 10:00, when the receptionist knows who'll be checking out and which rooms will be available.

RATES AND DEALS

I've described my recommended accommodations using a Sleep Code (see sidebar). The prices I list are for one-night stays in peak season, include a hearty breakfast unless otherwise noted, and assume you're booking directly with the B&B or hotel (not through a TI or online hotel-booking engine). Booking services extract a commission from the hotel, which logically closes the door on special deals. Book direct.

My recommended accommodations generally have a website (often with a built-in booking form) and an email address; you can expect a response within a day (and often sooner).

If you're on a budget, it's smart to contact several hotels to ask for their best price. Comparison-shop and make your choice. While B&B prices tend to be fairly predictable, large hotels use "dynamic pricing," a computer-generated system that predicts the demand for particular days and sets prices accordingly: High-demand days can be more than double the price of low-demand days. This makes it impossible for a guidebook to list anything more accurate than a wide range of prices. I regret this trend. While you can assume that hotels listed in this book are good, it's difficult to say which ones are the better value unless you email to confirm the price.

As you look over the listings, you'll notice that some accommodations promise special prices to Rick Steves readers. To get these rates, you must book direct (that is, not through a booking site like TripAdvisor or Booking.com), mention this book when you reserve, and then show the book upon arrival. Rick Steves discounts apply to readers with ebooks as well as printed books. Because I trust hotels to honor this, please let me know if you don't

Sleep Code

(£1 = about $1.60)

Price Rankings

To help you easily sort through my listings, I've divided the accommodations into three categories based on the highest price for a basic double room with bath during high season:

$$$	**Higher Priced**
$$	**Moderately Priced**
$	**Lower Priced**

I always rate hostels as $, whether or not they have double rooms, because they have the cheapest beds in town.

Prices can change without notice; verify the hotel's current rates online or by email. For the best prices, always book directly with the hotel.

Abbreviations

To pack maximum information into minimum space, I use the following code to describe accommodations in this book. Prices are listed per room, not per person. When a price range is given for a type of room (such as double rooms listing for £80-120), it means the price fluctuates with the season, size of room, or length of stay; expect to pay the upper end for peak-season stays.

S = Single room (or price for one person in a double)

D = Double or twin room. "Double beds" can be two twins sheeted together and are usually big enough for nonromantic couples.

T = Triple (generally a double bed with a single)

Q = Quad (usually two double beds; adding an extra child's bed to a T is usually cheaper)

b = Private bathroom with toilet and shower or tub

According to this code, a couple staying at a "Db-£90" hotel would pay a total of £90 (about $145) per night for a double room with a private bathroom. Unless otherwise noted, breakfast is included, and credit cards are accepted. For most places, the rates I list include the 20 percent VAT tax—but it's smart to ask when you book your room.

There's almost always Wi-Fi and/or a guest computer available, and it's generally free.

receive a listed discount. Note, though, that discounts understandably may not be applied to promotional rates.

In general, prices can soften if you do any of the following: Offer to pay cash, stay at least three nights, or mention this book. You can also try asking for a cheaper room or a discount, or offer to skip breakfast.

Staying in B&Bs and small hotels can save money over sleeping in big hotels. Chain hotels can be even cheaper, but they don't include breakfast. When comparing prices between chain hotels and B&Bs, remember you're getting two breakfasts (about a £25 value) for each double room at a B&B.

When establishing prices, confirm if the charge is per person or per room (if a price is too good to be true, it's probably per person). In this book, however, all room prices are listed per room, not per person.

TYPES OF ACCOMMODATIONS
B&Bs and Small Hotels

B&Bs and small hotels are generally family-run places with fewer amenities but more character than a conventional hotel. Most Scottish B&Bs have anywhere from three to eight rooms. The philosophy of the management determines the character of a place more than its size and facilities offered. I avoid places run as a business by absentee owners. My top listings are run by people who enjoy welcoming the world to their breakfast table.

Compared to hotels, B&Bs and guesthouses give you double the cultural intimacy for half the price. While you may lose some of the conveniences of a hotel—such as fancy lobbies, in-room phones, and frequent bedsheet changes—I happily make the trade-off for the personal touches, whether it's joining my hosts for afternoon tea or relaxing by a common fireplace at the end of the day. If  you have a reasonable but limited budget, skip hotels and go the B&B way.

Many B&Bs take credit cards, but may add the card service fee to your bill (about 3 percent). If you do need to pay cash for your room, plan ahead to have enough on hand when you check out.

B&Bs and small hotels come with their own etiquette and quirks. Keep in mind that owners are at the whim of their guests—if you're getting up early, so are they; and if you check in late, they'll wait up for you. Most B&Bs either have set check-in times (usually twice a day, in the morning and late afternoon), or will want to know when to expect you (call or email ahead to let them know).

B&B proprietors are selective about the guests they invite in for the night. Many do not welcome children. If you'll be staying for more than one night, you are a "desirable." In popular weekend-getaway spots, you're unlikely to find a place to take you for Saturday night only. If my listings are full, ask for guidance. Mentioning this book can help. Owners usually work together and can call up

The Good and Bad of Online Reviews

User-generated travel review websites—such as TripAdvisor, Booking.com, and Yelp—have quickly become a huge player in the travel industry. These sites give you access to actual reports—good and bad—from travelers who have experienced the hotel, restaurant, tour, or attraction.

My hotelier friends in Europe are in awe of these sites' influence. Small hoteliers who want to stay in business have no choice but to work with review sites—which often charge fees for good placement or photos, and tack on commissions if users book through the site instead of directly with the hotel.

While these sites work hard to weed out bogus users, my hunch is that a significant percentage of reviews are posted by friends or enemies of the business being reviewed. I've even seen hotels "bribe" guests (for example, offer a free breakfast) in exchange for a positive review. Also, review sites are uncurated and can become an echo chamber, with one or two flashy businesses camped out atop the ratings, while better, more affordable, and more authentic alternatives sit ignored farther down the list. (For example, I find review sites' restaurant recommendations skew to very touristy, obvious options.) And you can't always give credence to the negative reviews: Different people have different expectations.

Remember that a user-generated review is based on the experience of one person. That person likely stayed at one hotel and ate at a few restaurants, and doesn't have much of a basis for comparison. A guidebook is the work of a trained researcher who has exhaustively visited many alternatives to assess their relative value. I recently checked out some top-rated TripAdvisor listings in various towns; when stacked up against their competitors, some are gems, while just as many are duds.

Both types of information have their place, and in many ways, they're complementary. If a hotel or restaurant is well-reviewed in a guidebook or two, and also gets good ratings on one of these sites, it's likely a winner.

an ally to land you a bed. Many B&B owners are also pet owners. If you're allergic, ask about resident pets when you reserve.

Small places usually serve a hearty fried breakfast of eggs and much more (for details on breakfast, see the Eating section, later). Because your B&B or small-hotel owner is often also the cook, breakfast hours are usually abbreviated (typically about an hour—make sure you know when it is before you turn in for the night). It's an unwritten rule that guests shouldn't show up at the very end of the breakfast period and expect a full cooked breakfast. If you do arrive late (or need to leave before breakfast is served), most establishments are happy to let you help yourself to cereal, fruit or juice, and coffee.

B&Bs and small hotels often come with thin walls and doors, and sometimes creaky floorboards, which can make for a noisy night. If you're a light sleeper, bring earplugs. And please be quiet in the halls and in your rooms at night...those of us getting up early will thank you for it.

In the Room: Every B&B offers "tea service" in the room—an electric kettle, cups, tea bags, coffee packets, and a pack of biscuits. Your bedroom probably won't include a phone, but nearly every B&B has free Wi-Fi (if they don't, I'll note it in the listing). However, the signal may not reach to all the floors; you may have to sit in the lounge to access it.

Treat these lovingly maintained homes as you would a friend's house. Be careful maneuvering your bag up narrow staircases with fragile walls and banisters. And once in the room, use the luggage rack—putting bags on the bed can damage nice comforters.

Electrical outlets have switches that turn the current on or off; if your appliance isn't working, flip the switch at the outlet.

Americans sometimes assume they'll get new towels each day. The Scottish don't, and neither should you. Hang towels up to dry and reuse. You're likely to encounter unusual bathroom fixtures. The "pump toilet" has a flushing handle or button that doesn't kick in unless you push it just right: too hard or too soft, and it won't go. (Be decisive but not ruthless.) Most B&B baths have an instant water heater. This looks like an electronic box under the shower head with dials and buttons: One control adjusts the heat, while another turns the flow off and on (let the water run for a bit to moderate the temperature before you hop in). If the hot water doesn't work, you may need to flip a red switch (often located just outside the bathroom). If the shower looks mysterious, ask your B&B host for help...*before* you take your clothes off.

Hotels

Many of my recommended hotels have three or more floors of rooms and steep stairs. Older properties often do not have elevators. If stairs are an issue, ask about ground-floor rooms or choose a hotel with a lift (elevator). Air-conditioning isn't a given (I've noted which of my listings have it), but most places have fans. On hot summer nights, you'll want your window open—and in a big city, street noise is a fact of life. Bring earplugs or request a room on the back side or on an upper floor.

A "twin" room has two single beds; a "double" has one double bed. If you'll take either, let the hotel know, or you might be needlessly turned away. Most hotels offer family deals, which means that parents with young children can get a room with an extra child's bed or a discount for larger rooms. Teenagers are generally charged as adults.

An "en suite" room has a bathroom (toilet and shower/tub) attached to the room; a room with a "private bathroom" can mean that the bathroom is all yours, but it's across the hall.

If you want your own bathroom inside the room, request "en suite." If money's tight, ask for a room with a shared bathroom. You'll almost always have a sink in your room, and as more rooms go "en suite," the hallway bathroom is shared with fewer guests.

Note that to be called a "hotel," a place technically must have certain amenities, including a 24-hour reception (though this rule is loosely applied). TVs are standard in rooms, but may come with limited channels (no cable). Note that all of Britain's accommodations are now nonsmoking.

Modern Hotel Chains: Chain hotels—common in bigger cities all over Great Britain—can be a great value (£60-100, depending on location). These hotels are as cozy as a Motel 6, but they come with private showers/WCs, elevators, good security, and often an attached restaurant. Branches are often located near the train station, on major highways, or outside the city center. While most chain hotels have 24-hour reception, the service lacks a personal touch (at some, you'll check in at a self-service kiosk). Breakfast and Wi-Fi generally cost extra. For about the same price, you can get a basic room at a funkier and friendlier budget hotel or B&B in a more enjoyable neighborhood. But the chain hotel option is especially worth considering for families, as kids often stay for free.

Room rates change from day to day with volume and vary depending on how far ahead you book. The best deals generally must be prepaid a few weeks ahead and may not be refundable—read the fine print carefully.

The biggest chains are **Premier Inn** (www.premierinn.com, toll reservations tel. 0871-527-9222) and **Travelodge** (www.travelodge.co.uk, toll reservations tel. 0871-984-8484). Both have attractive deals for prepaid or advance bookings. Other chains operating in Britain include the Irish **Jurys Inn** (www.jurysinns.com) and the French-owned **Ibis** (www.ibishotel.com). Couples can consider **Holiday Inn Express**, which generally allow only two people per room. It's like a Holiday Inn lite, with cheaper prices and no restaurant (make sure Express is part of the name or you'll be paying more for a regular Holiday Inn; www.hiexpress.co.uk).

At the Hotel: If you're arriving early in the morning, your room probably won't be ready. Drop your bag safely at the hotel and dive right into sightseeing.

If you suspect night noise will be a problem (if, for instance, your room is over a noisy pub), ask for a quieter room in the back or on an upper floor. To guard against theft in your room, keep valuables out of sight. Some rooms come with a safe, and other hotels have safes at the front desk. I've never bothered using one.

Hoteliers can be a great help and source of advice. Most know their city well, and can assist you with everything from public transit and airport connections to finding a good restaurant, the nearest launderette, or a Wi-Fi hotspot.

Even at the best places, mechanical breakdowns occur: Air-conditioning malfunctions, sinks leak, hot water turns cold, and toilets gurgle and smell. Report your concerns clearly and calmly at the front desk. For more complicated problems, don't expect instant results.

Checkout can pose problems if surprise charges pop up on your bill. If you settle up your bill the afternoon before you leave, you'll have time to discuss and address any points of contention (before 19:00, when the night shift usually arrives).

Above all, keep a positive attitude. Remember, you're on vacation. If your hotel is a disappointment, spend more time out enjoying the city you came to see.

Hostels

Scotland has hundreds of hostels of all shapes and sizes. Choose your hostel selectively. Hostels can be historic castles or depressing tenements, serene and comfy or overrun by noisy school groups. A hostel provides cheap beds where you sleep alongside strangers for about £20-30 (about $30-50) per night. Travelers of any age are welcome if they don't mind dorm-style accommodations and meeting other travelers. Cheap meals are sometimes available. Many hostels offer kitchen facilities, guest computers, Wi-Fi, and a self-service laundry. Most hostels provide all bedding, including sheets. Family and private rooms may be available.

Official Hostels: The well-managed **Scottish Youth Hostelling Association** (SYHA, also known as Hostelling Scotland, www.syha.org.uk) has around 70 locations. They generally hit a fine balance: They're less institutional than many official hostels on the Continent, but not as grungy or party-oriented as many independent hostels. More than just about anywhere else in Europe, Scotland's official hostels are worth considering even for non-hostelers. Many have great family facilities. As part of Hostelling International (HI), SYHA hostels require that you either have a membership card or pay extra per night.

Independent Hostels: These tend to be easygoing, colorful, and informal (no membership required). A few chains have multiple locations around Scotland, including **MacBackpackers** (www.scotlandstophostels.com); others are listed on the **Scottish Independent Hostels** website, with a fun variety of well-established places (www.hostel-scotland.co.uk). Or you can check the typical

Making Hotel Reservations

Reserve your rooms several weeks in advance—or as soon as you've pinned down your travel dates. Note that some national holidays merit your making reservations far in advance (see page 490).

Requesting a Reservation: It's easiest to book your room through the hotel's website. (For the best rates, always use the hotel's official site and not a booking agency's site.) If there's no reservation form, or for complicated requests, send an email (see below for a sample request).

The hotelier wants to know:

- the number and type of rooms you need
- the number of nights you'll stay
- your date of arrival
- your date of departure
- any special needs (such as bathroom in the room or down the hall, twin beds vs. double bed)

Mention any discounts—for Rick Steves readers or otherwise—when you make the reservation.

Confirming a Reservation: Most places will request a credit-card number to hold your room. If they don't have a secure on-line reservation form—look for the *https*—you can email your card number (I do), but it's safer to share that confidential info via a phone call or two emails (splitting your number between them).

Canceling a Reservation: If you must cancel, it's courteous—and smart—to do so with as much notice as possible, especially for smaller family-run places. Be warned that cancellation policies

---

rundown of hostel sites: www.hostelworld.com, www.hostelz.com, and www.hostels.com.

Apartments

Renting an apartment (or "flat") can be a fun and cost-effective way to go local. Usually equipped with a modest kitchen and living room, apartments can be a good option for families and groups on a budget, and anyone looking for more space and the option of cooking your own meals.

Websites such as Booking.com, Airbnb, VRBO, and FlipKey let you browse properties and correspond directly with property owners or managers. Apartment prices vary depending on size, amenities, and location. Some places have a minimum-stay requirement (typically 4-5 nights). Read the contract carefully so you are aware of additional fees (a one-time cleaning fee is standard) and cancellation policies, which are usually less flexible than at a hotel (for example, a nonrefundable 50 percent deposit).

To find out more about an apartment's location, plot the ad-

From:	rick@ricksteves.com
Sent:	Today
To:	info@hotelcentral.com
Subject:	Reservation request for 19-22 July

Dear Hotel Central,

I would like to reserve a room for 2 people for 3 nights, arriving 19 July and departing 22 July. If possible, I would like a quiet room with a double bed and private bathroom inside the room.

Please let me know if you have a room available and the price.

Thank you!
Rick Steves

can be strict; read the fine print or ask about these before you book. Internet deals may require prepayment, with no refunds for cancellations.

Reconfirming a Reservation: Always call or email to reconfirm your room reservation a few days in advance. For B&Bs or very small hotels, I call again on my day of arrival to tell my host what time I expect to get there (especially important if arriving late—after 17:00).

Phoning: For tips on calling hotels overseas, see page 464.

dress on Google Maps and virtually "explore" the neighborhood using the Street View feature.

In most cases, you'll need to let the owner or property manager know your arrival time so they can meet you for check-in. Or they may give you a door code for self check-in.

Other Options: If a whole apartment is overkill, Airbnb and Roomorama also list rooms in private homes. Beds range from air-mattress-in-living-room basic to plush-B&B-suite posh. If you want a place to sleep that's free, Couchsurfing.org is a vagabond's alternative to Airbnb. It lists millions of outgoing members, who host fellow "surfers" in their homes.

Eating

The stereotype of "bad food in Scotland" is woefully dated. Scotland has caught up with the foodie revolution, and I find it's easy to eat very well here.

Scottish cooking has embraced international influences and

Haggis and Other Traditional Scottish Dishes

Scotland's most unique dish, **haggis,** began as a peasant food. Waste-conscious cooks wrapped the heart, liver, and lungs of a sheep in its stomach lining, packed in some oats and spices, and then boiled the lot to create a hearty, if slightly palatable, meal. Traditionally served with "neeps and tatties" (turnips and potatoes), haggis was forever immortalized thanks to Robbie Burns' *Address to a Haggis*.

Today haggis has been refined almost to the point of high cuisine. You're likely to find it on many menus, including at breakfast. You can dress it up with anything from a fine whisky cream sauce to your basic HP brown sauce. To appreciate this iconic Scottish dish, think of how it tastes—not what it's made of.

The king of Scottish **black puddings** (blood sausage) is made in the Hebrides Islands. Called Stornoway, it's so famous that the European Union has granted it protected status to prevent imitators from using its name. A mix of beef suet, oatmeal, onion, and blood, the sausage is usually served as part of a full Scottish breakfast, but it also appears on the menus of top-class restaurants.

Be on the lookout for other traditional Scottish taste treats. **Cullen skink** is Scotland's answer to chowder: a hearty, creamy fish soup, often made with smoked haddock. A **bridie** (or Forfar bridie) is a savory meat pie similar to a Cornish pasty, but generally lighter (no potatoes). A **Scotch pie**—small, double-crusted, and filled with minced meat, is a good picnic food; it's a common snack at soccer matches and outdoor events. **Crowdie** is a dairy spread that falls somewhere between cream cheese and cottage cheese.

And for dessert, **cranachan** is similar to a trifle, made with whipped cream, honey, fruit (usually raspberries), and whisky-soaked oats. Another popular dessert is the **Tipsy Laird,** served at "Burns Suppers" on January 25, the annual celebration of national poet Robert Burns. It's essentially the same as a trifle but with whisky or brandy and Scottish raspberries.

good-quality ingredients, making "modern Scottish" food quite delicious. While some dreary pub food still exists, you'll generally find the cuisine scene here innovative and tasty (but expensive). Basic pubs are more likely to dish up homemade, creative dishes than microwaved pies, soggy fries, and mushy peas. Even traditional pub grub has gone upmarket, with gastropubs that serve locally sourced meats and fresh vegetables.

All of Scotland is smoke-free. Expect restaurants and pubs to be nonsmoking indoors, with smokers occupying patios and doorways outside.

When restaurant-hunting, choose a spot filled with locals, not tourists. Venturing even a block or two off the main drag leads to higher-quality food for a better price. Locals eat better at lower-rent locales.

Tipping: At pubs and places where you order at the counter, you don't have to tip. Regular customers ordering a round sometimes say, "Add one for yourself" as a tip for drinks ordered at the bar—but this isn't expected. At restaurants and fancy pubs with waitstaff, tip about 10-12.5 percent. (Occasionally a service charge is added to your bill, in which case no additional tip is necessary—but this is rare in Scotland.)

BREAKFAST (FRY-UP)

The traditional fry-up or full Scottish breakfast—generally included in the cost of your room—is famous as a hearty way to start the day. Also known as a "heart attack on a plate," your standard fry-up is a heated plate with eggs, Canadian-style bacon and/or sausage, a grilled tomato, sautéed mushrooms, baked beans, and sometimes potatoes, kippers (herring), or fried bread (sizzled in a greasy skillet).  Here in Scotland, you may also get a salty, dense potato scone. Toast comes in a rack (to cool quickly and crisply) with butter and marmalade. The meal is typically topped off with tea or coffee. At a B&B or hotel, it may start with juice and cereal or porridge. Many progressive B&B owners offer vegetarian, organic, gluten-free, or other creative variations on the traditional breakfast.

Much as the full breakfast fry-up is a traditional way to start the morning, these days most hotels serve a healthier continental breakfast—with a buffet of everything you'd expect, such as yogurt, cereal, scrambled eggs, fruit, and veggies.

LUNCH AND DINNER ON A BUDGET

Even in pricey cities, plenty of inexpensive choices are available: pub grub, daily lunch and early-bird dinner specials, ethnic restaurants, cafeterias, fast food, picnics, greasy-spoon cafés, cheap chain restaurants, and pizza. On menus, adding "supper" to an item means it comes with fries (so "fish supper" is fish-and-chips).

I've found that portions are huge, and **sharing plates** is generally just fine. Ordering two drinks, a soup or side salad, and splitting a £10 meat pie can make a good, filling meal. If you're on a limited budget, share a main course in a more expensive place for a nicer eating experience.

Pub grub is the most atmospheric budget option. You'll usually get hearty lunches and dinners priced reasonably at £8-12 under ancient timbers (see "Pubs," later). Gastropubs, with better food, are more expensive.

Classier restaurants have some affordable deals. Lunch is usually cheaper than dinner; a top-end, £25-for-dinner-type restaurant often serves the same quality two-course lunch deals for about half the price.

Many restaurants have **early bird** or **pre-theater specials** of two or three courses, often for a significant savings. They are usually available only before 18:30 or 19:00. If you're bargain-hunting and willing to eat a bit earlier, inquire or check websites for details.

Ethnic restaurants add spice to the cuisine scene. Eating Indian, Bangladeshi, Chinese, or Thai is cheap (even cheaper if you do takeout). Middle Eastern stands sell gyro sandwiches, falafel, and *shwarmas* (grilled meat in pita bread). An Indian samosa (greasy, flaky meat-and-vegetable pie) costs about £2 and makes a very cheap, if small, meal. (For more, see "Indian Cuisine," later.) You'll find all-you-can-eat Chinese and Thai places  serving £6 meals and offering even cheaper takeaway boxes. While you can't "split" a buffet, you can split a takeaway box. Stuff the box full, and you and your partner can eat in a park for under £2 each.

Fish-and-chips are a heavy, greasy, but tasty English classic. Every town has at least one "chippy" selling a takeaway box of fish-and-chips in a cardboard box or (more traditionally) wrapped in paper for about £4-7. You can dip your fries in ketchup, American-style, or "go Scottish" and drizzle the whole thing with malt vinegar and fresh lemon.

Most large **museums** (and many historic **churches**) have handy, moderately priced cafeterias with forgettably decent food.

Picnicking saves time and money. Fine park benches and polite pigeons abound in most towns and city neighborhoods. You can easily get prepared food to go. The modern chain eateries on nearly every corner often have simple seating but are designed for takeout.

Bakeries serve a wonderful array of fresh sandwiches and pasties (savory meat pies, sometimes called bridies in Scotland).

Open-air markets and supermarkets sell produce in small quantities. The corner grocery store has fruit, drinks, fresh bread, tasty Scottish cheese, meat, and local specialties. Supermarkets often have good deli sections, even offering Indian dishes, and sometimes salad bars. Decent packaged sandwiches (£3-4) are sold everywhere. Munch a relaxed "meal on wheels" picnic during your open-top bus tour or river cruise to save 30 precious minutes for sightseeing.

PUBS

Pubs are a fundamental part of the Scottish social scene, and whether you're a teetotaler or a beer guzzler, they should be a part

of your travel here. "Pub" is short for "public house." It's an extended common room where, if you don't mind the stickiness, you can feel the pulse of Scotland. Smart travelers use pubs to eat, drink, get out of the rain, watch sporting events, and make new friends. Unfortunately, many city pubs have been afflicted with an excess of brass, ferns, and video slot machines. The most traditional, atmospheric pubs are in the countryside and in smaller towns.

It's interesting to consider the role pubs filled for Scotland's working class in more modest times: For workers with humble domestic quarters and no money for a vacation, a beer at the corner pub was the closest they'd get to a comfortable living room, a place to entertain, and a getaway. And locals could meet people from far away in a pub—today, that's you!

Though hours vary, pubs generally serve beer daily from 11:00 to 23:00, though many are open later, particularly on Friday and Saturday. Children are served food and soft drinks in pubs, but you must be 18 to order a beer. As it nears closing time, you'll hear shouts of "Last orders." Then comes the 10-minute warning bell. Finally, they'll call "Time!" to pick up your glass, finished or not, when the pub closes.

A cup of darts is free for the asking. People go to a public house to be social. They want to talk. Get vocal with a local. This is easiest at the bar, where people assume you're in the mood to talk (rather than at a table, where you're allowed a bit of privacy). The pub is the next best thing to having relatives in town. Cheers!

Pub Grub: For £8-12, you'll get a basic budget hot lunch or dinner in friendly surroundings. (For something more refined, try a **gastropub,** which serves higher-quality meals for £12-18.) The *Good Pub Guide* is an excellent resource (www.thegoodpubguide.co.uk). Pubs that are attached to restaurants, advertise their food, and are crowded with locals are more likely to have fresh food and a chef—and less likely to sell only lousy microwaved snacks.

Pubs generally serve traditional dishes, such as fish-and-chips, roast beef with Yorkshire pudding (batter-baked in the oven), and assorted meat pies, such as steak-and-kidney pie or shepherd's pie (stewed lamb topped with mashed potatoes) with cooked vegetables. Side dishes include salads, vegetables, and—invariably—"chips" (French fries). "Crisps" are potato chips. A "jacket potato" (baked potato stuffed with fillings of your choice) can almost be a meal in itself. These days, you'll likely find more pasta, curried dishes, and quiche on the menu than traditional fare.

Meals are usually served from 12:00 to 14:00 and again from 18:00 to 20:00—with a break in the middle (rather than serving straight through the day). Since they make more money selling beer, many pubs stop food service early in the evening—especially on weekends. There's generally no table service. Order at the bar, then take a seat. Either they'll bring the food when it's ready or you'll pick it up at the bar. Pay at the bar (sometimes when you order, sometimes after you eat). Don't tip unless it's a place with full table service. Servings are hearty, service is quick, and you'll rarely spend more than £12. If you're on a tight budget, it's OK to share a meal. A beer, cider, or dram of whisky adds another couple of pounds. Free tap water is always available. For details on ordering beer and other drinks, see the "Beverages" section, later.

GOOD CHAIN RESTAURANTS

I know—you're going to Scotland to enjoy characteristic little hole-in-the-wall pubs, so mass-produced food is the farthest thing from your mind. But several excellent chains with branches across the UK keep long hours and can be a nice break from pub grub. My favorites are Pret and Wagamama.

Pret (a.k.a. Pret à Manger) is perhaps the most pervasive of these modern convenience eateries. Some are takeout only, and others have seating ranging from simple stools to restaurant-quality tables. The service is fast, the price is great, and the food is healthy and fresh. Their slogan: "Made today. Gone today. No 'sell-by' date, no nightlife."

Wagamama Noodle Bar, serving up pan-Asian cuisine (udon noodles, fried rice, and curry dishes), is a noisy, organic slurpathon.

Portions are huge and splittable. There's one in almost every mid-size city in Britain, usually located in sprawling halls filled with long shared tables and busy servers who scrawl your order on the placemat.

Loch Fyne Fish Restaurant is a Scottish chain that raises its own oysters and mussels. Its branches offer an inviting, lively atmosphere with a fine fishy energy and no pretense (£12-20 main dishes, early-bird specials).

Marks & Spencer department stores have a new feature: inviting deli sections with cheery sit-down eating (along with their popular sandwiches-to-go section).

Ask and **Pizza Express** serve quality pasta and pizza in a pleasant, sit-down atmosphere that's family-friendly. **Jamie's Italian** (from celebrity chef Jamie Oliver) is hipper and pricier.

Yo! Sushi serves fresh and inexpensive Japanese food. You'll pick your dish off a conveyor belt and pay according to the color of your plate.

Carry-Out Chains: While the following may have some seating, they're best as easy places to grab prepackaged food on the run.

Major supermarket chains have smaller, offshoot branches that specialize in sandwiches, salads, and other prepared foods to go. These can be a picnicker's dream come true. Some shops are stand-alone, while others are located inside a larger store. The most prevalent—and best—is **M&S Simply Food** (an offshoot of Marks & Spencer; there's one in every major train station). **Sainsbury's Local** grocery stores also offer decent prepared food; **Tesco Express** and **Tesco Metro** run a distant third.

INDIAN CUISINE

You'll find Indian restaurants in most Scottish cities, and even in small towns. Take the opportunity to sample food from Britain's former colony. Indian cuisine is as varied as the country itself. In general, it uses more exotic spices than British or American cuisine—some hot, some sweet. Indian food is very vegetarian-friendly, offering many meatless dishes.

For a simple meal that costs about £10-12, order one dish with rice and naan (Indian flatbread). Generally one order is plenty for two people to share. Many Indian restaurants offer a fixed-price combination that offers more variety, and is simpler and cheaper than ordering à la carte. For about £20, you can make a mix-and-match platter out of several shareable dishes, including dal (simmered lentils) as a starter, one or two meat or vegetable dishes with sauce (for example, chicken curry, chicken *tikka masala* in a creamy tomato sauce, grilled fish tandoori, chickpea *chana masala*, or a spicy vindaloo dish), *raita* (a cooling yogurt that's added to spicy dishes), rice, naan, and an Indian beer (wine and Indian food don't really mix) or chai (cardamom/cinnamon-spiced tea, usually served with milk). An easy way to taste a variety of dishes is to order a thali—a sampler plate, generally served on a metal tray, with small servings of various specialties.

AFTERNOON TEA

While more of an English custom, afternoon tea is served in Scottish tearooms and generally includes a pot of tea, small finger foods (like sandwiches with the crusts cut off), homemade scones, jam, and thick clotted cream. A lighter "cream tea" gets you tea and a scone or two. Tearooms, which often serve appealing light meals, are usually open for lunch and close at about 17:00, just before dinner.

DESSERTS (SWEETS)

To the Scottish, the traditional word for dessert is "pudding," although it's usually referred to as "sweets" these days. Sponge cake, cream, fruitcake, and meringue are key players.

Trifle is the best-known Scottish concoction, consisting of sponge cake soaked in brandy or sherry (or orange juice for children), then covered with jam and/or fruit and custard cream. Whipped cream can sometimes put the final touch on this "light" treat.

The Scottish version of custard is a smooth, yellow liquid. Cream tops most everything that custard does not. There's single cream for coffee. Double cream is really thick. Whipped cream is familiar, and clotted cream is the consistency of whipped butter.

Fool is a dessert with sweetened pureed fruit (such as rhubarb, gooseberries, or black currants) mixed with cream or custard and chilled. Elderflower is a popular flavoring for sorbet.

Flapjacks here aren't pancakes, but are dense, sweet oatmeal cakes (a little like a cross between a granola bar and a brownie). They come with toppings such as toffee and chocolate.

Scones are tops, and many inns and restaurants have their secret recipes. Whether made with fruit or topped with clotted cream, scones take the cake.

BEVERAGES

Beer: The Scots take great pride in their beer. Many locals think that drinking beer cold and carbonated, as Americans do, ruins the taste. Most pubs will have **lagers** (cold, refreshing, American-style beer), **ales** (amber-colored, cellar-temperature beer), **bitters** (hop-flavored ale, perhaps the most typical British beer), and **stouts** (dark and somewhat bitter, like Guinness).

At pubs, long-handled pulls (or taps) are used to pull the traditional, rich-flavored "real ales" up from the cellar. These are the connoisseur's favorites and often come with fun names. Served straight from the brewer's cask at cellar temperature, real ales finish fermenting naturally and are not pasteurized or filtered, so they must be consumed within two or three days after the cask is tapped. Naturally carbonated, real ales have less gassiness and head; they vary from sweet to bitter, often with a hoppy or nutty flavor.

Short-handled pulls mean colder, fizzier, mass-produced, and less interesting keg beers. Mild beers are sweeter, with a creamy malt flavoring. Irish cream ale is a smooth, sweet experience. Try the draft cider (sweet or dry)...carefully.

Order your beer at the bar and pay as you go, with no need to tip. An average beer costs £3. Part of the experience is standing before a line of hand pulls and wondering which beer to choose.

As dictated by British law, draft beer and cider are served by the pint (20-ounce imperial size) or the half-pint (9.6 ounces). (It's almost feminine for a man to order just a half; I order mine with quiche.) In 2011, the government sanctioned an in-between serving size—the schooner, or two-thirds pint (it's become a popular size for higher alcohol-content craft beers). Proper ladies like a **shandy** (half beer and half 7-Up).

Whisky: While bar-hopping tourists generally think in terms of beer, many pubs are just as enthusiastic about serving whisky. If you are unfamiliar with whisky (what Americans call "Scotch" and the Irish call "whiskey"), it's a great conversation starter. Many pubs have dozens of whiskies available. Lists describe their personalities (peaty, heavy iodine finish, and so on), which are much easier to discern than most wine flavors.

A glass of basic whisky generally costs around £2.50. Let a local teach you how to drink it "neat," then add a little water. The easiest and perhaps best option for sampling Scotland's national drink is to find a local pub with a passion for whisky that's filled with locals who share that passion. Make a friend, buy a few drams, and learn by drinking. Keep experimenting until you discover the right taste for you.

Consider going beyond the single-malt whisky rut. Like microbrews, small-batch, innovative Scottish spirits are trendy right now. Blends can be surprisingly creative—even for someone who thinks they're knowledgeable about whisky—and non-whisky alternatives are pushing boundaries. For example, you'll find gin that's aged in whisky casks, taking off the piney edge and infusing a bit of that distinctive whisky flavor.

Distilleries throughout Scotland offer tours, but you'll often only learn about that one type of whisky. At a good whisky shop, the knowledgeable staff offer guided tastings (for a fee and typically by pre-arrangement), explaining four or five whiskies to help you develop your palate. If you don't care for a heavy, smoky whisky, ask

Whisky 101

Whisky is high on the experience list of most visitors to Scotland—even for teetotalers. Whether at a distillery, a shop, or a pub, be sure to try a few drams. (From the Gaelic word for "drink," a dram isn't necessarily a fixed amount—it's simply a small slug.) While touring a distillery is a ▲▲▲ Scottish experience, many fine whisky shops (including Cadenhead's in Edinburgh) offer guided tastings and a chance to have a small bottle filled from the cask of your choice.

Types of Whisky

Scotch whiskies come in two broad types: **"single malt,"** meaning that the bottle comes from a single batch made by a single distiller; and **"blends,"** which master blenders mix and match from various whiskies into a perfect punch of booze.

While single malts get the most attention, blended whiskies represent 90 percent of all whisky sales. They tend to be light and mild—making them an easier way to tiptoe into the whisky scene. Overseen by a master blender (a prestigious job, like a "nose" in the French wine industry), a neutral base of grain whisky (usually made from corn or wheat) is merged with a variety of single malts, and then aged in oak casks for just six months to a year of "marriage."

There are more than 100 distilleries in Scotland, each one proud of its unique qualities. The **Lowlands,** around Edinburgh, produce light and refreshing whiskies—more likely to be taken as an aperitif. Whiskies from the **Highlands** and **Islands** range from floral and sweet (vanilla or honey) to smoky (peaty) and robust. **Speyside,** southeast of Inverness, is home to half of all Scottish distilleries. Mellow and fruity, Speyside whiskies can be the most accessible for beginners. The **Isle of Islay** is just the opposite, specializing in the peatiest, smokiest whiskies—not for novices. Only a few producers remain to distill the smoky and pungent **Campbeltown** whiskies in the southwest Highlands, near Islay.

Making Whisky

Single-malt whisky has three ingredients: water, malted barley, and yeast.

To malt (or germinate) the barley, it's spread out on a floor, watered, and periodically turned. In about a week, when the barley starts to sprout, it's dried in an oven. Some distilleries (especially on the islands) use peat in their kilns, giving their whisky a distinctive smoky flavor.

Once malted, the barley is milled into a fine grist that's mixed with hot water to create mash. A sugary solution called wort is extracted from the mash, then cooled and mixed with yeast. For three or four days, the wort fizzes and ferments in big "washback" tubs as the yeast turns sugar into alcohol.

To boost the alcohol content, the wash is then double-distilled in tall, copper stills. First, in the "wash still," the liquid is

heated, to allow the alcohol to evaporate. Those gases are sent through coiled tubes to recondense them into a liquid called "low wines." That liquid flows through a second spirit still to create "spirit." No two stills are the same, and the copper in each brings about unique qualities in the spirit.

Distillers keep only the "heart" of the run; it has the most consistent alcohol levels and flavor profile. They snip off the "head" and "tail" (collectively called "feints") to be redistilled.

At the end of the distillation process, you have a concentrated, colorless liquid called "new make spirit"—but not yet "whisky." For that, the liquid must be aged for at least three years (more commonly eight or more years; the final product must register at least 40 percent alcohol by volume). This maturation typically takes place in casks made of American white oak, often recycled from the US. (American laws permit each cask to be used only once—but no such regulation exists in Scotland.) It's increasingly in vogue to use casks that have previously aged sherry, port, wine, or cognac, in order to infuse the whisky with faint echoes of those flavors.

During maturation, about 1 to 3 percent of the alcohol is lost to evaporation—what's poetically described as "the angel's share." For a long-aged whisky, it's more like the lion's share: A 25-year-old cask of whisky can end up being just over half full.

Finally, the aged whisky is bottled—or, in some cases, entire casks are sent to specialty stores.

Tasting Whisky

Tasting whisky is like tasting wine; you'll use all your senses. First, swirl the whisky in the glass and observe its color and "legs"— the trail left by the liquid as it runs back down the side of the glass (quick, thin legs indicate light, young whisky; slow, thick legs mean it's heavier and older). Then take a deep sniff—do you smell smoke and peat? And finally, taste it (sip!). What's the dominant first punch? The smooth middle? The "finish"? Swish it around and let your gums taste it, too. Adding a few drops of water is said to "open up the taste"—look for a little glass of water with a dropper standing by, and try tasting your whisky before and after.

A whisky's flavor is most influenced by three things: whether the malt is peat-smoked; the shape of the stills; and the composition of the casks. Even local climate can play a role; some island distilleries tout the salty notes of their whiskies, as the sea air permeates their casks.

for something milder. Some shops have several bottles open and will let you try a few wee drams to narrow down your options. I've listed both distillery tours and whisky shops in this book. Be aware: If they're providing samples, they're hoping you'll buy a bottle at the end.

For much more about whisky, see the "Whisky 101" sidebar.

Other Alcoholic Drinks: Many pubs also have a good selection of wines by the glass, a fully stocked bar for the gentleman's "G and T" (gin and tonic), and the increasingly popular bottles of alcohol-plus-sugar (such as Bacardi Breezers) for the younger working-class set.

Non-Alcoholic Drinks: Teetotalers can order from a wide variety of soft drinks—both the predictable American sodas and other more interesting bottled drinks, such as ginger beer (similar to ginger ale but with more bite), root beers, or other flavors (Fentimans brews some unusual options that are stocked in many pubs). The uniquely Scottish soft drink called Irn-Bru (pronounced "Iron Brew") is bright orange and tastes like bubble gum. Note that in Scotland, "lemonade" is lemon-lime soda (like 7-Up).

Staying Connected

Staying connected in Europe gets easier and cheaper every year. The simplest solution is to bring your own device—mobile phone, tablet, or laptop—and use it just as you would at home (following the tips below, such as connecting to free Wi-Fi whenever possible). Another option is to buy a European SIM card for your mobile phone—either your US phone or one you buy in Europe. Or you can travel without a mobile device and use European landlines and computers to connect. Each of these options is described below, and you'll find even more details at www.ricksteves.com/phoning.

USING YOUR OWN MOBILE DEVICE IN EUROPE

Without an international plan, typical rates from major service providers (AT&T, Verizon, etc.) for using your device abroad are about $1.50/minute for voice calls, 50 cents to send text messages, 5 cents to receive them, and $20 to download one megabyte of data. But at these rates, costs can add up quickly. Here are some budget tips and options.

Use free Wi-Fi whenever possible. Unless you have an unlimited-data plan, you're best off saving most of your online tasks for Wi-Fi. You can access the Internet, send texts, and even make voice calls over Wi-Fi.

Many cafés (including Starbucks and McDonald's) have hotspots for customers; look for signs offering it and ask for the Wi-Fi password when you buy something. You'll also often find

Tips on Internet Security

Using the Internet while traveling brings added security risks, whether you're getting online with your own device or at a public terminal using a shared network.

First, make sure that your device is running the latest version of its operating system and security software. Next, ensure that your device is password- or passcode-protected so thieves can't access your information if your device is stolen. For extra security, set passwords on apps that access key info (such as email or Facebook).

On the road, use only legitimate Wi-Fi hotspots. Ask the hotel or café staff for the specific name of their Wi-Fi network, and make sure you log on to that exact one. Hackers sometimes create a bogus hotspot with a similar or vague name (such as "Hotel Europa Free Wi-Fi"). The best Wi-Fi networks require entering a password.

Be especially cautious when checking your online banking, credit-card statements, or other personal-finance accounts. Internet security experts advise against accessing these sites while traveling. Even if you're using your own mobile device at a password-protected hotspot, any hacker who's logged on to the same network may be able to see what you're doing. If you do need to log on to a banking website, use a hard-wired connection (such as an Ethernet cable in your hotel room) or a cellular network, which is safer than Wi-Fi.

Never share your credit-card number (or any other sensitive information) online unless you know that the site is secure. A secure site displays a little padlock icon, and the URL begins with *https* (instead of the usual *http*).

Wi-Fi at TIs, city squares, major museums, public-transit hubs, airports, and aboard trains and buses. Another option is to sign up for Wi-Fi access through a company such as BT (one hour-£4, one day-£10, www.btwifi.co.uk) or The Cloud (free though sometimes slow, www.thecloud.net/free-wifi).

Sign up for an international plan. Most providers offer a global calling plan that cuts the per-minute cost of phone calls and texts, and a flat-fee data plan that includes a certain amount of megabytes. Your normal plan may already include international coverage (T-Mobile's does).

Before your trip, call your provider or check online to confirm that your phone will work in Europe, and research your provider's international rates. A day or two before you leave, activate the plan by calling your provider or logging on to your mobile phone account. Remember to cancel your plan (if necessary) when your trip's over.

Minimize the use of your cellular network. When you can't

How to Dial

Many Americans are intimidated by dialing European phone numbers. You needn't be. It's simple, once you break the code.

Dialing Rules

Here are the rules for dialing, along with examples of how to call one of my recommended hotels in Edinburgh (tel. 0131/667-5806). The 0131 is Edinburgh's area code.

Dialing Internationally to Scotland

Whether you're phoning from a US landline, your own mobile phone, a Skype account, or a number in another European country (e.g., France to Scotland), you're making an international call. Here's how to do it:

1. Dial the international access code (011 if calling from a US or Canadian phone; 00 if calling from any European phone number outside Scotland). If dialing from a mobile phone, you can enter a + in place of the international access code (press and hold the 0 key).
2. Dial the country code (44 for Scotland).
3. Dial the phone number (drop the initial 0).

Examples:

- To call my recommended hotel from a US or Canadian phone, dial 011, then 44, then 131/667-5806.
- To call from any European phone number (outside of Scotland), dial 00, then 44, then 131/667-5806.
- To call from any mobile phone (except a British one), dial +, then 44, then 131/667-5806.

Dialing Within Scotland

To make a domestic call (either from a Scottish mobile phone or landline), you'll generally dial both the area code (including the initial 0) and the local number. If you're calling within the same area code, you could drop the area code and just dial the local number. But because area codes can vary in length, and mobile phones utilize their own sets of prefixes, I keep things simple by always dialing the full phone number, including the area code or prefix.

---

find Wi-Fi, you can use your cellular network—convenient but slower and potentially expensive—to connect to the Internet, text, or make voice calls. When you're done, avoid further charges by manually switching off "data roaming" or "cellular data" (in your device's Settings menu; if you don't know how to switch it off, ask your service provider or Google it). Another way to make sure you're not accidentally using data roaming is to put your device in "airplane" or "flight" mode (which also disables phone calls and texts, as well as data), and then turn on Wi-Fi as needed.

Don't use your cellular network for bandwidth-gobbling tasks,

Example: To call my recommended hotel from any Scottish landline or mobile phone, dial 0131/667-5806. If dialing from a phone within the same 0131 area code, you can just enter 667-5806.

Calling from Any European Country to the US
To call the US or Canada from Europe (either from a mobile phone or landline), dial 00 (Europe's international access code), 1 (US/Canada country code), and the phone number, including the area code. If calling from a mobile phone, you can enter a + instead of 00.

Example: To call my office in Edmonds, Washington, from anywhere in Europe, I dial 00-1-425-771-8303; or, from a mobile phone, +-1-425-771-8303.

More Dialing Tips
Scottish Phone Numbers: Numbers beginning with 074, 075, 076, 077, 078, and 079 are mobile numbers, which are more expensive to call than a landline. For directory assistance, dial 118-500, but it's expensive (£3.99/call and £1.39/minute)—find the number online instead.

Toll and Toll-Free Calls: "Freephone" numbers, starting 0800 or 0808, are free for all callers, whether dialed from a mobile phone or a landline. Numbers beginning with 084, 087, or 03 are toll numbers that can be dialed from Scottish landlines or mobile phones, with per-minute prices that vary depending on who you're calling and which phone company carries the call (some as expensive as £0.45/minute). Numbers beginning with 09 are pricey toll calls, but you shouldn't encounter these unless you're calling chat lines. If you have questions about a prefix, call 100 for free help.

More Resources: The "Phoning Cheat Sheet" on the next page shows how to dial per country, or you can check www.countrycallingcodes.com or www.howtocallabroad.com.

such as Skyping, downloading apps, and watching YouTube—save these for when you're on Wi-Fi. Using a navigation app such as Google Maps can take lots of data, so use this sparingly.

Limit automatic updates. By default, your device is constantly checking for a data connection and updating apps. It's smart to disable these features so they'll only update when you're on Wi-Fi, and to change your device's email settings from "auto-retrieve" to "manual" (or from "push" to "fetch").

It's also a good idea to keep track of your data usage. On your

Phoning Cheat Sheet

Just smile and dial, using these rules.

Calling a European number

• **From a mobile phone** (whether you're in the US or in Europe):
Dial + (press and hold 0), then country code and number*

• **From a US/Canadian number:** Dial 011, then country code and number*

• **From a different European country** (e.g., German number to French
number): Dial 00, then country code and number*

• **Within the same European country** (e.g., German number to another
German number): Dial the number as printed, including initial 0 if there
is one

*Drop initial 0 (if present) from phone number
in all countries except Italy*

Calling the US or Canada from Europe

Dial 00, then 1 (country code for US/Canada), then area code and number;
on mobile phones, enter + in place of 00

Country	Country Code	Country	Country Code
Austria	43	Italy	39 [2]
Belgium	32	Latvia	371
Bosnia-Herzegovina	387	Montenegro	382
Croatia	385	Morocco	212
Czech Republic	420	Netherlands	31
Denmark	45	Norway	47
Estonia	372	Poland	48
Finland	358	Portugal	351
France	33	Russia	7 [3]
Germany	49	Slovakia	421
Gibraltar	350	Slovenia	386
Great Britain & N. Ireland	44	Spain	34
Greece	30	Sweden	46
Hungary	36 [1]	Switzerland	41
Ireland	353	Turkey	90

[1] For long-distance calls within Hungary, dial 06, then the area code and number.
[2] When making international calls to Italy, do not drop the initial 0 from the
phone number.
[3] For long-distance calls within Russia, dial 8, then the area code and number.
To call the US or Canada from Russia, dial 8, then 10, then 1, then the area
code and number.

device's menu, look for "cellular data usage" or "mobile data" and reset the counter at the start of your trip.

Use Skype or other calling/messaging apps for cheaper calls and texts. Certain apps let you make voice or video calls or send texts over the Internet for free or cheaply. If you're bringing a tablet or laptop, you can also use them for voice calls and texts. All you have to do is log on to a Wi-Fi network, then contact any of your friends or family members who are also online and signed into the same service. You can make voice and video calls using Skype, Viber, FaceTime, and Google+ Hangouts. If the connection is bad, try making an audio-only call.

You can also make voice calls from your device to telephones worldwide for just a few cents per minute using Skype, Viber, or Hangouts if you prebuy credit.

To text for free over Wi-Fi, try apps like Google+ Hangouts, WhatsApp, Viber, and Facebook Messenger. Apple's iMessage connects with other Apple users, but make sure you're on Wi-Fi to avoid data charges.

USING A EUROPEAN SIM CARD IN A MOBILE PHONE

This option works well for those who want to make a lot of voice calls at cheap local rates. Either buy a phone in Europe (as little as $40 from mobile-phone shops anywhere), or bring an "unlocked" US phone (check with your carrier about unlocking it). With an unlocked phone, you can replace the original SIM card (the microchip that stores info about the phone) with one that will work with a European provider.

In Europe, buy a European SIM card. Inserted into your phone, this card gives you a European phone number—and European rates. SIM cards are sold at mobile-phone shops, department-store electronics counters, some newsstands, and even at vending machines. Costing about $5-10, they usually include about that much prepaid calling credit, with no contract and no commitment. You can still use your phone's Wi-Fi function to get online. To get a SIM card that also includes data costs (including roaming), figure on paying $15-30 for one month of data within the country where you bought it. This can be cheaper than data roaming through your home provider. To get the best rates, buy a new SIM card whenever you arrive in a new country.

I like to buy SIM cards at a mobile-phone shop where there's a clerk to help explain the options and brands. Lebara and Lycamobile operate in multiple European countries and are reliable and economical. Ask the clerk to help you insert your SIM card, set it up, and show you how to use it. In some countries you'll be required to register the SIM card with your passport as an antiter-

The Language Barrier?

Yes, Scots speak English, but it has distinct qualities. Scottish people are known for their inimitable burr, and they're proud of their old Celtic language, Gaelic.

Scottish Gaelic thrives only in the remotest corners of Scotland—the Highlands and the Hebrides. In major towns and cities, virtually nobody speaks Gaelic on an everyday basis, but the language is kept alive by a Scottish population keen to remember its heritage. New Gaelic schools open all the time, and Scotland has replaced many road signs with new ones listing both English and Gaelic spellings (*Edinburgh/Dùn Èideann*).

Scotland has another language of its own, called Scots. Aye, you're likely already a wee bit familiar with a few Scots words, ye lads and lassies. A generation or two ago, Scots was denigrated in favor of the Queen's English. But in today's age of regionalism, Scots is enjoying a renaissance. Schoolchildren from Scots-speaking families once faced punishment for saying "youse" to mean "you all." Now a new generation of kids is being taught Scots. As you travel, you'll begin to collect Scots words (for starters, see below)...and enjoy the lovely musical lilt as well. One popular Scots saying is "Whit's fur ye'll no go by ye"—you'll get what's coming to you, good or bad.

As the old joke goes, "A language is just a dialect with an army and a flag." So Scots is halfway there. Linguists who argue that Scots is technically an ancient English dialect have clearly never heard a Scot read aloud the poetry of Robert Burns. He wrote in unfiltered (and often unintelligible) Scots, as in this opening line of "To a Louse": "Ha! Whaur ye gaun, ye crowlin ferlie?"

Fortunately, you're unlikely to meet anyone quite that hard to understand. Most Scottish people switch easily as the need arises, toggling between Scots (when they're hanging out with the lads or lassies) and the Queen's English (in professional settings). If you have a hard time understanding someone, ask them to translate: You may take home some new words as souvenirs.

Even within Scotland, there's a lot of regional variation. Lowland Scots is the most widespread dialect, although the language has evolved since Burns popularized it, and many of the poet's words are unfamiliar even to Lowland Scots today. Some cities have their own, very specific accents. For example, people in Dundee speak Dundonian, while in Aberdeen, they speak Doric, which replaces the word "what" with "fit." So a Doric speaker visiting a shoe store might say something that sounds like, "Fit fit fits fit fit?" (What foot fits what foot?) To sample the various regional dialects around Scotland, visit www.ayecan.com.

Scots Words

Scotch may be the peaty drink the bartender serves you, but the nationality of the bartender is Scottish; you could also call him a Scot, and the language he speaks is Scots. A sharp intake of breath (like a little gasp), sometimes while saying "aye," means "yes." And many Scots greet you with a cheery, "Aright!" (a compressed version of "Are you all right?").

Here are some Scots words that may come in handy during your time here:

auld	old
aye	yes
bairn, wean	child
blether	talk
bonnie	beautiful, handsome, good
braw	good, fine
cairn	pile of stones
close	an alley leading to a courtyard or square
ken	to know
kirk	church
nae	no (as in "nae bother"—you're welcome)
neeps	turnips
pend	arched gateway
ree	king, royal ("righ" in Gaelic)
tattie	potato
wee	small
wynd	tight, winding lane connecting major streets

Many Scots (or Gaelic) words relate to geography, and turn up often in place names:

aber	confluence or mouth of a river
bal	town
ben	mountain
blair	clearing
brae	slope, hill
burn	creek or stream
crag or craig	cliff, rocky ground, sea rock
dun or dum	hill fort
eilean	island
fell	hill
firth	estuary
glen	narrow valley
innis or inch	island
inver	confluence or mouth of a river
kyle	strait
loch	lake
sea loch	inlet
strath	wide valley

rorism measure (which may mean you can't use the phone for the first hour or two).

When you run out of credit, you can top it up at newsstands, tobacco shops, mobile-phone stores, or many other businesses (look for your SIM card's logo in the window), or online.

USING LANDLINES AND COMPUTERS IN EUROPE

It's easy to travel in Europe without a mobile device. You can check email or browse websites using public computers and Internet cafés, and make calls from your hotel room and/or public phones.

Phones in your **hotel room** can be inexpensive for local calls and calls made with cheap international phone cards (sold at newsstands, street kiosks, and train stations). You'll get a prepaid card with a toll-free number and a scratch-to-reveal PIN code; to make a call, dial the toll-free number, follow the prompts, enter the code, then dial your number.

Most hotels charge a fee for placing local and "toll-free" calls, as well as long-distance or international calls—ask for the rates before you dial. Since you're never charged for receiving calls, it's better to have someone from the US call you in your room.

Phones are rare in rooms in **B&Bs,** but if your room has one (or if you use your host's phone), the advice above applies.

Public pay phones are getting harder to find, and they're expensive. To use one, you'll pay with a major credit card (which you insert into the phone—minimum charge for a credit-card call is £1.20) or coins (have a bunch handy; minimum fee is £0.60). Only unused coins will be returned, so put in biggies with caution.

It's always possible to find **public computers:** at your hotel (many have one in their lobby for guests to use), or at an Internet café or library (ask your hotelier or the TI for the nearest location). If typing on a European keyboard, use the "Alt Gr" key to the right of the space bar to insert the extra symbol that appears on some keys. If you can't locate a special character (such as @), simply copy it from a Web page and paste it into your email message.

MAIL

You can mail one package per day to yourself worth up to $200 duty-free from Europe to the US (mark it "personal purchases"). If you're sending a gift to someone, mark it "unsolicited gift." For details, visit www.cbp.gov and search for "Know Before You Go."

The Scottish postal service works fine, but for quick transatlantic delivery (in either direction), consider services such as DHL (www.dhl.com).

Transportation

If you're debating between using public transportation and renting a car, consider these factors: Cars are best for three or more traveling together (especially families with small kids), those packing heavy, and those delving into the countryside—a tempting plan for this region. Trains and buses are best for solo travelers, blitz tourists, city-to-city travelers, and those who don't want to drive. While a car gives you more freedom, trains and buses zip you effortlessly and scenically from city to city, usually dropping you in the center, often near a TI. Cars are an expensive headache in places like Glasgow, but necessary for remote destinations not well served by public transport.

In Scotland, my choice is to connect big cities by train or bus and to explore rural areas (including most of the Highlands) foot-loose and fancy-free by rental car. The mix works quite efficiently (e.g., Edinburgh, Glasgow, Stirling, and Inverness by train or bus, with a rental car for the rest).

BY TRAIN

Scotland is served by Britain's great train system (15,000 departures from 2,400 stations daily), on which regular tickets are the most expensive per mile in all of Europe. For the greatest savings, book online in advance and leave after rush hour (after 9:30).

Since Britain's railways have been privatized, it can be tricky to track down all your options; a single train route can be operated by multiple companies. However, one website covers all train lines (www.nationalrail.co.uk), and another covers all bus and train routes (www.traveline.org.uk—for information, not ticket sales). For Caledonian Sleeper overnight trains, see www.sleeper.scot. Another good resource, which also has schedules for trains throughout Europe, is German Rail's timetable (www.bahn.com).

While not required, reservations are free and can normally be made well in advance. They are an especially good idea for long journeys or for travel on Sundays or holidays. Make reservations at any train station, by phone, or online when you buy your ticket. With a point-to-point ticket, you can reserve as late as two hours before train time, but rail-pass holders should book seats at least 24 hours in advance (see below for more on rail passes).

Buying Train Tickets in Advance: The best fares go to those who book their trips well in advance of their journey. Savings can be significant. For an Edinburgh-Inverness round-trip (standard class), the full fare is about £85; if you book online at least a day ahead, off-peak and advance-purchase discounts can combine for a rate closer to £65. An advance fare for the same ticket booked a couple of months out can cost as little as £25.

Public Transportation Routes in Scotland

50 Kilometers

50 Miles

- ⋯⋯ Rail
- --- Bus
- ⋯⋯ Ferry

Orkney Islands

Mainland
Stromness

St. Marg. Hope
Burwick
Scrabster ● Gills Bay
Thurso
John O' Groats
Wick

North Sea

Stornoway

Lewis
Ullapool
Harris ● Tarbert
Dingwall
Lochmaddy Uig
Elgin
Dunvegan Portree
Inverness
Uist Kyle of
Lochbolsdale Skye Lochalsh Culloden
Loch Ness
Arm- (Urqhart Aviemore Aberdeen
Mallaig Glen- Castle)
finnan SCOTLAND Ballater Stone-
Fort William haven
Ballachulish Glencoe Pitlochry
Craig- Dundee Arbroath
Staffa nure Perth
Mull Crian- Leuchars
Iona Fionn- larich St. Andrews
phort Oban Crail
Balloch Stirling Anstruther
Glasgow Edinburgh
Holy
Large Island
Arran Berwick
Ard. Kilmarnock
Troon
Prestwick
Cairnryan To York
Larne Dumfries & London
Hexham
Stranraer Carlisle ENGLAND
NORTHERN
IRELAND Penrith
Belfast Keswick
Irish
Sea Windermere To Liverpool
To Dublin To Isle & London
Liverpool of Man

The cheapest fares (minimum 7-day advance purchase) sell out fast. Especially in summer, it's often necessary to book six to eight weeks ahead. Keep in mind that "return" (round-trip) fares are not always cheaper than buying two "single" (one-way) tickets—thankfully National Rail's website will automatically display this option if it's the lowest fare. Cheap advance tickets often come with the toughest refund restrictions, so be sure to nail down your travel plans before you reserve.

To book ahead, go in person to any station, book online at www.nationalrail.co.uk, or call 0345-748-4950 (from the US, dial 011-44-20-7278-5240, phone answered 24 hours) to find out the schedule and best fare for your journey; you'll then be referred to the appropriate vendor—depending on the particular rail company—to book your ticket. If you order online, be sure you know what you want; it's tough to reach a person who can change your online reservation. You'll pick up your ticket at the station, or you may be able to print it at home.

A company called **Megabus** (through their subsidiary Megatrain) sells discounted train tickets well in advance on a few specific routes, though their focus is mainly on selling bus tickets (info tel. 0871-266-3333, www.megatrain.com).

Buying Train Tickets as You Travel: If you'd rather have the flexibility of booking tickets as you go, you can save a few pounds by buying a round-trip ticket, called a "return ticket" (a same-day round-trip, called a "day return," is particularly cheap); buying before 18:00 the day before you depart; traveling after the morning rush hour (this usually means after 9:30 Mon-Fri); and going standard class instead of first class.

Senior, Youth, Partner, and Family Deals: To get a third off the price of most point-to-point rail tickets, seniors can buy a Senior Railcard (ages 60 and up), younger travelers can buy a 16-25 Railcard (ages 16-25, or for full-time students 26 and older), and two people traveling together can buy a Two Together Railcard (ages 16 and over). A Family and Friends Railcard gives adults about 33 percent off for most trips and 60 percent off for their kids ages 5 to 15 (maximum 4 adults and 4 kids). Each Railcard costs £30; see www.railcard.co.uk. The Two Together Railcard can save you about £30 if you're traveling with a partner and doing most of your Scotland trip by train.

Rail Passes: There are three different Scotland-only passes (the Freedom of Scotland Pass, the Central Scotland Pass, and the Scottish Highlands Pass). But for a Scotland-only itinerary, these probably won't save you money over point-to-point tickets (especially if you buy tickets in advance or use a discount Railcard).

If your trip extends beyond Scotland, consider the BritRail Pass, which covers England, Scotland, and Wales. A rail pass offers hop-on flexibility and no need to lock in reservations, except for overnight sleeper cars. Passes come in "consecutive day" and "flexi" versions, with price breaks for youths, seniors, off-season travelers, and groups of three or more. Most allow one child under 16 to travel free with a paying adult. If you're exploring the backcountry with a BritRail pass, standard class is a good choice, since many of the smaller train lines don't even offer first-class cars.

BritRail passes cannot be purchased locally; you must buy your pass through an agent before leaving the US. Make sleeper reservations in advance; you can also make optional, free seat reservations at staffed train stations. For specifics, see www.ricksteves.com/rail.

BY BUS

Although buses are about a third slower than trains, they're also a lot cheaper. And buses go many places that trains don't, including destinations in the Highlands and the islands. For details on bus connections in the Highlands—where buses are the most useful—see page 238.

Most long-haul domestic routes in Scotland are operated by **Scottish Citylink.** In peak season, it's worth booking your seat on popular routes at least a day in advance (at the bus station or TI, online at www.citylink.co.uk, or by calling 0871-216-3333). At slower times, you can just hop on the bus and pay the driver. If you're taking lots of buses, consider Citylink's Explorer pass (£41/3 days in 5-day period, £62/5 days in 10-day period, £93/8 days in 16-day period).

Some regional routes are operated by Citylink's **Stagecoach** service (www.stagecoachbus.com). If a Stagecoach bus runs the same route as a Citylink one—such as between Glencoe and Fort William—it's likely cheaper (and maybe slower).

Longer-distance routes (especially those to England) are operated by **National Express** (tel. 0871-781-8178, www.nationalexpress.com) or **Megabus** (book far ahead for best discounts, info tel. 0871-266-3333, http://uk.megabus.com).

RENTING A CAR

Rental companies in Scotland require you to be at least 21 years old. Drivers under the age of 25 may incur a young-driver surcharge (depending on the class of car rented), and some rental companies will not rent to anyone 75 or older. If you're considered too young or old, look into leasing (covered later), which has less-stringent age restrictions.

Research car rentals before you go. It's cheaper to arrange most car rentals from the US. Consider several companies to compare rates. Most of the major US rental agencies (including Avis, Budget, Enterprise, Hertz, and Thrifty) have offices throughout Europe. Also consider the two major Europe-based agencies, Europcar and Sixt. It can be

Driving in Scotland

To Orkney Islands

Scrabster · John O'Groats

Durness · 70m · 2.25h · 20m .75h

120m · 3h

70m · 2.25h · 105m · 3h

120m · 3h (via Gairloch)

50m · 2h (Trotternish Loop)

Ullapool

m = miles
h = hours

Not exactly to scale

60m · 1.25h

85m · 2h

Skye · Apple-cross

Portree · 40m 1.5h · Inverness

35m 1h · 85m · 2h · 20m .5h · 60m · 1.5h · Dufftown (Speyside) · 105m · 2.75h

45m 1h · 75m 1.75h · 90m 1.75h · 75m ·2h · 45m 1.5h · 55m · 1.25h

Kyle of Lochalsh · Loch Ness (Urquart Castle) · 40m · 1.25h · Aberdeen

Armadale · Mallaig · 45m · 1.5h · 50m 1.25h · **SCOTLAND** · Ballater (Balmoral Castle) · 20m .5h

Ft. William · 20m · .5h · 55m ·1.75h · 45m 1h · Dunnottar Castle

Glencoe · 90m · 2.75h · Pitlochry · 50m · 1h

Mull · 35m ·1h · 80m · 1.75h · 45m · 1.25h · Dundee · 25m .5h

Iona · 35m · 1.25h · Oban · 60m · 1.5h · 70m · 1.5h · St. Andrews

Fionn-phort · Craig-nure · 75m · 2h · 85m · 2.25h · 30m .75h · Stirling · 50m · 1.5h

Loch Lomond (Balloch) · 25m .75h · 40m · 1h · Edinburgh

Glasgow · 50m · 1h · 75m · 2h · Holy Island

To Larne & Belfast (Northern Ireland) · 135m · 2.5h · 100m · 2.75h · 80m ·1.75h

90m · 2.25h · 130m · 3h · 100m · 2.5h · 125m · 2.75h

Cairnryan · 145m · 3h · Hadrian's Wall · 50m · 1h · 75m ·1.5h

Note: Your times may vary based on traffic, sheep, construction & road conditions. · 65m · 1.5h · Durham

Keswick · **ENGLAND**

100m 2.5h · To Liverpool · 120m · 3h · To York

cheaper to use a consolidator, such as Auto Europe/Kemwel (www.autoeurope.com) or Europe by Car (www.europebycar.com), which compares rates at several companies to get you the best deal—but because you're working with a middleman, it's especially important to ask in advance about add-on fees and restrictions.

Always read the fine print carefully for add-on charges—such as one-way drop-off fees, airport surcharges, or mandatory insurance policies—that aren't included in the "total price." You may need to query rental agents pointedly to find out your actual cost.

For the best deal, rent by the week with unlimited mileage. I normally rent the smallest, least expensive model with a stick shift (generally cheaper than automatic). Almost all rentals are manual by default, so if you need an automatic, request one in advance. An automatic makes sense for most American drivers: With a manual transmission in Scotland, you'll be sitting on the right side of the car, and shifting with your left hand...while driving on the left side of the road. When selecting a car, don't be tempted by a larger model, as it won't be as maneuverable on narrow, winding roads.

Figure on paying roughly $230 for a one-week rental. Allow extra for supplemental insurance, fuel, tolls, and parking. For trips of three weeks or more, leasing can save you money on insurance and taxes.

Picking Up Your Car: Big companies have offices in most cities, but small local rental companies can be cheaper. If you pick up your car in a smaller city or at an airport (rather than downtown), you'll more likely survive your first day on the road. Be aware that Scots call it "hiring a car," and directional signs at airports and train stations will read *Car Hire.*

Compare pickup costs (downtown can be less expensive than the airport) and explore drop-off options. Always check the hours of the location you choose: Many rental offices close from midday Saturday until Monday morning and, in smaller towns, at lunchtime.

When selecting a location, don't trust the agency's description of "downtown" or "city center." In some cases, a "downtown" branch can be on the outskirts of the city—a long, costly taxi ride from the center. Before choosing, plug the addresses into a mapping website. You may find that the "train station" location is handier. But returning a car at a big-city train station or downtown agency can be tricky; get precise details on the car drop-off location and hours, and allow ample time to find it.

When you pick up the rental car, check it thoroughly and make sure any damage is noted on your rental agreement. Find out how your car's lights, turn signals, wipers, radio, and fuel cap function, and know what kind of fuel the car takes (diesel vs. unleaded). When you return the car, make sure the agent verifies its condition with you. Some drivers take pictures of the returned vehicle as proof of its condition.

The AA: The services of Britain's Automobile Association are included with most rentals (www.theaa.com), but check for this when booking to be sure you understand its towing and emergency road-service benefits.

Navigation Options

When renting a car in Europe, for a digital navigator you can use the mapping app that's already on your cellular-connected device, or download a mapping app that's designed to be used offline. As an alternative, you could rent a GPS device—known as a "satnav" in Scotland—or bring your own GPS device from home. And of course, you can always refer to paper maps.

To use your mobile device for pulling up maps or routes on the fly, for turn-by-turn directions, or for traffic updates, you'll need to go online—so it's smart to get an international data plan (see page 462). But just using GPS to locate your position on a map doesn't require an Internet connection (and therefore doesn't require Wi-Fi or cellular data). This means that once you have the map in your phone, you can navigate with it all day long without incurring data-roaming charges.

Using Your Device's Mapping App: The mapping app you use at home (such as Google Maps or Apple Maps) will work just as well for navigating Europe.

The most economical approach is to download information while you're on Wi-Fi (at your hotel, before setting out for the day). Google Maps' "save map to use offline" feature is useful for this, allowing you to view a map when you're offline (though you can't search for an address or get directions). Apple Maps doesn't offer a save-for-offline feature, though it does automatically cache (save) certain data. So if you bring up the maps you need or plan your route while on Wi-Fi in the morning, the Apple Maps app may end up caching those maps and not using data roaming much during the day.

No matter which app you use, view the maps in standard view (not satellite view) to limit data use. And consider bringing a car charger: Even offline, mapping services gobble up battery life.

Using a Third-Party Offline Mapping App: A number of well-designed apps allow you much of the convenience of online maps without any costly cellular data demands. City Maps 2Go is popular; OffMaps and Navfree also offer good, zoomable offline maps—similar to Google Maps—for much of Europe. You need to be online to download the app, but once that's done, the maps are accessible anywhere (note that you won't get turn-by-turn directions, which require a data connection).

Using GPS: Some drivers prefer using a dedicated GPS unit—not only to avoid using cellular data, but because a stand-alone GPS can be easier to operate (important if you're driving solo). The downside: It's expensive—around $10-30 per day. Your car's GPS unit may only come loaded with maps for its home country—if you need additional maps, ask. And make sure your device's language is set to English. If you have a portable GPS device at home, you can take that instead, but you'll need to buy and download European maps before your trip. This option is far less expensive than renting.

Using Paper Maps: Several good road atlases cover all of Scotland. Ordnance Survey, Collins, AA, and Bartholomew editions are all available at tourist information offices, gas stations, and bookstores. The tourist-oriented Collins Touring maps do a good job of highlighting the many roadside attractions you might otherwise drive right past. Before you buy a map, look at it to be sure it has the level of detail you want.

Car Insurance Options

When you rent a car, you are liable for a very high deductible, sometimes equal to the entire value of the car. Limit your financial risk with one of these three options: Buy Collision Damage Waiver (CDW) coverage with a low or zero deductible from the car-rental company, get coverage through your credit card (free, if your card automatically includes zero-deductible coverage), or get collision insurance as part of a larger travel-insurance policy.

Basic **CDW** includes a very high deductible (typically $1,000-1,500). Though each rental company has its own variation, basic CDW costs $15-35 a day (figure roughly 30 percent extra) and reduces your liability, but does not eliminate it. When you reserve or pick up the car, you'll be offered the chance to "buy down" the basic deductible to zero (for an additional $10-30/day; this is sometimes called "super CDW" or "zero-deductible coverage").

If you opt for **credit-card coverage,** there's a catch. You'll technically have to decline all coverage offered by the car-rental company, which means they can place a hold on your card (which can be up to the full value of the car). In case of damage, it can be time-consuming to resolve the charges with your credit-card company. Before you decide on this option, quiz your credit-card company about how it works.

If you're already purchasing a **travel-insurance policy** for your trip, adding collision coverage is an option. For example, Travel Guard (www.travelguard.com) sells affordable renter's collision insurance as an add-on to its other policies; it's valid everywhere in Europe except the Republic of Ireland, and some Italian car-rental companies refuse to honor it, as it doesn't cover you in case of theft.

For more on car-rental insurance, see www.ricksteves.com/cdw.

Leasing

For trips of three weeks or more, consider leasing (which automatically includes zero-deductible collision and theft insurance). By technically buying and then selling back the car, you save lots of

British Radio

Local radio broadcasts can be a treat for drivers sightseeing in Britain. Many British radio stations broadcast nationwide; your car radio automatically detects the local frequency a station plays on and displays its name.

The BBC has five nationwide stations, which you can pick up in most of the country. These government-subsidized stations have no ads.

BBC **Radio 1:** Pop music, with youthful DJs spinning top 40 hits and interviewing big-name bands.

BBC **Radio 2:** The highest-rated station nationwide, aimed at a more mature audience, with adult contemporary, retro pop, and other "middle of the road" music.

BBC **Radio 3:** Mostly classical music, with some jazz and world music.

BBC **Radio 4:** All talk—current events, entertaining chat shows, special-interest topics such as cooking and gardening, and lots of radio plays.

BBC **Radio 5 Live:** Sporting events as well as news and sports talk programs.

BBC Scotland focuses on Scottish issues, and **BBC Gaelic** (or **BBC Gàidhlig**) broadcasts mostly in the Gaelic language. At the top of the hour, many BBC stations broadcast the famous "pips" (indicating Greenwich Mean Time) and a short roundup of the day's news.

Beyond the BBC offerings, several private stations broadcast music and other content with "adverts" (commercials). Some are nationwide, including **XFM** (alternative rock), **Classic FM** (classical), **Absolute Radio** (pop), and **Capital FM** (pop).

Traffic Alerts: Ask your rental-car company about turning on automatic traffic alerts that play on the car radio. Once these are enabled (look for the letters *TA* or *TP* on the radio readout), traffic reports for the area you are driving in will periodically interrupt programming.

money on tax and insurance. Leasing provides you a brand-new car with unlimited mileage and a 24-hour emergency assistance program. You can lease for as little as 21 days to as long as five and a half months. Car leases must be arranged from the US. One of many companies offering affordable lease packages is Europe by Car (www.europebycar.com/lease).

Driving in Scotland

Driving in Scotland is basically wonderful—once you remember to stay on the left and after you've mastered the roundabouts. Every year, however, I get a few notes from traveling readers advising me that, for them, trying to drive in Scotland was a nerve-racking and regrettable mistake. If you want to get a little slack on the roads, drop by a gas station or auto shop and buy a green *P* (probationary driver with license) sign to put in your car window (don't get the red *L* sign, which means you're a learner driver without a license and thus prohibited from driving on motorways).

Many Yankee drivers find the hardest part isn't driving on the left, but steering from the right. Your instinct is to put yourself on the left side of your lane, which means you may spend your first day or two constantly drifting into the left shoulder. It can help to remember that the driver always stays close to the center line.

Road Rules: Be aware of typical European road rules; for example, many countries require headlights to be turned on at all times, and it's generally illegal to drive while using your mobile phone without a hands-free device. In Scotland, you're not allowed to turn left on a red light unless a sign or signal specifically authorizes it, and on motorways it's illegal to pass drivers on the left.

STOP AND LEARN THESE ROAD SIGNS

Speed Limit (mph) — Yield — No Passing — End of No Passing Zone

One Way — Intersection — Main Road — Freeway

Danger — No Entry — No Entry for cars — All Vehicles Prohibited

Parking — No Parking — Customs — Peace

Ask your car-rental company about these rules, read the Department for Transport's *Highway Code* (www.gov.uk/highway-code), or check the US State Department website (www.travel.state.gov, search for your country in the "Learn about your destination" box, then click on "Travel and Transportation").

Speed Limits: Speed limits are in miles per hour: 30 mph in town, 70 mph on the motorways, and 50 or 60 mph elsewhere (though, as back home, many Scottish drivers consider these limits advisory). The national sign for 60 mph is a white circle with a black slash. Motorways have electronic speed limit signs; posted speeds can change depending on traffic or the weather. Follow them accordingly.

Note that road-surveillance cameras strictly enforce speed limits. Any driver (including foreigners renting cars) photographed speeding will

How to Navigate a Roundabout

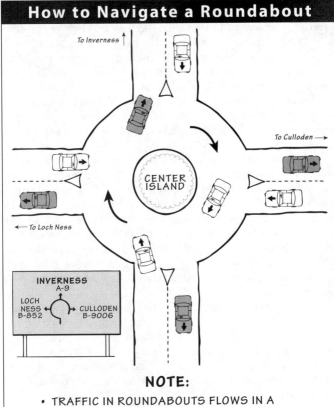

To Inverness ↑

To Culloden →

CENTER ISLAND

← To Loch Ness

INVERNESS
A-9

LOCH
NESS ← → CULLODEN
B-852   B-9006

NOTE:

- TRAFFIC IN ROUNDABOUTS FLOWS IN A CLOCKWISE DIRECTION.

- WHITE CARS ARE ENTERING THE ROUNDABOUT, GRAY CARS ARE EXITING.

- VEHICLES ENTERING A ROUNDABOUT MUST YIELD TO VEHICLES IN THE ROUNDABOUT.

- LOOK TO YOUR RIGHT AS YOU MERGE! ☺

get a nasty bill in the mail. (Cameras—in foreboding gray boxes—flash on rear license plates to respect the privacy of anyone sharing the front seat with someone he or she shouldn't.) Signs (an image of an old-fashioned camera) alert you when you're entering a zone that may be monitored by these "camera cops." Heed them.

Roundabouts: Don't let a roundabout spook you. After all, you routinely merge into much faster traffic on American highways back home. Traffic flows clockwise, and cars already in the roundabout have the right-of-way; entering traffic yields (look to your right as you merge). You'll probably encounter "double-roundabouts"—figure-eights where you'll slingshot from one roundabout directly into another. Just go with the flow and track signs carefully. When approaching an especially complex roundabout, you'll first pass a diagram showing the layout and the various exits. And in many cases, the pavement is painted to indicate the lane you should be in for a particular road or town.

Freeways (Motorways): The shortest distance between any two points is usually the motorway (what we'd call a "freeway"). In Scotland, the smaller the number, the bigger the road. For example, the M-8 is a freeway, while the B-8000 is a country road.

Motorway road signs can be confusing, too few, and too late. Miss a motorway exit and you can lose 30 minutes. Study your map before taking off. Know the cities you'll be lacing together, since road numbers are inconsistent. Scottish road signs are never marked with compass directions (e.g., *A-30 North*); instead, you need to know what major town or city you're heading for *(A-9 Inverness)*. The driving directions in this book are intended to be used with a good map. Get a road atlas, easily purchased at gas stations in Scotland, or download digital maps before your trip (see page 477).

Unless you're passing, always drive in the "slow" lane on motorways (the lane farthest to the left). The Scottish are very disciplined about this; ignoring this rule could get you a ticket (or into a road-rage incident). Remember to pass on the right, not the left.

Rest areas are called "services" and often have a number of useful amenities, such as restaurants, cafeterias, gas stations, shops, and motels.

Fuel: Gas (petrol) costs about $10 per gallon and is self-serve. Pump first and then pay. Diesel rental cars are common; make sure you know what kind of fuel your car takes before you fill up. Unleaded pumps are usually green. Note that self-service gas pumps and automated toll booths and parking garages often accept only cash or a chip-and-PIN credit card (see page 437).

Driving in Cities: Whenever possible, avoid driving in cities. Most cities have modern ring roads to skirt the congestion. Follow signs to the parking lots outside the city core—most are a 5- to 10-minute walk to the center—and avoid what can be an unpleasant grid of one-way streets or roads that are restricted to public transportation during the day.

Driving in Rural Areas: Outside the big cities and except for the motorways, Scottish roads tend to be narrow. In towns, you may have to cross over the center line just to get past parked cars. Adjust your perceptions of personal space: It's not "my side of the road" or "your side of the road," it's just "the road"—and it's shared as a cooperative adventure. If the road's wide enough, traffic in both directions can pass parked cars simultaneously, but frequently you'll have to take turns—follow the locals' lead and drive defensively.

Narrow country lanes are often lined with stone walls or woody hedges—and no shoulders. Some are barely wide enough for one car. Go slowly, and if you encounter an oncoming car, look for the nearest pullout (or "passing place")—the driver who's closest to one is expected to use it, even if it means backing up to reach it. If another car pulls over and blinks its headlights, that means, "Go ahead; I'll wait to let you pass." Scottish drivers—arguably the most courteous on the planet—are quick to offer a friendly wave to thank you for letting them pass (and they appreciate it if you reciprocate). Pull over frequently—to let faster locals pass and to check the map.

Parking: Pay attention to pavement markings to figure out where to park. One yellow line marked on the pavement means no parking Monday through Saturday during work hours. Double yellow lines mean no parking at any time. Broken yellow lines mean short stops are OK, but you should always look for explicit signs or ask a passerby. White lines mean you're free to park.

In towns, rather than look for street parking, I generally just pull into the most central and handy pay-and-display parking lot I can find. To pay and display, feed change into a machine, receive a timed ticket, and display it on the dashboard or stick it to the driver's-side window. Rates are reasonable by US standards, and locals love to share stickers that have time remaining. If you stand by the machine, someone on their way out with time left on their sticker will probably give it to you. Most machines in larger towns accept credit cards with a chip, but it's smart to keep coins handy for machines and parking meters that don't.

In some municipalities, drivers will see signs for "disc zone" parking. This is free, time-limited parking. But to use it, you must obtain a clock parking disc from a shop and display it on the dashboard (set the clock to show your time of arrival). Return within the signed time limit to avoid being ticketed.

Some parking garages (a.k.a. car parks) are totally automated and record your license plate with a camera when you enter. The Brits call a license plate a "number plate" or just "vehicle registration." The payment machine will use these terms when you pay before exiting.

FERRIES

Ferries link the Scottish mainland to its many islands. For most west coast routes, including the isles of Mull and Skye, you'll take a ferry run by Caledonian MacBrayne (tel. 0800-066-5000 or 01475/650-397, www.calmac.co.uk). Ferries to Orkney are operated by NorthLink (www.northlinkferries.co.uk) and Pentland

Ferries (www.pentlandferries. co.uk); Orkney Ferries runs the interisland routes (www. orkneyferries.co.uk).

Ferries can fill up in peak season—especially car spaces. During the summer, it's smart to reserve at least one day before (online or by phone). They'll hold a space for your car, but you must show up at least 30 minutes ahead, leave your car in line, and run into the ticket office to buy your ticket (have your confirmation number handy). Walk-on passengers don't need to reserve. Most car ferries have some kind of eatery on board.

FLIGHTS

The best comparison search engine for both international and intra-European flights is www.kayak.com. For inexpensive flights within Europe, try www.skyscanner.com or www.hipmunk.com; for inexpensive international flights, try www.vayama.com.

Flying to Europe: Start looking for international flights four to five months before your trip, especially for peak-season travel. Off-season tickets can be purchased a month or so in advance. Depending on your itinerary, it can be efficient to fly into one city and out of another. If your flight requires a connection in Europe, see my hints on navigating Europe's top hub airports at www. ricksteves.com/hub-airports.

Flying Within Europe: Several cheap, no-frills airlines affordably connect Scotland with other destinations in the British Isles and throughout Europe. If you're considering a train ride that's more than five hours long, a flight may save you both time and money. When comparing your options, factor in the time it takes to get to the airport and how early you'll need to arrive to check in.

Well-known cheapo airlines that serve Scotland include **easy-Jet** (Aberdeen, Edinburgh, Glasgow, Inverness; www.easyjet.com), **Ryanair** (Edinburgh, Glasgow; www.ryanair.com), **Thomson** (Aberdeen, Edinburgh, Glasgow; www.thomsonfly.com), and **Flybe** (Aberdeen, Edinburgh, Glasgow, Inverness; www.flybe.com).

But be aware of the potential drawbacks of flying with a discount airline: nonrefundable and nonchangeable tickets, minimal or nonexistent customer service, pricey and time-consuming treks

Begin Your Trip at
www.RickSteves.com

My mobile-friendly **website** is *the* place to explore Europe. You'll find thousands of fun articles, videos, photos, and radio interviews organized by country; a wealth of money-saving tips for planning your dream trip; monthly travel news dispatches; my travel talks and travel blog; my latest guidebook updates (www.ricksteves.com/update); and my free Rick Steves Audio Europe app. You can also follow me on Facebook and Twitter.

Our **Travel Forum** is an immense yet well-groomed collection of message boards, where our travel-savvy community answers questions and shares their personal travel experiences—and our well-traveled staff chimes in when they can be helpful (www.ricksteves.com/forums).

Our **online Travel Store** offers travel bags and accessories that I've designed specifically to help you travel smarter and lighter. These include my popular bags (rolling carry-on and backpack versions, which I helped design...and live out of four months a year), money belts, totes, toiletries kits, adapters, other accessories, and a wide selection of guidebooks and planning maps.

Choosing the right **rail pass** for your trip—amid hundreds of options—can drive you nutty. Our website will help you find the perfect fit for your itinerary and your budget: We offer easy, one-stop shopping for rail passes, seat reservations, and point-to-point tickets.

Want to travel with greater efficiency and less stress? We organize **tours** with more than three dozen itineraries and more than 900 departures reaching the best destinations in this book...and beyond. Our "Best of Scotland" tour covers just that in 10 days. You'll enjoy great guides, a fun bunch of travel partners (with small groups of 24 to 28 travelers), and plenty of room to spread out in a big, comfy bus when touring between towns. You'll find European adventures to fit every vacation length. For all the details, and to get our Tour Catalog and a free Rick Steves Tour Experience DVD (filmed on location during an actual tour), visit www.ricksteves.com or call us at 425/608-4217.

to secondary airports, and stingy baggage allowances with steep overage fees. If you're traveling with lots of luggage, a cheap flight can quickly become a bad deal. To avoid unpleasant surprises, read the small print before you book. These days you can also fly within Europe on major airlines affordably—and without all the aggressive restrictions—for around $100 a flight.

Flying to the US and Canada: Because security is extra tight for flights to the US, be sure to give yourself plenty of time at the airport. It's also important to charge your electronic devices before you board because security checks may require you to turn them on (see www.tsa.gov for the latest rules).

Resources

RESOURCES FROM RICK STEVES

Rick Steves Scotland is one of many books in my series on European travel, which includes country and regional guidebooks (including

Great Britain and England), city guidebooks (London, Paris, Rome, Florence, etc.), Snapshot guides (excerpted chapters from my country guides), Pocket Guides (full-color little books on big cities), and my budget-travel skills handbook, *Rick Steves Europe Through the Back Door.* Most of my titles are available as ebooks. My phrase books—for Italian, French, German, Spanish, and Portuguese—are practical and budget-oriented. My other books include *Europe 101* (a crash course on art and history designed for travelers); *Mediterranean Cruise Ports* and *Northern European Cruise Ports* (how to make the most of your time in port); and *Travel as a Political Act* (a travelogue sprinkled with tips for bringing home a global perspective). A more complete list of my titles appears near the end of this book.

Video: My public television series, *Rick Steves' Europe,* covers Europe from top to bottom with over 100 half-hour episodes. To watch full episodes online for free, see www.ricksteves.com/tv. Or to raise your travel I.Q. with video versions of our popular classes (including my talks on travel skills, packing smart, European art for travelers, travel as a political act, and individual talks covering most European countries), see www.ricksteves.com/travel-talks.

Audio: My weekly public radio show, *Travel with Rick Steves,* features interviews with travel experts from around the world. A complete archive of 10 years of programs (over 400 in all) is available at www.ricksteves.com/radio. Most of this audio content is available for free through my **Rick Steves Audio Europe app,** an extensive online library organized by destination. For more on my app, see page 10.

Maps: The black-and-white maps in this book are concise and simple, designed to help you locate recommended places and get to local TIs, where you can pick up more in-depth maps of cities and regions (usually free). Better maps are sold at newsstands and bookstores. The *Rick Steves Britain, Ireland & London City Map* covers Scotland and is useful for planning ($9, www.ricksteves.com).

APPENDIX

Useful Contacts

Emergency Needs
Police and Ambulance: Tel. 999 or 112

Embassies and Consulates
US Consulate in Edinburgh: 3 Regent Terrace, Mon-Fri 8:30-17:00, closed Sat-Sun, tel. 0131/556-8315; after-hours tel. 020/7499-9000, no walk-in passport services, http://edinburgh.usconsulate.gov
Canadian Consulate in Edinburgh: Mobile 0770-235-9916 (business hours); after hours call the High Commission of Canada in London at tel. 020/7004-6000, www.unitedkingdom.gc.ca

Directory Assistance
Operator Assistance: Tel. 100 (free)
Directory Assistance: Toll tel. 118-500 (£3.99/call and £1.39/minute)

Holidays and Festivals

This list includes selected Scottish festivals plus national holidays observed throughout Scotland (and Great Britain). Many sights and banks close on national holidays—keep this in mind when planning your itinerary. During July and August, book as far ahead as possible; Edinburgh is particularly jammed up in August during its festival season. Hotels also get booked up during Easter week; over the early May, spring, and summer Bank Holidays; and during Christmas, Boxing Day, and New Year's Day. On Christmas, virtually everything shuts down. Museums also generally close December 24 and 26.

Throughout the summer, communities small and large across Scotland host their annual Highland Games (like a combination track meet/county fair). These are a wonderful way to get in touch with local culture and traditions. For more on this phenomenon, see page 236.

Some Scottish towns have holiday festivals in late November and early December, with markets, music, and entertainment in the Christmas spirit (for instance, Stirling's Hogmanay party).

Before planning a trip around a festival, make sure to verify its dates by checking the festival website or the Visit Scotland website (www.visitscotland.com).

Here are some major holidays:

Jan 1	New Year's Day (closures)
Jan 2	New Year's Holiday (closures)
Jan 25	Burns Night (poetry readings, haggis)
Easter Sunday	March 27, 2016; April 16, 2017
Easter Monday	March 28, 2016; April 17, 2017
Early May Bank Holiday	May 2, 2016; May 1, 2017
Spring Bank Holiday	May 30, 2016; May 29, 2017
June	Edinburgh International Film Festival (www.edfilmfest.org.uk)
Mid-June	Royal Highland Show, Edinburgh (Scottish-flavored county fair, www.royalhighlandshow.org)
July	Edinburgh Jazz and Blues Festival (www.edinburghjazzfestival.com)
Summer Bank Holiday	August 1, 2016; August 7, 2017

Aug	Edinburgh Military Tattoo (massing of military bands, www.edintattoo.co.uk)
Aug	Edinburgh Fringe Festival (offbeat theater and comedy, www.edfringe.com)
Aug	Edinburgh International Festival (music, dance, shows; www.eif.co.uk)
Late Aug	Cowal Highland Gathering, west of Glasgow in Dunoon
Sept 3	Braemar Gathering, north of Pitlochry
Oct	Royal National Mòd; 2016 in Western Isles; 2017 in Lochaber (Gaelic cultural festival, http://ancomunn.co.uk)
Nov 5	Guy Fawkes Night (fireworks, bonfires, effigy-burning of 1605 traitor Guy Fawkes)
Nov 30	St. Andrew's Day (dancing and other cultural events)
Dec 1	St. Andrew's Day Bank Holiday
Dec 24-26	Christmas holidays
Dec 31–Jan 2	Hogmanay, Scotland (music, street theater, carnival, www.hogmanay.net)

Recommended Books and Films

To learn more about Scotland past and present, check out a few of these books or films.

Nonfiction

Crowded with Genius (James Buchan, 2003). This account of Edinburgh's role in the Scottish Enlightenment details the city's transformation from squalid backwater to marvelous European capital.

Edinburgh: Picturesque Notes (Robert Louis Stevenson, 1879). One of the city's most famous residents takes readers on a tour of his hometown.

The Emperor's New Kilt (Jan-Andrew Henderson, 2000). Henderson deconstructs the myths surrounding the tartan-clad Scots.

The Guynd (Belinda Rathbone, 2005). The marriage of an American woman and a Scottish man endures through cultural gaps and household mishaps.

How the Scots Invented the Modern World (Arthur Herman, 2001). The author explains the disproportionately large influence the Scottish Enlightenment had on the rest of Europe.

The Life of Samuel Johnson (James Boswell, 1790). Scottish laird Boswell's portrait of his contemporary is so admired that it inspired the use of Boswell's name to mean a close and companionable observer (Sherlock Holmes, for instance, at times refers to Watson as "my Boswell").

Scotland: The Autobiography: 2,000 Years of Scottish History by Those Who Saw It Happen (Rosemary Goring, 2007). Extracts from primary sources let a diverse cast of real-life characters, from Tacitus to Muriel Spark, tell the story of the nation.

Sea Room (Adam Nicolson, 2001). The owner of three tiny islands in the Hebrides contemplates their magical appeal and dramatic history.

A Traveller's History of Scotland (Andrew Fisher, revised 2009). Fisher probes Scotland's turbulent history, beginning with the Celts.

Fiction

For the classics of Scottish drama and fiction, read the "Big Three": Sir Walter Scott, Robert Louis Stevenson, and poet Robert Burns.

44 Scotland Street (Alexander McCall Smith, 2005). The colorful residents of an Edinburgh apartment house bring Scottish society to life.

Complete Poems and Songs of Robert Burns (Robert Burns, 2012, featuring work from 1774–1796). This collection showcases the work of a Scottish icon who wrote in the Scots language, including that New Year's classic "Auld Lang Syne."

The Cone Gatherers (Robin Jenkins, 1980). A staple of British secondary-school reading lists, this tragic novel about two brothers is set on a Scottish country estate during World War II.

Consider Phlebas (Iain M. Banks, 1987). In this first book in the popular *The Culture* science fiction series, Scottish author Banks describes a galactic war.

The Heart of Midlothian (Sir Walter Scott, 1818). This novel from one of Great Britain's most renowned authors showcases the life-and-death drama of lynchings and criminal justice in 1730s Scotland. Other great reads by Sir Walter include *Waverley* (1814), *Rob Roy* (1818), and *Ivanhoe* (1819).

Knots and Crosses (Ian Rankin, 1987). The Scottish writer's first Inspector Rebus mystery plumbs Edinburgh's seamy underbelly.

Lanark (Alasdair Gray, 1981). This eccentric, sprawling four-part novel set in Glasgow (and a fictional alt-Glasgow) tackles huge themes—capitalism, power, love—and earned Gray a reputation as a great Scottish writer.

Macbeth (William Shakespeare, 1606). Shakespeare's "Scottish Play" depicts a guilt-wracked general who assassinates the king to take the throne.

Outlander (Diana Gabaldon, 1991). This genre-defying series kicks off with the heroine time-traveling from the Scotland of 1945 to 1743. A popular TV adaptation began airing in 2014 (see page 494).

The Prime of Miss Jean Brodie (Muriel Spark, 1961). The story of an unconventional young teacher who plays favorites with her students is a modern classic of Scottish literature.

The Strange Case of Dr. Jekyll and Mr. Hyde (Robert Louis Stevenson, 1996). This famous Gothic yarn by a Scottish author chronicles a fearful case of transformation in London, exploring Victorian ideas about conflict between good and evil.

Sunset Song (Lewis Grassic Gibbon, 1932). Farm girl Chris Guthrie is rudely confronted by adolescence, modernity, and war in this lauded Scottish classic, the first book in the trilogy "A Scots Quair."

Film and TV

The 39 Steps (1935). This Alfred Hitchcock classic about a London man wrongly accused of murder is set in Edinburgh, Glencoe, and other parts of the Scottish countryside.

The Angels' Share (2012). In this working-class comedy, a Glaswegian ne'er-do-well discovers he has a great nose for whisky.

Braveheart (1995). Mel Gibson stars in this Academy Award-winning adventure about the Scots overthrowing English rule in the 13th century.

Brigadoon (1954). In this classic musical, an American couple visiting Scotland discover a magical village.

Highlander (1986). An immortal swordsman remembers his life in 16th-century Scotland while preparing for a pivotal battle in the present day.

A History of Scotland (2010). This BBC series presented by Neil Oliver offers a succinct, lightly dramatized retelling of Scottish history.

Local Hero (1983). A businessman questions his decision to build an oil refinery in a small Scottish town once he gets a taste for country life.

Loch Ness (1996). A skeptical American scientist is sent to Scotland to investigate the existence of the Loch Ness monster.

Monarch of the Glen (2000). Set on Loch Laggan, this TV series features stunning Highland scenery and the eccentric family of a modern-day laird.

Mrs. Brown (1997). A widowed Queen Victoria (Dame Judy Dench) forges a very close friendship with her Scottish servant, John Brown (Billy Connolly).

One Day (2011). Two University of Edinburgh students meet and fall in love on their graduation day, and their story continues to be told at each anniversary.

The Queen (2006). Helen Mirren expertly channels Elizabeth II at

Outlander Locations in Scotland

American novelist Diana Gabaldon's *Outlander* series spans continents and centuries, but the origin story—that of a Highlands laird and an English combat nurse caught up in the Jacobite rebellion—is grounded in Scotland. Much of the Starz television adaptation was filmed here. *Outlander* fans may enjoy splicing some of the following landmarks—both the real-life places described in the novel, and the locations used in the TV filming—into their travels.

The novel begins with Claire Randall on her honeymoon in 1945 **Inverness** (see page 296)—played on TV by the village of **Falkland,** near St. Andrews. Claire is mysteriously transported back in time to 1743 at **Craig na Dun,** a fictional stone circle inspired by **Clava Cairns** near Inverness (page 317). The TV version was filmed at **Dunalastair Estate,** between Pitlochry and Loch Rannoch.

In short order, Claire encounters British officer Jonathan "Black Jack" Randall, is rescued by the MacKenzie clan, and tends to injured Highlander Jamie Fraser. They travel to the fictional **Castle Leoch,** seat of the Clan Mackenzie (the real-life Mackenzie home is Castle Leod, near Strathpeffer). For the TV show, exterior scenes at Castle Leoch were filmed at **Doune Castle** near Stirling (page 194), and Leoch's grounds—where Claire gathers medicinal herbs—were filmed in **Pollok County Park** (near Glasgow's Burrell Collection; page 160).

Cranesmuir village, where Claire meets the "witch" Geillis Duncan, is fictional, but the village of **Culross,** with its distinctive mercat cross (page 192) is a fine onscreen stand-in. The stone-and-thatch village where the MacKenzies collect rents was filmed at the **Highland Folk Museum** (between Inverness and Pitlochry; page 337). Claire and Jamie visit the fictional Fraser family homestead, **Lallybroch,** which is played on TV by the deserted country estate of **Midhope Castle** (closed to the public).

In the novel, Black Jack Randall's stout stone fortress is at **Fort William** (page 286); for the TV show those scenes were filmed at **Blackness Castle** on the Firth of Forth. Nearby, **Linlithgow Palace** is the filming location for the fictional **Wentworth Prison** (where Black Jack imprisons—and Claire rescues—Jamie), and **Aberdour Castle** plays the monastery where Jamie recovers (the novel's monastery is in France).

Many of the show's interior scenes are filmed at **Wardpark Studios,** a former factory converted into Scotland's first permanent film studio for *Outlander* (and visible from the M-80 between Stirling/Falkirk and Glasgow). For more *Outlander* locations, see www.visitscotland.com/outlander.

her Scottish Balmoral estate in the days after Princess Diana's death.

Rob Roy (1995). The Scottish rebel played by Liam Neeson struggles against feudal landlords in 18th-century Scotland.

Skyfall (2012). In this James Bond film, we learn that 007 grew up in the Scottish Highlands, with a climactic scene at his childhood home (filmed near Glencoe).

Trainspotting (1996). Ewan McGregor stars in this award-winning, wild, gritty picture about Edinburgh's drug scene in the 1980s.

FOR KIDS

Always Room for One More (Sorche Nic Leodhas, 1965). This Caldecott Medal-winning picture book presents a Scottish folktale with evocative illustrations.

Bagpipes, Beasties and Bogles (Tim Archbold, 2012). This whimsical story about spooky creatures and bagpipes serves up Scottish culture in a package perfect for young readers.

Brave (2012). This Disney flick follows an independent young Scottish princess as she fights to take control of her own fate.

Greyfriars Bobby (2005). Based on a true story, this family-friendly film is about a terrier in Edinburgh who became a local legend after refusing to leave his master's gravesite.

An Illustrated Treasury of Scottish Folk and Fairy Tales (Theresa Breslin, 2012). Kelpies, dragons, brownies, and other inhabitants of the Scottish Isles come to life in this lovely volume of traditional lore.

Kidnapped (Robert Louis Stevenson, 1886). This fantastic adventure story is based on events in 18th-century Scotland.

The Luck of the Loch Ness Monster (A. W. Flaherty, 2007). A picky American girl on a boat to Scotland throws her oatmeal out the porthole every morning, unwittingly feeding the Loch Ness monster that follows her.

This Is Edinburgh (Miroslav Sasek, 1961, updated 2006). Vivid illustrations bring the Scottish capital to life in this classic picture book.

Queen's Own Fool (Jane Yolen and Robert Harris, 2008). A historical novel for 10-and-ups based on the girl who was a jester in the court of Mary, Queen of Scots, the first of the "Stuart Quartet" books.

The Story of Scotland (Richard Brassey and Stewart Ross, 1999). This humorous, comic-book style history book will engage young travelers.

The Water Horse (2007). In this film based on a book of the same name, a young boy in 1940s Scotland discovers an egg, which later hatches into the fabled Loch Ness monster.

Conversions and Climate

NUMBERS AND STUMBLERS

- In Europe, dates appear as day/month/year, so Christmas 2017 is 25/12/17.
- What Americans call the second floor of a building is the first floor in Scotland.
- On escalators and moving sidewalks, Scots keep the left "lane" open for passing. Keep to the right.
- To avoid the Scottish version of giving someone "the finger," don't hold up the first two fingers of your hand with your palm facing you. (It looks like a reversed victory sign.)
- And please...don't call your waist pack a "fanny pack" (see the British-Yankee Vocabulary list on page 500).

METRIC CONVERSIONS

Scotland uses the metric system for nearly everything. Weight and volume are typically calculated in metric: A kilogram is 2.2 pounds, and one liter is about a quart (almost four to a gallon). Temperatures are generally given in Celsius, although some newspapers also list them in Fahrenheit.

1 foot = 0.3 meter	1 square yard = 0.8 square meter
1 yard = 0.9 meter	1 square mile = 2.6 square kilometers
1 mile = 1.6 kilometers	1 ounce = 28 grams
1 centimeter = 0.4 inch	1 quart = 0.95 liter
1 meter = 39.4 inches	1 kilogram = 2.2 pounds
1 kilometer = 0.62 mile	32°F = 0°C

IMPERIAL WEIGHTS AND MEASURES

Scotland hasn't completely gone metric. Driving distances and speed limits are measured in miles. Beer is sold as pints (though milk can be measured in pints or liters), and a person's weight is measured in stone (a 168-pound person weighs 12 stone).

1 stone = 14 pounds
1 Scottish pint = 1.2 US pints
1 schooner = 2/3 pint
1 imperial gallon = 1.2 US gallons or about 4.5 liters

CLOTHING SIZES

When shopping for clothing, use these US-to-Scotland comparisons as general guidelines (but note that no conversion is perfect).

- Women's dresses and blouses: Add 4 (US women's size 10 = UK size 14)
- Men's suits, jackets, and shirts: US and UK sizes are the same
- Women's shoes: Subtract 2½ (US size 8 = UK size 5½)
- Men's shoes: Subtract about ½ (US size 9 = UK size 8½)

SCOTLAND'S CLIMATE

First line, average daily high; second line, average daily low; third line, average days without rain. For more detailed weather statistics for destinations in this book (as well as the rest of the world), check www.wunderground.com.

J	F	M	A	M	J	J	A	S	O	N	D
EDINBURGH											
42°	43°	46°	51°	56°	62°	65°	64°	60°	54°	48°	44°
34°	34°	36°	39°	43°	49°	52°	52°	49°	44°	39°	36°
14	13	16	16	17	15	14	15	14	14	13	13

FAHRENHEIT AND CELSIUS CONVERSION

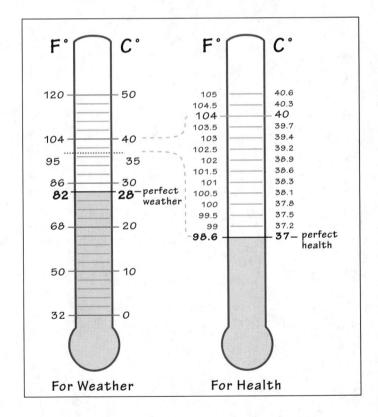

Scotland uses both Celsius and Fahrenheit to take its temperature. For a rough conversion from Celsius to Fahrenheit, double the number and add 30. For weather, remember that 28°C is 82°F—perfect. For health, 37°C is just right. At a launderette, 30°C is cold, 40°C is warm (usually the default setting), 60°C is hot, and 95°C is boiling.

Packing Checklist

Whether you're traveling for five days or five weeks, you won't need more than this. Pack light to enjoy the sweet freedom of true mobility.

Clothing

❑ 5 shirts: long- & short-sleeve
❑ 2 pairs pants or skirt
❑ 1 pair shorts or capris
❑ 5 pairs underwear & socks
❑ 1 pair walking shoes
❑ Sweater or fleece top
❑ Rainproof jacket with hood
❑ Tie or scarf
❑ Swimsuit
❑ Sleepwear

Money

❑ Debit card
❑ Credit card(s)
❑ Hard cash ($20 bills)
❑ Money belt or neck wallet

Documents & Travel Info

❑ Passport
❑ Airline reservations
❑ Rail pass/train reservations
❑ Car-rental voucher
❑ Driver's license
❑ Student ID, hostel card, etc.
❑ Photocopies of all the above
❑ Hotel confirmations
❑ Insurance details
❑ Guidebooks & maps
❑ Notepad & pen
❑ Journal

Toiletries Kit

❑ Toiletries
❑ Medicines & vitamins
❑ First-aid kit
❑ Glasses/contacts/sunglasses (with prescriptions)
❑ Earplugs
❑ Packet of tissues (for WC)

Miscellaneous

❑ Daypack
❑ Sealable plastic baggies
❑ Laundry soap
❑ Spot remover
❑ Clothesline
❑ Sewing kit
❑ Travel alarm/watch

Electronics

❑ Smartphone or mobile phone
❑ Camera & related gear
❑ Tablet/ereader/media player
❑ Laptop & flash drive
❑ Earbuds or headphones
❑ Chargers
❑ Plug adapters

Optional Extras

❑ Flipflops or slippers
❑ Mini-umbrella or poncho
❑ Travel hairdryer
❑ Belt
❑ Hat (for sun or cold)
❑ Picnic supplies
❑ Water bottle
❑ Fold-up tote bag
❑ Small flashlight
❑ Small binoculars
❑ Insect repellent
❑ Small towel or washcloth
❑ Inflatable pillow
❑ Some duct tape (for repairs)
❑ Tiny lock
❑ Address list (to mail postcards)
❑ Postcards/photos from home
❑ Extra passport photos
❑ Good book

BRITISH-YANKEE VOCABULARY

While Scotland has its own unique lexicon (see "The Language Barrier?" on page 468), most Scottish people also speak "British." Here are some words that may be unfamiliar. For a longer list, plus a dry-witted primer on British culture, see *The Septic's Companion* (Chris Rae). Note that instead of asking, "Can I help you?" many Brits offer a more casual, "You alright?" or "You OK there?"

advert: advertisement

afters: dessert

anticlockwise: counterclockwise

Antipodean: an Australian or New Zealander

aubergine: eggplant

banger: sausage

bangers and mash: sausage and mashed potatoes

Bank Holiday: legal holiday

bap: small roll, roll sandwich

bespoke: custom-made

billion: a thousand of our billions (a million million)

biro: ballpoint pen

biscuit: cookie

black pudding: sausage made with onions, pork fat, oatmeal, and pig blood

bloody: damn

blow off: fart

bobby: policeman ("the Bill" is more common)

Bob's your uncle: there you go (with a shrug), naturally

boffin: nerd, geek

bollocks: all-purpose expletive (a figurative use of testicles)

bolshy: argumentative

bomb: success or failure

bonnet: car hood

boot: car trunk

braces: suspenders

bridle way: path for walkers, bikers, and horse riders

brilliant: cool

brolly: umbrella

bubble and squeak: cabbage and potatoes fried together

candy floss: cotton candy

caravan: trailer

car-boot sale: temporary flea market, often for charity

car park: parking lot

cashpoint: ATM

casualty: emergency room

cat's eyes: road reflectors

ceilidh (KAY-lee): informal evening of song and folk fun (Scottish and Irish)

cheap and cheerful: budget but adequate

cheap and nasty: cheap and bad quality

cheers: good-bye or thanks; also a toast

chemist: pharmacist

chicory: endive

Chinese whispers: playing "telephone"

chippy: fish-and-chips shop

chips: French fries

chuffed: pleased

chunter: mutter

cider: alcoholic apple cider

clearway: road where you can't stop

coach: long-distance bus

concession: discounted admission

concs (pronounced "conks"): short for "concession"

coronation chicken: curried chicken salad

cos: romaine lettuce

cot: baby crib

cotton buds: Q-tips

courgette: zucchini

craic (pronounced "crack"): fun, good conversation (Irish/Scottish and spreading to England)

crisps: potato chips

cuppa: cup of tea

dear: expensive

digestives: round graham cookies

dinner: lunch or dinner

diversion: detour

dogsbody: menial worker

donkey's years: ages, long time

draughts: checkers

draw: marijuana

dual carriageway: divided highway (four lanes)

dummy: pacifier

elevenses: coffee-and-biscuits break before lunch

elvers: baby eels

face flannel: washcloth

fag: cigarette

fagged: exhausted

faggot: sausage

fancy: to like, to be attracted to (a person)

fanny: vagina

fell: hill or high plain (Lake District)

first floor: second floor

fiver: £5 bill

fizzy drink: pop or soda

flutter: a bet

football: soccer

force: waterfall (Lake District)

fortnight: two weeks (shortened from "fourteen nights")

fringe: hair bangs

Frogs: French people

fruit machine: slot machine

full Monty: whole shebang, everything

gallery: balcony

gammon: ham

gangway: aisle

gaol: jail (same pronunciation)

gateau (or gateaux): cake

gear lever: stick shift

geezer: "dude"

give way: yield

glen: narrow valley (Scotland)

goods wagon: freight truck

gormless: stupid

goujons: breaded and fried fish or chicken sticks

green fingers: green thumbs

half eight: 8:30 (not 7:30)

hard cheese: bad luck

heath: open treeless land

hen night (or hen do): bachelorette party

holiday: vacation

homely: homey or cozy

hoover: vacuum cleaner

ice lolly: Popsicle

interval: intermission

ironmonger: hardware store

jacket potato: baked potato

jelly: Jell-O

jiggery-pokery: nonsense

Joe Bloggs: John Q. Public

jumble (sale): rummage sale

jumper: sweater

just a tick: just a second

kipper: smoked herring

knackered: exhausted (Cockney: cream crackered)

knickers: ladies' panties

knocking shop: brothel

knock up: wake up or visit (old-fashioned)

ladybird: ladybug

lady fingers: flat, spongy cookie

lady's finger: okra

lager: light, fizzy beer

left luggage: baggage check

lemonade: lemon-lime pop like 7-Up, fizzy

lemon squash: lemonade, not fizzy

let: rent

licenced: restaurant authorized to sell alcohol

lift: elevator

listed: protected historic building

loo: toilet or bathroom

lorry: truck

mack: mackintosh raincoat

mangetout: snow peas

marrow: summer squash

mate: buddy (boy or girl)

mean: stingy

mental: wild, memorable

mews: former stables converted to two-story rowhouses

moggie: cat

motorway: freeway

naff: tacky or trashy

nappy: diaper

natter: talk on and on

neep: Scottish for turnip

newsagent: corner store

nought: zero

noughts & crosses: tic-tac-toe

off-licence: liquor store

on offer: for sale

OTT: over the top, excessive

panto, pantomime: fairy-tale play performed at Christmas (silly but fun)

pants: (noun) underwear, briefs; (adj.) terrible, ridiculous

pasty (PASS-tee): crusted savory (usually meat) pie from Cornwall

pavement: sidewalk

pear-shaped: messed up, gone wrong

petrol: gas

piccalilli: mustard-pickle relish

pillar box: mailbox

pissed (rude), **paralytic, bevvied, wellied, popped up, merry, trollied, ratted, rat-arsed, pissed as a newt:** drunk

pitch: playing field

plaster: Band-Aid

plonk: cheap, bad wine

plonker: one who drinks bad wine (a mild insult)

prat: idiot

publican: pub owner

public school: private "prep" school (e.g., Eton)

pudding: dessert in general

pukka: first-class

pull, to be on the: on the prowl

punter: customer, especially in gambling

put a sock in it: shut up

queue: line

queue up: line up

quid: pound (£1)

randy: horny

rasher: slice of bacon

redundant, made: laid off

Remembrance Day: Veterans' Day

return ticket: round-trip

revising; doing revisions: studying for exams

ring up: call (telephone)

rubber: eraser

rubbish: bad

satnav: satellite navigation, GPS

sausage roll: sausage wrapped in a flaky pastry

Scotch egg: hard-boiled egg wrapped in sausage meat

Scouser: a person from Liverpool

self-catering: accommodation with kitchen

Sellotape: Scotch tape

services: freeway rest area

serviette: napkin

setee: couch

shag: intercourse (cruder than in the US)

shambolic: chaotic

shandy: lager and 7-Up

silencer: car muffler

single ticket: one-way ticket

skip: Dumpster

sleeping policeman: speed bumps

smalls: underwear

snap: photo (snapshot)

snogging: kissing, making out

sod: mildly offensive insult

sod it, sod off: screw it, screw off

sod's law: Murphy's law

soda: soda water (not pop)

soldiers (food): toast sticks for dipping

solicitor: lawyer

spanner: wrench

spend a penny: urinate

spotted dick: raisin cake with custard

stag night (or **stag do**): bachelor party

starkers: buck naked

starters: appetizers

state school: public school

sticking plaster: Band-Aid

sticky tape: Scotch tape

stone: 14 pounds (weight)

stroppy: bad-tempered

subway: underground walkway

sultanas: golden raisins

surgical spirit: rubbing alcohol

suspenders: garters

suss out: figure out

swede: rutabaga

ta: thank you

take the mickey/ take the piss: tease

tatty: worn out or tacky

tattie scone: potato pancake

taxi rank: taxi stand

telly: TV

tenement: stone apartment house (not necessarily a slum)

tenner: £10 bill

tick: a check mark

tight as a fish's bum: cheapskate (watertight)

tights: panty hose

tin: can

tip: public dump

tipper lorry: dump truck

toad in the hole: sausage dipped in batter and fried

top hole: first rate

top up: refill (a drink, mobilephone credit, petrol tank, etc.)

torch: flashlight

towel, press-on: panty liner

towpath: path along a river

trainers: sneakers

treacle: golden syrup

Tube: subway

twee: quaint, cutesy

twitcher: bird-watcher

Underground: subway

verge: grassy edge of road

verger: church official

way out: exit

wee (adj.): small (Scottish)

wee (verb): urinate

Wellingtons, wellies: rubber boots

whacked: exhausted

whinge (rhymes with hinge): whine

wind up: tease, irritate

witter on: gab and gab

wonky: weird, askew

yob: hooligan

zebra crossing: crosswalk

zed: the letter Z

INDEX

MAP INDEX

Start your trip at

Our website enhances this book and turns

Explore Europe

At ricksteves.com you can browse through thousands of articles, videos, photos and radio interviews, plus find a wealth of money-saving travel tips for planning your dream trip. And with our mobile-friendly website, you can easily access all this great travel information anywhere you go.

TV Shows

Preview the places you'll visit by watching entire half-hour episodes of Rick Steves' Europe (choose from all 100 shows) on-demand, for free.

ricksteves.com

Radio Interviews

Enjoy ready access to Rick's vast library of radio interviews covering travel

tips and cultural insights that relate specifically to your Europe travel plans.

Travel Forums

Learn, ask, share! Our online community of savvy travelers is a great resource for first-time travelers to Europe, as well as seasoned pros. You'll find forums on each country, plus travel tips and restaurant/hotel reviews. You can even ask one of our well-traveled staff to chime in with an opinion.

Travel News

Subscribe to our free Travel News e-newsletter, and get monthly updates from Rick on what's happening in Europe.

Audio Europe™

Rick's Free Travel App

Get your FREE **Rick Steves Audio Europe**™ app to enjoy...

- Dozens of self-guided tours of Europe's top museums, sights and historic walks

- Hundreds of tracks filled with cultural insights and sightseeing tips from Rick's radio interviews

- All organized into handy geographic playlists

- For iPhone, iPad, iPod Touch, Android

With Rick whispering in your ear, Europe gets even better.

Find out more at ricksteves.com

Pack Light and Right

Gear up for your next adventure at ricksteves.com

Light Luggage

Pack light and right with Rick Steves' affordable, custom-designed rolling carry-on bags, backpacks, day packs and shoulder bags.

Accessories

From packing cubes to moneybelts and beyond, Rick has personally selected the travel goodies that will help your trip go smoother.

Shop at ricksteves.com

Rick Steves has

Experience maximum Europe

Save time and energy

This guidebook is your independent-travel toolkit. But for all it delivers, it's still up to you to devote the time and energy it takes to manage the preparation and logistics that are essential for a happy trip. If that's a hassle, there's a solution.

Rick Steves Tours

A Rick Steves tour takes you to Europe's most interesting places with great

great tours, too!

with minimum stress

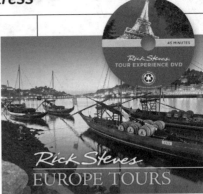

guides and small groups of 28 or less. We follow Rick's favorite itineraries, ride in comfy buses, stay in family-run hotels, and bring you intimately close to the Europe you've traveled so far to see. Most importantly, we take away the logistical headaches so you can focus on the fun.

customers—along with us on 40 different itineraries, from Ireland to Italy to Istanbul. Is a Rick Steves tour the right fit for your travel dreams? Find out at ricksteves.com, where you can also get Rick's latest tour catalog and free Tour Experience DVD.

Join the fun

This year we'll take 18,000 free-spirited travelers— nearly half of them repeat

Europe is best experienced with happy travel partners. We hope you can join us.

See our itineraries at ricksteves.com

Rick Steves

Maximize your travel skills with a good guidebook.

Photo © Patricia Feaster

RickSteves.com @RickSteves

Rick Steves books are available at bookstores and through online booksellers.

Credits

CONTRIBUTOR
Gene Openshaw

 Gene has co-authored a dozen *Rick Steves* books and contributes to many others. For this book, he wrote material on Europe's art, history, and contemporary culture. When not traveling, Gene enjoys composing music, recovering from his 1973 trip to Europe with Rick, and living everyday life with his daughter.

ACKNOWLEDGMENTS

Thanks to Jennifer Hauseman for the original version of the Glasgow chapter and to Colin Mairs for his help in Glasgow and throughout this book.

Avalon Travel
an imprint of Perseus Books
a division of Hachette Book Group
1700 Fourth Street
Berkeley, CA 94710

Printed in Canada by Friesens
Second printing July 2016

ISBN 978-1-61238-978-3
ISSN 2470-1904

For the latest on Rick's lectures, guidebooks, tours, public radio show, and public television series, contact Rick Steves' Europe, 130 Fourth Avenue North, Edmonds, WA
98020, 425/771-8303, www.ricksteves.com, rick@ricksteves.com.

Rick Steves' Europe
Special Publications Manager: Risa Laib
Managing Editor: Jennifer Madison Davis
Editors: Glenn Eriksen, Tom Griffin, Katherine Gustafson, Suzanne Kotz, Cathy Lu,
John Pierce, Carrie Shepherd
Editorial & Production Assistant: Jessica Shaw
Editorial Intern: Grace Swanson
Contributor: Gene Openshaw
Maps & Graphics: David C. Hoerlein, Sandra Hundacker, Lauren Mills, Mary Rostad

Avalon Travel
Senior Editor and Series Manager: Maddy McPrasher
Editor: Jamie Andrade
Associate Editor: Sierra Machado
Copy Editor: Judith Brown
Proofreader: Patrick Collins
Indexer: Stephen Callahan
Production & Typesetting: Tabitha Lahr
Cover Design: Kimberly Glyder Design
Maps & Graphics: Kat Bennett, Lohnes & Wright

Front Cover: Eilean Donan Castle, Loch Duich, Kyle of Lochalsh © P Lawrence /
Alamy Stock Photo
Title Page: Kiltmaker © Cameron Hewitt
Additional Photography: Dominic Arizona Bonuccelli, Rich Earl, Jennifer Hauseman,
Cameron Hewitt, David C. Hoerlein, Lauren Mills, Rhonda Pelikan, Rick Steves,
Gretchen Strauch, Wikimedia Commons (PD-Art/PD-US), p. 156 © Stephen C.
Dickson cc BY-SA 4.0. Photos are used by permission and are the property of the
original copyright owners.

Want more Britain?
Maximize the experience with Rick Steves as your guide

Guidebooks
London and England guides make side-trips smooth and affordable

Planning Maps
Use the map that's in sync with your guidebook

Rick's TV Shows
Preview where you're going with 9 shows on Britain

Free! Rick's Audio Europe™ App
Covering all the big sights and walks in London and more

Small Group Tours
Rick offers 4 great itineraries through Britain

For all the details, visit ricksteves.com